1980
Yearbook of Science and the Future

1980 Yearbook of Science and the Future

Encyclopædia Britannica, Inc.

Chicago Toronto London
Geneva Sydney Tokyo
Manila Seoul

THE UNIVERSITY OF CHICAGO
The Yearbook of Science and the Future
is published with the editorial advice of the faculties of
the University of Chicago.

1980 Yearbook of Science and the Future

Editorial Advisory Board

Contents

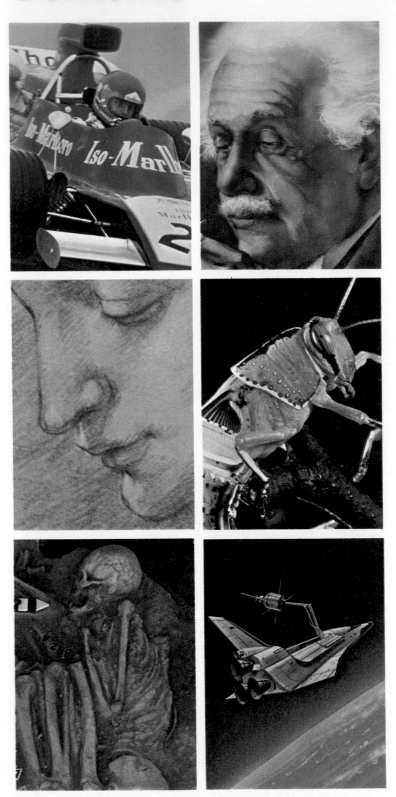

The Sky-High War

by Clarence A. Robinson, Jr.

In the arcane game of military satellites, the stakes are
national security, the players are superpowers, and
the winner will be the country whose spacecraft can best
spy, communicate, and raise the alarm.

It is late 1981. A U.S. space shuttle orbiter maneuvers into position 250 km (150 mi) above the Earth. Its crew listens intently as a low mechanical whine confirms the opening of the shuttle's white clamshell payload bay doors to the blue-black vacuum of space. Then, like the leg of a giant insect, the slender remote manipulator arm of the orbiter extracts an ungainly piece of cargo called Teal Ruby from the bay and releases it in orbit. A real-life drama of the near future, this action will signal the first military application of the shuttle transport system. Teal Ruby is a prototype satellite designed for low Earth orbit to detect infrared radiation emitted by the engines of strategic bombers and other aircraft flying within the Earth's atmosphere.

First mission-oriented flights with the shuttle will be nonmilitary and will begin in 1980. Running as many as 60 flights per year, this space workhorse not only will be capable of lofting 30,000-kg (65,000-lb) payloads into orbit but also will be able to return with as much as 14,500 kg, enabling satellite recovery in space for repair, refurbishing, and reuse. Eventually the stubby delta-wing orbiter will become the cornerstone for a U.S. space defense effort in the face of growing threats to its spacecraft from Soviet weapons.

The space shuttle is also the mechanism that will enable the U.S. Air Force and Army to take advantage of technological revolutions in the areas of electronic sensing, onboard computing, and exotic weaponry capable of destroying enemy spacecraft and intercontinental ballistic missiles (ICBM's). When coupled with a laser communications system now being tested, such technology will move the U.S. to the threshold of an adventure in space as imaginative as the Apollo flights to the Moon were a decade ago. The shuttle system will replace today's single-use, expensive launch vehicles to position satellites in low Earth orbit routinely for communications, timely high-resolution reconnaissance, and electronic eavesdropping and to park early warning spacecraft and defensive space weapons for boosting to more distant orbits. To meet these growing needs, the Air Force is planning to establish a major new Space Command and expects to begin a military man-in-space program in the 1990s.

Importance for peace

During the past decade the U.S. and the U.S.S.R. have so increased their dependence on military satellites in space that such devices are now the first line of defense. They act as the eyes and ears of the two nations to assure adherence to strategic arms limitation treaties limiting the development, testing, and deployment of nuclear weapons. Without these satellites, referred to euphemistically as "national technical means of verification," there could be no agreement on limiting strategic nuclear weapons. Without reconnaissance spacecraft each superpower would be virtually deaf and blind to the other's military preparations. Early warning satellites provide an alert for a nuclear attack and the necessary time to trigger a return strike to assure mutual destruction. It is upon this tenet that world peace now rests: either side will inflict unacceptable damage on the other regardless of which possesses the advantage of surprise.

In 1978 U.S. Pres. Jimmy Carter signed a directive to guide the conduct of U.S. activities in and related to space programs. He confirmed that the

CLARENCE A. ROBINSON, JR., *is Senior Military Editor for* Aviation Week & Space Technology *magazine, Washington, D.C.*

Illustrations by John Youssi

U.S. is committed to exploration and use of outer space for peaceful purposes and to increased development of useful commercial and government applications of space technology. In words that marked the first official U.S. admission of military reconnaissance space activities, he also affirmed that the U.S. has the fundamental right to acquire data from space and that no state can claim sovereignty over celestial bodies or any portion of space. U.S. space programs relating to national security, arms control, and economic and political objectives would be carried out within these principles.

Early warning satellites

Were a fleet of Soviet ICBM's and submarine-launched ballistic missiles (SLBM's) to be fired at the U.S., that country would have a maximum of 30 minutes to perceive the threat, prepare, and retaliate. Detecting these launches and relaying the information within 90 seconds to one of two ground stations is the critical function of the U.S. Air Force early warning satellite system. Dubbed the Defense Support Program within the government, the satellites also are known as Block 647 spacecraft based on their design by a California-based aerospace division of TRW, Inc.

The early warning satellite weighs more than 900 kg (2,000 lb) and is placed in a 24-hour synchronous, or geostationary, orbit about 36,000 km (22,300 mi) above a fixed point on the Equator. The Defense Support Program is composed of at least three satellites located above the Equator at any one time. One is positioned over the Indian Ocean, from which location it can monitor both Soviet and Chinese missile launches. Two are stationed over the Western Hemisphere, with one over the Pacific to detect submarine ballistic missile launches and the other over Brazil to cover the Atlantic for the same purpose.

In its equatorial orbit, the spacecraft is oriented such that its large widefield telescope points toward the Earth. The vehicle spins about its cylindrical axis at 5–7 rpm. The telescope's line of sight is offset from the satellite's spin axis so that the field of view rotates conically, generating an enlarged field of view. Light collected by the telescope is reflected onto the satellite's infrared sensor array, which detects the radiant heat emitted by ballistic missile boosters during the early stages of flight, typically spotting Soviet missile launches within the first 50 seconds.

The Air Force has provided a means to avoid interference from such natural phenomena as forest fires, blast furnaces, or breaks in natural gas pipelines. Each of the hundreds of component detectors that make up the sensor array can be commanded to trigger only above certain illumination levels, and logic in an onboard computer rejects phenomena not related to missile launches. The sensor must make a series of detections in successive scans to confirm a missile launch. A visible light sensor—a televisionlike device—is used with the infrared array to provide optical viewing of the exhaust plumes from ballistic missiles as they are launched and rise above the atmosphere. Using two types of complementary sensors on early warning spacecraft prevents false alarms that could otherwise occur from activation of the infrared sensors from cloud-reflected sunlight.

More than a thousand ICBM launches have been detected by early warning

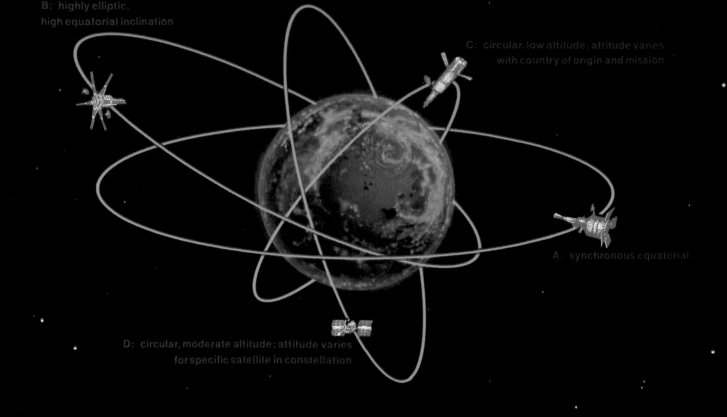

B: highly elliptic, high equatorial inclination

C: circular, low altitude; attitude varies with country of origin and mission

A: synchronous equatorial

D: circular, moderate altitude; attitude varies for specific satellite in constellation

General orbital characteristics for several categories of military satellite are listed in the table on the facing page and schematically compared above, with orbit types A through D keyed to the table. Satellites illustrated are (A) U.S. Block 647, (B) Soviet Molniya 1, (C) conception of U.S. Big Bird, and (D) U.S. NavStar.

spacecraft during Soviet research and development and operational testing since the first such satellite was put in orbit in 1971. Because of its scanning capability, the system can determine missile velocity and provide an indication of the path over which the missile will travel to the target area.

Air Force officials are concerned with providing some protection for the early warning system against enemy attack, and studies have been conducted to determine if and what steps might be taken to improve the present system or if a new satellite design is required. A passive warning device under development would provide a detector within the satellite's telescope

satellite	altitude (km)	orbit type
early warning		
U.S. Block 647	36,000 (synchronous)	A
Soviet (Cosmos)	apogee, 36,000; perigee, 400	B
reconnaissance		
Soviet (Cosmos)	apogee, 370; perigee, 180	C
Soviet (manned Salyut)	apogee, 270; perigee, 220	C
U.S. Big Bird	apogee, 290; perigee, 180	C
U.S. search and find	apogee, 320; perigee, 180	C
U.S. ferret	480	C
Soviet ferret (Cosmos)	similar to U.S. ferret	C
ocean surveillance		
Soviet (Cosmos)	240	C
U.S. Navy (White Cloud)	970	C
communications		
U.S. DSCS phase two	36,000 (synchronous)	A
U.S. Navy Fleet Satellite Communications System	36,000 (synchronous)	A
U.S. Air Force Satellite Data System	apogee, 40,000; perigee, 560	B
Soviet Molniya	apogee, 40,000; perigee, 550	B
navigation		
U.S. NavStar	20,200	D

to alert the ground terminals or to trigger a shutter to protect the optical and infrared sensors from the destructive light intensities of laser weapons. The two ground terminals, located in the U.S. and Australia, are even more vulnerable to attack than the spacecraft, and to reduce dependence on them the Air Force is developing mobile data readout facilities. Small processors can also be deployed in aircraft along with a communications module for relay to the president and other U.S. leaders in times of crises.

U.S. intelligence analysts believe the Soviet Union to be generally behind the U.S. in early warning satellite development. The Soviets use infrared sensors to detect ballistic missile launches, but their spacecraft operate in highly elliptical, nonsynchronous orbits. Apogee, or maximum distance from the Earth, is over the U.S. at some 36,000 km, allowing the satellites a 12-hour view of the U.S. as they climb to and descend from that altitude. At least two Soviet early warning satellites are always in orbit to keep the U.S. in constant view and to relay missile test-launch information to a satellite ground station in Cuba. Were the Soviet Union to place an early warning spacecraft in geostationary orbit over the Equator, resolution and coverage of some U.S. missile sites would be lost because of the Earth's curvature. By contrast, U.S. early warning satellites in equatorial orbit can adequately cover all such sites in the Soviet Union. Soviet operational control centers for early warning spacecraft are not automated like those of the U.S.; consequently they require round-the-clock staffing, which complicates the system.

Soviet reconnaissance spacecraft

The Soviet Union initiated what it termed the Cosmos program on March 16, 1962, "to continue the study of outer space." When the craft designated Cosmos 4 was recovered from orbit after only four days, it became clear to U.S. intelligence analysts that Cosmos was a blanket term covering a variety of missions. Systematic study of the orbits, launch times, launch sites, perigee, flight duration, and routine monitoring of radio transmissions revealed distinct military applications of some Cosmos spacecraft. Satellites that disappeared from orbit although their orbits were sufficiently stable to rule out natural decay indicated that they were brought down to recover reconnaissance film for processing. By the time Cosmos 247 was launched in 1968, nearly half of all Cosmos launches fell into this category. The figure rose above 50% by the time Cosmos 350 went up in 1970, but with a change to longer duration flights it decreased to about 47% by the end of 1975.

The first real evidence the U.S. had that these Soviet satellites might be concerned with the collection of intelligence information came during a detailed study of Cosmos 15 in April 1963, when it was observed that the satellite did not transmit on revolutions 19, 35, 51, and 67 as it passed north across Great Britain. At that time the ballistic missile early warning radar system at Fylingdales was going into operation. By plotting the ground tracks of orbits over a given area for the duration of the mission, it was possible to show that in eight days—the normal duration for this first-generation satellite—complete photographic coverage of the radar system was obtained. Cosmos 15 and other Soviet reconnaissance satellites also showed a correlation between launch times and sunset times in the Northern Hemisphere, pointing to a desire to maintain lighting conditions as nearly uniform as possible during photography.

In 1972, just after the first strategic arms limitation treaty was signed, the Soviet Union accelerated the pace of Cosmos launches in order to take inventory of U.S. nuclear weapons facilities for treaty compliance. A total of 29 spacecraft were launched during this period, about three times more reconnaissance satellites than the U.S. placed in orbit, but together they achieved only about 25% more time in orbit because of expanded use of new U.S. long-endurance Big Bird satellites, which will be discussed below.

From its geostationary orbit above the Earth, the U.S. Defense Support Program's Block 647 early warning satellite (opposite page) can detect ballistic missiles by their telltale electromagnetic emissions within the first 50 seconds after launch. Both infrared and visible light enter its large wide-field telescope and are reflected to separate, complementary sensor packages that convert them to electronic signals. Sensor output is analyzed by an onboard computer to confirm the launches and then is encoded, digitized, and relayed as a highly directional radio signal to one of two ground stations. The spacecraft also carries visual star sensors for satellite orientation and X-ray gauges and proton counters to detect nuclear radiation. Power for the satellite is generated by panels of photovoltaic cells on the main cylinder and on four supplementary "pedals."

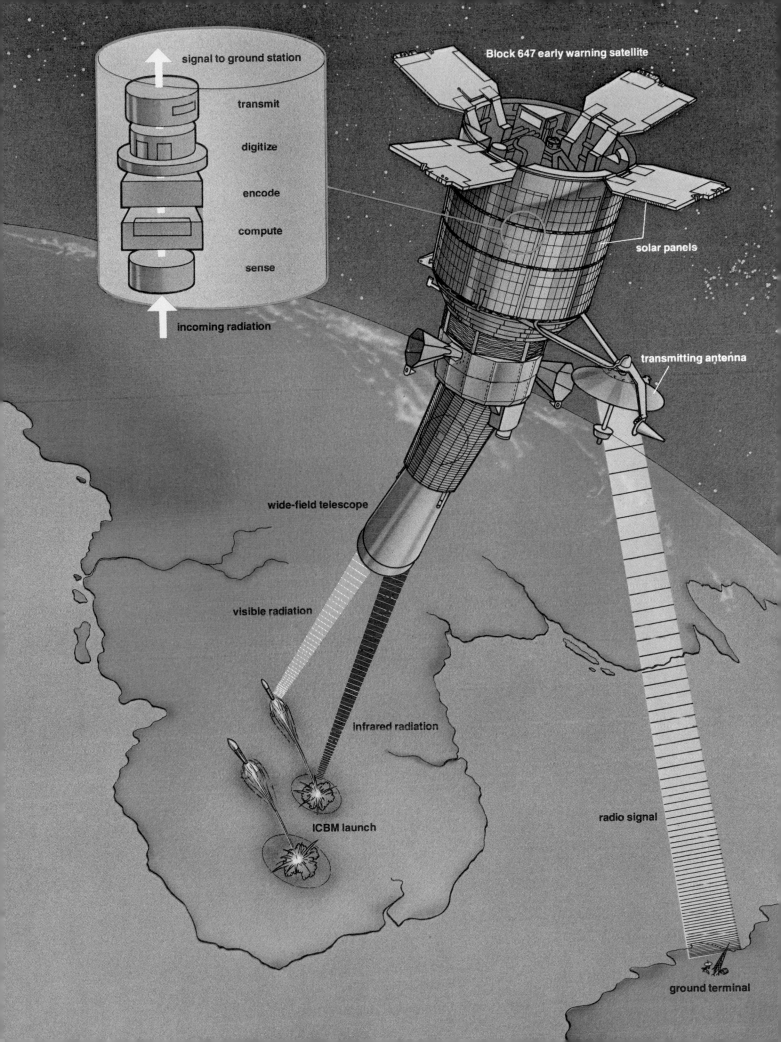

signal to ground station

transmit

digitize

encode

compute

sense

incoming radiation

Block 647 early warning satellite

solar panels

transmitting antenna

wide-field telescope

visible radiation

infrared radiation

ICBM launch

radio signal

ground terminal

Presently the Soviet Union fires approximately a hundred boosters each year to put various spacecraft including some 30 reconnaissance satellites into orbit, both manned and unmanned, and some boosters carry as many as eight communications spacecraft into orbit at one time. U.S. analysts believe that, of 120–130 Soviet spacecraft annually placed in orbit, at least 95% are for military missions. In comparison, the U.S. launches only 35–40 satellites each year with about 15% dedicated to military applications.

The U.S.S.R. has at least two unmanned satellites for photographic reconnaissance up at any given time. They generally operate in nearly circular orbit with an apogee of 370 km (230 mi) and a perigee, or minimum distance from the Earth, of 180 km (110 mi). The spacecraft is similar in design to the Soviet Soyuz transport system that has been employed for manned space missions; it has no film capsules which can be ejected separately for capture during a satellite pass over a given area, as do U.S. reconnaissance satellites. Instead the entire film load is returned with a reentry vehicle for processing. Each satellite has a lifetime of about 14 days. Recently the Soviets have tested a reconnaissance satellite with a 30-day lifetime, and it may have the capability to eject film pods for recovery before the end of the spacecraft's orbital lifetime.

The Soviet Union employs at least three types of photographic reconnaissance satellites. One is a system capable of high-resolution photography and can be differentiated from the other two by its maneuver capability in space and the type of telemetry signals it uses to communicate with ground stations. For several years the U.S. has had the capability to use low-energy lasers to illuminate the aperture of orbiting Cosmos satellite cameras and to determine from the reflected light the focal lengths of their lenses, the approximate type of film being used, and thus the resolution capability of the spacecraft.

The Soviets are prone to use manned spacecraft on high-resolution photographic missions of a military nature, permitting a high degree of flexibility in targeting the areas to be photographed. The space stations Salyut 3 and Salyut 5, which were launched in 1974 and 1976 respectively, were employed partly for this purpose and were manned several times each by military crews brought up in Soyuz spacecraft. Although there has been no launch of a military Salyut since 1976, the program is expected to continue in the future. There also is some evidence that the Salyut 2 spacecraft, which failed in orbit in April 1973, was on a military reconnaissance mission. This possibility emphasizes the early priority placed on manned military missions with satellites dedicated to that purpose at the earliest stages of the Soviet space station program.

Specific design differences have been noted in Salyuts 3 and 5. For instance, the military Salyut's docking port is at the rear of the spacecraft for docking with Soyuz transport vehicles. Primary docking for scientific Salyuts is at the forward end of the satellite. Solar panels are placed further aft on military Salyuts than on scientific Salyuts. Military Salyuts carry a large reconnaissance camera and at least one reentry vehicle designed to return film to Earth. Reentry vehicles were dropped with reconnaissance film from both Salyuts 3 and 5 after military crews had departed.

Shown in an artist's conception, the U.S. Big Bird reconnaissance satellite (opposite page) possesses two means of delivering photographs of extremely high resolution to the ground. Film taken of targets of normal interest is ejected from the satellite in one of six film pods (right sequence). Following reentry and parachute descent, the pod is either caught in midair by a specially equipped aircraft or retrieved from the ocean by frogmen. Film development takes place on the ground. For high-priority targets, exposed film is processed in the spacecraft itself (left sequence) and electronically scanned to convert the optical images into digital signals. A narrow radio beam transmits the information in this form to the ground, where it is computer processed to reconstruct the images.

16

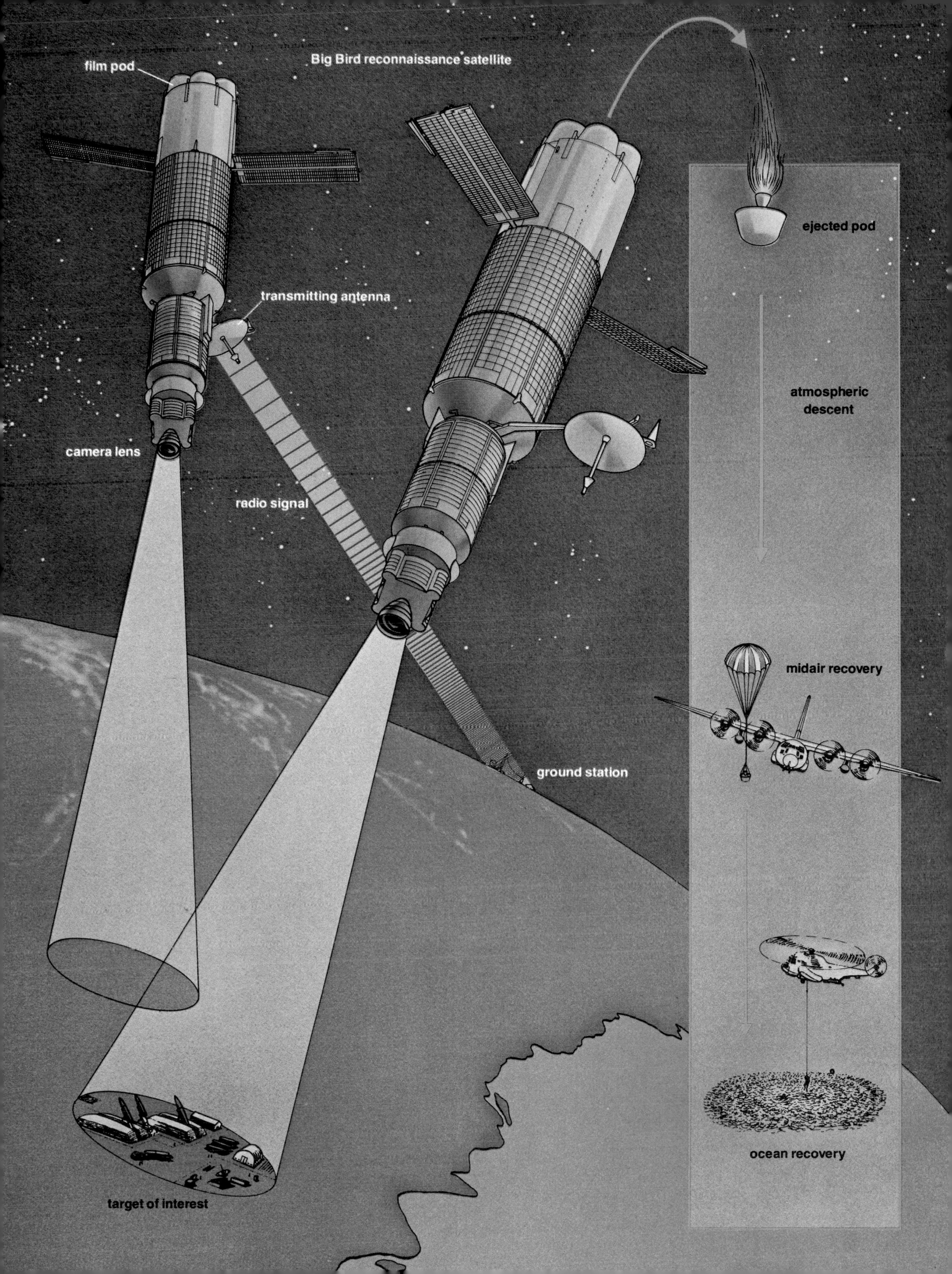

Big Bird reconnaissance satellite

film pod

transmitting antenna

camera lens

radio signal

ground station

target of interest

ejected pod

atmospheric descent

midair recovery

ocean recovery

U.S. reconnaissance satellites

The U.S. photographic reconnaissance satellite program is now in its fifth generation with a massive 11,350-kg (25,000-lb) system known as Big Bird. The Big Bird spacecraft is 3 m (10 ft) in diameter and 15 m (50 ft) long. It operates in low Earth orbit with an apogee of 290 km (180 mi) and a perigee of 180 km (110 mi) and is boosted periodically to higher altitudes to prolong its life in space to more than 200 days. Big Bird carries six film pods that are ejected at intervals from the satellite and plucked from the sky during parachute descent over the Pacific by specially configured Air Force YC-130 aircraft. Recovery is in midair whenever possible using a Y-shaped device on the nose of the aircraft to snag the parachute lines. If this fails, frogmen are sent into the ocean to recover the film from the floating capsule, which emits radio and sonar signals. If the capsule cannot be located in the water it self-destructs in a matter of hours.

From an altitude of more than 160 km (100 mi) Big Bird's film cameras can distinguish between objects on the Earth's surface that are separated as little as the span of a human hand and can discern the individual rivets on the wings of an aircraft. In addition, color television cameras and infrared photography are used on the spacecraft, with television images relayed to a communications satellite in synchronous orbit and from there to ground or shipboard terminals. This optical method is used to guide the spacecraft to targets that appear interesting from the video images. Photographic images of such high-interest targets need not wait for capsule recovery to be examined; they can be developed on the satellite itself and transmitted by digital signals to terminals for computer enhancement and printing. Big Bird's infrared capability enables detection of missiles in underground silos because of temperature variations and can be used to locate movement of missiles or mobile launchers at night or under cloud cover.

Another type of U.S. reconnaissance satellite for photography is the key component in a moderate-resolution search and find system. The film is developed on the spacecraft as it passes over one of its ground stations, scanned with a laser, and converted to a video signal for transmission to Earth. The U.S. orbits only one search and find satellite at a time and generally launches about two a year. Functioning at altitudes similar to Big Bird spacecraft, the system is designed to survey the Soviet Union for construction activity, particularly in missile fields and submarine shipyards.

A third type of U.S. reconnaissance satellite is the "ferret" spacecraft, carried into orbit piggyback style on Big Bird's Titan launcher. The system is designed to listen for and pinpoint enemy radars from its orbit some 480 km (300 mi) in space, which provides a lifetime of two to three years.

Detection of radar emissions and other forms of electronic reconnaissance are critical to implementation of the second strategic arms offensive-weapons agreement still being negotiated in early 1979 because this type of surveillance can be used to determine development plans for long-range weapons. It also can indicate whether plans are under way to prepare weapons systems and then to break or abrogate a treaty to gain a significant military advantage. Ferret spacecraft provide such valuable intelligence data on air-defense and ballistic-missile–defense radar systems, yielding not only

exact locations but radar characteristics as well. They also can determine if antiballistic missile (ABM) radars are being operated in violation of existing treaties, which prohibit testing of new-technology air-defense systems in an ABM mode. Such a case occurred recently when a type of sophisticated radar was detected operating on Kamchatka Peninsula in that mode; the Soviet Union subsequently was questioned about it in accordance with the 1972 ABM agreement.

The U.S. uses ferret satellites in much the same manner as photographic reconnaissance spacecraft. Two satellites are launched to work in pairs, with one in a lower orbit. One satellite covers wide areas of the globe to detect signals and determine rough locations of radar emissions. The other spacecraft is more sophisticated and larger and is used to obtain precise locations of targets of interest and detailed emission data.

Because of the large number of Cosmos satellite launches, it is more difficult to pinpoint Soviet ferret-type spacecraft. A number of Cosmos operate with collection equipment to relay stored electronic data to Earth terminals. There are usually eight Soviet ferret spacecraft operational at any one time. Recently the U.S.S.R. switched emphasis from smaller two-ton ferret electronic reconnaissance spacecraft to larger three-ton devices. Four of the larger craft were launched in 1978, compared with two of the smaller. These figures represent the largest number of big ferrets since 1970 and the lowest number of small ones.

Ocean surveillance satellites

Both the U.S. and the Soviet Union widely use ocean surveillance satellites. This fact came to public attention early in 1978 when Cosmos 954 reentered the Earth's atmosphere and broke apart, spreading radioactive material over a wide area of northern Canada. Equipped with an active radar system

Unclassified infrared photograph of a Texas airport, taken by a low-flying aircraft, provides some idea of the value of such imagery in satellite surveillance activities. The exposure was made about 10 PM local time; hotter areas, which emit infrared radiation more strongly, appear lighter. Not only are the silhouettes of several types of aircraft clearly discernible, but so also are areas of recently occupied pavement. Also visible are paths of heat created by engine exhaust as the aircraft taxied from place to place. Such imagery can likewise be used to track the deployment and movement of missile launchers and other military equipment at night or during cloudy conditions.

19

Telescope optics of a U.S. early warning satellite receives a crippling burst of light from a high-energy laser weapon mounted aboard a Soviet space station. The event is recreated in the background.

providing an all-weather, day-night capability, Cosmos 954 was one of a type of spacecraft that the Soviets have used for more than ten years to keep track of U.S. Navy ship movements.

The radar satellite weighs a hefty 2,700 kg (6,000 lb) and carries about 45 kg (100 lb) of enriched uranium-235 in a small nuclear reactor to provide electrical power for the radar system. It operates in low Earth orbit at approximately 240 km (150 mi) and usually in pairs to provide overlapping radar sweeps. Information on U.S. ships and fleet activities is transmitted back to the U.S.S.R. via relay from other satellites or directly to ground-based or shipborne terminals.

Formerly called White Cloud, a project name, the first U.S. system dedicated to ocean surveillance was launched in 1976 and uses three spacecraft, termed Navy observation surveillance satellites, which orbit at an altitude of about 970 km (600 mi). The craft are stationed about 80 km (50 mi) apart to detect radio and radar emissions from Soviet vessels and to pinpoint ship locations accurately. Another ocean surveillance system, launched in late 1977 to provide coverage of the world's oceans, operates with radar-intercept receivers and passive infrared sensors that can detect the heat emitted from nuclear powered ocean vessels.

In a program called Clipper Bow, the U.S. Navy is presently involved in developing a new ocean surveillance satellite equipped with an active radar for all-weather detection of surface vessels. However, a decision to produce a constellation of the spacecraft is not expected until 1984 at the earliest. The Air Force also is developing an active radar satellite for use in synchronous orbit to detect aircraft and aircraftlike cruise missiles.

Both the Soviets and the U.S. are developing blue-green lasers for use from spacecraft to penetrate the ocean in an effort to detect deep running ballistic missile submarines. Another Soviet development is a more powerful, narrow-beam radar to detect topographical changes in sea life caused by a nuclear-powered submarine gliding beneath the ocean surface.

Military communications satellites

Perhaps the most readily adaptable mission for artificial Earth satellites is that of communications, a concept first tested as early as 1958 with the U.S. launch of a radio relay satellite. Today, with the likelihood that any conflict in the world could draw the two superpowers into it, satellite communications have become paramount, and both sides are busily upgrading present systems and developing new technology.

One satellite communications network critical to U.S. security is the Defense Satellite Communications System (DSCS), consisting of four active spacecraft and two in-orbit spares. Scheduled to be fully operational in 1979, it is the present stage of a three-phase plan already spanning more than a decade. In phase one, 26 small satellites were launched into equatorial orbit between 1966 and 1968 to relay voice, imagery, computerized digital data, and teletype transmissions. Even though they were designed to last only 18 months, one was still operating ten years after launch.

Phase two began with two spacecraft launches in 1971. Phase-two satellites are built to carry many times the communications load of their predecessors with increased transmission power and double the lifetime expectancy. The first two phase two's are no longer operational, and of the second pair, launched in December 1973, one was still working over the Indian Ocean in early 1979. A third pair failed to reach orbit in 1975 because of a booster problem. A set of six phase-two DSCS satellites were ordered for launch between 1977 and 1979. The first two were placed in synchronous orbit in May 1977 and now provide service over the Atlantic and western Pacific.

Future plans call for phase-three DSCS spacecraft, which will have still more powerful capabilities and longer life in space than phase two's. They will have six active transmitter channels instead of the two now operational on phase-two spacecraft and an antenna design that allows the user to switch between a fixed wide-coverage antenna and a steerable parabolic antenna that can provide a narrow beam of increased power. This concept permits communications beams that can be tailored to suit the needs of different user terminals almost anywhere on Earth.

The present DSCS system allows the president of the United States to talk directly to commanders in the field, and it can handle coded information through ground stations. Wherever in the world the president goes he is never more than a few feet from an officer carrying a national command-authority telephone in case a nuclear war is triggered and the U.S. must respond. The telephone communicates with the nearest DSCS terminal, which relays the information around the world via this satellite network.

A separate satellite system, the NATO Integrated Communications System, has been used by the U.S. as a part of its DSCS network. Three satellites in the system operate in synchronous orbit above the Atlantic Ocean for rapid, secure communications among NATO nations through a network of ground and shipborne stations. The spacecraft are built and launched in the U.S. for alliance member nations.

The U.S. Navy and Air Force each possess or are in the process of establishing satellite communications systems. Operating jointly they will contribute to a near-global radio-frequency communications network for relaying high-priority military messages among ships, reconnaissance and command-post aircraft, and ground sites. The Navy's Fleet Satellite Communications System, the first satellite of which was launched in February 1978, will consist of four spacecraft placed into synchronous equatorial orbit and will make available 23 channels to Navy and Air Force commanders around the world. Other spacecraft, part of the Air Force Satellite Data System now in operation, occupy equatorially inclined, highly elliptical orbits that allow communication with strategic bombers flying over the North Pole. With an apogee of 40,000 km (25,000 mi) and a perigee of 560 km (350 mi) these latter spacecraft also spend about half of each 12-hour orbit over the Soviet Union doubling as reconnaissance satellites, most likely on communications-intercept missions.

The U.S. is keying its future satellite communications efforts to laser communications spacecraft, which in early 1979 were in developmental testing at ground facilities at White Sands Missile Range in New Mexico. The concept will soon be tested piggyback on another spacecraft, the shuttle-borne Teal Ruby scheduled for launch in 1981, following aircraft-to-ground tests.

One advantage of a laser communications network is its increased resistance to detection and jamming by an enemy. Because a beam of laser light diverges, or spreads out, very little even over great distances and emits no radio-frequency radiation, finding it or its source in space becomes extremely difficult. A narrow beam also allows its receivers to be designed with a very limited field of view, thus presenting a hard target for blinding devices. As another advantage, the intensity of narrow laser beams permits communications satellites to be positioned at altitudes beyond normal 36,000-km synchronous orbit and still maintain the high-quality transmission capabilities and high rates of data flow necessary for timely viewing of intelligence information. Using slower data rates, the system also can be used for secure jam-resistant conferences between command-post aircraft and battlefield commanders. In addition, the system can carry covert messages from U.S. bombers flying nuclear weapons on retaliatory strike missions. Directional laser signals transmitted from the aircraft can be passively received on the spacecraft by an optical device.

In the Soviet Union satellites of the Molniya designation perform both civilian and military communications functions. The first was launched in 1965 with a perigee 550 km (340 mi) above the Southern Hemisphere and an apogee 40,000 km (25,000 mi) over the Northern Hemisphere to provide line-of-sight communications with the U.S.S.R. for about nine hours a day. Molniya 1 satellites are for military communications, and Molniya 2s for civilian use. Four satellites are orbited 90° apart in the same plane. Some 35 Molniya 1s were launched from 1965 to 1976, and 15 Molniya 2s and six newer Molniya 3s, which are primarily for military use, from 1974 to 1977.

The Soviet Union also has launched Raduga satellites for communications in synchronous orbit over the Equator, and it has plans to orbit a network of synchronous spacecraft in the early 1980s for communications. A prelude to this system is believed to be the Statsionar series of three spacecraft launched in 1975 and 1976.

Navigation satellites

Military navigation satellites, which are highly useful when seeking to strike targets with tactical weapons, are employed by both the U.S. and the U.S.S.R. Through its NavStar Global Positioning System, a space-based radio navigation network, the U.S. will soon have the capability of providing extremely precise location fixes for its users. Four of the satellites in the network are already in orbit for tests, and they will become a part of a 20,200-km-high, 24-satellite constellation fully operational in the late 1980s.

NavStar provides an excellent example of the unique capability of spacecraft to enhance the conduct of military missions on Earth. With the fully operational system circling the globe every 12 hours, ships, aircraft, and ground-based users with proper equipment can receive and process the signals and determine their location in three dimensions within 9 m (30 ft), velocity within a fraction of a kilometer per hour, and time within a millionth of a second. By pressing a button users automatically select the four most favorably positioned satellites to lock on to their own navigation signals as a base for computations. The system will provide accurate blind-bombing capability for aircraft regardless of weather or visibility, and soldiers in the field will be able to get accurate locations from the NavStar network through a small portable manpack.

Killer spacecraft

Over the years the U.S. and the Soviet Union have tacitly accepted the other's use of satellites for military missions. This unspoken agreement was broken in 1977 when the U.S. clearly perceived that the Soviets had been testing antisatellite devices in space for the past several years, giving them the capability to destroy U.S. spacecraft in low Earth orbit. In response President Carter announced that the U.S. intended to seek verifiable, comprehensive limits on antisatellite capabilities and use, but in the absence of such an agreement, it would vigorously pursue development of its own antisatellite capabilities. He stated that the U.S. space defense program would include an integrated attack warning, notification, verification, and contingency reaction capability that could effectively detect and react to threats to U.S. space systems.

In its investigation of Soviet antisatellite activities the U.S. monitored a series of 16 tests with the most recent one in May 1978. Various intercept methods were attempted in the series, indicating exploration of new kinds of technology. The tests included maneuvering killer satellites alongside target craft in space on a fast flyby and then simulating an explosion to destroy the target's sensors with buckshotlike shrapnel. Another intercept technique involved a fast flyby of the target in an eccentric orbit with closing speeds of about 1,600 kph (1,000 mph) to simulate destruction of the target with a directed pattern of explosion fragments. Yet another intercept maneuver involved a fast "pop-up" mode to insert the killer vehicle rapidly into the target's orbit from a lower orbit. In all of the tests the killer satellite reached the target spacecraft within one or two revolutions of the Earth.

In response to the Soviet killer satellite capability the U.S. is now developing its own killer satellite, a small maneuvering intercept-technology vehicle under development by Vought Corporation. As a backup system it is investigating the use of high-energy laser weapons based both on the ground and in space. Developed originally as a nonnuclear warhead for the Army's Ballistic Missile Defense Command, the intercept system consists of a central unit or core surrounded by a cluster of small tubular rocket thrusters that not only provide maneuvering propulsion for the weapon but also function as the kill mechanism. The core contains an optical sensor to detect the satellite target and a small digital computer that homes the warhead by firing the thrusters. Once within range the rocket tubes detach and are launched into the path of the target to destroy it.

Lasers and particle beams

Air Force officials plan to begin a high-energy laser weapons program in 1983 by placing two ground-based laser weapons in the southwestern U.S. to destroy Soviet satellites in low Earth orbit in retaliation for any move against U.S. spacecraft. One laser weapon will be positioned in the desert area of California at China Lake and the other atop a mountain just outside

Soviet killer satellite begins to fragment from an internal detonation as it nears its U.S. counterpart. The U.S. version consists of a cluster of rocket tubes surrounding a central core equipped with an optical homing system. The rocket tubes are used initially for propulsion and maneuvering; once the satellite nears its target, the tubes detach and are fired into the target path as individual weapons. In the background a Soviet reusable shuttle positions a satellite in orbit while its piloted booster drops away to begin a return flight to Earth.

Kirtland Air Force Base, New Mexico, where laser weapons development is taking place.

Both the Air Force and the Army are pursuing development of high-energy laser weapons for use on spacecraft. Whereas haze, precipitation, particulate matter, and other phenomena in the Earth's atmosphere can absorb and reflect light and thus markedly reduce the effectiveness of ground-based laser weapons, the vacuum of space is ideal for laser propagation. Levels of energy sufficiently intense to destroy satellites can be beamed thousands of kilometers through space. Power units now exist that can provide the energy required for space-based lasers, and by using the space shuttle these and associated equipment can be carried into orbit in a series of loads for the construction of comparatively large, heavy-duty laser-weapon battle stations above the Earth.

As the U.S. prepares to meet antisatellite threats, which can provide political leverage in times of crises, the Soviets are continuing developmental testing of high-energy lasers at Saryshagan near the Chinese border and at Krasnaya Pakhra south of Moscow. U.S. intelligence specialists believe that the Soviets will seek to place a prototype laser weapon in space during 1979. Indeed, there is some evidence that high-energy laser tests were conducted on the Salyut 5 manned space mission, which began in 1974 and lasted some 14 months.

Beginning in 1977 controversial public disclosures revealed that the Soviet Union—and, to a lesser extent, the U.S.—were seeking to adapt the technology of subatomic particle accelerators to create beams of protons, electrons, or neutral hydrogen atoms capable of destroying orbiting satellites and in-flight missiles. Such weapons would be either Earth- or space-based and would be capable of being aimed, fired, and retargeted rapidly by computer. They also would have the advantage of reaching the target in milliseconds, making evasive maneuvers impossible. Pulsed continuously, a ground- or ship-mounted beam weapon would literally bore a hole for itself ever deeper through the atmosphere, rarefying gases in its path, and be capable of penetrating at least ten kilometers (six miles) to deliver a damaging jolt of energy to the electronics, structure, or explosive component of an incoming warhead. With a beam generator operating in space and away from atmospheric effects, the range and threat to missiles and spacecraft would be considerably increased. To create such weapons, however, many technological obstacles must be overcome, not the least of which is a practical method of meeting the immense power required for the beam.

Intelligence information gathered in recent years by U.S. reconnaissance satellites and other sources have left little doubt that the Soviets are pursuing development of novel power sources, energy storage equipment, particle generators, and other devices that could function as components of particle beam weapons. There exists a split within the intelligence and scientific communities, however, over specific Soviet intentions and current level of development. Some U.S. intelligence analysts believe that the Soviet Union is deeply committed to particle beam weaponry and that it could produce a ground-based antiballistic-missile defense weapon as early as 1980. A Soviet space-based particle beam weapon could be in orbit by 1986.

Some electron beam experiments have already been conducted by the U.S.S.R. from Cosmos, Soyuz, and Salyut spacecrafts to assess the effects of space and the Earth's magnetic field on beam propagation. In a joint Soviet-French program electron beams have been fired from Soviet-built accelerators onboard two French Eridan rockets sent into space with other equipment. The experiments are part of the Araks scientific program, and at least one more propagation test is planned for 1982.

In the U.S. the Army is doing exploratory technology development on two kinds of particle beam weapons. One is a ground-based system producing tremendous amounts of energy within a beam of protons and based on a concept called the autoresonant accelerator now under construction in Austin, Texas, for technology demonstration. As a weapon the system would be used to protect U.S. missile fields by intercepting incoming nuclear warheads from hostile ICBM's just as they reenter the Earth's atmosphere.

The Army's space-based neutralized hydrogen beam system is called Sipapu, an American Indian word meaning sacred fire. It will be at least the late 1980s before a space-based antiballistic-missile system could be deployed to intercept ICBM's just after liftoff or in midcourse trajectory out in space. In 1978 military officials told members of Congress that both the Army, which is developing Sipapu at the Los Alamos Scientific Laboratory in New Mexico, and the Air Force could use neutral beam technology from Sipapu to place an antisatellite variant in space within two or three years. Beam focusing and aiming and concentrated energy levels are not as difficult to obtain for satellite destruction as for use against the large numbers of reentry vehicles that would be encountered in a massive ICBM or SLBM attack. Moreover, reentry vehicles are "hardened" to withstand the intense heat of reentering the atmosphere and thus are more difficult to destroy.

The future

Like the U.S. the Soviets are deeply involved in developing a reusable space transportation system, which U.S. officials believe could be operational by the mid-1980s using a piloted booster capable of being flown back to Earth for reuse. The Soviet shuttle mated with the booster would take off horizontally from a runway. Once speed and altitude are sufficient for the orbiter to continue alone, the booster would separate and return to a Soviet airstrip for a horizontal landing.

In less than two decades satellites already have become key elements in military communications, reconnaissance, early warning, navigation, and meteorological systems. Soon the U.S. and Soviet shuttle transportation systems will accelerate the pace of development by making it possible to assemble large structures in the weightlessness of space. Using arrays of solar cells or nuclear fuel sources with power outputs many times the capability of today, new and possibly still unimagined machines will soon ply the skies above the Earth, ensuring continued security and peace for nations that, at least for the near future, must live in mutual mistrust.

N. Y. to L. A. in 54 Minutes– by Subway

by Robert M. Salter

Lightweight passenger trains traveling far underground in evacuated tubes may someday make a one-stop trip between New York and Los Angeles in less than an hour.

For several years a number of scientists and engineers have been envisioning an ultra-high-speed subway system called "Planetran" that will be able to provide coast-to-coast service in the United States in less than an hour. The system potentially can be extended to South America—and to Europe, Africa, and Asia via a link under the Bering Strait. Convenient, safe, quiet, and pollution-free service would be offered. Planetran is expected to be highly efficient, carrying passengers and light cargo using only a small fraction of the energy needed by aircraft and automobiles. Its cost would be high ($250 billion or more) but, its advocates believe, not high in comparison to the services it would provide, the economies it would enhance, or the energy it would save over the coming years.

Planetran "trains" would consist of lightweight cars which are "floated" by magnetic repulsion between vehicles and guideway. These repelling magnetic fields would be phased so as to produce a traveling wave along the guideway. This magnetic wave would provide both vehicle support and propulsion (or braking).

Planetran tunnels would follow the Earth's curvature and would be generally located several hundred feet below the surface in rock structures. Besides evacuated tubes for high-speed Planetran travel the tunnels would also house conventional railroad lines and power lines, communication links, and pipelines. This shared usage would help defray tunnel costs, which are the major element in Planetran's overall expense.

Early studies

The concept for Planetran evolved in 1957 from research at Lockheed Aircraft Corp. concerning the potential of space-derived systems for public transportation. It was readily apparent that the high-speed advantage offered by space vehicles (and ballistic transporters and hypersonic aircraft) could only be achieved after a lengthy climb to upper altitudes to find a rarefied enough atmosphere for low-drag operation. The idea of replicating such a low-pressure atmosphere in evacuated terrestrial tubes appeared as a ready alternative. It was known, based upon conventional electric motor technology, that repelling electromagnetic fields could be devised that could both "float" and propel a vehicle at high speeds. It was also known that with high currents made available through superconductivity, large enough repulsion forces could be achieved to levitate the Planetran vehicle as much as a foot above the guideway. What was not known at that time was a suitable method for providing the rigorous control needed to keep lateral accelerations within the guideway to an absolute minimum. Therefore, the project was abandoned until 1969, when it was determined that microelectric computing electronics would soon be a reality and could be employed to solve lateral acceleration control problems.

When consideration of the project was resumed, initial studies indicated possible nonstop times between Los Angeles and New York City of as little as 21 minutes. This would require a one G acceleration to midpoint and one G deceleration from there to the terminus. A "G," representing an acceleration of 32 feet per second per second, is equivalent to the gravitational force felt at sea level. A one-G horizontal thrust combined with an individual's

ROBERT M. SALTER is Senior Physical Scientist at the Rand Corporation, Santa Monica, California.

weight results in a force of 1.4G. With a properly inclined seating arrangement a passenger thus would "feel" 40% heavier. Later, more detailed research, however, was based upon slower speeds. The main corridor in this instance would provide for one stop in Dallas, Texas, and involve 1/3-G thrust schedules. At this level of acceleration/deceleration and with properly positioned seats a passenger would feel only 5% heavier during thrusting or braking periods.

Each link of this one-stop case (Los Angeles–Dallas and Dallas–New York City) would be 1,360 miles in length and would take 27 minutes to traverse. Through-cars from Los Angeles to New York City (or conversely) would pause for only a few seconds in Dallas so that the overall transcontinental passage would require 54 minutes. Passenger cars bound for Dallas or for connections to points from Dallas would be rapidly switched into the terminal and replaced in a few seconds by preloaded cars destined for New York City or Los Angeles.

Planetran routes

Selection of Planetran routes will require consideration of both terrain physiography and areas to be served. The particular links chosen in this discussion are for purposes of analysis. A future system could be somewhat different.

Care must be exercised in the process of laying out the route system, both to assure optimal passenger service and to be responsive to Planetran's impact on the nation's population growth patterns. This latter point raises interesting issues. One question might be whether to arrange the Planetran system to serve existing population centers or design it to encourage growth in other areas.

In the early days of the railroads, cities grew as clusters along the rail line right-of-way. It was a relatively straightforward process to provide local streetcar transportation as a simple extension of the railroad. With the advent of the automobile and later the airplane, people were no longer constrained to live and work along those corridors, and urban growth became more diffuse. One of the problems faced in attempting to institute local mass transit is that people presently live and work in much more random geographic distributions than in the past, so that local corridor-type service is now frequently unworkable.

The Planetran concept does not attempt to solve this problem. However, the system would be designed to fit those facilities that exist in the metropolitan centers served—freeways in Los Angeles, subways in New York City, etc. Besides coast-to-coast links Planetran would also have intermediate and local routes to provide for a completely integrated service.

Planetran would be designed with connections to airports and to complement rather than to compete with air service. Combinations of Planetran/air would in many instances improve service, even to areas not included in the Planetran network.

The overall system chosen for purposes of discussion generally covers the East, Central, and Pacific Southwest regions, with the Southeast, Northwest, and Rocky Mountain regions served only by aircraft. The system would

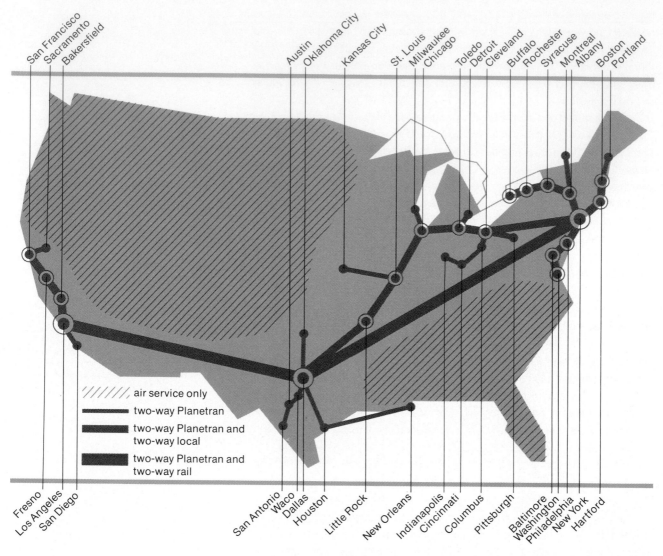

San Francisco
Sacramento
Bakersfield
Austin
Oklahoma City
Kansas City
St. Louis
Milwaukee
Chicago
Toledo
Detroit
Cleveland
Buffalo
Rochester
Syracuse
Montreal
Albany
Boston
Portland

/////// air service only

▬▬▬ two-way Planetran

▬▬▬ two-way Planetran and
two-way local

▬▬▬ two-way Planetran and
two-way rail

Fresno
Los Angeles
San Diego
San Antonio
Waco
Dallas
Houston
Little Rock
New Orleans
Indianapolis
Cincinnati
Columbus
Pittsburgh
Baltimore
Washington
Philadelphia
New York
Hartford

The proposed Planetran system offers a coast-to-coast main tunnel and intermediate feeder lines. The network would be designed to complement rather than compete with air travel.

have 7,800 miles of tunnels containing 21,000 miles of high-speed tubes and 2,700 miles of railroad lines. It would be arranged to serve approximately 80% of the U.S. population. It is anticipated that rail lines might be substituted for some of the local high-speed links in order to provide local rail passenger and auto/rail service.

It is assumed that most of the tunnels would be 40 feet in diameter and capable of containing either four evacuated tubes or two tubes and two rail lines. Because tunnel costs would comprise most of Planetran's overall expense, an optimum system would provide for maximum utilization of these tunnels. A total of 2,400 miles of the intermediate feeder lines would use two-tube tunnels approximately 28 feet in diameter. The Los Angeles–Dallas –New York City corridor would have the two-tube/two-rail arrangement. A second main corridor would extend from Dallas to Chicago to New York City and employ four high-speed tubes in a tunnel. Two of these would be for nonstop service from Chicago to New York City or Dallas, and two would be for local service to Little Rock, St. Louis, Toledo, and Cleveland.

Instead of two-way local service in a four-tube tunnel, planners have considered operating locals in one direction only. Because of the high speeds achieved, passengers could go the long way around to their destination. An example is the New York City–Boston link with local traffic to Hartford, Connecticut. By running local traffic only in the New York City to Boston direction, a traveler from Hartford to New York City would go by way of Boston. Hartford to Boston on the local would take 7 minutes, and Boston to New York City 11 minutes for a total time of 18 minutes. Traffic volume might be high enough to warrant two-way local service, but otherwise the extra tunnel space could be given over to local railroad service that, for the New York City–Boston link, would alternate in direction on a 75-minute cycle. Four-tube tunnels would also be deployed from New York City to Buffalo, New York, and to Washington, D.C., and from San Francisco to Los Angeles with two to three intermediate cities.

Energy utilization

Each Planetran car in any given link follows the same rigorously determined and controlled schedule. The superconducting current loops in the vehicle provide high magnetic dipole fields to repel the traveling magnetic waves in the track structure, which both levitate and propel (or brake) the vehicle. Planetran's precisely controlled electrical machinery is analogous to conventional synchronous electrical motors and generators, and thus can probably achieve the latter's efficiency.

Because Planetran cars do not need to be carried aloft to acquire an appropriately low-drag atmosphere (as do aircraft) and because magnetic levitation is highly efficient (lift-over-drag ratios perhaps 60 times those of aircraft), almost the only energy needed to be supplied would be that for kinetic energy of motion. Furthermore, just as in the conventional streetcar, Planetran's electrical braking would recover nearly all of this kinetic energy as electricity returned to the power lines.

It is estimated that with Planetran passengers and goods could be carried cross-country for a small percentage of the energy required by present-day aircraft. And because the future hypersonic aircraft transport will need a several-fold increase in fuel over existing planes, Planetran's energy-utilization advantage over the latter would be very high. Such advantage is further enhanced by the fact that Planetran would not need such mobile fuels as gasoline, which are likely to be scarce in the future. Furthermore, Planetran would not pollute the skies with heat, combustion products, and noise.

Recent analyses of the world's future energy supply situation forecast that the real limitation will not be on energy resources but on the money to develop them. Studies predict that world capital accumulation of $\$40 \times 10^{12}$ will be required to provide needed energy supplies by the year 2020, while only $\$10 \times 10^{12}$ will be available on a business growing-as-usual basis. To provide adequate capital accumulation will require a 12% reduction of the share of gross world product going into energy consumption—if a start to rectify the problem is made immediately. If there is a wait of 15 years to start the cut in consumption, the rate needed will be about 24%.

Brookhaven National Laboratory's prediction on U.S. energy flow in 1985 indicates that 28% will go into transportation, with three-quarters of this into automobiles and aircraft. Only 1% will be used by electrified rail systems. Because Planetran would use only a few percent as much energy per passenger mile as air and auto transport, replacement of half the traffic of these two modes by Planetran could achieve a 10% savings in total U.S. energy flow. Coupled with truck and rail freight energy savings via Planetran tunnel corridors, this would accomplish an overall energy consumption reduction by the Planetran system of approximately 12%—the reduction needed for adequate capital accumulation. Thus Planetran's mission to provide fast, convenient, nonpolluting service would be expanded to aid in the problem of conserving energy resources.

System control

Microprocessor control is a necessary part of the Planetran system. At speeds of thousands of miles per hour only small excursions from the prescribed paths of the vehicles can be permitted. Otherwise, with any kind of transverse motion, the passengers would experience high side forces.

By placing microprocessor computing elements at frequent intervals along the Planetran guideway, it is possible to provide this sort of control. Each of a number of periodic sensing stations along the tube wall would detect any departure of vehicle motion or position from a prescribed standard when Planetran cars pass its position. Information regarding any such departures would be transmitted along the tunnel in advance of the vehicle. Correcting stations would receive the error data and transform them into correction signals by high-speed microcomputer. If a particular departure is large, it may not be entirely corrected at the next station but perhaps at several along the way. Each station computer would have a built-in reference system that would provide the optimum set of precomputed corrections for any combination of Planetran position and velocity errors detected.

This correction system would also accommodate movements of the guideway (from Earth tremors or other sources). Inertial detectors placed on the evacuated tube wall would provide error data to the vehicle motion correction system. This would be done in such a way that even if the guideway structure moves, the magnetic field that it provides (to levitate the vehicle) would remain fixed in inertial space—a three-dimensional reference frame fixed in position relative to interstellar space. The evacuated tubes would be mounted on rollers and provided with sensor-controlled jacks in order to position them properly should the tunnel be displaced due to an earthquake.

Car and tube design

Planetran cars would be of lightweight construction similar to an aircraft fuselage. A large superconducting current cable located in the car bottom would provide for the vehicle magnetic field(s). This cable must be maintained at superconducting temperatures of a few degrees above absolute zero ($-459.67 °$ F) by means of liquid-helium cooling. The helium would be refilled at each vehicle turnaround.

The magnetic fields for the guideways could be supplied either by a triggered pulse-forming network (PFN) as in a linear accelerator or by continuously oscillating traveling waves from an alternating-current supply as in a linear-induction motor. The first choice has less electrical loss, while the second requires less expensive hardware. The second type of system has been assumed because it has greater flexibility for multicar trains.

Cars travel in a reduced atmosphere of 0.1% of sea level pressure (equivalent to that at about 170,000 feet of altitude). This level of vacuum is not difficult to achieve, requiring only "roughing pumps." (Vacuum systems employ large, mechanical pumps—piston or vane type—for initial reduction of pressure to a fraction of an atmosphere. Other, more sophisticated pumping systems are then employed to attain high heads of vacuum.) Large fusion power reactors and particle accelerators, for example, have internal densities less than one-billionth of Planetran's atmosphere. Drag losses are negligible. Total cost of vacuum systems (based on two 2,600 cubic feet per minute roughing pumps per mile) for all links is estimated at $320 million.

Prestressed high-strength concrete would probably be used both for the tube's vacuum shell and for tunnel lining. This would be based on concrete already used for defense purposes, which can withstand forces of 10,000 pounds per square inch. An approximate estimate of the cost is $63 billion for 21,000 miles of vacuum shell. Such concrete is dense enough for vacuum purposes, but a plastic or glaze wall coating would be added to provide a margin of safety. The joints would be simple sleeve clamps over O ring-type packing with some allowance for cocking of one tube section relative to the next for alignment changes.

Other Planetran features would include provisions for emergency system stopping, fail-safe design for the car life-support apparatus, quick-opening computer-controlled gates (valves) at tube ends, terminal car-handling networks, and tube vacuum pumping and sealing. To reduce longitudinal airflow in the vacuum locks airbaglike attachments at either end of a Planetran car would partially inflate as the vehicle moves into or out of the vacuum-tube region. These same bags, fully inflated, also would serve to seal off a portion of the tube in the event of an emergency stop for the vehicle. Periodically placed hatches in the tube wall would permit passenger emergency exits.

The Fast Rail System

The Planetran system routeway offers the potential for the establishment of an advanced Fast Rail System (FRS) in Planetran tunnels. FRS would be designed to interconnect with existing railroads and to carry semitrailers, container cargo, campers, and items too bulky to fit inside Planetran cars. FRS would share power and service installations with Planetran.

The FRS would consist of a two-way transcontinental link (via Dallas) plus potential substitutions in four-tube links. Computer-controlled trains would travel on rails at 100 miles per hour and would be electrically driven. Rail travel within Planetran tunnels would offer conditions of negligible curvature, grades limited to ½%, and no side winds or other weather problems. Original concepts were to place standard rail cars within self-powered, highly stream-

lined gondolas with steel wheels-on-rail support. It was found, however, that a conventional rail system utilizing Planetran's favorable tunnel conditions would probably be the best choice in trading off performance against convenience. One critical problem is the reliability of wheel bearings, particularly those of the old "journal" variety. FRS might have to be limited to "roller freight" cars, those that employ roller bearings in wheel journals.

FRS trains would be assembled at marshaling yards contiguous to an FRS/Planetran on/off ramp. Trains would be accelerated to tube speed and phased into a train in the tube under computer control. Train segments would be interconnected in the tunnel to form trains of length sufficient to reduce air resistance. Tunnel trains could be reformed with only slight speed changes in order to add or discharge cars to or from the system. Input/output maneuvers would be performed at any point where the roadway altitude is compatible with surrounding territory, making FRS available to cities and areas where no Planetran terminals would exist.

Trains would be closely spaced and under phase-locked control. Coast-to-coast service would take about a day in transit, obviating much of the need for transcontinental trucking and reducing many air-freight requirements. FRS would be a boon to container shipping, providing the long-sought "land bridge," coast-to-coast link and carrying seven million tons per day.

Tunneling requirements

Nearly all of Planetran's routes would be underground. Tunnels would be at least several hundred feet down in order to find solid rock. In some instances depths of a mile or so would be necessary when tunneling under mountains or ocean straits.

High-speed sections of Planetran would require large route curvatures, while with FRS all but the gentlest of grades (½%) must be avoided. This would place severe constraints on route siting, particularly in mountainous areas. Although one-mile depths are possible, extensive lengths far underground are not desirable because of additional access requirements. It is believed (although not assured) that routes can be found that meet the above objectives.

Tunnels would represent a major problem for Planetran, and most of its cost. The best system compromise would be one that minimizes tunnel costs at the expense of other system components. Placing several tubes in one tunnel is one economy measure. Planetran vehicles also should be narrow to minimize tube size. Smaller tubes are advantageous for reasons of vacuum pumping, tunnel packing, and use of smaller acceleration hardware.

Present-day tunneling techniques are expected soon to be greatly enhanced by more effective procedures. These would utilize advanced tunnel-boring machines, water-jet drills, laser and particle beam devices, hypersonic rock fractures, and the Los Alamos "Subterrene" heated tungsten probe that literally melts its way through hard igneous rocks.

In order to minimize lateral acceleration it is necessary to make the tunnels as straight as possible. This requirement would also affect route choice. Proper Planetran siting would involve detailed computer analyses of terrain contours and geological formations. These surveys along with the actual

Planetran tunnels could be adapted for several different purposes. One concept (opposite page) envisions a structure containing four tubes, two fitted with tracks for standard railway cars (top) and two designed as evacuated magnetic guideways for use by the Planetran vehicles (bottom). Such a tunnel would be about 40 feet in diameter and would probably be used for coast-to-coast service.

39

Planetran tunnel excavations would greatly contribute to a national inventory of subsurface resources.

Other tunnel uses

Sharing of facilities would help pay the high cost of Planetran tunnels. Included among these contemplated underground systems are pipelines for oil, water, gas, waste disposal, and slurries of materials such as coal and other bulk commodities; communication links, including fiber-optic channels for lasers and microwave waveguides; electrical power transmission lines such as superconducting cables; and passenger and freight-hauling systems.

Superconducting power cables require a controlled environment to protect the cryogenic refrigeration system that makes superconduction possible. A controlled-access tunnel is a virtual necessity for such a system. This type of power cable may alleviate many of the problems of siting of the future power station because it can be located at great distances from the user and yet suffer negligible power losses in transmission. Nuclear reactors, for example, could be located in cold regions and the thermal effects of their cooling effluent perhaps employed in useful ways.

Laser communication channels along with "repeater" stations will most certainly also require the protection of an enclosed channel. Future video-phone services will require millions of wide-band links. Thus, even though present fiber-optic laser links can carry up to 50 two-way video channels on a hair-sized filament, some 1,000,000 of these links might be needed. Along with signal boosters this communication system could by itself occupy a sizable portion of a tunnel. Tunnels might also be useful for the deployment of strategic nuclear weapon systems and to provide civil defense shelters.

Economics

The cost of the complete Planetran system (except for the FRS rail system and other tunnel uses) is estimated at $250 billion, which includes $122 billion for tunnels and terminals, $63 billion for evacuated tubes, and $65 billion for system hardware (in 1979 dollars). It is assumed that fares would be priced at $1 per minute in the system. Thus transcontinental passenger fares would be $54. Planetran-carried freight rates would be 15 cents per ton-mile. On the shorter links freight rates would be 40 cents per ton-mile. With 200 passenger or equivalent freight cars going both directions on one-minute headways and the assumed $1 per minute fare, revenues of $182,400 per minute or $96 billion per year are computed. Because energy costs are about 1% of the total, nearly all of this revenue can be applied to amortized investment cost.

Planetran's short transit times would make it possible for a businessman in New York City to travel to Los Angeles during his lunch hour, hold an afternoon meeting, and return at his regular quitting time. His desire to do this would be greatly enhanced if Planetran coast-to-coast fares were reduced to perhaps $6. This might be possible at a 15-fold increase in volume by using 500-passenger trains and ten-second headways.

Planetran's tunnel costs would also be reduced by sharing them with other underground system users. FRS contributions alone would be significant.

Will Planetran be built?

The construction of Planetran would require prodigious measures in system engineering management, but no scientific breakthroughs would be needed. Critical areas include tunnel alignment, vehicle lateral acceleration, vehicle control and damping, and the tunneling process itself. However, the technology needed to develop these already exists.

Will such a system ever be developed? The political outlook is much less optimistic than the technical one. History has shown that some projects, such as tunneling under the English Channel, proposed in the time of Napoleon, can be delayed for centuries because of political pressures. One aspect of the project that may be politically appealing is that the tunneling can be done in many places simultaneously, utilizing local resources.

How long would it take to build Planetran? Construction time would greatly depend upon the priority placed on the project. If such a development were pursued with the same diligence and vigor as the Manhattan Project for the atomic bomb or the U.S. Air Force's ballistic missiles and space program, then perhaps Planetran could be installed within a decade.

Both of these other programs were directed by special project teams. This so-called "skunk-works" approach (named after a special department at Lockheed where several advanced planes were produced) has been considered by the U.S. Department of Defense for some future high-priority programs. Such an approach is needed to cut through the bureaucratic red tape and overlapping jurisdictions that face any large undertaking.

Initially placing Planetran development under military sponsorship probably would be a necessity because most other governmental organizations have not had experience in procuring and managing large, complex projects. An exception to this was the management of the Apollo project by NASA (the U.S. National Aeronautics and Space Administration), but one should note that the Apollo's early development was directed by Air Force generals.

A formula for developing Planetran appears to be to utilize U.S. military skills in procurement and management, and in the development of the brick-and-mortar facilities, to team this with industry development of the innovative and advanced technological aspects of the problem, and to set up a special project organization composed of personnel drawn from both of these areas.

Are there reasons to develop Planetran? To many the answer is yes—perhaps not exactly in the form of the system described above but certainly something that closely resembles it and that satisfies Planetran's objectives. A system having Planetran's economy of operation and potential convenience to the public is a virtual necessity in the solution of future transportation and energy-supply problems. Planetran would also relieve pressures on the environment stemming from crowded highways and polluted skies.

The world population is growing rapidly. Projects to accommodate it should be started now. What is imminently required is a vigorous program of planning for the future that incorporates concepts for enhancing all facets of society—transportation, communication, education, energy, environment, etc. If we wait too long, our goal will no longer be that of achieving a better society but a desperate effort to preserve that which we have.

41

Spare Parts for People

by W. J. Kolff and John Lawson

The Bionic Man of television has his real-life counterparts in the thousands of people who have been furnished with artificial body parts, ranging from blood vessels and kidneys to arms and legs.

In a number of centers throughout the world groups of scientists are working on the development of a "bionic man." They are not trying to create the semihuman superman favored by writers of science fiction but instead are hoping to produce useful replacements for vital organs that have been damaged or destroyed so that recipients might lead comfortable and productive lives.

The basic concepts behind the creation of artificial organs can be traced back to ancient times when men first began to use wooden crutches as functional replacements for amputated legs. By the beginning of the 20th century, artificial arms, legs, teeth, and aids for defective vision were available. Stimulated by the development of the first artificial kidney and heart-lung bypass machine in the 1940s and 1950s, the American Society for Artificial Internal Organs was formed in 1955. Indicative of the expanding interest in bioengineering is the foundation of European, Japanese, and international societies for artificial organs within the last five years.

Perhaps the most important reason for this rapidly expanding interest is the recent progress in the fields of electronics, computers, chemistry, and materials sciences. Developments in these areas have provided the basic building blocks for numerous artificial organs.

A small but growing group of physicians has been trained in engineering as well as medicine. Bioengineering as a specific discipline is gaining acceptance at many schools of engineering. Nevertheless, most bioengineering projects are the result of collaborative efforts between several medical and engineering specialists and often demand input from materials scientists, physiologists, chemists, physicists, and various types of technicians.

Artificial eyes and ears

An illustration of the collaboration of disciplines and people in bioengineering is the artificial eye project headed by William Dobelle, a physiologist and director of the Artificial Organs Division at Columbia University. He uses a device developed by physicists and engineers at the Microcircuit Laboratory of the University of Utah. In turn, the device is implanted in blind volunteers by neurosurgeons at medical centers in the United States and Canada.

The artificial eye being developed by this group of scientists is based on direct electrical stimulation of points in the brain's visual cortex. Platinum electrodes are arrayed on a thin Teflon® plate that is inserted in a fold of the occipital lobe of the brain by the neurosurgeon. Each time a point is stimulated by a minute electrical charge, a dot of light appears in the blind volunteer's visual field. The electrode array consists of eight rows of eight electrodes for a total of 64 electrodes. Future plans call for arrays containing hundreds of electrodes, which would allow a patient to visualize a picture. One complication is that there is no correlation between the area of the visual cortex being stimulated and the location of the dot of light in the patient's visual field. Thus, every patient must have his visual cortex mapped on an individual basis. Once the map is completed, information can be transmitted visually to the patient. For example, the present 64-electrode array has been used to form Braille letters in the blind volunteer's visual field, allowing him to read Braille by seeing rather than feeling the letters.

W. J. KOLFF is Director of the Institute for Biomedical Engineering and JOHN LAWSON is Head of the Division of Artificial Organs, both at the University of Utah.

Paintings and drawings by Kinuyo Y. Craft. Photographs by Dan McCoy—Rainbow

44

In addition to the development of an electrode array and the neurophysiologic data necessary to provide the proper stimulation of the brain, the artificial eye will also demand the use of a viewing device, perhaps a miniature television camera, and a microcomputer to translate what the viewing device sees into the proper stimulation pattern for the visual cortex. There should be no barrier to miniaturizing all the elements of such a system to the extent that they would be easily portable by the blind person.

Direct electrical stimulation of the visual cortex has a close analogue in a proposed artificial ear that involves electrical stimulation in the inner ear. In some ways the artificial ear would be more complicated than the artificial eye. For example, the perceived pitch of a sound can be affected both by the placement of the electrode in the cochlea, the seat of the hearing organ, and by the frequency of the electrical stimulation. Experimental work on the artificial ear, as is the case with the artificial eye, is being carried on with the aid of sensorially deprived volunteers.

The kidneys, liver, and pancreas

Artificial kidneys, or dialysis machines, have been used for patients with kidney failure for more than 30 years. In 1978 approximately 38,000 patients were treated by dialysis in the United States. Dialysis machines replace the filtering function of the natural kidneys. Blood is taken from a patient's body and pumped over or through a membrane, usually made of a cellulose material, on the other side of which is a dialysis fluid. Waste materials carried in the blood plasma can cross the membrane and enter the dialysis fluid,

Eye, nose, and part of the cheekbone are all artificial, made from plastics and tinted to match the recipient's skin tones and iris color.

45

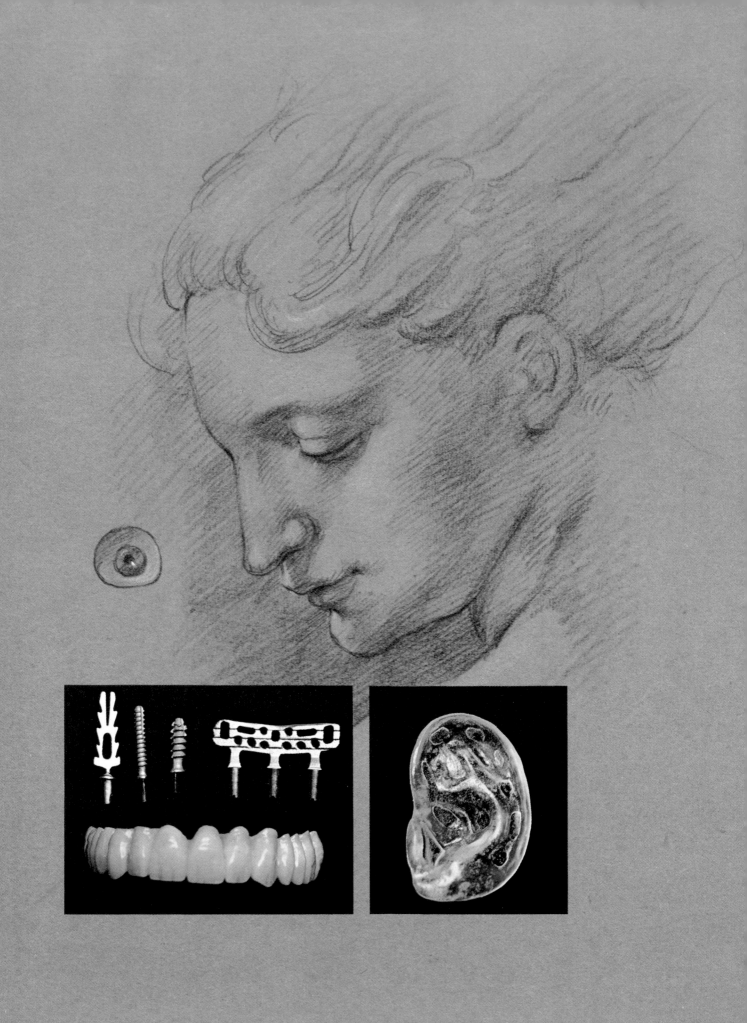

which is discarded when the dialysis is completed. The blood is returned to the patient.

An alternative to this process is to use the natural peritoneum as a membrane. In peritoneal dialysis the dialysis fluid is pumped into the peritoneal cavity and then pumped out again. The advantage of peritoneal dialysis is that blood does not have to be pumped out of the body. This advantage is especially important for elderly and/or atherosclerotic patients, where access to blood is particularly difficult, and also for diabetic patients who should not have their blood anticoagulated, as it must be if the blood is to be pumped to an extracorporeal membrane.

Both forms of dialysis necessitate attaching the patient to bulky equipment for about 12 hours every week. An important goal of bioengineering efforts to improve the artificial kidney is to develop a system that will be less disruptive of the patient's life. One way in which this might be done is to miniaturize the artificial kidney. If it were small enough, the patient could wear the kidney and use it while carrying on his normal daily routine. Several small kidneys have been developed, but each of them involves a certain period of time attached to some sort of large liquid container that is not easily portable. The small artificial kidneys utilize hemoperfusion, in which the blood is passed over some solid material such as coated charcoal, resin, or oxystarch, but none of the presently available materials removes sufficient amounts of urea to allow a completely wearable artificial kidney.

Many toxic substances can be removed from blood by a healthy liver, but even a healthy liver can be overwhelmed by massive amounts of toxic substances such as narcotics. A number of attempts have been made to create detoxification systems. These systems usually pass the blood over or through some material such as charcoal or a resin, but inherent in them are such difficulties as blood damage or the danger of having some of the detoxifying material enter the bloodstream. One possible solution to these problems might be to separate the plasma from the whole blood before passing the plasma over the detoxifying material and returning the detoxified plasma to the blood cells for reinfusion to the patient.

Detoxifying blood is only one of several vital functions of the liver, and the devices just mentioned are designed only for short-term emergency use. No feasible completely artificial liver has been developed, but scientists are working with so-called hybrid artificial livers. They are so named because they all use real liver cells in an artificial device; for example, liver cells are grown in capillaries made of plastic.

In the U.S. approximately 4% of the population suffers from some form of diabetes in which the pancreas does not produce the proper amount of insulin. A much smaller percentage of the population suffers from cancer of the pancreas, which may necessitate removal of the organ. Both groups of patients can survive if they observe certain dietary restrictions and take the proper amount of insulin. Bioengineers are developing an artificial pancreas, which, though it will not completely reproduce the functions of the natural pancreas, will automatically provide the proper amount of insulin for the patient's blood whenever it is needed. It will consist of some sort of sensing device, usually a glucose sensor, a pump, and an insulin supply. When the

Silastic®, trade name for a rubberlike substance containing silicone, is used to make cartilage for an artificial ear. The ear is sutured in place and then covered with skin grafts from adjacent areas. Metal implants set directly into the jawbone can support full artificial dentures.

47

glucose level in the blood rises to a predetermined level, the glucose sensor activates the pump, which then injects the insulin into the bloodstream. These devices have been used with some success in human volunteer patients, but long-term implantable versions have not yet been perfected.

Circulatory and urinary systems

One problem common to all the artificial organs described thus far is that they all need to have some connection between the recipient's body and a power source or controlling unit outside the body. In the case of the artificial kidney the machine must be connected to a fairly good-sized blood vessel. This is usually accomplished by creating a fistula or tube leading from an artery to a vein near the skin that can be punctured by a needle. A great deal of research has been devoted to developing materials that can be used for these artificial blood vessels.

Artificial blood vessels made of woven Dacron® have been widely used for more than 15 years, but they have been limited to replacements for the largest arteries. Small arteries are usually replaced with grafts from large veins in the leg. There is no entirely satisfactory replacement for veins, but there are several promising materials, such as Teflon® or graphite, that might be suitable for artificial veins if the proper method for weaving the graft material could be developed.

Siliconized rubber is a widely used implantable material, particularly in plastic surgery, because it is quite nonreactive to various body fluids. For this reason, it is often used as tubing whenever blood is circulated outside the body as, for example, in dialysis or in heart-lung bypass machines. There are instances, however, when it is not suitable. One of these cases is that in

Artificial breast for a post-mastectomy patient is a Silastic® bag filled with silicone gel. It is attached to the body with remaining skin from around the surgical wound.

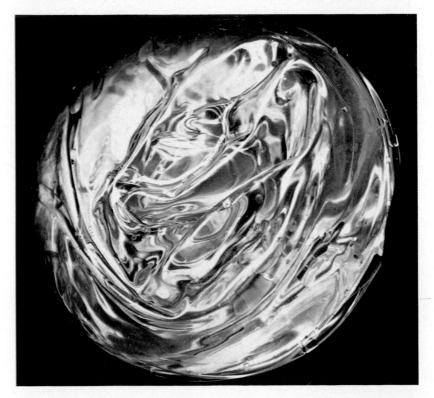

which the material is in contact with urine, as in artificial ureters, bladders, or urethras, because salts such as calcium tend to precipitate onto the surface of the siliconized rubber. More than 10,000 people in the United States lose their natural bladders every year, primarily because of bladder cancer. Usually, a new bladder is constructed surgically from a section of the patient's intestinal tract, but this is a time-consuming and sometimes difficult process that does not always result in a satisfactory bladder. Artificial bladders and ureters would be useful additions to the lists of artificial organs.

One necessary element of an artificial ureter-bladder-urethra system is a set of valves to insure that pressure does not build up in the kidneys and that bacteria cannot migrate to the kidneys. It would also allow the patient to control urination. A number of ingenious valves have been developed. Between the ureters and the bladder are usually duck-bill valves, so named because of their shape. Very small pressure differentials cause them to open, and they are closed in the absence of such differentials. Valves that serve to keep urine in the bladder must be mechanically opened by some voluntary movement by the recipient. One example is a valve that can be opened by digital pressure on a subcutaneously implanted, fluid-filled drum. The pressure on the drum forces the fluid into an implanted bellows, which expands and pushes an enveloping bellows; this, in turn, pulls fluid out of a balloon that serves as the valve at the outflow portion of the bladder.

A second essential element is a material that will not allow the buildup of calcium on the artificial surface. One such material is hydrogel such as is used in soft-lens contact lenses. Hydrogels resist calcification as long as urine is not allowed to form stagnant areas within the device, but they are not strong and are usually grafted onto some other material.

Diseased blood vessels, in this case the junction of the abdominal aorta with the two iliac arteries (left), are replaced with tubing made of Dacron® or Teflon®. Holes in internal organs can be repaired with a patch of synthetic mesh (right), which provides reinforcement until natural tissue eventually grows through it.

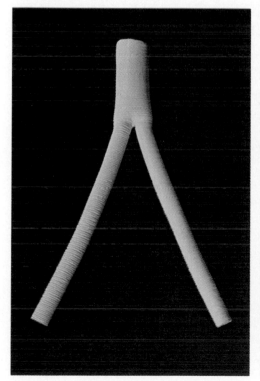

The final ingredient for a successful artificial urinary system is some method for completely emptying the urine from the system. If urine is allowed to remain, salts will tend to precipitate out and form deposits on the artificial material, and the opportunity for infection will be greatly increased. A number of methods for emptying the bladder have been developed, such as spring-powered pumps that can be activated by manned pressure. A unique device used to create a gentle pumping action in an artificial ureter was developed in France. It is powered by the natural movements of the recipient, such as breathing or walking, in much the same way that a self-winding wristwatch takes advantage of the natural movements of the arm. Artificial organs that need no outside power source would be a great advantage.

Cardiovascular system

A great deal of work in bioengineering has been directed toward solving cardiovascular problems. Heart disease is by far the number one cause of death and disability in the U.S. and Western Europe. The development of the heart-lung bypass machine in the middle years of this century has been described by some observers as the most important medical development of the 20th century. Not only did it allow open-heart surgery, which, in turn, enabled surgeons to correct problems that in earlier times would have led to death or disability, but the machine also served as a stimulus for numerous advances in bioengineering, medicine, and physiology.

Thousands of people have partially artificial hearts. The electrical system of the heart may be aided by a pacemaker. Artificial valves for the heart are commonplace. An aneurysm (a blood-filled dilatation of a blood vessel) or hole in the wall of the heart can be patched with a piece of Dacron® graft material. Clogged coronary arteries may be bypassed by new artificial blood vessels. Partially artificial hearts are beginning to be used to assist weak ventricles for limited periods of time, and a totally artificial heart will probably be available for human use within a few years.

The electrical signal that controls the contractions of the heart can

50

become defective. Implanted cardiac pacemakers mimic the natural electrical signal and are used to maintain regular heartbeats. Cardiac pacemakers have been available since the late 1950s and are constantly being improved. The batteries powering the pacemakers have been one area of improvement. Nuclear-powered pacemakers are available, but in the late 1970s lithium-iodide batteries were the most widely used. A recent development was the introduction of programmable pacemakers, which can be programmed by a radio signal to improve the performance of the pacemaker without having to go into the body. Early pacemakers were sometimes damaged by body fluids, particularly at the point where the electrical leads were attached to the heart. However, improved materials, such as siliconized rubber, and construction methods for the leads readily eliminated this problem.

Artificial valves can replace damaged natural valves, some people having as many as three of them. Materials are an extremely important consideration in the manufacturing of artificial valves. The ideal material must be strong enough to last through hundreds of millions of heartbeats yet gentle enough not to damage the blood cells; it also must be nonreactive to the blood and tissues that surround it. Pyrolytic carbon is one widely used material. It has provided the longest lasting valves, but it is usually used only when the recipients may be anticoagulated in order to avoid the probability of clots in the blood. Porcine heterografts (especially, treated pig valves) are becoming more popular. It is not yet clear if the porcine valves will last as long in the body as those made from pyrolytic carbon, but the former are less likely to induce the formation of blood clots.

The heart-lung bypass machine has allowed surgeons to stop a patient's heart so that they can repair a damaged or defective heart. However, in somewhat less than 4% of all open-heart surgery cases the patient's heart is simply too weak to take over the task of pumping blood once the operation has been completed. The earliest developed and most widely used device to assist such hearts is the intra-aortic balloon pump. It consists of a long, thin polyurethane balloon that is inserted into the aorta. The balloon is rapidly inflated during ventricular diastole, when the valve between the left ventricle and the aorta is closed. It is at this time that most of the blood flows into the coronary arteries. The inflating balloon increases the diastolic blood pressure and thus increases the blood flow to the coronary arteries. During systole, when the left ventricle is pumping blood into the aorta, the balloon is rapidly deflated, which lowers the blood pressure in the aorta and reduces the amount of work that the ventricle must do. The intra-aortic balloon pump is sometimes used for patients who must have some emergency support before undergoing open-heart surgery.

Another ventricular-assist device consists of a simple polyurethane tube inserted into the left ventricle or the left atrium. It allows the blood to flow into a roller pump, which then pumps the blood into the aorta. In this way the roller pump takes over the work load of the left ventricle, although the ventricle continues to beat. The theory is that if the ventricle is allowed to rest it will be able to regain its strength in a matter of hours or days. Initial results have tended to confirm this theory.

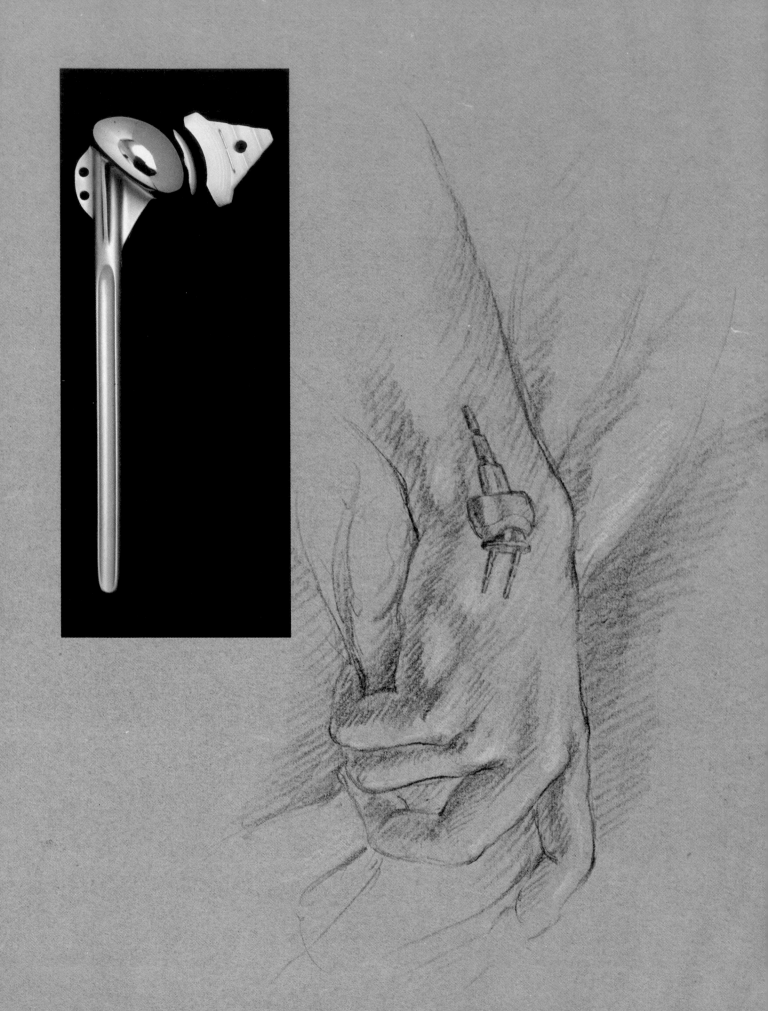

A similar left ventricular-assist device replaces the roller pump with an artificial ventricle. The artificial ventricle, usually made from polyurethane, consists of an air chamber and a blood chamber separated by a flexible diaphragm. As the blood flows into the blood chamber, the diaphragm collapses and the air is pushed or pulled out of the air chamber. When blood has filled the blood chamber, air is pumped into the air chamber; this expands the diaphragm, causing the blood to be pushed out of the artificial ventricle and into the aorta. Unlike the roller pump, this device has the disadvantage of needing artificial valves at the inflow and outflow portions of the artificial ventricle, but it provides a pulsating blood flow, which many believe is an advantage.

Ventricular-assist devices are meant for temporary use. A permanent replacement for the failing heart has been achieved only with a heart transplant. However, transplants are severely limited by the scarcity of donor hearts. There is no chance that there will ever be sufficient donor hearts for all heart-failure patients. Thus, a number of bioengineering centers are working on the development of an artificial heart. Experimental animals have been kept alive and in good health for more than 200 days after their natural hearts have been replaced with artificial hearts. Most of the experimental artificial hearts have been pneumatically powered in a manner similar to the left ventricular-assist devices. The pneumatic artificial hearts consist of two ventricles. Each ventricle has an air chamber and a blood chamber separated by pliant membrane. Sutured to the remnants of the recipient's natural atria, the ventricles are separated from the atria by artificial valves of the types presently used to replace damaged valves in human patients. Pneumatically powered artificial hearts could probably be ready for human implantation within the next year or two, but they are not likely to see wide-scale use because a pneumatically powered heart must remain attached to a source of compressed air; this would mean that the recipient of such a heart would be quite limited in mobility. Some experimental work has been done on a nuclear-powered artificial heart, but popular fears of nuclear power make such a device unlikely to be accepted within the next few years, and funding for such research is declining.

Perhaps the most realistic and practical artificial heart power source would be electricity. A number of devices have been developed for converting electrical energy into a pumping motion, and animal experimentation is under way. The great advantage of electrical energy is that in the form of batteries it is easily portable. Thus, a recipient of an electrically powered artificial heart should be able to lead a relatively normal life, including working at a job and doing moderate exercise.

Arms and legs

Artificial legs have been used for centuries, but only in the last few years has there been the possibility of an artificial leg that is more than a prop. Lightweight, strong materials with miniaturized electric motors controlled by microcomputers offer the possibility of artificial arms and legs that will be able to do what the recipient expects an arm or leg to do.

One experimental artificial arm comes with electrodes that can be taped

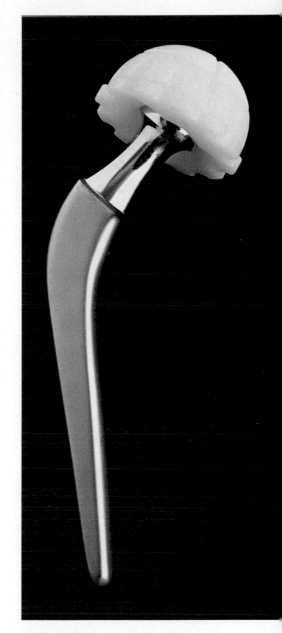

Artificial shoulder (opposite page, left) is a partial ball-and-socket joint that allows motion in at least two directions. A prosthetic wrist joint (opposite page) has been difficult to develop but is now in limited use. The ball in the artificial hip joint (above) is cemented into the natural cavity in the pelvic bone with Plexiglas® in gel form. The descending spike fits into the femur.

onto the shoulder. These electrodes can pick up the electrical signal sent by the central nervous system to control the movement of the muscles of the no-longer existing arm. These signals can be converted by a microcomputer into controls for small electric motors that move the arm. Thus, an amputee could move an artificial arm simply by thinking of moving it.

Future prospects

The entire field of artificial organs is rapidly developing and growing. This fact has been recognized by the U.S. government, which recently acted to put all new devices under the supervision of the federal Food and Drug Administration. The development and testing of all new artificial organs will thus be regulated by standards similar to those used for the development of new drugs. The advantage of this system is that patients will be protected to some degree from faulty devices. The disadvantage is that the development and testing of all new artificial organs will become much more expensive and time-consuming, and life-saving devices may be delayed in reaching the patients who could use them.

The development of artificial organs is only one of three major fields involving bioengineering. Bioengineers are also involved with the modeling of biological systems in mathematical or engineering terms in order to increase knowledge of how these systems work. This might be likened to the basic science of bioengineering as opposed to the applied science represented by the development of artificial organs. A third area involving bioengineering is in the development of diagnostic instrumentation. This is also a rapidly growing field. An instrument that can automatically analyze and measure as many as 20 of the constituent elements in a few drops of blood was unheard of 20 years ago, and yet nearly every hospital in the U.S. has such a machine today.

Silastic® finger joints (opposite page, top) can be implanted in any finger and will allow it to have natural bending motion. Myoelectric arms (below) contain electrodes at their upper ends that receive electrical impulses from the twitching of muscles in the patient's stump. These impulses are highly amplified in order to control motors that open and close the grip of the hand. A feedback vibration tells the wearer when the hand is fully opened or closed. The artificial skin covering the circuitry (opposite inset) can be obtained in various tones and simulates the appearance of natural human skin.

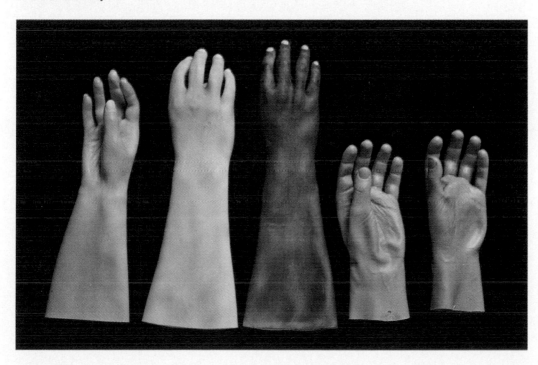

Those Strange New Racing Cars

by
Paul Van Valkenburgh

By experimenting with engines, tires, and chassis configurations, designers and engineers have in 30 years raised the record speeds of racing cars from about 140 to more than 200 mph.

The performance of modern-day racing cars borders on the incredible, even to blasé space-age, computer-age scientists. A supercharged dragster with a V-8 engine can accelerate to 250 mph in 5.6 seconds over a quarter of a mile, which is faster than it could free *fall* the same distance. In doing so it will consume 4.5 gallons of nitromethane (a rate of 18 gallons per mile) and develop well over 2,000 horsepower. A Formula One Ferrari has tires that permit it to corner at almost 2 *G*'s, a force equivalent to twice that exerted on the car by gravity. The same car, taking advantage of aerodynamic drag, also can reach peaks of almost 3 *G*'s in braking. Stock cars have roll cages and fuel systems that are so safe that it is not uncommon for drivers to walk away from 200-mph end-over-end crashes. (A roll cage is a frame-within-a-frame that surrounds the driver.) And the sports cars that compete in the annual race at Le Mans, France, are so durable that they can travel more than 3,000 miles in 24 hours, the equivalent of driving from Boston to Los Angeles in less than a day.

The average spectator, however, is not aware of the statistics and technical accomplishments. What makes automobile racing the third most popular spectator sport in the United States is the mind-wrenching drama, the assault on the physical senses, and, perhaps for some, the implication of impending tragedy.

PAUL VAN VALKENBURGH, a research engineer at Systems Technology, Inc., in Hawthorne, California, and formerly at the Chevrolet Motor Division of General Motors Corporation, is the author of Race Car Engineering and Mechanics (1976). He has also built and driven his own race cars.

There is nothing new in principle about auto racing. Given the competitive nature of humans, it has to be as old as the automobile itself. But, while people have been racing over roads, ovals, and straightaways since the first two motor vehicles met, the evolution of race cars has followed some curious paths. The most influential factor has been the sanctioning bodies.

While all international racing is governed by the Fédération Internationale de l'Automobile (FIA), in the U.S. there are several powerful local sanctioning groups. The United States Auto Club (USAC) is best known for Indianapolis-type cars; the National Association for Stock Car Auto Racing (NASCAR) handles stock car tracks; the Sports Car Club of America (SCCA) and the International Motor Sport Association (IMSA) deal with sports cars; and the National Hot Rod Association (NHRA) is responsible for drag racing. These sanctioning bodies determine the technology of race cars, the speeds that

The four major categories of racing cars include the Formula Ones (left), which compete in the grand prix events; stock cars (center left); sports cars (center right); and dragsters (bottom).

the cars reach, and the future of the sport. They determine what technological innovations will be permitted, and if speeds rise to an unacceptable level they restrict performance by regulations.

No matter what the rules, however, racing speeds inexorably climb. And, regardless of the sanctioning bodies, or the shape of race cars, or the rules, the basic fundamentals are essentially the same for all of them: (1) maximize engine power and driveline (transmission, differential, and axle) efficiency; (2) minimize the weight of the chassis, but maintain acceptable strength; (3) use the biggest, stickiest tires that will last; (4) minimize air drag and maximize aerodynamic downforce; and (5) optimize the driver's environment and controls. There are other constraints such as costs, reliability, and safety, but this discussion will concentrate on the technological factors.

Engines

A racing engine builder of the 1940s would not be confounded in 1979 by any radical advances in basic design. Pistons, rods, cranks, valves, and blocks are still identifiably the same. He would, however, be astounded at the gains in horsepower output. A U.S. seven-liter stock-block (valves actuated by conventional pushrods rather than overhead cams) V-8 engine can develop more than 750 horsepower. The three-liter Cosworth V-8's, when turbocharged for USAC racing, put out over 800 horsepower on methanol. (A turbocharged engine is one that has been supercharged—had air forced into it at a pressure higher than that of the surrounding atmosphere—by an exhaust-driven compressor.) The turbocharged 5.4-liter flat 12-cylinder engines that Porsche built for the Can-Am (Canadian-American) racing series

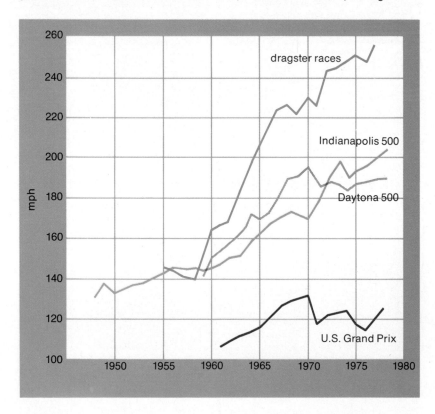

Speeds of various kinds of racing cars have increased considerably over the last 20–25 years. Imposed engine restrictions caused brief declines in speed of the Indianapolis cars in 1974 and in the Daytona 500 stock cars in 1965 and 1971. Changes in the track at the U.S. Grand Prix led to reduced speeds for the Formula One racers in 1971 and 1975.

were reported to produce 1,200 horsepower on gasoline. (A flat engine is one with opposing banks of cylinders lying at 180° to each other.)

The continued increase in horsepower is not due to revolutionary advances but to steady improvements in detail. For example, supercharging is not new, but increases in boost have been made possible by using pistons and valves with improved heat resistance, and by achieving better fuel control and elimination of waste heat. As a rule superchargers have been assumed practical only for straightaway and relatively constant rpm (revolutions per minute) use because of throttle response lag. In 1972, however, Porsche broke tradition by developing the turbocharged 917 Can-Am car. The firm tailored the fuel injection, response rates, and waste gates to produce cars that devastated all competition. Porsche subsequently started using turbochargers in its passenger cars.

Otherwise, engine advancements have come slowly and laboriously. Trial and experimentation have demonstrated that for a given displacement limit, the more cylinders the better. (Displacement is the total volume displaced

Bill Jennaro

Jeff Hutchinson

Innovations in engine design have resulted in greater horsepower. At left is a flat 12-cylinder engine developed by Ferrari for Formula One competition. Below is Ford-Cosworth's V-8 mounted in the rear of Mario Andretti's 1978 grand prix championship car.

Formula One
Exposed-wheel, open-cockpit, single-seater racing car with 3-liter racing engine or 1.5-liter supercharged engine

Formula Two
same as above with 2-liter racing engine

Formula Three
same as above with 2-liter stock-block engine

Formula 5000
same as above with 5-liter stock-block V-8 engine

Indianapolis car
same as above with 2.65-liter super-charged racing engine or 5.8-liter stock-block engine running on any kind of fuel

Stock car
Enclosed stock sedan body with 5.8-liter stock-block V-8 engine

Sports car
Generally two-seater, modified stock body with an open or closed cockpit; there are many classes, based on body and engine size

Dragster
Any vehicle intended for straight-line quarter-mile acceleration runs; there are many classes, based on body and engine size

by the pistons.) The four-cylinder Offenhauser lost out to the Cosworth V-8 at Indianapolis, and the Cosworth, in turn, was being seriously challenged by the Ferrari Flat 12 in Formula One competition. The same seems to be true in valves in that every serious racing engine now has four valves per cylinder. While there in no functional difference whether engine cylinders are arranged in a "V" or horizontally opposed as in the Ferrari and Porsche, the latter case has proved to be quite effective in racing. Although more material and weight are required for a given displacement and block rigidity in the horizontal configuration, it provides a lower center of gravity and reduced airflow blockage to rear wings.

Another area of refinement is increased rpm. For a given torque (rotational force), the higher the rpm available the greater the horsepower. Reducing displacements and increasing the number of cylinders reduces the mass of reciprocating and rotating components. In addition, more sophisticated high-strength materials and a better understanding of structural dynamic forces have resulted in engines that can be repeatedly revved in excess of 11,000 rpm. But, regardless of the strength problems, such engines never would have reached that point without the airflow science which developed fuel-air induction systems that can operate at such speeds.

Along with racing engines one should also consider the practice of modifying production stock-block engines from passenger cars. While this field has suffered from emission regulations and general reductions in size, materials science has recently made some advances. Over the past decade cast-iron V-8 engines such as those in Chevrolets and Chryslers have become available in low-wear, low-porosity aluminum alloys.

Chassis

As race car engineers have learned more about the science of vehicle dynamics, there have been some notable changes in chassis configurations. Low weight and low center of gravity have always been important considerations, but such questions as acceptable stiffness, ideal weight distribution, and proper suspension rates and geometry have been resolved gradually.

The first breakthrough was in the analysis of oversteer and understeer. Oversteer is the tendency of an automobile to steer into a sharper turn than the driver intends, with a consequent thrusting of the rear to the outside. Understeer is the tendency of a car to go straight ahead and turn less sharply than the driver intends. As racers discovered that a tail-out oversteering condition was not only harder on tires but harder to control, the more neutral four wheel drift became vogue. This occurs when a race car goes around a high-speed turn with apparently no steering angle at all. However, because the balance of the car changes as a function of speed, applied power, aerodynamics, braking, fuel load, and other factors, a slight amount of understeer has proven to be more practical.

Until this discovery rear-engine race cars had been relatively unpopular because of their uncontrollability at top speeds, and their tendency to break away into terminal oversteer (leading to a spin). The design transition began in Europe with the Formula One Coopers. Then, when Colin Chapman brought his rear-engine Lotus from Great Britain to Indianapolis in 1965 and

ran away from the front-engine cars, the lesson struck home.

The major advantage of rear-engine design is the increased rear weight distribution, which provides improved drive traction. The major disadvantage had been the necessity for independent rear suspension, which was associated with oversteer characteristics. Independent front suspension has proven to be superior in isolating steering interactions and reducing unsprung weight, which produced better road-holding characteristics. For a while, the deDion rear axle, which had a solid interconnecting axle going around the sprung differential, was tried. But eventually trial and error led to the almost universal acceptance of the unequal-length, double A-arm (double wishbone), independent rear suspension design. For a brief period designers had tried to solve the problems of weight distribution and traction with various four-wheel drive models, but their weight and complexity proved to be intolerable handicaps.

Control of oversteer and understeer turned out to be more than a question of weight distribution and the problem of keeping all four wheels vertical when the chassis rolled in a corner. The roll resistance had to be carefully balanced between the front and rear axles. Too much roll resistance at the rear leads to oversteer and vice versa. To distribute the roll resistance properly, engineers discovered that the chassis had to be torsionally stiff, a previously ignored consideration. Gradually, simple "ladder" frames of the chassis (longitudinal rails with cross members) gave way to the larger-cross-

Rear-engine Lotus (background) out-corners front-engine Offenhauser (foreground) in the 1964 Indianapolis 500. An Offenhauser won the 1964 race, but a Lotus triumphed the next year.

63

section "space frame" consisting of small-diameter tubing welded into fully triangulated structures. Construction costs and the necessity of an enclosing skin eventually led to the use of stressed skins, a type of construction in which the outer skin and the framework interact and most of the stresses are carried by the skin; this is called a monocoque chassis. Finally, the problems involved in getting a chassis around the engine in a narrow Formula car brought about the development of structurally stressed engines. In some instances the engine may actually be the only frame structure aft of the driver.

At the same time, ironically, stock car constructors progressed in the opposite direction. As more production cars were built with unit construction, the need for structural rigidity and impact protection led to the use of full roll cages. The interior of a NASCAR stock car is so heavily reinforced with a steel tube space frame that the body sheet metal is almost unnecessary. Recently, in open-wheel racing, designers found that the pure monocoque chassis is not as efficient as tube frames in accepting point loads such as shock absorber and engine mounts. Designers, consequently, are progressing toward the optimum utilization of both layouts.

Tires

In all the years of racing there never has been any revolutionary change in racing tires. But there has always been a continual increase in size and friction. As recently as 20 years ago, the laws of physics indicated that tire friction was independent of contact area and that it was impossible to get

Courtesy, Daytona International Speedway Corporation

a coefficient of friction greater than 1.0. At the time racing tires were primarily recaps on standard passenger-car cord bodies. (The coefficient of friction is the ratio of traction force to the perpendicular force on the tire.)

Eventually, however, tire engineers realized that spinning dragster tires were developing thrust coefficients greater than 1.0, and so they took another look at rubber mechanics. They discovered that rubber friction includes other dynamic effects. On rough pavement friction is increased by a mechanical gripping of small irregularities, and at high temperatures there is actually a momentary bonding of the rubber to the pavement followed by a shearing of the rubber from the tire. Serious drag racers were preheating their tires by doing warm-up "burnouts" through flaming bleach. The result was so effective that the tires generated an average coefficient of friction of almost 2.3 for a six-second quarter-mile run.

In races where tire life is important, however, such as road or oval racing, such self-destructive wear cannot be tolerated. Under these conditions the maximum coefficient of friction is currently about 1.4.

Most of the gains in race tire traction have been due to the black art of the rubber compounder. Tire rubber is made up of a half-dozen substances which come in hundreds of derivations and grades and which can be combined in an infinite combination of proportions. Added to the natural and synthetic rubbers are: carbon black for abrasion resistance, petroleum and synthetic oils for pliability, resins for resistance to deterioration, and sulfur and zinc oxide for vulcanization. Tire compounders face a continual trade-off

Stock car is readied for competition at Daytona Beach, Florida, in 1979 (opposite page). Richard Petty won the 1979 Daytona 500, driving his Oldsmobile at an average speed of 143.977 miles per hour. The coefficient of friction, the ratio of the tangential force needed to start or maintain relative uniform motion between two contacting surfaces to the perpendicular force holding those surfaces in contact, is seen (below) as a function of tire variables. Racing tires achieve a higher coefficient than street tires as a result of the rubber compounds with which they are made and the width of their treads.

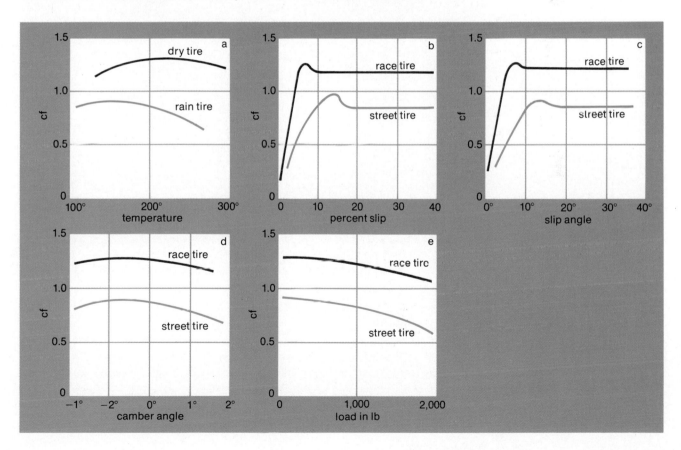

Wide tires of contemporary racing cars can be seen on the Formula One vehicle competing in the Dutch Grand Prix (above). On the opposite page is the type of rear tire used for sports car racing.

between traction and wear resistance, properties which can only be determined by years of experience and experimentation. The primary factors they must consider are total loading on the tire, its average velocity, operating temperatures, and the required lifetime (which may be no more than a few hundred miles).

Once tire engineers realized that increased contact area with the road surface was desirable, they began finding benefits in wider treads. In the early 1960s drag racers were surprised by the introduction of eight-inch-wide slick recaps. At the time cord bodies were a maximum of six to seven inches wide with an oval cross section. Therefore, tread width was limited by

the mass of rubber that could be cantilevered out on the tire's shoulders to create a flat contact area. These rubber shoulders were not reinforced with fabric, and they did not dissipate heat well; therefore, they tended to come unglued after a short time on road or oval courses.

Then engineers discovered the belt, or circumferentially wound cord body, from European radial-tire design. This belt restrained the tire from inflating into an elliptical cross-section by keeping it bound into an essentially cylindrical shape no matter how wide the section. As a result, some passenger car tires now are more than 12 inches wide, and race-tire width is limited only by the rules, currently about 21 inches in Formula One. Pure radial-tire construction was not well received by race drivers because of the lack of torsional stiffness about the steering axis, and so the bias-belted cord body remains most common.

While rubber-compound and cord-body technology can be applied directly to passenger-car tires, race-car tread design cannot. In fact, in the quest for maximum contact area, most current race-car tires have absolutely no tread grooves at all. Of course, such tires are extremely dangerous in rain, and so when rain racing is necessary totally different tires are used. The tread layer is much thicker, with significant longitudinal grooves, and the rubber compound is much softer. But even these tires are so specialized that they carry a label that is common to most race tires—"For Racing Purposes Only"—and they are illegal for street use.

Aerodynamics

Race car builders have worried about air drag from the very beginning. Even when cars had yet to break 100 mph, racers were intuitively streamlining them by removing windshields and fenders and by reducing frontal area. But until recently they ignored the tremendous body of knowledge generated by the aircraft industry. They seemed unaware of the fact that aerodynamic forces increase with the square of velocity. However, now that race-car speeds have doubled to well over 200 mph, where air drag is four times as great, much more attention has been paid to aerodynamics. Nothing has had as great an impact on race-car design in the last two decades.

Until the early 1960s most race cars had nicely rounded and tapered bodies. The ideal seemed to be an aircraft fuselage without wings. But about that time Ferrari brought out a curious innovation, the chopped-off Kamm tail with the rear lip spoiler. The spoiler broke up the smoothness of the airflow over the car's body and thus reduced aerodynamic lift at the rear wheels. Over the next few years other designers began to realize that instead of neutralizing the problem of lift they should exploit the potential of the aerodynamic downforce. Soon, many racing cars from Indianapolis 500 models to NASCAR sedans were sprouting turned-up tails, and today many passenger cars have adopted these designs.

Aerodynamic downforce has repeatedly proven to be of far greater value for increasing speed than shapes minimizing drag. By the late 1970s, ironically, race cars had the shape of an aircraft fuselage *with* wings. Another irony is that open-wheel racers were trying every trick within the rules to increase downforces by enclosing the wheels, and were trying to go faster by putting fenders back on.

In the late 1960s the Chevrolet/Chaparral coalition produced some spectacular innovations in race-car aerodynamics. First, they stumbled onto the realization that high pressures at the nose of the car were creating front-end lift, and so they developed a front-end "plow" to keep air from getting under the car. Then they improved upon the rear spoiler by making it movable, so that it could be aligned to produce less drag on straightaways. But the real revolution was in replacing the spoiler with an actual wing (airfoil) that was mounted above the body. Increased air loads on the body had been compressing rear suspension, so that was also countered by attaching the wing supports to the wheel hubs. There were occasional structural failures due to vibrations, however, which led the sanctioning bodies to require that all wings be attached to the body. But eventually, wings sprouted everywhere, on all types of race cars.

Aerodynamics reached its zenith of originality in 1970 with the Chevrolet/Chaparral "sucker" car. The designers sealed off the underside of the body with flexible plastic skirts and pumped the air out with fans. The sealing was not very good and the fans were not too efficient, but the result was amazingly effective. Considering the fact that the underside of the car covered about 30 square feet, even a pressure reduction of one pound per square inch could add over 4,000 pounds of traction. Unlike the situation with wings this suction traction increase was available even in the slowest corners and created no increase in air drag. As with all radical innovations, however, the concept suffered from lack of detail development, and the car never finished a race in spite of setting course records wherever it went. At the end of that season the concept was banned from racing by an international racing agreement that no movable aerodynamic devices would be permitted.

A recent innovation in wing technology was made by Lotus in the Formula One cars. As a variation of the principle of sealing off the bottom of race cars, most Formula cars adopted flexible plastic skirts at their fronts and sides. These skirts satisfy the rules by being rigidly attached, and yet maintain constant rubbing contact with the pavement by natural deflection. Lotus took

Chevrolet/Chaparral car of the late 1960s incorporates some remarkable innovations in race car aerodynamics. The "plow" at the front prevents air from getting under the car and thereby reduces front-end lift. The wing (airfoil) mounted above the body at the rear reduces drag on straightaways.

Petersen Publishing Company

A Formula One car manufactured by Renault makes a pit stop in the 1977 U.S. Grand Prix at Watkins Glen, New York (opposite page, top). Below it is the rear wing on a Renault Formula One car competing in the 1978 Watkins Glen race. A Chevrolet Monza competes in a 1977 sports car event in Ohio (above). At left, many of the features first tested in Porsche's racing car (background) have been incorporated into the firm's passenger vehicles (foreground).

Patrick Depailler drives the six-wheeled Tyrrell P34 in Formula One competition (top). Below, Niki Lauda drives to victory in the 1978 Swedish Grand Prix in a Brabham Bt46. The rear-end suction fan was later disallowed because it was believed to aid wheel grip unduly.

advantage of these "end plates" on the sides of the body by making the entire body a wing. The front wheels were moved out to the limit, the engine and cockpit were narrowed, and all the rest of the body, from nose to tail, was made one long continuous wing section.

The concentration on aerodynamic downforce, and the lack of concern with aerodynamic drag has had an unmistakable effect on race-car performance. Because of this emphasis straightaway speeds have remained relatively constant, while cornering speeds and average lap speeds have been rising dramatically.

Future prospects

There are two major factors in the future of auto racing. First and perhaps most important are the artificial restrictions of sanctioning bodies. Their primary interest is profit, which depends on attendance. This, in turn, depends primarily on close competition, and not necessarily on technological innovation. From that viewpoint one can expect better marketing and more show business in professional racing. There will probably be fewer design and engineering breakthroughs. However, one can never underestimate the imagination and creativity of competitors. Although racing is moving into an era of limits, in fuels, noise, and costs, someone will almost certainly be able to find a way to innovate successfully within the rules.

Tires are now restricted in width and diameter, but their other aspects are open to experimentation. Certainly there are some rubber compound combinations yet to be tried, using new materials. The same is true in cord materials and arrangements, including, perhaps, radials.

Aerodynamics will continue to be the greatest field for improvement, especially in the area of downforce from ground effect. Better ground seals and skirts will be likely to appear, and new methods for sucking the air out will be developed. If fuel economy is more closely regulated, air drag will again become important, and existing aerospace technology will transfer to cars such concepts as low-drag laminar airfoils.

Engines will probably be more frequently restricted by the use of fuel-consumption limits and plates on the induction orifice. But racers will be likely to counter these by making engines more efficient through a reduction in internal friction drag and better utilization of wasted heat.

The most likely productive area of innovation will probably be electronics. The auto industry's attempts to computerize the control of engine spark and fuel mixtures by using microprocessors will spill over into racing. Even now Formula One racers are experimenting with onboard electronic data recorders and instantaneous performance feedbacks. Eventually, aerospace engineers might even design an onboard inertial-guidance system that the driver simply turns on and monitors for other cars in its optimum path.

Einstein Revisited: A Centennial Evaluation

by Robert H. Dicke

The revolution in science generated by the work of
Albert Einstein is assessed on the one-hundredth
anniversary of his birth.

Albert Einstein was a revolutionary, a perceptive and highly original physicist who was not afraid to break new ground when he believed it to be necessary. In 1905 in a single volume of *Annalen der Physik* (vol. 17) he published three important articles, two of which were so revolutionary that they set physics moving on completely new pathways still being followed.

In these works Einstein seems to have been less influenced by the philosophical concerns that later were so important to him. Rather, it was the conflict between several observations and the physical theories and concepts of the time that drove him toward revolutionary change.

Special theory of relativity

One of these papers of 1905 was his first publication on the special theory of relativity. Einstein relates in his *Autobiographical Notes* how as a boy of 16 he had noted that according to the conventional interpretation of space and time an electromagnetic wave viewed by an observer who was traveling along with the wave at the velocity of light would have appeared to have properties inconsistent with the electromagnetic theory that had been propounded by Scottish physicist James Clerk Maxwell. He apparently puzzled over this for years, finally concluding that a completely new view of the nature of space and time was needed to eliminate the inconsistencies.

It is interesting to compare Einstein's approach to these inconsistencies with the approaches of other physicists. Instead of trying to reconcile the conflicts, as others attempted to do, Einstein saw clearly that a revolution was needed, that a completely new view of the nature of space and time was required.

Einstein's revolutionary ideas were not immediately accepted by all physicists. Some attempted to avoid the paradoxes by working within the framework of Hendrik A. Lorentz's concepts of electromagnetic matter composed of charged particles moving through an "ether." The paradoxes revealed in experiments by Albert A. Michelson, Edward W. Morley, and others were to be viewed as electromagnetic effects that could be resolved by giving matter the "right" electromagnetic structure. While this patchwork approach is not necessarily "wrong" in the sense of being unworkable, Einstein saw that the "preferred frame" required by this approach was without an observational basis.

Einstein's second revolution of 1905 involved the photoelectric effect, the effect due to the interaction of light or other radiation with matter. By noting several inconsistencies between the observations and the classical physical concepts of the time, he became convinced that the photoelectric effect resulted from electromagnetic energy in the form of particles being completely absorbed by single electrons. By ascribing particlelike properties to light while ignoring all the evidence from interference experiments for its wavelike character, Einstein set physics on a new path that ultimately led to quantum mechanics and to a quantum-statistical interpretation of microphysics. The paradoxical dichotomy between wavelike concepts of matter and particlelike concepts persists to this day.

The third great paper of 1905 provided an explanation for Brownian motion, the rapid motion of small, inanimate particles observed with a micro-

ROBERT H. DICKE *is Albert Einstein University Professor of Science and Professor of Physics at Princeton University.*

(Overleaf) Painting by Rob Sauber. Illustrations by William Biderbost

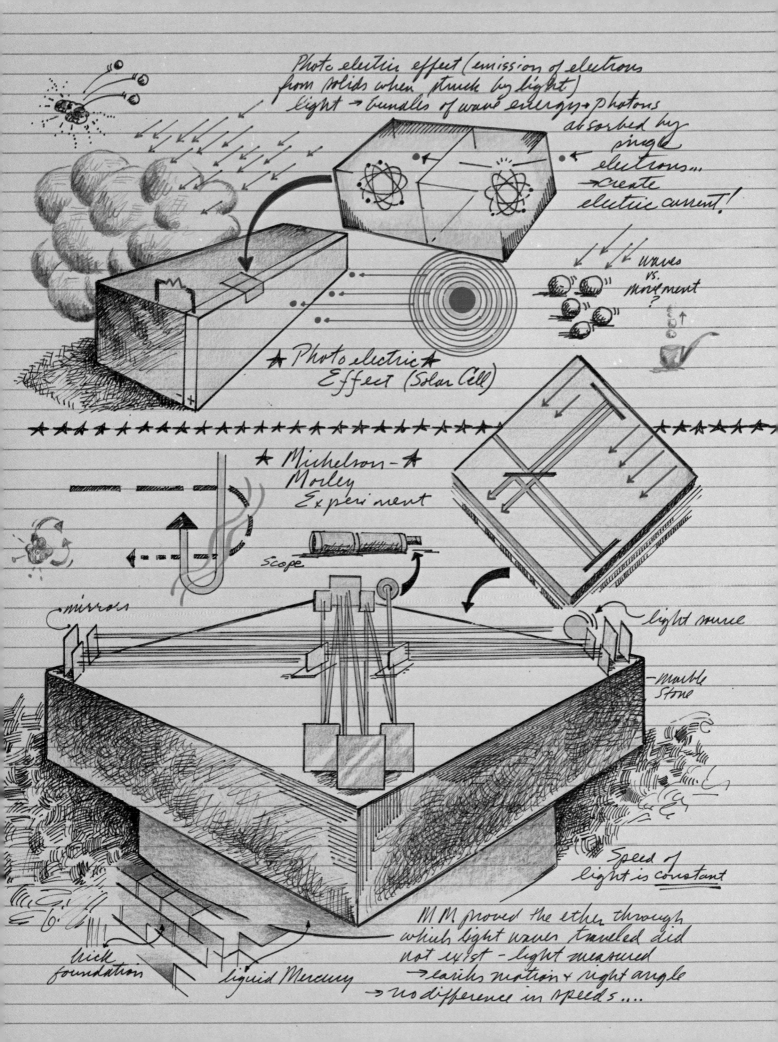

Photo electric effect (emission of electrons
from solids when struck by light)
light → bundles of wave energy → photons
absorbed by
single
electrons...
→ create
electric current!

waves
vs.
movement?

★ Photoelectric ★
Effect (Solar Cell)

★ Michelson — ★
Morley
Experiment

Scope

mirrors

light source

marble
stone

Speed of
light is constant

brick
foundation

liquid Mercury

M M proved the ether through
which light waves traveled did
not exist — light measured
→ earths motion & right angle
→ no difference in speeds....

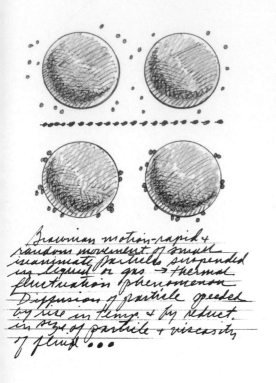

Brownian motion-rapid & random movement of small inanimate particles suspended in liquid or gas → thermal fluctuation phenomenon Diffusion of particle speeded by rise in temp. & by reduct. in size of particle + viscosity of fluid...

scope. From a present-day perspective it is difficult to realize how recent is the acceptance of the ancient kinetic theory of heat. Even as late as 1905 there were well known and respected physicists who doubted the existence of atoms. Einstein made important contributions to the statistical theory of heat, but his most important contribution in the 1905 paper was his explanation of Brownian motion as a thermal fluctuation phenomenon. Here for the first time one could see with one's own eyes the thermal motion of small particles, "molecules" so large that they were visible.

General theory of relativity

Einstein was virtually unknown to the general public until after 1916, when he published his general relativity theory, his relativistic theory of gravitation. (A relativistic theory is one based upon the postulate that the results of experiments are independent of the choice of the frame of reference.) But it was Sir Arthur Eddington's observation of the gravitational deflection of light in 1919, the apparent displacement from their normal positions of stars seen during an eclipse of the Sun, that supported Einstein's theory and made his name a household word.

With his theory of gravitation Einstein again showed his uncanny instinct for revolutionary change. But in this case there seems to be clear evidence that he found the right theory partly for the wrong reason. From his autobiographical notes and other publications it is clear that before 1908 Einstein had turned his attention to relativistic gravitational theory. The natural (and nonrevolutionary) approach was to apply his special relativity theory to Sir Isaac Newton's theory of gravitation.

Treated relativistically, Newton's theory exhibits some remarkable properties. Instead of propagating instantaneously the Newtonian gravitational potential propagates as a wave, with the velocity of light. The gravitational force acting on a particle is proportional to the rate of change of the "gravitational potential" with particle position. The masses of elementary particles interacting gravitationally are not constant but are functions of the gravitational potential. Owing to this mass change, rigid rods and clocks constructed of real atoms vary with the gravitational potential, and the resulting units of length and time vary when compared with the units of length and time provided by the adopted Minkowski flat-space geometry of special relativity. Measured by these real rods and clocks, the geometry is that of a curved (Riemannian) space. (This was noted later, by Einstein and A. D. Fokker, in 1913.)

Einstein seems to have rejected this relativistic theory of gravitation mainly because he believed that it would result in some laboratory-sized bodies falling with the wrong gravitational acceleration, that is, contrary to the observations. With this theory the gravitational acceleration of a massless particle (such as a photon) is zero. Thus it seemed almost self-evident that the electromagnetic energy contained in a complex body would not contribute properly to the weight of the body. But this self-evident conclusion was shown to be wrong. In a seemingly miraculous way the forces induced by the electromagnetic field on the charged particles of a bound system increase the weight of the rest of the system by precisely the right amount.

78

It had long been known that all kinds of matter fall with the same gravitational acceleration. Newton himself had made the first accurate experiment, and Hungarian physicist Lóránt Eötvös had demonstrated the universal character of the acceleration with an accuracy of 1 part in 10^8. It can be shown quite generally that in the relativistic-Newtonian theory all laboratory-sized bodies constructed arbitrarily of elementary particles coupled to Newton's gravitational potential fall with the same gravitational acceleration and that Einstein's concern about this was without foundation.

It is interesting to speculate about the possible course of scientific history if Einstein had not been misled by his concern about the universal gravitational acceleration. The gravitational red shift, a displacement of spectral spectroscopic lines toward the red (or longer wavelengths) for radiation emitted by atoms on the Sun or other massive bodies, is a prediction of both general relativity and the relativistic-Newtonian (scalar or Nordström) theory of gravitation. If this prediction had been made and the correct red shift had been observed, the latter, incorrect, theory of gravitation would have received strong support.

The relativistic-Newtonian theory would not have properly accounted for the excess rotation of the perihelion of Mercury's orbit, but this anomaly had long been known and had been blamed on possible, but unknown, complexities of the solar system. Because this theory does not predict a gravitational deflection of light, there would have been no incentive to look for one. Therefore, it might have been years before this unexpected effect was discovered and the incorrect relativistic-Newtonian theory was laid to rest.

Einstein's theory of gravitation describes gravitation as a purely geometrical effect. Bodies move gravitationally in a curved four-dimensional space-time along geodesic paths. Geodesics are the curved-space analogues of straight lines in flat space. Thus, the shortest distance between two points in curved space is the distance along the geodesic joining the points. The energy and momentum of matter (including a contribution from gravitation itself) are the sources of the space curvature. Even empty space is capable of propagating gravitational waves, gravitation generating new gravitation.

In his first (1916) publication on general relativity, Einstein suggested three observational tests of the theory. These were the gravitational red shift, the gravitational deflection of light, and the explanation for the excess 43 seconds of arc per century in the rotation of Mercury's perihelion.

The excess motion of Mercury's orbital perihelion had been discovered in 1859 by French astronomer Urbain-Jean-Joseph Le Verrier and had resisted all attempts to account for it. The U.S. astronomer Simon Newcomb had worked diligently on the problem for years and had considered a wide range of possible solar-system interactions. Einstein thus was overjoyed to discover that his gravitational theory could account for all of the excess. In Einstein's theory the transverse gravitational acceleration is increased by rapid motion (up to a factor of two at the velocity of light). At Mercury's perihelion (where it is closest to the Sun) Mercury is moving most rapidly, causing an increased acceleration and an increased curvature of the orbit. This causes the orbital ellipse to rotate in the direction of motion of the planet.

As mentioned above, it was the observation of the predicted gravitational

Mercury moves around sun → ellip. orbit
But never travels in same ellipse twice - Peri-
helion advances faster than predicted by Newton
— Relativity   by 43 seconds...
           Accounts
              for !!

Mercury
  Earth   Plane of
                                          Merc. orbit

Laser Light Experiments → laser beamed from earth
    to moon → reflected by cubes back to earth...
              yields distance within 6 inches
              Also - can compare gravitational
           acceleration of earth & moon toward
                                            sun

moon

cubes -
laser
set up?

Earth   Moon

deflection of light that projected Einstein into the public arena. In 1912 Einstein had inquired of George Hale, a U.S. astronomer, about the prospect of observing a small gravitationally induced shift in star positions. Hale suggested the use of an eclipse of the Sun for the observations. It was seven years before the observation was made. As Banesh Hoffmann pointed out, this was fortunate for in 1912 Einstein's expected deflection (based on a defective theory) was a factor of two smaller than the observed value, which agreed with the prediction of the general relativity theory.

The third test of general relativity suggested by Einstein was the gravitational red shift. This test is quite different from the other two, for the same effect is expected to occur for nearly all relativistic theories of gravitation. In fact, the magnitude of the red shift can be calculated from mass-energy equivalence, energy conservation, and the result of the Eötvös experiment. In retrospect, the early observations of the gravitational red shift of solar lines seem to have been overrated, for they did not take into account properly the large Doppler shifts associated with convection in the deeper lying outer layers of the Sun.

Quest for a unified field theory

Philosophical considerations seem to have been important in guiding Einstein toward general relativity, and they may have led him seriously astray in one important respect after 1918. He became convinced that general relativity was much more than a theory of gravitation and inertia (that property of matter by which it remains at rest or in relative motion unless acted upon by external forces) and that with suitable modification it should be capable of accounting for all of physical phenomena as purely geometrical effects. This started Einstein on his last and unsuccessful revolution, his attempt to construct a unified field theory.

This program was stimulated by the unsuccessful attempt by German mathematician Hermann Weyl in 1918 to generalize Einstein's theory to incorporate electromagnetism. The physicists' view of the physical world was then vastly simpler. Following Lorentz's ideas it appeared that one might be able to account for all physical phenomena in terms of electromagnetic and gravitational interactions. Hence, if electromagnetism could be given a purely geometrical explanation, so might all of physics.

Einstein pursued this revolution tirelessly until the end of his life. He showed the same tenacity that characterized his earlier striving for an acceptable theory of gravitation. His persistence in the face of a growing accumulation of experimental evidence that matter was much more complicated than the simple electromagnetic structure of Lorentz may have been influenced by his failure to come to a satisfactory resolution of the "observational paradoxes" of quantum mechanics. These paradoxes are very deep, and a number of the world's best physicists still believe that they have not been clearly resolved. For Einstein these paradoxes represented a serious stumbling block, and he felt uncomfortable about quantum mechanics. He did not find it a philosophically acceptable theory and consequently was uncomfortable with the new physics based on it.

Einstein died in 1955 without having reached his goal of a unified field theory. Some physicists have been critical of him for his single-minded devotion to this cause for so many years, but precisely the same criticism could have been leveled at Einstein in 1914 for his tenacity in searching so many years for an acceptable theory of gravity. But general relativity resulted from that search!

Decline and revival

After the early excitement raised by the discovery of general relativity, physicists began to lose interest in the theory. This occurred despite its widely recognized significance, mainly because of the difficulty in performing new experiments and because of the absence of contact of the theory with atomic physics, nuclear physics, and the other mainstreams of this rapidly developing science.

The post-Einstein era has, however, witnessed a substantial revival of interest in general relativity. This interest was stimulated in part by new observations. The gravitational acceleration experiment of Eötvös was repeated using improved techniques both in the U.S. and in the Soviet Union, and the universality of the gravitational acceleration of laboratory-sized bodies was established with a precision of 10^{-11} to 10^{-12}, three to four orders of magnitude better than Eötvös's value. Also, for the first time the "Eötvös experiment" was extended to astronomical-sized bodies when the laser-range measurements of the distance to three different reflectors on the Moon permitted the gravitational accelerations of the Earth and Moon toward the Sun to be intercompared with great accuracy.

The gravitational red shift was demonstrated for the first time in the laboratory and with considerable precision ($\sim 1\%$). Radio astronomy contributed greatly improved measures of the gravitational deflection. Planetary radar contributed improved measurements of the rotation of the perihelion of Mercury's orbit and a measure of the gravitational retardation of an electromagnetic wave (closely related to the deflection of the wave).

The significance of the excess rotation of the perihelion of Mercury's orbit as a completely relativistic effect was brought into question in 1966 when it was discovered that the Sun's surface had a distortion that could not be explained as a direct effect of the surface rotation. These 1966 observations seemed to require a distortion of the Sun's gravitational potential, a distortion that could account for 3 seconds of arc per century (out of the total of 43 seconds) as a nonrelativistic effect.

By 1978 this complication had not been satisfactorily resolved. However, it had become clear that the solar distortion was not a simple excess oblateness of the Sun. Rather, it was a more complex nonaxially symmetric distortion rotating on the surface of the Sun with a 12.2-day period (sidereal). It is conceivable that the shape of this solar distortion is not constant in time and that the time-averaged effect on Mercury's orbit is not the three seconds of arc per century derived from the 1966 measurements.

Another contributing factor to the revival of research on general relativity is the current interest in gravitational waves and their detection. It is now generally believed that such waves do exist, that they can be generated in substantial intensities by the gravitational collapse of stars or other large

82

systems, and that they have not yet been observed. A concerted effort is being made to develop instruments to detect these waves.

Black-hole physics is another new active subject. Under general relativity a sufficiently compact massive body cannot be supported by internal pressure and it collapses to a "black hole," a continuously imploding body (as viewed from the outside). One recently discovered remarkable property of a black hole is that according to the theory it acts like a thermally emitting hot body with a temperature determined by its mass.

Another recent source of interest in general relativity is astrophysics. Radio sources, quasars, possible black holes, pulsars, and close binary pairs of compact stars are all astrophysical objects for which relativity may play a significant, even dominant, role. In 1978 a close binary pair of stars, both probably neutron stars, yielded evidence for energy loss by the emission of gravitational waves.

Cosmology

Foremost among the astrophysical questions are those concerning relativistic cosmology, a science pioneered in large measure by Einstein himself. In this field one again can witness Einstein's uncanny ability, derived from his philosophical outlook, to drive a salient at the heart of a problem.

In his *Autobiographical Notes* Einstein emphasized the important role played by the work of physicist Ernst Mach in leading him to general relativity and also to his cosmology. Mach, building on Bishop George Berkeley's concerns about the nonobservability of the absolute space (space independent of what occupies it) of Newton, suggested that the inertial forces observed in an accelerated coordinate system represent forces induced by the distant matter in the universe. For example, in an automobile turning a corner one is free to imagine that the universe is wheeling about the car. According to Mach the inertial reaction, the centrifugal force experienced on the Earth, is to be interpreted as a force generated by the enormous accelerated mass of the universe that is acting upon the planet. This is the bare essence of the relativity principle.

Mach's principle guided Einstein to a generally covariant theory of gravity, that is, a theory for which all coordinate systems are equally permissible. But despite its origins general relativity does not seem to give a very satisfactory account of Mach's principle. In general relativity, the magnitude of an inertial force (expressed in terms of a standard based on a gravitational force) does not depend upon the amount of matter in the universe or its distance. By contrast, with the scalar-tensor theory of gravity the ratio of the inertial mass of an elementary particle to the fundamental gravitational mass depends upon the present structure and the past history of the universe. Thus this theory appears to be capable of giving a better account of Mach's principle than does general relativity.

Guided by Mach's principle, Einstein was led to consider as possible universes those that are finite, static, uniform, and isotropic (equal in all directions). He assumed that the average density of the matter distribution would be constant and uniform and that the properties of the universe would be independent of direction. In these assumptions he exhibited a remarkable

83

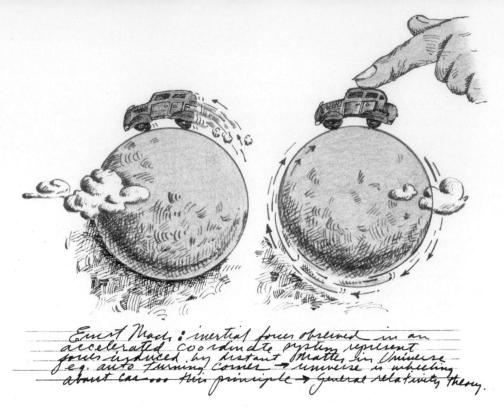

Ernst Mach: inertial forces observed in an accelerated coordinate system represent forces induced by distant matter in universe — eg. auto turning corner → universe is wheeling about car... this principle → General relativity theory.

anticipation of later observations, for at the time that he made these assumptions there was no believable observational basis for any of them. The stars seen with the naked eye seem to be reasonably uniformly distributed about us. But they are only nearby objects. With even a small telescope one sees that the Milky Way is more than a band of dim light. It is crowded with millions of stars. Thus, at that vantage point, matter seemed to be distributed in a way that was very far from uniform.

Some years later, however, it was shown that most of the nebulae, wispy faint clouds in the sky, were actually distant galaxies, collections of 10^{11} to 10^{12} stars, and that these galaxies were extremely numerous. Apparently most of the matter in the universe is located in these distant galaxies. Furthermore, these galaxies appeared to be uniformly and isotropically distributed in space, as Einstein had assumed.

Einstein's assumptions that the universe is finite, a closed spherical space, and that it is static were motivated by Mach's principle. As Einstein interpreted the principle, a static universe was needed to keep the inertial properties of matter constant in time. The finite universe was needed to avoid infinite inertial reactions.

The requirement that a universe containing uniformly distributed matter could be static was met by Einstein by introducing the "cosmological term" in his equations. This somewhat ad hoc modification of his equations acted like a negative pressure to permit the existence of a static solution to the cosmological equations. Later he was to abandon this term when it was found from the observations of the Doppler shifts of spectral lines from distant galaxies that the universe was actually expanding.

The observational basis for this relativistic cosmology has improved greatly in the 1960s and 1970s. Quasars are now observed at such great distances that the Doppler shifts increase the spectral wavelengths by more than a factor of two. New techniques for measuring luminosity in space have greatly improved our knowledge of the red shift/distance relation.

Nonetheless, much remains to be done. There is still not a decent value for the average density of matter in space, and the age of the universe is probably uncertain by a factor of two. Scientists still do not know if the universe is closed or open (finite or infinite).

The qualities that Einstein introduced to satisfy his interpretation of Mach's principle are not observationally established. Nonetheless, his assumptions of uniformity and isotropy in the universe seem to be strongly supported by the observations, particularly by those of the residual radiation left over from the "big bang."

Unresolved paradoxes

One should not conclude that all is now well with relativistic cosmology. In fact, there are paradoxes, unresolved and perhaps unresolvable, in the framework of Einstein's theory. Among these are the following:

(1) It has been shown that there is an unavoidable singularity in the solution to Einstein's equations at the start of the expansion of the universe and that as a result there is no way of continuing a conceivable previous history of the universe forward to the time immediately after the big bang. The "singularity" is a breakdown of the mathematics due to the occurrence of infinities.

(2) The universe started expanding with a remarkably carefully adjusted expansion rate. For a fractionally tiny increase or decrease in the expansion rate near the beginning of the expansion, conditions later would not have been such as to have led to the formation of stars.

(3) The start of the expansion was remarkably well synchronized over the whole universe, separate parts that were causally disconnected starting out together. (Causally disconnected parts are those that cannot communicate with each other in the time available from the start of the expansion.)

(4) In similar fashion the universe exhibits a remarkable global structure. Causally disconnected parts have similar densities and are otherwise similar.

(5) Another global peculiarity concerns the question of finiteness. Observed early in the expansion, the universe is remarkably close to "flat," the boundary between finite and infinite (a closed and open space). But why should it be so nearly flat without being precisely flat?

At this time, scientists can only speculate as to the meaning of these paradoxes.

FOR ADDITIONAL READING

Albert Einstein, *The Meaning of Relativity,* (Princeton University Press, 1955).

Banesh Hoffmann (with Helen Dukas), *Albert Einstein, Creator and Rebel,* (Viking, 1972).

Paul A. Schilpp, (ed.), *Albert Einstein, Philosopher-Scientist,* (Cambridge University Press, 1951).

D. W. Sciama, *Modern Cosmology,* (Cambridge University Press, 1971).

Steven Weinberg, *The First Three Minutes,* (Basic Books, 1977).

The Structure
of the Universe
by Robert M. Wald

Cosmologists are applying newly won knowledge in astronomy and physics to understand how the universe began, if and when it will end, and what makes it as it is today.

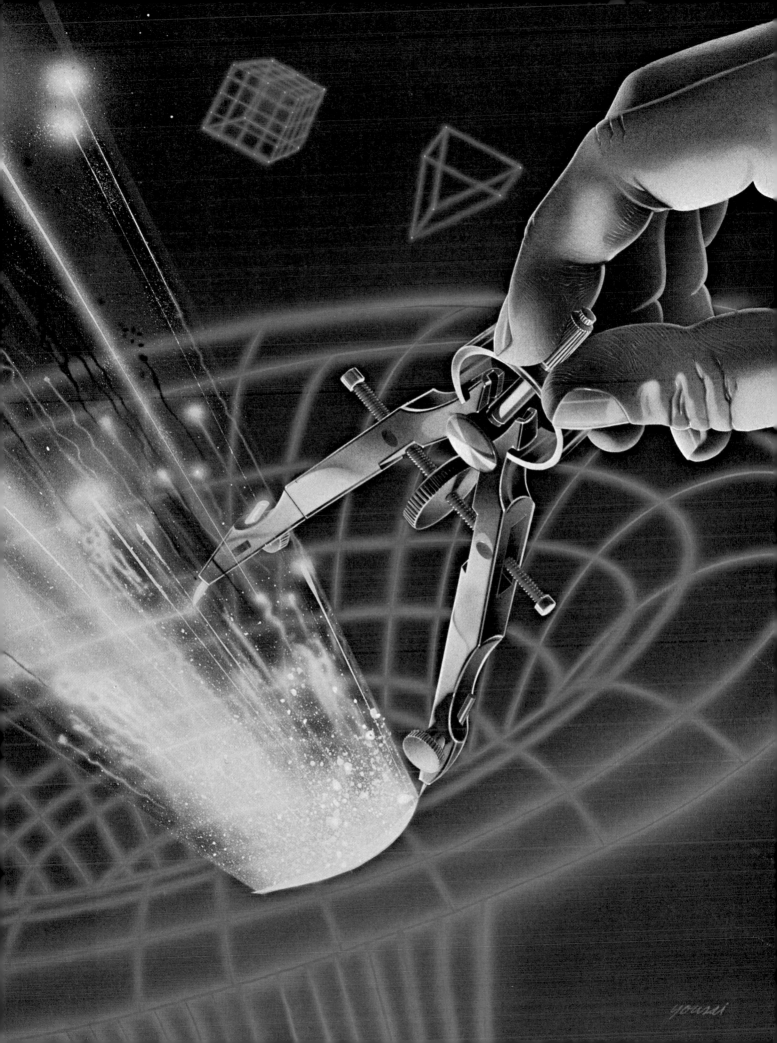

At the beginning of the 20th century two revolutionary ideas transformed man's notions of space and time—Albert Einstein's theories of special relativity and general relativity. Published 11 years apart, these profound mathematical statements upended longstanding conceptions of the structure of the universe. Their challenge to modern astronomy—to verify further (or to disprove) these ideas and to determine precisely which of the possible structures admitted by theory best describes the universe—remains a major scientific goal.

The marriage of space and time

Prior to the appearance of the theory of special relativity, in 1905, it was generally believed that all observers would agree in their determination of the interval of time between two events. That these observers might be moving in relation to each other made no difference. Likewise, the measured distance between two events happening at the same time was thought to be independent of the observers, and the spatial relations between such events to satisfy Euclid's laws of geometry. Space and time were regarded as distinct, unrelated entities. Special relativity demonstrated that space and time must be regarded as aspects of a single entity: space-time. Neither time intervals nor space intervals between events are independent of which observer measures them; two observers in relative motion will obtain different answers for these quantities. The quantity about which all observers do agree, however, and thus one that must be basic to the structure of space and time, is a certain combination of the time interval and space interval between events. Remarkably this combination, called space-time metric, has much of the mathematical character of the concept of distance in ordinary geometry. Thus, in special relativity the structure of space-time can be described in much the same way that the structure of an ordinary surface is described by its geometry.

In special relativity Einstein postulated the geometry of space-time to have a particular, simple structure analogous to Euclidean geometry for ordinary surfaces. However, two key ideas—together with his desire to incorporate gravitation into the theory—motivated him to drop this assumption and replace it with the theory of general relativity, which included the special theory only as a special case applicable when gravitational fields are absent. The first idea stems from the fact—known as the equivalence principle—that all bodies fall exactly the same way in a gravitational field regardless of their masses, elemental compositions, shapes, or other characteristics. This was first demonstrated in Galileo's famous experiment at the Leaning Tower of Pisa, and modern experiments have verified it to very high precision. This universality of gravity, with its complete independence of the nature of the falling bodies, suggested the possibility of ascribing the properties of the gravitational field to the structure of space-time itself.

The second motivating idea was the philosophical belief, known as Mach's principle, that the notion of what constitutes inertia and motion should not be fixed, absolute concepts but rather should be determined or at least influenced by the matter present in the universe. For example, if a dinner plate were thrown spinning into the air, and then suddenly somehow

ROBERT M. WALD *is Assistant Professor at the Enrico Fermi Institute and in the Department of Physics, University of Chicago.*

Paintings by John Youssi

88

the entire universe of matter except for the plate were made to vanish, according to Mach's principle the plate's rotation and movement through space would no longer exist. They would not simply be immeasurable quantities because of the absence of objects to which the plate's motions could be related; more fundamentally, a universe devoid of matter would have no structure of space-time against which the plate could move. In general, the space-time structure of a "Machian" universe is dependent upon the presence and distribution of the matter within it.

In the mathematics of general relativity, presented in 1916, the presence of a gravitational field is shown by the differing of the space-time metric from the form it was assumed to have in special relativity. All physical effects of a gravitational field are now described in terms of a non-Euclidean space-time geometry. This geometry is not invented independently; rather it evolves naturally from an equation, postulated by Einstein, relating it to the distribution of matter throughout space-time. Thus, general relativity beautifully incorporates both the equivalence principle and some (though not all) aspects of Mach's principle by describing gravity in terms of the space-time metric and by relating the space-time metric to matter distribution. It is in the light of general relativity that modern notions of the structure of the universe are described.

A choice of geometries

General relativity allows for many possible structures of space-time. To determine the structure of the universe from these possibilities, information must be supplied from further assumptions or, preferably, from observations. Since the Copernican revolution it has been assumed that the Earth does not occupy a preferred position in the universe. Thus, a natural assumption to make is that the universe is homogeneous; *i.e.,* such basic properties as the average density of matter (the mass in a given volume of space) do not vary greatly from place to place. Similarly, it is natural to assume that the universe is isotropic; *i.e.,* that the nature of what an observer sees does not depend upon which direction in space he or she looks. Although there was little observational support for these assumptions a half century ago when they were first made in a modern cosmological context, today there is strong evidence for them.

When these two assumptions are applied to Einstein's equation relating space-time structure to matter distribution, the range of possible structures for the universe is reduced considerably. Remarkably, all of the possibilities still in the running are dynamic: the universe must be expanding or contracting. The nature of this expansion or contraction is illustrated in figure 1 on pp. 90–91. The volume-filling cubes in figure 1 represent various stages of an expanding universe in three spatial dimensions, and the front surface of each cube presents a simplified two-dimensional view. The spiral and elliptical bodies, representing galaxies, are, by assumption, distributed in a roughly homogeneous manner throughout the universe. Einstein's equation requires that at later or earlier times the distribution of matter will remain homogeneous but the distance scale between objects will change, as illustrated in the succession of cubes. In effect, space itself expands or contracts! The

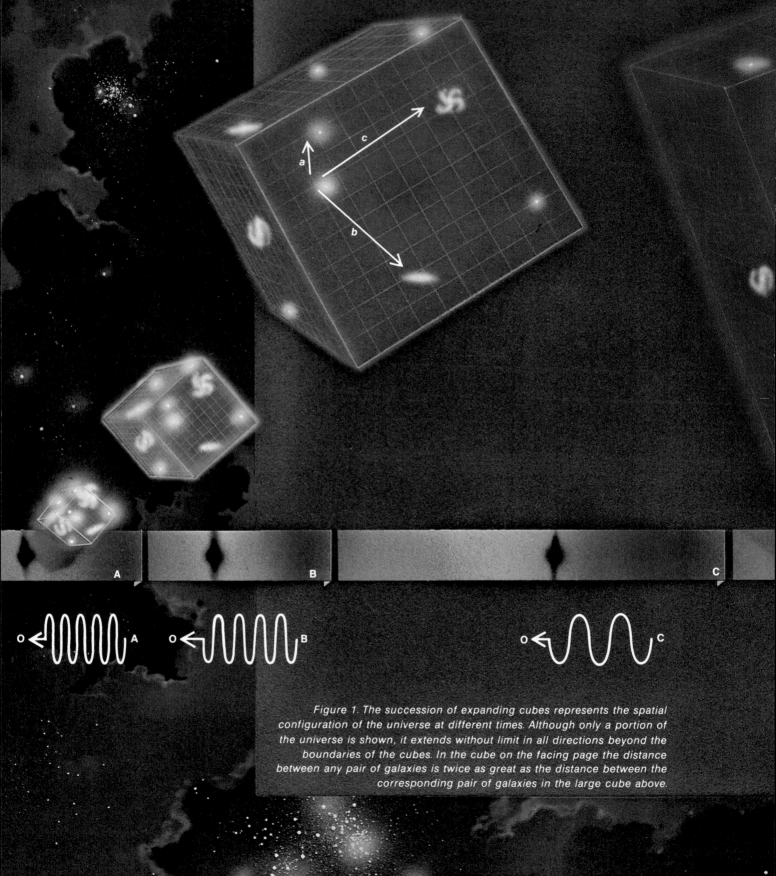

Figure 1. The succession of expanding cubes represents the spatial configuration of the universe at different times. Although only a portion of the universe is shown, it extends without limit in all directions beyond the boundaries of the cubes. In the cube on the facing page the distance between any pair of galaxies is twice as great as the distance between the corresponding pair of galaxies in the large cube above.

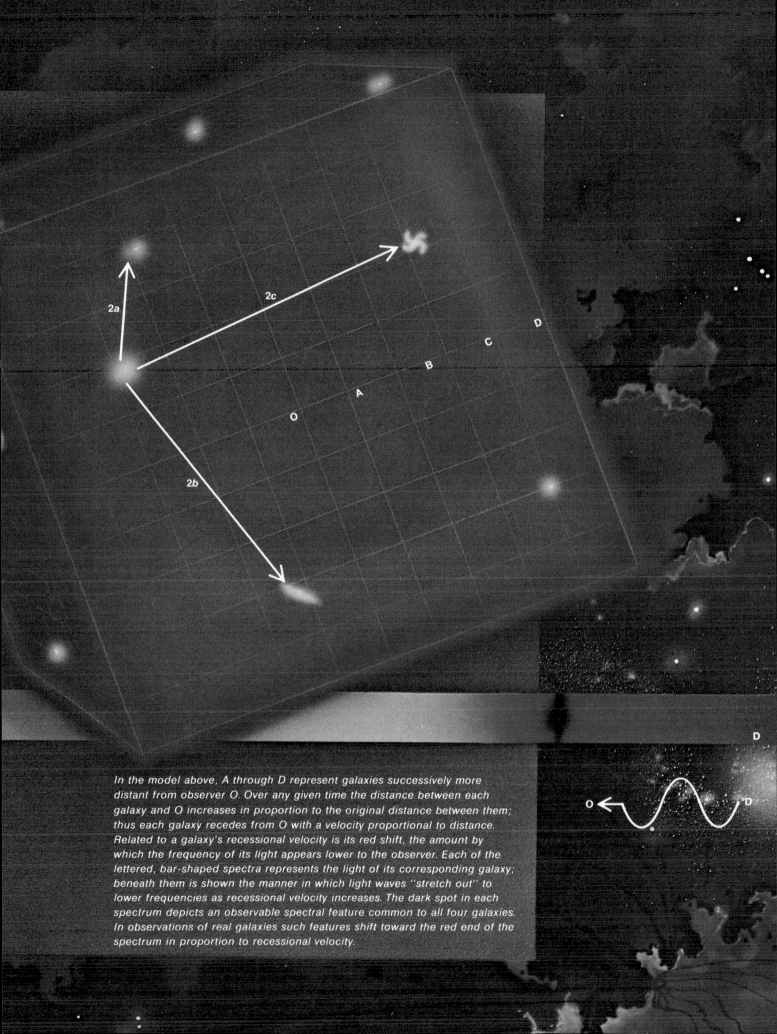

In the model above, A through D represent galaxies successively more distant from observer O. Over any given time the distance between each galaxy and O increases in proportion to the original distance between them; thus each galaxy recedes from O with a velocity proportional to distance. Related to a galaxy's recessional velocity is its red shift, the amount by which the frequency of its light appears lower to the observer. Each of the lettered, bar-shaped spectra represents the light of its corresponding galaxy; beneath them is shown the manner in which light waves "stretch out" to lower frequencies as recessional velocity increases. The dark spot in each spectrum depicts an observable spectral feature common to all four galaxies. In observations of real galaxies such features shift toward the red end of the spectrum in proportion to recessional velocity.

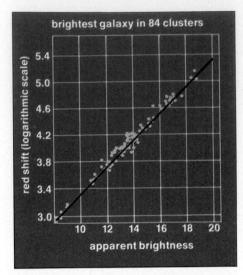

brightest galaxy in 84 clusters

red shift (logarithmic scale)

5.4
5.0
4.6
4.2
3.8
3.4
3.0

10 12 14 16 18 20

apparent brightness

Figure 2 (above). The red-shift–distance relationship, as derived from recent measurements. The brightest galaxy in a cluster of galaxies is thought to have an intrinsic brightness that varies little from cluster to cluster. Hence its apparent brightness can be used as a measure of its distance: the fainter its appearance, the more distant. When the apparent brightnesses of many such galaxies are plotted against their red shifts, all the data points lie very nearly on the same line, in excellent agreement with the prediction of the expanding universe. Hubble's original, more limited, measurements are represented in the graph by the small box in the lower left-hand corner. Figure 3 (facing page). In Euclidean geometry, depicted on a flat surface, the sum of the angles of a triangle (a + b + c) is always 180°, and initially parallel straight lines always remain so. In hyperboloid geometry, shown on a saddle-shaped surface, a + b + c is always less than 180°, and initially parallel "straight lines," or geodesics, diverge. In spherical geometry, shown on a spherical surface, a + b + c is always greater than 180°, and initially parallel geodesics converge and eventually cross.

galaxies, as well as such smaller objects as planets and human beings, easily resist the small driving forces and remain unchanged in size.

In an expansion of the kind shown in figure 1, over any given time the distance between each pair of points increases in proportion to the original distance between them. Thus, if such an expansion takes place continuously, each point would recede from every other point with a velocity proportional to its distance. Expressed as an equation,

$$v = Hr \qquad (1)$$

in which v denotes velocity, r denotes distance, and H is a constant valid for the present day (which, as will be discussed below, may actually change with time). If this effect were occurring in the universe, its consequences should be observable. Just as the pitch, or frequency, of a train whistle lowers as the train moves away from a listener, the frequency of light from a receding galaxy should appear lower to an observer than if the galaxy and observer were motionless relative to each other. This kind of change is called a "red shift" because visible light is shifted downward in frequency toward the long-wavelength, red end of the electromagnetic spectrum. For velocities much smaller than the speed of light the size of such a shift is proportional to the velocity of the source of light.

Historically, prediction of a dynamic universe was not accepted immediately. In 1922 the Soviet mathematician Alexander Friedmann described an expanding universe based on Einstein's equation, but his work was largely ignored. Einstein himself found the idea of a dynamic universe sufficiently unpalatable that he proposed a modification of his original equation—the addition of a new term called the cosmological constant. With this new term his equation could describe static universes, although it later became apparent that these models were unrealistic. They were unstable in much the same sense as a pencil standing on its point is unstable; the slightest deviation from the conditions required for exact equilibrium causes the system to become dynamic.

The philosophical aversion to a dynamic universe was overcome in 1929 by U.S. astronomer Edwin Hubble, who showed from an analysis of the red shifts of distant galaxies that they are indeed receding from our Galaxy and with velocity of recession proportional to distance—exactly the characteristics predicted by the expanding universe model of unmodified general relativity. Hence, the universe is expanding. A graph of modern data is shown in figure 2.

Figure 1, illustrating the spatial configuration of the universe, was drawn in a manner indicating that Euclidean geometry applies; for example, that the sum of the angles of a triangle is always 180°. As previously mentioned, however, in general relativity the geometry depends on matter distribution and is not fixed arbitrarily. The assumptions of homogeneity and isotropy restrict the spatial geometry to three possibilities: ordinary Euclidean geometry, hyperboloid geometry, and spherical geometry. Some characteristics of each of these possibilities are discussed in figure 3. With Euclidean and hyperboloid geometries, the universe extends infinitely in all directions; its total volume and content of matter are infinite. However, the three-dimensional space of spherical geometry "closes in" on itself just like its two-

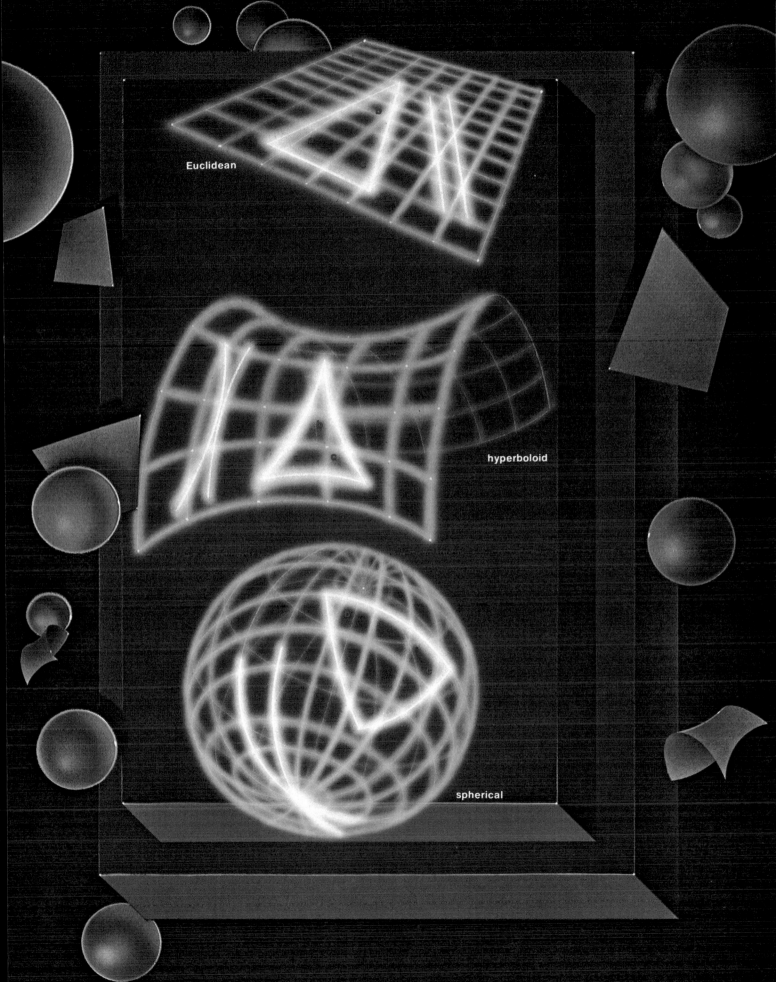

dimensional analogue, the surface of an ordinary sphere. Thus, with this possibility the total volume and matter content of the universe are finite, yet there is no boundary or "edge" to the universe, just as there is none on the surface of a sphere. (Such an "edge" would violate the assumption of homogeneity.) Just which of these three geometries is to hold for the real universe depends upon the amount of matter present, as represented by its average density. According to Einstein's equation, Euclidean geometry will hold if the average density d is related to the expansion rate by the equation

$$d = \frac{3H^2}{8\pi G} \qquad (2)$$

in which G is the gravitational constant and H is Hubble's constant (or v/r) as defined by equation 1. If d is smaller than this critical value, hyperboloid geometry holds, whereas if d is greater, spherical geometry applies. One of the important questions of modern cosmology is to determine which geometry holds and, in particular, whether the universe is "open" (infinite in extent) or "closed" (finite). On aesthetic grounds, most theorists have favored a closed universe, but as will be discussed below, the observational evidence presently favors an open one.

The big bang

Whichever of these possibilities holds, Einstein's equation allows one to predict the future evolution of the universe and to trace its early behavior. When a mathematical excursion into the past is made, a very striking thing happens. For all three spatial geometries, the farther back one goes in time, the more contracted was the universe and the more rapid was the rate of expansion. In fact, general relativity indicates that approximately 15 billion years ago the universe was infinitely contracted: the distance between any two points was zero, the density of matter was infinite, and, for a closed universe, the volume of the entire universe was zero! According to this picture the universe came into being in a highly singular state, the moment of its origin being referred to as the "big bang."

A common misconception is that the theory envisions a previously empty universe into which, 15 billion years ago, matter suddenly poured from an explosion at a point. This is not the case. Not only did matter come into existence at the big bang, but so also did the structure of space-time; space itself, in effect, was shrunk to zero size at the time of the big bang, and "before" the big bang time was meaningless. Note that this concept is very difficult to express in common language since the word "before" presupposes a notion of time.

What caused this big bang to take place? Unfortunately, this is not a question that cosmologists are equipped to answer at present. In science, one is accustomed to having general laws and specific initial conditions; when the initial conditions are prescribed, the laws predict consequences. Thus, questions of causation are usually answered in terms of the initial conditions operating within physical laws. Similarly, given the present conditions of the universe, Einstein's equation "predicts" that the big bang must have occurred. This is not a very satisfying "explanation" of why the big bang occurred, but it is really all that can be said at present.

94

A word of caution should be given concerning the prediction of a singular beginning for the universe. Like basic physical laws, one expects general relativity to be valid over a very wide range of conditions, but at the extreme conditions within a very small fraction of a second of the big bang there is reason to believe that the theory is not applicable. This is because general relativity presently is an incomplete theory in the sense that it neglects certain effects in the realm of quantum mechanics, that branch of physics that deals with the properties of matter on the atomic and subatomic level. Under normal conditions these effects would be extremely small, but very near the big bang they could become large and invalidate the predictions of general relativity. So it is not really known what happened prior to the first tiny fraction of a second.

After this first fraction of a second, however, the predictions of general relativity are believed to be valid. Combined with present knowledge of elementary particle interactions and the best observational evidence to date, they yield the following picture of the evolution of the universe. For the first second or so after the "big bang" the matter in the universe was very hot and dense. Extremely energetic elementary particles, both stable and unstable, were present in large numbers. Following that second, however, expansion and cooling of the universe proceeded so rapidly that most of the unstable particles decayed away. During the next 15 minutes nuclear reactions took place between individual protons (hydrogen nuclei) and neutrons producing helium nuclei (two protons and two neutrons) and a small proportion of deuterium nuclei (one proton and one neutron) but essentially no heavier elements. The relatively few neutrons that did not react soon decayed into protons and electrons. Theory indicates that about one-quarter of the original mass of protons and neutrons in the universe was converted to helium at this time. This fraction of helium is in good agreement with its observed abundance in the present universe. After 15 minutes the density and temperature of matter had dropped sufficiently that no further nuclear reactions could occur until much later in the evolution of the universe when stars were formed.

All this time, matter was everywhere absorbing and emitting electromagnetic radiation in the same way as an ordinary hot body, and the early universe was filled with a homogeneous "soup" of matter and radiation. Just as the color, or frequency, of thermal radiation emitted by a hot body is associated with its temperature, so also was the frequency of this cosmic radiation associated with the temperature of the early universe. As the universe expanded and cooled, the frequency of this primordial radiation lowered until by the present era it should correspond to a temperature only a few degrees above absolute zero. Thus, if the big-bang theory predicted by general relativity is correct, the universe should be filled with a uniform sea of very low temperature electromagnetic radiation.

Exactly such a "cosmic background radiation" was discovered in 1965 by U.S. radio astronomers Arno A. Penzias and Robert W. Wilson in work that earned them the 1978 Nobel Prize for Physics (see SCIENTISTS OF THE YEAR). Later measurements confirmed the thermal nature of this radiation and established to a very high accuracy that it reaches the Earth equally from

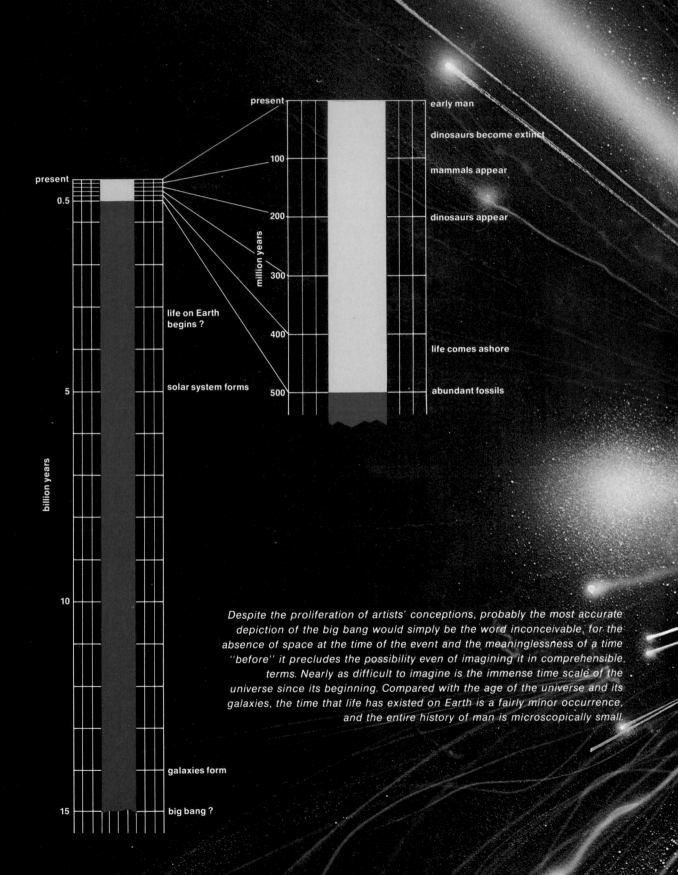

present
0.5

5

billion years

10

15

present

100

200

million years

300

400

500

life on Earth
begins ?

solar system forms

galaxies form

big bang ?

early man

dinosaurs become extinct

mammals appear

dinosaurs appear

life comes ashore

abundant fossils

Despite the proliferation of artists' conceptions, probably the most accurate depiction of the big bang would simply be the word inconceivable, for the absence of space at the time of the event and the meaninglessness of a time "before" it precludes the possibility even of imagining it in comprehensible terms. Nearly as difficult to imagine is the immense time scale of the universe since its beginning. Compared with the age of the universe and its galaxies, the time that life has existed on Earth is a fairly minor occurrence, and the entire history of man is microscopically small.

Photos, courtesy, Halton Arp and Francesco Bertola

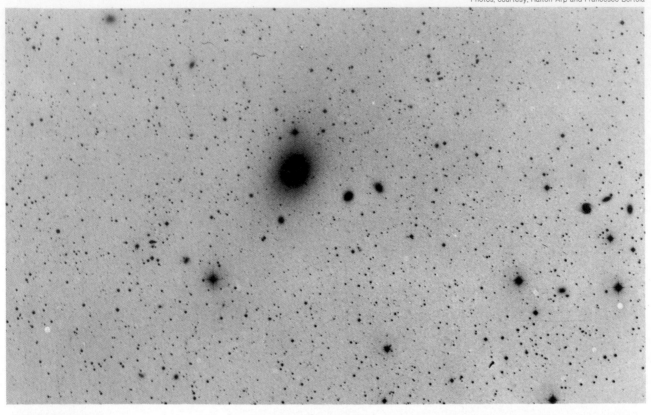

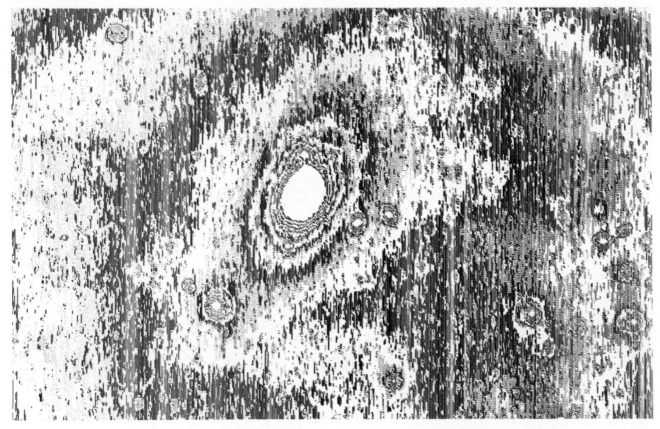

all directions. The existence of this radiation is very strong confirmation of the big-bang theory, which predicts it and accounts for it in the simplest way. Furthermore, the high degree of isotropy of the radiation provides strong evidence that the universe is homogeneous and isotropic, as was assumed.

Open or closed?

General relativity also predicts the future evolution of the universe, much of it dependent upon the geometry that applies. Regardless of whether the universe is open or closed, the expansion rate will continue to decrease. If the universe is open the expansion rate never reaches zero; the universe continues to expand forever. On the other hand, Einstein's equation predicts that, for a closed universe, expansion will eventually come to a halt. The universe will then contract and eventually end, though no earlier than 20 billion years from now, in a "big crunch" analogous to its origin in the big bang. Hence one of the most important questions in modern cosmology is the determination of whether the universe is open or closed. Information on this issue has been obtained thus far in several ways.

As mentioned above, if the present mass density of the universe is greater than the critical density given by equation 2 above, the universe is closed; otherwise, the universe is open. There is evidence that essentially all of the mass in the universe resides in galaxies—with little, if any, matter between galaxies. For many years a disturbing problem has hampered efforts to develop a consistent picture of galactic masses. Clusters of galaxies are believed to be stable, long-term systems held together by gravitational attraction. When mass calculations are made based on this assumption, however, for many clusters the amount of mass that must be present is many times the mass actually observed. In general, mass estimates for individual galaxies have been consistently lower than the masses derived for galaxies occurring in clusters. Many astronomers now believe that this "missing mass problem" can be explained by galaxies having a massive halo composed of stars too faint to see. Using this higher estimate of the mass of galaxies, the mass density of the universe is still about 20 times smaller than the critical density. Although this provides strong evidence that the universe is open, the possibility of significant amounts of matter between galaxies cannot be completely ruled out.

A second method for determining whether the universe is open or closed is to measure the age of the universe; *i.e.,* the time elapsed since the big bang. The reciprocal of Hubble's constant $(1/H)$, called the Hubble time, can be considered a measure of the time required for a galaxy to achieve its present distance from our Galaxy assuming the present, relatively slow rate of expansion; in other words, the maximum time since the galaxies separated, or the upper limit of the age of the universe. For a universe—either open or closed—whose expansion rate was higher in the past, the actual expansion time must be shorter than the Hubble time. Einstein's equation shows that a closed universe evolves faster than an open universe. Specifically if the age of the universe is less than two-thirds of the Hubble time, or $2/(3H)$, the universe must be closed; otherwise it is open. See figure 4 on p. 100.

The age of the oldest known star clusters can be estimated from the

The appearance of galaxy M87 in a conventional photographic negative (facing page, top) is of a small, central, fuzzy-edged object. However, when its photo image is scanned with a device called an isodensity tracer that amplifies and maps imperceptible variations in light around the image, an enormous halo appears (bottom). Presumably accounting for this halo is an envelope of stars that are too faint to see yet add significantly to the mass estimate of the galaxy. When similar estimates are made for other galaxies, the mass density estimate for the universe increases, though not enough to provide evidence for a closed universe.

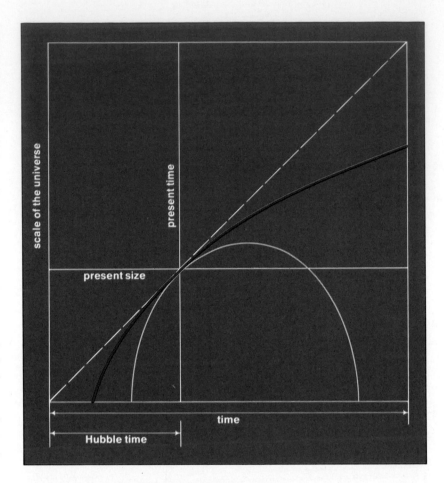

Figure 4. Three fates for the universe are charted on a graph that plots the size of the universe against time. All curves converge at the present time and present size because each fate must describe the situation observed today. If the present expansion rate has remained unchanged since the galaxies separated (dashed line), then the Hubble time is the actual age of the universe, and expansion can be expected to proceed forever in direct proportion to time. For a universe whose expansion rate was higher in the past, the age of the universe must be shorter than the Hubble time. With comparatively slow deceleration of the expansion rate, expansion will still continue forever, but increasingly more slowly (red line); it can be shown that such a universe must have begun during the first third of the Hubble time. Greater deceleration of the expansion rate signifies a still younger universe, which must eventually stop expanding and then contract toward a "big crunch" (yellow line); the age of this kind of universe must be less than two-thirds of the Hubble time.

theory of stellar evolution, and the age of long-lived radioactive elements can be determined by measuring the fraction of the atoms that have decayed. Assuming that the universe itself is not significantly older than the ages of these objects, the oldest whose age can be determined, one arrives at the above quoted estimate of 15 billion years as the present age of the universe. This number, however, is rather uncertain; the correct age quite possibly could be as little as 10 billion or as much as 20 billion years.

To compare this with the critical age, $2/(3H)$, one needs to know the numerical value of Hubble's constant (v/r). This requires a determination of the absolute distances (r) to faraway galaxies. Such a determination is made using the simple principle that if one knows the intrinsic brightness of an object, one can find how far away it is by observing how bright it appears to be. Although this principle makes it easy to determine relative distances to objects of the same intrinsic brightness (which, of course, is all that is needed to establish that velocity is proportional to distance), the calibration of absolute distances of distant galaxies relies on a rather complicated chain of reasoning whereby the distances to nearby objects are used to calibrate the distances and intrinsic brightnesses of more distant objects, which, in turn, are used to calibrate these values for yet more distant objects. Several important errors were made in this distance determination in the past, probably the most famous of which was the error in calibrating the brightness of Cepheid variable stars, an important link in the distance determination chain. Consequently, the value of Hubble's constant is now believed to be about ten times smaller than Hubble's original estimate. With this new value, the critical age of the universe is about 13 billion years. Although this value is in good agreement with the observed age, the uncertainties in both are too great to conclude from this test whether the universe is open or closed.

A third observational test concerns the decrease, or deceleration, of the expansion rate. Although Hubble's constant decreases with time whether the universe is open or closed, it decreases more rapidly for a closed universe. The light reaching Earth from very distant galaxies was emitted long ago and its red shift is affected by the expansion rate at earlier epochs. Thus, for very distant objects one expects to see deviations from Hubble's law caused by the change in the value of Hubble's constant with time. From these deviations, the deceleration of the universe can be measured. Unfortunately, it is quite likely that the intrinsic brightness of a galaxy varies significantly during its evolution and may have been quite different at the early epoch during which the light from distant galaxies was emitted. If so, such methods of distance calibration break down, and the deceleration cannot be determined—at least until astronomers develop a much better understanding of the evolution of galaxies.

A fourth test concerns elemental synthesis during the first 15 minutes after the big bang. As mentioned above, a substantial amount of helium and a little deuterium should have been produced during that time. The amount of synthesized helium predicted by the general relativity model of the universe is fairly independent of the variables within the model, but the amount of deuterium produced depends rather sensitively on the density and expansion rate during this era, which, in turn, correlate with whether the universe is open or closed. Recent measurements of cosmic deuterium abundance yielded results in line with an open universe, although this test is also not conclusive because the possibility exists that deuterium could be made, destroyed, or both by processes other than big-bang nucleosynthesis.

Thus, in total the present observational evidence points to an open universe. It may well require another half-century of observational data, however, before a firm conclusion can be drawn on this question.

Alternatives to the big bang

The above discussion focused on the big-bang theory and the many good reasons for which nearly all astrophysicists today believe in its validity. However, observational data relevant to cosmology is not easy to obtain, and misinterpretations can be and have been made. It is worthwhile, therefore, to examine other cosmological theories. Those described below are by no means a complete list, but they should give a flavor of some of the possibilities that have been considered in the past and that undoubtedly will be again if new observational data should yield discrepancies with big-bang predictions.

(1) Models within general relativity: The big-bang model follows from general relativity under the assumption of exact homogeneity and isotropy. Clearly, the universe is not exactly uniform; matter is clumped into galaxies

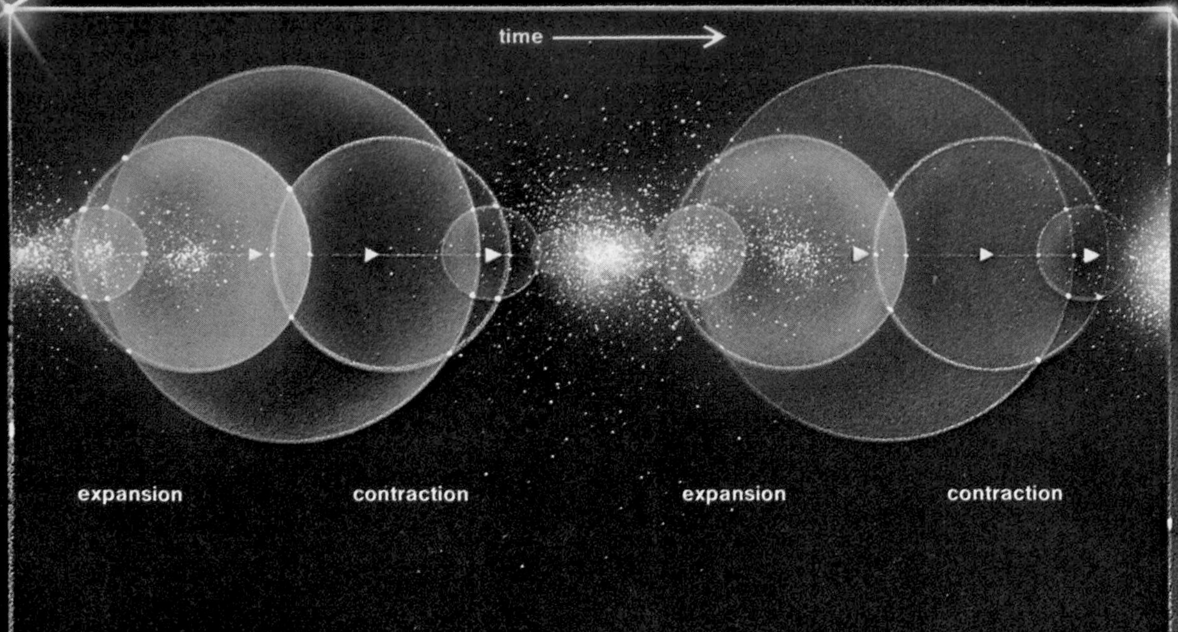

time ⟶

expansion   contraction   expansion   contraction

Accordion model: The universe proceeds through an infinite number of cycles of expansion and contraction. Infinite mass densities, such as that thought to have existed at the instant of the big bang, do not occur.

real position

apparent position

Brans-Dicke theory: In this modification of Einstein's equation, the gravitational constant may vary with time. Like general relativity, it predicts that starlight passing near the Sun will be gravitationally deflected; hence, as seen from Earth, the star's image will occupy an apparent position that differs from its real position. Brans-Dicke theory, however, disagrees with general relativity in the predicted amount of deflection.

Steady-state model: The universe has always been expanding at a uniform rate and will continue to do so. Matter is continually being created throughout the universe to maintain a constant mass density.

"Tired-light" theories: The red shift does not arise from the velocity of receding galaxies but from other mechanisms such as the interaction of light with matter between galaxies or the decay of photons due to their interaction with the structure of curved space-time. Hence, the universe is not expanding at all.

and other bodies, making the model an approximation at best. However, the high degree of isotropy of cosmic background radiation as well as the correct predictions of helium production indicate that it is probably a very good approximation for the universe from the first few minutes onward. The possibility certainly remains, nevertheless, that the universe was not very nearly uniform at first but was soon "homogenized" and "isotropized" by some mechanism. The ability to theoretically investigate this possibility is greatly hampered because it is extremely difficult to solve Einstein's equation unless one makes such strong mathematically simplifying assumptions as homogeneity and isotropy. At one time it was widely believed that the absence of uniformity in the very early universe could circumvent the prediction of a singular beginning of the universe. In particular, whereas the exactly homogeneous, isotropic model has a singular beginning and end for a closed universe, some theorists felt that relaxation of these assumptions could give an "accordion model" of the universe, with an infinite number of cycles of contraction to a highly condensed state followed by reexpansion, without infinite densities ever being reached. However, some mathematical results proved within the last 15 years by theorists Roger Penrose and Stephen Hawking in Great Britain show that this cannot occur in the context of general relativity—although, of course, it remains a possibility if general relativity breaks down in the very early universe.

(2) Modification of Einstein's equation: The simplest modification of Einstein's equation is the introduction of the cosmological constant. Einstein strongly advocated abandonment of this modification after the expansion of the universe was discovered, but it has been reintroduced nearly every time an apparent discrepancy of theory and observation has been found, only to be abandoned again when the discrepancy has been resolved. At present, there are no clear-cut discrepancies, and only a few astrophysicists believe that the cosmological constant should be kept in Einstein's equation.

An interesting modification of Einstein's equation was proposed nearly 20 years ago by physicists Carl Brans and Robert Dicke in the U.S. Part of the motivation for their work stemmed from an idea of British theoretical physicist P. A. M. Dirac called the large number hypothesis. In it certain fundamental constants of nature, such as the gravitational constant, G, must vary with time as the universe expands in order to account for numerical relationships seen among certain measurements taken in the present universe. In Brans-Dicke theory, the gravitational "constant," like space-time geometry, is affected by matter distribution and can vary with time. Brans-Dicke theory, however, predicts a different value than general relativity for a well-known phenomenon elegantly explained in the context of space-time geometry: the gravitational deflection of light passing near a massive body such as the Sun. Recently a very precise measurement of this effect was made using radio signals from a quasar as it was being eclipsed by the Sun. The results agreed with high accuracy with the prediction of general relativity. Thus, it appears that Brans-Dicke theory can be ruled out.

(3) The steady-state model: The attempt of this model, proposed 30 years ago by Hermann Bondi, Thomas Gold, and Fred Hoyle in Great Britain, was to retain the notion of an expanding universe but avoid the notion that it

104

changes with time and had a singular origin in the big bang. In the steady-state model the universe has always been expanding and will continue to expand forever at a uniform rate. Such a postulate eliminates the need to answer such questions as what caused the universe to begin and why did it begin when it did. In order to keep the density of matter from decreasing, continual creation of matter is postulated. A new form of matter, the "C-field," must also be postulated in order to make the steady-state model compatible with Einstein's equation. Although these ideas are highly speculative, at one time the steady-state model had many adherents. The model was largely abandoned, however, after the discovery of cosmic background radiation, which cannot be accounted for in a natural way in the steady-state model.

(4) "Tired-light" theories: Direct evidence that the universe is expanding comes from the fact that the frequency of light emitted from distant galaxies is red-shifted. As discussed above, the most natural interpretation of this red shift is that the distant galaxies are receding from our Galaxy. According to tired-light theories the universe is, in fact, not expanding, and the red shift arises from some other mechanism. Examples of such mechanisms are the interaction of light with matter between galaxies and the decay of photons (the energy packets, or quanta, of light). These explanations, however, both assume and predict physical phenomena that have not been observed and thus have had very few advocates.

The future: proceed with caution

Although neither the theories discussed above nor any others are presently serious competitors of the big-bang model, the great difficulty in obtaining foolproof cosmological data should make one very cautious. After all, one can only observe a tiny fraction of the universe, and interpretations of the observations that can be made often involve many implicit assumptions. Compared with other cosmologies, the big-bang theory is solidly grounded, but in view of the magnitude of its predictions more work must be done to assure its correctness. The subject of modern cosmology has existed for only half a century and yet has seen several major breakthroughs, including discoveries of the expansion of the universe and of cosmic background radiation. Even if no comparable breakthroughs occur in the next half century, it is likely that improvements in both observations and theory will either uncover a serious discrepancy with the big-bang theory or conclusively confirm it.

But even if there were no doubt whatsoever that the big-bang theory is correct, all questions about cosmology would not be answered. At present no one knows how to answer—or in some cases even properly formulate—such questions as: Why did the big bang occur? Why is the universe apparently composed of matter rather than antimatter? How did the universe make its choice between the possibilities of being open or closed? Although quantum effects should be important very near the big bang, again no one knows how to incorporate them into general relativity. Should this last problem be solved, man may well witness the next major revolution in cosmology.

See also Feature Article: EINSTEIN REVISITED: A CENTENNIAL EVALUATION.

Building to Save Energy

by Richard G. Stein

In recent years conscientious architects have applied their insights to the design and modification of buildings to reduce energy expenditure without sacrificing function.

In the early 1970s, when the United States began to consider its growing energy use an important national issue and when the term energy crisis became common, studies were undertaken to delineate energy use more accurately. After some initial disbelief, government officials, economists, and other concerned parties were compelled to realize that about one-third of the nation's total energy was consumed in the operation of its stock of buildings. Of this figure about 20% accrued from direct use of fossil fuels and 6% each from lighting and from operation of the other electrical systems built into buildings, such as cooling systems, heating systems, ventilation fans, elevators, pumps, and miscellaneous motors.

Whereas early responses to the energy crisis involved looking to technological means to solve the dilemma caused by the Arab oil embargo of 1973 and 1974, it soon became apparent that none of these solutions could be achieved quickly or economically. Nuclear power, once portrayed as the major new energy source of the late 1980s, has been downgraded to a far less pivotal role. Its cost per kilowatt of capacity has soared, the time for completing a plant has stretched out, and the reliability of the plants has dropped below expectations. In addition, the scope of safety and security problems has become more widely recognized, and the method of disposal of radioactive wastes still awaits a sound solution.

A gentler alternative, solar energy, has also been reevaluated, primarily on the basis of cost of installation and on the time needed to install a statistically significant number of units. Originally put forward as immediately available because of the omnipresent Sun, exploitation of solar energy is now considered to require the time to build an industry, educate the construction professions, and slowly gain acceptance for incorporation in new buildings. Development of new technology to increase domestic supplies of fuel has

RICHARD G. STEIN is Senior Partner in the architectural firm of Richard G. Stein & Partners and an Adjunct Professor at Cooper Union, New York City.

(Facing page) Illustration by Marilyn Shimokochi

Housing offices, restaurants and shops, and a church, New York City's 59-story Citicorp Center is an amalgam of innovative concepts, including a computerized energy-use system that recycles the heat generated by people and lighting within the building. The structure is designed to use 42% less energy for heating, ventilation, and air conditioning than comparable high-rises. A solar collector has been suggested for the south-facing, wedged top, but a final decision on installation awaits state-of-the-art improvements in solar power technology.

not advanced rapidly. Gasifying coal, extracting petroleum from tar sands, moving coal slurries through pipelines, and other large-scale techniques affecting supply have been found to be expensive and in most cases ecologically questionable. The shift to a greater dependence on coal has required costly investments in stack scrubbers to reduce hazardous chemicals that would otherwise be released into the air during combustion.

Economists, government agencies, and the Organization of Petroleum Exporting Countries and other international groups have made numerous projections of the rate of growth of energy use in the U.S. and other countries and of the time and cost of alternative energy sources. Typically these studies indicate that, given even the most restrained prediction of growth rate in energy use, consumption will continue to outstrip production.

Significance of energy efficiency

To put the various available options into perspective, it must be realized that none of the proposed technical alternatives will substantially alter present patterns of energy use, although in combination they can have an important cumulative effect. For example, hydroelectric power produced by the extensive dam constructions of the Tennessee Valley Authority and on the Colorado and Columbia rivers and elsewhere in the U.S. represented one-eighth of total generating capacity in 1975, producing about 3% of total national energy. To increase this by 50%, provided that water sources were available, would entail an expenditure of at least $40 billion. The time for implementation would be measured in decades. If the other high-technology options were pursued concurrently, it is apparent that virtually all construction capabilities in the U.S. would be devoted to providing energy capacity and that the rate of increase in capacity would closely parallel the rate of increase in energy use, leaving the problem no closer to solution.

On the other hand, the efficiency with which energy is used can have enormous implications. For instance, about the same time that energy use became a major concern, some architects and engineers suggested cautiously that in most buildings the consumption of energy might be reduced as much as 20%. It soon became clear that this savings, which translates to a reduction of 6% of overall energy use in the U.S., could be achieved almost immediately if everyone took advantage of all available options. As a result of such thinking, which has application not only to the operation of buildings but to transportation, industry, and virtually all other activities that consume energy, "energy conservation" rose in the list of strategies until by 1974 it had become the most important and least expensive choice.

Before proceeding further, the concept of energy conservation should be given an accurate description. When one speaks of conserving energy, one is actually still describing ways to expend it. By using energy more efficiently, less is needed to do a given job. Nevertheless, it is being used—converted from one form to another. Hence, a more descriptive term would be increasing the efficiency of energy use, and this reality should be understood wherever "conserving energy" is encountered. With respect to buildings, this concept has deeper implications than merely cutting down on overuse of systems and plugging up heating leaks through the building skin. It has

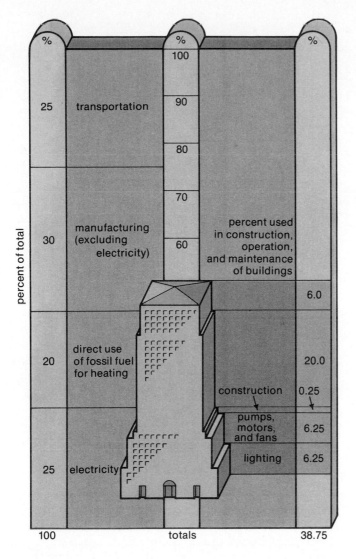

%		%	percent used in construction, operation, and maintenance of buildings	%
25	transportation	100		
		90		
		80		
		70		
30	manufacturing (excluding electricity)	60		6.0
20	direct use of fossil fuel for heating			20.0
			construction	0.25
			pumps, motors, and fans	6.25
25	electricity		lighting	6.25
100		totals		38.75

percent of total

become the key to understanding the true functioning of buildings and has led directly to a fundamental reexamination of many of the attitudes, methods, and techniques that were considered to be architectural axioms. An examination of conservation targets will serve as a demonstration.

Four broad categories account for virtually all of the energy consumed in the U.S. Building-related activities make up about a third of this total.

Recognizing waste

Because it was the present stock of buildings that had been found to be such important energy consumers, and because many of these buildings had a life expectancy of at least 50 years, the first responsibility was to understand how they used electricity, fuel oil, gas, and coal. This led to detailed information that had never before been assembled about buildings. Architects and engineers had believed that they were producing functional, high-performance buildings; the studies proved otherwise. Even the housekeeping options available to the operations and maintenance staffs were shown to have the potential for savings of 20–25%.

For example, if one examines the most characteristic new building form developed through modern technology—the high-rise office building—rec-

109

Lighting represents more than half the total energy use in many commercial office buildings.

Peter Vandermark—Stock, Boston

ords of the quarter century following World War II reveal a steady increase in the average amount of energy required for their operation. A study conducted by Charles Lawrence, then New York City's public utility specialist, of 86 city office buildings built between 1950 and 1970 established that each five-year period showed an average increase of energy use per square foot above the previous one and a doubling over the 20-year range. The highest energy user consumed more than seven times the energy value per rentable square foot per year established by the federal General Services Administration as a reasonable level for an efficient office building.

A factor that upon first inspection appears primarily to affect energy accounting methods actually influences decisions and choices as well. Used on the site, one kilowatt-hour (kw-hr) of electrical energy has a value of 3,413 British thermal units (BTU). It requires an energy input between 10,000 and 11,500 BTU to generate it at the utility's power station and about 10% more to transmit it over power lines and transform its voltage up and down. If electricity is considered only at its site value, it would be a system of choice for space heating or hot-water heating. On the other hand, if all of the energy that is wasted in generation and transmission is considered, electricity in most cases will be one of the least efficient alternatives. Other related drawbacks include the facts that electricity is generally much more expensive than other choices and that it is an inappropriate use of high-grade energy. If the underlying purpose of an energy conservation program is the actual reduction of overall energy use, then it is quite logical and informative to consider the efficiency of the energy source.

There is a further advantage in cutting down unnecessary electrical use.

110

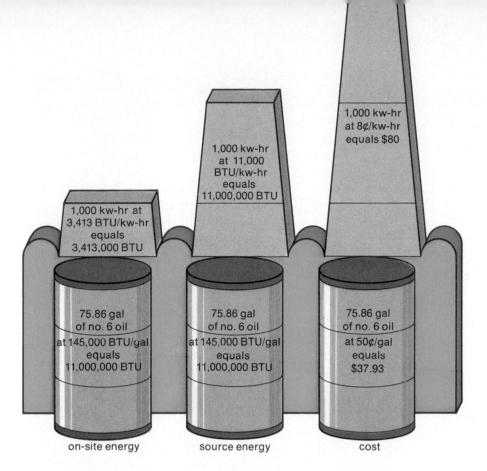

1,000 kw-hr at 3,413 BTU/kw-hr equals 3,413,000 BTU

1,000 kw-hr at 11,000 BTU/kw-hr equals 11,000,000 BTU

1,000 kw-hr at 8¢/kw-hr equals $80

75.86 gal of no. 6 oil at 145,000 BTU/gal equals 11,000,000 BTU

75.86 gal of no. 6 oil at 145,000 BTU/gal equals 11,000,000 BTU

75.86 gal of no. 6 oil at 50¢/gal equals $37.93

on-site energy   source energy   cost

Although electricity is generated by a number of different types of generators, including steam turbines, water-powered turbines, diesel motors, and wind-driven turbines, that are fueled with a variety of substances (coal, gas, petroleum, lignite, and uranium among them), reduction in electrical use will reduce the use of the least efficient generators because these units are brought on-line only after the base loads are provided by the more energy-efficient equipment. Thus, although benefits from elimination of unnecessary electrical use are computed from the average BTU rate to generate the electricity, the savings will be greater because the least efficient units, generally oil-fired ones, will be the generators taken off-line.

The trouble with lighting

Detailed energy-use profiles of hundreds of buildings revealed the enormous range of differences from one building type to another and even within a single building type. For example, lighting, which represents more than half the total energy use in many commercial office buildings, may account for only 15% in a hospital or 30% in an elementary school. Building code requirements and industry-wide standards that call for excessively high ventilation rates may in themselves be responsible for one-third of the total energy requirements in a school. In a typical New York City school, for instance, 35% of all the energy used is to heat the air that will then be exhausted to satisfy air-change requirements. A bit more energy is expended in the electricity necessary to operate the fans. Conservatively, two-thirds of this is wasted. Not until building codes are changed, however, will this use be cut back to a more reasonable level.

The generation of 1,000 kw-hr of electricity at a utility power station requires a total energy investment of about 11 million BTU, which is the energy equivalent of nearly 76 gallons of number 6 oil. Consumed on the site this quantity of oil still yields 11 million BTU whereas the value of on-site electrical energy is less than one-third of this amount. If the costs of energy-equivalent quantities of electricity and oil are compared, electricity in general is much more expensive.

111

Electric light switching for New York City's World Trade Center is controlled by a computer that turns on or off a quarter of a floor at a time. Air conditioning is zoned to control 33 floors on a facade as a unit. Consequently, accommodations for even one late-working individual require that an entire quarter of a floor be lighted and 33 floors of one facade be cooled. Recent changes in the building's systems have allowed more individualized control.

In the past five years, the single category of lighting has been recognized as an immediately available reservoir for savings. It is now commonplace in schools, commercial buildings, airports, and markets to find half the overhead lights turned off in work spaces, corridors, and recreational areas. Yet, the activities in the spaces proceed much as they always have, and there is no impression of deprivation. A systematic examination of activities that take place in the buildings offers the possibilities of still further reductions. In fact, within a category that represents 6% of all energy use, reductions in lighting use alone can save 20–50% of this value.

Following the Blackwell report, a 1958 lighting study that recommended a significant increase in light levels, electrical engineers and architects began designing such levels into their projects. Although other studies demonstrated that these levels offered no appreciable gain in human performance or benefits to health, they were completely accepted and often far exceeded on the theory that if more is better, still more is still better. So much heat was introduced by the lighting system that it was able to provide the entire heat requirement of the building in winter; yet it introduced the same amount of heat in the summer, increasing enormously the work and size of air-conditioning systems. Presence of this excessive lighting load has allowed many of the first-level energy reductions in modern buildings.

Refinements of the lighting systems offer the potentiality for other significant cuts. One effective means is through the use of task lighting, the application of light specifically to the area of work, in place of high levels of lighting throughout the space. Selective switching that permits lighting to be turned off when there is no activity in the space is another means. The use of fixtures that permit changes in light intensity according to the particular use of the space is a third. The replacement of inefficient light sources and fixtures is still another choice.

Scheduling and decentralized control

The minimum energy requirements for any given set of services have been determined, and when efficient systems have been identified or devised to accomplish them, the next steps in conservation studies are to determine where specifically these services are needed, and when. For instance, although the systems of many hospitals are designed to provide carefully controlled conditions 24 hours of every day, many services are in use only part of the time and generally on a scheduled basis. The operating-room schedule might call for its use 35 of the 168 hours per week. Because its systems are designed to provide as many as 25 complete changes of expensively conditioned air every hour, with all of it exhausted to the outside after it has been through the operating suite, measures that can be instituted to provide these conditions only when needed will save both energy and money. A recently analyzed 114-bed hospital had the potential to reduce its energy use by 12,750 gallons of oil and 250,000 kilowatt-hours of electricity annually by modifying the air-handling systems to operate in harmony with scheduling of the different medical services.

For simplicity of installation and decreased cost during construction, the number of control points introduced into mechanical systems, including

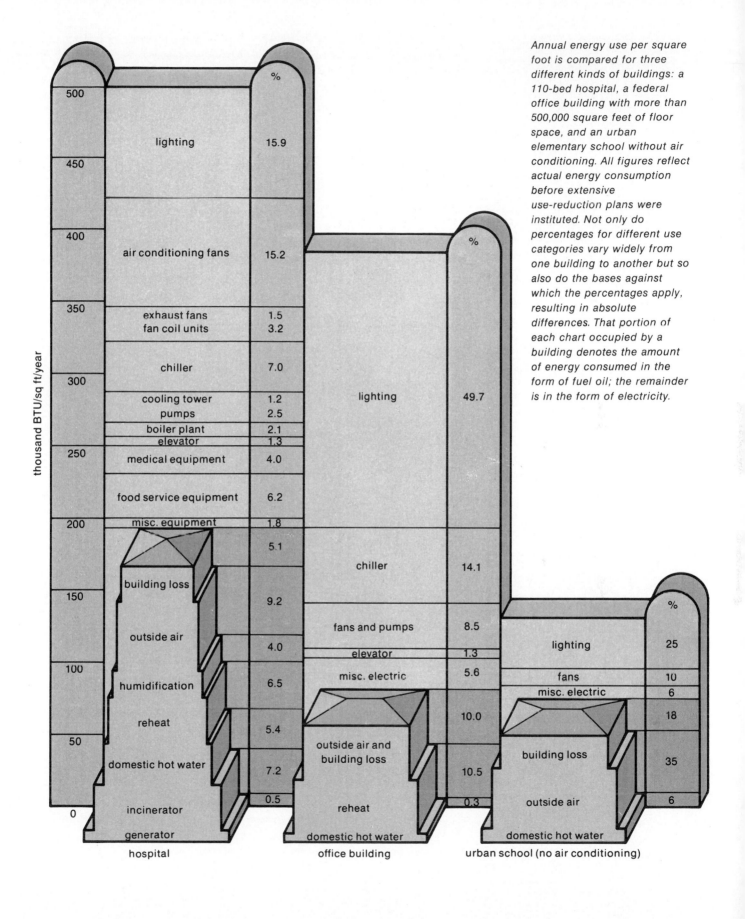

thousand BTU/sq ft/year

hospital

	%
lighting	15.9
air conditioning fans	15.2
exhaust fans	1.5
fan coil units	3.2
chiller	7.0
cooling tower	1.2
pumps	2.5
boiler plant	2.1
elevator	1.3
medical equipment	4.0
food service equipment	6.2
misc. equipment	1.8
building loss	5.1
outside air	9.2
humidification	4.0
reheat	6.5
domestic hot water	5.4
incinerator	7.2
generator	0.5

office building

	%
lighting	49.7
chiller	14.1
fans and pumps	8.5
elevator	1.3
misc. electric	5.6
outside air and building loss	10.0
reheat	10.5
domestic hot water	0.3

urban school (no air conditioning)

	%
lighting	25
fans	10
misc. electric	6
building loss	18
outside air	35
domestic hot water	6

Annual energy use per square foot is compared for three different kinds of buildings: a 110-bed hospital, a federal office building with more than 500,000 square feet of floor space, and an urban elementary school without air conditioning. All figures reflect actual energy consumption before extensive use-reduction plans were instituted. Not only do percentages for different use categories vary widely from one building to another but so also do the bases against which the percentages apply, resulting in absolute differences. That portion of each chart occupied by a building denotes the amount of energy consumed in the form of fuel oil; the remainder is in the form of electricity.

lighting, was greatly reduced during the two decades of intensive building after World War II. Part of it was justified as providing greater flexibility; since one did not actually know where the maximum requirement of a system would be needed, it would be safest to provide it continuously everywhere. A second reason for centralizing control points was to make the system more compatible with computer control.

Although central computerized control can turn lights and other systems on or off according to prearranged schedules, wiring for each connection is quite expensive. In addition, when there are thousands of lights and hundreds of offices with different uses, different schedules, and different requirements for practical reasons, the temptation is high to gang together large numbers of systems. The results are familiar: the entire floor of a commercial building that is either all lighted or all dark, or the entire face of a building that is either totally air conditioned to a single level of comfort or totally without treated air. Aside from the broadness of the system, it was also discovered that predetermination of the times that systems were to be turned on or off, as required for computer control, was only realistic if the work performed was absolutely undifferentiated from day to day. One corporation, IBM, found that in many of its buildings it was more energy efficient to allow individuals to turn lights on and off as they came in or left. Consequently it has taken many of its lighting systems off computer control in favor of space-by-space switching.

Among the energy-reducing options that have been developed has been the introduction of additional controls. In lighting this means simply more switching, either on a fixture-by-fixture or space-by-space basis. To be entirely successful as an energy-reduction tactic, it requires the cooperation of the user, a highly significant variable. Either one optimistically assumes that users who understand the underlying reason for seeking these reductions will comply conscientiously with requirements, or it becomes inevitable that the only reductions one can count on are those that can be achieved by technological means.

The following instance is representative of the kinds of unexpected problems that can arise with user-controlled systems. In schoolrooms laid out with a panel of separate switches near the door to operate rows of lights both near and far from windows, it has been observed that all the lights are almost always turned on as a group, usually with one upward gesture of the hand. One method of overcoming this is to place those lights nearest the window on an automatic, light-level–controlled switch. Another, perhaps more preferable solution is to locate the switch for these lights away from the door and on a wall close to the windows where an immediate and obvious cause-and-effect relationship appears when the lights are turned on or off.

The extra personal effort required to turn systems on or off can be offset by motivations that arise from the very process of decentralization. In place of the prevailing sense of alienation and of frustration at having no control over the conditions of one's surroundings, these changes reintroduce a quality of individualism and differentiation into the physical environment. In existing buildings, which are the targets for these savings, it is difficult and expensive to achieve all potential reductions. At one end of the range of choices are cost-free modifications that can be introduced with no changes in equipment. At the opposite end are major modifications or replacements of built-in systems that are partially buried in walls and floors. Where to draw the justifiable cut-off line between these extremes must be based on such factors as the cost and efficiency of other fuel-reduction choices, cost and scarcity of the type of fuel that will be saved, and governmental tax incentives and other financial benefits that will accrue to the owners and users of the buildings affected. A tax benefit for the addition of insulation and storm sash is an example of this kind of incentive. A massive government-financed program for the inspection and adjustment of all home-heating oil burners would be another.

Design for the future

In addition to fostering extensive benefits and improvements to the more than 100 million existing buildings in the U.S., this concentrated examination of building performance has deeply affected attitudes toward architectural theory and building design. In the early 1950s the functional, rational direction of architectural design was somewhat submerged by a stress on easily-built structures with relatively undifferentiated facades, sealed to avoid the complexities of operable openings for light and air and totally dependent on increasingly large and expensive mechanical plants. The necessity for new buildings to operate with lessened dependency on these energy-consuming internal systems—and possibly in emergencies to operate in a limited way with no consumption of fuel whatsoever—offers an immediate challenge to apply the knowledge recently gained.

After a transitional period of construction, new buildings will have more floor space in close proximity to the outdoors. The various systems that make up the exterior wall will have a far greater performance capability. When insulation requirements are high, the wall will be able to prevent most unwanted heat from entering the building and, conversely, to keep heat in during cold weather. On the other hand, when heat transfer is desirable, it will be able to provide for it. Such a wall will introduce natural light and distribute it deep into the space, using different methods on the different exposures. It will be able to introduce necessary air into the spaces within the building but will keep out unwanted particulates and noise. It will allow the Sun's rays to contribute to winter heating but reflect them (or intercept them for other purposes) when solar heat would create discomfort. Winds will be used for cooling but will be diverted when they are too strong, too cold, or too pollutant-laden.

All of these environmentally responsive characteristics would differ from one climatic region to another and would be applied differently to each building according to its needs. As these buildings became a larger and larger part of the entire building stock, the quality of towns and cities would change, with buildings that are richer in scale and detail and more representative of the complex life going on behind their facades. The path to this change has been opened by the extensive work being done in energy conservation—the more efficient use of energy—and can be expected to extend into the future.

Built in 1890–94 and still in use, the Reliance Building in Chicago (facing page, top) provides guidance for modern energy-conscious architects. The street-facing facades are composed of large fixed windows that provide ample natural light and small narrow side windows that open for ventilation. Architect Le Corbusier's Unité d'Habitation (facing page, bottom), a hotel-apartment building in Marseille, France, incorporates design features called sun breaks that had their precedents in Mediterranean and tropical structures. Windows on the long facades facing east and west and on the end facade facing south are set back into concrete wells to keep out the Sun's heat. The building has no windows facing north. At Le Corbusier's chapel (above) at Ronchamp, France, daylight illuminates the interior through deep wall recesses and through a gap between ceiling and wall. Candles provide the only light at night.

115

Saving the Sacred Stones

by Roy Davies

Scientists and restorers with daring imagination and technological skill are working to rescue the "timeless" stone monuments of the world's cities from the ravages of weather and pollution.

In Athens a Greek struggles to return a huge area of powdery gypsum to solid marble. North of Rome an Englishman coaxes the growth of a stone statue. In a score of European cities scientists expose the surfaces of every kind of building stone to chemicals, laser beams, gamma rays, and even bacteria in a desperate race against time. The nightmare they all face is that largely because of industrial pollution most of the ancient buildings left in the world are crumbling away, and as yet there is no agreement on how the deterioration should be stopped. The magnificent carvings, sculptures, facades, spires, towers, gargoyles, buttresses, arches, walls, and foundations of mankind's architectural history comprise an awesome inheritance. To pass it on in a worse condition than it was received could forever attract the scorn of future generations.

Recognizing the problem

Stone has always decayed. It decays in ordinary atmospheric conditions free from industrial pollution. Be it marble, limestone, sandstone, granite, or basalt, stone begins dying from the moment it is hewn from its quarry bed. The specialists of earlier centuries, however, saw no problem worth discussing. Rotting stone was cut away and replaced by the armies of stonemasons who proliferated near towns which could boast anything from antiquity. This process of renewal was thorough; as an example, it has been estimated that only eight original stones remain on the exterior of Westminster Abbey, one of London's most eminent medieval buildings. As late as the 1940s, apart from well-thumbed works on the destruction of stone buildings by the Austrian Alois Kieslinger, only a handful of articles on weathering and the preservation of monuments, stone, and buildings indicated the possibility of a problem and how it might be tackled.

By the mid-1960s attitudes had changed. A world grown more conscious of its obligations to preserve the works of both nature and man found that the decay of stone had become a ruthless enemy in a very short space of time. Major symposia on stone and its problems were held at Turin, Brussels, and Warsaw in 1966 and in New York three years later. In Venice in 1970 UNESCO brought experts from all over the world to discuss the conservation of stone, and similar meetings took place in La Rochelle, France, in 1972, Athens in 1976, and Paris in 1977. Today in every country chemists, biologists, nuclear physicists, and geologists are eagerly offering original ideas on how and when to proceed with solutions.

But enthusiasm alone is no substitute for agreement and cooperation. In addition, a philosophical difference effectively divides some of the very people who could assist each other. Restorers and conservationists argue that unless something is done to prevent the present stock of inheritance from rotting it will not exist much longer in any recognizable state. On the other hand, some architectural and artistic aficionados contend that everything has a natural life span and should not be preserved artificially. Such polarization reduces to a simple choice: keep it up or let it crumble.

There is one point, however, about which no one argues. The industrial by-products of sulfur dioxide, hydrogen sulfide, and carbon dioxide are directly to blame for the extent and acceleration of the deterioration of stone

Frank Siteman—Stock, Boston

Once rich in surface detail, a gargoyle's blunted and pocked visage glowers over the streets of Paris from its perch on the Cathedral of Notre-Dame.

ROY DAVIES is a Television Producer for the Archaeology and History Unit, British Broadcasting Corporation, London.

Illustrations by John Craig

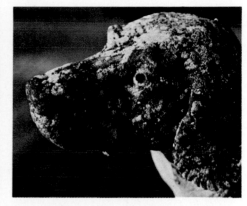

Effects of stone decay are evident in a nearly featureless waterspout from St. Peter's in Wantage, England (top left), in a huge eroded face at Tivoli in Italy (top center), and in details from the Arch of Constantine in Rome (left). Lichen, a composite of two symbiotic organisms, decorates a castle ornament in Loches, France (above). If and to what extent lichen damages or protects stone are questions under active investigation.

Two weathered carvings adorn a wall of the cathedral at Chartres, France. The entire face of the figure on the right has spalled as the result of internal pressure from decay products that penetrated the stone surface in solution and then recrystallized.

monuments in the past half century. Falling rain dissolves these gases, forming sulfuric and carbonic acids, which have an indisputable effect on stone. Carbonic acid, for instance, is responsible for the formation of stalactites and stalagmites in limestone caves and for the caves themselves.

Initially, when these acids come into contact with building stone, part of the surface is transformed chemically and dissolves, and soluble salts form. These salts are carried in solution by capillary action from the surface into the pores of the masonry. When the water evaporates, salt crystals form in large spaces between mineral granules. When moisture invades these spaces again, the crystals often redissolve and travel deeper into the stone. In this, the second stage of the decay process, the large accumulation of crystals exerts increasing pressure on the granules of stone around them, forcing crystal formation even in the very fine pores of the stone. In these tiny passages even greater stresses mount, eventually causing the breakdown of granule adhesion. As a result whole areas near the surface of the stone flake off in a phenomenon known as spalling. This kind of decay has attacked stone on the Athenian Acropolis, the cathedrals at Reims in France and Cologne in West Germany, York Minster in England, and many other beautiful buildings of the world. Near their walls a grainy dust bears witness to the silent destruction going on continuously overhead.

Although the problem is relatively simple to define, the search for and discovery of a universal solution has not proved the routine scientific task some people had expected. Controlled laboratory simulations involving sulfur dioxide, water, and stone have not successfully reproduced the kind of reaction that is taking its toll every day on ancient buildings. Something is missing, an unknown factor apparently acting as a catalyst in natural conditions. Scientists do not yet know exactly what has accounted for their failure, but some believe it is related to the presence of bacteria in the stone. Consequently, the kinds and number of bacteria on deteriorating stone are being assessed, and plans are under way to infect test materials in the laboratory with bacteria to simulate actual conditions more closely.

Scientists from the Central Institute of Restoration in Rome recognized some time ago that the presence of nitrate and sulfate salts in decaying stone may have been produced by enzymatic reactions of specific organisms. In an attempt to determine the role of these microorganisms, they found no relevant differences in bacterial development between urban environments, where automobile emissions are heavy, and rural environments. In their opinion the bacterial population of stone that would thrive on atmospheric pollutants is always present, regardless of pollution levels.

In related work, Richard Lallemant and Serge Deruelle of Pierre and Marie Curie University in Paris have examined the effect that lichens—symbiotic associations of algae and fungi—might have on ancient buildings, where they are often permitted to remain for aesthetic reasons. Lallemant and Deruelle concluded that, although in certain cases the chemical characteristics of lichen by-products might lead to stone damage, in other cases their attack is negligible. The investigators suggested that lichens may even help protect stone against the more serious attacks of air pollution.

Apart from the influence of living organisms, there are other puzzling

Deruelle S., Lallemant R. et Roux C.: la vegétation lichénique de la Basilique Notre-Dame de l'Epine (Marne). *Documents phytosociologiques*, nouvelle serie

complications. For example, a group of Italians working as a research unit to study the statues in the Boboli Gardens in Florence discovered that air pollution affects stone in different ways even in cases where objects are relatively close together—sometimes only meters apart. In Venice the atmosphere is known to deteriorate stone more severely than that in London even though rainfall and sulfur dioxide levels are lower in Venice than in London. But studies also have shown that condensation of atmospheric moisture on building surfaces is greater in Venice than London. Whether condensation patterns induce the formation of sulfuric acid more easily in Venice than in London, and more broadly, whether humidity variations play an important role in unexplained deterioration are questions still to be answered.

Chemist Maria Serra and physicist Giuseppe Starace, both from the University of Rome, studied how sulfur dioxide actually reacts with calcite, the major component of marble and limestone, to form gypsum. They discovered that the quantity of sulfur dioxide absorbed and transformed in the oxidizing phase of the reaction between acid and stone is dependent upon the relative humidity and the characteristics of the stone surface. Their results could be useful for understanding the open-air phenomena of attack in the absence of rain and surface condensation and for understanding decay processes that go on even in such closed environments as atmospherically controlled museums.

In addition to acid attack, the action of frost in some countries is a strong influence on the deterioration of stone. Again, laboratory simulations of the heat-freeze-thaw cycle do not seem to approach the phenomenon that produces stone decay in nature. As scientific research continues, new and stranger reasons for stone decay continue to emerge, but airborne pollution is still the greatest hazard to be faced.

Perhaps the best known example is the well-publicized acid decay of the beautiful caryatids, the graceful ladies supporting part of the Erechtheum

Lichen encrusts stones of the Basilique Notre-Dame de l'Epine, located in an agricultural region in Marne département, France. Recent research has related changes in the composition of such overgrowths to the combined effects of humidity and fertilizer use in the vicinity.

temple on the Acropolis. Carved from the marble of Mount Pentelicus near Athens nearly 2,500 years ago, the stance of the statues from afar is as delicate as it was in antiquity. But from a few meters away, the faces of the five original statues left standing are unrecognizable, decaying lumps of stone. Ironically, the unseen backs of the statues, protected from the damaging rain, still show the actual marks of the sculptors' chisels. The cathedrals of York, Lincoln, and Wells in the U.K.; Chartres, Reims, and Strasbourg in France; Cologne in West Germany; and Milan in Italy are also under severe acid attack. There are many other examples in these countries as well as in Belgium, Poland, Yugoslavia, and Czechoslovakia.

Early conservation work

Every great cathedral still has its stonemasons, and upkeep of the great minsters requires them fully all year round. Yet theirs is the centuries-old job of restoration, whereas the role of the conserver has evolved very quickly. Before World War II one or two people experimented with primitive methods of conservation, but their work hardly made an impact on the vast amount of stone waiting to be treated. One of those who tried was Arthur R. Warnes, recognized at the time as the expert in stone decay in the British Isles.

Warnes attempted to harden and consolidate the surface of stone with a chemical that precipitated silicon dioxide within the pore space of the stone. He treated and repaired the Angel Frieze above the Christchurch Gate in Canterbury before World War II, and about the same time he removed two and a half tons of rusting iron bars from the flying buttresses of the Market Cross at Chichester and replaced them with a half ton of nonrustable alloy.

Although restoration efforts on the ancient Parthenon (below) have continued throughout the 20th century, the structure owes much of its reconstructed appearance to the early work of Nicholas Balanos. Balanos used iron beams to reinforce the caryatid-supported porch roof of the Erechtheum (facing page, left) and throughout the rest of the Parthenon. By the late 1970s severe rusting and swelling of the iron had cracked the marble around it. In a detail of the Parthenon (facing page, right), deterioration of the lintels progresses despite the use of reinforcements.

A. F. Kersting

As Warnes was removing the rusting metal, Nicholas Balanos, a Greek architect, was nearing the end of a mammoth project of inserting hundreds of iron bars and beams into the marble pillars and walls of the temples of the Acropolis in Athens as part of a successful reconstruction for the Greek Department of Antiquities. The task had taken him more than 30 years to finish, but in that time he re-erected much of the fallen Parthenon, rebuilt the ancient gateway and the adjacent Temple of Athena Nike, and strengthened huge areas of the Erechtheum. His work was highly praised, but disaster followed. In the past ten years the iron bars Balanos used in his reconstruction have rusted and swollen in their marble beds and are cracking their unique housings throughout the famous rock. Balanos had no way of knowing that iron would behave so viciously when confronted with the corrosive maritime atmosphere of Athens. But he can be faulted for failing to copy the practice of the ancient Greeks, who had covered their iron dowels and joints with a layer of corrosion-resistant lead.

The techniques available to Balanos were few: stone masonry and metal reinforcements, and for such features as the broken drums of the huge Parthenon columns, entirely new sections made from concrete, which at the time was thought to resemble the color of marble. However, it was the discovery of polymers in the early 20th century that was to revolutionize the whole concept of stone conservation.

Polymer coatings

Silicone, or polysiloxane, polymers are products of chemical research that, by the nature of their composition, find their place between organic and inorganic chemistry. Like other polymers they consist of chains or networks of smaller molecules chemically linked together. They differ from most of their genre, however, in that their structural backbones contain no carbon but instead are made up of siloxane chains, in which silicon and oxygen atoms alternate. Today silicones are employed in numerous production processes and as components of finished products. But it was only when scientists began searching for a solution to stone decay that they discovered another use for these versatile chemicals. Mixed silicone polymers are

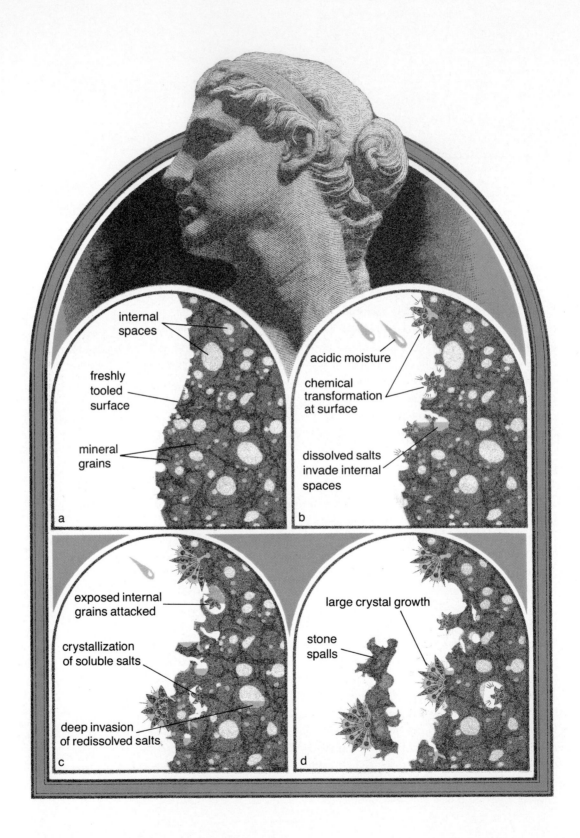

manufactured by combining certain silicones with other, organic polymers.
As a result, one of their outstanding attributes of value to stone preservation
is a certain resistance to water and other solvents and chemicals. Unfortunately there is a problem. According to one system of classification—and
one now vastly important in the field of stone conservation—polymers that
exhibit a high degree of resistance to erosion and chemical change, such
as the silicones, are termed ''hard,'' whereas those based on acrylics and
other less inert materials are termed ''soft.'' The Venice convention of 1970
is remembered for one thing more than anything else. That convention drew
up a fundamental rule that today in the discipline has the force of a com-
mandment. The Venice delegates agreed that from that moment no conservation treatment should be undertaken which could not be reversed if

*The progress of acidic attack on a
stone surface, as described on p. 120,
is depicted in sequence (facing page):
(a) unweathered stone, (b) initial
decay, (c) decay penetrates more
deeply, and (d) recrystallizing salts
fracture stone. Electron micrograph
(above) of the surface of decaying
Pentelic marble from the Acropolis
reveals the structure of individual
gypsum crystals. Deteriorating
caryatids (left) bear part of the
Erechtheum porch roof. A caryatid
head is molded to make plaster
copies (top).*

necessary at some time in the future. Effectively this cancelled out any use of hard polymers, including the potentially fruitful silicones.

In Venice itself, however, Kenneth Hempel, formerly of the Victoria and Albert Museum in London, recently removed the statues of the four virtues from the Porta della Carta, the entrance to the Doges' palace on St. Mark's Square and, in defiance of convention, cleaned and treated them with hard silicone polymer. Nearing the end of his task in late 1978, he was waiting for the opportunity to reinstall them, confident in their future ability to survive any attacks from airborne acids of the industrial areas across the lagoon.

Hempel began experimenting with polymers more than a decade ago. After working to conserve the treasures of Florence following flooding in the Po Delta in 1966, Hempel was invited to advise the "Venice in Peril" organization on stone conservation. He has since consolidated several statues and the Loggia, the marble base of the massive brick tower in St. Mark's Square. At first, working with hard silicones he restored the marble monuments simply by painting the material onto the cleaned surface. In the past few years, however, he vastly improved this technique by adapting industrial equipment to suck the resin further into the pores of the stone. The process subjects the stone to a powerful vacuum, ensuring that all air and moisture is dragged from the internal spaces. When pressure is allowed to return, silicone is drawn from a reservoir into the vacated spaces. Once set deep inside the stone, the polymer ensures that moisture, the killer element in stone destruction, is unable to reenter.

Hempel's work can never be reversed, a fact clear both to him and to the Venetian authorities. In Hempel's view the statues of the four virtues were in a terminal condition as a result of air pollution. If they were ever to be replaced in their original positions, they had to be completely protected, and the only way was by deep impregnation with a silicone or an acrylic resin. Reversible in theory, acrylic resin is impossible to remove entirely from the pores of a stone building. Hence, Hempel reasoned that relatively little would actually be risked by the use of silicone. His argument was accepted and so

Industrially polluted 20th-century Venice (above) exacts a heavy toll from the city's artistic heritage. Statuary decorating a portal of the Doges' palace (top) underwent recent cleaning to remove a dark crust of acidic decay. During a restoration of the facade of Saint Mark's Cathedral (left), one of the famous horses above the main entrance at the lower right was removed to the mezzanine to serve as a test object for various preservation methods. (Facing page) Battered stone refugees of the 1966 flood in Florence lend their tortured expressions to a modern disaster.

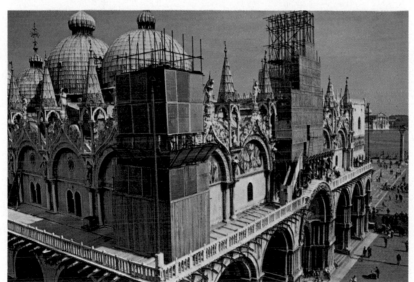

(Above) Dmitri Kessel; (top, right) © Ronald Sheridan; (bottom, right) Dmitri Kessel

was his solution. When finally replaced on the ornately carved doorway, the four virtues will be their original pink color, and every pore will be filled with a material set as hard as the original marble.

Hempel's method of completely and irreversibly sealing the stone pores does have a serious disadvantage, particularly if used to treat stone in large volumes or on building exteriors where only the exposed portion of the stone can be sealed. Such treatment hampers the ability of stone to "breathe," or to allow water to migrate outward. Water that remains trapped behind the treated zone or that has come from elsewhere in the building will eventually cause the stone to decay from within. Recently, other silicon-containing formulations have appeared on the market. These have the potential to waterproof and strengthen stone while still allowing it to breathe. However, even with the most promising of these materials, a formulation called Brethane, the general lack of experience with polymer coatings makes its use a risky business at present.

Brethane is a polymerizing compound developed by Clifford Price and Lesley Arnold at the Building Research Establishment in the U.K. Applied by a spray technique on small areas at a time, it will trap soluble salts and consolidate stone to a depth of a few centimeters, or more than an inch, by lining the pores. Because it does not seal the surface, more consolidant could be added at a later date if necessary.

In the absence of support for any irreversible method, perhaps the most encouraging technique is that of epoxy impregnation, the development of two U.S. investigators, K. Lal Gauri and Seymore Lewin. Gauri and Lewin have suggested that the cavities of the stone be filled with deep-penetrating epoxy resin and covered with a float of fluorocarbon polymer. The epoxy resin is reversible and has great adhesive powers for consolidating the damaged crystal system of the stone, but it is sensitive to ultraviolet radiation and would soon deteriorate with exposure to sunlight, allowing resumption of decay. The fluorocarbon-polymer float, which is also reversible, ensures that water cannot penetrate the stone surface and also acts as a filter against ultraviolet light.

In West Germany the problems of stone consolidation have been treated entirely differently on some of the country's municipal buildings. To the purists who are appalled at the measures taken by Hempel in Venice, one technique used in West Germany in particular is unspeakable. The principal aim of most stone conservers is to retain as much surface detail of the original stone as possible. Yet on fabrics of some of their most beautiful buildings, German restorers begin with a wire brush and scrub back to the undecayed stone, reducing the surviving details to dust. Then they consolidate the sound fabric with a resin specially developed for sandstone, and finally build up the surface with a compound of sand, silicones, and acrylics to the immaculate detail it displayed before the rotting process began. The method may be unacceptable in other countries, but the artwork of the German restorers, who apparently have been able to reconstruct the thinking of the original stonemasons and carvers, is so good that it is difficult to fault from the vantage point of the scaffolding platforms, much less from the pavements and squares below.

(Top) John F. Asmus, University of California, San Diego; (below) photos by K. Lal Gauri, SCIENTIFIC AMERICAN, June 1978

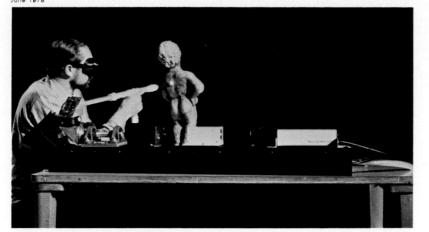

Restorer (left) uses a laser to selectively evaporate black encrustation from a marble sculpture of the Doges' palace in Venice. Two electron micrographs of polymer-impregnated Georgia marble reveal differences between treatments that partially (below) or entirely (bottom) plug the pores between mineral grains. Incomplete filling is desirable because it slows penetration by water while still allowing the stone to breathe.

Many ideas, little daring

The explosion of concern over stone conservation in the past 20 years is reverberating around every ancient building, monument, carving, and sculpture in the Western world, but the science is still relatively new and the warnings against proceeding with uncertainty are a great restriction. This need not be a bad philosophy for the discipline in the long run, but stone is crumbling now. In the absence of any internationally accepted solution, various conservers have begun work with some trepidation in the face of potential international criticism.

In comparison to the boldness of Hempel, other plans for preservation often seemed guarded and tentative, as if their proponents sensed that the world of conservation would peer over the shoulder of a man or woman who dared to paint protective material on any speck of stone. However, in Great Britain restorers under the guidance of John Ashurst and Bob Bennett of the Department of the Environment are planning to conserve the ancient Romanesque porch of Malmesbury Abbey in Wiltshire using a fine spray technique to wash the building to remove encrustation, followed by spray application of irreversible Brethane as a consolidant. Another Briton, Robert Baker, has been using a limestone wash on Wells Cathedral to replace the lime released from the stone over many years. Many experts see his treatment as an advantage because it peels off after about 15 years, leaving the stone available either for rewashing or for application of a conservation agent yet to be developed.

On the fringe of the central problem are ingenious innovations that may prove quite helpful once they are refined for general use. A French firm, for example, is investigating the use of gamma rays to transform small molecules introduced into the pores of the stone into large-molecule, hard-set polymers. Having lower viscosity, small molecules are better able to penetrate the stone, providing for improved consolidation.

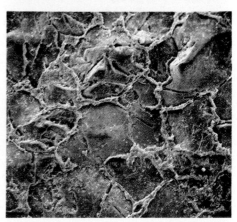

U.S. physicist John Asmus and Lino Marchesini of the University of Padua in Italy have used laser beams to remove the black encrustation caused by acid attack from decayed stone before consolidation. Again, however, there is a problem, one inherent in the nature of a laser. The most successful present method of cleaning away the encrustation is by use of an air-powered abrasive pencil that fires tiny glass or aluminum oxide beads at the affected area. In the hands of experts, such as the Italians working on the Porta della Carta in Venice, the pencil is an extremely satisfactory tool that can be manipulated over nooks and crannies of the most delicate sculptures with no more protection for workers than a dust mask. By contrast, the laser beam must be focused at a precise distance from the stone surface and the movement of the beam extremely carefully controlled. In addition, burns and blindness from the intense light are serious hazards.

In dealing with problems of surface cleaning, Hempel again has shown himself an innovator. At a conference in 1978 he explained that, mainly because of the time taken to clean a relatively small area and the cost of the process, he had applied himself to finding a "digestive pack" to remove encrustation from stone. He described how a formula for the pack was devised in the hope that the slight solubility of the crust in glycerol plus the slow liberation of ammonia from degrading urea would be effective. Experiments with the pack included a test on a piece of Istrian stone in Venice, in which it was shown that the area of black crust treated by the pack was much easier to clean, needing only half the time required for untreated areas. An additional bonus was that such traces of original paint as remained were unaffected and were revealed again.

Despite the pack's proven success, Anne Moncrieff, senior scientific officer at the Victoria and Albert Museum in London, had doubts about the mechanics of the cleaning action. Her tests showed that the nature of the activity in the pack was not chemical but bacterial. By late 1978, it was still not clear which types of bacteria were involved or how they produced their effects. Appealing for assistance, Hempel suggested that a strain of bacteria might be bred specifically for the task of removing encrustation.

In addition to receiving an invitation to demonstrate his pack in Athens, Hempel has intrigued the Greeks with another idea that, if successful, could ensure the future of the caryatids. While restoring the treasures of Florence, Hempel heard of the sulfurous springs of the village of San Filippo in the mountains of Tuscany between Rome and Siena. From deep underground, mineral-laden water gushes up in the vicinity, and the village seems to be built on and surrounded by massive calcite deposits that give a strange appearance to the rolling Tuscan hillside.

In San Filippo new deposits of calcite are laid down by the springs to a depth of a centimeter in less than six months. Hempel's idea was to place a latex rubber mold of a caryatid in one of the village streams so that water running through the mold deposited an ever increasing thickness of calcite within. In half a year he would have "grown" an exact copy of one of the original caryatids. With the right color and close-knit calcite crystal structure, exact copies of the caryatids could stand on the Acropolis while their originals rested free from attack in a new Acropolis museum.

Hempel's first attempt did not work. When the mold in its aluminum container was taken from the water in September 1977 it revealed no growth at all. Hempel realized almost at once what had gone wrong: in setting the mold in the stream he had succeeded in cutting off the air supply to the water inside the mold, a crucial factor in the growth of the calcite. A new attempt

Kenneth Hempel's method for "growing" stone copies of statues is illustrated on the facing page. (a) A latex mold of the statue—open at the top and bottom—is made, encased in an aluminum box, and placed in a San Filippo stream. (b) Mineral-laden water running through the box with access to air builds up an ever thickening deposit of calcite on the inside surface of the mold. (c) When the process is complete, the mold contains an exact duplicate of the statue, which can be erected in place of the original. In a series of laboratory tests, two marble samples (below) were treated with a material under evaluation as a protective agent. The sample on the right was then exposed to an atmosphere of sulfur dioxide and water vapor. The powdery decay product is gypsum.

Theodore Skoulikidis, National Technical University of Athens

Marvin Newman—Woodfin Camp & Associates

It is generally recognized that the condition of stone art and architecture in the Soviet Union is better than that in Western nations. Details of this achievement, however, await improved information exchange among restorers.

at San Filippo has taken this factor into account, and Hempel and the Greeks have their fingers firmly crossed.

In the absence of Hempel's new stone copies, Greek researchers are attempting another solution. Theodore Skoulikidis, a chemist at the National Technical University of Athens, has studied the transformation under acid attack of the surface marble of the caryatids into a film of gypsum, which in some places is now four millimeters (about one-sixth of an inch) thick. Eventually this film will flake off, taking surface detail with it forever. Skoulikidis wishes to reverse the chemical transformation in a process that involves placing each caryatid in a high-temperature environment and exposing its surface layer of gypsum to carbon dioxide under pressure. His idea should work, but the public outcry that would emanate if anything went wrong with a caryatid makes any move impossible until success is a certainty.

An anxious future

Care and conscientiousness apart, costs of conservation are formidable and have been a major obstacle to progress. Sufficient consolidant for a cubic foot of crumbling stone can cost £7, or about $14. To preserve a small statue would cost more than ten times as much for materials alone, and such an expense for just the west front of Wells Cathedral could run as high as £65,000. On an individual basis such sums have been and can be raised, but to solve its own problems nationally each country needs a much more concentrated and expensive program than it is willing to mount at present. In the U.K., for example, the Building Research Centre, a government agency of 800 people, employs only one to deal with conservation techniques.

Left alone, the problem of stone decay can only worsen. Perhaps it will require a blow to national pride, such as the collapse of Cologne Cathedral or York Minster, before the right kind of attention can be commanded. There are no easy answers. Fitting a protective dome over the entire Acropolis now seems a ludicrous concept, yet this was one of the suggestions made to the Greeks when they first announced their plight. One such dome implies hundreds or thousands for every building in the world worth conserving.

Today once again the Acropolis is the focus of interest. The condition of its revered structures is known worldwide, and if nothing can solve the problems at Athens, then there is very little hope indeed for lesser monuments. Conservationists are especially attentive, for the method of conservation that will be permitted for the marbles of the ancient Greeks will be legitimized for use almost everywhere else. In the world of conservation the suspense mounts as all wait for that first splash of consolidating compound against the sacred stone.

"Construction of a Cathedral," a manuscript illustration by 15th-century painter Jean Fouquet. Debate continues today concerning not only how to preserve the monumental works of such builders but also whether they should simply be allowed to crumble with the passage of time, in accordance with the "natural order" of all material objects.

Corrosion–The Silent Scourge
by Jerome Kruger

National economies, defense, medical technology, public safety, and much of man's cultural heritage depend upon the continued efforts of scientists to understand metallic corrosion and to develop new protection techniques.

Corrosion is the cancer of materials. Just as human cancer silently and ruthlessly destroys living tissue, corrosion quietly and methodically devours the materials that underpin the technology of the 20th century. Although in recent years the term corrosion has come to refer to the destruction of all kinds of materials caused by their exposure to a variety of environments, more conventionally it is limited to the degradation of metals, the definition used in this article.

Rusted and pitted surfaces and gaping holes on automobiles, boats, gutters, screens, plumbing, and countless other metal items are a bane of everyday life. But corrosion has consequences much more serious than these casual encounters with it would indicate. Its effects profoundly influence the economy, health, safety, technology, and culture of society.

The price tag

Concerned about the waste of money and resources, the U.S. Congress requested in 1976 that the National Bureau of Standards produce a study of the economic effects of metallic corrosion in the United States. The project enlisted the help of Battelle Columbus Laboratories in Ohio and used input–output analysis, an economic tool developed by Nobel laureate Wassily W. Leontief that enables the complex interactions of all sectors of the economy to be considered. The overall cost of metallic corrosion to the U.S. economy was found to be $70 billion per year. This figure represents about 4% of the gross national product and is more than one and a half times the amount spent in 1977 to import crude oil into the U.S. The study also determined that $10 billion of the total cost could be avoided if currently available corrosion prevention measures were applied.

In recent years increasing use of metal implants in the body in the form of hip joints, pacemakers, pins, plates, and other prosthetic devices has

Weakened by stress corrosion, in 1967 part of the Silver Bridge (above) failed under the weight of rush-hour traffic and plunged into the Ohio River, killing 46 persons. Offshore oil-rig worker stands on steel pipe casings (facing page, top), which have begun to rust in the maritime atmosphere even before they are used. Inspector surveys nuclear waste containers (facing page, lower left), which must be made to withstand the heat and radioactivity of their contents as well as environmental attack. Photomicrographic cross section (facing page, lower right) reveals damage to the inside surface of a carbon steel waste container after undergoing compatibility tests for more than a year in contact with simulated waste sludge. The region on the right consists of a sludge-cement mixture; the steel on the left shows evidence of intergranular attack.

JEROME KRUGER *is Group Leader of the Corrosion and Electrodeposition Group, National Bureau of Standards, Washington, D.C.*

Illustrations by Dave Beckes

made corrosion an important consideration in the field of health. Implant corrosion problems typically appear as broken electrical connections, tissue inflammation caused by corrosion products around implants, and fracture of weight-bearing prosthetic components. For example, although the situation has now improved, first applications of metallic hip joints to alleviate arthritis were limited to persons over 60 years of age. It was decided that if these devices were used in younger patients, corrosion and other failure mechanisms could necessitate removal of the joints 10–15 years after implantation, a time when the individuals would likely be old and infirm.

Usually even more injurious to health than implant corrosion are problems that affect safety and cause severe injuries and loss of life. A dramatic instance is the collapse of the Silver Bridge over the Ohio River in 1967. This failure, attributed to stress corrosion, which will be discussed below, resulted in the deaths of 46 persons. Certain gas pipeline explosions have also been attributed to stress corrosion. Less dramatic and frequently unrecognized as corrosion problems are the sudden failures of aircraft, autos, bicycles, cable-supported platforms, and other metal structures and devices that serve the modern world. Finally, the possible corrosion of metallic containers for nuclear wastes is a health and safety concern that must play a crucial role in the formulation of any national plan for waste disposal.

Corrosion-resistant alloys, stainless steels, high-nickel alloys, and special thermally resistant formulations called superalloys are indispensable elements of industrial technology and modern defense systems. A number of the constituents making up these alloys have few or no sources of supply within the U.S.; most notable is chromium, major producers of which are Rhodesia (Zimbabwe), South Africa, and the U.S.S.R. Without the corrosion-resistant properties imparted by chromium, the foundations of an advanced industrial society and its defense would crumble.

The economic and strategic consequences of corrosion cannot be divorced from its technological effects, which often stand as barriers to new developments. Problems arise in the requirement for materials that can withstand increasingly high temperatures and pressures and highly corrosive environments; many times all of these extreme conditions are present simultaneously. The important field of energy generation offers a host of examples of corrosion as a hindrance to technological development. The success of controlled nuclear fusion will require solution of many materials problems, including the development of metals able to withstand corrosion at high temperatures. Similarly, the generation of energy from coal by magnetohydrodynamic systems, which pass hot ionized gas through magnetic fields, makes use of temperatures and environments that can obliterate materials in contact with the gas in surprisingly short times. Less demanding but still dependent on the solution of corrosion problems are solar energy systems that require alloys to withstand hot circulating heat-transfer fluids for long periods. Likewise, geothermal systems call for materials that resist highly concentrated solutions of corrosive salts at high temperatures and pressures. Drilling for oil in the sea and ever deeper on land requires overcoming such problems as stress corrosion, microbiological degradation, and a vast array of difficulties encountered in the highly corrosive marine environment.

Comparatively recent disclosures of the serious deterioration of artistically and culturally important gilded bronze statues in Venice, Italy, have aroused international concern. The corrosive processes responsible for the destruction of these priceless artifacts had been accelerated by the highly polluted atmosphere of the modern city. Similar or worse conditions exist in most such cities of the world. Even within the protected environments of the world's museums, conservators and restorers must fight to protect cultural treasures from the ravages of corrosion.

In the realm of art, corrosion can have beneficial as well as detrimental effects. Corrosion is responsible for the beautiful green, black, and brown

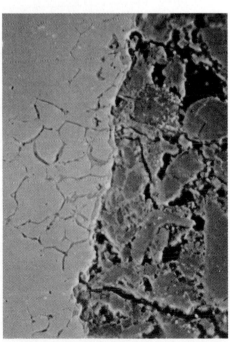

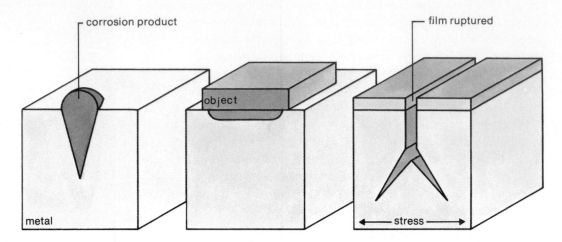

pitting corrosion   crevice corrosion   stress corrosion

corrosion product

film ruptured

object

metal

stress

patinas that form on bronze statuary and copper roofs. The corrosion of "weathering steels" produces a dark brown protective layer that is considered beautiful by some and ugly by others. Used more and more by artists and architects, such material is found, for example, in the large abstract sculpture by Picasso in Chicago. Interestingly, the formation of the patina on these steels is aided by polluted atmospheres.

Causes

The corrosion of metals has its origins in a very basic fact: with the exception of gold the metallic state is an unnatural and hence unstable condition of matter. Uncombined metal atoms must be wrested from their naturally occurring compounds, or ores—a stable condition of matter—by enormous expenditures of energy in the smelting process. Corrosion results from the overwhelming tendency of metals to react with oxygen, water, and other nonmetallic substances present in the Earth's environment and thereby return to the more natural stable state of an ore.

Fortunately, the conversion of crucially important metals is arrested by the beginning stages of the very process that seeks to return them to their natural state. Paradoxically, the initial reaction of a metal with an environment in which it can survive usually produces a very thin but protective film. This film, which in some cases can be only ten atomic layers thick, seals the metal surface from further attack and allows the metal beneath it to remain perfectly stable as long as the protective ability of the film is not compromised. Corrosion results from a breaching of the film barrier.

To illustrate, aluminum metal has an overwhelming tendency to react with atmospheric oxygen and become aluminum oxide. The aluminum oxide that first forms on an aluminum surface, however, very effectively seals off the aluminum from further contact with oxygen, and hence aluminum can be extensively used by itself or alloyed to make all kinds of objects from cooking pots to jet aircraft skins. Yet, if a metal is exposed to a corrosive environment

Deborah Collings—Stock, Boston

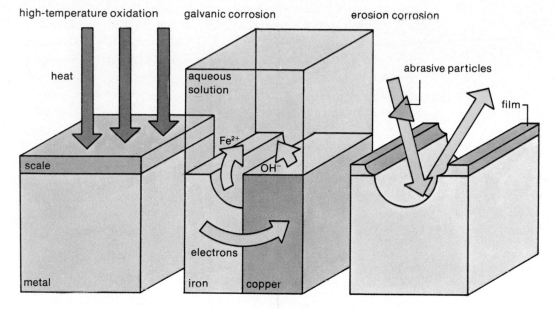

high-temperature oxidation   galvanic corrosion   erosion corrosion

heat

abrasive particles

film

scale

aqueous
solution

Fe²⁺

OH⁻

electrons

metal   iron   copper

such as seawater, its film may be breached by dissolution of the oxide or by penetration at weak spots. The metal then begins to revert to its natural state—a crumbling corrosion product or a dissolved salt.

Dissolution of the entire protective film and uniform degradation of the metal is called generalized corrosion. By contrast, an attack that takes place because of a breakdown of the protective film at defective sites results in a highly localized form of corrosion called pitting. Pitting corrosion can drill holes in thick sheets of metal. Pitting usually occurs not only because of the breakdown of the film at discrete sites but also because of the formation of crusts or piles of solid corrosion products at those sites. Under this loose cover a concentration of damaging chemical species that make a pit grow can develop. Corrosion products are not alone in providing such a covering over metal surfaces; a pile of sand, a barnacle, a gasket, or a collection of leaves in a gutter likewise can serve as the canopy under which highly corrosive environments evolve. The corrosion resulting on such covered surfaces is called crevice corrosion.

Nature's protective films may also fail to stop corrosion when metals are exposed to high-temperature environments. High temperatures accelerate corrosive chemical reactions and enhance the movement of reactive species through the film. High-temperature corrosion or oxidation taken to its extremes is the literal burning of a metal. Another way protective films can be defeated is by mechanical processes. If a metal structure is distorted by pulling or bending, the protective film may break and allow corrosive environments to attack the metal at the exposed sites. This type of attack leads to a kind of degradation called stress corrosion. Similarly, if a metal surface is bombarded with fast-moving abrasive particles—for example, windblown sand—bare spots are exposed and erosion corrosion results.

One form of corrosion, an electrochemical process called galvanic corrosion, is especially worthy of explanation because most aqueous corrosion results from the existence of a "corrosion battery." A metal surface corrod-

Several types of corrosion that are discussed in text on pp. 139–140 are diagrammed schematically on the facing page and above. In the example shown for galvanic corrosion, iron and copper are in contact in an aqueous solution. Iron, the more active of the two metals, becomes the anode of a corrosion battery; it corrodes by dissolving and does so more readily than it would alone. Bronze statue (facing page) owes its aesthetically desirable green color to corrosion products.

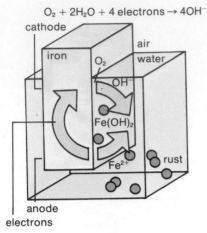

$$O_2 + 2H_2O + 4 \text{ electrons} \rightarrow 4OH^-$$

Corroding electrochemically in a salt solution like seawater open to the air, a metal such as iron possesses both anodic and cathodic surface sites. At the anodes electrons are liberated from neutral iron atoms, leaving behind positively charged ions (Fe^{2+}), which pass into solution. The electrons flow in a current through the metal to the cathodes; there they enter into a reaction in which water (H_2O) and dissolved oxygen (O_2) from the air combine to form hydroxyl ions (OH^-). The cathodic reaction is summarized in the equation at the top of the illustration. Eventually Fe^{2+} and OH^- meet, forming the corrosion product ferrous hydroxide, or $Fe(OH)_2$, which may transform further to the iron oxides commonly called rust.

ing in an aqueous solution like seawater possesses two distinctly different sites: negative sites called anodes, at which the metal is dissolving, and positive sites called cathodes, at which dissolved oxygen in the seawater reacts with molecules of water to produce hydroxyl ions (OH^-) while leaving the metal surface intact. This combination of positive and negative sites constitutes the corrosion battery. The flow of electrical current between them is called the corrosion current, a measure of how fast the corrosion process is taking place. Galvanic corrosion results from contact between a more active metal like steel or aluminum and a less active metal like copper or gold. The more active metal has a greater tendency to become the anode of a corrosion battery, and the less active metal to become the cathode. Thus, if aluminum comes in contact with copper in a corrosive aqueous environment, the aluminum will corrode and will do so more readily than it would alone under the protection of its naturally formed oxide film.

Basic approaches to prevention

Understanding the different types of corrosion and their causes has led directly to ways of preventing or slowing down the destructive process. One major way is to add constituents to a metal to improve the effectiveness of its protective film. Adding chromium and nickel to ordinary steel, for example, produces a form of stainless steel, an alloy considerably more resistant to attack than ordinary steel. The additional elements in the film make it a more resistant barrier even at high temperatures.

Another approach toward corrosion control is to apply an artificial barrier to the metal surface rather than to depend on an ineffective natural barrier of the sort that forms on unalloyed steel. Various kinds of protective coatings are used, the most important being organic materials including a multitude of paints, lacquers, waxes, and greases. Chrome plate and other metallic coatings produced by electroplating work because the metal in the coating is more corrosion-resistant than the metal that it protects. Ceramic coatings composed of porcelain enamel, glass, or similar fired materials also provide effective corrosion resistance. These materials resist attack because they are usually oxides, the stable compounds that make up many metal ores.

Rather than protect a metal by improving the effectiveness of surface barriers, it is possible to prevent corrosion by affecting the tendency of a metal to corrode. One way this can be done is by taking advantage of galvanic corrosion. For instance, when zinc—an active metal—is coupled to steel, the zinc acts as the anode of a corrosion battery and consequently suffers galvanic corrosion, but in so doing it protects the steel by making it the cathode. Somewhat poetically, the zinc used in this way is called a sacrificial anode. This protection scheme, termed cathodic protection, was invented in the early 19th century by the English chemist Sir Humphry Davy to preserve the copper bottoms of battleships of the British Navy. The excellent corrosion resistance of galvanized iron and steel, which are coated with zinc either by dipping in the molten metal or by electroplating, owes much to the process of sacrificial corrosion. As breaches occur in the zinc coating, a corrosion battery develops and the ferrous metal receives cathodic protection at the expense of the zinc.

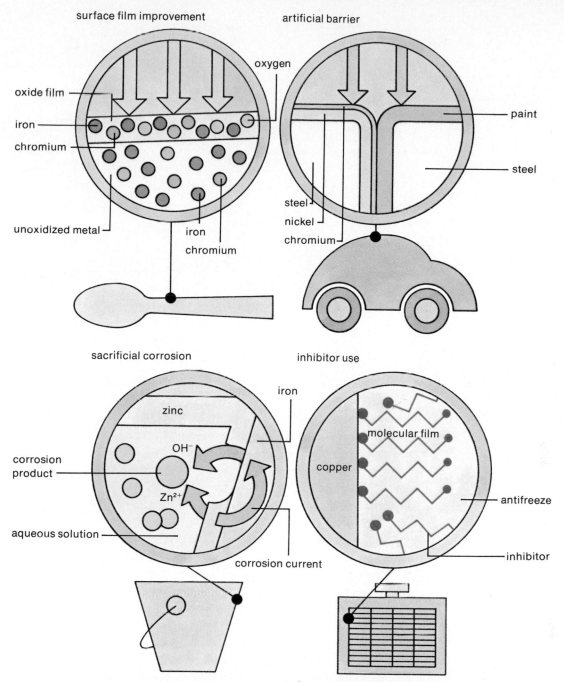

surface film improvement

oxide film
iron
chromium
unoxidized metal
iron
chromium
oxygen

artificial barrier

paint
steel
steel
nickel
chromium

sacrificial corrosion

zinc
iron
OH⁻
Zn²⁺
corrosion product
aqueous solution
corrosion current

inhibitor use

molecular film
copper
antifreeze
inhibitor

Another protection scheme, to alter the environment encountered by a metal, is made possible through the use of chemicals called inhibitors. Some kinds of inhibitors adsorb on the metal surface, forming a single layer of inhibitor molecules that acts as a barrier to the environment. These include chainlike organic molecules, such as imidazoline derivatives, which possess a "head" end that attaches itself to the metal surface and a "tail" that projects outward to present an oily or greaselike surface to the environment. Other inhibitors prevent corrosion by keeping the environment from becoming more corrosive (usually more acidic) by providing what is called a buffering action. The chemicals ammonia and morpholine are examples of this latter type. They are used to maintain a mildly alkaline environment in the boilers used in power plants.

Examples of basic approaches to corrosion control include (1) adding chromium to ordinary steel to create a type of stainless steel, which forms an especially tough surface film; (2) coating steel with paint or with a corrosion-resistant metal plating; (3) coating iron with a more active metal such as zinc, which undergoes sacrificial galvanic corrosion while protecting the iron; and (4) adding a film-forming inhibitor to the environment of a metal surface.

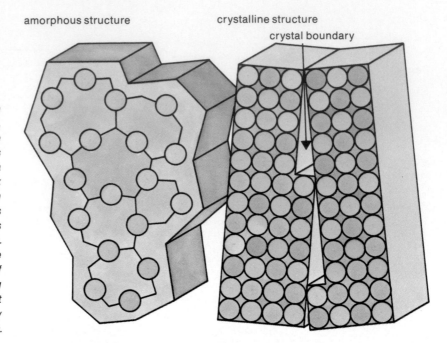

amorphous structure   crystalline structure

crystal boundary

Protective surface films that have an amorphous, or noncrystalline, structure may provide a more effective corrosion barrier for metals than crystalline films. Arranged as a broad but very thin molecular network of interconnected metal and oxygen atoms, an amorphous film possesses comparatively few unrestricted paths for diffusion of corrosive substances. By contrast, a crystalline film is made of a jigsaw-puzzle arrangement of separate crystals whose ill-fitting boundaries create long gaps that could allow easy penetration by damaging chemical species.

New research

Promising approaches currently under development could result in considerable advances in corrosion prevention technology in the future. They involve new concepts, new research tools, and new materials, of which only a sampling can be discussed below.

A good way to look at the most significant concepts is to examine corrosion processes that occur in the microworld of a corroding metal surface. As pointed out above, of paramount importance in any corrosion microworld is the thin protective film that stands between a metal surface and a potentially destructive environment. One new concept, still to be proved, is that those films which have a noncrystalline, or glassy, structure provide the most effective barriers against the environment. Crystalline films, it is reasoned, are made up of many small crystals, or crystallites, that must fit together like the pieces of a jigsaw puzzle. The boundaries between crystallites provide paths for aggressive species in the environment to penetrate the protective film and do their damage. On the other hand, a noncrystalline film does not have such boundaries but is instead a more monolithic structure, a giant but very thin molecule made up primarily of metal and oxygen atoms. Such noncrystalline films of silicon oxide provide excellent protective films for the silicon that comprises the integrated circuits of modern electronic devices. Attempts are under way to develop concepts that will allow one to predict what can be added as alloy constituents to promote the formation of protective glassy films on alloy surfaces.

Essential to an understanding of the relationship between a film's structure and its protective ability is an accurate picture of the destructive microenvironment that exists inside pits, cracks, and crevices. It is now generally recognized that the ambient environment to which a metal may be exposed is not necessarily the same as the environment that really counts, the one

142

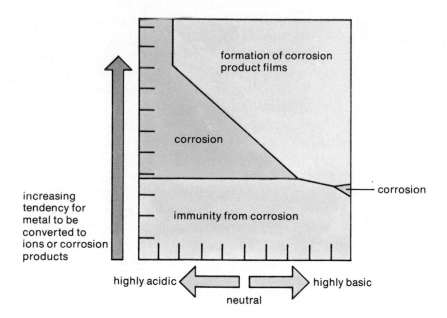

increasing tendency for metal to be converted to ions or corrosion products

formation of corrosion product films

corrosion

corrosion

immunity from corrosion

highly acidic ◁◁ ▷▷ highly basic

neutral

Simplified Pourbaix diagram for iron (left) plots the tendency of the metal to ionize or form corrosion products (which is dependent upon the kinds and concentrations of chemical species in the microenvironment of the metal) against the acidity or alkalinity of the environment. Such a graph delineates the conditions under which iron can be expected to corrode. The formation of a corrosion product film may or may not influence the rate of corrosion. (Below) A ship may nominally be immersed in seawater of typical salt concentrations, but in the microworld created beneath barnacles and other objects adhering to the hull, chemical concentrations and acidity can be considerably higher.

that exists in a tiny pit or crack. Thus, whereas a steel piling exposed to seawater nominally may be immersed in 3.5% solution of sodium chloride (salt) along with other chemicals, in the microworld crevice created beneath a barnacle chloride solutions become much more highly concentrated and considerably more acidic than ordinary seawater. The recognition of the important role played by these unusual environments has spawned the development of very sensitive microanalytical techniques designed to characterize extremely small quantities of aqueous solutions. Knowing the compositions of these solutions, corrosion scientists can use a map of the corrosion microworld, called a Pourbaix diagram, to determine if a destructive situation can exist.

A third intriguing concept involves the suspicion that the protective film of metals is engaged in continuous breakdown and repair. One hint that such a dynamic process is occurring is the observation of a phenomenon called corrosion noise. Using sensitive electronic equipment, researchers have detected tiny electrical signals that appear to indicate a rapid and repetitive starting and stopping of corrosion. Furthermore, adding inhibitors into an environment appears to decrease this corrosion noise.

If the concept of a dynamic breakdown-repair of the protective film is valid, ways can be explored to minimize the breakdown stage of the process by promoting the formation of films with improved resistance. It may prove possible to modify environments and alloys to promote a more rapid and effective film repair process. The existence of a corrosion noise pattern, perhaps indicative of a particular type of corrosion, also offers the possibility of a monitoring technique capable of detecting the onset of dangerous corrosion conditions in such inaccessible places as the heat exchangers of nuclear energy systems.

To help establish and apply these concepts and others, a large array of

Hank Morgan—Rainbow

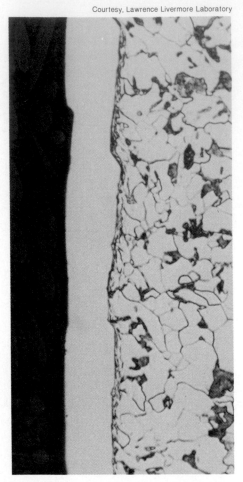

Highly magnified cross section of a steel plate reveals the effects of a controlled explosion in bonding a razor-thin ribbon of metallic glass to a thicker sheet of ordinary steel. The light, featureless appearance of metallic glass, which possesses an amorphous structure, contrasts sharply with the graininess of the steel, which is made up of discrete crystal regions. The improved corrosion resistance of metallic glass may be due to the presence of an amorphous surface film.

new surface analytical techniques are entering the battle against corrosion. In the past two decades an explosive increase in such tools has created a veritable alphabet soup: AES (Auger electron spectroscopy), AP (atom probe), ESCA (electron spectroscopy for chemical analysis), FIM (field ion microscopy), SIMS (secondary-ion mass spectrometry), STEM (scanning transmission electron microscopy), XPS (X-ray photoelectron spectroscopy), and many others. These new techniques can examine films and surfaces in exquisite detail, detecting and identifying the atoms that constitute 1% of a layer one atom thick or, with the atom probe, even identifying individual atoms. Other techniques can visually resolve individual atoms or atom planes. The techniques listed above rely heavily on the complex interactions of electrons, ions (charged atoms), or electromagnetic radiation (*e.g.,* X-rays or laser beams) to identify and measure amounts of constituents and to determine forms and structures. Obviously such tools will remain of great value in determining how extremely small amounts of key elements in an alloy or environment can alter the properties of protective films.

New concepts and techniques frequently lead to practical applications, and corrosion scientists are actively pursuing at least three novel protection schemes. Although not yet in wide use, they are regarded as having promise for the future.

The first is the use of glassy metals, or metallic glasses, as corrosion-resistant materials. These special metal alloys are produced by extremely rapid cooling of metal from its molten state. The material that results is an alloy which has virtually no crystalline structure; that is, the atoms in the alloy are not arranged in the extensive ordered array found in conventional alloys. Instead, there exists a random, or amorphous, arrangement of atoms somewhat characteristic of a glass.

Laboratory studies of metallic glasses have shown them to exhibit corrosion rates that are 100–1,000 times slower than similar alloys having crystalline structures. One reason suggested for their superior corrosion resistance is that a noncrystalline protective film will form on a noncrystalline surface. As discussed above, some scientists believe that a noncrystalline film provides a more effective barrier to the environment than a crystalline one.

Since their discovery, metallic glasses have been manufactured almost exclusively in the form of powders, wires, and thin ribbons because of the need to avoid the high temperatures of ordinary welding and casting operations. Such intense, prolonged heating would devitrify them, or return them to their crystalline state. One method used for ribbon production involves spraying a jet of molten metal onto a cold rotating drum, which acts to quench the metal at a rate of millions of degrees per second. Recently investigators have found that controlled chemical explosions can be used to compress metallic glass powders into strong solid shapes and weld thin ribbons to plates of ordinary crystalline metal to form corrosion-resistant coatings. A precisely arranged explosion squeezes the glassy material into shape so rapidly that devitrifying levels of heat do not build up.

Another way to promote the formation of a noncrystalline metal surface is called "laser glazing." This process creates a thin coating of amorphous metal on a bulk metal object by subjecting the metal surface to the intense

Dan McCoy—Rainbow

heat of a laser beam for a short time. The beam melts the outermost layer of metal, and the rapid cooling that results when the laser beam is removed produces a glassy metal coating.

A third surface treatment that promises to provide improved corrosion resistance is ion implantation. The treatment involves bombarding a metal surface with an ion beam in a vacuum chamber, thereby driving thousands of atoms into the surface layers of a metal. This process accomplishes two ends. First, the composition of the metal surface is altered, creating a new alloy in the outer layers of the metal. Because the ions can be of almost any element, quite exotic alloy surfaces can be produced, containing atoms that under ordinary procedures will not go into solution in the base metal. In addition, because very small quantities of atoms are needed for ion implantation, thin coatings of rare and costly surface alloys can be made relatively inexpensively. The second way the ion-implantation process may alter a surface is to disorder its atomic structure and thus render it glassier. At present it is not clear how and to what extent ion implantation accomplishes this effect; some ion-implanted surfaces have exhibited superior corrosion properties, but not all.

Meeting the challenge

The metals upon which modern technology so critically stakes its future owe their integrity to a microscopically thin surface layer of simple molecules. Penetration of this natural armor by but a few damaging atoms can lead to serious corrosion—not only of the metal beneath it but also of national economies and societies. Despite its ubiquity such protection has many shortcomings that need to be eliminated, and it is this work that challenges the corrosion scientists of the future, who must keep the wheels of civilization quite literally from rusting solid.

Steel samples are tested in the laboratory for their ability to resist rusting.

FOR ADDITIONAL READING

Economic Effects of Metallic Corrosion in the United States: part 1 by L. H. Bennett *et al.,* part 2 by J. H. Payer *et al.;* National Bureau of Standards special publications 511-1 and 511-2 (U.S. Government Printing Office, 1978).

U. R. Evans, *The Corrosion and Oxidation of Metals*, 2nd suppl. vol. (Edward Arnold, 1976).

M. G. Fontana and N. D. Greene, *Corrosion Engineering* (McGraw-Hill, 1967).

M. Pourbaix, *Lectures on Electrochemical Corrosion* (Plenum Press, 1973).

J. C. Scully, *The Fundamentals of Corrosion*, 2nd ed. (Pergamon Press, 1975).

L. L. Shreir (ed.), *Corrosion*, two vols. (Newnes-Butterworths, 1976).

H. H. Uhlig, *Corrosion and Corrosion Control*, 2nd ed. (John Wiley & Sons, 1971).

Antarctica– The Living Legacy

by George A. Llano

Recent studies of the organisms that inhabit the "bottom of the world" have increased respect for their importance in the food web that sustains the higher forms of life on Earth.

January 19th [1828].—To-day, being in latitude 83° 20 '[S], longitude 43° 5' W. (the sea being of an extraordinarily dark color), we again saw land from the mast-head. . . . The shore was precipitous, and the interior seemed to be well wooded. . . . After searching about for some time. . . we saw four large canoes put off from the shore, filled with men who seemed to be well armed. . . a hundred and ten savages in all. . . . We saw but few wild animals, and none of a large size, or of a species with which we were familiar. One or two serpents of a formidable aspect crossed our path. . . .

—Edgar Allan Poe, from *The Narrative of Arthur Gordon Pym* (1838)

Heavy vegetation, strange animal forms, bloodthirsty native tribes, deep chasms resembling letters of ancient scripts, and a volcanically heated south polar sea confronted the unwilling traveler Pym in Poe's bizarre Gothic tale. To Poe and his readers of the early 19th century the Antarctic regions held much the same awe and mystery that the universe beyond the Earth does today. The extreme environment and isolation of the region made it the final frontier, of which virtually nothing was known and about which the wildest speculations could not be disproven.

Presently Antarctica is no longer the most unknown region on Earth. Topographic mapping, aerial photography, satellite surveillance, and visits by teams of explorers and scientists—practically all of it within the past half century—have replaced the imaginings of an earlier age with a scientifically sound outline of Antarctic geography, geology, and biology. Since the mid-1950s scientific studies have given Antarctica a reputation as a unique biological laboratory. On land the scarcity of life and simplicity of interdependence among its forms provide exciting opportunities for the study of a biological community at the limits of adaptability to a harsh environment. In the sea the staggering abundance of life promises a challenge to man's full appreciation for years to come. Recently, mounting international pressures to exploit the Antarctic region of its vast food resources and potential mineral wealth have presented scientists—and world leaders—with yet another issue: the protection of Antarctica's delicate terrestrial and marine ecosystems from human activity. To this end a thorough understanding of Antarctic biology is a fundamental requisite.

The land and its life

The Antarctic continent is a generally circular landmass that, with the exception of the northward flare of the Antarctic Peninsula, lies almost wholly within the South Frigid Zone. It resembles an oceanic island and has been isolated geographically and climatically from other continents for at least 20 million years. Less than 5% of the land is visible; the rest lies buried under a vast glacial sheet that accounts for 90% of the world's store of ice. The formation of winter sea ice may double or even triple the total area of ice. This creates a heat sink and is the cause for strong interactions among air, sea, and ice. The position of Antarctica is pivotal in the development of weather systems and oceanic circulation and in the evolution and distribution of land- and ocean-dwelling life.

Antarctica is divided by the Transantarctic Mountains into two regions,

GEORGE A. LLANO is a consultant with the Marine Mammal Commission, National Marine Fisheries Service, and other organizations, and former Program Manager, Polar Biology and Medicine, Office of Polar Programs, National Science Foundation, Washington, D.C.

(Overleaf) © W. Curtsinger—Rapho/Photo Researchers, Inc. Illustrations by Leon Bishop

148

(Top) Popperfoto; (bottom) courtesy, NOAA, National Climatic Center

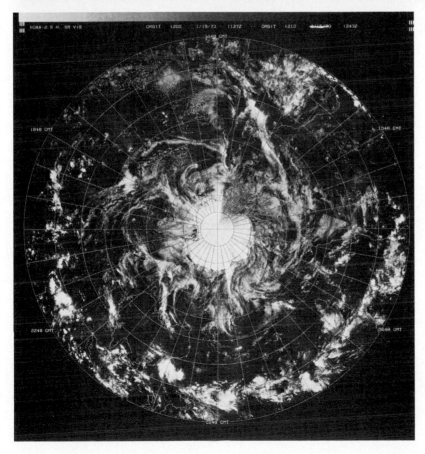

On Jan. 17, 1773, British explorer James Cook's vessel "Resolution" became the first known ship to cross the Antarctic Circle. The engraving above portrays its grim-faced, ill-equipped crew in its efforts to hunt food and collect ice for drinking water. Exactly two centuries and two days later, the sophisticated optical sensors of an orbiting satellite, NOAA 2, recorded cloud patterns above the Antarctic continent and the entire Southern Hemisphere from quite a different perspective (left). South America lies at the top of this photo mosaic, which was assembled from a day's set of orbits.

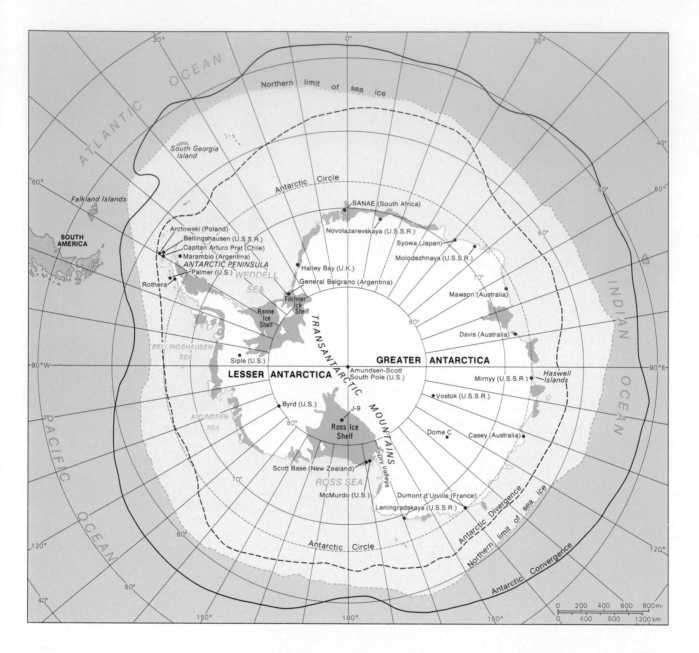

Greater and Lesser Antarctica. The former, about the size of Australia, consists of rocks of ancient geological age. Its coal beds and the remains of characteristic plants of Permian age (about 250 million years old), as well as the first evidence of ancient terrestrial amphibians and reptiles from the Triassic Period that followed, tell of past land ties with India, South America, Australia, and southern Africa. Such evidence also points to a seasonal and more temperate past climate and indicates that Antarctica once occupied a different position on the Earth's surface. Lesser Antarctica is an ice-covered archipelago of mountainous islands separated by deep channels under the ice that would interconnect the Weddell, Bellingshausen, Amundsen, and Ross seas if the ice were to melt. Characteristic of Antarctica are the extensive, undulating ice shelves hinged to coastal glaciers and extending sea-

150

ward over the continental shelf. The Ross, Filchner, and Ronne ice shelves are striking features of Lesser Antarctica, overlying sunless marine habitats that are only now being studied. Another impressive feature of Antarctica is its tabular icebergs, which are massive slabs that have broken away from the barrier face of the ice shelves. These bergs rise as much as 60 meters (200 feet) above the sea surface and may extend more than 65 kilometers (40 miles) in length.

Contrary to Poe's fanciful description, the variety of land-dwelling life in the Antarctic is extremely limited. There are no native terrestrial vertebrates; the seals, penguins, and seabirds that abound along the coasts must be considered denizens of the ocean, where they find their food. Virtually the entire animal population of the continent consists of a limited array of mites, springtails, midges, lice, and other land arthropods as well as lesser microscopic forms of lower life. Antarctica has saline and freshwater ponds that thaw partially or completely during the summer months. There the highest forms of animal life are minute crustaceans called copepods; fish, snails, shellfish, and aquatic insects are absent. There are no rivers, marshes, or bogs.

Except for two flowering plants that live on the Antarctic Peninsula, plant life consists typically of algae, mosses, liverworts, and lichens, which are found on ice-free land or exposed rock where conditions favor plant growth. In sheer mass the most abundant plant forms are the algae, including the blue-green algae. These extremely primitive organisms thrive in water, on exposed land, and even in ice and snow. Lichens, which consist of species of algae and fungi in symbiotic association, are widely distributed and have been observed within four degrees of the South Pole at an elevation of nearly 2,000 meters (6,560 feet). Mosses are the most commonly observed plant form and in the upper Antarctic Peninsula form extensive stands that are often composed of single species. Liverworts are common in the peninsular region and rare on the continent. Together these plants form an important habitat for the springtails, mites, and other forms of multicelled, microscopic animal life.

Rugged mountains rise behind the exposed shoreline of the Antarctic Peninsula. Orange lichen clings in patches to the bare rock in the foreground. The map on the facing page depicts the Antarctic continent, major ice shelves, and surrounding waters. Also shown are locations of scientific research stations and outposts of various countries that supported active Antarctic programs in the late 1970s. Dome C is the site of an international effort to study Antarctic glaciers. J-9, on the Ross Ice Shelf, is the location of the ice shelf drilling project described on pp. 165–167.

151

Terrestrial plant life of the Antarctic leads a meager but tenacious existence on snow-free land of the Antarctic Peninsula (top). Both lichens (center) and mosses (bottom) are common sights in the comparatively benign environment of the peninsular region, but some species of lichen have even been found near the South Pole.

Most Antarctic meltwater lakes and ponds support communities of algae, usually in the form of felts along their bottoms. In some lakes and pools water-dwelling mosses and terrestrial species that have become adapted to the watery environment are an important component of bottom plant communities. Bacteria, fungi, and yeasts occur throughout the water. On the whole phytoplankton—the collective name for the diverse assortment of minute plant life found at and near the water surface—are poorly represented compared with the bottom community; blue-green algae are the dominant group, forming 70% of species present.

Demands of a brutal environment

The scarcity and simplicity of Antarctic terrestrial life are due to several interrelated factors. Historically Antarctica has been isolated by wide stretches of ocean and insulated by a massive ice cap, both of which have made introduction and survival of organisms difficult. Even under present-day conditions of reduced ice cover, much recently exposed land area still lies uncolonized. This is in large part due to the severity of the climate. Precipitation over the continent is so low that the region is classified as a polar desert. With the possible exception of the upper Antarctic Peninsula, this precipitation occurs mostly as ice or snow and varies considerably from year to year. Wind-propelled ice and snow granules also abrade plant tissues, and until melted they are unavailable as water for plant growth. The lack of water, prevailing humidity, and drying winds restrict normal plant growth during the brief Antarctic summer.

Another important influence is the wide and rapid daily fluctuation of temperature near the land surface, which may rise or drop as much as 35° C (63° F) in just a few hours. Bare rocks and exposed earth absorb considerable solar radiation, and additional warming of the layer of air over the ground by long-wavelength, reradiated energy often creates a thin summer-like "microclimate" even when the ambient temperature may be below the freezing point of water. In fact, the severe drop of winter temperatures to as low as −70° C (−94° F) on the continent actually may be less stressful to plant metabolism than these daily freeze-thaw cycles.

The character of Antarctic soils, which exhibit wide microbiological, chemical, and physical variations, is another influencing factor. Although devoid of plants easily visible to the eye, some soils contain culturable microorganisms. These forms of life occur predominantly at ice-cemented surfaces where summer warming provides liquid water for the upper surface. Availability of soil nutrients for plant growth varies between coastal and inland sites. Organic nitrogen—i.e., nitrogen combined in such chemical compounds as ammonia and nitrate that living organisms can use—often reaches high concentrations and has several sources. Blue-green algae found with mosses and lichens have been shown to transform, or fix, atmospheric nitrogen into organic forms. Nitrogen and phosphorus are also supplied by birds and seals. For example, Soviet scientists have estimated that the bird population of the Haswell Islands (about 67° S, 93° E) deposits as much as 100 tons of organic material in the form of guano and other debris each nesting season. The well-developed stands of lichen found

153

Stranded near Livingston Island off the tip of the Antarctic Peninsula, an iceberg impregnated with living algae glows like a mountain of jade (above). Eroded rock in the Olympus Range (right; about 77° S, 162° E) testifies to the severity of wind abrasion on the continent and suggests its detrimental effect on plant tissue.

Penguins clustered at the base of a large iceberg discolor its surface with their excrement (above). Compounds of nitrogen and phosphorus provided by birds and seals are an important source of nutrients for terrestrial plant life. (Left) Scientists examine a pair of seals seemingly stranded on a vast flat of ice overlying McMurdo Sound on the western edge of the Ross Sea. Sun illuminates the landscape, yet the time is 3 AM, a reminder of the alternating six-month cycles of light and darkness that tax the adaptive capacity of Antarctic inhabitants.

on the exposed peaks of ice-buried interior mountains owe their luxuriant growth to the presence of guano nutrients from cliff-dwelling birds. In addition, recent research has shown that significant quantities of nitrogen compounds, formed in the upper atmosphere through the action of solar radiation, are precipitated upon the continent in snow.

Antarctic terrestrial and freshwater organisms also must function under other severe environmental constraints. The alternating six-month periods of light and darkness make uncommon demands on forms of life that have evolved under the 24-hour day-night cycle of lower latitudes. The elevation of the Antarctic continent intensifies wind and blizzard conditions, and the open, warmer ocean surrounding it favors continental cooling. In fact, it is believed that Antarctic glaciation predated that in the Arctic by more than 20 million years.

Because of all these environmental hardships, only the right combination of conditions will allow an organism a foothold at any particular site. Adaptation is obviously essential for survival. Some Antarctic mosses have moved underwater where, protected from desiccation, daily temperature changes, and wind abrasion, they develop a luxuriant growth. One kind of lichen has adapted to a similar habitat under the ocean along the shore of the Antarctic Peninsula. Plants have met the problem of great seasonal light and temperature changes in various ways. The minute phytoplankton near the surface of lakes and pools appear adapted to low light intensities, whereas bottom-dwelling forms respond to high light intensities. Plant survival during the intense winter is believed dependent largely on low rates of respiration accompanied by an ability to manufacture food through photosynthesis at very low light levels. Algae in both freshwater and saltwater ponds are tolerant of water temperatures that can rise as high as 14° C (57° F) under the summer Sun. Antarctic algae also have a better ability to revive after freezing than temperate forms. Reproduction of freshwater crustaceans coincides with the peak of phytoplankton development; their predilection for eating what comes to hand, including dead organisms, reflects the lack of a reliable food supply.

Bounty of the southern ocean

The Antarctic marine environment is a deep ocean system with a well-developed atmospheric and oceanic circulation. Its distinctive currents, which completely circle the continent, play an important role in the general oceanic circulation and contribute to the living bounty found in Antarctic waters. Except for some regions very near the continent, the Antarctic surface waters (see diagram on facing page) are driven clockwise by prevailing westerly winds in an eastward, circumpolar movement. Along their northern limit these waters sink beneath the less dense and warmer subantarctic waters. This marks a natural boundary, the Antarctic Convergence or Polar Front, which influences the distribution of fish, birds, and the assemblage of minute plants and animals that constitute plankton.

The Antarctic Convergence is a region across which temperature and nutrient salt concentrations change abruptly. Surface water temperatures south of the convergence average 1°–2° C (about 34°–35.5° F) in winter and

Schematic representation on the facing page depicts the character of the water masses surrounding the Antarctic continent; see text at lower right. Magnified sample of plankton from McMurdo Sound (below) reveals the rich, varied nature of its composition. Prominent near the center is a euphausiid, surrounded by other crustaceans.

156

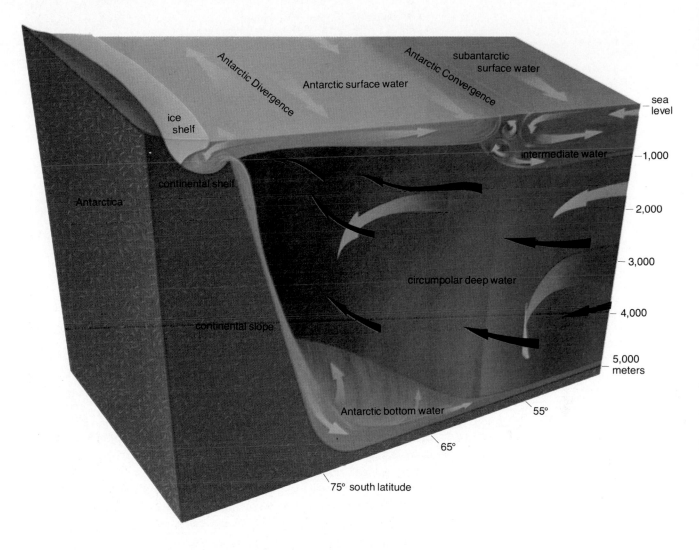

Antarctic Divergence
Antarctic surface water
Antarctic Convergence
subantarctic surface water
sea level
ice shelf
intermediate water
—1,000
continental shelf
Antarctica
—2,000
—3,000
circumpolar deep water
continental slope
—4,000
5,000 meters
Antarctic bottom water
55°
65°
75° south latitude

3°–5° C (37.5°–41° F) in summer; north of the convergence these temperatures average about 5° C higher. Near the ice-bound continent the water
remains close to −1.9° C (28.5° F) throughout the year; this cold mass sinks
sharply to the bottom and flows northward along the seafloor, even extending north of the Equator into the oceans of the Northern Hemisphere. Between the bottom water and Antarctic surface waters lies a relatively
warmer, more saline, and nutrient-rich zone, the circumpolar deep water,
which upwells toward the surface around Antarctica where it contributes to
the luxuriant growth of marine life. This upwelling is a basis for the high
abundance of Antarctic marine phytoplankton, the primary producers or
foundation of the food web that sustains all higher forms of life in the region.

The formation and breakup of winter ice cover over the ocean are important stages in the annual cycle of the marine ecosystem. Winter ice reduces
by half the area of open water south of the convergence, screening out
about 90% of light required by photosynthesizing phytoplankton. Scientists
now believe that these seasonal variations in light and sea ice cover and the
nearly uniform temperature of Antarctic surface waters may be more signifi-

157

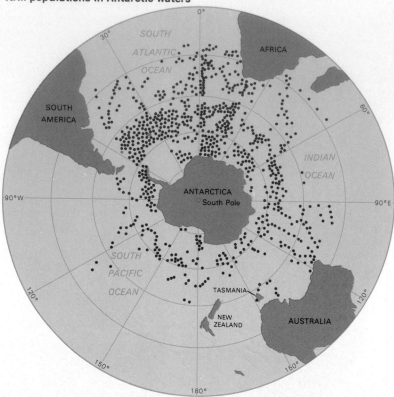

Map (above) depicts reported concentrations of krill in Antarctic waters; greatest concentrations are found in the Atlantic sector. The diagram on the facing page shows predator-prey relationships in the open ocean surrounding the continent. A food chain is a simple linear arrangement of organisms in ascending or descending order of predation; one example in the diagram would be the pathway from phytoplankton to krill, to baleen whale, and to man. Many interlocking food chains form what is termed a food web.

cant than the regeneration of nutrients by upwelling. Recent evidence also indicates that the undersurface of the ice cover supports photosynthetic life under low light intensities to the extent that it plays a major role in food production. At breakup, these primary producers are released into the water; depending on the timing this may affect the total seasonal production of life.

Both early investigations and more recent work have shown that there are conspicuous geographic and seasonal variations in the distribution of phytoplankton. Coastal waters off Antarctica and the subantarctic islands appear to have a greater abundance of life than oceanic regions. Phytoplankton south of the convergence are dominated by diatoms; these single-celled algae, which possess delicate skeletons of silica, are represented in Antarctic seas by almost 100 species. There are also about 60 species of algalike dinoflagellates.

An important step up in the Antarctic food web from the primary producers are the zooplankton, the animal component of plankton. The dominant forms are the crustaceans, including eight species of *Euphausia* distributed in the Antarctic and subantarctic zones. One of these, the krill (*E. superba*) of Antarctic waters, is the principal food of baleen whales and a vital component of the Antarctic ecosystem. The translucent body of *E. superba* reaches a length of about five centimeters (two inches) and is tinged with patches of reddish brown. Krill occur in large swarms, dense enough to discolor the surface of the sea; the largest concentrations are in the Atlantic sector, and such a swarm may have been observed by an astronaut who reported seeing red splotches south of the Falkland Islands. The biomass

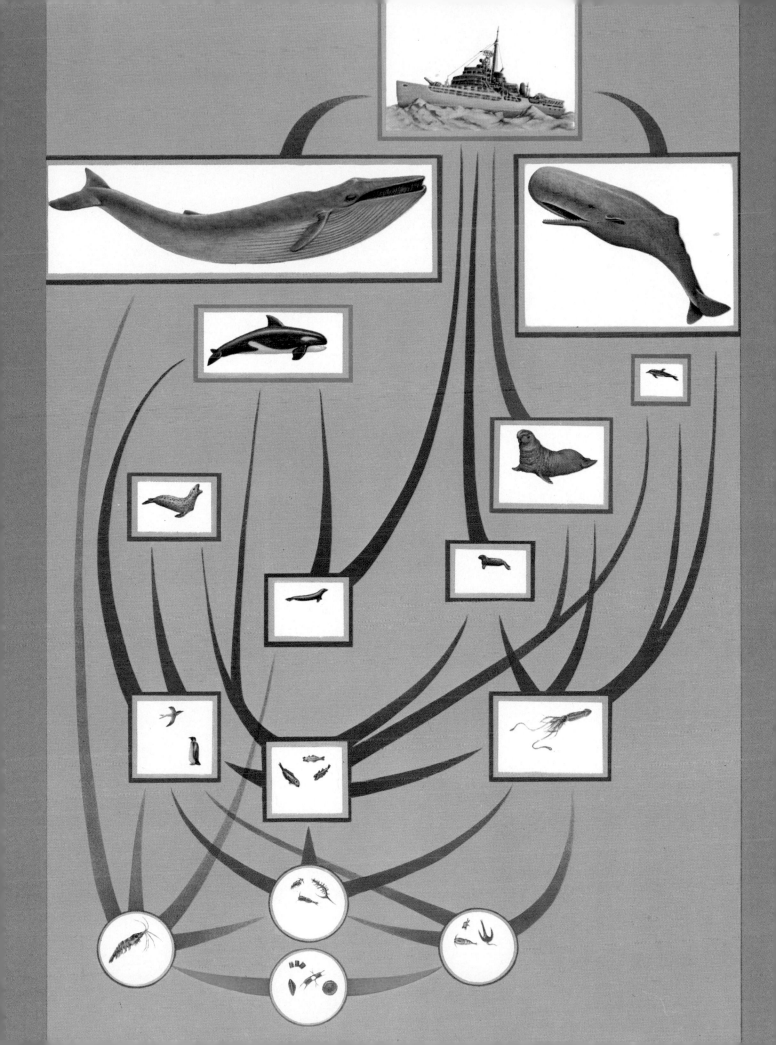

(Top) Peter Kettle—G. R. Roberts, Nelson, N.Z.; (bottom) Frank S. Todd, Sea World, Inc.

In the continual struggle for survival in the Antarctic, an animal's status in a food chain—as predator or prey—may suffer a sudden and fatal reversal. An Adélie penguin (top) feeds its chicks with regurgitated krill taken in a recent ocean foray. (Left) Under the surprised stares of several Adélie penguins, a killer whale—an active feeder on the birds—abruptly breaks the water's surface. The formidable teeth of the leopard seal (above) are well suited for taking both penguins and seals and are also somewhat modified for feeding on krill.

Blanketing the Antarctic shores in vast numbers, king penguins (top) incubate their eggs by placing them on their feet and then covering all with a fold of skin. Each bird's brooding territory is measured by the distance over which it can peck its neighbor. Two chinstrap penguins (bottom) engage in courtship behavior.

of krill has been estimated as high as five billion tons. From January to April a cubic meter of ocean may hold as much as 20 kilograms of these animals —about 35 pounds per cubic yard.

Five species of baleen, or whalebone, whales migrate into Antarctic waters during the southern summer. Over a period of 120 days, grazing almost exclusively on krill, they increase their body weight about 50%. The large blue whales feed four times a day, each taking about four tons of krill daily; smaller whales each consume about two tons daily but feed more frequently. Their specially modified sievelike mouth structure is well adapted for taking krill, and their tendency to fast out of Antarctic waters suggests a special dependence on high populations of zooplankton. Since the beginning of the 20th century, Antarctic baleen whale populations have been reduced by about 85–90%. The current stocks, estimated at about 351,500, consume

162

about 33 million tons of krill yearly. This implies a huge surplus of krill that some Antarctic observers feel has favored an increase of birds and seals. The remaining baleen whales also appear to be eating more as a result of the surplus, growing faster, and reproducing earlier.

More than half of the world's seal population occurs in the Antarctic. It represents a natural resource of potential usefulness that since historic time has attracted commercial interests. The leopard, crabeater, Ross, and Weddell seals are truly Antarctic species, largely confined to the sea ice around the continent. In addition, fur and elephant seals are found in the peninsular region. Crabeater seals, estimated to number about 15 million, feed largely on krill; their tooth structure is remarkably developed to form a retaining sieve. The leopard seal, a predator on seals and penguins, also feeds on krill and its teeth are somewhat modified for the purpose.

Fur seals (top) are commonly found basking on the rocky shores of the Antarctic Peninsula. The black-browed albatross (bottom) is a migratory Antarctic dweller that breeds on islands and exposed coasts.

163

Penguins, petrels, and albatross are conspicuous Antarctic dwellers, breeding on islands and ice-free coastal areas; the snow and Antarctic petrels also nest on exposed mountain peaks hundreds of kilometers from open water. The majority of seabirds are migratory, and their distribution, like that of most Antarctic marine organisms, is circumpolar. An estimated 188 million birds inhabit the region, consuming about 39 million tons of food annually. As krill consumers they are about equal in importance to baleen whales and about half as important as seals. The most striking behavioral characteristic of Antarctic birds, and of mammals as well, is that in the absence of terrestrial predators they have become less alert and more approachable and docile. Penguins, whether alone or in groups, show little fear of man; this trait and their flightlessness have allowed scientific investigators new insights into the social behavior, navigational abilities, and physiology of marine birds.

The ocean bottom

Recent U.S., British, French, and Soviet investigations of Antarctic life on the continental shelf reveal a varied and rich assemblage of marine organisms. These studies show it to be an efficient, stable community structure composed of a small number of species, many of which are found nowhere else, and characterized by an extraordinarily high abundance of such invertebrates as sponges, starfish, corals, sea anemones, mollusks, bryozoans, and tunicates. Many of these animals grow slowly, tend to remain in one place, and feed by straining organic matter from the water. The dependence of such organisms on suspended food particles in bottom currents becomes critical in winter when algal photosynthesis is sharply reduced. This brings about a general trend toward scavenging, opportunistic feeding, decrease in activity, and even reduction in biomass. Marine invertebrates are protected against freezing by specialized body fluids. One species of limpet, a kind of snail, is believed to excrete a protective mucus that inhibits formation of ice crystals over its body down to −10° C (14° F).

The Antarctic fish population numbers about 100 species, few of which

Trematomus nicolai, a bottom-dwelling fish of Antarctic waters, recently was shown to possess compounds in its blood which enable it to survive in water temperatures that ordinarily would crystallize its blood serum.

Arthur DeVries, University of Illinois

live outside of Antarctic waters. The Nototheniiformes, predominantly coastal fish, make up the majority of species, and most are under 25 centimeters (10 inches) in length. Among the larger ones the Chaenichthyidae, commonly called icefish, are unique by the absence of red blood cells containing the oxygen-carrying pigment hemoglobin. Apparently oxygen taken from the water dissolves directly in their whitish blood. Most Antarctic fish are sluggish, large-headed, tapered-bodied creatures of diverse habitats. In recent years their ability to accommodate to near-freezing conditions has attracted considerable scientific attention, and it has been shown that various "antifreeze" compounds in the blood enable some nototheniids to survive in −1.9° C seawater. Thus, where a fish lives may be dictated by its blood serum freezing point, although high metabolic rates also play a large part in cold adaptation.

Recent research

The world's largest permanent ice shelves are the Ross Ice Shelf and those of the Weddell Sea. The former is approximately the size of France with a seaward ice cliff 20–70 meters (65–230 feet) high and an average thickness of about 400–450 meters (1,300–1,475 feet). The sunless sea below, capped by glacial ice for millennia, is the last of Earth's major ecological

The sheer barrier face of the Ross Ice Shelf rises as high as 70 meters (230 feet) above the sea surface. Mt. Terror, more than three kilometers in altitude, ascends from Ross Island in the background.

165

Kenneth G. Seaburg/Bruce C. Parker, Virginia Polytechnic
Institute & State University

James D. Brandt—ANIMALS ANIMALS

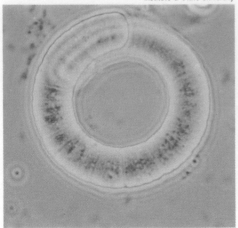

*Antarctic freshwater and saline lakes
and ponds often support
phytoplanktonic life. In December
1977 the filamentous alga shown
above, a species of Arthrospira, was
taken in samples from Lake Miers at
the floor of a dry valley bordering
McMurdo Sound. View from a tip of
Erebus Glacier (right) near McMurdo
research station on Ross Island
presents an unworldly appearance.*

communities to be explored. In December 1977, after several years of set-backs, an international research team used a special drill tipped with a jet of hot gas to bore a 420-meter hole through the sheet about 450 kilometers (280 miles) from its nearest seaward edge. Observation with television cameras and lights and direct sampling revealed the presence of life despite the absence of sunlight and direct contact with the atmosphere.

Jere Lipps and co-workers from the University of California, Davis, reported finding bacteria as well as living phytoplankton, diatoms, and dinoflagellates in the 237-meter water depth below the drill site. Crustaceans, amphipods, and other marine arthropods and a few fish were also observed.

166

There were also bacteria in the bottom sediments but no large organisms. All the species thus far seen resembled those in the open sea; their principal source of food appeared to be organic matter swept under the shelf by ocean currents.

McMurdo Sound, a bay of the Ross Sea, lies under the western edge of the Ross Ice Shelf. The land bordering this region is carved with dry, snowless valleys that may aptly be described as frigid desert, with soils high in soluble salts and devoid of visible plant and animal life. So hostile are these regions that some scientists have compared the environment with that thought to exist on the surface of Mars. Their studies of the microbiology of the dry valleys have sought clues as to what characteristics Martian life might have and where to look for it. Roy Cameron and colleagues of the U.S. National Aeronautics and Space Administration found significant differences in environmental tolerance among species of microscopic life growing in the soil. Bruce Parker of Virginia Polytechnic Institute and State University noted a predominance of pigmented bacteria in the upper surface of soils, suggesting that this might be some type of adaptation to high exposure to ultraviolet light. Parker also found that many Antarctic soil microorganisms delayed their growth and reproduction when cultured with nutrients, a phenomenon he interpreted as a resting stage or means for conserving energy.

Despite the many seasons of field work in the dry valleys, it was only recently that investigators reported sampling rock for evidence of bacterial or algal organisms in the Antarctic desert ecosystem. In 1977 E. I. Friedmann and co-workers of Florida State University discovered the presence of photosynthetic life inside crystalline marble and sandstone rocks. An assemblage of bacteria, fungi, and blue-green algae, as yet not identified, were seen growing about two millimeters beneath the rock surface in a visible, blue-green layer that filled the spaces between mineral grains. In such a habitat the internal air space constitutes a closed system; transparency of the overlying minerals allows light to penetrate to the algal layer where humidity and temperature ensure a hospitable microenvironment. Rocks with northern exposures were more readily colonized apparently because they received more light and heat. Moisture was thought to be provided by meltwater from snow.

Friedmann discovered that identical habitats below rock surfaces and the same general collections of organisms also existed in the Negev of Israel and in California deserts. Dissimilarities in temperature offer a sharp contrast; that of the hot deserts ranges from freezing to 50° C (122° F) while in the cold deserts it varies from subfreezing to 10° C (50° F). Variations on such habitats have been reported by G. A. Llano in South Victoria Land in Antarctica and by G. Follmann of the University of Chile, Santiago, in the Chilean deserts. Llano observed a sparse but compact and moist vegetation of mosses, lichens, and blue-green algae concealed beneath a layer of snow-white marble chips. The chips were apparently frost-shattered fragments from marble outcrops; the vegetation grew best where the chips lay thinnest. Follmann reported lichens growing beneath translucent pebbles.

The rapid expansion of Antarctic biological research has been distinguished by the rising sophistication of field investigations. One particularly

Photos, E. Imre Friedmann, Florida State University

Survival abilities of microbial life in the hostile dry valleys, including Anderson and Beacon valleys (above), have been the focus of recent Antarctic research. In 1977 algae and fungi in primitive lichen association and colorless bacteria were discovered growing in multicolored layers beneath the surface of Beacon Valley sandstone (right). The space between mineral grains of the stone formed a protected, hospitable microclimate in which the organisms could thrive.

Mary Alice McWhinnie, DePaul University

The tiny krill may one day rival the soybean in importance as a source of protein.

significant study in molecular biology has been the identification and elucidation of biochemical antifreezes in both Arctic and Antarctic fish by University of Illinois scientists Arthur L. DeVries and Y. Lin. They discovered that antifreeze appears not only in blood but also in body tissues and consists of large but simple molecules ranging from 2,600 to 33,000 in molecular weight. In Antarctic fish these substances are glycopeptides, which according to the researchers "are expanded molecules and appear to have a structure which presents a large surface area that can interact with ice or water." The exact mechanism of protection is still under study. The impressive results of this research are even more remarkable because the major, highly complex experimental work was carried out in the field, about 13 degrees from the South Pole.

Historically man's knowledge of the Antarctic marine ecosystem has had practical application for the management and harvesting of its biological products. Indeed, the classic "Discovery" studies by British scientists prior to and after World War II were initiated by the activity of the whaling industry. In turn, information gained on the distribution of whales and their food and the identification of the water movements and sharp thermal boundary of the Antarctic Convergence provided scientists a better understanding of the southern ocean.

Today the world seems poised to reap on a large scale another of the Antarctic's treasures, the krill, which with an estimated potential annual harvest of 50 million to 200 million tons may someday rival the soybean as a source of protein for humans and livestock. Despite the long voyages, the bitter cold, and the short "keep" period of krill, countries already known or

169

reported to be harvesting the crustacean include the Soviet Union, Japan, Poland, Chile, and West Germany. Because of the pivotal role of the krill in the Antarctic food web, many scientists and other concerned citizens are fearful that its unregulated harvesting will have an incalculable and serious effect on most Antarctic life. Again, a sound grasp of the marine ecosystem and of krill biology can help ensure safe, efficient exploitation.

One of the first intensive studies of the krill is a U.S. effort now being conducted both in the open ocean and in a laboratory at Palmer Station on the Antarctic Peninsula. Mary Alice McWhinnie of DePaul University, Chicago, who succeeded for the first time in raising krill in laboratory aquariums throughout the Antarctic winter, made many potentially important findings that overturned previous beliefs. Krill were seen to be both omnivorous and cannibalistic, and not exclusively feeders on phytoplankton as had been formerly thought. This implied that krill could grow significantly even under a cover of winter ice and in the absence of photosynthesis. Krill also have a very high spawning potential, about 2,000 eggs per female, and do not die after spawning but molt and revert to a younger stage of maturity to spawn again. Development of *E. superba* was found to progress more slowly than that of related species, requiring perhaps as much as four years to reach the adult stage.

McWhinnie found differences in krill taken from different segments of ocean, indicated by variations in temperature tolerances, respiration rates, and growth patterns. This could be due to a decided racial, or genetic, difference or simply to different age classes. Another discovery was that krill are subject to a parasitic infection, especially with the advance of the Antarctic summer, that affects the abdominal limbs and possibly the reproductive organs. McWhinnie's initial success with aquarium-raised krill opens a vista for future long-term observation of living material that previously had been almost impossible to monitor carefully in its natural habitat.

Future prospects

In the last two decades Antarctica, so long isolated by time, distance, and ignorance, has been swept precipitously into the technological mainstream of the 20th century. The forces were initiated by the first major world scientific effort of the Third Polar Year of 1957–58, widely acclaimed as a successful international cooperative geophysical event. It produced lasting political and scientific effects, climaxed by the Antarctic Treaty of 1959, and led directly to the opportunity for life scientists to take a role in Antarctic research. Article IX of the treaty ensures the preservation of living resources and forms the basis for later agreements concerning the conservation of Antarctic life, designation of specially protected species and areas, and the conservation of Antarctic seals in the event of future sealing activities. More recently it was proposed to mount an international biological investigation of marine Antarctic systems and stocks under the acronym BIOMASS. The objective of BIOMASS would be to gain a better understanding of the structure and functioning of the Antarctic marine ecosystem as a basis for the future management of potential living resources.

Widely praised as an international scientific laboratory, Antarctica is now

A garbage dump, the refuse of Antarctic visitors, covers part of a penguin rookery. Though merely a smudge on this vast pristine land and its life, it serves to remind humankind of the consequences of gross carelessness and indifference.

being hailed as a bank of mineral and biological wealth. This sudden change in status, sparked by interest in the Antarctic krill and in the potential mineral and hydrocarbon reserves of the continent and the seabed, has momentous ecological implications. Although the Antarctic Treaty is silent on mineral reserves, its signatories were not blind to the commercial potential of the continent. Fear of the effects of exploitation of the land and seabed has aroused environmentalists and conservationists, underscoring the difficult role of biologists and the need for a high degree of biological competence. There is also concern that commercial activities may restrict the traditional Antarctic freedom of scientific inquiry or may divert important scientific inquiry to resources exploitation.

Notwithstanding, Antarctica's unique features will always offer opportunities for those interested in basic biological research. The most pressing and challenging problem is the need for a better understanding of ecological processes, energy flows, production rates, and food chains of the Antarctic marine ecosystem. This calls for the services of a wide spectrum of biological specialists and the cooperation of other scientific disciplines on an international scale. It will require application of satellite techniques and sophisticated monitoring systems for essential seasonal measurements. The U.S. Nimbus 7 atmospheric satellite, for example, which was launched in October 1978, is instrumented for remote sensing of chlorophyll a as an indicator of phytoplankton biomass. South African and U.S. scientists are cooperating in an experiment with airborne acoustic sensing gear to locate krill shoals and collect data for estimating stocks. In the final analysis, it is the living resources of Antarctica that are at stake. Their preservation is dependent on assertive and imaginative leadership by life scientists.

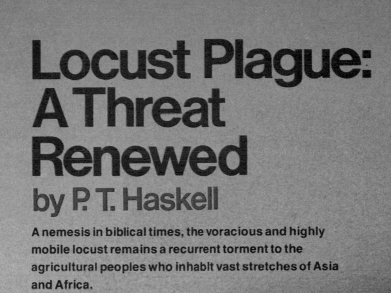

Locust Plague: A Threat Renewed

by P. T. Haskell

A nemesis in biblical times, the voracious and highly mobile locust remains a recurrent torment to the agricultural peoples who inhabit vast stretches of Asia and Africa.

In the biblical book of Exodus, Moses asks God to send a plague of locusts to punish the Egyptians for their enslavement of the Israelites.

P. T. HASKELL *is Director of the Centre for Overseas Pest Research in the British Ministry of Overseas Development.*

(Overleaf) Painting by Eraldo Carugati

The enemy is poised to invade. Its armies contain billions of individuals, each one a highly efficient flying machine that can strike into a territory from a hundred miles away across a neighbor's border and then vanish without trace except for enormous damage to crops. Such was the problem facing the ministers of agriculture of some 55 countries in early 1978. Their common enemy is an insect, the desert locust, historically the most infamous insect pest in the world.

Locusts have plagued man since the origins of agriculture 8,000–9,000 years ago. Celebrated in fact and fable throughout much of recorded history, they appear in the annals of religion and mythology, are portrayed on tombs of the 6th dynasty (*c.* 2345–2181 BC) at Saqqarah in Egypt, and are described in several books of the Bible and in the Koran. Locust plagues have been exorcised by the Christian church, and laws about destruction of locusts appear in ancient Chinese, Greek, and Roman texts. In recent times they have been the subject of intensive scientific research and experiment—in 1970, for example, some 720 scientists in more than 66 countries were engaged in research on locusts and grasshoppers—and probably more money has been spent on research to understand and control this group of pests than any other. Yet, in 1979 the world once again faced the possibility of a plague, which might last several years and which would cost millions of dollars to control. What these plagues are, how they occur, and whether they can be controlled are questions to be asked only after a consideration of the locust itself.

174

Anatomy of an enemy

Locusts are insects of the order Orthoptera, meaning "straight-winged," so called for their two pairs of long narrow wings. Locusts and grasshoppers are closely related, and indeed there is no completely clear-cut distinction between them. But the name locust is applied commonly to about 16 species of Orthoptera found all over the world that show in extreme form two behavioral characteristics: gregariousness and the urge to migrate.

Locusts react to and are stimulated by the presence of other locusts, both male and female, and they behave so as to keep together in a crowd. This can be effectively shown by a very simple experiment in which a number of locusts are introduced into a featureless arena in which heating and lighting are uniform. In about half an hour the locusts are found to have grouped together; if disturbed and separated, the group re-forms quite quickly.

Names and distribution of 16 species of Orthoptera that are commonly called locusts are listed in the table at bottom. Other members of the order include (below, left to right) the bush locust (Phymateus leprosus); lubber grasshopper (Brachystola magna); and green locust (Locusta viridissima).

(Left) Anthony Bannister—Natural History Photographic Agency; (center) J. E. Henry, Rangeland Insect Laboratory, USDA; (right) Hans Reinhard—Bruce Coleman Inc.

common name	species	distribution
desert locust	*Schistocerca gregaria*	most of Africa north of the Equator, the Middle East, India, Pakistan
African migratory locust	*Locusta migratoria migratorioides*	Africa south of the Sahara
Asiatic migratory locust	*Locusta migratoria migratoria*	basins of Black, Caspian, and Aral seas; central Asia as far as northern China
Oriental migratory locust	*Locusta migratoria manilensis*	eastern and southern China, Japan, Philippines, Celebes, Borneo, Malaya
Madagascar locust	*Locusta migratoria capito*	Madagascar
red locust	*Nomadacris septemfasciata*	southern and central Africa
South American locust	*Schistocerca paranensis*	South America
Central American locust	*Schistocerca americana*	Central America
brown locust	*Locustana pardalina*	southern Africa
Australian plague locust	*Chortoicetes terminifera*	Australia
Australian spur-throated locust	*Austracris guttulosa*	Australia, New Britain
Bombay locust	*Patanga succincta*	India, southeastern Asia, Philippines, Malayan archipelago
Javanese grasshopper	*Valanga nigricornis*	southeastern Asia, Malayan archipelago
Moroccan locust	*Dociostaurus maroccanus*	southern Europe, north Africa, Cyprus, Turkey, Middle East, south-central Asia
Italian locust	*Calliptamus italicus*	southern Europe, Middle East, central Asia, southern Siberia
Sahelian tree locust	*Anacridium melanorhodon*	western and eastern Africa, southwestern Arabia

The second important type of locust behavior is a drive always to be on the move. Even in their early growth stages, when the young locusts have no wings and are called hoppers, this locomotor urge pushes them in long marches across country in groups known as hopper bands. When they reach the adult stage and develop wings, they migrate by flying—still maintaining their gregariousness and thus giving rise to vast airborne populations known as swarms, the typical manifestation of a locust plague.

Before the 1920s, studies had shown that swarms of some species of locusts seemed to appear and disappear in a mysterious, unpredictable manner. It was noticed, however, that when swarms were absent another insect, a solitary and nonmigratory grasshopper, often could be found in large numbers where locust swarms had last been seen. Eventually it was discovered that these two kinds of insects, which differed markedly in size, body shape, color, physiology, and behavior, were in reality two forms, or phases, of the same species. Laboratory experiments proved that one locust phase could be completely transformed into the other in a matter of weeks simply by changing the population density; for example, by crowding together large numbers of the solitary phase in a cage. Recent research has suggested a flow of sensory stimulation between individual insects by way of vision, touch, and smell to be important in inducing the phase change. Investigations also point to the balance of insect hormones in the body as the controlling factor in the transformation process itself.

Apart from gregariousness and a migratory urge, locusts have a simple life cycle. The eggs are laid in a group or pod, which can contain 30–100 eggs according to the species. The pods are normally deposited in moist soil because they need water to develop; the incubation period depends on the temperature but is about 10–14 days. After emergence, the young hoppers molt through five or six growth stages called instars. The period of time spent in each instar varies a great deal with environmental conditions, particularly temperature, and can be as short as 20 days at 42° C (108° F) or 45 days at 24° C (75° F). In the last couple of instars wing buds form, and

176

Photos, Stephen Dalton—Natural History Photographic Agency

A female locust (facing page, left) deposits a pod of about 70 eggs in moist sand. White froth secreted above the pod protects the eggs from drying out and keeps open a tunnel to the surface for the hatchlings. Desert locust hatchling (facing page, right) rests by rice-sized egg. Two hoppers (left, bottom) confront each other in their ceaseless search for food; their stubby, undeveloped wing buds are incapable of flight. Bright pink adult locust (top) allows its flight wings to uncurl and stiffen after final molt. Its dark discarded husk remains attached to the branch.

at the final molt to adult the four long wings become fully developed. The new adult is sexually immature; maturation takes another week or more. During this time the locust feeds voraciously, its flight muscles increase in size, and fat—which serves as its flight fuel—is stored in a mass of specialized tissue called the fat body.

When young hoppers emerge from the egg they show at once the behavioral characteristics of gregariousness and locomotion, forming bands that move across country foraging for food. These bands vary greatly in size, depending on the size of the parental population; some contain only a few hundred hoppers, although large populations of parents can produce hopper bands of enormous size. The largest band ever recorded had a front of 34 kilometers and was 3 kilometers in depth, thus covering an area of more than 100 square kilometers with some 20 million individual hoppers. (A kilometer is about 0.62 miles; a square kilometer is 0.38 square miles.)

When these hoppers transform into adults, they form flying swarms. These

177

swarms again vary in size—from about one-half or one square kilometer in surface area, containing perhaps 50–100 million locusts, to the largest recorded, which was 1,300 square kilometers in size and probably contained about 50,000,000,000 locusts. Such figures begin to suggest the magnitude of the problem, which is further clarified when one considers the question of the damage that locusts can do. Individual locusts weigh two or three grams and can eat their own weight of food every 24 hours. If a square kilometer of swarm contains 50 million locusts, then a simple calculation shows that a swarm covering 100 square kilometers can eat more than 10,000 metric tons of food every day. Although this is the maximum potential damage figure and is not often reached, clearly locusts do cause enormous destruction. In 125 BC, for example, a locust invasion of North Africa, then a major granary of the Roman Empire, resulted in the death of 80,000 people from starvation. In 1931 approximately 20% of the subsistence crops of Kenya were destroyed, and in Ethiopia in 1958 locusts attacked cereal crops and destroyed the food of a million people for a year. Again in 1978 newspaper headlines announced the same story: "locust plague decimates Ethiopia," "locust swarms threaten crops," and so on. A serious complication is that, in general, locusts live in the drier and arid regions of the world, where subsistence farming is paramount. The destruction of crops in such locations puts the human population immediately at risk of famine.

Distribution and movement

The basis of any war plan—and the fight against locusts has been just that for more than a thousand years—is intelligence about the enemy: Where are his bases and his lines of communication? How far and how fast can he move from them? Where is he most vulnerable and to what sort of attack? Although locusts had been recognized as a major pest on an international scale for years, it was not until the 1920s that any coordinated action was taken against them. Then, on the initiative of Boris Uvarov of the Imperial Bureau of Entomology in London, an international effort was begun in Africa; teams were sent out into the field to establish the details of the life and movements of the most harmful locust species. As a result of this work two major types of locust were recognized, the "outbreak area" type and the "invasion area" type.

An example of the former is *Locusta migratoria,* the African migratory locust, which caused great damage in many countries in Africa between 1928 and 1941. At the height of that plague, most of the southern part of the continent was infested, but research showed that the swarms initiating this invasion all came from a small area situated in the flood plains of the Niger River in West Africa (see figure 1). Even when all swarms had disappeared from the rest of Africa, locust populations could still be found in this region. This observation led to the hypothesis that, when due to favorable conditions these populations increased in numbers, they underwent a phase change to the migrant form and swarmed to favorable territory outside the originating region. There they bred, and more swarms were produced that flew still further and invaded more territory, thus spreading the plague to the

178

limit of favorable conditions. These populations, however, could not maintain themselves indefinitely outside the outbreak area when environmental conditions became adverse, and eventually they died out. The residual population, nevertheless, remained in the Niger outbreak area and obviously could start another plague when conditions permitted.

The suggested solution to this particular problem was to set up a control organization in the outbreak area to keep watch on the resident population and, when it showed signs of increasing above certain limits, to control it with pesticides. Accordingly, in 1949 the British, French, and Belgian governments jointly initiated what was to become the International African Migratory Locust Organisation (OICMA). The scientific reasoning proved correct, and since OICMA was established there have been no plagues of this species. The OICMA organization is now run by 17 independent African countries and offers an excellent example of achievement through international cooperation. This success was followed by others, resulting in the widespread control of locusts that begin their reign of destruction in a relatively small, well-defined area.

But what of the other type of locust, the "invasion area" type? *Schistocerca gregaria,* the desert locust, exemplifies this kind. This species, as figure 2 shows, can inhabit a vast region of Africa and Asia, stretching from the Atlantic across northern Africa and the Middle East to the Bay of Bengal, and it has no restricted outbreak area. It can both live and breed anywhere within this invasion area of approximately 29 million square kilometers, or one-fifth of the world's land surface. In this region live several hundred million people in some 55 countries; most of them rely on subsistence agriculture, and thus to them a plague of the desert locust can mean hunger and perhaps famine.

The desert locust

The desert locust is now threatening a new plague; to understand how this has come about and the enormous problems of dealing with it, one needs to consider this species and its distribution in more detail. Although the desert locust infests the whole of the vast area mentioned above, its populations show marked fluctuations, and it was discovered in the 1940s that the

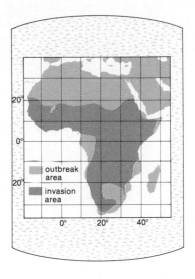

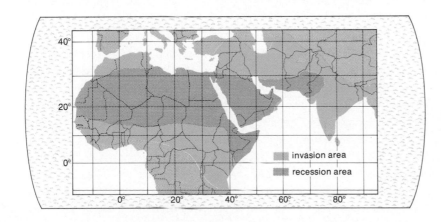

Figure 1 (above) maps the maximum area invaded by swarms of the African migratory locust between 1928 and 1941 and pinpoints their outbreak area. Figure 2 (left) shows the distribution of the desert locust: the maximum area liable to invasion and a smaller, but still extensive, region in which locusts are found when environmental conditions are unfavorable. (Facing page, top to bottom) African migratory locust; desert locust; locust swarm during an invasion of French Morocco (now part of Morocco) in 1954.

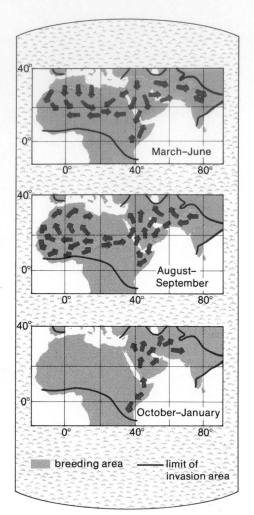

breeding area — limit of invasion area

migration and breeding of swarms followed a marked seasonal pattern. This characteristic is illustrated in figure 3, which shows the regions in which the main populations are found during spring, summer, and winter, and the main directions of migration for swarms that breed in those areas.

This work suggested the basis of a strategy to control the desert locust. If the main locust populations are confined to definite areas at certain times, then a major international control effort concentrated on those areas might be able to destroy a large part of the population and interrupt the plague. But even these breeding areas, although much smaller than the whole invasion area, are vast and present formidable logistic and organizational problems for any control body. In order to work out control tactics it is necessary to know, for example, how far and fast and in what precise direction swarms fly and at what time of year.

Further research produced some answers to these questions. First of all, in both the laboratory and the field, studies of the flight capacity of the desert locust showed that the fuel used for its flight muscles was fat, stored in the insect's fat body. A flying desert locust operates at a metabolic rate of 75 kcal/kg/h (kilocalories of energy per kilogram of body weight per hour), and its hourly consumption of fuel is only 0.8% of its body weight. A modern jet fighter, running on gasoline or kerosene, operates at a rate of between 500 and 4,000 kcal/kg/h and consumes between 4 and 36% of its weight in fuel in an hour—far less efficient. With an average fat load, a desert locust can fly continuously for ten hours a day. Research has demonstrated that the maximum air speed in still air is of the order of 19–24 kilometers per hour; hence, the maximum unassisted flight range in still air would be about 250 kilometers. Yet it was known from direct measurement of swarm movements from light aircraft which flew with the swarm that desert locusts could travel much further, and other work then showed that swarms moved with the prevailing winds.

Driven by the migratory urge, the locusts in a swarm take off, fly up into the air, and orient their flight downwind. Swarms maintain their gregarious cohesion even in flight because the insects have developed a number of visual and acoustic methods to keep them together. As a result of such behavior swarms generally move at or at slightly less than the speed of the prevailing wind and in its direction. A dramatic example is offered by one swarm in Kenya that was tracked over a period of six days. Because of changes in wind direction, it went around in a large distorted circle, and although it actually flew some 180 kilometers—in fact, over the Kenya-Tanzania border and back—ultimately it displaced only five kilometers.

This seems an inefficient mechanism, but it is now known that the whole flight behavior of downwind movement is in itself an adaptive behavior pattern. As mentioned above, the eggs of the desert locust need water for their development and hatching. Furthermore, when the young hoppers emerge, they need fresh vegetation on which to feed. These requirements can only be fulfilled in areas of rainfall. But the area in which the desert locust lives is characterized by very low, erratically distributed rainfall, and to breed the locust needs to locate and move into an area of moisture. The fact that the desert locust appears to have this ability had been observed for many

180

Anthony Bannister—Natural History Photographic Agency

years, because its appearance in an area is very often associated with rainfall—so much so that in some parts of its invasion area it is called locally the "rain locust."

Downwind flight behavior explains this correlation, since the major wind systems in which locusts fly move toward regions that meteorologists term "convergence zones." These zones are precisely those in which rain is most likely to occur, so that going with the wind constitutes for the desert locust a method of survival. One of the most important zones in Africa is the Intertropical Convergence Zone, which crosses the northern portion of the continent at roughly latitude 20° N; swarms are trapped in this zone between cool northerly and warm southerly winds.

Such knowledge of how and in what direction locusts move affords the basis for a system to forecast the behavior of swarms. In the 1940s scientists of the British Anti-Locust Research Centre (since 1971 the Centre for Overseas Pest Research) in London, where much of the original research on locust movement had been done, set up an international desert locust forecasting service. This consisted of a monthly summary of known desert locust populations throughout the area, together with a forecast of possible breed-

Figure 3 (facing page) maps migratory movements of main populations of the desert locust in spring (March–June), summer (August–September), and winter (October–January). Brown locust hoppers (above) feed on fresh vegetation.

181

Analyst examines satellite imagery of cloud patterns over the Indian Ocean (top). Accurate assessment of future weather conditions is a valuable aid in forecasting locust breeding grounds and swarm movements. Tethered adult locust (bottom) undergoes wind tunnel experiments at the Centre for Overseas Pest Research in London. Such tests help in understanding locust flight characteristics and the effect of insecticides on flight efficiency.

ing locations and swarm movements for the next month. Such a forecast was obviously of the utmost value to control organizations in the deployment of their forces and soon was launched as an international service under the aegis of the Food and Agriculture Organization (FAO) of the United Nations. These monthly forecasts were distributed to the locust control organizations of those countries threatened by the desert locust, which carried out the actual control operations described below.

Locust control measures

In ancient times there was little to be done about locust swarms other than to ask the local church for prayers—and many instances of this are recorded —or to send boys banging drums and shouting to drive the locusts on to a

A PLAGUE OF LOCUSTS IN SYRIA.

neighbor's field. Only with the advent of insecticides did practical control become a possibility. The earliest poisons were substances like sodium arsenate, mixed with a bait such as bran and scattered on the ground in front of hopper bands. Although this method, now improved by the use of modern insecticides, is still practiced in some countries, it suffers from logistic and organizational problems of transporting large amounts of bait in trucks over difficult terrain. In the 1950s a simple sprayer was developed that was driven by back pressure from a vehicle exhaust. This device laid a barrier of a persistent insecticide such as dieldrin on vegetation eaten by hopper bands and swarms. It proved to be very efficient and is still widely used.

The mobility of the flying swarms, however, required control forces to acquire a similar capability, and in the 1940s research began into the use of aircraft spraying against locusts. Special atomizers were developed to produce sprays of fine drops that caught locusts in flight or on the ground, and special formulations of new insecticides were produced. So effective was this research that, whereas in 1945 a liter, or a little more than a quart, of insecticide killed only 2,000 locusts, by 1968 a liter killed one million locusts at one-fiftieth the cost.

At the same time that research improved the efficiency of control techniques, logistic and organizational problems were being studied and solved. Restraining the desert locust poses above all a problem in international cooperation; a flying swarm respects no border and may move as much as 5,000 kilometers in its lifetime. A swarm may form in one country, fly into neighboring territory to damage crops, and then move on to another country to breed. Thus it is obvious that interchange of information between countries is fundamental to successful control. The basis of this intelligence service is the forecasting system described above, but some arrangement for international flexibility is also required. For instance, if an aircraft from one country is spraying a swarm, it must be able to follow its target over the border of neighboring countries to complete the job. This at once raises political problems, which can only be resolved by international agreements.

Early locust control measures involved literal hand-to-hand combat between man and insect. Tree branches served as giant swatters, and drums were beaten in hopes of frightening the pests away.

183

Atomizer-equipped plane sprays locust swarm area in Ethiopia as part of DLCOEA control program.

International cooperation

In 1952 the FAO assumed the role of international coordinator for campaigns against the desert locust. Under FAO aegis campaigns have been organized on a regional basis, sometimes under regional locust commissions. For example, the FAO South West Asia Regional Locust Control Commission covers India, Pakistan, Iran, and Afghanistan; these countries cooperate in the exchange of information and have set up a trust fund to provide insecticides and machinery, including aircraft, for control. In other regions independent international locust control organizations exist, funded by the countries concerned. There are two of these, one being the Desert Locust Control Organization for Eastern Africa (DLCOEA) supported by Kenya, Uganda, Tanzania, Ethiopia, Somalia, Sudan, and Djibouti; the other, an organization in West Africa called OCLALAV, is supported by the countries of that region to control both locusts and bird pests.

Three major FAO commissions and two independent international control organizations together cover the entire desert locust area. With the support of the UN Development Program a massive research, development, and training program was carried out over a number of years to train personnel

184

of the regional and national control units as research scientists, pilots, pesticide experts, forecasters, and administrators. In 1973 the FAO felt the time was ripe for its regional offices to assume the responsibility for the desert locust forecasting system, hitherto based in London. This large locust control network has been in general very successful. Although it is known that populations fluctuate considerably over the years due to variations in the weather, especially rainfall, nevertheless there is evidence to show that the reduction in infestations that has been seen in recent years has been considerably assisted by international control efforts. If such has been the case, it is reasonable to ask why many susceptible areas presently face the strong possibility of another plague.

The new threat

From another examination of figure 3 it will be seen that the shore of the Red Sea is a key area for locust breeding in winter as well as the spring and summer. This then is an area that must be kept under constant surveillance, both from the ground and the air, to ensure that all locust breeding is detected and controlled before swarms are formed. This task is important because at the appropriate seasons swarms bred near the Red Sea can move into Arabia, down into eastern Africa, or across it to infest western Africa, and in any one of these new areas swarms can breed again and maintain the plague. It is also true that once swarms form and invade the mountainous area of Ethiopia and the Horn of Africa they are very hard to find and control. This region, therefore, is of critical importance in the desert locust story; for many years now it has been successfully surveyed and controlled by DLCOEA.

Recently, however, hostilities in Ethiopia between the Eritrean Liberation Front and the Ethiopian government have prevented surveys from being made on the Red Sea coast, even by aircraft. In October and November 1977 exceptionally heavy rains fell in Ethiopia, Somalia, and southwestern Arabia, creating highly favorable breeding conditions that led to rapid multiplication and swarm production. The rains continued unabated in December 1977. Swarms formed and some moved out, and on Dec. 26, 1977, the first swarm was reported in Saudi Arabia, followed by reports of swarms in Yemen (San'a'). In all some two dozen swarms were reported from the area between January and May 1978.

Vigorous control campaigns were waged in the Arabian Peninsula in Saudi Arabia and Yemen (San'a'), and the situation seemed to have been contained. But on the other side of the Red Sea conflicts between Ethiopia and neighboring Somalia also curtailed survey and control activity, and by May 1978 there were some 50 reports of swarms covering an area of 2,000 square kilometers in Ethiopia, as well as 17 swarms in Somalia between March and June; many more were believed to exist in inaccessible areas. Hopper bands invaded Sudan from the Ethiopian province of Eritrea. Locusts invaded India at the beginning of June over the Arabian Sea; five swarms were seen but were controlled.

In July 1978 the FAO called an emergency session of its Desert Locust Control Committee, in which representatives of all countries involved with

185

Stephen Dalton—Natural History Photographic Agency

the desert locust, together with locust experts from Great Britain, the U.S., and the international locust control organizations, decided on a number of actions to facilitate reporting and forecasting and to build up the control potential, particularly the stock of insecticides, that might be needed. Appeals were made to the international community to provide assistance through the FAO to the regional and national control units. The aid agencies of many governments responded with aircraft, vehicles, insecticides, and equipment, and locust experts were lent to survey key areas.

Presently it still is not possible to say with certainty that a full-scale plague will start; as usual, much will depend on the weather, but long-range forecasts predict more rain in the key breeding areas, which could lead to population increases and swarm escapes. In preparation the FAO has issued emergency warnings to all countries to increase their locust survey activity; if timely action can be taken in all areas, then a plague can be averted, but latest odds by locust experts are 60–40 that a plague will occur. Its duration and severity will depend again basically on international cooperation. It seems likely that all necessary material aid will be provided; if it can be used then chances are good that the plague can be brought under control reasonably quickly.

The future

It seems clear that the present situation was brought about by a combination of unprecedented heavy rainfall in the region of the Red Sea and related areas and a political situation that prevented essential survey and control activity at the crucial time. There is little doubt that the control techniques now in use, provided they can be deployed in time, are highly effective and generally sufficient to deal with locust situations that can lead to a plague. As always, however, there remains the problem of gathering information on the exact position of locust hopper bands, swarms, and egg fields and of obtaining weather information from what are often still inaccessible areas, in order to predict the likely occurrence and success of breeding.

Research in recent years has brought about the development of sophisticated techniques to help gather this data. Several years ago the Centre for Overseas Pest Research in London pioneered the use of weather pictures of locust breeding areas obtained from Earth satellites, notably Landsat and more recently Meteosat, to improve forecasting techniques. The Remote Sensing Unit of the FAO is now trying to develop further the use of these techniques. Joint research carried out by British and Australian scientists has resulted in development of a radar unit that can detect locust swarms as much as 50 miles away. Subsequently engineered to fit in aircraft, it now can be used in air-to-air search, thus extending the range of detection. In theory, deployment of such devices could provide an effective early warning system, but both initiation and maintenance costs would be very high.

Expense is a category in which the desert locust sets another problem. Owing to the correlation of breeding and weather, there can be long periods, perhaps as much as seven or eight years, when locust populations remain very low. Experts call these "recession periods," during which are needed only minimal survey and no control activities. This poses problems for the poorer, less developed countries that fund the control organizations. During recession there is a tendency to cut funds and staff, equipment and vehicles are not renewed, and a general loss of efficiency and morale ensues. Then when the locusts return, much time and money is required to bring the service back to its normal efficiency.

In addition, there are continuing difficulties with international cooperation. Nevertheless, the record of African countries has been remarkably good in that despite political differences they generally have maintained their support for the international locust effort. In late 1978 the FAO initiated a study to find a new system that could overcome the problems of information and survey for locust control. The lesson of recent months is clear: the desert locust is still an enemy to be reckoned with, and the international community must continue to improve its efforts to combat it.

Of little threat individually, the desert locust (facing page, bottom) migrates in swarms large enough to engulf the crops and buildings of an entire agricultural community, as it did to the town of Keren in Ethiopia (facing page, top). Desert locust control scout (above) counts the toll after aerial spraying along a streambed outside Keren.

The Science of Growing a Tree

by Jonathan W. Wright

New planting techniques and genetic research are increasing the productivity of forests and of farms set aside for the cultivation of economically useful trees.

In spite of substitutes the demand for wood throughout the world continues to increase, spurred on by growing populations and the development of many new wood-based products. The increase in demand is shown by the consumption figures for industrial (nonfuel) wood, which were 29, 42, and 48 billion cubic feet per year for 1950–52, 1967–69, and 1976, respectively. To the 1976 figure should be added another 43 billion cubic feet used for fuel by the people in less developed countries who cook and heat with charcoal. Total consumption in 1976 was enough to make a pile of wood 10 feet high and 114 feet wide around the Equator, and consumption is expected to double by the year 2000.

That demand must be met from a decreasing forest area because woodlands are being lost to agriculture or urbanization. Therefore, intensified forest management and, especially, a great increase in the rate of forest planting are necessary. Planting increases production in two ways. First, less productive forest types can be replaced by more productive ones, as in the southeastern United States where oaks are being replaced by faster-growing pines. Second, rotations can be shortened: planted forests start growing immediately whereas reliance on natural regeneration may entail a wait of several years.

Although most forests are still reproduced naturally, planting is gaining in importance. In the United States tree plantations in 1978 occupied approximately 37 million acres, or 6% of the nation's forest area. Of the other major forest countries, the Soviet Union has a plantation area similar to that of the U.S., but Canada has only about two million acres. As of 1976 China reportedly had the largest plantation area, 120 million acres.

Forest planting is having the biggest impact on forestry in Southern Hemisphere countries, where fast-growing subtropical pines from the Northern Hemisphere grow exceptionally well and produce long-fibered wood of great value for pulp and building materials. Also, the very-fast-growing (up to 20 feet per year) eucalypts from Australia are suited to large areas in Africa and South America. South Africa is an extreme example of what may be accomplished by planting. That country's two million acres of forest plantations comprise only 25% of its forest area yet produce nearly all of its forest products.

189

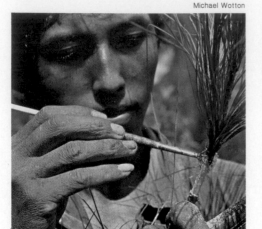

A research technician in Indonesia (above) applies growth hormone to the stem of the conifer Pinus caribaea. *Tree farming in Japan is exemplified by the grove of bamboo trees in various stages of growth (right).*

JONATHAN W. WRIGHT is Professor of Forestry at Michigan State University, East Lansing.

(Overleaf) Photo by Dan Morill

Nursery and planting practices: the old and the new

Some reforestation is done with direct seeding, particularly with the longleaf pine in the southeastern U.S. Most, however, is done by planting seedlings that are 6–12 inches tall, small enough to be carried easily and planted quickly in large numbers. In the United States most such seedlings are begun in outdoor nurseries located on sandy soils. In the Southeast plantable seedlings are produced in one year, but in colder climates two to three years are required.

During the past 50 years some aspects of nursery practice have changed little, but others have changed markedly. Weed control, for example, is now accomplished by chemicals that are usually applied a few weeks before the seeds are sown. Several different chemicals are in use, most of which will kill fungi and insects as well as weed seeds and disintegrate rapidly in the soil. Except in very small nurseries all tilling and seedbed preparation are done by machine. When the seedlings are ready for planting, they are usually loosened by machine (actually a long, tractor-drawn knife set at an angle that simultaneously cuts roots and loosens soil). The actual pulling and packing, however, are done by hand in most regions. In large industrial nurseries in the southeastern U.S. there are complex machines to do the whole lifting operation from soil loosening to packing. Increased use of chemicals and mechanization in itself often has resulted in better-quality nursery stock.

In Finland, with its short growing seasons and slow-growing trees, the large-scale use of greenhouses for tree seedlings began during the past decade. The greenhouses are made of lightweight materials and are commonly quite long, 30 feet wide, and 15 feet tall. Seedlings are grown in the same way as in outdoor nurseries and are transplanted in a bare-root condition. Most of these production greenhouses are unheated and without supplemental light. Even so, the protection against the outside cold results in lengthening the growing season by six to eight weeks. Because of this birch seedlings can be raised in one year and pine or spruce seedlings in two years, a year's saving in each case.

In many subtropical countries seedlings are grown in containers and planted with a core of soil around their roots. The containers may be of wood veneer, plastic bags with aeration holes punched in the base, or tarpaper. Unless biodegradable, they are removed at planting time. Such containers are usually 1½–2 inches in diameter and 6–8 inches long, and are filled with soil. The seeds may be sown directly in the containers or sown in flats and transferred to the containers when a few weeks old. Such containerized seedlings are usually field-planted when five to eight months old.

There are advantages to the use of containerized seedlings. The roots are not damaged during lifting, and one is permitted greater leeway as to time of planting. These advantages have prompted much research on containers in the northern United States and Canada. In most cases the work has been done in heated greenhouses given supplemental light. Results have often been spectacular. Spruces, for example, grow as tall in six months under continuous light as they do in three years outdoors. In the early 1970s some Pacific Northwest industries erected large greenhouses to produce containerized and accelerated growth seedlings on a commercial scale. Because of cost and survival problems, however, some of these were being phased out in 1978 with a return to bare-root seedlings.

Even in developed countries many trees are still planted by hand. With bare-root seedlings this involves making a slit in the ground with a spade or special heavy bar, just as might have been done 50 years ago. With seedlings in containers holes must be dug. In open land, machines may be used with bare-root stock. A planting machine is relatively simple. Tractor-drawn, it consists of a u-shaped shoe that makes a slit eight to ten inches deep, a seat above and behind the shoe for the person doing the planting, and two diagonally placed packing wheels. In operation the person doing the planting places the roots of a tree in the slit and holds the top until the packing wheels close the slit and cause the soil to grasp the roots. This type of machine was developed some 25 years ago, yet it seems to work better than more sophisticated models developed later.

The biggest recent advances in planting technique have been in the area of weed control. In the northeastern United States, where grass and herbaceous weeds are the problem, chemicals are used. These are usually of the same types used in agriculture. In the southeastern United States, where woody vegetation is the problem, weed control is usually accomplished by means of bulldozers that scrape the ground and leave the brush in long piles or windrows. Where wage rates are low, as in many parts of the subtropics, the machete and hoe are still the primary weed-control tools.

Eggs of the shieldback pine seedbug are laid on the cone of a loblolly pine. Both nymphs and adults of this insect inflict damage to forests by feeding on the pine seeds.

191

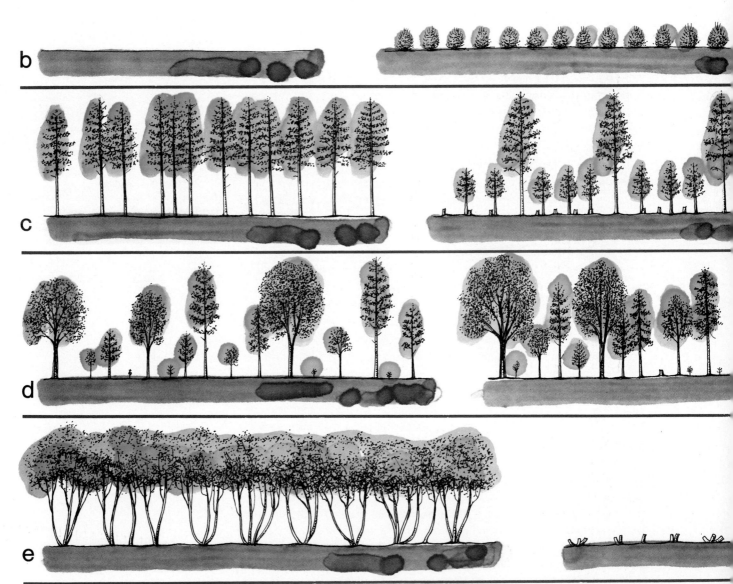

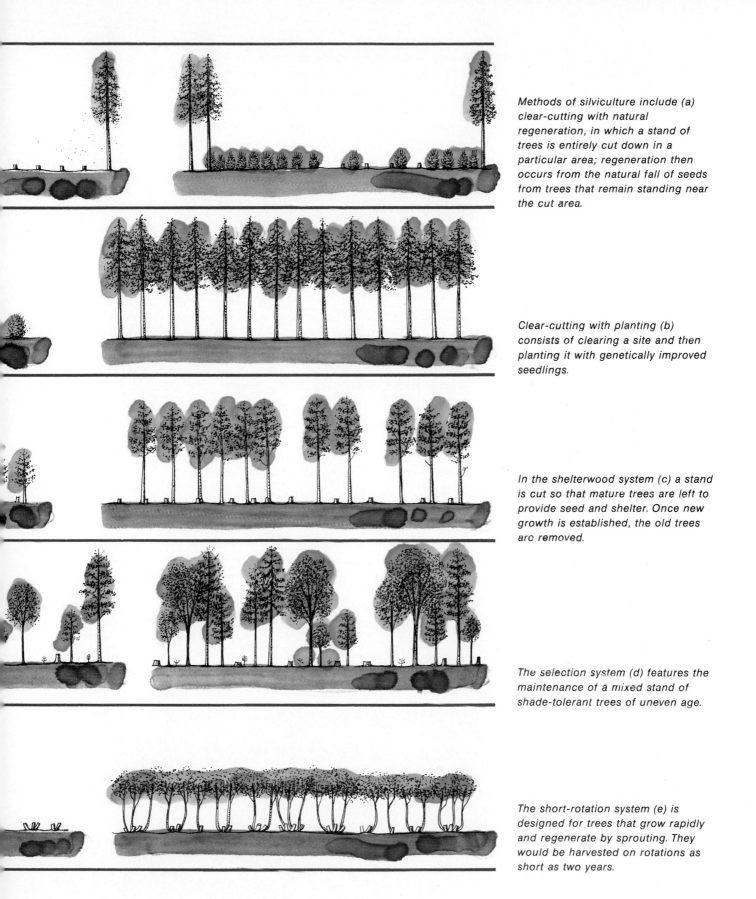

Methods of silviculture include (a) clear-cutting with natural regeneration, in which a stand of trees is entirely cut down in a particular area; regeneration then occurs from the natural fall of seeds from trees that remain standing near the cut area.

Clear-cutting with planting (b) consists of clearing a site and then planting it with genetically improved seedlings.

In the shelterwood system (c) a stand is cut so that mature trees are left to provide seed and shelter. Once new growth is established, the old trees are removed.

The selection system (d) features the maintenance of a mixed stand of shade-tolerant trees of uneven age.

The short-rotation system (e) is designed for trees that grow rapidly and regenerate by sprouting. They would be harvested on rotations as short as two years.

Development in the southeastern U.S.

The rate of forest planting in the U.S. climbed from very little in the 1930s to a half million acres per year in 1950 and 2 million acres per year in 1960. Then it dipped, but rose again to 1.9 million acres per year in 1977. Of that amount two-thirds was planted in a 200-mile-wide strip along the Atlantic and Gulf coasts, from Virginia to Texas. Most of this planting involved two native pines, loblolly and slash. These are long-fibered and make a strong pulp. Also, they are planted more easily than hardwoods and grow rapidly on a variety of sites.

Genetic research on tree improvement started on a small scale in Florida in the 1930s and was intensified and spread throughout the southeast in the 1950s. During the past quarter century the forest industry in that region has devoted more energy to breeding work than to any other type of research on tree growing. Much of this has been done by three large consortia between universities and industries, though the states and federal government have also been active. Among the reasons for the interest in this research is the permanence of the results. Once developed, a new variety of tree can be planted ever afterward at no extra cost, whereas a new development in nutrition requires the addition of expensive fertilizers each year. Also, breeding of new varieties offers the easiest answer to some problems in tree growing. That is true, for example, for the damage caused by fusiform rust, a serious disease of plantation-grown pines. The rust can be controlled by spraying but only at prohibitive cost. By contrast, the breeding of resistant varieties promises to be a relatively simple undertaking.

The improvement program practiced in the Southeast is mainly one of selecting and crossing the best trees. Foresters scour the woods for exceptional trees, from which small branches ("scions") are clipped and then grafted onto small seedlings or "rootstocks." These grafted trees are then placed in seed orchards, where they can cross-pollinate one another. The earliest orchards contained only a few dozen clones (a clone in this context is all the grafted offspring of a single tree). In modern programs breeders work with hundreds or thousands of clones.

Fusiform rust, seen in close-up (below) and affecting the foreground trees in a grove (right), is a serious fungal disease of plantation-grown pines. Controlling the rust by spraying is expensive, and so geneticists are attempting to breed resistant varieties.

William Cibula

Harry R. Powers, USDA, Forest Service

Some selected trees produce offspring that are only average or even inferior in the traits for which they were selected. To identify such trees progeny testing is now standard practice. By this procedure seeds are collected from each selected parent, and the offspring are grown in specially designed experiments called progeny tests. In the 15-year period from 1964–78, participants in the North Carolina State University-Industry progeny testing program established 3,400 acres for such tests. Every few years these experiments are measured to show which parents are producing the best offspring. The results are then used to show which clones should be removed from the seed orchards. The progeny testing often results in a fourfold increase in the amount of genetic improvement.

To enhance seed production the trees in seed orchards are spaced 20–30 feet apart and intensively cared for. Most orchards are either mowed or cultivated. They are regularly fertilized, especially with nitrogen, and a few are irrigated.

Some trees in the oldest plantations are 75 feet tall. For this reason in the pine orchards cone collection is a problem. The tree shakers developed for the fruit industry proved useful with slash pine, in which the cones drop quickly to the ground if given a sharp rap. The shakers are not useful with loblolly pine, however. Some orchard managers have turned to renting tall lift trucks for the cone-collecting season. Some allow the cones to open naturally and harvest the seeds from cloths placed on the ground, while others are experimenting with large vacuum cleaners. Cone insects are among the other problems faced by orchard managers. In some years pests cause heavy damage to the seed crops.

A different type of improvement program has been practiced in Mississippi and Louisiana, where seeds were collected from many natural stands of trees. This experiment showed that trees that were growing in one county produced offspring that were exceptionally resistant to fusiform rust and also grew rapidly. In this case the wild trees in that county can be considered to comprise a very large seed orchard.

In 1977 the seed orchards in the Southeast produced about 70,000 pounds of loblolly pine seed and about 55,000 pounds of slash pine seed. That was enough to supply all the needs of some companies and about one-third of the needs for the entire region. Estimates of the exact amount of genetic improvement obtained vary widely, from as low as 7% to as high as 20%. Already work is under way on second-generation orchards, which promise an additional 7–20% gain.

Replenishment in Brazil

Brazil is nearly as large as the United States. At one time most parts of the nation were covered with trees, but extensive forests remain only in the inaccessible Amazon region. Most of the land in the southern part of the country, where the majority of the 110 million people live, has been cleared for agriculture or production of charcoal. The nation has, therefore, undertaken a vast reforestation program. By 1975 approximately 5.2 million acres had been planted and the rate of forestation was increasing. Nearly all of this was done by private companies, with the impetus supplied by a 1966

Cones are collected from a pine forest in Georgia. Seeds from such cones are used in progeny tests, specially designed experiments for breeding improved trees.

195

Trays of Douglas fir seedlings grown under controlled conditions in a large greenhouse in the state of Washington are moved for planting outside (above). At the right, 12-year-old trees grown at a U.S. Forest Service test site in Wisconsin demonstrate the results of progeny testing of families of white spruce. Ribbons connect trees representing the same family. Differences in the growth potential of fast-growing (yellow ribbon) and slow-growing families (blue and red ribbons) can reach 25–35%.

law offering income tax credits for money spent on reforestation.

Slash and loblolly pines from the United States have been the principal species planted. In recent years pines from the Caribbean area have proved successful in frost-free areas. Eucalypts from Australia and nearby islands have also been grown extensively. These are evergreen trees with narrow leaves similar to those of the willow. They can thrive on mineral-deficient soils and can grow in areas having too little rainfall to support other types of large trees. Many grow 10 feet and some even 20 feet per year.

The first reforestation was begun by a railway in São Paulo in the early 1900s to supply fuel for its wood-burning locomotives. Although the need for that fuel is long past, the reforestation work continued and led to the development of a pulp industry in the four southernmost states of the nation. Actually, more wood is being grown in those states than the pulp mills can use. The surplus pine wood is a bonus because it can be used for many other purposes, but the surplus eucalypt wood is a problem because eucalypt lumber has a tendency to become bowed and crooked during the curing process. If the curing problem can be solved, the extra eucalypt wood can be put to good use in plywood and furniture.

Like the more southern states the seacoast state of Espírito Santo was once densely forested. It now consists mostly of grazing land. Two companies started a 500,000-acre reforestation program in 1968, planting mostly *Eucalyptus grandis.* Even though there was almost no previous experience to guide the work, the program was successful enough to warrant the establishment of a pulp mill, which began operation in 1978.

The mid-southern state of Minas Gerais faces a difficult challenge. It contains rich iron mines that are the basis for a steel industry producing ten million tons of steel nationally per year. Because Brazil has only one coal mine, charcoal has been used for all the smelting. This has led to widespread cutting of forests, and the very future of the steel industry is now in danger unless new supplies of charcoal can be grown quickly. The original ground cover throughout most of the state was a scrub forest the Brazilians called

196

"cerrado," and research on planting it was begun during the year.

Brazil's tree improvement program consists mostly of a series of field trials of different species or different races of the same species. Most were started after 1972 and are concentrated in the southern states. Although this program is simple, it has been effective in showing that some previously neglected species could grow 15–20% faster than the ones now planted most commonly. These tests become especially important in the regions such as Minas Gerais and Espírito Santo where there is little past experience.

Growth rates in Brazil often surpass those for the same species planted elsewhere. Judging from the rapid progress of the last decade and the large areas suited to tree growth, Brazil may develop enough forest plantations to change from a timber importer to a nation with a large wood surplus.

The reforestation efforts in the southeastern United States and Brazil exemplify the work being done in many parts of the world to meet the ever increasing demand for wood and its products. The steady loss of woodlands to agriculture or to the expanding urban areas makes it imperative to use the land that remains for forests as productively as possible.

The tropical rain forest in Brazil's Amazon River basin is estimated to contain approximately $1 trillion worth of timber. Some 20% of that has been cut, with little replacement. A 16-story floating paper mill (bottom), owned by U.S. businessman Daniel K. Ludwig, is towed up the Jari River to process wood from some 81 million fast-growing trees planted in the rain forest. Unlike earlier harvesters of the forest, the Ludwig enterprise planned to replant the cut areas.

197

Mining
the Ocean
by Robert E. Burns

In the face of dwindling resources on land, mankind is
looking to river deltas, volcanically active seabeds, and
the deep ocean for manganese, copper, zinc, diamonds,
and other valuable materials.

Thirteenth-century Chinese woodcut (above) depicts the extraction of salt from seawater-filled evaporation ponds. (Overleaf) Grand Isle mine, one of two offshore sulfur operations in existence, stands in 50 feet of water off the Louisiana coast. The three drilling/production platforms in the background lie above sulfur beds, from which sulfur is extracted using the Frasch process and then pumped ashore through an insulated underwater pipeline.

ROBERT E. BURNS is Project Manager, Deep Ocean Mining Environmental Study, U.S. National Oceanic and Atmospheric Administration.

(Overleaf) Courtesy, Freeport Minerals Company. Illustrations by Leon Bishop

The deep ocean, with its tremendous pressures, sunless landscape, unbreathable "atmosphere," and near inaccessibility, must rank with the Moon as one of the most inhospitable environments ever explored. Like much of the habitable land surface that man considers home, the seafloor and overlying water possess a wealth of exploitable resources, including a reserve of minerals at least equivalent to that which has been the historical source of mining on land. Compared with conventional mining, however, dipping into the ocean's well-guarded treasury of minerals has been intermittent until the last decade, when increased demands, higher costs, and threatened depletion of mineral reserves ashore have given man a powerful incentive to push his activities forward and seaward to the limits of present-day technology. Excluding oil and gas, the mineral resources of the ocean include many types of material that occur in several forms: chemicals dissolved in seawater, unconsolidated deposits which have accumulated on or near the seafloor, and consolidated ore bodies similar to those commonly mined on land.

Minerals in solution

Although recovery of dissolved minerals from seawater is not commonly considered mining, such recovery processes account for a production of minerals with a market value approaching $250 million per year worldwide. The ocean is the ultimate reservoir of material dissolved by rain and carried

to the sea by streams and rivers. It is also a region into which hot solutions are introduced by submarine volcanic activity, adding to the store of dissolved metals. Throughout the open ocean, several dissolved elements—magnesium, sodium, calcium, bromine, potassium, sulfur, strontium, boron, and uranium—occur in concentrations large enough to be considered possible mineral resources. In some localized areas—such as the major mountain chain that forms the Mid-Atlantic Ridge and the tectonically active region of the Red Sea, where molten rock from deep within the Earth is rising to form new seafloor—high concentrations of metal-rich solutions provide possible sources of zinc, copper, lead, and silver.

The many elements dissolved in seawater are the source of the ocean's salinity, and among the first materials extracted from the sea was common salt. As early as 2000 BC, the Chinese recorded their efforts to obtain salt by solar evaporation of seawater. Today, salt from the sea is a major source in China and India and is of increasing importance in Europe, where almost all of the maritime nations produce some salt by solar evaporation. In addition to table salt the extraction process provides industrial pickling brines and bitterns from which potash, bromine, and epsom salts are recovered.

Although present in extremely low concentrations, the volume of dissolved gold in the ocean is immense, and one of the earliest attempts to extract it was prompted by the outcome of World War I. Following the war

Mechanical shovel carves from a mountain of salt during modern extraction operations along the Mediterranean coast of France.

201

Standing in evaporation ponds, mineral-rich water from the Dead Sea produces a whitish residue (above) that yields potash for fertilizer, bromine, magnesium, calcium chloride, and other chemical products. An Israeli company operates the installation at Sedom. Schematic diagram (facing page) illustrates one proposed method for extracting minerals from the seabed using a modified form of the Frasch process. Conventional or nuclear explosives would be used to fracture the ore deposit prior to solvent extraction.

Germany was faced with the repayment of a heavy debt, the equivalent of about 50 tons of gold. One of the world's foremost chemists, Fritz Haber, who is best remembered for his industrial process for synthesizing ammonia, conceived a plan to acquire gold by extraction from seawater. An early oceanographic expedition, the cruise of the ship "Meteor," was a German effort to assess the extent of the gold resource and to determine whether some parts of the ocean were more highly enriched with the metal than others. Unfortunately for both Germany and marine mining, this program proved that, although there was far more than enough gold in the ocean to settle the war debt, the cost of extraction would be far too great.

Efforts to extract dissolved minerals met with more success in the United States when shortages of critical materials developed during World War II. The wartime aircraft industry required enormous quantities of magnesium; out of necessity the ocean became the source. Although magnesium makes

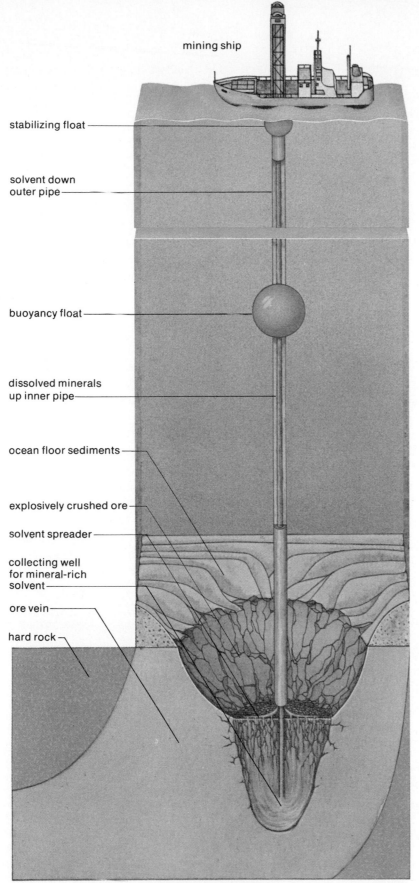

mining ship

stabilizing float

solvent down
outer pipe

buoyancy float

dissolved minerals
up inner pipe

ocean floor sediments

explosively crushed ore

solvent spreader

collecting well
for mineral-rich
solvent

ore vein

hard rock

modified Frasch process

up only 0.13% of the sea's dissolved materials, an extraction process was developed which provided the bulk of the U.S. requirement for this critical material. As a result magnesium from the ocean has become a viable and continuing source for today's industry. A similar wartime shortage of bromine forced the petroleum industry, which uses bromine as an additive in processing, to develop large plants in North Carolina and Texas; these, too, continue to produce bromine by extraction from seawater.

Nearshore underground deposits

A number of mining activities which are sometimes considered marine are more properly classified as land mining. In many parts of the world, minerals are mined underground from solid rock near the coast, and frequently the ore deposit is followed seaward under coastal waters. Submarine mining of coal accounts for production of almost half a billion dollars per year from mines in Nova Scotia, Taiwan, Japan, Turkey, and the United Kingdom. Iron ore valued at $20 million per year is mined under the coastal waters of Newfoundland and Finland. Although such activity presently is confined to accessible coastal regions, similar deposits probably occur farther out on the continental shelf and slope. Until there are significant improvements in the technology of both finding the deposits and mining them, however, this type of marine mining will be slow to develop.

One of the techniques developed on land, and now moved offshore, may be a key in the eventual development of mining consolidated deposits at sea. The Frasch process for mining sulfur involves drilling and inserting a set of concentric pipes into an underground deposit containing solid elemental sulfur. Hot water pumped down one of the pipes melts the sulfur, which is then pumped up another pipe and recovered. This type of mining is being carried out extensively in coastal regions of the Gulf of Mexico, and some limited offshore activity in the U.S. contributes a sulfur production valued in excess of $50 million per year.

Although the Frasch process relies upon both the low melting temperature of elemental sulfur and molten sulfur's immiscibility in water, the general technique may be considered a precursor in developing marine mining of consolidated ore bodies below the seafloor. The hot water can be replaced with appropriate mineralizing fluids that will leach, dissolve, or otherwise react with the ore. Recovery will involve pumping the resultant fluid back to the sea surface for collection or initial processing.

Unconsolidated deposits

Compared with the occurrence of dissolved minerals in seawater and of ores buried beneath the seafloor, unconsolidated deposits of mineral sands, shell, and other material represent the most diverse source of marine minerals. Normal processes of erosion, deposition, and reworking have resulted in accumulation of many commercially valuable deposits on the seafloor and exposed to the overlying water. These unconsolidated materials include sands, gravels, shells, and phosphate rock; concentrations of iron- and tin-bearing minerals; and even exploitable placer deposits containing diamonds, gold, platinum, and other rare and precious minerals.

204

Historically offshore mining of these unconsolidated deposits is a natural outgrowth of the mining of similar deposits in river valleys and coastal beaches. Frequently the operations began with mining of placer deposits and developed into a dredging activity that followed the deposit seaward into the nearshore water of the continental margin. Such mining characteristically is conducted from ships using some type of dredging, in which the ore is removed from the seafloor, carried to the surface, and separated as necessary from unwanted material.

The dredges used for nearshore mining are quite similar to those that work in rivers and harbors. In general there are two basic types: scraper dredges, which drag buckets along the bottom and then hoist them to the surface to be unloaded at the mining ship, and hydraulic dredges, which utilize a hydraulic suction tube to raise a mixture of material and water to the ship. Most such dredges can be used without major engineering modification in water as deep as 30–40 meters (one meter is about 3.3 feet).

Recovery of nonmetallic minerals from the seafloor is not commonly regarded as a mining industry, yet nonmetallics presently are a major product of offshore activity. Sand and gravel required for construction and for beach replenishment have become increasingly difficult to mine from land sources. This has led to development of offshore mining in the North and Baltic seas and along the coasts of Japan such that it now provides about 20% of the annual requirements of the U.K., Japan, and The Netherlands. In the U.S. the principal sources of these materials are still on land, but offshore mining is on the rise off New England and the Middle Atlantic States. The Bureau of Mines has estimated a steady increase in demand for sand and gravel at a rate of 3% per year, with demand to double by AD 2000.

A gold-mining bucket dredge in operation off the California coast weighs 3,750 tons and can dig to a depth of 32.6 meters (107 feet). Each of its 110 wear-resistant manganese buckets excavates one-half cubic meter (18 cubic feet) of material.

In addition to sand and gravel for construction purposes, offshore mining operations are recovering localized concentrations of sand-sized particles of heavy minerals. Several million tons per year of magnetite sands, a source of iron, are hauled from water depths of 25–30 meters off the southern tip of Kyushu island in Japan. Many tin deposits of southeast Asia are mined from placers along the coast. The mineral cassiterite, the source of tin, is very resistant to normal weathering processes and tends to accumulate in placer deposits that frequently extend seaward along submerged river valleys. These deposits are being mined, using scraper dredge techniques, in 30-meter depths off Sumatra in Indonesia. Similar operations off Thailand are recovering cassiterite from water between 30 and 40 meters deep at distances as far as eight kilometers (five miles) offshore. These operations produce several tens of millions of dollars worth of tin annually and are fully competitive with land mining, costing just about half of the amount needed to produce similar tonnage from older mine sites ashore.

Rare and precious minerals are also generally quite resistant to weathering processes and hence are found frequently in placer deposits. One of the very earliest offshore mining operations took place in the waters off Nome, Alaska, during the gold-rush days of the early 1900s. Using a very simple bucket dredge, miners recovered the gold from sands that extended seaward across the shelf from Anvil Creek. The operation was short-lived be-

206

cause the problems of winter ice and stormy seas made the neighboring beaches and emergent beach terraces more attractive to the miners. This area, across the shallow continental shelf of the Chukchi Sea, is still considered a high-potential site for marine mining of gold. Similarly the submerged valley of the Salmon River through Kuskokwim Bay, Alaska, has been mined intermittently for platinum, but the economics of the operation have been marginal in the past. In another part of the world, mining of diamonds has been carried out on deposits accumulated in the submerged extension of the Orange River off southwest Africa.

Exploiting the deep ocean

In contrast to mining on the continental shelf, mining in the deep ocean has not yet been operationally productive. Although the deep-ocean resources of some minerals are at least equal to those which have been exploited on land, both technological and legal problems have precluded early development of a deep-ocean mining industry. Continued increases in the demand for and price of metals, however, have prompted two innovative plans. These are the collection of manganese nodules from the floor of the eastern equatorial Pacific and the mining of metal-rich muds from deep brine-filled depressions in the Red Sea.

Indigenous to the deep floor of the world ocean, manganese nodules occur in economically promising quantities in a broad belt extending east–west between 5° and 20° N in the eastern Pacific. These black and brown lumps of golfball to baseball size are predominantly oxides of manganese and iron. Although their existence had been known for more than a century, they remained a scientific curiosity (there is still no consensus on their origin) until increasing demand for nickel and copper resulted in an assessment of the nodules as a possible source of these and other metals.

Low dam under construction isolates a stretch of South African shoreline from the ocean. Once the water is removed from this artificial pond, the exposed shore, which contains diamond deposits, is amenable to conventional surface-mining techniques.

In order to mine the nodules, several international consortia have been conducting exploration and engineering development of mining systems during the past ten years. Their investigations defined several areas within the eastern Pacific where the concentration of manganese nodules on the seafloor averages about ten kilograms per square meter (two pounds per square foot) and where nickel and copper are each present in the nodules in amounts of about 1%. Further, in some localities these deposits extend over several hundred square kilometers of topographically subdued seafloor that is generally free of steep cliffs or valleys. Regions where all of these criteria are met have been identified as tentative mining sites.

Compared with the mining of materials from relatively shallow water of the continental margin, technology has been a limiting factor in plans to recover nodules from a water depth of four to five kilometers (two and a half to three miles) at which the mining sites are located. Because the nodules are characteristically found on the seafloor, they are readily recoverable by dredges, which skim only the upper few centimeters of bottom material. But mining operations far from land require large seagoing ships to carry and stabilize all of the equipment required to lift the nodules to the surface.

One type of deep-ocean mining system is similar in principle to the scraper dredge used near shore but is greatly complicated by the extremely long

Basic elements of continuous line bucket and hydraulic dredge systems are compared in the diagram on the facing page. A description of each technique appears in the text at right. Snared in webbing, a "grab sampler" (above) used to collect manganese nodules for grade and abundance determinations is hoisted aboard a research ship operated by Kennecott Exploration, Inc. Ship crew (right) inspects a sample of nodules brought up by a model test collector from a depth of more than 4.5 kilometers (15,000 feet).

(more than ten-kilometer) loop of cable on which the buckets are fastened. In a configuration resembling a large flexible Ferris wheel, a continuous cable lowers a series of strainerlike buckets to the bottom where they scrape up nodules and sediment. En route to the surface, water flowing through the buckets washes out the smaller, unwanted particles of sediment. As the buckets pass across the ship they unload their cargo and begin another descent to repeat the cycle. These systems, called continuous line bucket or CLB systems, were developed relatively early, and a major deepwater test was conducted in 1972 from the mining ship "Kyokuyo Maru II" at a site about a thousand kilometers southeast of Hawaii.

Slower to be developed, but generally favored by those mining consortia in which U.S. participation is prominent, are the hydraulic mining systems. In these systems a sledlike collector is towed along the bottom at the end of a long vertical pipe. As the collector moves it gathers the nodules and upper few centimeters of bottom sediment. An initial separation drops most of the sediment back to the seafloor and moves the nodules into the lower end of the vertical pipe. The pipe is the lift system, carrying nodules to the surface by means of a rapid upward movement of water through the pipe. This lift may be provided by powerful submerged pumps, by air injected at depth into the pipe, or by a combination of the two techniques.

Early testing of a hydraulic system was accomplished on the Blake Plateau off the southeast coast of the U.S. This effort, in August 1970, demonstrated the feasibility of air-lift hydraulic systems to raise nodules from deep water. More recently, pilot mining runs were conducted by a Canada-U.S.-West Germany-Japan consortium in early 1978. These tests demonstrated additional deepwater capability by recovering almost a thousand tons of nodules from a mining site in water more than 5,200 meters (three and one-quarter miles) deep. Additional pilot mining tests were conducted in the autumn of 1978; others were scheduled for the late winter of 1979.

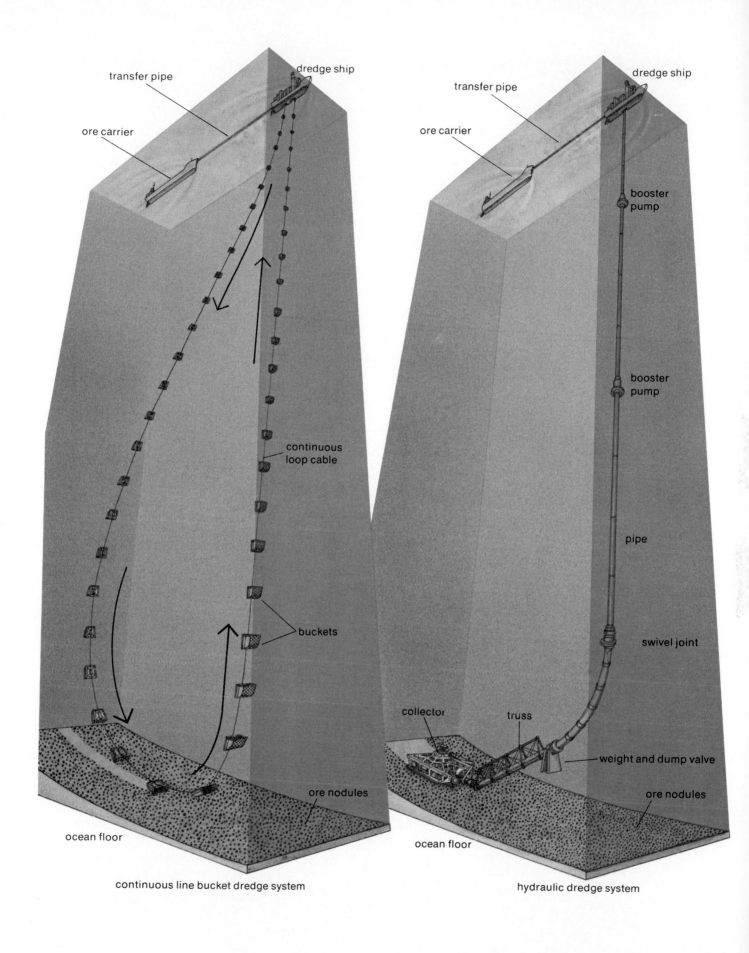

transfer pipe

ore carrier

dredge ship

continuous
loop cable

buckets

ocean floor

ore nodules

continuous line bucket dredge system

transfer pipe

ore carrier

dredge ship

booster
pump

booster
pump

pipe

swivel joint

collector

truss

weight and dump valve

ore nodules

ocean floor

hydraulic dredge system

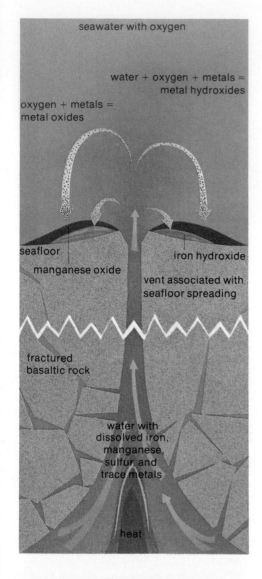

seawater with oxygen

water + oxygen + metals =
metal hydroxides

oxygen + metals =
metal oxides

seafloor

manganese oxide

iron hydroxide

vent associated with
seafloor spreading

fractured
basaltic rock

water with
dissolved iron,
manganese,
sulfur, and
trace metals

heat

seawater

stagnant brine

sulfur + metals = metal sulfides

metal
sulfides

hot water with dissolved iron,
manganese, sulfur, and trace metals

Jose J. Honnorez, University of Miami

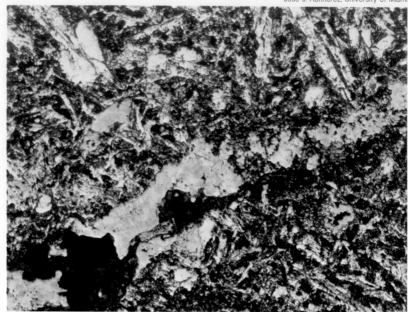

Many metal deposits on the seafloor are associated with regions of seafloor spreading, such as the Mid-Atlantic Ridge and the Red Sea. Hot water driven upward through fractured basaltic crust leaches iron, manganese, and other elements and carries them in solution to the seafloor surface (left). There, mixing of the solution with cold, oxygenated seawater favors precipitation of iron and manganese as insoluble oxides and hydroxides. This mechanism produces deposits of other trace metals (e.g., copper and zinc) in economically attractive quantities only under conditions that prevent contact of the hot solution with oxygen, thus allowing formation of insoluble sulfides. Such conditions exist in the Red Sea, where stagnant brine pools occupy low spots on the rifting seafloor (lower left). Metal sulfides may also precipitate, protected from oxygen, in the crust itself. In the photomicrograph above, which is of a thin slice of crustal basalt from the Mid-Atlantic Ridge, copper-iron sulfides appear as reddish-black particles in a light green vein of another mineral.

Another mineral resource on the seafloor is associated with deep depressions that occur along the long axis of the Red Sea. These basins, originally discovered by the oceanographic research vessel "Atlantis II" in 1963, are unusual in that they contain water of extremely high salinity. Because of their density, these relatively hot brines occupy low spots in the seafloor; they are associated with submarine volcanism that occurs along the axis of the Red Sea in a region of active seafloor spreading. At the seafloor the sediments in the depressions frequently contain high concentrations of metals.

Mining of these sediments will involve recovery from depths in excess of two kilometers. Mud deposits several tens of meters in thickness contain the desired metals, but these are frequently found on very irregular bottom and will be very difficult to collect with dredges. In contrast with the collector used to mine manganese nodules by skimming the seafloor, the collector for these sediments must remove material from a deposit that has some thickness and consists of relatively compact mass. For this type of deposit the

210

mining system involves a process of mechanical agitation that breaks up and loosens the mud, mixes it with bottom water, and collects the liquefied mixture for pumping to the surface for recovery and initial processing. Pilot tests of this system were planned for the late winter of 1979 under the auspices of the Saudi Arabian-Sudanese Red Sea Joint Commission.

Effect on oceanic life

One factor that will affect future development of marine mining is growing public concern about possible effects on the marine ecosystem. Although historically it has been a dumping ground for all manner of man-made wastes, it is apparent that man cannot continue to use the ocean in a haphazard manner. In spite of its volume, the ocean is part of a vast global mechanism and is subject to stress and possible alteration. Consequently,

"Deepsea Miner II," (upper left) a research ship chartered by Deepsea Ventures, Inc., is a converted ore carrier fitted to operate a hydraulic dredge system for collecting manganese nodules from the seafloor. Behind the white, T shaped midship house is storage space for 450 sections of 36-foot pipe used to connect the collector on the seafloor with the ship. Housed in the white dome is a hoist and other pipe deployment equipment. Two 1,600-horsepower compressors, painted red and located forward of the midship house, supply air to the pipe at depth to lift the nodules. Computers and other electronics to monitor and control the undersea equipment are located in a large container on the raised deck at the aft end of the ship; an interior view of the control center is shown at the lower left. Manganese nodules (above) spill from a collection basket of the "Prospector," a deep-ocean survey and exploration vessel operated by Deepsea Ventures.

Part of NOAA's Deep Ocean Mining Environmental Study involves the sinking and recovery of a heavy box core sampler (top) that preserves an entire volume of manganese nodules, seafloor sediment, and any marine organisms present in their original arrangement. From this core smaller samples can be carved out for individual examination (above).

new activity in marine mining must adhere to various national and international regulations, which require an adequate environmental assessment. In contrast with former concern about pollution, which was rarely expressed until after the fact, new marine mining will not be developed without reasonable probability of minimal environmental effect.

Several examples can be cited in which studies of potential environmental threat were conducted during formative stages of development of the new industry. Project DOMES (Deep Ocean Mining Environmental Study) of the U.S. National Oceanic and Atmospheric Administration (NOAA) has been investigating probable effects of deep-ocean mining of manganese nodules for several years. The most urgent concern is with the effect of sedimentary particles and abraded nodule fragments, which will be stirred up at the seafloor and discharged at the surface of the ocean. Such activity forms plumes of turbid water that are not normally found in the open ocean. At the seafloor there are questions about the amount of resedimentation and its effect on the bottom-dwelling population. At the surface it is necessary to evaluate the effect of increased turbidity both on the feeding habits and behavior of surface organisms and on light penetration and consequent changes in the growth of phytoplankton, the mass of minute oceanic plant life that depends on sunlight for photosynthesis. Preliminary studies have been supplemented with information obtained during monitoring of pilot mining tests in 1978 and early 1979. Additional information will be obtained by monitoring the industry as it develops, and guidelines will be formulated on the basis of these data. Although findings to date do not indicate any serious detrimental results, continued collection of information will provide a means of minimizing possible effects.

Similarly, proposed mining of the Red Sea muds has had an environmental impact assessment program incorporated in its planning from the start. Working under the auspices of the Saudi Arabian-Sudanese Red Sea Joint Commission, environmental scientists are examining the possible effects of discharged muds on the reef life of the area. In the coastal regions of New England the potential effect of sand mining has been the subject of NOAA's Project NOMES (New England Offshore Mining Environmental Study). A similar study is currently under way as a preliminary to possible mining of sand needed for construction in the Virgin Islands and Puerto Rico.

An uncertain future

The future of marine mining depends upon three factors: the comparative economics of marine mining and conventional activity on land, the development of technology to permit efficient recovery of marine minerals, and the legal framework of permits and regulations that pertain to marine mining.

In general, mining of the seafloor under the relatively shallow waters of the continental shelf has been an expansion of shoreside activities into offshore regions. The cost of many of these operations is competitive, and the technological capability that is required to mine many of these minerals is already developed and being improved. Little problem exists in the realm of international law since "ownership" of the continental shelf has been well defined by international legal experts.

Ronald K. Sorem, Washington State University

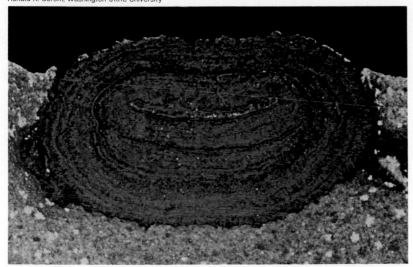

By contrast, national laws and regulations are frequently a check on uncontrolled development of offshore mining. For example, offshore mining for sand and gravel does not suffer from a lack of adequate technology but is subject to uncertainty associated with the problems of possible environmental damage that the mining could cause. Most of the coastal states of the U.S. presently have some type of moratorium on offshore dredging, which will probably delay mining until there is a better understanding of its probable effects on the nearshore environment.

In international waters of the open ocean, both exploration and mining-system development have reached a stage where successful pilot mining tests demonstrate the possibility of deep-ocean mining. The beginning of commercial mining, however, will be determined by several nontechnological factors. A critical economic factor is the price of nickel and copper. Although costly, today's marine mining systems are capable of supplying raw material at a marginally competitive price. With increasing demand and higher prices, manganese-nodule mining should be competitive with land-based sources of nickel and copper.

A second factor causing uncertainty about commercial-scale mining is the absence of any logal framework within which the mining companies can operate. In contrast to the relatively well-defined laws that govern development on the continental shelves, historically the open oceans have been international; in 1967 the Malta proposal stated that the resources of the deep-ocean floor were a common resource for all mankind.

Attempts are continuing to define the legal framework within which the mining of the manganese nodules can be accomplished. Law of the Sea conferences have been held periodically over the past two decades, and the "ownership" of the nodules has been a central theme in recent years. To date no agreement has been reached on the manner in which the profits earned from seafloor minerals will be divided among the nations of the world. Until some solution is accepted, countries eager to begin operational or commercial-scale mining must content themselves with improving their technologies and looking to brighter days ahead.

Cross section of a single manganese nodule in its natural position in sediment reveals a typical growth-shell structure. Many scientists believe that nodule growth on the seabed probably occurs slowly over millions of years, although much about the formation process and about factors that influence growth rates is not known.

213

Children Who Have Trouble Learning

by Robert O. Pihl

Finding causes, developing comprehensive therapies, and even formulating accurate definitions are the problems confronting medical scientists and psychologists who grapple with afflictions common to millions of schoolchildren.

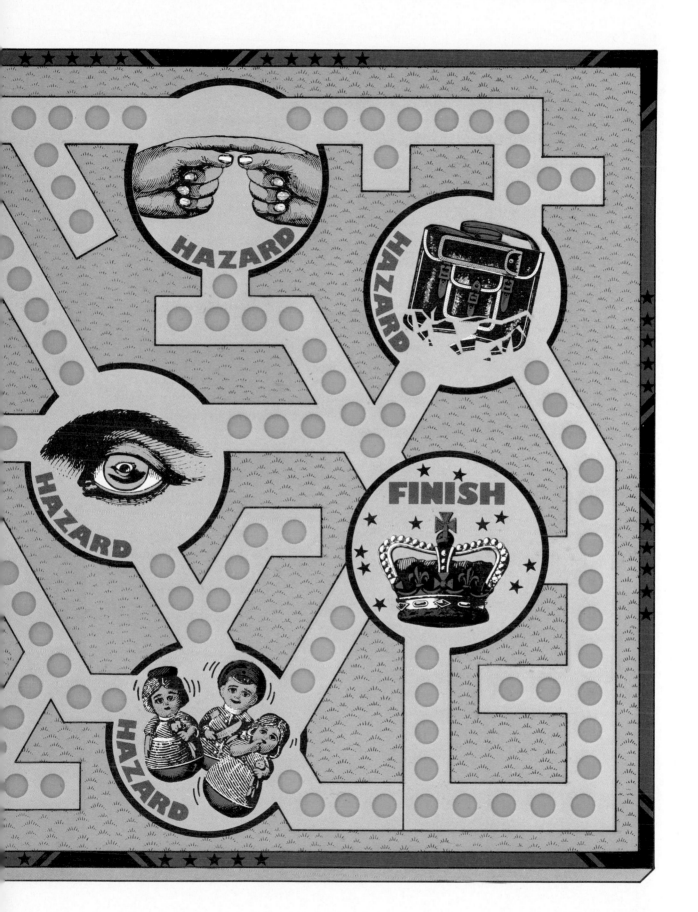

"What's the use of their having names," the Gnat said, "if they won't answer to them?" "No use to *them*," said Alice; "but it's useful to the people who name them, I suppose. If not, why do things have names at all?"

In Lewis Carroll's *Through the Looking-Glass,* the revealing discussion between the Gnat and Alice quite appropriately describes the present confusion rampant in the field of learning disabilities; that is, there is a general consensus that learning disabilities exist, but there is also great debate over an explicit definition.

The U.S. Congress, for example, seems convinced of the existence of learning disabilities, for afflicted children were included under the Education for All Handicapped Children Act, passed in 1975. Definitional problems, nevertheless, forced Congress to seek specific learning-disability guidelines so that children would not be labeled inappropriately. The Office of Education of the Department of Health, Education, and Welfare, which was saddled with the task of producing these regulations, naturally solicited the help of those working in the field. What followed was a cacophony of responses from which three things were concluded: that a consensus of definition did not exist, that rigorous formulas were inappropriate and far ahead of observed fact, and that affixing labels should be a multidisciplinary task.

The problem in definition stems from the fact that the concept of learning disability is relatively new, is behavioral rather than physiological, and is primarily a catchall for otherwise unclassifiable problems. Even the actual term learning disability is quite new, although the phenomena are quite old. As early as 1911 the problem of "word blindness" appeared in the professional literature, followed in 1928 by "dyslexia," "organic brain stem syndrome" in 1934, "the disabled learner" in 1962, "learning disabilities" in 1963, "the minimally brain-dysfunctioned child" in 1966, and "learning dysfunction" in 1967. With the growing divergence in terms there has been a concomitant increase in the breadth of the population covered by these concepts. So, for example, whereas word blindness referred specifically to difficulty in differentiating words, the present concept of learning disability includes all children who fail to learn any subject in school yet are seemingly intelligent and healthy.

It is the consensual view that learning-disabled children have average or above-average intelligence. Although seldom is it clear exactly what intelligence tests measure, the general belief is that learning disability characterizes the seemingly able child who does not achieve in school. Similarly, healthy implies that such obvious problems as disturbances of vision, hearing, or the central nervous system are not evident. For many professionals in this field healthy also implies the absence of emotional problems prior to the appearance of the learning disability. Psychologically disturbed individuals, of course, function well below their optimum performance level and often act in a manner incompatible with achievement. The definitional problem at this point, however, seems irresolvable because most learning-disabled children do have emotional problems. One survey, for instance, found that only 4% of children referred for treatment because of a learning disability displayed average or better emotional adjustment. Although the learning-

ROBERT O. PIHL is Associate Professor in the Department of Psychology, McGill University, Montreal.

Illustrations by William Biderbost

216

disabled child suffers emotional harm from perpetual conflicts and frustrations in the school setting, it is strictly an assumption to state that the child's emotional problem is secondary to the learning disability.

Finally, because such early experience factors as cultural deprivation and lack of opportunity are known to have a profound effect on learning, these possible explanations are also excluded from the definition.

Characteristics of the disabled child

The term learning disability encompasses many characteristics, with no single characteristic typical of all afflicted individuals. Learning, behavioral, and attitudinal problems all occur; some children display a single characteristic, and others are heavily burdened. Needless to say, of the numerous lists of characteristics that have appeared in the literature many reflect personal opinion. The following list and its ordering are no exception.

Difficulty in focusing and maintaining attention seems to be the most frequently found characteristic in children with learning disabilities. Certainly this is the most obvious characteristic of those excessively active and impulsive children labeled hyperactive, of whom approximately 80% have a learning disability. Poor attentiveness is similarly frequent in learning-disabled children with normal impulsivity. Low-scoring performance in tests involving reaction time, specialized listening tasks, matching familiar figures, and vigilance in general bear out the presence of this problem. Peculiarities in brainwaves and cardiac response to stimuli also strongly support the importance of this characteristic.

It is possible that some attentional deficits are a consequence of a learning disability rather than a cause. Such a case is also usually argued for the second predominating characteristic of the problem, a loss in self-esteem. Numerous studies have demonstrated that the major effect of failure is self-deprecation. The learning-disabled child usually attributes failure to lack of ability, which often is generalized to a negative attitude about himself or herself and then evolves into a poor expectation for learning in new situations or perhaps even an avoidance of these situations. It has been reported that these children are at high risk of becoming school dropouts or drug abusers, and over half of them show conduct problems. Not only do these children think less of themselves, but this feeling is also corroborated by peers, who find them less attractive than unafflicted children.

A third characteristic, which may in fact be responsible for the two just mentioned, is a deficit in information processing. For example, it is becoming apparent that what many researchers had thought to be a problem in perception actually is a processing problem, such as an impairment in the use of memory strategies. Studies show, for example, that learning-disabled children are often lacking in their use of rehearsal as an aid to memorizing. Other processing difficulties are seen in symbolization, where perception and memory are integrated, and in verbal and auditory processing.

A fourth characteristic, perceptual deficit, is probably the most frequently quoted. Current research, however, seems to demonstrate that this deficit is less significant than generally thought. Problems in identifying, discriminating, and sequencing sensation make up this category, which in learning-disabled children is manifested typically as reversal and rotation of printed letters, distortion in copying geometric figures, difficulty in separating figures from their backgrounds, and difficulty in differentiating or recognizing sounds. Adults tend to overreact to these problems in children, often failing to recognize that perceptions of adults and children differ greatly and thus failing to consider age in defining what is or is not a perceptual deficit. Even when these problems persist beyond age limits and are related to learning disability, their explanation in terms of deficits in attention and information processing is often more satisfactory.

A fifth characteristic comprises problems in coordination. The importance of this characteristic is highly argumentative, with many experts contending that motor behavior has nothing to do with learning a scholastic task like reading. Nevertheless, learning-disabled children are often awkward, have trouble maintaining balance, perform poorly in tasks requiring fine eye-hand skills, and display gross movement peculiarities. The main effect of this observation has been the development of programs to train coordination skills in order to improve learning ability. A second outgrowth is the infamous "skipping test" of many kindergarten teachers in which a child who literally trips the light fantastic is apt to be labeled as potentially learning disabled.

Other characteristics have been suggested, although it is felt that the more important of these are encompassed in the five listed above. What must be obvious, however, is that learning disability is not a single syndrome.

In spite of the definitional confusion, the label of learning disability is affixed with professional regularity. The exact number of learning-disabled individuals, of course, is limited by the scope of one's preferred definition. Surveys suggest that between 4 and 25% of the school-age population is affected. Perhaps the most meticulous study was carried out in 1969 in the Chicago area in which 2,767 third- and fourth-grade children were administered a battery of psychoeducational tests. Of this population 15% were underachieving, and intensive study of a portion of these children suggested that only half of them could be excluded because of medical or emotional causes. Consequently, even with stringent exclusion criteria, 8% of the population must bear the label learning disabled.

Models and causes

A number of often divergent views have evolved to explain the existence of learning disabilities. Without doubt the most widespread, covetously held, and consequential of these models is the physiological approach, in which the problem is seen as neurological. With the exceptions of some very recent work demonstrating peculiarities in electrical brain activity and the presence of abnormal levels of toxic elements in the hair of learning-disabled children, the existence of a neurological condition typically has been inferred. Specifically, because afflicted children are more likely to be male, left-handed, uncoordinated, and awkward; to have had a history of early illness with neurological aftereffects; and to have been the result of a difficult pregnancy and delivery, a condition is assumed that forms the basis for concluding the existence of brain dysfunction. However, until physiological processes are routinely and directly measured as part of the diagnosis,

Perceptual deficit: The most frequently quoted, it seems less significant than generally thought.

rather than measuring effects and inferring processes, this thinking can be criticized as being circular.

Recent work in "neurometrics," which is a methodology for gathering and combining data from recordings of brainwaves and of sensory-evoked transient electrical responses from various regions of the brain, revealed consistent variations in populations of learning-disabled children. To date, this approach has allowed discrimination of disabled children from normal children with 93% accuracy. Further, the technique has proved superior to a battery of psychometric (mental measurement) tests in separating the populations and has revealed at least five subgroups of brain abnormality within the learning-disabled population. Related to behavior, the findings show that children with verbal problems reflect abnormalities in the left hemisphere of the brain, whereas those with problems in arithmetic demonstrate right-hemisphere dysfunction. Another interesting report found that a sample of learning-disabled children could be discriminated from a nondisabled group with 97% accuracy on the basis of the levels of lead, cadmium, lithium, cobalt, and manganese contained in their hair. It seems that hair is a kind of recording filament for nutritional and health histories, and if stringent collection and measurement procedures are followed, these histories can be read. Both of these quite new research approaches are open to question and reservation until they are more adequately demonstrated.

Recent, popular variations of this model have focused on the diet of the learning-disabled child, reflecting current concerns about proper nutrition and the effects of food additives. Hypersensitivity to food or the substances in food is a clear and indisputable problem for approximately 3% of adults and between 10 and 15% of children. Allergies, of course, result in a large range of bothersome symptoms and have been implicated in psychic disturbances. Recent work in this field does relate food allergies to learning disorders and hyperactivity, although investigators have experienced great difficulty in differentiating satisfactorily between behavioral changes caused by the removal of substances from the diet and those brought about by psychological factors—e.g., placebo effects and changes in life-style—affecting the children, their parents, and even their evaluators.

A second model, the educational model, looks to the educational system rather than within the individual to explain the problem. Thus, the system is seen as not ready or able to cope with the needs of the individual. This view does not obviate physiological factors that could have produced some lag in development, but rather steadfastly asserts that schools should be able to teach all. Those who fail to learn represent a failure for the system. Schools, of course, are not flexible and typically are as arteriosclerotic as any bureaucracy, holding to specified sets of expectations that the learning-disabled child cannot fulfill. Then, too, problems can exist long before the child sets foot in school. Children from lower socioeconomic classes often reflect cognitive, fine-motor, attentional, and curiosity deficiencies seemingly because of deprived early experiences. In school these difficulties are perpetuated by the emotional and self-defeating characteristics of the disadvantaged and learning disabled and by the general failure of society to develop appropriate and effective treatments.

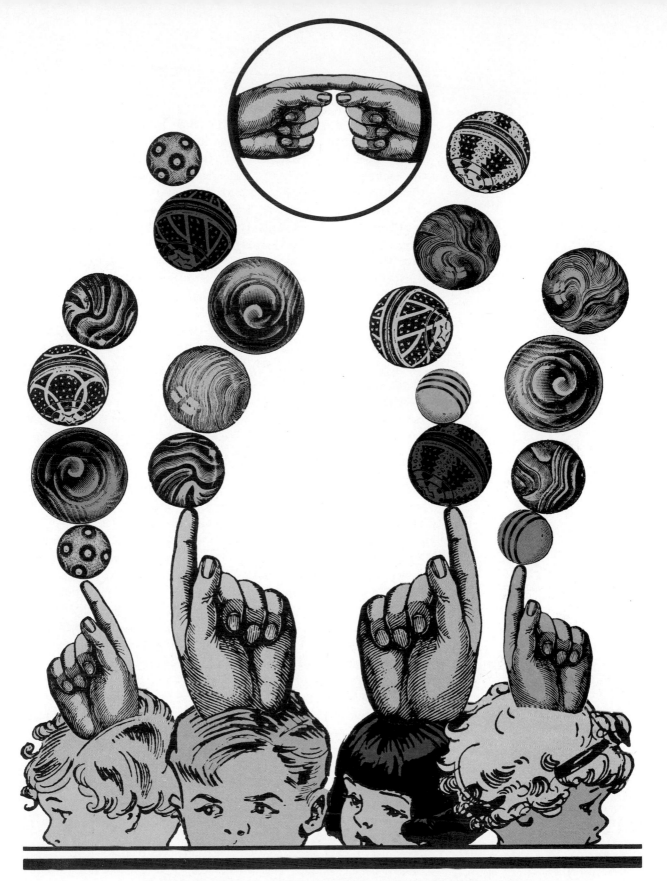

Coordination problems: A child who literally trips the light fantastic is apt to be labeled as potentially learning disabled.

Effectiveness of current treatments

Professionals in the field of learning disability tend to view events through a theory-tainted lens; thus, choice of treatment strategy is often predicated upon belief in causation. It is at this point that mayhem is often created, albeit in the name of logic. For example, it has been alleged that between 5 and 10% of the children in Omaha, Nebraska, were victims of a wave of enthusiasm for the stimulant drug methylphenidate (Ritalin). Just how many children were—or still are—so "treated" nationwide is unknown. It is a fact, however, that Ritalin use results in growth changes involving reduced weight and increased height and in variations in heart rate. Evidence also shows that typically prescribed dosages have been unnecessarily high and that the drug often has become a palliative for harried and self-doubting parents.

Evidence does exist for the effectiveness of Ritalin and other drugs with similar properties in the treatment of hyperactivity. Paradoxically these stimulants seem to settle hyperactive children and improve attentiveness; they have also proved more effective than such other forms of treatment as behavior therapy. Unfortunately, not all hyperactives respond well to treatment with stimulants; successes range from 40 to 70%. In addition, follow-up studies after two years report no differences in intelligence and academic achievement between treated and untreated hyperactives. Treatments that draw their justification from pragmatism or theory warrant considerable caution. The success of a treatment can occur for a myriad of reasons. To cite an absurd example, the mobility of hyperactive children can be readily reduced by amputation of both legs. Unless one can specify exactly how and upon what behavioral factor a drug works, one must also consider the possibility of a kind of pharmacological amputation.

The accusational finger, however, does not point solely at drug treatments. School systems seem to go through paroxysms every few years in which new strategies of education are enthusiastically embraced. In less than five years, for example, the "enlightened" approach to educating hyperactive children swung from isolating them from distracting stimuli in three-sided carrels to placing them in open classrooms that traded off the benefits of isolation for significant freedoms.

Some physical treatments of considerable currency rest on recent, controversial theories of causation. Typical of these are the nutritional and vitamin-supplement programs designed as treatment for learning disabilities. The Feingold diet, for instance, calls for the complete avoidance of foods containing naturally occurring salicylates and such additives as dyes and flavors. Whereas claims of 50–85% success for the diet are frequently heard, recent controlled research offered much less optimism—with best success figures around 20%—and much less certainty that the observed effects can be attributed solely to the deletion of dietary substances.

Whereas the Feingold diet is not proving to be the panacea that was first announced, at least it presently is the target of high-quality research that eventually should determine if certain children would do well to avoid some food substances. Proponents of other ideas have been far less earnest in testing notions experimentally. Vitamin-supplement treatments can be thus accused. Yet, it is a fact that only 16% of children receive a balanced diet,

Hyperactivity: Follow-up studies report no differences in intelligence and academic achievement between drug-treated and untreated hyperactives.

and evidence shows that learning-disabled children consume more junk food than the nondisabled.

Straightforward remedial educational therapies would seem the most parsimonious approach for helping children who are having difficulties learning. The guidelines would seem simple; for example, if the child is having trouble learning to read, provide extra opportunity. Unfortunately, considerable evaluation of this strategy has been most pessimistic in its conclusion. Short-term gains do accrue, but long-term changes seem unattainable. Poor readers tend to remain poor readers in spite of the heroic efforts of specialized teachers and a wide assortment of educational techniques. Noteworthy is the fact that just as there is little understanding of what is happening in the brain of the learning-disabled child, there is similar deficiency, or perhaps confusion, in understanding the reading process. Making reading an educational fetish for all often ignores the basic intelligence of the child and the fact that learning still goes on if the individual is left to his or her own devices.

Because perceptual and coordination difficulties have been viewed as primary characteristics of learning disability, it is easy to understand why many treatments focus on correcting these problems. Unfortunately, although such problems are correctable, the level of improvement is not consistently related to learning level. Some studies which report decreases in copying errors and awkwardness and improvements in balance, visual tracking, and the dominant use of the hand, foot, eye, and ear on the same side of the body also report significant improvement in certain scholastic tasks, yet other studies do not.

Treating the emotional effects of a learning disability, that is, restructuring an individual from self-defeated rubble, is possible and is a priority. Simply attending to the general needs of these individuals in a nonspecific manner is helpful, as is the teaching of coping strategies to handle the stresses they must endure. As long as the vicious circle of defeatism remains, other interventions are jeopardized. Physically, for example, the child may be better able to attend but psychologically will remain distracted.

Learning disability and the future

Future projections to a certain degree depend upon the camp of experts from which the crystal ball is borrowed. For example, the proselytizers for physiological causation would foresee sophisticated laboratory diagnostic procedures followed by corrective drug treatments, controlled diets, and even brain-stimulation procedures. Adherents to the educational model, on the other hand, might predict individualization of instruction, perhaps even to the level of home-based education. Given that the past and present is usually the best predictor of the future, one might factitiously conclude that learning disabilities are doomed to remain a ubiquitous label, applied to amorphous problems, with unpredictable outcomes. Such a conclusion, however, would represent a misreading of the present confusion.

Learning disabilities are in fact many phenomena. There is no logical reason why an individual who has difficulty learning mathematics should be like one who has trouble reading. Further, the very task of reading may comprise a multiplicity of divergent systems or skills; such a possibility may

224

Processing problems: What many researchers had thought to be a problem in perception is apparently an information processing deficit.

well explain the present difficulties both in understanding the reading process and in dealing with reading problems.

In spite of good evidence that perceptual-motor training, remedial education, gross-motor exercise, and special diets are far from being universally effective treatments, they most likely contain kernels of truth that when explicated may allow differentiated forms of treatment for various learning disabilities. Unfortunately, the characteristic single-mindedness with which definitions and explanations in this field are held will probably continue to stunt progress. Nevertheless, some relatively sound prognostications concerning the near future can be made.

As people become increasingly reliant on pharmacology as a solution to all manner of problems, the use of drugs to treat learning disabilities will grow substantially. One can readily envision daily use of drugs that affect the transmission of specific kinds of nerve impulses in localized regions of the cerebral cortex, counteract junk-food diets and contaminant-laden environments, and buoy mood in the face of frustration. Neurometrics methodology has begun to focus on specific regions of brain tissue in hopes of relating them to specific forms of learning. Perhaps neurometrics will become the diagnostic procedure of the future, pointing to the region of the brain in need of intervention with neuroregulating drugs.

The high levels of elemental contaminants found in some children with learning and behavior problems, as well as the suggestion that some individuals exhibit a specific allergic reaction to diet, seem also to be problems to be resolved pharmacologically. Chemicals that bind to unwanted contaminants and remove them from the body are available, and as increasing attention is directed to these sources of the problem, this form of intervention is sure to follow. Similarly, drug treatment for food allergies seems more plausible than attempting to control what a child eats. Finally, "better living through chemistry" is for much of modern culture a description of its pill-popping philosophy, designed to soothe and fortify battered psyches. For the learning disabled, who are especially embittered and frustrated, such preoccupation with the pharmacological alleviation of stress will mean a growing arsenal of mood-altering chemicals to placate their ruptured egos.

Perhaps the greatest hope of the learning-disabled child resides in the practical growth of computer technology. For the most part, a learning disability is a school-produced problem: educational demands are not met. Afflicted individuals do learn; they just do not do so in the manner prescribed by educational bureaucracies. Hence, individualized instruction can be a positive approach. But such instruction often yields to collective demand, financial restraints, and fears of stigmatized children who are "different" in the eyes of their peers. However, once the price of individual computer terminals drops to a level that principals and teachers cannot resist, then specialization will occur for everyone. Some students might read questions from displays, others hear them through headphones, and yet others "read" them tactilely like Braille through special, heat-sensitive digital displays.

Eventually primary schools and nursery schools will combine, and tailored computer learning will start much earlier than kindergarten. Children will attend school from age two, not only to protect teachers' jobs, which are

226

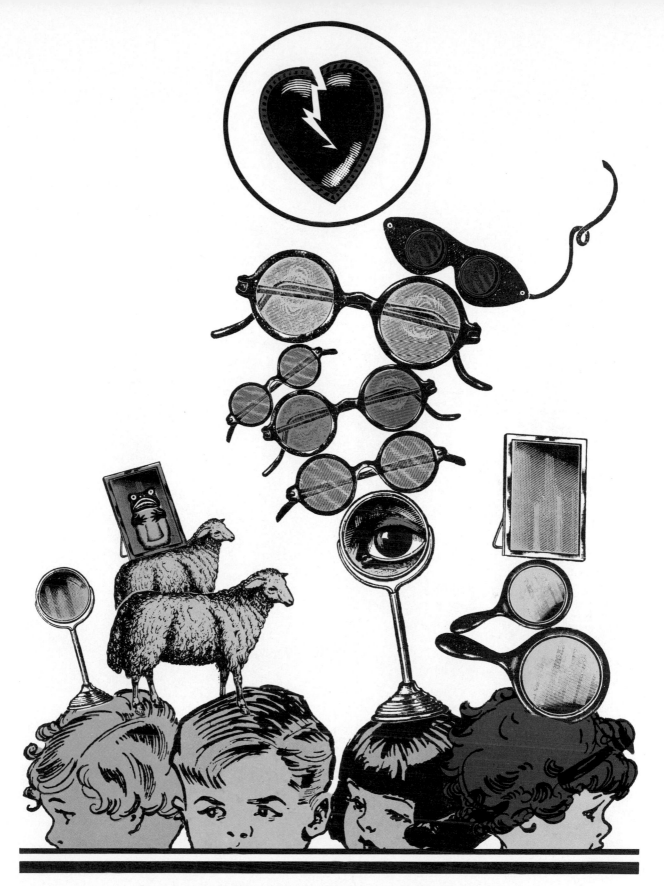

Emotional complications: Only 4% of children referred for treatment for a learning disability display average or better emotional adjustment.

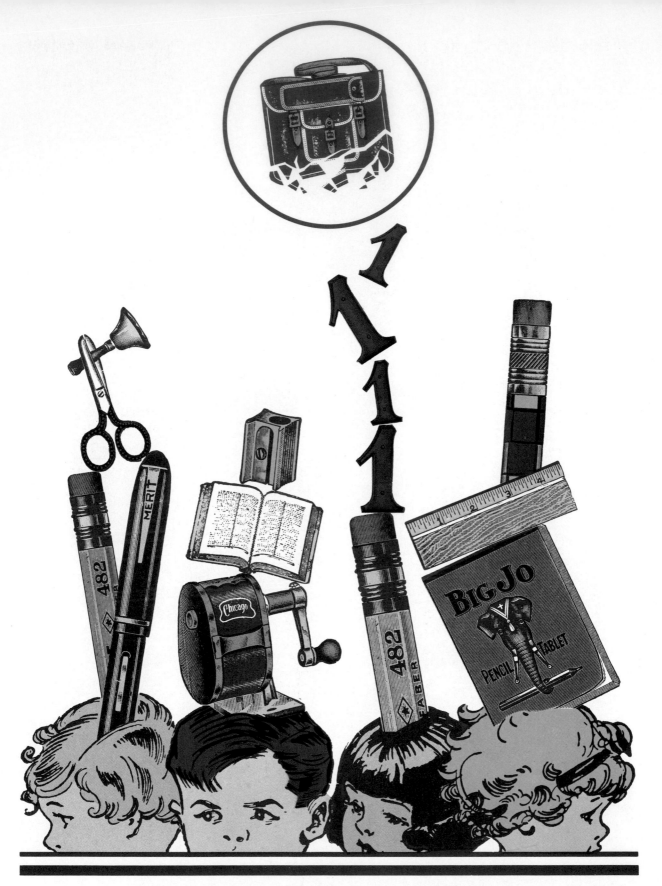

Educational shortcomings: Schools are not flexible and typically are as arteriosclerotic as any bureaucracy.

being jeopardized by the shrinking school-age population, but also to meet the absolute societal necessity of providing child-care facilities when both parents are employed outside the home. Such a system will provide an earlier start to the educative process and a more individualized and leisurely approach to learning. Both of these occurrences, in turn, will significantly ameliorate the substantial problem that learning disabilities have become.

The ramifications of inflexibility, however, cannot be ignored. The consequences of doing so are illustrated in the following fable written by Canadian psychologist Sam Rabinovitch, a man who cared for and empathized deeply with the learning disabled.

Once upon a time, the animals decided they must do something heroic to meet the problems of a ''new world.'' So they organized a school.

They adopted an activity curriculum consisting of running, climbing, swimming, and flying. To make it easier to administer the curriculum, all the animals took all the subjects.

The duck was excellent in swimming, in fact, better than his instructor. But he made only passing grades in flying and was very poor in running. Since he was slow in running, he had to drop swimming and stay after school to practice running. He continued this until his web feet were badly worn and he was only average in swimming. But average was quite acceptable, so nobody worried about that—except the duck.

The rabbit started at the top of his class in running, but had a nervous breakdown because of so much make-up work in swimming. The squirrel was excellent in climbing, but he developed frustrations in flying class because his teacher made him start from the ground up instead of from the treetop down. He developed charlie horses from overexertion and then made a C in climbing and a D in running.

The eagle was a problem child and was severely disciplined. In climbing classes he beat all the others to the top of the tree, but insisted on using his own way of getting there.

At the end of the year an abnormal eel that could swim exceedingly well and could also run, climb, and fly a little had the highest marks and was class valedictorian.

The prairie dogs stayed out of school and fought the tax levy because the administration would not add digging and burrowing to the curriculum. They apprenticed their child to a badger and later joined the groundhogs and gophers to start a free school.

FOR ADDITIONAL READING

E. Roy John et al., ''Neurometrics,'' *Science* (June 24, 1977, pp. 1393–1410).

Robert Knights and Dirk Bakker, *Rehabilitation, Treatment and Management of Learning Disorders* (University Park, 1979).

Helmer R. Myklebust, *Progress in Learning Disabilities,* vol. iii (Grune & Stratton, 1975).

R. O. Pihl and Muriel Parkes, ''Hair element content in learning disabled children,'' *Science* (Oct. 14, 1977, pp. 204–206).

Ronald Rosenthal and Terry Allen, ''An examination of attention, arousal, and learning dysfunctions of hyperkinetic children,'' *Psychological Bulletin* (1978, pp. 689–715).

Alan Ross, *Psychological Aspects of Learning Disabilities and Reading Disorders* (McGraw-Hill, 1976).

Courtesy, Northwestern University;
photo by Robert Pickering

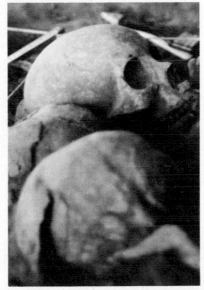

Koster and the New Archaeology

by Stuart Struever and Felicia Antonelli Holton

At the Koster site in southern Illinois archaeologists are excavating the remains of American Indian settlements that originated about 7500 BC. They are using new analytical techniques in an effort to learn more about these people.

Six thousand years before the first American pioneers headed westward to explore their country's frontiers, people lived the good life in what is now the Middle Western United States. In 3900 BC a group of Amerindians (ancestors of the North American Indians of today) established a village in the lower Illinois River valley, in what was to become Greene County, Illinois. Chance played no part in their choice of a homesite. They deliberately settled in one of the great river valleys of the midcontinent. They knew that in the long, narrow riverine strip and its immediate environs nature offered them an incredible abundance of nutritious food resources. For thousands of miles on either side of the valley stretched environments that could not begin to provide the kinds and amounts of food resources which throve in the river valley itself.

Before the pioneers

Having selected their homesite with a calculating eye, this band of 100 to 150 people built permanent houses (among the earliest in North America) at the base of 150-foot-high bluffs that gave them shelter from wintry blasts. The forests in the nearby uplands were excellent sources of firewood. A few yards from the houses meandered a spring-fed stream, which yielded not only water but also, in its rock beds, all the chert the people needed to make stone tools.

Within a radius of a few miles enough wild animal and plant resources flourished to sustain the group on a year-round basis. Along with wild deer and turkeys, they consumed more than 35 different kinds of freshwater fish and mussels, 15 varieties of waterfowl, basketsful of hickory and other nuts, and numerous wild plants. For all this bounty, they probably worked about 20 hours a week—less than half the time most people in our highly technological society work to put food on the table. They had ample leisure time to domesticate dogs and to turn out handsomely decorated bone hairpins.

Their technology was simple; their intelligence was not. Almost 5,000 years before their descendants first shifted to an agricultural way of life in the lower Illinois River valley, these people were sufficiently organized to obtain their yearly supply of food through a highly organized program of hunting, collecting, and fishing. They harvested annual "crops" of fish, ducks, geese, hickory nuts, and cereal-like seeds from such plants as the marsh elder (*Iva annua*) and goosefoot (*Chenopodium*). By following this strategy, these early Amerindians were able to gather food in

STUART STRUEVER *is Professor of Anthropology and Archaeology in the Department of Anthropology, Northwestern University, and Chairman of the Board of the Foundation for Illinois Archaeology. He is co-author, with* **FELICIA ANTONELLI HOLTON,** *of* Koster: Americans in Search of Their Prehistoric Past.

232

quantities that usually are associated only with agricultural production.

Most archaeologists have assumed that people did not become sedentary until they were able to produce surplus food to tide them over the winter. These people, however, established permanent villages long before agriculture was practiced in the region.

A unique discovery

The group we have described was one of a series of cultures which once flourished at the Koster site, named for Mary and Theodore Koster on whose farm it was discovered. The Koster site is located in rural Illinois, about 270 miles southwest of Chicago and about 50 miles northwest of St. Louis, Missouri. The people who lived at Koster in 3900 BC have been named Helton after the Kosters' next-door neighbor, Harlin (Alec) Helton, a farmer who in 1968 led archaeologists to the cornfield where he had discovered artifacts.

Koster has turned out to be one of the most important archaeological sites ever discovered in North America. People lived at Koster, off and on, over a 9,000-year span, from about 7500 BC to AD 1200. Some, like the Helton people, established permanent villages; others used the site briefly as a hunting-butchering camp. It is not yet known why people abandoned the site from time to time; in some cases it may have been because they had used up all the available firewood within a comfortable walking distance from their settlement.

Each time Koster was abandoned, soil washed down from the bluffs behind the site, creating a protective layer of earth that preserved the underlying ruins. This particular type of soil, called loess, preserves bones and plant remains very well. Most of the 26 human habitation levels or horizons at Koster are separated from the ones above and below by a layer of sterile soil. In North America it is very rare to find such a well-preserved site, with a stack of intact village remains representing such a long time span. In addition, most of the horizons were occupied during the Archaic time period in American prehistory, about which very little had been known before Koster was discovered. Archaeologists have designated several time periods in North American prehistory: Pre-Paleo-Indian (from about 30,000 BC to 12,000 BC), Paleo-Indian (12,000 BC–8000 BC), Archaic (8000 BC–500 BC), Woodland (500 BC–AD 1200), and Mississippian (AD 900–AD 1673). Woodland and Mississippian overlap.

Exploring ancient Illinois

Koster is the largest, oldest, and most complex of a series of sites being excavated in the lower Illinois River valley by the Foundation for Illinois Archaeology (FIA), in collaboration with faculty of Northwestern University, Evanston, Illinois. Over the past 14 years, the activities of the FIA and the Northwestern [University] Archaeological Program (NAP) have been closely interwoven. Together they sponsor a variety of educational and research programs in archaeology. Some of these programs, like grant-supported research and field schools for university students (including 15 Northwestern University courses), are conducted under Northwestern sponsorship. Oth-

233

ers, like the rescue archaeology program and the excavation field schools for high school students, are funded and staffed by the FIA. Some members of the FIA's scientific staff hold joint appointments with Northwestern.

Since it was established in 1956, the FIA has excavated 21 prehistoric sites, including Koster. Seventeen of these have been in the area of Kampsville, Illinois, which serves as headquarters for the Koster dig. Koster is about nine miles southeast of the town, on the opposite side of the Illinois River. The FIA also conducts research in the Chicago metropolitan area, particularly in the vicinity of the Fox, Des Plaines, and Du Page river valleys that lie west of the city.

In the late 1960s the FIA formed the Kampsville Archaeological Center as the first permanent archaeological teaching and research field campus in North America. The FIA-NAP researchers, working out of the center, are conducting a long-term study of more than 10,000 years of North American Indian life. For this purpose, the FIA-NAP has staked out a research "universe," which includes a 2,800-square mile area of western Illinois lying immediately north of St. Louis.

Kampsville is centrally located within this "universe," which encompasses sections of the Illinois and Mississippi river valleys. The region is rich in archaeological sites, and because it is a rural area they have remained relatively undisturbed. More than 1,800 ancient sites have been mapped. The FIA-NAP archaeologists plan to excavate enough of them over the next 25 to 30 years to create the first comprehensive picture of pre-European history in any area of the United States. The intense focus that is being given to this region of the Illinois-Mississippi valley is unique in American archaeology.

The new archaeology

Archaeology in North America underwent a revolution in the 1960s that was both methodological and intellectual in nature. A small group of archaeologists maintained that their discipline, as it was then practiced, was outmoded in 20th-century America. They introduced advanced statistical methods and computers and insisted that data should be rigorously tested, following the scientific method, as are data in other scientific disciplines. They argued, furthermore, that archaeologists should try to understand the causes of cultural changes over time and to derive, from these, universal laws governing all cultural changes. This group came to be known as the "new" archaeologists, to distinguish them from their colleagues who held more traditional views.

The new archaeologists define culture differently from traditional archaeologists. They recover more data as they dig, and they ask different questions of their data.

Traditional archaeologists define culture as a body of ideas, values, and beliefs shared by a group of people. One generation passes these ideas, values, and beliefs on to the next. The archaeologist looks at the material remains of an extinct culture in an effort to define the concepts that were in the minds of the ancient people.

New archaeologists define culture as a nonbiological system which hu-

The huge excavation in the field where Theodore Koster once grew corn (opposite page, top) began in 1969 with a few test holes (below, left). The horizontal divisions of the site (below, right) are sometimes based on statistical sampling and computer analysis, sometimes on the archaeologists' educated guesses.

235

The loess covering the Koster site is a highly porous type of soil, probably wind-deposited in origin, that is particularly well suited for the preservation of organic remains. The soil is removed from the site and then carefully sifted and inspected for artifacts.

man beings develop to cope with their environment. Culture is seen as a series of interlinked behavior systems and material items. All parts of the cultural system—economic, social, political, religious—are interdependent. The total cultural system serves as a buffer between the people who developed it and their environment. It permits them to shape the environment to their ends, to protect themselves from danger, and to exploit potentially valuable aspects of the environment, including animals and plants. It also enables them to adapt to other cultures that impinge on them.

In setting their goals, traditional archaeologists have been influenced by psychology. They ask: What were the mental modes of the people who made these artifacts? In contrast, new archaeologists employ a set of concepts derived from evolution and ecology. Cultural systems go through a set of changes, in the course of which they become increasingly complex. As a system becomes more complex, it develops more parts, with each part performing fewer tasks but performing them more efficiently. Through this process the total cultural system enables human beings to meet their needs better within their environment. New archaeologists ask: What are the reasons for these changes? When, why, and how do cultures become more complex? How do human beings interact with their environment as the changes occur?

Traditional archaeologists excavate sites in order to find formal representations of the ideas held by the ancient people, as embodied in their artifacts and other material remains. They believe that by examining material remains and making up a trait list of standard forms—of houses, spearheads, knives, pots, and burials—they can infer what basic ideas, values, and beliefs these people once shared.

236

New archaeologists also study artifacts, but they analyze them in order to gain an understanding of how the early people used the cultural system to cope with their environment. They try to reconstruct on paper three extinct systems—the human biological system (from human skeletal remains); the environmental system (from bits of charred seeds and nuts, animal bones, fishbones, soil studies); and the cultural system (from artifacts). By determining how these three systems interacted in a given culture, they attempt to explain changes in any, or all, of the systems.

As they excavate, new archaeologists collect various kinds of material that traditionalists have ignored. All of us, as we move through the day, create various kinds of debris, much of it unnoticed. We drop gum wrappers, tabs from beverage cans, broken shoelaces, paper clips. On a prehistoric site people may have dropped bits of half-finished or broken stone or bone tools, fish scales, and the like. Earlier archaeologists tossed out this debris. New archaeologists, however, call it the by-products of everyday maintenance, and they collect it. They also collect bits of evidence that might yield clues to the extinct environment, such as pollen, snail shells, and mineralized plant cells called opal phytolites.

Reconstructing the game plan

New archaeologists try to reconstruct the behavior of an extinct people. To do this, they study the subsistence settlement system of the prehistoric culture, or the group's "game plan" for getting along in its environment.

All of us have game plans, although we may be unaware of it. We set aside certain portions of the day for work and for play. We eat in our kitchens or dining rooms, work in offices, play games in a gym or in a park. In 7500 BC the environment around Koster consisted of prairies, forests, floodplains, bluff tops, rivers, lakes, and streams. Like modern people, Koster residents had to plan where to invest their time, but in their case the decisions concerned where to live, hunt, fish, gather plants, and make tools.

To determine exactly where the early people carried on all these activities, archaeologists, like all good detectives, start with the smallest clues and then match them or add onto them. For example, in the Helton village at Koster Horizon 6 (3900 BC–2800 BC), an excavator came across a stone scraper. Dirt taken from that immediate spot was then put through the flotation process, in which dirt is washed through solutions of water and chemicals to float out tiny food remains. Dozens of fish scales were found, and from these and the wear marks on the scraper, it was clear that someone had been cleaning fish at that spot. This is called an "activity set." Two or more activity sets (such as the fish-cleaning set and a meat-butchering set) comprise a settlement type. The Helton village was a settlement type. Two or more settlement types constitute a settlement system.

While Helton people lived at Koster all year round, at different times of the year work parties camped away from home to procure food for the group. In the fall a group of women, taking infants and small children along, may have moved down to the river floodplains for several days to harvest the seeds of such wild plants as the marsh elder (*Iva annua*) and pigweed (*Amaranthus*). During the winter some of the Helton men may have moved

Whether the artifacts are as large as a limestone floor or as small as a chert projectile point, great care is required to distinguish the manifestations of man from the surrounding soil deposits.

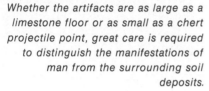

into the uplands or out onto the prairie for two or three weeks to hunt American elk and white-tailed deer. The carcasses would have been brought back to the hunting camp to be skinned and butchered, and some of the meat would have been dried before it was carried back to the village.

All three settlement types—the Koster village, the seed-processing camp, and the hunting-butchering camp—would be part of the subsistence settlement system of the Helton people. As part of their long-term goal the Northwestern archaeologists will be attempting to excavate examples of sites representing each of the above settlement types used by the Helton people some 6,000 years ago.

Querying the data

The archaeologists working at Koster are continually experimenting with new ways to make the data "talk," and they have encouraged other scientists to join the effort by bringing techniques from their disciplines to bear on the archaeological evidence. With the establishment of the Kampsville Archaeological Center, these scientists can be offered laboratory space, some of it on a year-round basis, for long-term research.

For example, Frederick C. Hill, a zoologist, has used fish scales and mussel shells to help discover what the climate was like in Archaic times. The ratio of strontium to calcium in mussel shells is determined by conditions in the river or lake where the animal lives. By studying this ratio in mussel shells found in some of the Koster villages, Hill was able to determine that during the Helton people's occupation of Horizon 6 (3900 BC) there was a great deal more rainfall than there had been a thousand years earlier, when people lived at the Horizon 8 level. Analysis of the mussels that lived in the Illinois River during Horizon 6 times revealed that streamflow then was swifter than in the earlier period, indicating heavier rainfall. Furthermore, the fish that were consumed by Horizon 6 people were species that prefer somewhat sluggish habitats, suggesting the existence of many backwater lakes formed when receding floodwaters were caught in pockets of land in

Among the most revealing finds in any dig, human burials, by their method and location, tell the archaeologist much that is important about the culture of the people who made them.

At the end of the summer field season, workers at Koster cover the site to protect it through the winter.

the floodplains. Such lakes also would have resulted from heavy rain.

Christopher Carr, a doctoral candidate at the University of Michigan, is experimenting with resistivity surveys in some lower Illinois River valley archaeological sites in an effort to identify the most promising digging sites with greater accuracy. Since the archaeologists' aim is to recover a full range of human activities in the region, the ideal method would be to dig all the sites that exist, but this is not economically feasible. The usual system is to do a surface survey at a site. First a string grid is placed on the surface, and all artifacts within the marked-off squares are picked up. These are then plotted on graphs, and the resulting information is used to help decide where to dig for the richest source of buried data. This method, however, does not reveal the location of some important human activities that would have caused disturbance in the soil, such as the digging of storage pits or house floors.

In resistivity surveying, the variation in the electrical resistance of the soil is mapped and measured. The electrical property of the soil depends on its moisture content; the amount of ions in the soil water (potassium, hydrogen, or magnesium, which may be natural to the soil or may be the result of human occupation); the temperature of the soil water; and the arrangement of the particles in the soil, which determines the arrangement of water film around the particles. By measuring all these indexes in soil on sites and in surrounding off-site soil, Carr found that the prehistorically disturbed soil can

240

be distinguished from undisturbed soil. Therefore, areas occupied by prehistoric man can be distinguished from the surrounding region, thus helping to identify the specific location of human activities in ancient villages. These experiments are being continued with the aim of refining this method so as to make it a more useful tool for archaeologists.

Another important aspect of the work at the Kampsville Archaeological Center deals with human remains from prehistoric times. Archaeologists have largely focused on the cultural remains of ancient populations, giving little attention to growth, nutrition, disease, heredity, and other aspects of ancient human biology. In the past decade, however, the field of bioarchaeology has begun to emerge. Research in this field—aspects of which can be termed medical archaeology—examines the relationship of prehistoric people and their environment. Thus Jane E. Buikstra of Northwestern University has excavated and studied ancient cemeteries with the goal of identifying and measuring the effects of the environment on prehistoric Amerindian groups. This has included the study of ancient diseases and their relationship to prehistoric diet, daily work patterns, living conditions, and climate.

Using a site for education

One of the major functions of the Kampsville Archaeological Center is education, and programs are offered at several levels. Few scientific disciplines can allow untrained university undergraduates to enter a research project

Among the first lessons a worker at Koster learns is to exercise patience and care in handling remains. Here brushes are used delicately to remove soil from a skeleton.

and begin immediately to participate in information recovery. Archaeology is an exception. Annual summer field schools, each involving approximately 70 to 90 university students, have been conducted each year at the Kampsville Center since 1968.

Archaeology in America does not have a public constituency like those that rise to the defense of endangered species or wilderness areas. One of the aims of the Kampsville Center is to build such a constituency, to educate people so they will understand and support archaeological research. The age level of people invited to dig has been extended both upward and downward. Field schools for high-school and junior high-school students down to the age of 11 are offered, and post-college adults are invited to attend special field schools. Since 1974 some 4,831 students from 422 schools and colleges and about 1,000 post-college adults have helped dig at lower Illinois River valley sites. The policy of allowing young students to participate in research at a site is proving to be a powerful educational tool. They are taught that data, if destroyed, is irretrievable and must be handled with great care. Very rapidly, they learn to work as responsible scientists.

Another special feature of the Kampsville Center is the Native American Studies Program run by John White, a scholar of Cherokee and Scots descent. Workers connected with museum and historic sites, primary and secondary school teachers, students, and lay persons study Amerindian culture at Kampsville by making and using replicas of items of prehistoric technology. They collect clay and make pottery, manufacture stone artifacts, weave fabrics, and collect and process traditional Amerindian foods. They have built replicas of three types of prehistoric houses—Archaic, Woodland, and Mississippian. The goals of the program are to help those responsible for the interpretation of prehistoric people in their own work and to enhance students' insights into the people whose remains they are excavating.

The Kampsville Archaeological Center is also used to inform the general public, to educate Americans about their own prehistory. Members of the public are invited to visit a site under excavation, the Kampsville Archaeological Museum, a laboratory, and Native American workshops. And it is hoped that, as the public becomes educated about archaeology, it will lend its support. More than 60% of the funds for operating the Kampsville Center are raised through public donations.

Archaeology today is asking the most significant questions in its history, and its capacity to answer these questions will depend in large measure on the character of its research efforts. During the past two or three decades major advances have been made in the physical and biological sciences. But this growing knowledge of chemistry, physics, mathematics, medicine, and other sciences plays only a limited role in archaeological research. The expertise involved takes years of specialization to acquire, and many of the procedures require capital expenditures that are beyond the resources of conventional archaeological research efforts. The archaeologists at the Kampsville Center hope to combine the specialized expertise, technology, and funding necessary to sustain meaningful methods-oriented research, particularly research involving the efforts of several scholars and technicians over substantial periods of time.

Science
Year in Review

Science
Year in Review
Contents

Anthropology

The death of Margaret Mead (*see* OBITUARIES) on Nov. 15, 1978, marked a transition and a challenge for anthropology. She was a staunch opponent of the parochialism in science accepted today as a fact of academic life. She became something of a national and international oracle at a time when anthropologists were experiencing difficulty communicating even among themselves. Mead was a master of anticipating things to come; her social antennae would be missed by a discipline that allows itself to follow worn patterns and to be surprised by new ones. No wonder Mead could ask, "What is there for the young anthropologist to do? In a sense everything. The best possible work has not yet been done."

Margaret Mead maintained a broad perspective and addressed the largest possible audience. Not all anthropologists agreed on the correctness of her perspective, and many have chosen to neglect her audience. Now that she is gone, however, the profession as a whole is realizing that it must attempt to accomplish as a body what one outstanding member had been required to undertake practically by herself.

Unity in anthropology. In an open letter appearing in the American Anthropological Association's (AAA's) newsletter, Paul J. Bohannan, the association's president, advised his colleagues that anthropology is "constantly on the verge of shattering into its components." He urged his membership to "defend the unity of anthropology," an exhortation repeated by the association's Committee on Anthropology as a Profession: "The committee regards the present fragmentation [of anthropology] as working against the maintenance of the broad approach that underlies anthropology's unique role through the years both in application and theoretical understanding of man."

Anthropology indeed attempts more ambitious coverage than any other social science. Every facet of human life in every locale in which human life is found —or is found to have been—is introduced into the anthropological gristmill. Anthropologists have always had this holistic perspective to fall back on, even if individual anthropologists were gaining their expertise in extremely limited areas. Now, amid observations that the field was fragmenting, that the total picture had been lost, the fear was that pressures of specialization had preempted the comparative tasks of anthropology.

The trend toward greater specialization affected the anthropological job market, in which applicants had to respond to notices with increasingly specific job descriptions. Another sign was the year's rejection rate for manuscripts submitted to the *American Anthropologist*, an AAA journal that emphasizes the unity of anthropology. In 1978 the editors rejected 51 of 57 manuscripts submitted, many on the grounds that the audiences they addressed were too specialized. The trend was further identified by a 1979 *Yearbook of Science and the Future* article that reported highly concentrated activity in several specialized subfields, such as medical anthropology, ecological anthropology, and sociobiology.

There were indications in 1978 of an imminent swing back to "grander theory." Marvin Harris and Marshall Sahlins, for example, debated the importance of nature versus culture in several highly visible publications. However, the tendency for anthropology to shrink back from a confrontation with important world issues continued to resist correction.

In a related issue, *The Chronicle of Higher Education* (Nov. 27, 1978) reported that, despite the shortage of teaching positions in anthropology, few scholars seriously look elsewhere for employment. *The Chronicle* reported: "Work outside departments of an-

This footprint, one of a series of five preserved in volcanic ash at Laetolil, Tanzania, may have been made by a direct ancestor of man 3.5 million years ago. The print, discovered by Mary D. Leakey and co-workers, is about 6 inches long and 4.4 inches wide, and is believed to have supported an individual approximately 4 feet tall.

Courtesy, © National Geographic Society

After looking at a picture of an angry mother cat scolding her three crying kittens, Koko, a 140-pound lowland gorilla, makes the hand signal for "bad." Under the tutelage of Stanford University doctoral candidate Francine Patterson (left), Koko has become the first gorilla to learn sign language. Koko has a vocabulary of about 375 signals.

thropology in the arts or sciences or museums is considered second-class. Jobs in government or business organizations are even farther out on the status scale."

This disdain for nonacademic involvement was indicative of the prevalent attitude among anthropologists that their discipline has little connection with the "real" world. Anthropologists were finding this attitude increasingly difficult to defend and more and more in need of defense. Nevertheless, the academic position in a department of anthropology, with its traditional separation from direct application and with its sense of distance from other disciplines, continued to provide the basic model from which most anthropologists operated. Although there was a noticeable out-migration of anthropologists to contract research and similar settings, it was not clear that anthropology at its disciplinary center would profit from the variety of experiences and insights these migrants were gaining.

American culture. In response to the continuing lack of money for fieldwork, many anthropologists were choosing to conduct research at home. There was still a bias in anthropology, however, in favor of those individuals who had done fieldwork, and for some traditional academic departments and research-granting agencies, American culture did not qualify. Work in America, it was argued, makes few intellectual demands and is incapable of providing culture shock, an important rite of passage for the anthropologist.

The scholarly reputations of anthropologists who go away to do fieldwork rest with their knowledge of the people studied and not with their understanding of their own culture. In essence, an anthropologist gains expertise and accomplishment from the study of another culture without necessarily ever analyzing his or her own.

The mass suicide and murders in Guyana in 1978 in which more than 900 members of the People's Temple died may have upset the complacency with which many anthropologists had viewed the workings of their own culture. The horror of the demise of the Rev. Jim Jones and his followers strains all comprehension and shakes the untested certainty that we know our own culture. The investigation of cultism must reckon with the cultural construction of the person in America if it is to explore the dynamics of such an event. The crucial question is why recruits to the People's Temple and other cults are willing to surrender a large measure of their personal responsibility and potential for growth in order to gain group membership and a sense of security. Inside or outside the context of cults, Americans were intensifying the search for meaning and direction in their lives. The Guyana tragedy illustrated a tremendous miscalculation of the risks involved in that search.

No doubt anthropologists would redouble their efforts to study the dynamics of leadership, cultism, and group process in the wake of the Guyana catastrophe. Continued inquiry into the fundamentals of American culture was also called for. It was to be hoped that, rather than devoting all their energies to well-delineated areas of inquiry established by social science tradition, anthropologists would respond to this event with a careful examination of urgent issues.

The program of the AAA's 1978 meeting indicated a growing interest in the study of American culture. One group of papers, entitled "Studying Up," reported research conducted on powerful groups in America, such as physicians, police, and government bureaucrats. Reports such as these point up the blind spots resulting from the omission of the study of power from much social science research. Because of the inherent difficulties, anthropologists generally have shied away from research in highly politicized settings. It was becoming apparent, however, that research in settings of power and politics is a foremost priority.

Anthropologists and government. Anthropologists were becoming increasingly watchful of the power structure that determines availabilities and priorities for their own research. During 1978 anthropologists closely monitored the deliberations in the U.S. House of Representatives and Senate over reauthorization of the Archeological and Historic Preservation Act of 1974, commonly known as the Moss-Bennett Act. The AAA presented testimony before the Senate Energy and Natural Resources Committee urging continuation of support for archaeological salvage funds and opposing amendments that would have cut reauthorization back from five to two years and reduced funding levels. In the end, Congress approved funding for five more years. Under the terms of the reauthorization, the secretary of the interior was empowered to make discretionary appropriations for archaeological salvage work through designated federal agencies beyond the 1% figure provided for in the 1974 act. As a result,

Bodies of his dead followers lie in front of the chair used by the Rev. Jim Jones at his People's Temple settlement in Guyana. The mass suicide of Jones and his followers focused attention on cults.

contract archaeology would continue to be an important activity for several more years.

In a related development, cultural anthropologists coined the term salvage ethnology in relation to proposed government financing for ethnographic projects. The goal was to guarantee the security of cultural systems (*e.g.,* tradition, language, history) threatened by development projects. These anthropologists were seeking a definition of environmental impact that would include cultural as well as natural resources.

Among the objections to the idea of salvage ethnology was the argument that, once the salvage work was completed, "people can be bulldozed out of their existence." Other anthropologists disagreed with the emphasis on preservation, believing instead that peoples can best be helped by introducing them into mainstream national economies. These issues were not new to anthropology in 1978, nor were they likely to be resolved in the coming years. But they were clearer and more loudly debated during a period of increased governmental determination of research priorities and goals.

Systems theory. Systems theory, derived from a variety of sources, has had a significant impact on anthropology for 20 years, and it promises to be of consequence for the discipline in the future. Its attraction for anthropology is due in part to the congruence of systems theory and traditional holistic orientations in anthropology. General systems theory continued to be the most widely utilized systematic approach in anthropology, although there was no single systems theory in anthropology or elsewhere.

The development of systems theory in no way reduces the responsibility of the anthropologist in making sensible decisions regarding what to study. The identity of the boundary between a system and its environment, for example, is very much a matter of judgment. Third world anthropologists who resent mathematical expressions of cultural phenomena as both dehumanizing and reductive should oppose the cultural uses of the theory rather than its mathematical look. Well-articulated cultural goals can be achieved through formal analyses in which system boundaries incorporate the important areas of history and ideology.

Systems theory tends, however, to assume a Durkheimian view that permeates British and American anthropology and which in its consensus-oriented approach overlooks contradictions in society and nature. Systems theory has the potential to contribute to the study of power and ideology, two topics of the highest importance to third world anthropologists. Western anthropologists are constantly being reminded by their third world colleagues and by world events to establish appropriate priorities.

Ethics. The complexity of ethical issues in anthropology increases with the changing nature of anthropology and the growing self-awareness of peoples

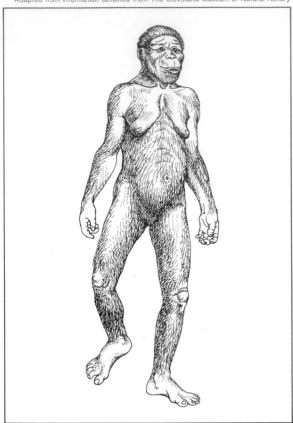

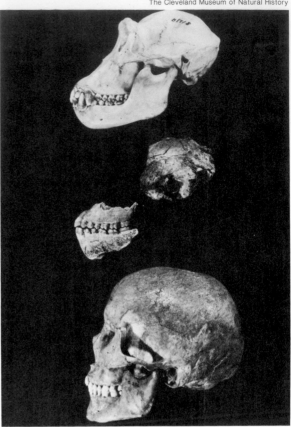

Australopithecus afarensis was reconstructed (left) from three-million-year-old remains from Ethiopia. Its bones (right center) more closely resemble those of a chimpanzee (top) than of modern man (bottom).

throughout the world. Earlier statements on problems in research and ethics by the AAA and equivalent bodies in other countries emphasized problems within the traditional anthropological context. In a document drafted in 1967, the AAA emphasized protection for informants and people studied: "In research an anthropologist's paramount responsibility is to those he studies." The assumption was that all people studied would be from "simpler" societies, bounded by non-progressive traditions, and dominated by the powerful nation-states in which they were located.

The notion of paramount responsibility is complicated, however, when the anthropologist cannot offer his or her personal support to the ideology or goals of the group under study. What is the paramount responsibility, for example, of the anthropologist studying racist or sexist groups? In even the most traditional research settings anthropologists have complex involvements where differences of opinion and conflicts of interest prevail within the group under study. Anthropologists were learning that ethical issues are not easily resolved and that some of the most vexing dilemmas derive from contradictions within the anthropological charter itself—a charter that emphasizes theory over practice without ever committing itself to a merger of the two.

Paleoanthropology. Interest continued in the archaeological evidence from the Pliocene-Pleistocene in East Africa. As Glynn Isaac reported (in *Scientific American*, April 1978), Pleistocene archaeology no longer depends primarily on the analysis of stone artifacts. Human evolution is being studied from a variety of perspectives, including anatomy, comparative ecology and ethology, and population genetics, sometimes within a sociobiological framework. Archaeological theory provides a core discipline for evolutionary theory which promises to bring together anatomical, economic, and behavioral evidence in meaningful ways.

Recent research in paleoanthropology has demanded reconstruction of land-use patterns, subsistence patterns, and ecological inference. Within this framework the term culture has been deemphasized, no longer serving as the absolute distinguishing feature between human and nonhuman behavioral repertoires. For example, food-sharing behavior and not culture, per se, has assumed importance in recent archaeological inquiries.

Furthermore, definitions of culture, when employed, emphasize aspects of culture as behavior (*e.g.,* language, technology) and do not view culture as a system of meanings and symbols, a perspective endorsed by a growing group of influential symbolic anthropologists. The symbolic approach has been shown to have analytic utility for studies of the ethnographic present, but the lack of agreement between paleoanthropologists and cultural anthropologists on important issues such as this demonstrates the perseverance of tensions within the discipline and belies the accuracy of pronouncements of unity in anthropology.

—Lawrence E. Fisher

Archaeology

The study of living human societies in order to gain information useful for interpreting archaeological records has made important advances in the last several years. Among the detailed studies that have appeared recently are those by John E. Yellen, dealing with the behavior of the Kung Bushmen of southern Africa; by Richard A. Gould, treating the Australian Aborigines; and by Lewis R. Binford, describing the activity patterns of the Nunamiut Eskimo. These studies provide significant new insights into the ways in which residues deposited by human groups reflect the patterns of daily living, and they strengthen the interpretative base of archaeological methods for understanding the remains of the past.

The matching of obsidian artifacts to the geologic sources of the raw material through geochemical measurement of trace elements has opened up a whole new understanding of the nature and extent of ancient trade and exchange relationships. New work on the trace-element analysis of chert, another kind of stone commonly used for toolmaking and found widely in archaeological sites around the world, promises to expand this understanding even further. The problems of adequately characterizing archaeological specimens and matching them with geologic sources are complex. However, results of a major project carried out by the Museum of Anthropology, University of Michigan, over a period of several years suggest that this form of analysis has genuine promise.

Concern for the preservation of prehistoric sites, once largely confined to archaeologists, continued to grow, particularly in the United States. A series of federal laws and rulings provides for the preservation of important historic and archaeological sites. Widespread implementation of these acts by public and private agencies appeared to be moving archaeologists more and more into multidisciplinary preservation efforts combining archaeological, historical, architectural, and ethnologic points of view.

The development of domesticated plants and animals in prehistoric times continued to interest many archaeologists. The question of whether people of the western European Upper Paleolithic kept domesticat-

ed animals, of major concern some decades ago, was reopened by Paul G. Bahn. He pointed out, for example, that lines suggesting a harness are indicated on some horse representations in Upper Paleolithic cave art; furthermore, abnormal wear patterns on horse teeth from the Mousterian site of La Quina in France are like those found in modern horses that have been tied up or stabled and have worn down their teeth by biting at their restraints. Such indicators are far from conclusive. However, given the current scientific recognition that domestication was not a single event or invention but rather the outcome of a long-continued pattern of association between humans and other species, the time may have come to reconsider seriously the question of very early domestication.

Important new surveys and excavations at Lower Paleolithic sites in the Hungsi Valley of peninsular India were reported by K. Kaddayya. Some 13 localities, of Acheulean Age, have been identified. Three were manufacturing sites, situated in a foothills zone closely associated with sources of limestone that served as raw material for toolmaking. Six others were evidently habitational locations, and the remaining four were associated with water-laid gravels. All the sites discovered so far are located on the valley floor, near perennial water, while the drier uplands flanking the valley seem not to have been occupied. These discoveries establish a broad potential for developing regionally

Archaeologists measure the entrance to an arched tunnel in Greece. Dating from about 320 BC, it is the oldest known continuous arch in the Western world.

oriented behavioral studies of Paleolithic peoples in peninsular India.

A combination of evidence from archaeological excavations and ethnologic research in the Lake Victoria region of eastern Africa added importantly to knowledge of prehistoric iron smelting in sub-Saharan Africa. Excavations at the KM 2 site show that smelting furnaces and techniques comparable to those found in the region today were in use at least 1,500 to 2,000 years ago. Ethnologic research among traditional iron workers in the area indicates the high degree of sophistication of the processes involved, which allows the production of high-quality carbon steel. These discoveries, reported by Peter R. Schmidt and Donald H. Avery, add a new dimension to the history of metallurgy as well as the history of technological development on the African continent.

The implications of recent excavations at Tepe Yahya, Tal-i-Malyan, Susa, and Godin Tepe on the Iranian Plateau were synthesized by C. C. Lamberg-Karlovsky. New Proto-Elamite sealings and tablets, together with other evidence, suggest political consolidation and an expansion of Proto-Elamite political control over much of the Iranian Plateau around 3400 BC. This was apparently intended to guarantee access to the raw materials and manufactured goods of the region surrounding the Proto-Elamite center at Susa.

Evidence suggests the breakdown of this political hegemony after about a century, probably because of the excessive economic and social burden of maintaining political and administrative control over so broad an area. The Proto-Elamite case is one of the culture-historical developments that must be traced if we are to develop a full understanding of the internationalism that linked the Iranian Plateau to Mesopotamia and the Persian Gulf in the late 4th millennium BC.

In China's Shensi Province, in the Yellow River valley, work continued on uncovering a huge subterranean vault containing an army of some 6,000 life-size men and horses, modeled realistically in clay. This was the spectral army of Ch'in Shih Huang Ti, the first emperor of China and builder of the Great Wall along the country's northern frontier. When he died in 210 BC he was buried under a great earthen mound not far from where this vast guardian army waited. Historical chronicles relate that the emperor ordered construction to begin on his tomb complex when he first ascended the throne at age 13, and the work continued for 36 years.

The vault containing the army lay 4 to 6 m (15 to 20 ft) below ground, extending some 215 m (700 ft) east–west and 60 m (200 ft) north–south. As of early 1979 only a small portion of the area had been cleared, but test excavations revealed its extent. The army was arrayed in marching order, in 11 great columns. Four-horse chariots accompanied by groups of foot soldiers comprised six of the columns, while the rest consisted of rank on rank of foot soldiers, armed with real crossbows, spears, and swords of an alloy of copper, tin, and 13 other elements. The traditional histories describe the imperial sepulcher itself as a place of great magnificence. It seemed certain that spectacular treasures awaited the archaeologists' attention there.

Excavations in Tonga, western Polynesia, reported by Patrick V. Kirch, provided valuable new evidence on the subsistence economy of the so-called Lapita people. The Lapitans' distinctive pottery and other artifacts are believed by many archaeologists to represent the earliest incursions of the ancestors of modern Polynesians into the western Pacific. Pottery of Lapita type has been dated between about 1600 and 500 BC.

Haya men in Tanzania make carbon steel in a preheated forced-draft furnace, a process that they first perfected about 2,000 years ago according to recent archaeological discoveries. Not until almost 19 centuries later was such sophisticated steel-making technology developed elsewhere.

Sites on the island of Niuatoputapu yielded food scrapers of shell and a number of pits apparently used for the fermentation and storage of starch paste made from root crops. This is a storage technique known from historic times in the southwestern Pacific, and the Niuatoputapu evidence suggests that it may date back to the time of the earliest Polynesian occupation. A broad-spectrum marine-based economy was indicated by the remains of many species of fish, sea turtle, and shellfish. Bird bones included those of domestic chickens and several species of aquatic fowl native to the area. Evidence such as that from Niuatoputapu increasingly points to the settlement of all the major island chains of western Polynesia, and many of the smaller and more isolated islands as well, by the Lapitans during the early 1st millennium BC.

A newly reported underwater site at Little Salt Spring, Fla., gave evidence of a vast array of human remains, artifacts, and fossils in a remarkable state of preservation. Little Salt Spring was a great sinkhole up to 80 m (260 ft) across and 60 m (195 ft) deep. The earliest evidence of human activity at the site consisted of the overturned, collapsed shell of a giant land tortoise belonging to a now-extinct species. A sharply pointed wooden stake, which evidently had killed the tortoise, was found thrust into the body cavity. Wood from this stake was radiocarbon-dated to about 10,000 BC. The bones of other species, including giant ground sloth and mammoth or mastodon, also came from the site. Artifacts included a socketed antler projectile point, the base of a carved oaken mortar radiocarbon-dated about 7000 BC, and a fragment of a well-preserved nonreturning boomerang carved of oak. This was the first specimen of its kind reported for the Paleo-Indian period in the Western Hemisphere and the oldest dated boomerang in the world.

A very large cemetery, estimated to contain perhaps 1,000 individuals, was also discovered. A pointed oak digging stick, radiocarbon-dated at nearly 5000 BC, was found with the burials, and some of the human bone was directly dated to about 4000 BC. It was expected that further investigation at Little Salt Spring would provide abundant evidence of material culture, as well as new insights into the subsistence practices and environmental adaptations of these early Floridians.

The Hoko River site, on western Washington's Olympic Peninsula overlooking the Strait of Juan de Fuca, was yielding a remarkably well-preserved record of ancient Northwest Coast culture, dating back to about 500 BC. Because the site deposits are waterlogged, greatly retarding normal processes of decay, fishing equipment, basketry, cordage, woodworking tools, stone knives set in wooden hafts, and other normally perishable items were being recovered.

A clear picture of a rich and flourishing culture, probably directly ancestral to that of the Makah Indians who inhabit the area today, was emerging from the excavations, which were being conducted by a team from Washington State University. Hoko River is only a few miles from the site of Ozette, which yielded similarly spectacular evidence. The materials from these sites were being preserved at the Makah Cultural and Research Center at Neah Bay.

There was a resurgence of interest in the possibility of early Celtic occupation of northeastern North America. That Viking adventurers reached American shores in pre-Columbian times is now well established, but an old question, recently reopened by Barry Fell, of a migration of pre-Christian-era Celtic peoples into New England remains hotly disputed. It has been claimed that certain rocks with detailed markings on them are Celtic records, but skeptical archaeologists have coun-

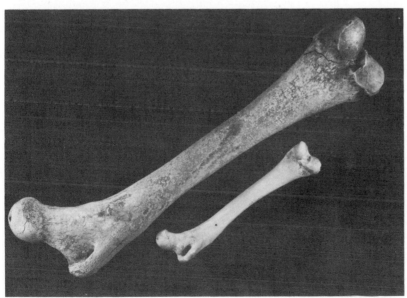

A femur of an ancient bear found in Utah measures about two and a half feet in length (left), more than double that of a present-day small black bear (right). The ancient animal lived about 18,000 years ago and when upright stood nearly 12 feet tall, 3 feet taller than a polar bear and 5 feet taller than an average grizzly.

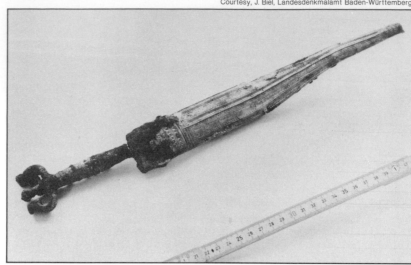

A gold dagger was among the many ornate objects found near Stuttgart, West Germany, in the tomb of a Celtic chieftain who died about 550 BC.

tered that the so-called symbols probably represent simply a biased selection of a few suggestive markings chosen from a vastly larger number of markings of natural or accidental origin. Many stone structures claimed by Fell and others to be of early Celtic origin are alternatively identified as belonging to the much later Colonial American period. In a critical review of the problem, Anne Ross and Peter Reynolds stated their opinion that the evidence presented thus far in support of the theory of an early Celtic migration to the New World is totally inconclusive.

Investigations by Michael J. Snarskis at the site of Turrialba in central Costa Rica produced significant new evidence of Paleo-Indian occupation in Central America. Large leaf-shaped projectile points, thinned at their bases by the removal of long slender fluting flakes from either surface, were found, along with raw materials, cores, and working debris indicating that the artifacts were made on the spot. Some of the Paleo-Indian points are of the North American Clovis fluted type, while one clearly represents the South American stemmed fishtail type, which is also fluted. This suggests that Central America was a boundary zone between two major early North American and South American lithic traditions. Further excavations at Turrialba were expected to be of great importance in evaluating early Paleo-Indian cultural relationships.

At Taima-taima in Venezuela excavations reported in 1978 by a combined North American-South American archaeological team uncovered the skeleton of a juvenile mastodon associated with artifacts of the El Jobo complex. The mid-section of an El Jobo type lanceolate projectile point was found among the pelvic bones of the animal, and other stone tools, as well as the bones of horse and sloth, were found nearby. Radiocarbon assay of small woody fragments associated with the mastodon bones indicated that the finds date between 11,000 and 12,000 BC. These discoveries add to the evidence for a distinctive early Paleo-Indian big-game hunting tradition in South America.

Abrigo do Sol in the state of Mato Grosso, Brazil, on the southwestern edge of the Amazon basin, produced evidence suggesting human occupation in the tropical jungles of South America perhaps as early as 7000 to 10,000 BC. The excavations, which had been extended to a depth of several meters, uncovered well-made, surface-modeled and incised, unpainted pottery in the upper levels. A few small gold artifacts also occurred there. In lower levels crudely chipped flakes, cores, scrapers, and grinding tools were found. Many incised markings, including animal representations and female symbols, occur on stones found both at the surface and at considerable depth, suggesting that the site may have a long history as an important ceremonial location. The excavations were being carried out by Eurico Miller of the Archaeological Museum of the state of Rio Grande do Sul.

—C. Melvin Aikens

Architecture and civil engineering

How people react to new architecture is a lively topic of debate among architects, engineers, social scientists, and almost everyone who uses buildings. What do people like about their new buildings?

Some of the structures which received professional attention in 1978, designed for diverse uses and in different settings, also received popular acclaim. These buildings attract people by the thousands. They are already called "landmarks," and they are playing major roles in revitalizing their cities.

What do these buildings have in common? They are, first and foremost, places where people enjoy seeing other people. They are brightly lit, with colorful signs and graphics. They are well connected to urban streets and subway systems, encouraging use by many people; they glorify the open, public realm, as if the street life of the historical piazza and boulevard had now found its counterpart in contemporary architecture.

Opened in downtown Boston in 1978 was Quincy Market's North Building, the third structure of the historical trio of Greek Revival-style buildings that comprise the Faneuil Hall Marketplace. Originally a political forum as well as a wholesale marketplace, the area was developed by Mayor Joseph Quincy in 1826 as Boston's first public food market. It remained active as a produce trade center for 130 years, but then began to show signs of urban decay associated with its crowded location between the waterfront and deteriorating downtown areas. Beginning in 1968, under the leadership of the Boston Redevelopment Authority, the buildings were acquired for restoration and adaptive reuse by the Rouse Co., urban developers, and Benjamin Thompson & Associates, Inc., architects. The central building, featuring Greek-temple porticos and a copper-roofed dome, was expanded by glazed porches along the sides and its twin companions, the North and South buildings, had their granite facades refurbished. The three structures now splendidly house a great variety of small shops and restaurants, which attract some 30,000 people on an average day. The major contribution of modern architecture has been the glazed side porches, with orange canvas canopies and doors that slide up into the roof, opening the market in the summer months. The effect is like sitting in a lively sidewalk cafe alongside a medieval market square.

People also throng the Gallery on Market St., the central east-west thoroughfare of downtown Philadelphia as laid out in William Penn's 1683 plan. In 1978 the viability of that plan was expressed by the popular success of this new urban marketplace, which marries the best qualities of a typical suburban shopping mall and the main retail core of a city. The Gallery at Market East is located along the north side of Market St., directly above the public subway lines and almost in the shadow of City Hall's 512-ft tower that marks the center of Philadelphia. The Gallery is a new element in the center of town—an enclosed, skylit, colorful, multilevel set of walkways. Unlike a typical modern street, the Gallery gives predominance to communication over transportation; like a medieval street, it promotes face-to-face contact, casual interaction, and exchange. It contains 405,000 sq ft of building area and has been tremendously successful, attracting more than 50,000 people a day to its 125 shops and restaurants on four levels.

Like the Faneuil Hall Marketplace, the Gallery at Market East was developed by the Rouse Co. The architects were Bower Fradley Lewis Thrower, Philadelphia, and RTKL Associates, Inc., Baltimore. Their work has succeeded in achieving some of the civic intentions of Philadelphia's planners and architects, especially those of the late Louis Kahn, whose images of the good life and the good society were focused on a lively, open, democratic city center.

The new Eaton Centre in Toronto, which contains stores, offices, and an enclosed gallery, looks like a white luxury liner docked on Yonge St. The gallery is a

Faneuil Hall Marketplace in Boston, originally completed in 1826 (above), has recently been restored and now houses many shops and restaurants (left). Added in the restoration were glazed side porches that can be opened up in the summer.

glistening white, as are the enclosing wall panels of the stores and office buildings. The result is startling. But even more startling are the size and complexity of the Centre. Its 15-ac site encloses an area comparable in size to New York's Times Square. The Galleria Mall is 860 ft long and 90 ft high. When completed, the multiuse complex will have six million square feet, including a new department store and two office towers. The developers are the Cadillac Fairview Corp. Ltd. and the Eaton Co.; the architects are Bregman + Hamann and the Zeidler Partnership, Toronto.

Eaton Centre is strategically located between two subway stops, and the gallery will connect two department stores in the now classic plan of suburban malls. But, despite its dramatic impact on downtown Toronto, questions remain concerning the Centre's relationship to Yonge St., Toronto's traditional entertainment and shopping street. Will Eaton Centre siphon off all public life, or will it stimulate new vitality in its neighborhood?

New York City is famous for its skyscrapers and their spectacular silhouettes. Since the development of open-air plazas at Lever House (1952) and the Seagram Building (1958), the ground level of skyscrapers has attracted attention as well. During recent months a major new concept emerged in the heart of Manhattan at the base of the 59-story, 915-ft-high office headquarters of Citicorp. The new Citicorp Center raises the first floor of its office building more than 100 ft above the street and encloses under the building an open plaza and a skylit atrium. Directly open to the subways, the atrium is an entrance portal to the city; it is also, like a public square, a place for people to meet and to pursue such urban recreations as window-shopping and people-watching.

Since the 1960s the New York City Planning Commission has encouraged the creation of public spaces.

In the Citicorp Center, the public realm is magnificently served in this respect by the private owner. The chief architects, Hugh Stubbins & Associates, and the structural engineers, LeMessurier Associates, responded to the challenge to urban architecture and building technology by bringing the building's tower to the ground on only four points and by developing a complex system to counteract the forces of both gravity and wind. The structure has four columns located, not at the corners of the building, but at the center line of each facade; from the street level the building seems almost completely open to the skylit atrium and plaza.

The year was also notable for the opening of the new East Building of the National Gallery in Washington, D.C., which brought to the world of art museums some of the qualities of public life that characterize the urban galleries of Philadelphia, Toronto, and New York. Unlike its neighbor, the National Gallery's main building, designed in 1941 in noble Roman style with a grand flight of 40 steps up to a main floor, the East Building sits flat on the ground and is easily entered by one and all. The central space is a triangular court, 80 ft high and lit by a glass roof. The roof structure, a triangulated space frame covering more than a third of an acre, is given dramatic impact by its creation of dappled light on smooth surfaces. The building itself is so dynamic that it encourages exploration of the small galleries that surround the court. The new wing was designed by I. M. Pei & Partners, architects, and Weiskopf & Pickworth, structural engineers, New York.

Perhaps the most significant public structures in cities are not visible above ground at all. The new Washington, D.C., subway, "The Metro," has been hailed by architectural critics as "one of the few new places in Washington that has true grandeur architecturally; it manages to be at once monumental and gracious."

The Gallery at Market East in downtown Philadelphia is an enclosed, skylit, multilevel set of walkways that combines features of a suburban shopping mall with those of the retail center of a large city.

Eaton Centre in Toronto is a multiuse complex that includes stores, offices, and an enclosed gallery 860 feet long and 90 feet high.

Indeed, the Metro is a splendid addition to the public realm. The architectural design evokes the vaults of the great interiors of the Roman public baths, which also inspired the waiting rooms of such railroad terminals as New York's Pennsylvania Station (demolished in 1965) and Grand Central Station, and Chicago's Union Station.

In the Metro the vaults are grand, soaring elements of space and structure; they are also an economic merger of architecture and civil engineering. The subway architects, Harry Weese Associates, and the engineers, DeLeuw Cather and Co., were given parallel credits for the design. After studies of other subways in Europe and the United States they recommended, instead of the conventionally framed box, an unimpeded vault because of its economic and aesthetic advantages. The architects sought to "treat the envelope as the sky," and therefore kept the platforms, mezzanines, and even the escalators away from the vault walls. The resulting spaces are at their most exciting at Metro Center, where two lines, the Red and the Blue, cross and the vaulted ceilings cut through each other to form a great new civic room. The lighting is generally soft and indirect, except at the platform's edge, where small lights are set into the granite paving. These intense lights define the edge for 600 ft; they remain on all the time as a safety measure but pulsate when a train approaches, making its arrival a dramatic event. As of early 1979 about 15 mi of the Metro had been completed, carrying 135,000 riders a day. It is planned to eventually be a 100-mi system extending from the center of the city to suburban areas.

—Robert Geddes

See also Feature Article: BUILDING TO SAVE ENERGY.

Astronomy

The many fronts on which astronomy advanced in 1978 ranged from the inner solar system to cosmology, testifying to the continually broadening horizon of this science and also to the application of new methods to solve classic problems. An event of popular interest was the solar eclipse of Feb. 26, 1979. Its path of totality extended through the northwest corner of the United States and across Canada. Not until 2017 would another total solar eclipse be visible from any part of the U.S.

Ra-Shalom. Systematic photographic searches with the large Schmidt telescopes at Hale Observatories in California and at the European Southern Observatory in Chile revealed that there are many more Apollo-type asteroids (minor planets that cross the Earth's orbit) than anyone had suspected a few years ago. There are even three known asteroids that revolve around the Sun in less than one year and that have orbits largely inside that of the Earth. These are called Aten-class asteroids, after 2062 Aten, the first example.

The asteroid Ra-Shalom was discovered on a photograph taken in September 1978. Revolving around the Sun in 277.20 days, it has the shortest period of any known asteroid.

The most extreme case is minor planet 2100 Ra-Shalom, which has a mean distance from the Sun of 124.5 million km (1 km = 0.62 mi) and completes a revolution around it in 277. 20 days; this is the shortest period of any known asteroid. It was discovered by Elinor Helin of Hale Observatories on a photograph she had taken Sept. 10, 1978, with the 18-in Schmidt telescope on Palomar Mountain. At the time Ra-Shalom was a 13th-magnitude object 24 million km from the Earth and speeding southwestward about two degrees per day. After a first orbit had been calculated, it was realized that this asteroid was identical with another observed on two nights only in October 1975 at the European Southern Observatory. These early positions, in conjunction with 18 positions measured in September 1978, permitted the calculation of accurate orbital elements. The distance of Ra-Shalom from the Sun ranges between 70.1 million and 178.8 million km. It is among the smallest asteroids known, with a diameter of less than five kilometers. Helin made calculations showing that there is a 50% probability of Ra-Shalom colliding with the Earth during the next 165 million years.

Chiron. Chiron is the unusual solar-system member discovered in October 1977 by Charles Kowal at Hale Observatories (see *1979 Yearbook of Science and the Future* Year in Review: ASTRONOMY). Chiron moves around the Sun in a 50.7-year elliptical orbit that comes inside of that of Saturn and goes out almost as far as that of Uranus. Although this faint, slow-moving body has been designated asteroid 2060, uncertainty remains as to whether Chiron is planetary or cometary in nature.

Shio Oikawa and Edgar Everhart of the University of Denver recently studied the projected motion of Chiron over a span of several million years. At present, the changes in Chiron's orbit are chiefly controlled by the gravitational attraction of Saturn. Whenever a close approach to Saturn occurs, as happened about 2100 BC, very large perturbations of Chiron take place and its orbit is altered in a manner that is sensitive to the precise geometrical circumstances of the encounter. The present orbit of Chiron, though well determined, is not known accurately enough to calculate what the orbit will be after one or more close approaches to Saturn.

Oikawa and Everhart overcame this seeming impasse by a statistical method that involved extensive calculations with a large electronic computer. They assumed 60 very slightly differing sets of elements for the present orbit of Chiron, and then in each of the 60 cases they took the starting elements as exact and traced mathematically the motion of Chiron into the remote future or past, as perturbed by Saturn.

In these 60 numerical experiments it was found that there is about one chance in eight that Saturn's attraction will eventually accelerate Chiron enough to eject it from the solar system. In a typical case, ejection will happen in 3,000,000 years. There are about seven chances in eight that the perturbations by Saturn will cause Chiron's orbit to shrink gradually until after typically 106,000 years Chiron will be under the gravitational control of Jupiter. In that case its ultimate fate also will be ejection from the solar system, either by Jupiter's action alone or by the joint action of Jupiter and Saturn.

These results show that Chiron's orbit is not stable over very long time spans, and Chiron is unlikely to have been an original member of the solar system. As far as the dynamical evolution of its orbit is concerned, it resembles a comet.

Pluto's satellite. The unexpected discovery of a close satellite of the planet Pluto was announced by the U.S. Naval Observatory in July 1978. Pluto is routinely photographed with the observatory's 155-cm astrometric reflector at Flagstaff, Ariz., in order to determine precise positions of the planet. While measuring these plates, J. W. Christy noted that on some of them the planet's image appeared to have a slight elongation not detectable in neighboring star images. This elongation was then found on plates exposed on five more nights in 1978, and on five in 1970 and two in 1965. It was also confirmed on photographs taken in 1977 with the McDonald Observatory's 208-cm reflector and in 1978 with the Cerro Tololo Inter-American Observatory's four-meter telescope in Chile.

On the photographs in question Pluto resembles an unresolved double star, with a maximum elongation of about 0.9 sec of arc in position angles 170° and 350°. The probable interpretation is that Pluto has a satellite

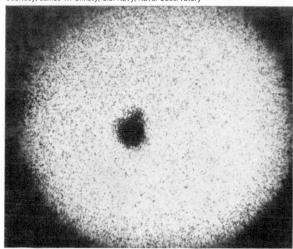

A photographic image of Pluto reveals a slight elongation at the upper right. Astronomers attribute this to the presence of a satellite of the planet.

two to three magnitudes fainter than itself, moving around the planet in a nearly circular orbit of about 20,000-km radius with a period of 6.3867 days—the same as the rotational period of Pluto. Such an equality could have resulted from long-continued tidal friction.

The mass of Pluto, as calculated from its satellite's motion, is only $1/140{,}000{,}000$ that of the Sun. If this value is even approximately correct, Pluto is a small object hardly worthy of being called the ninth planet and incapable of producing significant perturbations in the motions of Uranus and Neptune. It would follow that Percival Lowell's prediction of Pluto's existence from such perturbations was unfounded, and that the discovery of Pluto in 1930 was the fortunate result of an extensive but blind search. The name Charon has been proposed for Pluto's satellite by its discoverer.

The Tunguska event. A Czechoslovakian astronomer, Lubor Kresak, recently proposed the most plausible explanation of the remarkable event of June 30, 1908, when an object collided with the Earth in a remote area of central Siberia, near the Tunguska River. A brilliant fireball was seen; a deafening explosion was heard at distances of up to 1,000 km, and a large tract of forest was devastated.

For some years it was supposed that the impacting object was an unusually large meteorite or a small asteroid. But examination of the site by E. L. Krinov several decades ago revealed no large craters, nor was any considerable amount of meteoritic material found thereabouts. Therefore, several astronomers, including Kresak, suggested that the Tunguska object had been a small comet.

According to Kresak the body that collided with the Earth was an extinct fragment separated from the nucleus of Comet Encke. He supported his contention by noting the absence of major cratering, which indicates that the impacting object was of low density, as comet nuclei are supposed to be. The direction in space from which the object approached is known from eyewitness reports and from the pattern of fallen trees. It agrees well with the radiant of the annual Beta Taurid meteor shower; this shower is caused by debris from Comet Encke and peaks at the time of year of the Tunguska event.

The probable mass of the impacting body before it entered the Earth's atmosphere was about 10^8 to 10^9 kg, according to the Soviet astronomer V. A. Bronshten. This corresponds to a diameter of roughly 100 m for the object, which was completely destroyed before reaching the ground. A comet nucleus this small would be extinct rather than active, Kresak noted; that is, it would no longer yield appreciable amounts of gas when warmed by solar radiation. For several weeks in June (shortly before striking the Earth), the object was so placed in the evening sky that it might have been observed as a comet if it had been active instead of extinct.

All the evidence, said Kresak, is consistent with the Tunguska object having been a dead fragment of Comet Encke and moving in nearly the same orbit. There is thus no need for the speculations about the event involving a nuclear explosion, antimatter, a black hole, or an alien spacecraft.

Novae. On the night of Sept. 9–10, 1978, visual observers in Canada, Arizona, and Japan discovered a new 7th-magnitude star near Rho Cygni. Nova Cygni 1978 was brightest (magnitude 6.1) on September 12 and then faded steadily, reaching 11 by mid-January 1979. Before it exploded the nova had been recorded as an extremely faint star (magnitude 20) on photographs taken in the 1950s. Shortly after maximum light the spectrum of the nova showed interstellar absorption lines of sodium and ionized calcium; from the strength of these lines the nova's distance from the Earth could be estimated at about 1,300 parsecs (1 parsec = 19.2 trillion miles).

WZ Sagittae is a recurrent nova, normally of magnitude 15.5, which temporarily brightened to 7.0 in 1913 and to 7.7 in 1946. The third observed outburst occurred in 1978, with maximum light (magnitude 7.9) about December 1. By early January the star had dimmed to 13. This rapid fading characterized all three outbursts.

Attention was called in 1978 by British astronomer David A. Allen to an unusual star, AS 239, which he suggested might be a very slow nova that reached maximum light around 1940. It is located on the boundary between the constellations Ophiuchus and Sagittarius. It was first recorded in the early 1940s as a 12th-magnitude star with bright hydrogen lines in its spectrum. During the following three decades AS 239 faded dramatically, in 1950 being magnitude 15 and in 1976 magnitude 18 or 19; in February 1978, it was only

19–20. Its spectrum also changed drastically. Spectrograms of 1943 and 1945 show AS 239 as a very hot blue star, with many high-excitation emission lines. In 1978, using the 3.9-m reflecting telescope of the Anglo-Australian Observatory, Allen found that AS 239 was spectroscopically a cool star of class M, much redder than in the 1940s. This reddening is attributed to dust grains that have been condensing in the star's neighborhood to form a thick circumstellar shell.

AS 239 may be either a peculiar slow nova or else a symbiotic star, a binary having a red and a blue component, with the blue component undergoing occasional major novalike outbursts. Several such symbiotic systems are already known. The present extreme faintness of AS 239 gravely hampers its detailed study.

Interstellar matter. The space between the stars is pervaded by an extremely rarefied gas and a thin sprinkling of small solid grains that dim the light of background stars. By the beginning of 1979 radio astronomers had recognized a total of about 40 species of organic molecules in the interstellar gas from their characteristic microwave absorption lines. These molecules range from such simple ones as hydrogen (H_2) and hydroxyl (OH) to acetaldehyde (CH_3CHO), ethanol (CH_3CH_2OH), and methyl formate (CH_3COOH).

The presence of complex molecules in interstellar space is puzzling. It is difficult to imagine them having been built up from atoms or simpler molecules, since the gas density is so low that encounters between individual atoms or molecules are far too infrequent. A challenging suggestion as to how these complex molecules originated was advanced by Carl Sagan and Bishun N. Khare of Cornell University. It was an outgrowth of their extensive laboratory experiments intended to throw light on the origin of life by simulating processes in the solar nebula from which the Earth and planets are believed to have formed. In these experiments mixtures of cosmically abundant gases such as methane (CH_4), ammonia (NH_3), and water (H_2O) are subjected to ultraviolet light or electric discharges. The results of such treatment are tarry brown residues that Sagan and Khare named tholins. Tholins are complex mixtures the properties and composition of which depend on the energy source used and the precursor materials. The analysis of these mixtures is difficult but was being actively pursued in the Cornell University laboratory. The investigators found in the tholins a majority of the kinds of molecules detected in interstellar space.

On the basis of this research the Cornell group proposed that the interstellar solid grains are composed of tholins and that the more complex interstellar gas molecules are their degradation products. The grains, Sagan maintained, were ejected from solar nebulae by radiation pressure and by stellar winds from cool stars during their early evolution. Several processes could gradually destroy such grains, such as ultraviolet starlight and collisions with cosmic rays.

Sagan and his co-workers pointed out that the connection of this picture with the origin of life on Earth is at most indirect. While complex organic molecules could have formed abundantly in the primitive solar nebula, the Earth's surface was probably molten during its early history, and so any extraterrestrial molecules on the surface would have been destroyed. Only after the Earth had cooled down could the organic syntheses take place in the oceans and atmosphere that led eventually to terrestrial life.

Gamma-ray line. Mapping the sky at gamma-ray wavelengths with satellites and balloon-borne instruments revealed a diffuse general flux from extragalactic space against which the narrow, brilliant band of the Milky Way stands out, brightest at the center of our Galaxy. These features are observed by their continuum radiation (that showing continuous, nondiscrete changes in intensity). However, astrophysicists have long anticipated that gamma-ray emission lines should also appear, resulting from the interaction of matter

A multilens telescope containing 80 small apertures gathers laser light reflected from the Moon. Its design enables it to collect much light from a small area.

The spiral shapes of most galaxies may be caused by localized chain reactions of exploding stars. Basing their theoretical model on observations of two galaxies, astronomers used a computer to simulate the evolution of galactic forms. The computer-generated symbols at the left match well with a superimposed photograph of galaxy M81.

and antimatter. In particular, when an electron and positron annihilate each other, their masses are completely converted into energy that is radiated, usually in the form of two gamma-ray photons of 511 kv energy. (The corresponding wavelength is 0.0024 Å.)

Thus, a major event of 1978 in gamma-ray astronomy was the unambiguous detection of the 511-kv emission line from the center of our Galaxy, by Marvin Leventhal and his colleagues at Bell Laboratories and Sandia Laboratories. Their observations were made with a gamma-ray telescope flown in a balloon from Alice Springs, Australia. It collected data for 17.3 hours at a level above 99.7% of the Earth's atmosphere. This telescope, which was pointed alternately at the galactic center and at a comparison area of the sky, had a field of view 15° across. The gamma-ray detector consisted of a large crystal of pure germanium, which included electronic components that allowed it to provide a plot of the number of gamma-ray photons detected at different photon energies. The success of the experiment hinged on the excellent energy resolution of the telescope.

The gamma-ray spectrum of the galactic center was found to show, superimposed on the continuum of gamma-ray emission, a sharp line at an energy of 511 ($\pm$1) kv. The strength of this line indicated a flux of 12 ($\pm$2) photons per square meter per second at the top of the atmosphere.

The line indicates the presence of large numbers of positrons near the galactic center. A small number of the positrons are without doubt the result of cosmic-ray collisions with interstellar particles, but as of 1979 the origin of most of them remained an unresolved question. An attractive possibility is that they were produced

as a result of supernova explosions. In such explosions heavy elements are synthesized on a large scale. Many of the stable atomic species are produced first as unstable radioactive elements that often decay with the emission of a positron. A second suggestion involves radio pulsars, rapidly rotating neutron stars like that in the Crab Nebula, the radiations of which are powered by a gradual loss of rotational energy. Some models of radio pulsars predict a copious ejection of positrons.

Other, more exotic suggestions for the origin of the positrons at the galactic center involve black holes. An eventual decision among these possibilities was expected to be made possible from observations of other gamma-ray lines predicted. Groups at the University of New Hampshire and in France made gamma-ray balloon experiments to detect the 511-kv line, but detailed results had not been published as of early 1979.

Gravitational waves. An important astronomical confirmation of Albert Einstein's general theory of relativity was reported in late 1978 by Joseph H. Taylor, Lee Fowler (both at the University of Massachusetts), and Peter McCulloch (of the University of Tasmania). According to general relativity, gravitational waves should be radiated by massive objects during close encounters with other massive objects. Traveling at the speed of light, these waves would reveal themselves as an alternate expansion and contraction of space as they pass by. But so weak is this gravitational radiation that laboratory experiments to detect it from cosmic sources have led to no sure result. In particular, the bursts of gravitational radiation reported since 1968 by University of Maryland researchers have not been detected in careful searches by other groups.

The most promising astronomical test object for confirmation of the theory is the pulsar PSR 1913 + 16 in the constellation Sagitta, discovered in 1974 by Taylor and R. A. Hulse. This is a binary system composed of a neutron star that emits sharp radio pulses every 0.059 second and an unobserved companion star. The pulse period varies slightly in a cycle of 0.3230 day, being shorter when the radio pulsar in its orbital motion is approaching the Earth and longer when the radio pulsar is receding from it. General relativity predicts that the binary system PSR 1913 + 16 should emit gravitational waves. The energy loss should cause a contraction of the orbit and therefore a very gradual decrease in the orbital period. The observational test applied by Taylor's group was the measurement of this period decrease.

The necessary observations were made with the 305-m radio telescope at Arecibo, P.R., over a 4.1-year span, and consisted of precise timings of pulses at frequencies of 430 and 1,410 MHz. The large number of observations and high accuracy permitted evaluation of several other effects from which a complete specification of the orbit could be derived. The orbital period was found to be shortening at the rate of 0.00010 second per year, in good agreement with expectations from general relativity theory.

This investigation resulted in the first determination of the mass of a radio pulsar, 1.39 ($\pm$0.15) solar masses. The companion, at 1.44 ($\pm$ 0.15) solar masses, is probably a neutron star also, although there is a possibility of its being a white dwarf.

Over the years theorists have proposed that gravitational radiation could be produced by such violent events as a supernova explosion or by stellar collapse leading to the formation of neutron stars or black holes. New theoretical work by several groups suggests that the formation of neutron stars provides an efficient mechanism for generating gravitational waves.

As a slowly rotating massive star collapses, it spins faster and faster, eventually becoming strongly flattened. When the collapse ends at a density of 10^{15} g per cc the star has shrunk to 1% of its original radius. The new calculations show that the star lingers long enough in this stage, before further collapse, to develop the correct shape to be a highly effective gravitational-wave radiator.

—Joseph Ashbrook

See also Year in Review: PHYSICS: *General developments.*

Chemistry

Major achievements of the past year in chemistry included the synthesis of the antibiotics erythromycin B and monensin and of a promising antitumor agent, maytansine. Lasers continued to be used to separate isotopes of elements, and new methods were devised for separating deuterium from hydrogen. In a major breakthrough research scientists induced bacteria to manufacture human insulin.

Inorganic chemistry

The number of scientific publications in inorganic chemistry continued to increase at a dramatic rate. For example, in 1978 the journal *Inorganic Chemistry* issued a total of 3,772 pages, compared with 2,714 pages ten years earlier. It was conservatively estimated that the world's publications in inorganic chemistry exceed this number tenfold. Most reports continued to describe basic research, although much of it related to such practical topics as energy.

Caged metal ions. In 1967 C. J. Pedersen at E. I. Du Pont de Nemours and Co. in the U.S. reported the preparation of 33 cyclic polyethers and some of their metal complexes. These complexes are extremely stable, including those that contain alkali metal cations (*e.g.,* Na^+, K^+, and Rb^+), which generally form only very weak complexes. Since that time some of the polyethers have become commercially available and have come to be called crown ethers because of the appearance of their molecular models and their ability to "crown" metal cations by binding them into the centers of their rings.

A schematic representation of 18-crown-6 is shown in (1). Six —CH_2CH_2— groups connect the six oxygen atoms to form the ring, and the name 18-crown-6 signifies a total of 18 atoms (12 carbon and 6 oxygen) in the molecule and 6 oxygen atoms that attach to a central metal ion in the formation of a metal complex. In 1970 J. M. Lehn and co-workers at the University of Strasbourg in France reported the syntheses of related compounds containing both nitrogen and oxygen atoms that bond to the central metal ion. These compounds have properties similar to the crown ethers and are called cryptands.

Recently A. M. Sargeson and his collaborators at the Australian National University in Canberra were able to go one important step beyond the crown and cryptand metal complexes. Whereas these two systems encircle the metal ion, the Australian group was able to prepare a type of molecule that completely encapsulates the metal to produce a complex called a metal sepulchrate. The method of synthesis of the cobalt sepulchrate is shown in (2). The first step in this multiple-step

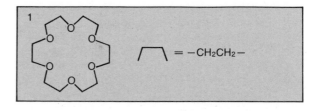

synthesis requires the condensation of formaldehyde (CH_2O) with a bound amine (a) to give the coordinated carbinolamine (b; $—NCH_2OH$), followed then by elimination of water. The resulting imine (c; $CH_2 = N—$) is attacked by ammonia (NH_3) to yield the gem diamine. Addition of another formaldehyde and imine formation allows intramolecular condensation of the gem diamine with the imine, and the first six-membered ring system is formed (d). Doing this again (e) leads to the completed cap (f), and the process is then repeated on the opposite octahedral face to give the completely encapsulated metal ion (g). This process involving a metal that brings organic reactants together for reaction in a specific manner is called a template reaction. The metal serves as the template to direct the building blocks for the final molecule.

Examination of the crystal structure of the complex cation $[Co(sepulchrate)]^{3+}$ shows that cobalt is captured and held inside the sepulchrate cage. This accomplishment makes it possible for the first time to study metals isolated in extremely stable, controlled, caged environments. As of early 1979 it was too early to assess the importance of this class of metal complexes, but it was certain that they would be extensively studied during the years ahead. Already a most significant observation was reported regarding the stereochemistry and the redox (reduction and oxidation) properties of the cobalt complexes. These systems provide the only known stable optically active cobalt(II) complex. (Cobalt(II) and cobalt(III) are the ions Co^{2+} and Co^{3+}, respectively.) Compounds are said to be optically active if they can exist in similar but different forms, much the same as do one's left and right hands. If a solution of right-handed or *dextro*-$[Co(sep)]^{2+}$ is mixed with an exactly equal amount of left-handed or levo-$[Co(sep)]^{3+}$, the optical activity, which for each of the complexes separately would persist for days, is very rapidly lost. In fact, the rate of loss of optical activity, caused by electron transfer between Co(II) and Co(III), is 100,000 times faster than it is for the classical example of $[Co(en)_3]^{2+/3+}$, in which en $=$ $NH_2C_2H_4NH_2$. This observation indicates that there may be some serious shortcomings in the theory used to account for the slow electron transfer in the classical example, because the complexes $[Co(sep)]^{2+/3+}$, which exchange electrons rapidly, have the same electron structure and almost the same Co—N bond distances as do the complexes $[Co(en)_3]^{2+/3+}$.

EXAFS. Applications of the fine structure of spectra found above the absorption edges of X-ray absorption spectra (called extended X-ray absorption fine structure, or EXAFS) are about to revolutionize structural chemistry, in particular inorganic and bioinorganic chemistry. No longer will it be necessary to resort to single-crystal X-ray studies to determine some of the structural aspects of molecules. EXAFS does not require the use of single crystals but can determine the structure of molecules in any physical state and in solution. It can also determine local structures in molecules too large to be determined by X-ray crystallography. Fortunately for inorganic chemistry, EXAFS spectroscopy has proved particularly powerful for studying the environment of metal atoms, specifically the number and kinds of atoms attached to the metal and metal–atom distances.

Unfortunately, high-resolution EXAFS spectra can be obtained only from high-intensity X-ray sources, particularly synchrotron radiation sources, which in 1979 were available in fewer than a dozen laboratories in the world. Synchrotron radiation is produced from beams of high-energy electrons or positrons such as are available at the Stanford Positron Electron Accelerating Ring (SPEAR) of the Stanford Linear Accelerator Center at Stanford University. Investigators from laboratories around the world provide samples for study to the Stanford Synchrotron Radiation Laboratory (SSRL), where work on inorganic and bioinorganic samples has largely been the responsibility of Keith O. Hodgson.

Two examples of significant research reported recently on bioinorganic systems, which could not have been done without the use of EXAFS, are discussed below. The first concerns hemoglobin, a hemoprotein made up of four subunits each containing the protein globin and the metal complex heme. Heme in turn consists of an organic nitrogen-containing, ring-shaped molecule called a porphyrin and an iron atom, which is bound to the porphyrin via its nitrogen atoms. The role of hemoglobin in animal respiration depends on the ability of its iron atoms to reversibly bind molecules of oxygen. Robert G. Shulman and his collaborators at Bell Laboratories, Murray Hill, N.J., studied differences in the bond distances between iron and porphyrin nitrogen in oxygenated and deoxygenated hemoglobin. Unlike information from earlier crystallographic studies, their EXAFS studies show that the iron atom moves much less than 0.7 Å away from the plane of the porphyrin ring, or heme plane, on deoxygenation (one angstrom, Å , is 10^{-8} cm). This significant find suggests that the observed phenomenon of "cooperativity," in which the oxygen affinity of hemoglobin increases with an increase of bound oxygen, cannot be explained by a model which postulates that cooperativity is caused by motion of the iron atom relative to the heme plane on oxygenation. Consequently, factors remote from the iron site seem to be responsible.

The second example involves nitrogen fixation, an important area of very active research by inorganic and bioinorganic chemists (see *1979 Yearbook of Science and the Future* Feature Article: FOOD, FAMINE, AND NITROGEN FIXATION). This is understandable, because the very life cycles of plants and animals depend on nitrogen fixation, the process of converting nitrogen in air to compounds of nitrogen. Chemists have been intrigued but puzzled by the ease with which certain bacteria readily convert the extremely stable nitrogen molecule N_2 into ammonia. During 1978 EXAFS provided important information on the structure of the iron- and molybdenum-containing FeMo (or Mo-Fe) protein component of nitrogenase, which is the metalloenzyme responsible for nitrogen fixation. At present, investigators are optimistic that this could be the breakthrough needed for a detailed understanding of how nitrogenase really works. The research reported was a collaborative effort of Hodgson, R. H. Holm, and coworkers at Stanford University. EXAFS spectroscopy of the FeMo protein and of its cofactor, FeMo-co, showed that the molybdenum environments in these species are similar. Furthermore, the spectra indicated that molybdenum is attached to iron and to sulfur in a MoFeS cluster that was not identified in detail. This information, together with their previous experience with the "simple" syntheses of iron-sulfur clusters somewhat analogous to natural metalloproteins called ferredoxins, prompted the investigators to attempt the preparation of a corresponding cluster containing two species of metal atoms; namely, Fe and Mo. Nature

was kind to them, allowing a specific mixture of $[Et_4N]_2MoS_4$, $FeCl_3$, and $NaOCH_3$ in methanol solution to yield black crystals whose composition is consistent with the formulation $[Et_4N]_3[Mo_2Fe_6S_9(SEt)_8]$, in which $Et = C_2H_5$. The structure (3) of the metal-containing portion of the complex was determined by X-ray crystallography, and it shows two distorted $MoFe_3S_4 (SEt)_3$ cubes connected through a $MoS(SEt)_2Mo$ bridge. Most exciting about this double cluster is that its molybdenum EXAFS spectrum is identical to that for the FeMo protein found in the nitrogenase of the bacterium *Clostridium pasteurianum*. Thus for the first time chemists may well have the structure of the molybdenum sites in nitrogenase, which should assist in better understanding its role in nitrogen fixation.

Solid-state chemistry. Solid-state chemistry, long a subfield of research in inorganic chemistry, has been actively pursued at industrial laboratories in the U.S. and in other countries and at several European universities. In the past decade research activity has increased greatly as a result of interest in new materials having unusual and useful electrical, optical, or magnetic properties.

One group of inorganic compounds known to produce solid materials with important electrical properties are the solid electrolytes, also known as fast-ion conductors or super-ionic conductors. In the most highly conducting of these solids, the cation or occasionally the anion has mobility approaching that of ions in aqueous solution. Thus these materials owe their conductivity to ion migration rather than to the electron migration characteristic of metals and semiconductors. Fast-ion conductors have existing and potential applications in various devices including chemical sensors and batteries. For example, in 1967 Joseph T. Kummer and Neill Weber of Ford Motor Company Research Laboratories introduced the concept of the sodium-sulfur battery. In this high–energy-density battery, molten sodium and molten sodium polysulfide are separated by a solid sodium-ion electrolyte called sodium β-alumina. This development sparked interest in the synthesis of improved sodium-ion solid electrolytes. A very promising one was developed recently at the Lincoln Laboratories by John B. Goodenough (now of the University of Oxford) and his associates. A careful consideration of structures led this group to synthesize a new solid having intersecting tunnels of a diameter appropriate to allow ready passage of sodium cations (Na^+). Because the formula and systematic name are cumbersome, they coined the name nasicon, for Na^+ super-ionic conductor.

In addition to the synthesis of better ionic conductors, there is considerable interest in a fundamental description of how ions achieve high mobility in solids. One way in which solid-state inorganic chemists contribute to this understanding is through the synthesis of a series of closely related solids in which the mobile ion differs. For example, the first In⁺ (indium) and Tl⁺ (thallium) halide conductors were discovered by Duward F. Shriver and Donald H. Whitmore and co-workers at Northwestern University, Evanston, Ill. They were guided in their search for new ionic conductors by variable-temperature Raman spectroscopy, which displays spectral-line broadening at temperatures where disordered phases occur. (Good ionic conductors are characterized by disordered arrays of the mobile ions and vacancies over the possible sites in the crystal lattice.) Their studies indicate that the In⁺ and Tl⁺ ions, which have $d^{10}s^2$ electronic configurations, are less mobile than Cu⁺ (copper) and Ag⁺ (silver) ions, which have d^{10} outer electron configurations. The mobility difference is attributed to a shape difference between the two types of electron clouds.

—Fred Basolo

Physical chemistry

At the core of physical chemistry, as with other disciplines, lies instrumentation, the tool of the scientist's trade. But two factors, inflation and the increasing complexity of modern scientific instruments, are rapidly driving the price of doing research beyond the reach of many scientists. Finding solutions to this ever more serious dilemma was a preoccupation of those involved in physical chemistry research in 1978. The importance of financial restrictions was well illustrated by the many new research techniques relying heavily on expensive equipment. Several techniques based on the use of particles and waves to probe the properties of physical systems either were developed or matured into widely used tools.

One possible answer to the problem posed by high prices of new instruments came from the U.S. National Science Foundation. Established in 1978 were six regional research centers to provide access to instruments needed but not affordable by chemists in many academic and industrial institutions. The six centers were Colorado State University and the University of South Carolina (nuclear magnetic resonance), Johns Hopkins University, Baltimore, Md., and the University of Nebraska (mass spectrometry), the University of Arizona (carbon-14 dating), and the University of Pennsylvania (lasers). Typical of the facilities provided were those at the University of Pennsylvania, where a $1.4 million grant was made to pay for salaries and equipment purchases over a four-year period. The Pennsylvania center was to have lasers for ultrafast (picosecond or faster) spectroscopy, for ultra-high-resolution spectroscopy, for infrared laser-induced chemistry, and for conventional flash photolysis.

Laser-induced chemistry. The Pennsylvania laser center is a good example of these new facilities because laser-induced chemistry continued to be a major research topic during 1978. An application of it that

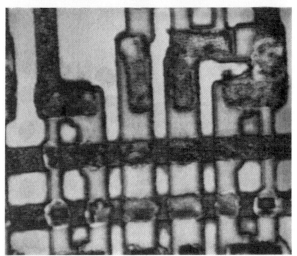

Transistors on a silicon-on-sapphire wafer are viewed through an optical microscope (top) and a newly developed acoustic microscope (bottom). A kind of microscopic sonar, the acoustic instrument reveals internal structure to a depth of one or two microns.

was receiving considerable attention was the separation of isotopes, forms of the same chemical element with different atomic masses. Lasers are thought to be ideal for this task because the frequency of the light they emit can be precisely adjusted to match frequencies absorbed by atoms or molecules containing the isotopes of interest. The laser-excited species can then be separated from the others because they have different physical or chemical properties. If they had been ionized by having absorbed photons from the laser beam, for example, the excited species could be collected by an electric field.

The overriding interest in laser isotope separation has been as a possibly inexpensive means of obtaining uranium-235 for use in nuclear power plants (naturally occurring uranium is mainly uranium-238 from which

M. Hohenstatt, W. Neuhauser, and P. E. Toschek, Institut für Angewandte Physik

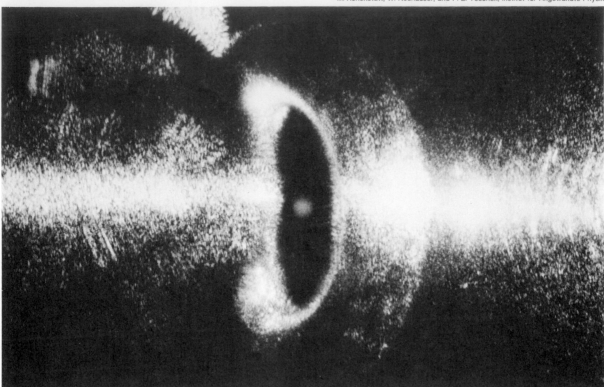

A photomicrograph reveals resonance fluorescence from a cloud of about 50 barium ions (center) confined in an electric field and irradiated by laser light, aimed at developing precise frequency standards.

uranium-235 must be separated). But the separation of other isotopic species is also of interest. For example, experiments in 1978 also provided ways of separating deuterium, the heavy isotope of hydrogen, from ordinary hydrogen. Deuterium oxide (heavy water) is used in large amounts in some types of nuclear reactors as a moderator to slow down energetic neutrons produced when uranium fissions. The reactor can use natural uranium as a fuel, thus avoiding the need for making uranium-235; because the latter can also be used in weapons it contributes to worries about nuclear proliferation and terrorism.

One of the new methods for obtaining deuterium was devised by Sidney W. Benson of the University of Southern California. Benson used a carbon dioxide infrared laser to irradiate dichloroethane. About one in 2,000 molecules of this substance contains an atom of deuterium in place of hydrogen, and only those molecules absorb the laser light and subsequently dissociate. An attractive feature of Benson's process is that billions of pounds of dichloroethane are used each year in the manufacture of polyvinyl chloride, and therefore heavy water could be available as a by-product from chemical plants simply by burning the separated, deuterium-containing material.

Researchers Jack Marling and Irving Herman of the U.S. Department of Energy's Lawrence Livermore (Calif.) Laboratory made use of a different molecule, Freon 123 (CF_3CHCl_2), to obtain deuterium. The Livermore team was able to obtain a 1,400-fold enrichment (increase in deuterium concentration) in one irradiation with a carbon dioxide laser. Marling claimed that Freon 123 meets many of the requirements for economical enrichment of deuterium.

Another feature of lasers is the high flux of energy in a laser beam. Such a flux can influence the way colliding molecules interact with one another and thereby influence the course of chemical reactions. Thomas F. George of the University of Rochester, N.Y., proposed, for example, the use of lasers to intervene in the reaction between two or more species by lowering the energy barrier between them. This process is to be distinguished from the more commonly considered alternative, that of boosting reactants over a barrier by injecting them with energy from a laser beam. As of 1979 George's idea had yet to be demonstrated in interactions between molecules, but a similar effect had been seen in collisions between atoms.

In 1977 Stephen Harris, Jim Young, and their coworkers at Stanford University first reported what have been termed laser-induced collisions in their studies of a mixture of strontium and calcium vapors. The Stanford researchers observed that the probability for the transfer of energy from a strontium atom already in an excited state to a calcium atom during a collision between them increased, for all practical purposes, from zero to a measurable value when laser light of a frequency not absorbed by either strontium or calcium was present. In 1978 this finding was confirmed in an experiment with europium and strontium vapors by Ph. Cahuzac and P. E. Toschek of the Institut für Angewandte Physik der Universität Heidelberg. By monitoring fluorescence emitted from atoms excited during collisions that then decay to lower energy states, both groups of researchers were able to obtain information about the interaction energies of the colliding species.

Methods based on the use of collisions between atoms or molecules in collimated (parallel) beams in a vacuum have for many years been a workhorse for chemists studying the kinetics of reactions. With the addition of lasers that excite the atoms or molecules to specific energy states, even more detailed information has been collected, so-called state-to-state chemistry. One problem with molecular beams has been the low concentration of particles in the beams, so that distinguishing between particles scattered into a detector by way of the collisions of interest and by accident (background) was difficult and experiments were time-consuming.

In 1977 W. Ronald Gentry and Clayton F. Giese of the University of Minnesota modified the molecular beam source (consisting of a furnace to produce the species of interest in vapor form and a collimated orifice through which the particles escaped into an evacuated chamber) by adding electromechanical valves

A pulsed supersonic beam of naphthalene at a temperature of almost absolute zero is produced by adding electromechanical valves (nozzles) to a conventional molecular beam source.

(nozzles) that allowed the creation of pulsed beams about ten microseconds in duration and two centimeters in length. These virtually instantaneous beams may be many orders of magnitude (factors of ten) more intense than a continuous beam, in the same way that the light from a pulsed laser is much more in-

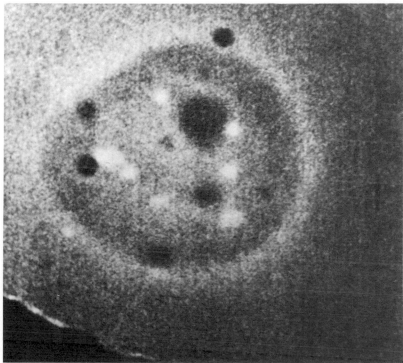

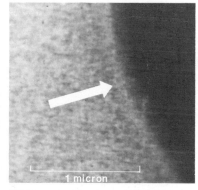

Electron energy-loss spectroscopy can locate minute quantities of low-atomic-weight elements (see text, p. 266). At the left the bright spots are areas in a human blood platelet with high concentrations of a form of serotonin containing fluorine, a tracer used to determine its distribution. In the cross section of a microelectronic circuit (above) the arrow points to a string of carbon atoms (white line).

Courtesy, Argonne National Laboratory

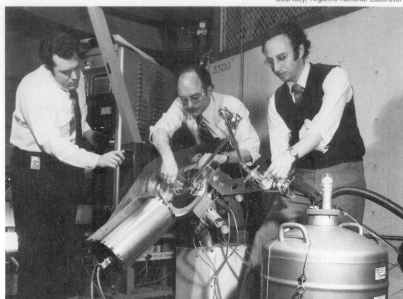

Richard K. Brown, Jack M. Williams, and Arthur J. Schultz (left to right) align components of a neutron diffractometer at Argonne (Ill.) National Laboratory. With other colleagues the three used the neutron diffraction method to study the molecular structure of a large and complicated organometallic complex (see text below).

tense than that from a continuous-wave laser.

A second advantage of the modified source is that the pulsed-nozzle method emits beams with an effective temperature near 0 K (absolute zero); that is, all the particles in the beam have nearly the same vibrational and rotational quantum numbers. Richard E. Smalley of Rice University, Houston, Texas, took advantage of this feature to study, for example, the redistribution of energy into the various vibrational modes of naphthalene following its excitation by the absorption of laser light. Determining where and how fast energy injected into a molecule by a laser is redistributed is a topic of intense interest to laser chemists.

Electron microscopy. An increasingly interesting instrument for electron microscopy is the scanning transmission electron microscope (STEM), developed in the early 1970s by Albert V. Crewe of the University of Chicago, because it combines the high resolution of conventional transmission electron microscopes with the versatility associated with the scanning variety. Recently, a new feature was added to the STEM by David C. Joy and Dennis M. Maher of Bell Laboratories, Murray Hill, N.J., and by Michael S. Isaacson and Crewe at Chicago. The conventional instrument forms images by measuring the intensity of electrons transmitted through a sample. Contrast is formed when electrons are scattered out of their paths by such objects as imperfections in crystalline materials. But another fate of some electrons is that they lose energy as they pass through, and the energy losses are characteristic of the specific elements in the material with which the electrons interact. Thus by using a detector that can measure the energy of the transmitted electrons, researchers can determine the spatial distributions of specific elements in a sample.

In a report in 1978, for example, Joy, Maher, and Jonathan L. Costa of the National Institutes of Health Clinical Center, Bethesda, Md., applied the energy-loss method to the mapping of the distribution of difluoroserotonin in human blood platelets. The researchers were able to detect less than 10^{-20} g of fluorine in an area of ten square nanometers and thus could localize fluorinated tracer molecules with biological activity (one nanometer=one billionth of a meter). This capability is of particular interest because fluorine is difficult to detect by other methods. The technique was developed at Bell primarily for assessing the concentrations of low-atomic-weight impurities that can be detrimental to the operation of microelectronic circuits.

Neutron diffraction. Neutron diffraction, the scattering of neutrons by the atoms within solids, liquids, and gases and the study of the phenomena that arise from this process, is a technique with a steadily growing following. At present, the use of neutrons requires journeying to a reactor, the only source of intense beams. But a new, very-high-intensity pulsed neutron source based on the use of a proton synchrotron (accelerator) will soon become available at Argonne (Ill.) National Laboratory. Construction is to begin in 1979. This pulsed source will enable new types of experiments to be done and will greatly reduce the time needed to collect data in presently feasible studies. More important, the availability of the pulsed source is expected to increase interest in neutrons and draw more researchers into the field.

One demonstration of the usefulness of neutrons was provided in 1978 by Jack M. Williams of Argonne and his colleagues there and at Oak Ridge (Tenn.) National Laboratory. These chemists used neutron diffraction to study the molecular structure of an unusual organometallic complex, $\{Th[(CH_3)_5C_5]_2H(\mu\text{-}H)\}_2 \cdot$ $C_6H_5CH_3$, the largest and most complicated structure yet determined entirely by neutron diffraction. The experiment considerably expanded the range of the neutron technique; in the past, some crystallographers had argued that redundant X-ray data also had to be used in determining such structures. Moreover, neutrons are much more sensitive to the presence of hydrogen atoms than are X-rays, a feature that enhances the technique's usefulness when examining organic materials.

This by no means covers all the new techniques employed by physical chemists during the past year. Others involved the use of an elementary particle, the muon, to probe the properties of molecules and solids. Refinements of nuclear magnetic resonance, the absorption by atomic nuclei in a static magnetic field of energy from a radiofrequency field at characteristic frequencies, allowed its use in elucidating the features of solids. And the use of ultraviolet radiation and X-rays from synchrotron radiation sources to study the atomic geometry of solid surfaces was extended.

—Arthur L. Robinson

Applied chemistry

During the past year scientists made advances in the prevention of cancer by identifying potential carcinogens, testing the preventive effects of vitamins and antioxidants, and developing new diagnostic tests for early detection. In the relatively new field of genetic engineering, researchers induced bacteria to manufacture human insulin; a large enzyme was sequenced; and a gene was cloned. Other important studies carried out during 1978 involved developments in cosmochemistry.

Cancer prevention. Because as many as 90% of all cancer cases can be traced to environmental factors (air and water pollution, type and content of diet, food additives, etc.), a noticeable shift in emphasis was taking place in the battle against this disease. Physicians and researchers began stressing "chemoprevention" of cancer before it occurs. Thus, cancer epidemiologists cited the Western high-fat, low-fiber diet as a major contributor to the high rate of colon and breast cancer in the U.S. and suggested changes in nutritional habits.

In investigations of food, nitrogen compounds called N-nitroso compounds were shown to induce cancer in laboratory animals. When tested in a modification of the bacterial assay developed by Bruce Ames of the University of California at Berkeley, they were found to be mutagenic (disruptive to the bacteria's genetic system). Because nitrosamines (in which a nitroso group is attached to nitrogen) may form on frying meats preserved with nitrites, in May the U.S. Department of Agriculture requested the immediate reduction of nitrite

A miniature pilot plant is being used by polymer chemists in an effort to determine the feasibility of reclaiming usable chemicals from wastes of mixed plastic materials.

in meat products from 200 ppm (parts per million) to 120 ppm and ultimately to 40 ppm.

According to two studies reported in June, the conditions under which potentially carcinogenic (cancer-inducing) nitrosamines may form inside the body may be more common than has been realized. William Lijinsky, director of the Frederick Cancer Research Center in Maryland, found that rats and mice fed several common drugs (such as chlordiazepoxide, the active ingredient in the tranquilizer Librium; and oxytetracycline, an antibiotic) will convert them into nitrosamines if their diets also contain nitrites. The conversion occurs frequently enough to cause a significant increase in tumors when those animals are fed these drugs for most of their lives. Based on such studies, the U.S. Food and Drug Administration proposed banning the antihistamine methapyrilene from nonprescription sleeping pills.

The second study, carried out by nutrition researchers including Steven R. Tannenbaum of the Massachusetts Institute of Technology and W. R. Bruce of the Ontario Cancer Institute, found that the nitrites needed for nitrosamine formation can be synthesized in significant concentration in the human intestine. Scientists had previously thought that nitrites had either to be present in the diet or to be formed by bacteria in the saliva. The study showed that the fecal matter of healthy men fed a high-fat, low-fiber diet contained greater amounts of nitrites and nitrates than they ingested with their food, leading Tannenbaum and Bruce to suggest that diet along with natural conversion processes can help explain the high incidence of colon cancer in Western countries. Bruce also detected mutagenic N-nitroso compounds in the fecal matter, but these could be reduced by two- to threefold by adding vitamin C (ascorbic acid) and vitamin E (tocopherol) to the diet. These vitamins are antioxidants that inhibit the formation of N-nitroso compounds from nitrites. The Canadian researchers were able to reduce the fecal mutagen content by increasing the protein and fiber content of the diet.

Like Bruce, John Weisburger, vice-president for research at the American Health Foundation, Valhalla, N.Y., suggested that vitamin C prevents conversion of dietary nitrites to N-nitroso compounds. Weisburger proposed a correlation between vitamin C intake and the decline in stomach cancer in Western countries. As an example, when Japanese migrate to the U.S. and switch to an American diet, their stomach cancer rate declines from the high level of their native country and approaches that of U.S. natives.

Evidence that antioxidants other than vitamins may prevent cancer was reported by Elizabeth K. Weisburger of the National Institutes of Health, Bethesda, Md., who found that the antioxidant butylated hydroxytoluene (BHT) prevents tumors in animals fed powerful carcinogens (N-hydroxy–2-acetylaminofluorene, acetylaminofluorene, and azomethane). Following a study by Michael Sporn at the National Cancer Institute showing that 13-cis-retinoic acid (a form of vitamin A), inhibits bladder cancer in rats and that large doses of natural vitamin A inhibit breast tumors in rats, Warren Koontz and co-workers at the Medical College of Virginia in Richmond began clinical studies to learn if 13-cis-retinoic acid will prevent recurrence of bladder cancer in patients from whom tumors had been removed surgically.

There was increasing emphasis during the year on the search for new methods to detect cancer at a stage early enough for effective treatment. Georg Springer of Northwestern University, Evanston, Ill., developed what may prove to be the earliest chemical warning signal for breast cancer yet devised, a simple skin test that is more than 90% reliable in detecting the cancer. In this procedure a protein called T-antigen, obtained from outdated blood from blood banks, is injected in the skin of the arm. A hard, red patch that forms around the injection site within 24–48 hours indicates adenocarcinoma of the breast, the most common form of the disease.

In June Robert L. Longmire of the Scripps Clinic and Research Foundation, La Jolla, Calif., described a simple blood test useful in monitoring and evaluating the success of therapy for various forms of cancer (breast, lung, stomach, pancreas, and blood-producing organs). In studies of about 200 patients Longmire concluded that blood levels of the serum protein C3DP are usually found in normal individuals in concentrations below 150 micrograms per milliliter (1 microgram=1 millionth of a gram), while in cancer patients, regardless of type of cancer present, levels may be as high as 400 micrograms per milliliter. The C3DP assay can detect a recurring cancer one or two months before the onset of other clinical symptoms.

Genetic engineering. In 1978 federal, state, and city regulatory bodies in the U.S. developed guidelines for recombinant DNA (deoxyribonucleic acid) research in order to avoid the possibility that insertion of a gene from one life-form into an ordinary harmless bacterium might result in a previously unknown deadly or otherwise undesirable pathogen against which man

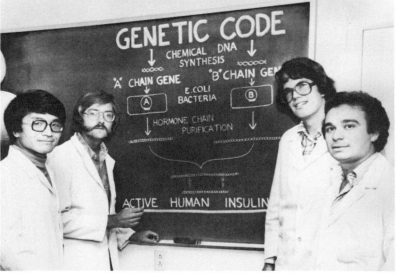

Scientists from the City of Hope National Medical Center and Genentech, Inc. explain how they utilized recombinant DNA techniques to "trick" the common intestinal bacterium Escherichia coli into manufacturing human insulin.

UPI Compix

has no defense. Scientists adhered to these guidelines, maintaining that recombinant DNA technology would prove beneficial in the long run.

Probably the most spectacular triumph of genetic engineering in 1978 was the announcement in September that scientists at the City of Hope National Medical Center, Duarte, Calif., and Genentech, Inc., in South San Francisco, Calif., had employed recombinant DNA techniques to induce the common intestinal bacterium *Escherichia coli* to manufacture human insulin. In the first step City of Hope chemists Arthur Riggs, Keiichi Itakura, Roberto Crea, Tadaaki Hirose, and Adam Kraszewski synthesized separately the two genes that control the production of the two amino-acid chains of the human insulin molecule. This involved piecing together in the correct order the genes' nucleotide building blocks. Next Genentech scientists David Goeddel, Dennis Kleid, Francisco Bolivar, Daniel Yansura, and Herbert Heyneker introduced the synthesized DNA strands—again separately—into rings of bacterial DNA called plasmids. The plasmid gene chosen as the site of insertion was one coding for the synthesis of β-galactosidase, an enzyme *E. coli* employs for the digestion of the sugar lactose. Specifically the gene for each insulin chain was attached near that portion of the plasmid gene called the *lac* operon, which functions as an "on-off" switch for producing β-galactosidase. Consequently, when the altered plasmids were returned to their bacterial hosts and lactose was provided as a nutrient, the genes for both β-galactosidase and insulin chain were switched on together, producing a hybrid molecule composed of both proteins. Finally, to produce an intact, double-chain insulin molecule, the experimenters extracted and purified the two chains from separate bacterial cultures and then joined them chemically.

Although human insulin production by bacteria is presently limited to milligram (about 1/28,000 oz) quantities, Eli Lilly & Co. of Indianapolis planned to scale up the bacterial process for commercial production. If successful, within two to five years human insulin may become available for the first time. It will be especially beneficial to diabetics allergic to insulin derived from cattle and pigs.

After research taking eight years Audree Fowler and Irving Zabin of the University of California at Los Angeles finally succeeded in determining the precise arrangement of amino-acid building blocks in the largest protein yet sequenced, the enzyme β-galactosidase, which consists of a chain of 1,021 amino-acid units. Some idea of the difficulties involved in this work as well as of the advances recently made in protein chemistry may be gained from the fact that in 1958 Frederick Sanger received the Nobel Prize for chemistry for determining the amino-acid sequence in bovine insulin, a molecule consisting of only 51 amino-acid units. Fowler and Zabin claimed that researchers can now learn

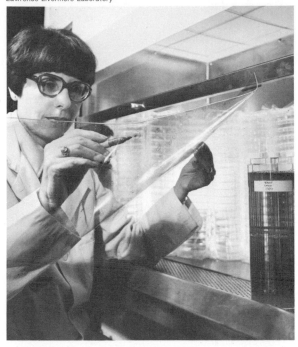

Biologist counts hamster embryo cell colonies grown in polystyrene container that can hold as many cells as 150 culture dishes could. Many cells are needed to test the ability of exhaust pollutants to alter DNA.

more about the connection between genes and protein production by comparing the sequences of the β-galactosidase enzymes produced by different genetic mutants of *E. coli*. They also claimed that knowledge of the enzyme's structure will lead to more detailed knowledge of its functions within the cell.

While rumors of the first cloning of a human being abounded in the news media, a cloning project of more modest but more realistic proportions actually succeeded. After five years of research Bert O'Malley, Savio Woo, Achilles Dugaiczyk, and other scientists of the Baylor College of Medicine, Houston, Texas, purified and cloned for the first time a hormone-regulated gene. It was the gene for ovalbumin, a major chicken egg glycoprotein the synthesis of which is under steroid hormone control in the oviduct of the hen. Until the Baylor scientists' recent success the amount of ovalbumin DNA available was too small to permit close scrutiny of its action, but afterward the amount was increased by a factor of 10^{15} (one followed by 15 zeros). One of the major goals of molecular biologists is to learn how hormones facilitate specific protein syntheses. O'Malley believes that such knowledge will lead within the next decade to cures for hormone-defect diseases, which will be treated by inserting the correct genes back into cells.

Another exception to molecular biology's central dogma that DNA begets RNA (ribonucleic acid), which then begets proteins was found when Heinz Fraenkel-

Courtesy, R. Ganapathy, J. T. Baker Chemical Company

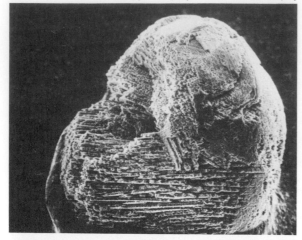

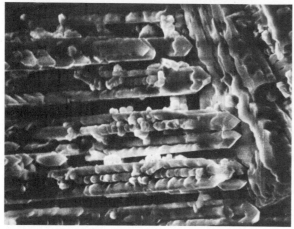

Silicate spherule recovered from sediments at the bottom of the Pacific Ocean was determined by chemical analysis to be a remnant of space debris probably formed when the solar system originated. Scale bars measure 100 (top) and 10 micrometers.

Conrat and Masato Ikegami at the University of California at Berkeley discovered in normal cells an enzyme that makes RNA copies from other RNA molecules. Scientists previously had believed that such enzymes are made only when certain viruses, which rely on RNA instead of DNA for their genetic material, infect plant cells.

Cosmochemistry. A major unsolved problem in cosmochemistry is the determination of the factors that led to the origin of life on the Earth, which occurred about 3½ billion years ago. One of the most recent attempts to simulate the conditions that generated the amino acids, proteins, and other biological building blocks on the primitive Earth was reported in July by Noam Lahav, David White, and Sherwood Chang of the University of Jerusalem, the University of Santa Clara, Calif., and the National Aeronautics and Space Administration's (NASA's) Ames Research Center at Moffett Field, Calif., respectively. The researchers tested

their theory that under fluctuating conditions of temperature and humidity single amino acids formed into long chains called peptides on the surface of clay particles that act as a catalyst. They did so by repeatedly exposing different clay minerals treated with solutions of glycine, the simplest amino acid, sequentially to dehydration at 60° C (140° F), heating at 94° C (201.2° F), and rehydration with water in order to reproduce the daily and seasonal fluctuations on the primitive Earth. Extraction of the products from the clay and determination of their chemical composition with an amino-acid analyzer showed that long amino-acid chains were produced more easily at a given temperature with clay than in the absence of it and that peptide production was greater when moisture and temperature fluctuated. Lahav, White, and Chang proposed that in the primitive Earth the same moisture and temperature fluctuations could have led to formation of complex peptides and ultimately to the precursors of the giant protein molecules required for the maintenance of life.

By using neutron activation analysis and other modern analytical techniques R. Ganapathy of the J. T. Baker Chemical Co., Phillipsburg, N.J., Paul W. Hodge of the University of Washington at Seattle, and Donald E. Brownlee of the California Institute of Technology demonstrated that the tiny silicate spherules found buried in sediments from the Pacific Ocean bottom are almost certainly remnants of space debris probably formed at the same time that the solar system originated, a conclusion suspected but previously unproven. Neutron bombardment of the spherules followed by measurement of the characteristic gamma radiation emitted from them by each element showed that the concentrations of several trace elements (including strontium, scandium, osmium, and iridium) were almost exactly the same as their calculated concentrations in the primitive solar system.

Ever since the Italian astronomer Giovanni Virginio Schiaparelli reported the peculiar markings on Mars in 1877, the origin of these *canali* (erroneously translated into English as "canals" rather than "channels") has been a subject of speculation. A century later in 1978 Yuk Ling Yung of the California Institute of Technology and J. P. Pinto of the Goddard Institute for Space Studies in New York City, proposed that the channels were formed by the action of liquid hydrocarbons. Assuming that the original Martian atmosphere contained methane, hydrogen, and nitrogen in the ratio of 60:6:1 by volume along with water vapor at 100 millibars atmospheric pressure (1.45 psi), Yung and Pinto calculated that photochemical reactions could have converted the methane to a hydrocarbon layer one meter thick in the relatively short geological time span of ten million years. As the Martian atmosphere became depleted of hydrogen (the lightest element known), the oxygen formed by photochemical decomposition of water vapor would gradually oxidize the hydrocarbons to carbon monoxide, carbon dioxide, and other gases. Thus the hydrocarbons would escape but the channels that they cut would remain.

—George B. Kauffman

Organic chemistry

The year 1978 marked the 150th anniversary of Friedrich Wöhler's discovery that the animal product urea is produced by heating ammonium cyanate, an inorganic compound. Urea formed in this way is indistinguishable from urea produced during protein metabolism. Wöhler's simple experiment signaled the birth of organic chemistry as a science because it overthrew the widespread belief that compounds produced in a living cell were somehow different from those of synthetic origin. Since 1828 the laboratory synthesis of natural products has become an industry and a remarkably sophisticated science. In fact, the most notable achievements in organic chemistry during the past year were the syntheses of several exceptionally complex natural products. This article briefly describes a few of these impressive accomplishments.

Natural product synthesis. Monensin is one of a class of polyether antibiotics produced by *Streptomyces* microorganisms. It has the peculiar property of enhancing the passage of ions through cell membranes because the ether oxygens are strategically placed along the molecular backbone so as to wrap comfortably around a cation such as Na^+ or K^+ (1). The exterior coating shields the central ion from the nonpolar (lipid) environment of a cell membrane and allows the ion to pass through. Molecules of this sort are called ionophores or ion-bearers.

The laboratory synthesis of monensin presented a formidable challenge. The problem was especially difficult because the molecule possesses 17 chiral centers on the backbone of 26 carbon atoms; this means that there are 131,072 conceivable structures with the

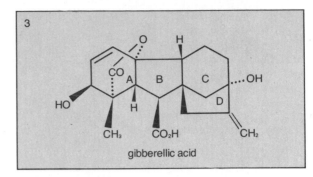

gibberellic acid

same molecular skeleton as monensin but with different arrangements of the atoms in space (stereoisomers). (Chiral molecules exist in mirror-image forms that differ in the manner of left- and right-handed gloves. Chirality is due usually to the presence of one or more carbon atoms to which are attached four different substituent groups.) How to obtain monensin and not the 131,071 other structures was the problem. Despite the difficulty, Yoshito Kishi and his associates at Harvard University succeeded in the synthesis. Their strategy was first to synthesize the left half (2A), then the right half (2B), and finally to patch the two halves together.

Each step of the synthesis was controlled to give at best only one isomer and at worst a mixture from which the desired isomer could be separated as the major product. Further, the synthesis was developed using chiral precursors to ensure that the final product was monensin and not its mirror image or a mixture of the two. Indeed, the final step led to a synthetic substance that was identical with monensin in every respect. This synthesis represented the culmination of untold hours of effort, outstanding intellectual and experimental skills, and the utilization of all the physical tools available to the modern chemist.

Gibberellic acid is a metabolite of the fungus *Gibberella fujikuroi* and is produced commercially there-

monensin (as an ion-bearer)

monensin

maytansine

N-methylmaysenine

6

erythronolide B (R and R′=H;
when H is replaced by sugars, the
molecule becomes erythromycin B.)

from for agricultural purposes (it promotes plant growth and hence plays a central biological role in the plant kingdom). After extensive efforts from many different laboratories the total chemical synthesis of gibberellic acid (3) was achieved during the past year by Elias J. Corey and his associates at Harvard University.

The synthesis proved more difficult than was anticipated, as Corey explained, ". . . largely because the combination of overall molecular complexity, centers of high sensitivity toward many reagents, and a singularly diabolical placement and density of functionality serves to thwart all but the most sophisticated of approaches." The approach used was arrived at by extensive antithetic analysis, which means that, in the planning stage, the structure was artificially unravelled into smaller pieces that could be reconstructed by chemically viable reactions. The synthesis was then executed according to the overall plan, which started with ring C intact and built onto it rings B and then D, and finally attached ring A to B.

Gibberellic acid and many other natural products are easier to obtain from natural sources than by chemical synthesis. The measure of achievement in a complex synthesis is not then the few milligrams of product obtained but the chemistry that unfolds en route. Crucial new synthetic methods, increasingly selective reactions, and greater chemical insight are the long-term benefits that derive from many syntheses of natural products. However, when the demand for a natural product outstrips the supply, chemical synthesis may be the solution. The motivation to synthesize maytansine (4) lies in its promise as an antitumor agent and in its short supply—not to mention the challenge to the chemist of achieving the synthesis of such a complex molecule. Corey reported in 1978 the first synthesis of a part of maytansine, the maytansinoid ring system, as in *N*-methylmaysenine (5).

Corey also reported in 1978 the first total synthesis of erythronolide B (6), the biological precursor for the erythromycins. As a class the erythromycins are macrocyclic lactones produced naturally by the fungus *Streptomyces erythreus*. They constitute one of the most important of all known families of antibiotics, and their application to medicine has resulted in the saving of countless numbers of human lives. The Corey synthesis of erythronolide B, and, effectively, erythromycin B, is a great achievement. It is fitting that this anniversary year in organic synthesis was marked by the synthesis of the erythromycin and maytansinoid ring systems.

Unnatural product synthesis. Not all synthetic endeavor has been directed toward natural products, as is obvious from the current abundance of man-made materials. Many chemists are intrigued by the synthesis of the unusual. Indeed, two new compounds of particular interest were reported in 1978. One of these, tetra-*tert*-butyltetrahedrane (7), is the first example of

tetra-*tert*-butyltetrahedrane

8

A kekulene (annulenoid form)

B kekulene (benzenoid form)

Earth sciences

A yearlong investigation of the atmosphere, a large-scale study of the crust and upper mantle, and new discoveries about deep-ocean currents were among the major developments of the past year in the Earth sciences. An earthquake in Mexico was significant in that it fulfilled a forecast almost perfectly.

Atmospheric sciences

During December 1978 scientists and engineers from many countries began a massive, yearlong international program to observe the Earth's atmosphere in great detail. It was the culmination of more than a decade of planning and preparation. Also over the past year there were significant activities in other areas of atmospheric sciences research. Among the most important were studies of the nature of climate, particularly global climate; atmospheric chemistry, especially the chemistry of the ozone layer; and medium-scale precipitation phenomena in the form of organized thunderstorms and within large cyclonic storms.

Global Atmospheric Research Program. In 1966 a panel of experts assembled by the U.S. National Academy of Sciences under the leadership of Jule Charney of the Massachusetts Institute of Technology published a report entitled "The Feasibility of a Global Observation and Analysis Experiment." It concluded that by means of satellites, instrumented balloons, and buoys it would be feasible to obtain global observations sufficient to define the entire atmosphere as "a single physical entity." It also was noted that, given sufficiently accurate observations of the atmosphere, it might be possible by means of numerical models to make skillful weather predictions for periods up to about two weeks. The Charney report was influential in the formulation of an international effort to observe the atmosphere.

During 1979 the first global weather experiment was to become a reality. It was to be an international effort of truly staggering proportions that, for the first time, will obtain unique and valuable sets of observations of essentially all of the Earth's atmosphere and of the upper layers of the oceans. The standard surface and upper air observations taken on a daily basis at weather stations throughout the world will be supplemented in a variety of ways. Particular emphasis has been placed on obtaining data over the vast ocean areas occupying about 70% of the Earth's surface.

Satellites will play principal roles in the global experiment, both for observing the atmosphere and for gathering and transmitting data to receiving stations in the United States, the Soviet Union, and other countries. If all goes according to plan, there will be four polar-orbiting satellites and five geostationary satellites stationed over the equator at various longitudes around the globe.

the synthesis and isolation of a small molecule having the carbocyclic framework of a tetrahedron. Synthesized by Günther Maier and his colleagues at Marburg, West Germany, the compound is remarkably stable considering that the C—C ring bonds are enormously strained and expected to open readily to a biradical (a compound with two unpaired electrons). It appears that the structure owes its stability to the bulky groups at the corners of the tetrahedron. Their very size prevents the ring bonds from opening readily. The restriction is a sort of "corset effect." As the bulky groups move apart on breaking a ring bond, they are forced back together by the pressure of the other two bulky groups.

A second intriguingly unnatural product, called kekulene, was prepared by Heinz A. Staab and his colleagues at the Max Planck Institute for Medical Research in Heidelberg, West Germany. Its synthesis was first attempted in 1965 but was thwarted until the development of methodology for creating large rings. The compound is of interest because, on the one hand, it was predicted to resemble two concentric polyenes (annulenes, 8A) and, on the other hand, to resemble benzene (8B). In fact, it turned out to be a highly insoluble compound with properties that support the benzenoid form. It is a kind of "superbenzene."

—Marjorie C. Caserio

The observational program will also include the following components: 43 specially instrumented ships (from 22 countries); about 10 research airplanes; 285 drifting ocean buoys in the Southern Hemisphere; and about 300 instrumented, constant-level balloons in tropical areas.

An international structure was established for collection and management. Several years of intense study by scientists in many countries will be required in order to analyze the observations. The result should be a fuller understanding of climate and improved weather services, particularly weather forecasts.

Atmospheric chemistry. Extensive research continued on the gaseous and particulate substances in the atmosphere. The term biogeochemistry was being more widely used to designate the science of the chemical interactions associated with biological and geophysical processes. Special attention was being given to the factors governing the formation, destruction, and transport of ozone, carbon dioxide, and nitrogen compounds.

Investigators were seeking to obtain better measurements of the global distribution of ozone. In addition to the use of ground-based spectrophotometric techniques and balloon-borne instruments, greater use was

Protection from the bitter winter of 1977–78 is afforded by appliance boxes as three men walk home through snow and high winds in Cumberland, R.I.

being made of high-flying airplanes equipped with instruments for measuring the concentration of ozone and of many other atmospheric constituents. The flights were particularly valuable in making measurements over oceanic areas. Observations by the U.S. National Center for Atmospheric Research revealed much greater variations in ozone levels over the Pacific Ocean than had been expected.

A 1978 report from the U.S. National Research Council supported earlier predictions that stratospheric ozone can be destroyed as a result of the release of fluorocarbons. These substances have been widely used as refrigerants and as propellants in aerosol spray cans. Recent laboratory studies yielded new estimates of the rates at which ozone-related chemical reactions proceed. Current estimates of the rates of ozone destruction by fluorocarbons exceed those made in 1976. On the other hand, it now appears that nitrogen oxides generated by high-flying aircraft will have smaller effects on the ozone layer than was thought to be the case in 1975.

There has been some uncertainty about whether or not nitrogen fertilizers, over a period of many decades, would increase or decrease stratospheric ozone. A National Research Council report published in 1978 estimated that the nitrogen compounds would decrease the ozone amounts by perhaps one-fourth the rate of reduction by fluorocarbons. The report concluded that if its predictions are correct major effects would not be experienced until the 22nd century. In the meantime, for many decades into the future, the value of the increases in agricultural production resulting from the use of nitrogen fertilizers would be expected to exceed the cost to society of ozone reductions.

In a recent publication four California scientists, L. A. Capone, I. G. Poppoff, L. C. Whitten, and R. P. Turco, concluded that nitrogen oxides emitted from aircraft and derived from fertilizer could increase the ozone in the stratosphere. They employed a complex set of chemical equations similar to those used by earlier investigators, but they used what they regarded as more up-to-date values for the rates of reaction.

It has been believed that atmospheric ozone is created principally in the stratosphere as a result of photochemical reactions involving ultraviolet radiation, and that ozone is transported to the lower atmosphere in certain weather situations. From an analysis of the ozone in the Northern and Southern hemispheres, Paul Crutzen at the National Center of Atmospheric Research and Jack Fishman at Colorado State University concluded that a significant amount of it is produced in the troposphere, the lower atmosphere. The production can be caused by reactions involving carbon monoxide, nitric oxide, and hydrocarbons.

Large-scale fossil-fuel combustion, smelting, and refining emit large quantities of sulfur dioxide (SO_2) into the atmosphere. Volcanoes are also prolific natural

Instrument boom extends from the front of an Electra aircraft used by the U.S. National Center for Atmospheric Research to measure the global distribution of such trace constituents of the atmosphere as ozone, carbon monoxide, sulfur dioxide, and nitric acid.

sources. The gas undergoes various reactions leading to sulfate compounds, including sulfuric acid droplets. Debates continued concerning the rate of sulfate formation. A recent analysis by J. Freiberg at Rutgers University concluded that "the oxidation occurs almost wholly near the source of the SO_2."

It is clear, however, that the sulfur compounds, once put into the atmosphere, can travel long distances before being carried out of it by rain and snow. In many parts of the world, particularly Scandinavia, Western Europe, and the northeastern United States, it has been observed that rain and snow are more acidic than pure water. There is growing concern that the consequences of such a trend could be costly to acid-sensitive plant and animal life.

Carbon dioxide and climate. Measurements at several stations around the world show that atmospheric carbon dioxide (CO_2) is increasing at the rate of about one part per million (ppm) per year with its present value at about 332 ppm. According to calculations by Charles Keeling and Robert Bacastow at the University of California at San Diego, atmospheric carbon dioxide in the year 2050 will be about twice the 1900 value if fossil fuels continue to be major energy sources. Syukuro Manabe and Richard Wetherald at the Geophysical Fluid Dynamics Laboratory at Princeton University made calculations indicating that this could cause about a 2° C increase in average global air temperature near the ground. Such a result would be accompanied by changes in the distribution of temperature and precipitation in many parts of the world. It is important to remember that the Manabe-Wetherald model does not adequately account for a number of important relevant factors, particularly interactions of the atmosphere with land and sea. Until such uncertainties are removed, predictions of substantial global warming should be treated with caution.

John Mercer at Ohio State University concluded that the warming that might result from a doubling of atmospheric CO_2 would be magnified in polar regions. His calculations showed that warming over western Antarctica would cause widespread melting of ice with a consequent increase of sea level amounting to five meters. Such a result would produce a geophysical disaster of unprecedented proportions throughout the world, as coastal cities would be flooded. By monitoring global CO_2 concentrations and temperatures as well as the ice sheets in Antarctica, it should be possible to establish whether the predicted chain of events is realistic. Mercer recommended that the ice shelves on both coasts of the Antarctic Peninsula be observed regularly by means of satellites. Breakup of these ice shelves would be a warning sign of a dangerous warming trend in Antarctica.

Other climate studies. All aspects of climatology were receiving considerable attention in many countries. During the year U.S. Public Law 95-367 created a National Climate Program calling for research on the nature of climate, its prediction, and its effects on food production, water supplies, energy consumption, and other human activities. On an international scale the World Meteorological Organization and the International Council of Scientific Unions were working on cooperative programs having goals similar to those of the National Climate Program.

Analyses of tree rings continued to be sources of climatic information. In the past much work has been done by Harold Fritts and his colleagues at the University of Arizona in relating tree-ring widths to rainfall and temperature (see *1976 Yearbook of Science and the*

Future Feature Article: DENDROCHRONOLOGY: HISTORY FROM TREE RINGS). In recent years geochemists have begun to analyze isotopes of elements in the wood to infer climatic information. Samuel Epstein and C. Tapp at the California Institute of Technology measured the ratio of deuterium (heavy hydrogen) to hydrogen because this ratio can be used to estimate the temperature at the time the cellulose in the wood was formed. They found that from 14,000 to 22,000 years ago, when there was maximum glaciation, average annual temperatures in ice-free regions of the Earth were milder than they are today.

Temperature information obtained from oxygen isotopic analysis of the layered sediments in cores drilled in the seafloor supports the theory advanced some 40 years ago by Milutin Milankovich that, over time scales of tens of thousands of years, changes in the Earth's orbit around the Sun can account for climate changes. Manabe and his associates at the U.S. National Oceanic and Atmospheric Administration used a mathematical model of the global atmosphere to test this concept and found it to be feasible. Mathematical models were also used to recreate atmospheric conditions during the last major ice age, some 18,000 years ago.

Recently, A. P. Kershaw at Monash University in Australia obtained a core drilled into Lynch's Crater, located in Queensland at about 146° E and 17° S. By analyzing the pollen existing in various layers, he was able to estimate rainfall amounts during the last 120,-000 years. During this period deviations of rainfall and sea-surface temperature (in the North Atlantic Ocean) from long-term averages were positively correlated. For example, over the last 15,000 years temperatures and rainfall have both been substantially higher than during the preceding 60,000 years.

The extent to which changes in weather and climate can be attributed to changes in emissions from the Sun continued to be debated. After a critical review of most of the relevant literature A. Barrie Pittock, an Australian climatologist, concluded that "little convincing evidence has yet been produced for real correlations between sunspot cycles and the weather/climate on the 11- and 22-year time scales." Pittock recently indicated, however, that the results of J. Murray Mitchell, Charles Stockton, and David Meko relating drought conditions in the western United States to the 22-year sunspot cycle may have statistical validity.

Mesometeorology. Dealing with weather systems that extend over areas from ten to hundreds of kilometers across, mesometeorologists are particularly interested in the organized bands of thunderstorms that sweep across the Great Plains of North America during the spring and early summer. These storms are prolific sources of hail and tornadoes.

Scheduled to begin in the spring of 1979 was a major effort to observe characteristics of organized thunderstorms in Oklahoma. Through the use of airplanes, closely spaced radiosondes, Doppler radars, and ground stations, scientists planned to make detailed observations of thunderstorms and their surroundings.

During the year Peter Hobbs and his associates at the University of Washington studied the small- and medium-scale precipitation phenomena within large-scale cyclones moving over the coast near Seattle, Wash. They found it possible to describe the precipitation-formation sequences in different parts of the cyclones. This research was concerned not only with the processes of cloud and precipitation formation but also with their effects on the evolution of the cyclone itself. It verified earlier findings in other parts of North Ameri-

Floor-to-ceiling tornado simulator (above) at Purdue University can generate room-sized twisters. Swirling air currents inside the simulator (right) are made visible by piped-in smoke.

Photos, courtesy, C. R. Church and E. M. Agee, Purdue University, under sponsorship of the National Science Foundation

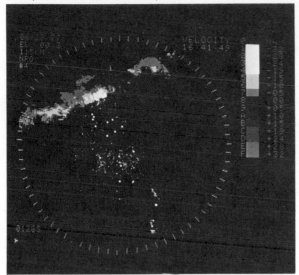

Image generated by Doppler radar shows squall line approaching Oklahoma City. Unlike conventional radar the Doppler form can detect motion by comparing the frequencies of the original and reflected pulses. The lighter the shading, the higher the wind speed.

ca that rain at the ground under warm fronts may originate as streamers of ice crystals that are generated at altitudes above ten kilometers (six miles). The crystals collide and adhere, producing snowflakes that continue to grow as they fall through warm air at low elevations.

Downbursts. Thunderstorms are characterized by updrafts and downdrafts. The latter often extend to the ground and bring cool air that serves to improve the comfort index on a hot, humid, summer day. Unfortunately, under certain conditions vigorous thunderstorms grow to great altitudes and intensity and develop violent characteristics. The most common are torrential rains, frequent cloud-to-ground lightning, hail, tornadoes, and strong downdrafts. In some cases the descending air comes through the cloud base at speeds exceeding 20 mph. Such a downward surge of air can pose a serious threat to airplanes, particularly if they are in the process of taking off or landing. T. T. Fujita at the University of Chicago, who coined the word "downburst" to designate such strong downdrafts, showed that they were responsible for a number of commercial airplane accidents. During recent months he led a team of scientists and engineers in studying means of detecting and predicting the onset of downbursts. Doppler radars capable of measuring the air motions in storms were used to observe thunderstorms in northern Illinois. The researchers found that some downburst-producing storms could be identified in sufficient time to allow traffic controllers to route airplanes around dangerous regions.

—Louis J. Battan

Geological sciences

A large-scale study of the Earth's crust and upper mantle, an accurate prediction of an earthquake, and continued investigation of plate tectonics were among the year's highlights in the geological sciences. Geologists also joined in efforts to discover new sources of energy throughout the world.

Geology and geochemistry. Almost everyone in the geological community agrees that man's knowledge of the Earth was fundamentally changed as a result of important discoveries during the 1960s. It is, in fact, quite common to hear geologists speak of that decade as a period of "scientific revolution." The revolution resulted in the widespread acceptance of the view, previously strongly resisted by most geologists, that the continents had moved with respect to one another during the history of the Earth. It was also suggested that the Earth's crust consisted of a number of more or less rigid plates, which had formed several billion years ago and had been in a state of continuous lateral motion since that time.

This hypothesis of continental drift and plate tectonics, which together with related hypotheses such as seafloor spreading is often termed the "new tectonics," has without question profoundly influenced the geology of the 1970s. It has served to organize and synthesize a great deal of knowledge from such seemingly diverse fields as geophysics, structural geology, petrology, oceanography, and paleontology. And, even more significant, the direction of research in the 1970s has to an important degree been determined by attempts to lend support to these theories of the 1960s. One should not expect then that 1978 would have been marked with great theoretical breakthroughs. It was a year of intense and significant research activity nonetheless.

There is another, equally significant influence upon contemporary geological investigation. Geology has been closely allied with economic interests since its beginning in the 18th century, and so in the 1970s it turned to the attempt to solve problems relating to the immediate and long-range needs of society, particularly, but by no means exclusively, those problems that have risen from the "energy crisis."

A remarkable aspect of geological research in this decade is the extent to which the attempt to solve problems of social and economic significance has been guided by the theoretical framework provided by the new tectonics. An example was provided by the July 1978 issue of the *Journal of the Geological Society of London*, which was devoted to papers on the development of metal deposits in various parts of the world. P. W. Guild's paper on metallogenesis, the formation of ores, in the western United States begins, "Plate-tectonic theory has greatly improved our understanding of geological processes, including metallo-

R. Kientzy, T. Juteau, CNEXO, photo, courtesy, J. Francheteau

Mechanical arm of the deep-sea submersible "Cyana" reaches out toward sulfide deposits on the ocean floor. These deposits are rich in zinc and silver.

genesis." Although he recognized the significance of other factors, Guild emphasized the role of plate tectonic phenomena in providing the energy necessary for the concentration of ore deposits. In a discussion of the metallogenesis of southeast Asia the authors also regarded plate tectonics as an important factor, pointing out "that there is a broad convergence between metallogenic provinces and the plate tectonics of SE Asia." These papers are primarily concerned with a theoretical understanding of metallogenesis, but such studies will no doubt guide the search for economically significant ore deposits in the future.

Sedimentation. The study of the accumulation of sediments and the formation of sedimentary rocks, so important as a basis for an understanding of the origin and migration of petroleum, now presupposes a tectonic framework provided by continental drift and sea-floor spreading. The examination of modern environments of sedimentation, so enthusiastically pursued in recent years, continued during 1978. Studies of the Alaska shelf by the Marine Geology Branch of the United States Geological Survey provided one particularly notable example. J. Douglas Glaeser's ingenious attempt to correlate the worldwide distribution of barrier islands with the plate tectonic setting, published in the *Journal of Geology,* illustrates the significance of the

new tectonics as a theoretical precondition in contemporary sedimentology.

A seeming preoccupation with modern environments of deposition did not signal a neglect of the traditional study of ancient sediments. Important studies of both Cretaceous carbonates (Texas Bureau of Economic Geology) and Paleozoic carbonates (American Association of Petroleum Geologists) were published during 1978. Clastic sediments, those made up of fragments of preexisting rocks, also received attention. A paper in the *American Journal of Science,* for example, attempted to explain the widespread occurrence of Lower Paleozoic black shale facies and the scarcity of similar facies in the later Paleozoic on the basis of a variation of dissolved oxygen in the open ocean. Facies are the features present in a sedimentary rock that characterize it as having been deposited in a particular environment.

The study of evaporites has been of interest to economic geologists not only as a source of economically significant minerals but also because of the long-established association of evaporite deposits and petroleum. Recently the geological setting and physical properties of salt deposits have been studied with renewed interest because they have come to be regarded as the most promising sites for the disposal of radioactive wastes. A report on the problems of radioactive waste disposal in salt deposits was published by the U.S. Department of Energy.

Diagenesis, the process by which sediments are transformed into sedimentary rocks, continued to be an active area of investigation, at least in part because it is so important a factor in understanding the development of petroleum reservoirs. In 1978 an issue of the *Journal of the Geological Society of London* was devoted to papers on sandstone diagenesis.

Energy sources and environmental geology. Activity in petroleum exploration was at a high level in every corner of the world during 1978, but the search for sources of energy was not confined to petroleum. Possible sources of geothermal energy were investigated in the hope that they might meet a significant, if small, proportion of future needs. Some new impetus was given to geothermal exploration in the U.S. by a program initiated by the Department of Energy to share the cost of drilling deep exploratory wells. Exploration was not, of course, limited to the U.S. In a few places, such as geothermally active Iceland, it appeared that geothermal sources would provide a significant contribution to energy resources in the near future.

Despite the uncertain future of nuclear reactors as a source of power the price of uranium continued to rise, and the mining industry responded with intensive uranium mining and exploration. Porous sandstone and conglomerate deposits in the western U.S. remained the major source of that nation's supply, with mines of uranium-bearing veins in Washington and southeast-

The research submersible "Alvin" investigated the Mid-Atlantic Ridge during two months of deep dives in mid-1978.

ern Alaska providing a much smaller but still significant resource. The development of less conventional uranium-bearing deposits such as, for example, the Chattanooga shale, awaited advances in technology that would make it economically feasible. Largely as a result of exploration in the San Juan Basin of New Mexico, the estimated uranium reserves in the U.S. recoverable at $50 a ton or less rose from 762,000 tons as of Jan. 1, 1977, to 807,400 tons as of Jan. 1, 1978.

Activity in environmental geology, a discipline born in response to the "environmental crisis," was still growing during 1978. The Office of Environmental Geology of the United States Geological Survey undertook studies on such diverse topics as site location for dams and nuclear power plants, the hazards of earthquakes and landslides, and the environmental impact of mining. But the attempts to solve environmental problems were not confined to offices and departments of environmental geology. Aided by the ever increasing sophistication of their techniques, geochemists continued studies reflecting concern over the alteration of the atmosphere and the Earth's crust by man.

Plate motion. While some geologists regarded the framework provided by plate tectonics as a background against which to view geological processes, others pursued the question of the ultimate source of plate motion. While it is widely accepted that convection in the mantle provides the principal mechanism of plate motion, many problems remain to be solved before a satisfactory explanation can be achieved. Frank Richter discussed these problems and how they might be solved in his paper "Mantle Convection Models," in the *Annual Review of Earth and Planetary Sciences* for 1978. He concluded that the convection system needed to account for plate motions may be much more complicated than previously supposed.

Investigations fundamental to understanding the Earth's crust and mantle continued to be sponsored by the Deep Sea Drilling Project. The main objective of leg 55 of the project was to test the "hot spot" hypothesis of the origin of the Hawaiian Islands and Emperor seamount chain. According to this hypothesis volcanic activity was successively induced as the oceanic crust drifted over a persistent "hot spot" in the mantle that is now located beneath the still volcanically active island of Hawaii. The hypothesis was confirmed to the extent that the ages of volcanic extinction along the Emperor chain were consistent with a crustal movement over the hot spot of about nine centimeters per year. This rate of extinction closely matches that previously determined for the Hawaiian chain. It is interesting to note that the ages of extinction were arrived at by estimating the age of the fossils in the lowest sediments above the volcanic basalts obtained in drilling into the seamounts. These estimates were to be checked against the radiometric dating of the underlying basalts.

Despite the general acceptance of the new tectonics and its enthusiastic application it is clear that much work remains to be done, and notes of caution were sounded here and there. A. R. McBirney reported in the *Annual Review of Earth and Planetary Sciences*, for example, that he sees "little direct relation, other than a spatial one, between volcanism in the Pacific Northwest and the subduction that is commonly thought to be associated with it." (Subduction in tectonic theory is the downthrusting of one plate under another when the two meet.)

Paleontology. Though paleontology has not shown a dramatic expansion in recent years, research in the field remained active. Micropaleontology was playing a decisive role in the interpretation of the complex history

Adapted from Roy Andersen, © *National Geographic*, August 1978, pp. 160–161

The small dinosaur Deinonychus, *standing about four feet tall and weighing about 150 pounds, had characteristics that support the theory that some dinosaurs were warm-blooded. Its powerful hind limbs for running down its prey, good vision for coordination, and hands articulated for grasping, all suggest an animal with agility and speed, more similar to a warm-blooded flightless bird than to the slow cold-blooded reptiles.*

of the ocean basins and continental margins. The investigation undertaken in the aforementioned leg 55 of the Deep Sea Drilling Project provided but one example. Invertebrate fossils were playing an important role in biostratigraphic studies, but invertebrate paleontologists were increasingly preoccupied with the study of phylogenies (evolutions of genetically related groups of organisms), particularly with the early history of major groups. This interest was reflected in John W. Durham's discussion of the Precambrian metozoan biota published in the *Annual Review of Earth and Planetary Sciences.* Vertebrate paleontology continued to place primary emphasis upon phylogenetic rather than stratigraphic studies. Dinosaurs attracted the attention of both paleontologists and the general public in 1978. John Ostrom published an account of the biology and phylogeny of dinosaurs in which he advanced the theory that at least some of them were warm-blooded.

Future prospects. The vigorous state of the geological profession during the year was reflected in an increased demand for qualified geologists. Enrollments in geology courses in colleges and universities were higher than they had been since early in the 1960s. Despite the large enrollments many geologists, along with other scientists, expressed concern over what they considered to be a deemphasis of science instruction at all educational levels.

Although this review has been presented in terms of more or less traditional fields, an aspect of geology that was clearly manifested in 1978 was the extent to which in the everyday practice of the discipline the boundaries separating these traditional fields have become blurred. Contemporary geology often takes as its organizing themes not the methods characteristic of traditional disciplines but rather some problems whose solutions are sought in these methods. Thus geochemists, structural geologists, hydrologists, petrologists,

geophysicists, and engineering geologists all joined in an effort to solve the critical problem of the disposal of radioactive wastes.

Geological activity during 1978 was probably at an all-time high. The effort to secure the geological revolution and the search for answers to pressing social and economic problems has sustained this high level of activity. When will the next revolution occur? No one can answer that question, but one thing is plain. The geological community has just begun to exploit the revolutionary advances of the recent past.

—David Kitts

Geophysics. During the last year a large earthquake in Mexico fulfilled a scientific forecast nearly perfectly, and a geological study produced an impressive record of prehistoric earthquakes. Large cooperative projects cast light on the deep structure of the Earth's crust, and instruments were deployed which promised to help resolve many important problems in Earth science.

The most destructive earthquake of the year occurred in eastern Iran on September 16, killing some 15,000 people. It had a magnitude of 7.7 and was accompanied by fault breakage of the ground surface over a distance of at least 55 km (33.5 mi). Earlier, on June 20, a shock of magnitude 6.4 killed at least 50 people and caused considerable damage in the vicinity of Thessaloniki, in Greece. It was felt widely throughout Greece, Bulgaria, and southern Yugoslavia. Shocks on January 14 (magnitude 6.5) and June 12 (magnitude 7.5) were responsible for a total of at least 39 deaths and 438 injuries on Honshu Island, Japan.

History of southern Californian earthquakes. The ability of scientists to assess seismic hazards in North America has always been severely hampered by the shortness of the historical record there. On the San Andreas Fault of California, for example, only two great earthquakes have occurred since Europeans arrived, and these were on different segments of the fault (near

Los Angeles in 1857 and near San Francisco in 1906). Such an incomplete record provides little useful information on the frequency of these potentially catastrophic events.

During recent months, however, this record suddenly was extended back in time more than a millennium by studies of recent sedimentary deposits in the Mojave Desert in California. The site of these deposits, on Pallett Creek near Pearblossom, combined several unusual characteristics from which the seismic history of the area can be deduced: it lies astride the San Andreas Fault; it has been subjected to rapid sedimentation (about 30 cm per century) at least since the beginning of the Christian era; large earthquakes have disturbed the sediments in recognizable ways; peats and other carboniferous materials in the sediments can be dated by the carbon-14 method; and Pallett Creek has recently cut through the deposits, exposing them for study. Disturbances caused by the 1857 earthquake and eight earlier ones, dating back to the sixth century AD, are preserved. Six of these events were great earthquakes like that of 1857, and the other two may have been as well.

What does this new information portend for southern California's future? The average interval between earthquakes at Pallett Creek has been about 160 years; the shortest interval was about 60 years and the longest about 275 years. Because it has been 122 years since the last great earthquake, seismologists have received confirmation of their opinion that another is likely within the next several decades. On the other hand, there is a hint that long intervals alternate with short ones, and that the region is now experiencing a long one. On this assumption the next earthquake is still 80–150 years away. The range of uncertainty is disturbingly large. The need to find precursory signals of earthquakes thus remains as urgent as ever.

Oaxaca earthquake. An important earthquake occurred on Nov. 29, 1978, in the Mexican state of Oaxaca. Its significance stems neither from its size (magnitude 7.8) nor from its destructiveness; earthquakes as large occur about twice a year and when centered in continental areas they often cause more damage. Interest in this event stems from the fact that its occurrence was anticipated by seismologists and its location and magnitude accurately forecast.

The prediction had been published in 1977 by three scientists from the University of Texas, who noted that an unusual period of seismic quiescence began in 1973 in an area ordinarily subject to many small earthquakes. Similar periods of quiescence had preceded two earlier large earthquakes in the Oaxaca region, and the scientists concluded that an earthquake of magnitude 7.5 (±0.25) was impending. They gave a probable location for it which was within about 50 km (30 mi) of the actual epicenter. Its exact time could not be foreseen, although it appeared to be imminent.

The prediction caused controversy among seismologists, some of whom doubted the statistical significance of the purported "seismic gap" or questioned the physical soundness of basing a prediction upon it. Matters were made worse by sensational and irresponsible coverage of the prediction by some newspapers, which led to social disruption in Oaxaca said to have been worse than the actual effects of the earthquake. The accuracy of the forecast cannot be denied, however, and is sure to increase interest in using seismicity patterns to anticipate large earthquakes.

Survivors of the most destructive earthquake of 1978 huddle in front of a ruined building in a village in eastern Iran. The earthquake, which struck on September 16 and registered 7.7 on the Richter scale, killed approximately 15,000 people.

Alain Keler—Sygma

Sidney Harris

Southern Californian uplift. An elaborate program of surveying southern California was carried out early in the year, aimed at understanding the anomalous uplift that has occurred there, beginning in 1961. The cause of the uplift is unknown, and many scientists fear that it may be a precursor of an impending earthquake, but interpretation of the anomaly was hampered by a lack of high-capacity data. The history and pattern of vertical motion had to be pieced together from surveys conducted at different times and places by various agencies and for various purposes.

The 1978 resurvey was carried out by the National Geodetic Survey and covered the entire area of the anomaly within a short period, so as to provide a "snapshot" of the state of the deformation. Elaborate corrections must be applied to reduce surveying data of this sort to usable form, and this process consumed most of the year, with the reduced data becoming available in late January 1979. As of early 1979 there was not yet any geophysical interpretation to be given to these results.

Global digital seismic network. A network of 13 seismic research observatories (SRO's) distributed throughout the world approached completion in 1978. The seismometers at these observatories are emplaced in 100-m-deep boreholes to isolate them from wind-generated vibrations; the data are recorded in digital form so that they can be read and processed on computers. The SRO's and a similar network of eight high-gain long-period stations supplement the World-wide Standardized Seismograph Network (WWSSN), which was installed in the early 1960s and which contributed much of the evidence confirming the theories of plate tectonics and continental drift. The WWSSN was scheduled to be modernized over the next few years by the addition of digital recording at 15 sites.

In addition, another network called IDA (International Development of Accelerometers) by 1979 consisted of 14 ultra-low-frequency instruments and was providing data on tides and free oscillations in the solid earth. Together, these digital instruments provided scientists with a network greatly superior to anything previously available in terms of sensitivity, accuracy, dynamic range, and frequency response. It is difficult to predict in detail what discoveries will be made using the new data, but the fields of Earth structure and earthquake mechanisms seem certain to benefit.

Studies of crustal structure. During the year there was increasing activity in the U.S. in the study of the structure of the Earth's crust and upper mantle. This had been a field of vigorous activity in the early 1960s, when, as part of the program to learn to distinguish earthquakes from underground nuclear explosions, several institutions (notably the U.S. Geological Survey, the Carnegie Institution of Washington, and the University of Wisconsin) conducted experiments on the refraction of seismic waves at several places in the

"I don't know what it measured. The Richter scale is down there."

U.S. Then, for about ten years the initiative shifted to other countries, especially West Germany and the Soviet Union, where vigorous theoretical and experimental programs were pursued. Some of the motivation for these programs has apparently come from the search for mineral deposits. By the middle of the 1970s more was known about the structure of Eurasia than of the U.S. About that time a Consortium for Continental Reflection Profiling (Cocorp) was formed in the U.S. to apply seismic exploration techniques developed in the oil industry to scientific problems. These techniques provide good resolution of small-scale features and are ideally suited to detailed studies of small regions.

Two of the most interesting experiments yet conducted by Cocorp were completed in 1978 and the data made available to the scientific community. These were profiles of the reflection of seismic waves across the Rio Grande rift zone near Socorro, N.M., and across the Wind River Mountains in Wyoming. Analysis of the results from these studies was expected to continue for some time, but some preliminary interpretations were made. The Wyoming profile clearly shows a thrust fault dipping at an angle of 35° beneath the range and extending to a depth of 24 km (14.5 mi). The fact that this thrust persists to such depths indicates that the range was created by horizontal compression, accompanied by motion on the fault and crustal thickening. Previously, some had hypothesized that purely vertical motions had raised the mountains.

The Cocorp results also showed complex folded structures at great depths which resemble folds seen at the surface in the Precambrian core of the range.

Love Canal neighborhood in Niagara County, New York, suffered polluted groundwater because of the long-term burying of chemical wastes in the region. More than 200 families had to be evacuated from their homes in the neighborhood and relocated in other areas.

This is apparently the first time that geologically recognizable structural details have been resolved at such depths, and it proves that the continental crust was already 30 km or more thick when the rocks were folded, some three billion years ago. In the Rio Grande rift zone strong seismic reflections were found from features at midcrustal depths. These lend support to earlier theories that a chamber of magma (molten rock) underlies the area.

Results from a seismic profile across the San Andreas Fault in central California proved to be quite complicated, and their analysis was continuing. Preliminary results, however, indicate that the fault can be detected at least as deep as ten kilometers (six miles). Researchers hoped that results from this profile will shed light on the mechanism of faulting.

Another indication of a revival of interest in structural studies was a large seismic refraction experiment that was carried out during the autumn in Wyoming, Montana, and Idaho. This experiment was an international effort, involving the cooperation of universities and government agencies from the U.S., Switzerland, and West Germany. It concentrated on the region of Yellowstone National Park and the Snake River plain southwest of Yellowstone and had several objectives. These included determining the pattern of wave velocities in a seismically active area and attempting to detect magma chambers that may underlie the Yellowstone volcanic area. The experimenters also hoped to gain an understanding of how the structure in the deep crust and upper mantle is related to surface tectonic and volcanic features. Results from this project were being analyzed and were scheduled to be published late in 1979.

—Bruce R. Julian

Hydrological sciences

Increased attention to the problem of man-made contamination of groundwater, research on forecasting river floods, and new discoveries concerning currents near the ocean floors were among the significant developments in the hydrological sciences during the past year.

Hydrology. A turning point in public awareness to the problem of groundwater contamination was reached in 1978. The publicity surrounding the chemical waste disposal in the Love Canal, Niagara County, N.Y., sensitized the public to the effects of pollution from landfill sites. Groundwater experts had recognized the problem for many years, but only recently had government agencies stepped up support for further study and data collection.

As of 1979 polluted groundwater resources were small in comparison with total available groundwater, but the problem could not be minimized. In the United States the Environmental Protection Agency (EPA) estimated that there are at least 17 million waste disposal facilities disposing more than 1.7 trillion gal (6.44×10^{12} l) of contaminated liquid into the ground each year. In addition, the EPA identified 32,254 hazard waste sites, of which 638 were estimated to contain wastes that may pose significant, imminent hazards to public health. The most serious of the contaminants are trace organics. Many are carcinogenic, and others such as dioxin are deadly toxic. In the Niagara County area, where the Love Canal is situated, it was estimated that 3,700 tons of trichlorophenol waste contains 2,000 lb of dioxin (of which 141 lb had been buried in Love Canal). Three ounces of dioxin is a sufficient quantity to poison one million people.

The problems are not unique to the United States. Groundwater contamination from landfills and waste disposal sites can be found throughout Europe. Unfortunately, the nature of the problem does not yield to a quick solution. Once the contaminants reach the groundwater system, they can remain there for decades polluting larger and larger parts of the aquifer system. Cleaning up existing landfills may not be feasible either; not only are such efforts expensive but also decayed containers may rupture during removal.

The response to the growing concern of groundwater contamination was an increase in activity and support for research, monitoring, and data collection. In the U.S. a national symposium on groundwater quality was held Sept. 20–22, 1978. While concentrating on defining the extent of the problem in the U.S. and the impact of new U.S. federal regulations, the symposium had implications beyond the United States. Countries that lack effective regulations concerning waste disposal were expected to study experiences in the U.S. when trying to find remedies for their problems.

The main regulatory powers in the U.S. come from the Safe Drinking Water Act of 1974 and the Resource Conservation and Recovery Act of 1976. On Dec. 18, 1978, the EPA published proposed guidelines and regulations on identification and listing of hazardous wastes as well as performance standards for hazardous-waste management. Prior to this there had been few regulations controlling groundwater contamination.

One development from the new regulations was increased research in modeling groundwater contamination. These models were based on the physics of groundwater flow and contaminant transport, and on equations that describe chemical reactions that take place between the pollutants and the soil. The models try to mimic mathematically what occurs or will occur in the ground.

Because groundwater systems are extremely complex, with variations in soil type and hydrologic characteristics over short distances, the models are simplified. Extensive field data must be collected to estimate model parameters and to verify that the model is mimicking the real system correctly. The collection of these data is expensive and time-consuming, especially when the more hazardous trace organics are included. During 1978 the EPA increased its support for monitoring. Data were being collected at a few test sites, and these data were expected to assist in developing better predictive models.

Applied research. Research into the application of hydrological models to important and pressing water resources problems continued to hold high priority. The emphasis was on taking results from basic hydrologic research and developing better models for general applications, or taking new models and applying them to complex case studies to investigate their usefulness as general tools.

A new hydrological model was being developed under a cooperative effort among the Institute of Hydrology (Wallingford, U.K.), SOGREAH (Grenoble, France), and the Danish Hydraulic Institute. The first version of the model, completed during 1978, was being tested. Known under the acronym SHE (Système Hydrologique Européen), it describes the entire land phase of the hydrologic cycle. No such system had previously been available for large-scale practical applications.

The model is based almost entirely on knowledge of measurable physical parameters, the reliance on empirical or semiempirical parameters with uncertain physical interpretation being minimal. This physical basis makes the modeling system appropriate for the prediction of impacts from structural and land-use changes in the watershed. Furthermore, it is believed that a physically based model facilitates application to watersheds for which little or no data are available, physical parameters being much easier to estimate than empirical or semiempirical ones.

SHE is structured to allow flexibility in its application. This is provided by allowing the individual hydrologic components to be modified or omitted in any given application, depending on the actual conditions and data availability. Furthermore, the individual components are structured as separate units that can be used independently. Because SHE is intended as a general hydrologic modeling system, this flexibility is crucial.

Another applied research area that has received high priority is hydrologically based flood-forecasting systems. The purpose of such systems is to forecast the magnitude and timing of flood peaks during the occurrence of a storm, and to use model predictions for flood warnings or reservoir operations. Traditional hydrological models were not able to effectively utilize incoming data that were collected as the storm occurred. New techniques being investigated combine hydrological modeling with statistical estimation procedures traditionally found in other fields of engineering and science. Such forecasting models are most effective in areas where floods occur rapidly and flood warnings can reduce loss of life.

In the United States during 1978 flood fatalities exceeded 120, with the majority occuring in "flash" flood situations. Consequently, the National Weather Service was conducting and coordinating the development of better flood-forecasting models. It saw a growing need for these models, as building continued in and around small rivers that respond quickly to precipitation. U.S. flood damage in 1978 exceeded $1 billion, with much of the destruction occurring along small rivers that do not lend themselves to flood-protection works such as levees, walls, or dams. Studies by the NWS revealed that the most cost-effective method for reducing lives lost and flood damage is a more effective flood warning system based on better hydrological forecasting models.

Providing emergency first aid to France's inland waterways, each of the two vessels carries up to 1,000 kilograms of oxygen. The gas is used to treat water that has suffered sudden excesses of pollutants.

Similar research was conducted in the United Kingdom, where the Institute of Hydrology completed a study for the South West Water Authority. The British forecasting models also utilized statistical procedures that enabled them to efficiently incorporate data on precipitation as it occurred. The results showed that such models could achieve substantial improvements over more traditional hydrologic forecasting techniques. Similar techniques were being applied to the Ombrone River (Italy) and the Ohre River (Czechoslovakia).

During the past year the Egyptian Master Water Plan study provided an opportunity to apply some research tools. These included better procedures for analyzing long-term persistence of the flow of the Nile River; dynamic models of water balance for the swamps in the upper Nile basin and the impact of their future development on the whole Nile basin hydrology; and linkages between groundwater utilization in the delta and potential contamination from saltwater intrusion from the Mediterranean Sea into the freshwater aquifer.

Basic research. Two important trends evident in recent basic hydrologic research were the integration of surface-water and groundwater concepts and the integration of stochastic (involving chance or probability) and deterministic techniques (those not incorporating

an element of randomness). These trends were evident in the research connected with the generation of runoff from hillsides. Essentially, these studies tried to understand the relationship between precipitation, infiltration, and surface runoff over a wide area where soil properties and slopes vary significantly. Some researchers supported the idea that in humid regions a relatively small area of a watershed generates the flow observed in the stream. Given this hypothesis, the occurrence of runoff is governed by near-surface, saturated-unsaturated hydrogeologic regimes that exist on the hillsides near the channel. Other researchers support the notion that runoff is generated when precipitation rates exceed the infiltration capacity of the soil, causing surface saturation. When surface saturation occurs, additional precipitation results in runoff, and, therefore, runoff can be generated from all parts of the hillslope. Additional work was required before these concepts concerning runoff generation could be interpreted in terms of observed historical streamflow records.

The integration of stochastic and deterministic techniques was most evident in recent research on groundwater systems. Traditionally, groundwater research concentrated on solving the partial differential equations that describe groundwater-flow physics. During the past year, however, a number of papers, representing work in Israel, the United States, and Canada, analyzed the effect of variability in soil properties. Because the actual soil properties are unknown due to high variability, the analyses considered soil properties as stochastic processes and studied the effects of such uncertainty on groundwater flow.

Most hydrologic systems are dynamic systems; that is, they vary with time. One important study published during 1978 analyzed dynamically the influence of climate, soil, and vegetation on the annual water balance. The study combined the stochastic nature of precipitation and the deterministic interaction of water with the effects of vegetal cover and soil type. Expected annual values of the major components of the water balance system—evapotranspiration, surface runoff, water yield—could be estimated as a function of precipitation statistics, vegetal cover, and soil properties. Such research is relevant for large-scale hydrologic studies where hydrological records such as evaporation or streamflow are either scarce or nonexistent.

—Eric F. Wood

Oceanography. Studies of the ocean involve not only a spectrum of disciplines, ranging from descriptive biology to geophysical fluid dynamics, but also a variety of approaches, both theoretical and experimental. Another dimension is added by the uses to which the results are put. These include the location and harvest of resources, both living and nonliving, the protection of the marine environment from the activities of man, and the forecast of atmospheric events determined by the nature of the ocean. The findings of recent investigations in some of these fields are described below.

The ocean and climate. The storage and transport of heat in the ocean are thought to contribute in an important way to determining changes in atmospheric circulation and, thus, to establishing weather and climate. The magnitude of oceanic heat storage is illustrated by the fact that a column of surface water only three meters deep contains as much heat as an equivalent air column extending from the sea surface through the entire height of the atmosphere.

Satellite measurements of solar radiation at the top of the atmosphere permitted estimates to be made of the total poleward heat transport. The atmospheric component of this transport can be calculated by using the standard meteorological observational network; the magnitude of the oceanic heat flux can then be determined by subtracting the atmospheric component from the total. This estimate was different from that derived from oceanographic calculations, and a large-scale experiment to reconcile the difference was proposed. This would involve measuring the north-south component of flow and the water temperature across an entire ocean basin, for example between

Seasat 1 oceanographic research satellite is prepared for sound and vibration tests in an acoustic chamber (left). At the right is a radar image obtained by the satellite showing the coast of Baja California (right), a chain of islands (center), and the Pacific Ocean (left).

(Left) Courtesy, Lockheed Missiles & Space Company, Inc.; (right) Courtesy, NASA

Miami, Fla., and a point in Africa just south of the Canary Islands.

It was shown during the International Geophysical Year (1957–58) that heat storage is a major determinant of seasonal variations in sea level. The satellite Seasat 1, which operated for a few months in late 1978, carried a radar altimeter that measured the distance between the satellite and the sea surface with sufficient accuracy to permit determining the elevation of the sea surface and associating that level with the heat stored in the surface layer. This pilot study demonstrated that satellite altimetry may eventually make possible the global mapping of oceanic heat storage.

The ocean is characterized not only by its high heat content but also by the fact that its density is nearly a thousand times that of the atmosphere. Thus changes in the ocean take place much more slowly than in the atmosphere. If it can be demonstrated that atmospheric events are controlled by those in the ocean, prediction of oceanic changes can lead to longer-range forecasts of weather and climate than are possible using the present models.

A number of attempts were made to examine these interactions. For example, an analysis of the Northern Hemisphere showed that during the winter variations in ocean temperatures in much of the Central Pacific are coupled with those of air temperatures in distant regions; when ocean temperatures in the Central Pacific are colder than normal, so are air temperatures in the southeastern United States and in northern Europe, while abnormally warm regimes prevail along the west coast of North America and in the eastern Mediterranean. In view of this relationship several prediction schemes were tested. One involved an objective selection of analogues in the historical record of sea-surface and atmospheric anomalies, and the other linked a predicted anomaly in sea-surface temperature with atmospheric flow at the 700-millibar level (an altitude of about 9,500 ft). Both were successful in predicting recent severe winters.

With the link between anomalies in the ocean and atmosphere becoming more clearly established, attention turned to an attempt to understand the dynamics of the ocean anomalies. A large-scale, five-year study was under way in the North Pacific to measure wind-driven surface flow, thermal structure in the upper 500 m of the ocean, and the surface wind and heating parameters. Ships, U.S. Navy aircraft, and buoys were being used as observation platforms. By examining the temperature anomalies in three dimensions and over a long period of time, scientists were discovering the effects on ocean temperature of such weather events as the passage of large winter pressure depressions. Of particular interest was the use of satellite-tracked buoys to measure the wind-driven surface currents. Early results showed that the buoys move somewhat to the right of the wind and do not change their relative positions until they approach the coast, where they separate and move into the major gyres (ring-shaped elements of circulation) in the Gulf of Alaska and off the west coast of the U.S.

Planktonic exile. Ring-shaped vortices of water are commonly pinched off from meanders, fluctuations of the flow, in the Gulf Stream. Rings extruded to the south contain cold water from the slope region inshore of the Gulf Stream. From 8 to 15 may be observed at a time, and they may survive as discrete units for one or two years or longer. There are also warm rings of Sargasso Sea water that are trapped on the landward side of the Gulf Stream.

Because the marine environment is so different north and south of the stream, the fauna also differs. The rings serve to introduce animals from one environment to the other. A study was recently made of the fate of a euphausiid plankton species that had been isolated within a cold core ring and transported into the Sargasso Sea. Collections from several rings showed how the abundance of this euphausiid decreased as the rings decayed, with extinction taking place in one or two generations.

One ring was observed at ages of 6, 9, and 17 months; at the last observation extinction of the plankton had occurred. The earlier observations showed the populations had moved deeper by several hundred meters each three months. As the rings decayed, surfaces of constant temperature and salinity also descended, and it appeared that the creatures were attempting to stay in a favorable environment. Ultimately, available food was inadequate to maintain growth and reproduction. In the last stages before extinction suitable food is so scarce that the animals metabolize some of their own proteins and fats.

One could speculate that both the cold and warm rings are used by this and other species to explore distant environments. Most of these journeys end in extinction. But eventually when a suitable environment is found, the explorers are ready to establish new population centers.

The ocean depths. Because they are the location of man's maritime activities, it is not surprising that the surface waters of the ocean receive the most attention. But the great depths have always fascinated scientists and have been the subject of recent intensive studies. Tradition has these dark and cold regions nearly devoid of motion and life; the new findings challenge these assumptions.

While physical oceanographers had proposed near-bottom flows in the deep ocean of a few tenths of a centimeter per second (a few kilometers per month), geologists found the bottom sediments in many places sculptured in ways that could only be explained by much stronger flows. A consequence of these strong motions became evident with the discovery of near-bottom mixed layers in many parts of the ocean. New

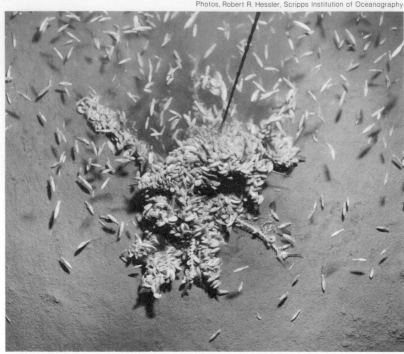

Bait of dead fish (above) is placed near cameras at the bottom of the Philippine Trench, more than 30,000 feet beneath the ocean's surface. After about six and a half hours the fish have been devoured by amphipods (right).

instruments that permit continuous profiling of temperature and salinity near the bottom showed turbulent boundary layers some tens of meters thick; simultaneous current measurements indicated flows of 10–15 cm per second.

The bottom mixed layer, the so-called benthic boundary layer, is often cloudy with resuspended sediment forming a "nepheloid" layer; such layers form where strong near-bottom currents are present. Particles are also abundant in surface waters, many arising from the biological process of primary production. Away from the coast and river discharge and runoff, most inorganic particles are carried to the sea by winds.

The surface and deep particle layers are connected through the fallout of particles from the surface. This fallout determines the nature of marine sediments and provides food for benthic animal communities. Particle formation, transport, and dissolution processes also determine the fate of many pollutants. It was previously believed that most particles travel to the deep seabed in the form of fine debris, a few micrometers in diameter, and fall at a speed of only a few hundred meters per year. Now, however, sedimentation is seen to be much more rapid. Sediment traps placed at great depths near the seafloor collect large particles consisting of the remains of various calcareous organisms and of fecal pellets falling at speeds a hundred times as fast as previously believed. Thus materials introduced in the surface ocean can be taken up by living and inorganic particles and rapidly transported to the abyss.

Once particles have reached the bottom, they are subject to the burrowing activity of seafloor organisms. The mixing of sediments is called bioturbation and reaches to depths of ten centimeters or more. Only in a few regions where bottom waters are devoid of oxygen, such as the Black Sea, is the process suppressed so that undisturbed sediments occur.

Bioturbation is accomplished by many organisms, such as clams and worms, that pass sediment through their gut and extract its edible organic content. The extent of bioturbation can be studied by looking at the distribution in sediment core tops of tracers such as microtektites, plutonium, and isotopes such as lead-210 and silicon-32. Measurements of bioturbation-mixing rates are important for interpretation of the distribution of microfossils in sediments. For example, with a sedimentation rate of three centimeters per 1,000 years and a mixing depth of eight centimeters, sedimentary information on paleoclimate changes cannot be resolved to less than about 2,500 years.

As in other branches of oceanography, deep-sea biology is being transformed by new sampling and measuring devices. For example, improved trawls equipped with fine screens and closing doors are capable of obtaining single samples that contain more animals than were collected on the entire four-year expedition of HMS "Challenger" 100 years ago. Most of the animals are small, but their diversity is comparable to that of a coral reef or a tropical rain forest. Experiments conducted on the deep seabed are intended to throw light on the reason for this high diversity.

These experiments revealed that colonization of

Peter Bruchhausen, Lamont-Doherty Geological Observatory

Courtesy, U.S. Navy, photo by Paul Dearing

A fish, the Trematomus (loennbergii?), *is photographed near the seafloor beneath the Ross Ice Shelf (above). Bait is attached to a cylindrical weight suspended below the camera. Very little light ever penetrates this region. At the right snow is cleared from ice cores taken from the Ross Ice Shelf. Scientists drilled a hole through 420 meters of ice.*

unoccupied sediments is very slow, a factor of interest in evaluating recovery of the seafloor fauna from proposed mining or ocean dumping operations. While some species grow very slowly—a tiny bivalve, *Tindaria,* takes 50 years to reach maturity—others, such as a wood-boring bivalve, have been reported to mature in three months.

In the deep sea the environment is constant and life is monotonous, but some species have evolved to seize on the rare event and to take full advantage of it. Food events are exploited even in the deepest parts of the ocean. Recently, cameras baited with frozen fish were placed on the bottom of the Philippine Trench at depths of 9,600–9,800 m. One species of mobile scavenger, the amphipod *Hirondellea gigas,* appeared within 5–20 minutes. After half an hour there were too many amphipods to count; in another 4–12 hours the fish flesh had been completely consumed, and the amphipods had dispersed. Different rates of adaptation and the rare and haphazardly distributed disturbances and events have led to a heterogeneous patchwork of diverse populations on the deep seafloor.

Beneath the Ross Ice Shelf. Much of the Ross Sea, a huge indentation in the Pacific sector of the Antarctic continent, is permanently covered by thick ice. After trying for several years to drill through this ice shelf to determine its effect on the underlying ocean, scientists in December 1977 finally completed a hole half a meter in diameter through 420 m of ice. From the ice-water interface, the water column extended an additional 237 m to the seabed.

Virtually no light can penetrate the ice shelf. One of the first questions was whether life would be present under such unusual conditions and so far from the productive open sea. Visual observations and collections soon revealed an unusual assemblage of bottom organisms, including amphipods, an isopod, and fish. These animals must depend on food brought by ocean currents from the open sea, hundreds of kilometers away. This exchange was confirmed by measurements of tritium and carbon-14 in the waters beneath the ice.

Remarkably, the bottom sediments themselves appear to be devoid of animal life, unlike the situation in most parts of the ocean. There are, however, abundant fossil diatoms in deeper sediment layers, suggesting that in the middle Miocene Epoch (from about 20 million to 14 million years ago) the Ross Sea was not covered with permanent ice. (*See also* Feature Article: ANTARCTICA—THE LIVING LEGACY.)

—Warren S. Wooster

Electronics and information sciences

Information and communications systems continued to become faster and more efficient during the past year. Among the major achievements were the development of a silicon chip that can store more than 64,000 binary units (bits) of information, the introduction in Great Britain of an experimental service providing data to homes through adapters attached to television sets and telephones, and the fabrication of a microprocessor that can handle data 16 bits at a time.

Communications systems

Information is most useful if it is accurate and current. Timing is so important for some forms of information, such as a weather forecast, that they may lose all their value if seriously delayed. Communication and computer systems of the future will contribute in a major way to efficient collection and distribution of many new forms of information.

During the past 30 years computers and associated equipment such as display terminals, printers, and magnetic storage devices have been installed in a large number of organizations to provide accurate data of all kinds, from airline reservations to tax receipts. During the past five years inexpensive, handheld calculators have provided individuals with more accurate arithmetic data than can be obtained by hand calculation. Yet much information must be gathered at one location, manipulated and reduced at a second location, and consumed at a third location. To move such information rapidly and efficiently from one location to another while keeping it current and useful, a communication system that has been designed specifically for data is needed.

In response to this need information services for businesses and homes are expected to become widely available during the next two decades. The former will become available first. Then, as prices decline due to the effects of technological advances, economies of scale, and competition, such systems will gradually become available for home use. Access to most of them will be provided by means of a terminal consisting of a keyboard and a display akin to a television screen. Eventually, printers are expected to become inexpensive enough to be used in the home as well, stimulating a growth of electronic communication that will largely replace the less efficient mail service of today.

Confidence that such systems will soon be developed grew substantially during the past year. In fact, the significant events of the past year are a harbinger of things to come. These events took place within the framework of three major developments: new applications made possible by technology were providing a growing demand for current information; new technologies being developed were supplying the underlying system at reduced cost; and a changing worldwide regulatory environment was permitting and even encouraging modern information systems.

Technologies. The term "technology" frequently elicits a mental image of a component such as a vacuum tube or a transistor. Yet, many of the most important technologies of the future communications system will not be component technologies but, instead, will be system technologies. System technologies are techniques for designing and assembling communications systems (in this case) from components.

A tiny silicon chip, measuring only one-quarter of a centimeter on a side, can store more than 64,000 binary units of information.

IBM Corp.

Component technologies are nonetheless extremely important. The two most significant to future communications systems will be the microprocessor and the microelectronic storage chips. The microprocessor, first developed in the early 1970s, is a single thin slice of silicon, called a chip, with about the same area as a fingernail. Printed on it are thousands of devices (similar to transistors or diodes) and interconnecting circuits. Its significance lies in the fact that it is very cheap and provides a major portion of the arithmetic and logical functions of a computer on a single chip with only a few wires needed to attach it to the other components. Similarly, microelectronic storage relies on the random access memory chip, which contains a great deal of information storage on a small, inexpensive piece of silicon. One of the most advanced memory chips can store more than 64,000 binary units of information (see *Computers*, below).

An information system of the future will use microprocessors and random access memory throughout. Microprocessors in the television or typewriterlike terminals will reduce the data for most efficient transmission through the network, and microprocessors in the network itself will route the data through the network to the destination in an efficient and reliable way.

Marked improvements in component technologies make sophisticated communications systems possible and shift the emphasis of research toward the problems surrounding the assembly and operation of the system: the system technologies. One of the first major experimental test beds for such technologies was Arpanet, developed by the U.S. Department of Defense's Advanced Research Projects Agency (ARPA) in the closing years of the 1960s. This network, which uses minicomputers to switch data between various communication paths and to interconnect the most complex computers and the simplest terminals, experimented with a number of novel techniques such as switching small packets of data, routing data, and controlling the flow of data in the network. It also provided experience with new applications such as message exchange among individual users of the network; in effect, this was a limited version of electronic mail.

Other experiments stimulated study of one of the most popular system technologies, distributed processing. The fundamental concept of distributed processing is that information storage and information processing are resources which are provided in a number of geographically separated computers in such a way that they can be accessed by a user from any location in the system. Generally, there is also a certain amount of independence of location built into all the components of the system. A distributed processing system can be particularly valuable if, for example, it is designed such that if one computer center should fail, the programs that are normally run there can be moved to another without disruption and possibly even without the knowledge of the users of the system. Highly distributed processing in the sense in which the term is used by research scientists is not expected to be practical for a number of years. By 1979, however, more elementary forms were available from a number of computer manufacturers.

Applications. There is almost no limit to the number of possible applications for information systems that provide accurate and current information. Many of these will become possible in the near future. Furthermore, almost everyone in the computer and computer-related industries has been surprised by the particular applications which have been spawned by the drastic

Microprocessor used in a data communications network provided by the Telenet Communications Corp. The printed circuit boards are representative of the central processing unit and the line processing unit.

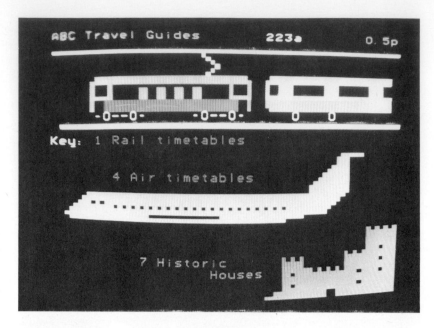

Information is displayed on a home television screen in Great Britain by means of an adapter attached to the subscriber's set and telephone. The experimental Prestel system provides this service, which permits a subscriber to have access to data from many sources.

improvements in semiconductor circuitry. Some examples, such as the citizens band radio and the hand calculator, are well known. In 1978 many stores were sold out of electronic toys long before the peak of the holiday buying rush.

Prototype systems such as Arpanet indicate that electronic message exchange may be more valuable than anticipated. Many researchers are taking advantage of the network to perform joint research and to author joint papers without ever meeting in person. Other studies show that many of the functions of a business office, which have been carried out manually for years and for which productivity gains have been limited, will provide the next major application area for information systems. A number of recent requests to the Federal Communications Commission (FCC) proposed new communications systems or facilities that are intended to meet the needs of the automated office of the future. Among these was a request by Xerox Corp. to modify radio frequency allocations to permit a network that would accommodate a much greater data flow than is possible over the telephone lines available to most businesses today. Also during 1978 American Telephone & Telegraph Co. announced plans for a business-oriented data network service called "Advanced Communications Service."

These proposed networks and services all have the potential to be used in a number of business applications, including office systems and electronic mail. Other similar networks and services in the U.S., announced in previous years, include a service provided by Telenet Communications Corp. that uses many of the ideas of Arpanet and a proposed high-speed voice and data service based on satellites to be offered by Satellite Business Systems.

These announcements were part of a worldwide trend to provide new public data communications networks. During the past year such service was scheduled to begin in a number of national and regional public data networks, such as those in Japan, France, Canada, and the Scandinavian countries (Sweden, Norway, and Denmark).

Most applications which will use public data networks are directed toward business needs. Yet, major systems were being studied and built to provide similar benefits to the individual consumer. Notable among these was the experimental Prestel system, providing services to about 1,500 subscribers in the United Kingdom. Prestel was furnished to the home through a special adapter attached to the television set and telephone, permitting a subscriber to have access to data provided by many information suppliers (see *Information systems and services*, below).

As new applications are developed, particularly those that involve the transmission of personal data such as bank balances of individuals, it becomes necessary for the suppliers of the services to protect such data from purposeful or inadvertent disclosure to unauthorized persons. Techniques and products to protect information advanced rapidly in recent years and were expected to continue to receive much research attention.

Regulatory questions. The regulatory environment for public data transmission systems varies widely in countries throughout the world. In countries where the telephone company is part of the government, the development of advanced networks is heavily influenced by political and social considerations. Governmental directives have established advanced experiments such as Prestel in the United Kingdom and similar systems in West Germany and Japan. However, experiments such as these have sometimes failed in the past and can result in an extra tax burden to the citizens of the country.

In the U.S. such experiments are usually carried out by private firms with private venture capital, although regulatory hurdles can and frequently do discourage such ventures. Efforts directed toward decreasing such hurdles by increasing unregulated competition in the communication industry resulted in a bill referred to as the Communications Act of 1978, introduced during the second session of the 95th Congress. Parallel efforts were under way in the FCC and in an agency of the U.S. Department of Commerce, the National Telecommunications and Information Administration.

The regulatory environment will be influential in determining the rate of progress and its initial direction in communication systems. In the long term, however, technological improvements and the demand for applications are certain to produce better practical information facilities whether or not regulatory constraints influence the early solutions to information distribution problems. New systems that improve the productivity of people, provide new applications not previously possible, and simplify the complexities of life at home and work will emerge quietly but persistently during the next two decades.

—Robert F. Steen

Electronics

A major thrust in electronics during recent years has been to increase the number of electronic components in an integrated circuit (IC) and to increase the capacity

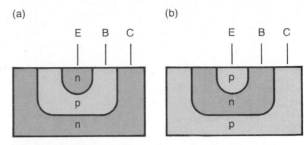

(a)   (b)

Figure 1. In these cross sections of npn and pnp transistors the n regions contain electrons (negative-charge current carriers) and the p areas have holes (positive-charge current carriers).

of IC's used for memories in computers. Concomitant with these efforts has been the development of the microcomputer, a computer with circuitry on a single chip of silicon having an area of only some six square centimeters. The applications for these devices are legion. In addition to their industrial and military use, the integrated circuit and microcomputer are finding increasing application in commercial products that range from the electronic watch to the automobile.

The transistor. The basis for this burgeoning activity is the transistor, invented in 1947. Prior to that year electronics was synonymous with vacuum tubes. These are the devices that made amplifiers, radio, television, and other electronic equipment possible. The vacuum tube can amplify a minute signal to a level where, for example, it may actuate a loudspeaker, provide a TV picture, or control the position of a rudder on aircraft. It functions by controlling the flow of electrons from a heated filament in the tube (which lights the tube). The power required to heat the filament is typi-

IBM Corp.

Scanning electron micrograph reveals a portion of a programmable logic array with locations for as many as 4,000 logic elements. Reducing the minimum dimensions of the device to one micrometer achieved an increase in speed and a reduction in power dissipation.

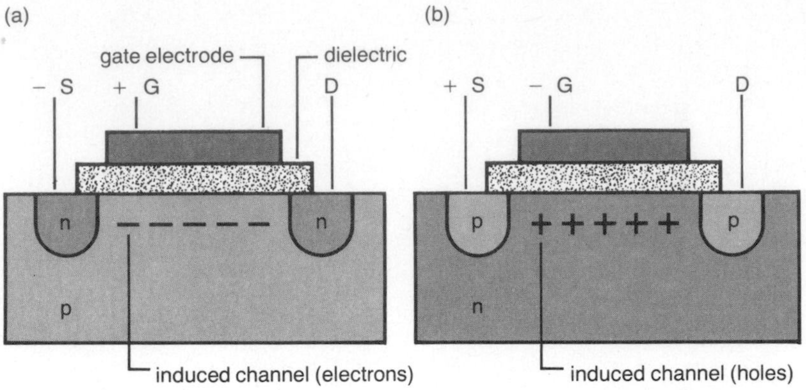

(a)

gate electrode — dielectric

− S + G   D   + S − G   D

n   n   p   + + + + +   p

p   n

Figure 2. Cross sections of two types of field-effect transistor (FET), the N-MOSFET (a) and P-MOSFET (b). For each device the signal to be amplified is connected across the gate (G) and source (S) terminals (see text below).

└ induced channel (electrons)   └ induced channel (holes)

cally two watts. A TV set containing, for example, 20 tubes would require 40 w of power, all wasted as heat. The transistor, by contrast, does not require filament power. Other advantages of the transistor over the vacuum tube include its much smaller size and longer life. Today, the transistor and integrated circuit have replaced the vacuum tube in virtually all electronic equipment.

The transistor, like the vacuum tube, is capable of amplification. It is a solid-state device, generally made of silicon (figure 1). The region labeled n contains electrons, and the region labeled p contains holes. Electrons are negative-charge current carriers, and holes are positive-charge current carriers. Because both types of carriers partake in its operation, the transistor often is called a bipolar junction transistor. Usually, a signal to be amplified is connected across the base (B) and emitter (E) terminals. The amplified output signal is taken across the collector (C) and base terminals. Two types of transistor are the npn (figure 1a) and the pnp of figure 1b.

Another type of transistor enjoying wide application is the field-effect transistor (FET). Important versions of these devices are the N-MOSFET and the P-MOSFET. As shown in cross-section views in figure 2, these transis-

tors are fabricated in a silicon chip. Terminal G, the gate, is insulated from the chip by a dielectric (insulator) material, such as silicon dioxide (glass). The n regions serve as the source (S) and drain (D) terminals in figure 2a; in figure 2b, the p regions serve as the source and drain terminals. For each device the signal to be amplified is connected across the gate and source terminals; the amplified output signal is obtained across the drain and source terminals.

If, for the N-MOSFET a voltage is applied across the gate and source terminals, electrons will be induced in the channel if the gate is more positive than the source. This enhances the flow of electrons between the drain and source terminals. If the gate is made less positive with respect to the source, the electron flow in the channel is reduced. Similarly, if for the P-MOSFET the gate is more negative than the source, holes are induced in the channel. The number of holes varies with the magnitude of the gate voltage. Owing to this behavior, both devices are capable of amplification, like the bipolar junction transistor.

The integrated circuit. In an integrated circuit, elements that are used in electronics, such as the transistor and resistor, are fabricated together in a single chip of silicon. (Resistors are elements that limit the flow of current. The resistor and transistor are key components found in electronic circuits.) The number of such devices per unit area, called the packing density, is many thousands per square centimeter.

A cross-section view of an integrated circuit containing two npn transistors is illustrated in figure 3. The two transistors are formed in a p-type substrate, about 0.001 cm thick. The collector of each transistor is the n region; the base is the p region; and the n^+ the emitter. The designation n^+ indicates that this region has more electrons than the n region.

The necessary electrical isolation of the two transistors is realized by returning the p-substrate to a voltage that is less positive than the voltage at the collector (n region). This results in a reverse-biased p-n junction. A reverse-biased p-n junction may be thought of as acting like an open switch. In this manner the two npn

Figure 3. Cross section of an integrated circuit that contains two npn transistors. The designation n^+ indicates that this region contains more electrons than the n area (see text, this page).

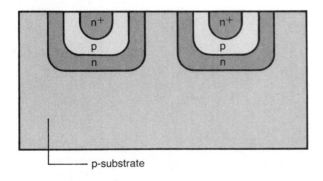

└ p-substrate

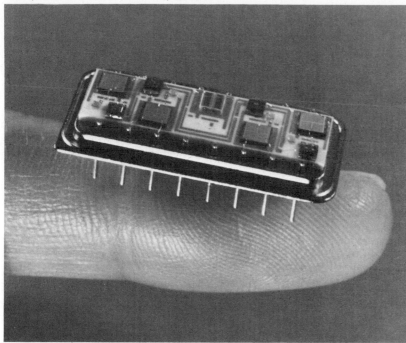

Solid-state relay developed to replace and upgrade electromechanical switches contains such components as a light-emitting diode, a photodiode array chip, and a field-effect transistor.

transistors are electrically separated from each other.

For N-MOSFET and P-MOSFET devices electrical isolation is realized without the need for establishing reverse-biased p-n junctions. This results in a greater packing density than achieved with the bipolar junction transistor. Using such techniques as electron-beam lithography, it is possible to achieve, for example, a gate length as small as 0.000001 m. This permits a packing density of some 200 circuits on an area of one square millimeter and some 50,000 circuits in a chip of silicon. This high packing density is an example of very large-scale integration (VLSI). (*See* Year in Review: PHYSICS: *Solid-state physics.*)

Microprocessors, microcomputers, and memories. The microprocessor is a device that on a single chip of silicon contains the essential circuits of a digital computer, those that perform arithmetic and control the sequence of operations. In a digital computer numbers and alphabet characters are represented by a string of 1s and 0s, called bits. An eight-bit microprocessor processes data that is eight bits long (or one byte long). For example, number 15 is represented by the eight bits 00001111. In 1978 a 16-bit microprocessor was introduced. A larger bit capacity of a microprocessor or computer increases its precision.

In addition to the arithmetic and control circuits a microcomputer contains in a single chip a memory and input/output devices for communicating with the outside world. The microcomputer is equivalent to a basic digital computer in a single chip of silicon having an area of some six square centimeters.

Two basic memories are employed in microprocessors and microcomputers. These are the random-access memory (RAM) and the read-only memory (ROM). The RAM allows data to be read from, and written into, the memory. For the ROM, however, only reading of data is possible. During the past year RAM memories capable of storing 64,536 bits of information (referred to as a 64-K memory) were introduced.

A major development of 1978 was the introduction of a magnetic-bubble memory capable of storing 250,-000 bits of information. In this type of memory storage is accomplished by the movement of minute magnetized particles, or "bubbles." In the near future magnetic bubble memories for storing a million or more bits of information are expected to become a reality. (*See* Year in Review: MATERIALS SCIENCES: *Ceramics.*)

Medical electronics. Microprocessors and microcomputers in recent months were finding increasing applications in medicine in two prime areas: diagnostics and the development of aids for the handicapped and disabled. Applications in diagnostics included early diagnosis of glaucoma, in which the blood circulation of the optic nerve head was monitored for physical changes. In addition, a microprocessor-based system was used in the determination of cognitive skills in brain-damaged victims, and a data system, Medical Display Analysis and Recording Systems, was developed for use during heart surgery and intensive-care monitoring.

Among the applications for the handicapped and disabled were a keyboard and display unit that enabled a deaf person to communicate by telephone. Also, a microcomputer was used to send signals to a knee

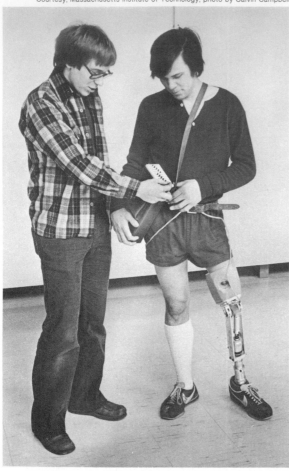

By adjusting a microcomputer slung over his shoulder, an amputee can "tune" his artificial knee joint to the gait that he desires for a particular circumstance, such as climbing stairs.

mechanism that permitted amputees with above-knee prostheses to walk with a natural gait. Finally, by using a microcomputer a nonspeaking person could observe and correct messages that were then translated into instruction for a voice synthesizer that delivered the message.

Consumer electronics. Recent emphasis in consumer electronics was directed toward the lowering of energy consumption, the introduction of digital techniques for the processing of data, and the use of large-scale integrated circuits. One example of such activity was the development of the digital audio record. The audio signal is converted to a string of 0 and 1 bits, the number of bits being proportional to the amplitude and frequency of the signal. Both the recording and playback are done with laser light. Use of this technique increases the dynamic range, reduces distortion to less than 0.03%, and results in virtually no flutter or record wear.

The bulkiest item in a television set is the picture tube (cathode-ray tube). In 1978 flat-screen TV sets were demonstrated. One had a 50-mm-thick electroluminescent screen, while another was a pocket-size black-and-white TV set using a liquid-crystal display, the same type of display used in many electronic watches and calculators.

A number of educational toys based on electronics were introduced in the market during 1978. Perhaps one of the most interesting was a machine that talks. It contains a large semiconductor memory in which are programmed more than 200 words that are frequently misspelled. The user is able to go through spelling drills without the drudgery of such activity.

Because the U.S. Environmental Protection Agency has required automobile manufacturers to improve gas mileage, the microprocessor is making a significant impact on that industry. For example, it is being used by Ford Motor Co. to optimize timing, the air/fuel ratio, and exhaust-gas recirculation, all for the purpose of increasing gas efficiency. The microprocessor was also used by General Motors Corp. to improve the performance of the catalytic converter.

Other developments. In 1978 design studies were conducted by a number of aerospace companies to determine the feasibility of launching solar collectors in space. Once the collectors are in orbit, the collected energy would be converted to radio waves of very high frequency (microwaves) and aimed toward the Earth. The received waves would then be converted to electrical energy.

The factory production line also was influenced by electronics. For increased productivity, several microcomputers, each dedicated to control a specific process on the line, are controlled by a larger computer, called the minicomputer. The first commercial microcomputer-controlled robot, for use in the assembly of small parts, was unveiled in 1978.

—Arthur H. Seidman

Computers

Programming languages, computer chess programs, and microcomputers were among the areas in which there were major developments in the computer field in 1978.

Programming languages. Computer programs are written in many different programming languages. Hundreds and perhaps even thousands of these languages have been introduced since general-purpose electronic computers were first developed in the late 1940s. Only a few of these languages have survived and become important.

A significant event in June 1978 was the Conference on the History of Programming Languages in Los Angeles. It was organized by Jean Sammet, who was one of the leading figures in the development of COBOL (Common Business Oriented Language) in the early

Using one of the world's most powerful computers, researchers view two computer-simulated galaxies set on a collision course. The width of the television screen represents a distance of 100,000 light-years. In such applications computers may help scientists increase their understanding of the dynamics of the universe.

1960s. Among the leading participants were John Backus, who had major responsibility for the development of FORTRAN (Formula Translation) in the mid-1950s, and Alan Perlis and Peter Naur, who, along with Backus and others, designed ALGOL (Algorithmic Language) in 1957–60.

FORTRAN quickly became the standard programming language for scientific computation, and COBOL became the standard programming language for business data processing. ALGOL was designed by a committee of computer scientists from Europe and the United States whose goal was to produce a language that would be the standard international programming language. ALGOL became a popular language for scientific computing outside the U.S., but its use has been diminishing, and it is expected that the original ALGOL language will soon be only of historical and theoretical interest.

Over the years since ALGOL was introduced there have been a number of efforts to change and extend and improve the language. One of the most successful was the development of the programming language PASCAL by Niklaus Wirth of the Eidgenössische Technische Hochschule in Zurich. A complete definition of PASCAL was published in 1971. Since that time it has received widespread acceptance, especially by the academic computer science community.

PASCAL is in many ways a simpler language than ALGOL. It leaves out features that have proved difficult to understand and difficult to implement in compilers (that is, in programs that translate the programming language into machine language). On the other hand, PASCAL goes beyond ALGOL in providing the user the ability to define and manipulate fairly arbitrary "data structures." Thus, while ALGOL was mostly limited in its use to calculations involving the numbers and arrays that appear in mathematical computation, PASCAL provides a convenient tool for writing well structured programs that manipulate much more general types of data such as alphabetic strings and records and lists. The language most used on microcomputers and small minicomputers has been the elementary and unstructured language BASIC. A major advance in 1977–79 was the development of PASCAL compilers suitable for use on very small computers. A number of companies making small computers adopted PASCAL as the language that they use internally and that they promote among their users. A powerful microcomputer software system based on PASCAL was developed at the University of California at San Diego and was distributed to and used at a number of other universities.

The U.S. Department of Defense (DOD) is an important user of computers, and many computer languages were developed in connection with the thousands of defense-oriented computer systems. There are, however, advantages to having just one standard computer programming language, provided of course that the language is suitable for use in all of the areas in which it would need to be used. There are huge costs associated with the existing diversity of languages.

In 1975 the DOD initiated a formal effort to develop a programming language that would become the standard for its future computing systems. This effort achieved a major step toward completion with the publication by the DOD of a language requirements document entitled "Steelman" in June 1978. "Steelman" is the most recent in a series of language requirements specifications that started with "Strawman" and con-

297

tinued through "Woodenman," "Tinman," and "Iron-man." Each successive specification was the result of a major effort to refine and improve the preceding one. Along with the more recent versions of the language requirements, contracts have been let to computer software companies to develop detailed specifications for languages satisfying these requirements.

As the process has continued, it has become clear that the eventual language that is developed will have a great deal in common with PASCAL. PASCAL was not discussed in the 1978 Conference on the History of Programming Languages because it is too recent a language to have been included there. However, PASCAL and its extensions will almost certainly be included among the most important and widely used computer languages of the 1980s.

Computer chess. In 1978 a chess-playing program running on a high-speed computer and playing under standard chess tournament rules won a game from a chess player who held the rank of International Master. This was a truly remarkable accomplishment.

Efforts to build a machine that can think and act like a human being, and in particular a machine that can play chess, began long before the development of the modern electronic computer. One interesting instance was a chess-playing automaton, "The Turk," which was designed and built by Baron Wolfgang von Kempelen in 1770. First demonstrated at the Royal Palace in Vienna, it was exhibited in Europe and the U.S. for many years. "The Turk" was an ingenious device built with many gears and very elaborate clockwork. The most ingenious part of the design was the way in which a small human chess player could be hidden inside and could remain hidden even while the spectators thought that they were being allowed to examine all of the internal workings of the automaton.

In 1835 a British mathematician and scientist, Charles Babbage, designed and started the construction of an "analytical engine," which, if it could have been completed, would have been the world's first general-purpose digital computer, more than 100 years before such a computer was actually built. In his writings about the analytical engine Babbage pointed out that it would be possible to program it to play games of great complexity, including the game of chess. Babbage was right in principle. The idea of the general-purpose digital computer would indeed make it possible for a machine to play chess, but Babbage's mechanical version of such a machine would have been too limited in capacity and much too slow.

There is no Nobel Prize in computer science, but in 1978 a computer researcher, Herbert Simon of Carnegie-Mellon University in Pittsburgh, Pa., won the Nobel Prize for Economics. Simon was one of the early workers in the area of computer science known as artificial intelligence. The field of artificial intelligence is the modern counterpart of, and to some extent the realiza-

Herbert Simon of Pittsburgh's Carnegie-Mellon University, winner of the 1978 Nobel Prize for Economics, pioneered in the area of computer science known as artificial intelligence.

tion of, earlier efforts to make a machine that can think and act like a human being. Pattern recognition, problem solving, and language translation are examples of the kinds of intelligent behavior that have been programmed on computing systems with varying degrees of success. From the beginning, workers in the field of artificial intelligence have been interested in developing chess-playing programs. Aside from their intrinsic interest, such programs provide a vehicle in which useful ideas for the simulation of other intelligent human behavior can be developed and tested.

Much progress was made in the then-new field of artificial intelligence in the 1950s, and there was a great deal of optimism about results that were soon to be achieved. Simon expressed this optimism in a talk that he delivered in 1957 in which he made a number of predictions of accomplishments that were to be expected in artificial intelligence in the next ten years. One of his predictions was that within that time period a computer program would be chess champion of the world.

By 1968 it was clear that this result had not been achieved, and that it would not be achieved for a very long time, even though some fairly good chess-playing programs had been written. During that year a wager involving a fairly significant sum was made between several computer scientists and David Levy, an International Master who was then chess champion of

Scotland. Levy bet that no computer chess program would be able to beat him in a chess match in the next ten years. The end of that ten-year period was 1978.

For a number of years prior to 1978 chess tournaments between computer chess programs had been featured at conferences of the Association for Computing Machinery, and at meetings of IFIP, the International Federation for Information Processing. The most consistently successful program was one written by Larry Atkin and David Slate at Northwestern University. The most current version of their program, Chess 4.7, running on the most powerful computer on which it could be run, the Cyber 176 of Control Data Corp., was the logical choice for a match against David Levy. The match was played in Toronto in August 1978. Levy won by a score of 3½ to 1½, but in the course of the match the computer program won one game and drew another, a respectable showing.

Chess players are rated according to a rather complicated formula by national and international chess federations. A chess master is a player with a rating of 2200 or more. David Levy, who is an International Master, has a rating in the 2300 range. A player of world championship stature would have a rating close to 2700. The Cyber 176, running Chess 4.7, would probably be rated close to 2000. A great deal of the success of the program is due to the tremendous speed of the Cyber 176. However, the speed of the computer is not the only factor that determines the performance of a chess playing program. A faster computer makes it possible for the program to look farther ahead and to consider a very large number of possible variations before it selects its move. However, the number of possible variations in chess is so large that it is impossible to consider all variations, and any brute-force approach that uses a simple step-by-step procedure to select the variations to be considered is doomed to failure even on the fastest possible machine.

Serious chess programs use ingenious and complicated procedures to select and analyze variations that are important and worth considering in the limited amount of time available. In so doing they implement chess strategies and tactics analogous to those used by human chess players. Chess 4.7 has probably reached the chess master level in its tactical play, but it is much weaker on the level of strategy. Future versions will probably perform much better in this area, but the development of strategic planning ability comparable to that of a human chess master is a task of great difficulty. New advances in artificial intelligence implemented on computers very different from those now in use will probably be needed in order to produce a chess-playing program of world championship caliber. Even though tremendous progress has already been made, the human world chess champion seems safe from defeat by a machine, at least in the 20th century. It would be foolish to predict any limitations on what

IBM Corp.

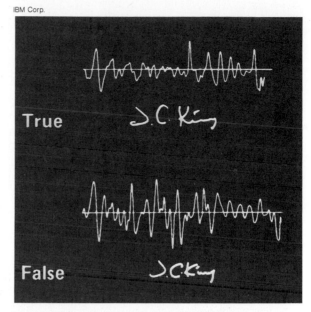

New signature verification system has detected forgeries. Each name above was written with a special pen connected to a computer. Differences in the speed of the writing and pressure on the pen revealed the fake.

computers might be able to do beyond the year 2000.

Microcomputers, microprocessors, and memory chips. Techniques in the design and fabrication of large-scale integrated circuits continue to improve from year to year, and each year brings with it a number of impressive new developments. Two of the important new computer developments in this area in 1978 were 16-bit microprocessors and 64K-bit (K = 1,024) random access memory chips.

A microprocessor is a computer central processor on a single small silicon chip whose area is usually less than 0.25 sq cm (less than 0.04 sq in). With circuits of given speed the power of a computer is directly related to the number of bits (binary digits) that can be transmitted to and from memory and processed in parallel. Up to 1978 the most powerful microprocessors in widespread use were designed to handle data eight bits at a time. They are the central processors of the microcomputers and intelligent terminals that were introduced in 1976–78.

It seemed almost miraculous that the very large number of complex circuits needed for an 8-bit computer central processor could be fabricated on a single chip, but by the time the first 8-bit microprocessors were being delivered in 1972–73, the technological advances had already been made that would lead to the introduction of 16-bit microprocessors a few years later. A number of integrated circuit manufacturers started producing and delivering 16-bit microprocessors in 1978, and a number of others announced some even more powerful 16-bit microprocessors for delivery in

1979. The 16-bit microprocessors are at least ten times more powerful than the earlier 8-bit microprocessors.

Computer memory sizes are usually expressed in terms of multiples of K bits, with K = 1,024. The cost of computer memory has been declining rapidly as the number of chips needed for a memory of given size has decreased. Between 1976 and 1978 the standard density for high-performance random access memory chips has gone from 4K to 16K bits per chip. In 1978 a number of manufacturers announced the production of 64K-bit memory chips.

It takes a large investment in new technology and in engineering design to produce high-density microprocessors and memory chips, but the production cost per chip is then almost independent of the density or circuit complexity. Thus, if the development costs can be distributed over very large production runs, the cost per chip will eventually be little if any higher than the costs of the earlier generation of low-density chips. For some computer systems this can mean an order of magnitude increase in performance at essentially no increase in cost.

The more powerful microprocessors and denser memory chips will affect all levels of the computer field, but they will have their greatest impact on microcomputers, computers that use a microprocessor as the central processing component. Microcomputers are relatively inexpensive computer systems ranging in price from a few hundred dollars up to about ten thousand dollars. Many are sold in retail stores as personal computers used by hobbyists and computer enthusiasts. Others are used as data-processing computers for small businesses. The early microcomputers were regarded by many as expensive toys that would have limited use in the world of serious computer applications. The new very powerful microcomputers based on 16-bit microprocessors should do much to change that outlook. Significant computing power is becoming available at very low cost, and this will have a profound effect on the way computing power is distributed and used.

—Saul Rosen

Satellite systems

Earth-orbiting satellites that utilize their vantage points in space are called applications satellites, as distinct from scientific research satellites. Used for economic benefit and military purposes, there are three general classes of such satellite systems: communications, Earth observation, and navigation. Users are nations, groups of nations, and private industrial concerns.

The U.S. and the Soviet Union continued to dominate such activities because of their large booster rockets, which they also used to launch satellites for other nations. However, France, Japan, and China, as well as the European Space Agency (ESA), continued

progress in developing their own launch capabilities. ESA, a consortium comprised of Belgium, Denmark, France, West Germany, Ireland, Italy, The Netherlands, Sweden, Switzerland, the United Kingdom, and Spain, planned to use the French-developed booster (Ariane) for communications and weather satellites. Japan was using the N-1 launcher, which had U.S. rocket-propulsion systems for its first and third stages, but had its own launch vehicle under development. China announced the development of a high-energy rocket booster.

Communications satellites. The International Telecommunications Satellite Organization (Intelsat), a consortium of more than 100 nations of which the Communications Satellite Corp. (Comsat) is the U.S. member, continued to grow in size and capability. Global transmission of telephone, television, facsimile, and digital data was provided by Intelsat 4 and 4A spacecraft in geostationary orbit. (A geostationary, or geosynchronous, orbit is at an altitude of 35,900 km (22,300 mi) above the Equator. At that height a satellite travels at the same angular velocity as the surface of the rotating Earth, and thus remains at a constant point above the Earth. Three such satellites can provide global coverage except at the highest latitudes.) Two Intelsat 4A satellites were launched by the U.S. National Aeronautics and Space Administration (NASA) in January and March 1978.

Three domestic satellite systems were operational in the U.S. Western Union owned and operated Westar satellites to transmit telegrams, mailgrams, Telex, and high-speed facsimile data. In March the Public Broadcasting Service (PBS) began to use the Westar 1 satellite to transmit noncommercial television programs to some two dozen stations in the southern U.S., from Florida to Texas. By January 1979 more than 200 public television stations were linked by satellite in nearly every state, as well as in Puerto Rico and the Virgin Islands.

RCA Corp. operated a Satcom satellite system for commercial leased lines, as well as cable and pay-television distribution services. Comsat General Corp., a subsidiary of Comsat, leased the capacity of Comstar satellites to the Bell systems of American Telephone and Telegraph Co. (AT&T). A third Comstar satellite was launched by NASA in June.

Satellite Business Systems (a partnership of IBM Corp., Aetna Life and Casualty Co., and Comsat General) was scheduled to begin all-digital services in 1980 to the U.S. government and large business firms. Three satellites were on order. In 1978 the Xerox Corp. applied to the Federal Communications Commission for a telecommunications network to be used for document distribution, data transmission, and teleconferences. Ground stations would be located in 200 metropolitan areas, and service would begin in 1981.

In March 1978 Comsat signed a one-year contract

with the U.S. Postal Service to plan and demonstrate international electronic mail in 1979. To be investigated were the feasibility of scanning mail messages, converting this information into digital data, encrypting, sending data via satellite to another ground station outside the U.S., processing the received signal, and producing a facsimile of the original message. The advantages of such a system would be reduced delivery time and decreased amount of handling.

The three Marisat maritime communications satellites, operated by Comsat General, provided high-fidelity voice, data, Telex, and facsimile service to some 150 merchant ships that were equipped with Marisat antennas. Users throughout the world included some U.S. naval vessels.

In May the U.S. officially joined the International Maritime Satellite Organization (Inmarsat), comprised of 40 maritime nations. A thorny political situation developed during the last half of 1978. The existing Marisat satellites have a five-year design lifetime, and so Comsat General proposed a follow-on Marisat 2 (Leasat) system that would begin operation in 1981. With the exception of the U.S., however, the 22-member board of Inmarsat unanimously supported purchase of ESA's Marecs maritime satellites, currently under development. Also planned was the installation of maritime packages on three future Intelsat 5 satellites. To cloud matters further the Soviet Union offered to launch an ESA Marecs satellite.

In April NASA launched a developmental Japanese broadcast satellite into synchronous orbit. Its purpose was to conduct experimental broadcasts of color television to small user terminals in urban and remote areas of Japan.

Late in 1978 China sent a space delegation to the U.S. for discussions that resulted in an informal agreement between the two countries to cooperate in the development of a Chinese domestic communications satellite system. China would be permitted to purchase a U.S. spacecraft and a ground station. Launching was to be by the U.S. space shuttle.

In May NASA launched an ESA developmental communications satellite, a forerunner of an operational satellite system to be operated by the European Conference of Postal and Telecommunications Administrations. Other NASA launches included a new U.S. Navy satellite in February, a second NATO III secure communications satellite for the North Atlantic Treaty Organization in November, and Anik B, a Canadian domestic communications satellite.

Earth observation satellites. This category of applications satellites consists of three major types: meteorological, Earth resources, and military reconnaissance.

Weather satellites. By 1979 weather, or meteorological, satellites had become an integral part of weather reporting systems throughout the world. In June

Satellite designed to orbit over the North and South poles and observe auroras (above) was launched from Japan by the University of Tokyo's three-stage rocket Mu-3H No. 2 (below).

Photos, Authenticated News International

NASA launched the third Geostationary Operational Environmental Satellite (GOES 3) for the U.S. National Oceanic and Atmospheric Administration (NOAA), which operates the U.S. weather satellite system. It was placed in geostationary orbit at longitude 135° W. The GOES 1 weather satellite, previously situated at that longitude, was moved to longitude 60° E. Five geostationary weather satellites throughout the world were reporting weather data at half-hour intervals.

The NOAA polar-orbiting operational satellite system was joined in October by NASA's Nimbus 7 and TIROS-N developmental weather satellites. Nimbus 7 carried eight complex sensors to monitor global atmosphere, color gradations of lakes and oceans (important to monitoring pollution), and the Earth's heat radiation. These data contribute to the understanding of climate, oceanography, atmospheric pollution, and regional and global weather patterns. TIROS-N, the first of a third generation of operational NOAA weather satellites, carried advanced instrumentation, including a scanning radiometer for visible and infrared images and a vertical sounder designed to provide temperature readings and moisture data from the Earth's surface through the stratosphere. A heat-capacity mapping satellite launched by NASA in April provided a new source of data of temperature variations on the Earth's surface.

Structural thermal model of the Intelsat 5 communications satellite, complete except for its solar panels, is prepared for an environmental test. The first launch of an Intelsat 5 is scheduled for 1979.

Courtesy, Ford Aerospace & Communications Corporation

Images of the surface were processed in as many as nine colors, indicating relative temperatures within a few degrees.

In June NASA launched Seasat 1 into polar orbit. The first satellite to study oceans, it carried five instruments to obtain data on surface winds and temperatures, tides and currents, wave heights, ocean topography, and coastal storms in all-weather and day and night conditions. After functioning well for three months the satellite became inoperative as a result of a power failure.

Earth resources satellites. In January Landsat 1 was shut down after its performance had degraded. The first satellite of its kind, it had produced more than 300,000 pictures since its launch in 1972. Landsat 2 continued to be operational and was joined in March by Landsat 3; the latter carried an improved vidicon recorder, and image resolution was improved greatly (from 80 m to 40 m). In addition, Landsat 3 carried a system capable of collecting data transmitted directly from as many as 1,000 remote ground platforms.

The three important potential uses of Landsat multispectral images are location of energy supplies, assessment of food production, and large-scale environmental monitoring. After three years of the "large area crop inventory experiment" (LACIE) by the U.S. Department of Agriculture, NASA, and NOAA, the feasibility of such study and forecasting seemed proved. The accuracy of its prediction of the Soviet wheat crop in 1977 was, remarkably, within a few percent. In addition to the three U.S. Landsat ground stations capable of receiving satellite data, Canada, Brazil, Italy, and Iran had operational ground receivers and India was planning to build one.

Military reconnaissance satellites. Although the existence of such military satellite systems of the U.S. and U.S.S.R. has been well known for years, the first public acknowledgement was made by U.S. Pres. Jimmy Carter in October. He stated that satellite photo reconnaissance had become an important stabilizing factor in world affairs in monitoring arms agreements. A third nation, China, was apparently developing reconnaissance spacecraft. Of the eight satellites launched by that nation since 1970, three returned reentry packages that were recovered.

The U.S. Navy developed ocean surveillance satellites designed to monitor electronic intelligence from surface vessels and submarines. Originally known by the name White Cloud, the first of an operational series of these satellites was expected in 1979. (*See also* Feature Article: THE SKY-HIGH WAR.)

Navigation satellites. The U.S. Navy navigational satellites system, Transit, continued the operations it began in 1960. The first in a series of improved navigation spacecraft, Nova, was scheduled to be launched in 1979. Initial development tests with three U.S. Air Force NavStar Global Positioning Satellites proved

Marisat communications satellite is inspected in a laboratory after a radio frequency test. Marisats are used as instant links between ships and shore for the transmission of various types of data.

highly successful. Tests were performed on fighter and transport aircraft and on a portable manpack mounted on a truck moving up to 50 mph. Positional accuracies within about one meter were achieved. With three such satellites latitude and longitude only could be obtained. A fourth GPS satellite would be required for altitude measurement.

The NASA Nimbus 6 weather satellite was used in a series of demonstrations of position determination in remote land and airborne travel. During the solo trek by Japanese explorer Naomi Uemura to the North Pole and across Greenland, a ten-kilogram beacon transmitter tracked his movement. Signals relayed from his dogsled to the satellite were then relayed to NASA's center at Greenbelt, Md., where a large-scale map marked progress with an accuracy of one to two kilometers. Similar beacons tracked the first balloon crossing of the Atlantic Ocean in August, and a geological expedition in Egypt's western desert in September and October.

—F. C. Durant III

Information systems and services

A key element in all automated information systems and services is the data base, the computer-searchable file that contains records of data and bibliographic citations to documents in specialized fields. According to a market survey, revenue from the information data base industry will grow from $740 million in 1976 to $1.6 billion by 1985. This expansion will be due to declining costs of computer hardware, new data base production, and the entry of additional firms into the data base marketing sector.

One effect of the increased availability of computer-

based information systems is a change from paper to nonprint, electronic forms of information distribution. Another is a shift from a nearly total reliance on local information sources to an extensive use of commercial services for gaining access to large, remote sources of information. In this postindustrial era information systems and services are thus becoming ever more important and efficient.

Health care. The fight against disease is a major concern for physicians and researchers throughout the world. The International Cancer Research Data Bank sought to promote the exchange of information among cancer scientists by keeping them aware of completed and ongoing projects taking place in laboratories throughout the world. The program included three computerized data bases collectively referred to as CANCERLINE. Of the three, CANCERLIT contains more than 156,000 abstracts of published literature dealing with all aspects of the disease. Updated monthly, it was expected to grow by approximately 30,000 items per year. CLINPROT is a specialized data base containing about 1,000 protocols, or summaries, of clinical investigations relating to new therapeutic agents and procedures. It is updated quarterly and was designed to remain small. CANCERPROJ contains some 21,000 descriptions of cancer research projects in progress during the preceding two years. Project descriptions are contributed by scientists throughout the world. The data base is updated every three months, at which time the descriptions are modified or removed as the research projects are changed or completed.

CANCERLINE data bases are computerized and can be searched by typewriterlike terminals located in medical, scientific, and academic institutions anywhere in the world and connected by a telecommunications network to the central computer facility located at the National Library of Medicine in Bethesda, Md. Search results can be printed at the user's terminal or at the central computer and mailed to the user.

High blood pressure, or hypertension, is another killer disease. It is estimated that more than 23 million people in the U.S., or one out of every seven adults, has high blood pressure. In spite of the research and the new treatment methods that are available, hypertension is the direct cause of more than 20,000 deaths each year and is a contributing factor to many more fatalities. To combat this disease the secretary of health, education, and welfare initiated the National High Blood Pressure Education Program, of which the High Blood Pressure Information Center is a major component. The center serves as a national clearinghouse for the collection, evaluation, and dissemination of information on the disease. The primary mission is an educational one, and information is disseminated to the general public, health educators, health planners, and health care providers. The center maintains an extensive collection of printed and audiovisual materials and provides information on community programs and activities. Each month it receives almost 2,000 requests and inquiries and distributes approximately 200,000 educational publications.

Health care implies rehabilitation as well as treatment, and the National Rehabilitation Information Center maintains and provides access to a definitive collection of published materials resulting from research and evaluation grants awarded by the Rehabilitation Services Administration. The collection includes books, journals, conference proceedings, and selected nonprint materials. Information services are provided to rehabilitation professionals, handicapped individuals, and concerned members of the public in order to contribute to the improvement of rehabilitation pro-

grams serving the physically and mentally disabled members of the community.

Research results do not improve health care; physicians do when they apply these results in practice. Recognizing this, the National Library of Medicine developed a unique health information system for practitioners, a system that translates new research findings into a form that the physician can use. This data bank is designed to contain substantive answers to questions posed by practitioners, answers that reflect the current consensus of a group of experts and which include citations to primary publications for more detailed study, if desired.

An Information Exchange System on Aging was established by the Social Development Division of the United Nations (UN) Secretariat for the purposes of collecting and disseminating information on aging, of promoting the development of policies and standards, and of encouraging practical action in the field of aging at both national and international levels. The system serves as both a clearinghouse and a referral center for governments, agencies, and individuals. It contains more than 1,000 items collected and cataloged from material published by UN agencies, offices, and legislative bodies. A network of national correspondents collects relevant material from sources outside the UN. In addition to documents, the information exchange maintains an index of resource persons, classified by country and specialization, who can advise and consult on specific projects relating to the needs of the aged.

In addition to the development of new accident reporting, treatment, and rehabilitation methods, medical researchers continued to be concerned with bioethical issues. Bioethics can be defined as a systematic study of value questions which arise in the biomedical and behavioral fields. It includes such topics as euthanasia, psychosurgery, human experimentation, genetic inter-

Two researchers view the video display screen of INTERNIST, an experimental medical diagnostic system on computer. A physician can supply information to the computer, which then will ask additional questions. On the basis of the original data and the answers to the questions INTERNIST will then provide a diagnosis.

vention, abortion, the definition of death, and the allocation of scarce medical resources. Over the past few years bioethics has become increasingly important, and by 1979 there were more than 70 primary journals that published English-language materials discussing bioethical issues. The Center for Bioethics at the Kennedy Institute of Bioethics at Georgetown University in Washington, D.C. established a data base, known as BIOETHICSLINE. It is maintained at the National Library of Medicine and contains approximately 6,800 citations to print and nonprint materials dating from 1973 to the present.

Public services. Not all information systems need to be complex, computerized, or designed to be used by experts. A case in point is the National Center for Appropriate Technology. Appropriate technology is a technology that is sensitive to the needs of people and to the resources of the community. The technical issues addressed by the center include energy conservation, waste management, food production, local resource utilization, and economic development. Information is collected on community action agencies, research and technology groups, and individuals, with the objective of connecting people and information by responding to queries and providing assistance and by encouraging the transfer of appropriate technologies to low-income communities. As of 1979 the data base was manually operated and consisted of index cards and files organized by geographical area and subject. A computerized system was planned for the future.

A nationwide, toll-free telephone travel planning service called the U.S. Travel Service was sponsored by the U.S. Department of Commerce. Travel counselors supply information on a wide variety of the U.S. Travel

Service's publications which are available to the public. They also answer specific questions on what sights to see in a given location, and the availability of rental car companies, local mass transit facilities, hotels, and motels. The center does not make bookings or reservations. For prices and local information, callers may be referred to state and city tour offices.

An innovative information-communication system called Prestel was developed by the British Post Office. To use the system, patrons call the Prestel Computer Center on a telephone linked to their home television sets. Having established contact with the computer, they consult an index and then select the information pages they wish to see. A small handheld programmer codes and transmits the selection to the computer. These pages are displayed on the home television screen.

Prestel is operational in the U.K. but only to a limited extent, and various groups were examining and testing techniques for expanding and improving its use. One project team was studying the use made of Prestel terminals located in public libraries and their effect on reference services, users, and library management. Another was concerned with Prestel's potential as a conveyor of community information, including procedures for adding local information to the data base and monitoring its use. Similar systems were being developed in West Germany and France, and arrangements were being discussed for marketing Prestel in the U.S.

Research and future developments. In the U.S. research and development in information science receives major support from the Division of Information Science and Technology of the National Science Foundation (NSF). This division has been reorganized

"Oh, you press the button down.
The data goes 'round and around,
Whoa-ho-ho-ho-ho-ho,
And it comes out here."

and its program expanded to include support for (1) fundamental information science research with emphasis on strengthening the conceptual and theoretical foundations of the discipline; (2) applied information science research with emphasis on increasing knowledge about human, social, economic, and technological factors affecting the transfer and use of scientific and technical information; and (3) descriptive and analytical research with emphasis on studies of the major changes in the operation of scientific and technical communication systems. More specifically, the division was supporting research on the development of measures and standards for assessing the effectiveness of information-processing procedures and systems, on the behavioral aspects of information transfer, on the statistical and structural properties of information, and on the development and testing of existing and planned information systems.

Under NSF sponsorship the Stanford Research Institute began testing the effectiveness of electronic alternatives to the traditional paper-based communication systems. The study was concentrating on aerospace-related information that loses value with age and for which rapid dissemination is important. The experiment was designed to validate a set of hypotheses regarding the time value of information, the reduction of information overload, and the increased usefulness of electronically distributed information resources. At the same time, the American Institute of Physics was conducting an experiment to evaluate the effectiveness of using remotely located data bases via satellite link. Participating users are NASA scientists and engineers of the U.S. National Aeronautics and Space Administration. The documents they request are sent by facsimile transmission if hard copy is needed or by slow-scan TV transmission for video scanning.

An applied research project at Syracuse University was studying different schemes for arranging or ranking the output of computer-based information-retrieval systems. Such systems generally provide the user with a list of references to documents that are likely to contain the information requested. Generally this list is unordered or perhaps ordered alphabetically by author name. The Syracuse study was seeking to rank the output according to the relevance of the retrieved items to the user's query. The validity of many ranking schemes, under different operating conditions, was being evaluated.

The core constructs and basic laws of information science were being identified and studied at the Georgia Institute of Technology. In order to chart the future course of information studies as a scientifically based, empirical discipline, the investigators are evaluating the present level of development of information science, its theoretical foundations, and its technical achievements.

—Harold Borko

Energy

Events affecting energy occurred at a rapid pace during the past year. Highlighted in this review are energy legislation in response to U.S. Pres. Jimmy Carter's National Energy Plan in the United States; the decisions of the Organization of Petroleum Exporting Countries (OPEC) on petroleum prices during 1979; the revolution in Iran and its implication for crude-oil marketing and supplies; difficulties in the organization and performance of the new U.S. Department of Energy; the clouded future of nuclear energy in the U.S.; and a review of energy production and consumption.

Legislation. After 18 months of debate the U.S. Congress enacted five bills in response to President Carter's National Energy Plan, submitted in April 1977. The legislation finally enacted by the Congress was different from that proposed by Carter. The Carter plan had contained seven principal elements: the crude-oil equalization tax; continued price controls on natural gas; conversion to coal; conservation; electricity pricing; nuclear power policy; and the strategic petroleum reserve (enacted in 1977). The legislation enacted by

New wind-energy generator promises to produce more electrical power than windmills. Its open-top tower captures a large quantity of wind, and adjustable vertical slots create a strong tornado-like vortex.

Courtesy, Grumman Aerospace Corporation

Table I. U.S. Energy Production, Consumption, Imports, and Exports, 1972–78
(10^{18} BTU)

Year	Production	Consumption	Imports	Exports
1972	62.8	71.6	11.5	2.1
1973	62.4	74.6	14.7	2.1
1974	61.2	72.7	14.4	2.2
1975	60.0	70.7	14.1	2.4
1976	60.1	74.4	16.8	2.2
1977	60.2	76.3	19.9	2.1
1978	61.0	77.7	18.5	1.9

Source: U.S. Department of Energy.

Congress consisted of five bills: Natural Gas Policy Act of 1978; Public Utility Regulatory Policies Act of 1978; National Energy Conservation Policy Act; Energy Tax Act of 1978; and Powerplant and Industrial Fuel Use Act of 1978.

By far the most significant of these bills was the Natural Gas Policy Act. The thrust of this legislation was threefold. First, intrastate gas that had previously been unregulated was brought into the regulatory framework. Second, the established control price of natural gas during the next few years was to be adjusted for the rate of inflation. Third, natural gas prices were to be deregulated beginning in 1985 through 1987 unless price controls are reimposed at that time. The determination of the actual ceiling price on any given unit of gas depends upon a large number of factors and requires a complicated formal regulatory process. The act was a compromise between the House of Representatives, which wanted continued price controls on a nationwide basis for all natural gas, and the Senate, which wanted to decontrol all natural gas prices.

The Public Utility Regulatory Policies Act established federal standards with respect to rates, electrical system interconnections and pooling, retail policies for natural gas utilities, federal loans and other incentives for small hydroelectric power projects, and permissions to operate crude-oil transportation systems. The National Energy Conservation Policy Act was designed to reduce the growth of demand and energy in the U.S. without inhibiting economic growth. It provided various incentives for energy conservation in homes, schools, and hospitals, established energy efficiency standards for automobiles and certain appliances, and provided for federal energy initiatives to demonstrate solar energy. The Energy Tax Act provided a series of tax credits for certain energy conservation expenditures, imposed a gas guzzler tax, and contained many other tax provisions relating to energy consumption. The Powerplant and Industrial Fuel Use Act was designed to encourage the conversion of facilities from oil and gas to coal as the primary fuel source.

This package of legislation differed from that proposed by President Carter in his National Energy Plan. The key element of the Carter proposal, to raise through taxes the cost of energy to the level of that represented by imported oil, was rejected by Congress. The legislation did reflect some of the president's proposals, however, including the provisions to convert to coal, some of the tax measures to encourage conservation, and regulatory reforms in electrical energy.

OPEC and Iran. During the first three quarters of 1978 world crude oil supplies were ample, and OPEC, led by Saudi Arabia, was reducing production to balance the supply and demand situation. Under these circumstances Saudi Arabia took the position that price increases in 1979 should be held to a low level. However, by late in the year the political situation in Iran had deteriorated. As a result, by the time the OPEC ministers met in December 1978, Iranian production had been reduced and the supplies of crude oil had become tight. In response to this new situation the OPEC ministers agreed upon a series of quarterly price increases during 1979 that would result in an increase in crude-oil prices of about 14.5% by the end of that year. By late

Oil workers in Iran engage in a sitdown strike at a refinery in Abadan. The political turmoil in Iran in 1978 and 1979 caused temporary shutdowns of the nation's oil production.

Philippe Ledru—Sygma

Solar collectors on the roof of the Frenchman's Reef Holiday Inn at St. Thomas in the Virgin Islands are part of the world's largest solar energy cooling system. The 13,000 square feet of the collectors heat about 450 gallons of water per minute to about 230° F in order to drive absorption chillers that air condition much of the 300-room hotel.

March 1979, however, it had become clear that this price decision would not be maintained throughout the year. The tight supply situation created by the closing down of Iranian production resulted in price increases by some members of OPEC well in excess of those agreed upon in the December conference.

In a series of rapid developments the Iranian government changed from a constitutional monarchy to a regency government to control by Ayatollah Ruhollah Khomeini, whose aim was to establish an Islamic republic. As of early 1979 the political situation in Iran remained unsettled. The effect on the energy situation of the industrialized nations was great. Iranian production, which through October 1978 was about 5.6 million bbl per day, declined to almost zero by January 1979; by March it was approaching the diminished target of 3 million bbl per day. Iranian production normally accounts for half of the non-Arab OPEC production and about 17% of total OPEC production.

The oil-importing countries of the world would suffer considerably from a sustained loss of Iranian crude oil. In the U.S. the loss of Iranian imports could cause a series of mandatory conservation measures ranging from gasoline allocations and closing of service stations to gasoline rationing. As an immediate response to the Iranian production cutback, other members of OPEC increased production. Saudi Arabia, whose capacity of 10.7 million bbl a day represents almost one-third of total OPEC capacity, increased its production but indicated that it might not be able to sustain the increased levels of output. By March the Iranian government had announced resumption of production for export but at a rate of only about one-half of that in 1978 and under a completely different marketing system, whereby the oil would be sold on the spot market at whatever price it would bring rather than through the mechanism of oil marketing companies at fixed prices under the OPEC regime.

Table II. U.S. Energy Production by Source, 1972–78
(10^{18} BTU)

Year	Coal	Crude oil and natural gas liquids	Natural gas	Hydroelectric power	Nuclear electric power	Other	Total
1972	14.5	22.6	22.2	2.9	0.6	...	62.8
1973	14.4	22.1	22.2	2.9	0.9	0.1	*62.5
1974	14.5	21.0	21.2	3.2	1.3	0.1	*61.2
1975	15.2	20.1	19.6	3.2	1.8	0.1	60.0
1976	15.9	19.6	19.5	3.0	2.0	0.1	60.1
1977	15.9	19.6	19.6	2.3	2.7	0.1	60.2
1978	15.1	20.6	19.3	3.0	3.0	0.1	*61.0

*Totals may not equal yearly sum due to independent rounding.

Source: U.S. Department of Energy.

The most significant result of the Iranian crisis was not the temporary loss of oil production but the hastening of a fundamental change in marketing procedures by the Middle Eastern members of OPEC. As the oil fields of the Middle East were nationalized, the governments of the region had continued to use the international oil companies as the marketers of their oil and the oil continued to move under firm long-term arrangements. By offering its crude oil to a spot market, the new Iranian government broke that marketing arrangement. Libya began systematically to reduce the proportion of its production that it would market under those arrangements. Exxon Corp., one of the largest of the world's oil companies, announced that it would phase out the marketing of oil to other customers and would concentrate on purchasing oil for its own refineries.

The implications of these new marketing arrangements could be profound. It has long been argued by Morris A. Adelman of the Massachusetts Institute of Technology that the cohesiveness of the OPEC cartel is directly related to the marketing functions of the large international oil companies. Adelman argued that if such functions were interfered with or ceased to operate the potential for price competition and price breaking would be greatly increased. Thus, the cartel could be progressively undermined by price competition

Table III. Crude Oil Consumption for Selected Major Non-Communist Countries, 1973–78
(000,000 bbl per day)

Year	Japan	West Germany	France	United Kingdom	Canada	Italy
1973	5.0	2.7	2.2	2.0	1.6	1.5
1974	4.9	2.4	2.1	1.9	1.6	1.5
1975	4.6	2.3	1.9	1.6	1.6	1.5
1976	4.8	2.5	2.1	1.6	1.7	1.5
1977	5.0	2.5	2.0	1.6	1.7	1.5
1978	5.0	2.6	2.0	1.7	1.7	1.5

Source: U.S. Central Intelligence Agency.

among the members. It is much too early to observe whether or not the results predicted by Adelman will, in fact, take place. However, there were some indications early in 1979 that they were occurring as spot prices appeared to be falling and other members of OPEC moved to change their marketing arrangements.

Department of Energy. It was widely recognized when the U.S. Department of Energy was established that the bringing together of such a large organization from so many diverse existing agencies would create serious management problems. Aside from the expect-

Carbon dioxide laser amplifier is under construction at the Los Alamos (New Mexico) Scientific Laboratory. It will be part of an eight-beam laser fusion system that might someday form the basis of an electrical power plant.

Courtesy, Los Alamos Scientific Laboratory, photo by Johnnie S. Martinez

Under construction (left) is the nuclear power plant at Seabrook, New Hampshire, the site of a major antinuclear demonstration in June 1978. At the right protesters against the Seabrook plant demonstrate at United Nations headquarters in New York City.

ed amount of partisan and politically inspired criticism, there emerged during the past year several major areas of difficulty in the administration of the department and in the conduct of its programs. Chief among these was the continued delay and difficulty in establishing the strategic petroleum reserve. Also, it was not possible to extract the oil already stored because the equipment for extraction was not scheduled to be installed until 1980. Thus, the stockpile is not available if needed to cushion the loss of oil from Iran.

In the regulatory area it became evident that there had been substantial "laundering" of old oil to create new oil after the imposition of price controls in 1973. Under price controls old oil can sell for only about $5.50 per bbl, but new oil brings a much higher price. Fraudulent activity to change the category obviously pays. Although the Department of Energy substantially stepped up its referrals of such cases of fraud to the Department of Justice, it was evident that the scope of this cheating was much larger than earlier believed.

Finally, the research program directed toward developing alternative sources of energy was moving much more slowly than planned. Budget requests for 1980 reflected substantial reductions in this area of activity, related to performance below expectations. But perhaps the most difficult task facing the department was the implementation of the new natural gas legislation, which, as discussed above, creates a complex regulatory situation that will place additional burdens on an already overburdened regulatory framework.

Nuclear energy. The nuclear power industry in the U.S. continued to encounter difficulties. Although actual generation from domestic nuclear power plants increased 10% in 1978 compared with 1977, this rate of increase was much lower than that envisioned by

President Carter in his energy plan submitted in 1977. The rate of increase in 1978 was also much lower than during most of the preceding five years. Those rates were: 1974, 49%; 1975, 51%; 1976, 10%; 1977, 32%; and, as stated above, 1978, 10%. Of even more importance than a slowdown in the rate of increase were the continued difficulty in completing plants under construction and the severe decline in new orders.

The difficulty with converting rapidly to nuclear energy was perhaps best illustrated by the renewed questions about the fundamental safety of light-water nuclear reactors. The so-called Rasmussen report, which had served as one of the major guidelines for the Nuclear Regulatory Commission's licensing procedure was, in December 1978, found by that Commission to be less conclusive than it had earlier believed. This was followed in March 1979 with the forced closing of five operating nuclear reactors upon discovery of a design error in their construction that may invalidate the safety systems of those reactors under earthquake conditions. The Nuclear Regulatory Commission ordered the plants shut down until design modifications could be undertaken. Finally, on March 28, a combination of equipment malfunctions and human errors at a pressurized-water nuclear plant near Harrisburg, Pa., forced a shutdown of the plant and caused radiation to escape through the facility's concrete walls into the atmosphere, to be vented in steam, and to be discharged into a nearby river. Apparently no one had received more than low-level contamination, but the accident was a setback for nuclear power.

The continued uncertainty of the future of nuclear power in the U.S. was beginning to have an effect on the producers of nuclear power reactors. Many manufacturers indicated that they were considering dropping out of the nuclear reactor business because of the lack of new orders. The Westinghouse Electric Corp. closed the facility it had started for the construction of floating power plants, which had been hailed as a way of greatly reducing the siting problems inherent in nuclear power. The closing was based upon the failure of these plants to receive permits and the withdrawal of orders by the public utilities concerned.

Production and consumption. Table I summarizes the production and consumption of energy and the levels of energy imports and exports for the last seven years in the United States. Domestic energy production declined from 1972 until 1975, but then began a slow increase. Table II presents the production of energy by source in the U.S. over the seven-year period. The increase in 1978 was almost entirely due to the increased production of crude oil, reflecting the flow of Alaskan crude to markets in other parts of the U.S.

Domestic consumption declined in response to the rapidly escalating prices of energy during 1974 as well as to the recession of 1974 and 1975; by 1976, however, domestic consumption had returned to its 1973 level and after that date continued to increase. The increases through 1977 were supplied by energy imports. In 1978, however, imports declined slightly, and the rise in consumption was satisfied by increased domestic energy production.

Petroleum consumption in the major non-Communist industrialized countries continued to rise during 1978. Table III summarizes the data for selected countries. In response to the Iranian cutback the International Energy Agency met in March 1979 and established a target for a 5% reduction in crude-oil consumption by the member states. Each country, of course, would achieve that reduction by whatever means it chooses.

Table IV. OPEC Production by Country, 1978
(000 bbl per day)

Country	Year average	% change from 1977
Saudi Arabia	8,059	−10.7
Kuwait	1,865	+ 4.6
Neutral Zone	466	+27.7
Iran	5,207	− 8.1
Iraq	2,629	+18.7
Qatar	485	+11.5
United Arab Emirates	1,833	− 8.9
Algeria	1,225	+12.3
Libya	1,993	− 3.5
Nigeria	1,910	− 9.0
Gabon	225	...
Indonesia	1,637	− 2.9
Venezuela	2,163	− 3.2
Ecuador	202	+12.2
Total OPEC	29,899	− 3.8

Source: Tippee, Bob, "Iran Shutdown Slashes Global 'Feast' of Crude," *Oil and Gas Journal*, Feb. 26, 1979.

U.S. Navy divers inspect a snakelike bladder more than 73 yards long and made of synthetic rubber-coated nylon fabric and cord. It is being tested to determine whether it can be used for open-ocean oil storage.

Crude-oil production for the world increased slightly in 1978, rising to a level estimated at 22 billion bbl from the 21,950,000,000 bbl estimated for 1977. Of more significance was the substantial decline in total OPEC production. Table IV shows the average daily production for the OPEC countries in 1978 and the percent change from 1977. The total output dropped by 3.8% in spite of significant increases by some of the OPEC countries. During the Iranian shutdown Saudi Arabia, Kuwait, Iraq, and the United Arab Emirates increased production substantially. The decline for the year would have been larger except for increased demand in the attempt to build stocks as the Iranian situation became more uncertain and except for the substantial increases in production to offset the Iranian decline. Significant production increases were registered by the two major North Sea producing countries, the United Kingdom, up 41%, and Norway, up 27%.

Perhaps the major disappointment in the United States during 1978 was the negative result from exploratory drilling in the Baltimore Canyon outer continental shelf area in the Atlantic Ocean off the New Jersey coast. The poor results from exploratory drilling were reflected in the lack of interest in the leases of-

Table V. Installed Nuclear Power in Major Non-Communist Countries

Country	Number of reactors		Capacity (000 of gross electrical kilowatts)	
	9/77	12/78	9/77	12/78
Canada	7	8	3,960	4,790
France	11	14	3,970	6,840
West Germany	10	10	6,410	6,410
Great Britain	31	32	8,040	8,790
India	3	3	620	620
Italy	3	4	630	1,490
Japan	13	18	7,970	11,500
Spain	3	3	1,120	1,120
Sweden	6	6	3,880	3,850
Switzerland	3	3	1,060	1,060
United States	64	71	47,073	54,120
Total	154	172	84,733	100,590

Source: U.S. Department of Energy.

fered in the second Baltimore Canyon sale in early 1979. Although there were some shows of gas in several of the exploratory wells, as of early 1979 there were no confirmed findings of oil and gas in commercial quantities from the leases initially issued.

The natural gas outlook in the U.S. in 1978 changed substantially from what it had been a year earlier. Although marketed production of natural gas was somewhat lower in 1978 than in 1977, production after the passage of the new natural gas act increased to levels virtually identical to those achieved in late 1977. Of more importance natural gas supplies increased to such an extent that gas utilities were once again offering new hookups to customers, and the Department of Energy was urging consumers to switch from oil to gas in order to ease the pressure on oil imports.

For the first time since 1973 domestic production of coal in the U.S. declined. This was primarily due to the coal strike, which reduced production substantially during the first quarter of the year. By the end of the year coal production was running at monthly levels well above those for 1977, but this increased output was not able to overcome the decline registered during the first quarter of the year.

Future prospects. The world energy economy was jolted by the Iranian revolution. Once again the economic and political implications of industrial world dependence on Middle Eastern oil became a major concern. In this context President Carter announced his decision to gradually decontrol crude-oil prices when controls expired on May 31, 1979. Also in the U.S. major federal decisions must be made on methods of moving oil from the West Coast to the Midwest markets

Magnetohydrodynamic (MHD) generator channel, along with a combustor, will form the core of a 1.7-megawatt generator to be used in the development of coal-fueled MHD power plants. Such plants are expected to burn coal with little pollution and greater efficiency than conventional facilities.

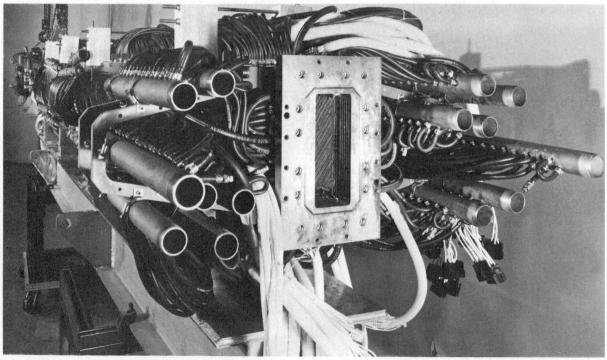

and on transporting Alaskan natural gas to the other states. Implementation of strip-mine reclamation regulations and the leasing of western coal deposits raise major environmental and economic issues.

Similar problems face the other industrial countries. World oil and, therefore, energy supplies will remain uncertain and subject to disruption for as long as internal political unrest exists in the major oil-producing countries and the overall political situation in the Middle East, centering on the conflict between Israel and the Palestinian Arabs, remains unsettled.

From the point of view of North America the discovery of large volumes of oil and gas in Mexico and in Canada has the potential of reducing the region's dependence on Middle Eastern, African, Asian, and South American oil. However, political and economic arrangements between the North American countries must be made, and they raise many thorny issues. Meanwhile, European countries were gaining increased supplies from the North Sea, but over the next decade must still import much of their energy. In Asia Japan must remain dependent on imported energy.

Many analysts were foreseeing a major shortage of world oil by 1990. This prospect creates pressures to develop alternative energy sources, such as solar, wind, and geothermal energy, and makes it imperative to face the issue of the viability of nuclear power. As shown in Table V, installed nuclear power for selected countries rose by 19% over the past year, but these were plants ordered five to ten years ago. New plants are not being planned and are not likely to be in areas where nuclear power is politically unacceptable.

—William A. Vogely

Environment

Two developments were of paramount importance during the year. A great deal of scientific analysis appeared on intensely controversial and little understood issues. Also, a curious development of great significance became clear in the literature for the first time: it began to appear that ecology, environmental science, and economics are the same science. Retrospectively, this equivalence seems to have been veiled previously only because of two historical accidents, the effects of which were vanishing as described below.

Three highly controversial issues in the United States are the appropriate approach to dealing with coyotes on sheep ranches; the use of pesticides to control insects; and the best way to manage the agricultural sector of the economy so as to ensure both fair incomes for farmers and fair food prices to consumers. An important multiauthored compendium on each of these issues was published during the year. It is particularly interesting that while these works could all be interpreted as highly critical of existing government

Exterminating the coyote, favored by many sheep ranchers, might allow the proliferation of small animals that compete with sheep for range food.

policies and operations, they developed from symposia funded by government agencies. The book on coyotes evolved out of a National Coyote Workshop sponsored by the U.S. Fish and Wildlife Service; the book on insect pest control developed from a conference supported by the Council on Environmental Quality and the Environmental Protection Agency; and a book on agriculture and energy reported on a conference funded by the National Science Foundation.

Coyote control. Sheep ranching has a low profit margin. The percentage of sheep, and particularly lambs, that appear to have been killed by coyotes is sufficient in many instances to completely eliminate the profit in the business. Accordingly, and quite reasonably, sheep ranchers have intense feelings about coyotes. Indeed, most sheep ranchers would perceive complete extermination as the appropriate means of dealing with the wild coyote population. One of the other political constituencies in the coyote controversy is the conservationist-naturalist-wildlife group, which objects to both the mass killing of coyotes and the methods (cyanide and strychnine baits or devices, for example) used to kill them.

The new book on coyotes discusses two aspects of this controversy that previously had received inadequate attention. Studies show that sheep make up no more than 8% of the coyote diet and usually much less. Scientists who study coyote diets mention that some part of the livestock component consists of carrion. Also, a very high proportion of the diet of coyotes consists of herbivores that compete with sheep—mice, rabbits, hares, and deer. This finding raises a disconcerting question: What would happen if all coyotes were in fact to be eliminated from sheep country?

Chamber with contoured walls designed to be completely nonreflective allows Canadian researchers to deliver precisely measured doses of low-level microwave radiation to test animals.

The issue is especially important because the area-wide techniques often used to kill coyotes also kill many other species of mammal and bird predators. Clearly, if the sheep ranchers got their wish and coyotes were exterminated, the other predators would also probably be exterminated as a side effect. The ultimate result would be sheep range overrun by rodents, hares, and rabbits, all competitors for the food of the sheep, which would be driven from the range. The ultimate irony is that the small herbivores would be enormously more difficult to exterminate than the coyotes because of their extraordinary reproductive potential. In short, coyote control could ultimately be counterproductive.

Another aspect of new coyote research revealed a more immediate counterproductive effect of coyote control. Four different computer studies simulating the effect of control on coyote populations produced the same result: coyote populations can withstand high levels of mortality. This happens because high mortality rates elicit compensatory population responses; survival and reproductive rates increase among the surviving coyotes, which now have less competition for food. To illustrate how large these compensatory reactions can be, one study indicated that the coyote population would increase slightly when mortality rates were 80% for pups and 40% for adults. Thus it is scarcely cause for surprise that, although over four million

coyotes have been killed in "damage control programs" since 1916, the U.S. coyote population is still large and apparently growing and spreading.

From this evidence it is clear that indiscriminate killing of coyotes is not a feasible means of reducing their populations over large areas, given presently available techniques and budgets likely at any time in the foreseeable future. Only selective killing of individual coyotes particularly dangerous to sheep seems to be a rational or economically feasible method of protecting the interests of sheep ranchers.

The pesticide controversy. Since the reproductive potential of insects is much greater than that of coyotes, it might be expected that area-wide attempts to control insects by using pesticides may not necessarily turn out as planned. David Pimentel of Cornell University, Ithaca, N.Y., and his associates have concluded that if crops in the U.S. were not treated with pesticides but some alternate forms of control were used instead, losses to pests (insects, diseases, and weeds) would increase from the currently estimated 33% to 37%. In other words, there would be no serious food shortages here if pesticides were eliminated. The effect on all foods would not be the same, however. For example, terminating the use of pesticides would have a greater than average impact on the availability of apples, peaches, plums, onions, tomatoes, and peanuts. Helga and William Olkowski and their associates made the interesting discovery that, in the urban environment, different trees are differentially susceptible to plant diseases and insect pests. This means that economies in pesticide use can be effected by treating only those trees that need it. This relates to a more general issue: that of an injury-level concept. Under this concept pests are controlled only when the level of injury resulting from their activities surpasses a threshold intensity. Such a system saves a great deal of money as compared with the alternative strategy of routinely following a control "calendar" or "schedule."

The pest control controversy is typical of those surrounding environmental issues generally. There has been an immense amount of research and discussion about the problem; meanwhile, from 1947 to 1975, the amount of pesticide produced in the U.S. increased by a factor of 14 and the proportion of crops lost to pests rose by roughly a factor of 2. Many reasonable people would have to conclude from these facts that the problem contains some elusive element that has not yet been adequately analyzed. Thomas Grumbly, who has held senior executive positions in the federal government, arrived at the sort of conclusion that is being proposed more and more frequently: the problem is basically cultural.

He points out three common beliefs that jointly produce the current approach to pest control. It is widely believed that the appropriate agricultural strategy is to produce the maximum amount of food at the lowest short-run cost. Also, most people are committed to simplicity as opposed to complexity; bureaucrats are particularly wary of doing anything too complex. Finally, our culture has an almost overwhelming desire for the great technological fix. To be acceptable, Grumbly argues, any pest control plan must be compatible with this trio of beliefs.

From this argument, Grumbly draws a number of specific suggestions for changes in the overall management of agriculture that must come about if there is to be rational pest control. Among these suggestions are marginally higher "income support rates" for farmers who adopt specified pest management plans; broadening of agricultural education to include computer methods and systems analysis; and strong, continuous, and systematic evaluation of agricultural extension programs by universities. Also, he states that complex technological menus will not work; thus, development of host-plant resistance is more likely to win wide acceptance than biological control using parasites and predators.

Management of agriculture. Another body of research, from the Center for the Biology of Natural Systems of Washington University, St. Louis, Mo., produced important findings derived from systems analysis. Two groups of 14 farms in the Corn Belt were studied (in Illinois, Iowa, Minnesota, Missouri, and Nebraska). In one group, the farmers practiced organic agriculture, using no chemical pesticide or fertilizer. Each of these farms was paired with a conventional farm in a control group of 14 that was roughly similar in every respect except for the use of chemicals. Over a two-year period the average net economic return from the two groups of farms was exactly the same to the nearest dollar per acre. The market value of the crops from the organic farms was only $164 per acre, as opposed to $183 per acre for the conventional farms. However, this was exactly compensated by reduced operating costs: $31 per acre for the organic farms, compared with $50 for the conventional farms.

This is important for several reasons. In early 1979 the almost total shutdown of the Iranian oil industry as a result of political upheavals brought renewed fears of

A truck enters the Three Mile Island nuclear power plant near Harrisburg, Pa., on March 30, 1979, two days after the plant suffered a dangerous accident. The tank on the truck was to be used to help drain off radioactive nuclear wastes.

a world energy shortage. This raises the question of what fossil fuel energy shortages would do to U.S. agricultural production. The results just mentioned suggest that the effect might not be very serious. But if that is so, it leads to the further question of just how chemical fertilizers and pesticides help the average farmer. According to the findings, they only allow him to supersaturate the market with his produce and drive down the price. If farmers saved themselves the work involved in distributing chemical agents, there would be a gain, not a loss. It should be noted that this counterintuitive result is in accord with the conclusions reached on coyote control and insect pest control. In all three instances, doing away with agricultural chemicals would have far less effect than is generally realized.

In his book *The Pesticide Conspiracy* (1978), the late Robert van den Bosch presents one of the most complete discussions yet published of the institutional background to the use of agricultural chemicals. According to his thesis, the conventional wisdom that pesticides are highly effective has its origins, in part, in a large array of institutional phenomena. Most of the advisers with whom a typical farmer has contact are committed to the notion that pesticides are a panacea. This commitment is also found in Congress, the executive branch of the government, the media, corporations, universities, and professional societies. Furthermore, it is very difficult for those branches of government that are supposed to regulate pesticide use on behalf of the public to operate free from political interference and pressure. Still another question emerges from this study: Might the regulatory function in society be better managed by the private rather than the public sector? In this case, regulation would come about through the free availability of information. The credibility and survival of the agency would depend on the objectivity and trustworthiness of the information provided to subscribers.

At the very least, all the new studies on controversial environmental issues raise searching questions about the institutional arrangements currently being used to deal with those issues.

A merger of sciences. On the face of it, the notion that ecology, environmental science, and economics are actually the same field in different guises seems farfetched. Yet a number of recent studies all point in that direction. The seed for this idea comes from *Living Systems* (1978) by James Grier Miller, in which the author argues convincingly, with many examples, that living systems at seven different hierarchical levels of organization, from the cell to the supranational system, have basically similar structures and dynamics. From this perspective, it is apparent that ecology, environmental science, and economics all deal with a small number of fundamental problems.

To illustrate, one of these problems is: What is the response of a living system when confronted with changing absolute and relative availability of its inputs? This is the general statement of a problem that can show up in a variety of specific instances. For example, how does a population of insect parasites or predators adjust when confronted with increased density of a particular host or prey species? How does a corporate management team respond to an increase in the cost of energy relative to the average cost of labor? How does Seattle, Wash., adjust to an increase in the amount of money available for the construction of Boeing aircraft? In short, the scientific principles in each of these fields "map onto" principles in the others.

If, in fact, all these fields are really the same field, why has it taken so long for this to be apparent? Two historical accidents provide the answer. In economics the dominant paradigm of the last several decades has been that of John Maynard Keynes, which argues for government intervention to stimulate a flagging economy. Because this strategy tends to obscure the regulatory effect of natural economic phenomena, it has tended to veil the basic parallels between economics and other disciplines. However, in its Dec. 31, 1978, issue, *Fortune* magazine reported on a poll of professors of economics at 55 American universities. Eighty-two percent of the respondents indicated that their confidence in the ability of government to fine-tune the economy was decreasing. Clearly, the hold of Keynes is weakening. What remains is called the rational expectations school of economics, which is much more obviously related to other academic disciplines than was the case with Keynesian economics.

While economics is moving closer to ecology and environment, those fields are also moving closer to economics. In the past they were preoccupied with conceptual models concerned with the number of events per unit time. This concern is now shifting to the costs and benefits of alternate strategies and how particular strategies affect the number of events per unit time.

One important example shows how thinking has changed. One means of controlling insect pests is through biological control—using insect parasites or predators of the pest species. From the 1930s to about 1970 there was a great deal of research on the searching behavior of insect parasites and predators and its effect on the percentage of pests killed. Now this problem is viewed in economic terms. Thus in 1978, in an important representative paper, M. P. Hassell and T. R. E. Southwood considered the costs and benefits for species that forage individually and group-foraging species.

The only two remaining differences between economics and the other two fields concern money—which, in the absence of intervention in the money supply, serves the basic purpose of communicating the relative availability of various resources to the marketplace—and international or interregional trade, which

Waves wash over the wrecked oil tanker "Amoco Cadiz" (above), which ran aground and broke in two off the Brittany coast of France in 1978. Volunteers (right) help to clean the tanker's spilled oil from the Brittany beaches.

has no parallel in ecology. As resources used by humans, such as crude oil, become short, there will be interresource substitutions (coal and solar power for oil, for example), just as a bear would respond to a shortage of berries by shifting to salmon. Both economics and ecology have developed theories dealing with such adjustments, but it is really all one body of theory, not two separate ones. As these fields undergo a natural merger, it can be expected that each will be stimulated by new ideas received from the other.

There was also evidence during the year that political science is beginning to merge with a new systems science of resources. For example, R. E. Johannes explained how the management of reef and lagoon resources in Pacific islands responds to differences in the way rights to the resource are assigned. In traditional cultures the right to fish in a particular part of a lagoon was controlled by a clan, chief, or family. It was in the best interest of the tenure holder for a particular area to harvest in moderation so as to make the resource last.

However, with the coming of Western cultural influences to Oceania—including the concept of free and open access to all common property resources, which were assumed to be infinite in abundance—the resources around the islands dwindled. As the theory argued by Garrett Hardin (*Managing the Commons*, 1977) and others suggests, there is evidently a relationship between the system of assigning rights to a limited resource and the extent to which the resource can survive.

Other studies in 1978 went even further in exploring the relationships between political arrangements, economic arrangements, and environmental consequences. For example, Alfred Levinson, Charles Rosenberg, and Aguibou Yansane presented an analysis of the Sahel countries of Mali, Niger, and Upper Volta. In it, they showed that use of energy in agriculture in those countries is dependent not only on the internal political systems but also on the relationships between the internal systems and those of other nations, such as France. In their complete conceptual model, the international political arrangements affect international and intranational economic phenomena, and these in turn affect the environmental situation in the Sahel.

To illustrate, roughly 55 million tons of wood are used annually in the Sahel-Sudan for cooking. If solar cookers were used half of the time and solar water heaters and solar distillation were utilized for public service needs, this wood would be saved. In addition, solar pumps could be used for pumping irrigation water from the large groundwater reserves. These developments are not occurring because of the shortage of supporting domestic industries and the shortage of foreign exchange. Furthermore, innovations are biased toward the export crop sector rather than the subsistence crop sector. The root cause of all these phenomena is the pattern of political relationships between Sahel countries and other nations. In actuality, according to a number of studies, these countries have the carrying capacity to feed their populations.

In sum, the year saw the rapid development of a highly interdisciplinary way of viewing environmental problems, in which political, economic, and environmental-ecological phenomena are seen as components in an interlinked system. In order to make wise policy decisions about how to manage such systems, it is necessary to understand how all parts of the system function together. The considerable complexity of this system implies increasing interest by scientists in the use of large computer systems models for exploring the consequences of various policies, even though the culture at large is still emotionally committed to simple, quick-fix, technological solutions.

—Kenneth E. F. Watt

Food and agriculture

The principal developments concerning food and agriculture during the past year included an improvement in world food supplies; growing concern about the possible effects of chemical additives in food and of herbicides and pesticides used in food production; and renewed efforts by research scientists to find new or improved sources of human nutriments. These efforts included studying items such as the cotton plant, not normally considered a food source.

Agriculture

World grain production rose about 6% in 1978–79, and stored grain stocks were expected to grow substantially. With a record harvest in 1978–79 supplies of most food grains were likely to equal or exceed global requirements, although consumption levels were also reaching all-time highs. Trade levels changed only marginally, and there was a slight buildup of yearend stocks. India, the subject of concern over hunger in 1974, had a record grain crop, making that country self-sufficient in grain and providing some surplus for export.

The excellent world grain harvest caused the volume of U.S. grain exports to dip slightly. Good harvests in the U.S.S.R. and the European Economic Community could trim demand again in 1979. Sales to most other regions of the world increased, however. This was true particularly for China, which bought a considerable amount of corn. U.S. wheat exports to Latin America, the U.S.S.R., and both Eastern and Western Europe were lower than in 1977. Rice exports to western Asia, Africa, and Western Europe increased.

Food production had risen faster than population for the world as a whole; per capita production increased 4% between 1974 and 1977. This was true even in the less developed countries. Such populous nations as India and Pakistan recorded significant gains in production and stocks of grain, a marked improvement for

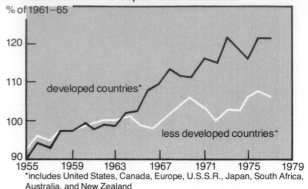

Index of World Per Capita Food Production

*includes United States, Canada, Europe, U.S.S.R., Japan, South Africa, Australia, and New Zealand
†includes Latin America, Asia (except Communist Asia), and Africa (except South Africa)

Courtesy, U.S. Department of Agriculture

an area where as much as two-thirds of U.S. food aid had gone in recent years. There were, of course, exceptions to this generally favorable trend. In Bangladesh and most of Africa, per capita food production declined during the same period.

Agricultural exports continued to represent the United States' principal weapon in its battle against a balance of payments deficit. In 1977 agricultural products reduced the U.S. trade deficit by more than $10 billion. Three times since 1960—the last time in 1975—the agricultural surplus had been more than enough to offset the deficit in nonagricultural trade. If all this surplus had been sold overseas, it would have given the U.S. a surplus balance in its total trade account.

After rising approximately 10% in 1978, retail food prices in the U.S. were expected to increase between 8 and 10% on average in 1979 with grocery store food prices being at the lower end and prices at away-from-home eating establishments at the higher end of the range.

The 1978 trend toward improved financial conditions for most U.S. farmers should continue in 1979. Consumers were expected to spend $207 billion for domestic farm foods (not including imported items such as coffee), 11% more than in the preceding year. The farm value of this food was expected to rise 17%. This was the first significant increase in farm value since 1973. About 75% of the gain was due to higher prices of livestock products, resulting chiefly from a reduction in breeding stock during the mid-1970s.

Chemicals in agriculture. For more than a decade, consumers had expressed concern over the use of chemicals and additives by the food industry and the use of herbicides and pesticides in the production of crops and livestock. Bacon had been identified as a problem because it consistently contains a low concentration of nitrosopyrrolidine after it is fried. This compound, derived from nitrite which is used to cure the meat, reacts with amines to produce carcinogenic (cancer-causing) nitrosamines. Components of meat curing usually include salt, sugar, and nitrate and/or nitrite, along with other chemicals such as ascorbates and phosphates. Curing produces a characteristic pink, heat-stable color that is different from that of fresh meat, and a typical flavor, as well as a unique texture. Furthermore, curing prevents spoilage by organisms including *Clostridium botulinum*, the causative agent of botulism.

During 1978 the U.S. Senate held hearings to discuss the relative safety of nitrite. The hearings were prompted by results of a study conducted by Paul Newberne of the Massachusetts Institute of Technology for the Food and Drug Administration (FDA). Newberne reported indications that nitrites themselves may be carcinogenic. Other scientists pointed out, however, that two studies in Denmark and The Netherlands showed no adverse effects on rats fed nitrite-treated meat. In addition, scientists had found that nitrite effects are counteracted by vitamin C, and therefore ascorbic acid often is added in the curing process.

Many scientists also pointed out a potential danger of botulism if nitrites were banned. Richard V. Lechowich of Virginia Polytechnic Institute and State University argued that regular outbreaks of botulism are reported in France and Spain, resulting from consumption of home-cured meats. Nitrite and nitrates are either not used in those countries or are used with poor control. Numerous authors argued that the financial consequences of restricting or discontinuing the use of nitrite in meat curing would lead to higher meat prices and increased spoilage, with adverse consequences for the meat-processing industry, the meat-production industry, and the consumer.

Three questions were critical: (1) Are the results of experiments using nitrite with laboratory animals applicable to the mixture of compounds used in curing meats that are cooked before being consumed by humans? (2) Is the occasional small exposure that humans experience comparable to the relatively large doses that cause cancer in laboratory animals? (3) Is the risk associated with low levels of such compounds in meat a reasonable risk in comparison with the risk of botulism? Complicating the situation was the so-called Delaney Amendment to the Food and Drug Act, which says that no substance that produces cancer in laboratory animals may be added to foods.

One option might be to preserve meat by irradiation, a method studied by the U.S. Army for some 25 years. Irradiating meat involves exposing it to ionizing radiation. The ionized molecules form unstable secondary products that kill microorganisms, sterilizing the meat and giving it a shelf life equivalent to that of canned foods. Meats could be put in a flexible vacuum pack, heated to 70° C (160° F) to deactivate enzymes, and then frozen, irradiated, and thawed. The Army studies show that the procedure could virtually eliminate *Salmonella* contamination and would drastically reduce

the need for nitrites to destroy the botulism toxin. A major question was whether consumers, who may have a misunderstanding about the meaning of the term "irradiated food products," would buy them. The net effect of the controversy was a tendency by the industry to reduce the amount of food additives, especially nitrite.

Scientists also were working on ways to reduce pesticide use in food production. During 1978 the U.S. Department of Agriculture and the land-grant universities initiated a substantial program called Integrated Pest Management. IPM involves the application of virtually everything known about pests and crops to manage pest populations in a safe, effective way. Among the possible techniques are changing planting dates and practices to avoid pests, using insect-resistant crops, and relying partially on biological control of pests, including the introduction of predator insects or insect diseases. By monitoring the insect population and carefully selecting pesticides and specific dates for spraying, farmers can reduce markedly the volume of pesticide applications. The use of such techniques in apple orchards in parts of the western U.S. lowered the

Wind erosion of topsoil from a field in Arizona would have been prevented if the field had been protected by rough tillage or crop residues.

USDA—Soil Conservation Service

number of sprayings from an average of 16 per season to 2 or 3. The approach holds much promise.

Although the value of limiting the use of chemicals in food production is widely appreciated, there are costs associated with it. In a recent address former secretary of agriculture Clifford Hardin pointed out that paperwork associated with governmental regulation of chemicals in agriculture had more than quadrupled in the last seven years. He emphasized that while paperwork and red tape are nuisances, the real concern is that they add to the cost of consumer goods. He argued further that they discouraged innovation, delaying or preventing the introduction of new products that appear to have limited market potential because prospective profits would not cover the cost of obtaining federal approval.

Improving on Mother Nature. Between 1950 and 1979 beef output in the U.S. increased more than 70% while the number of beef cows rose only 16.7%. This was due to a number of technological advances. One of the most recent of these is superovulation. The basic technique involves the use of follicle-stimulating and luteinizing hormones to induce multiple-egg ovulation or release by cows of high genetic quality. After the eggs are fertilized they are transplanted to incubator cows, the genetic quality of which is not important.

In one of the most spectacular embryo transplant operations on record, 28 fertilized embryos were obtained from a single donor in one nonsurgical recovery. The embryos were transplanted into 28 recipients with a 71% success rate. The result was that 20 calves were born within a few days of each other, all full brothers and sisters. Ova transfer allows cows with superior genetic characteristics to reproduce at a more rapid rate than had been possible previously. The cost of performing ova transfers has been lowered markedly in recent years. Such a technique could lead ultimately to stabilization of the number of food-producing animals, thus avoiding the peak-and-trough cycles that have occurred in the U.S. for many years. This, in turn, should bring about greater stabilization in the market price of meats to the consumer.

Scientists at Tuskegee Institute in Alabama developed an instrument that detects early pregnancy in meat-producing animals. The method involves directing high-frequency sound waves through body tissue. Because the fluid-filled pregnant uterus is denser than other tissues, it produces a strong echo, which is displayed on a screen. The technique, which has been used in cattle, sheep, and hogs, should help farmers reduce the number of barren or nonproducing female food animals, thus lowering production costs.

Another way to lower the cost of processing meats is by introducing "boxed beef." The beef is cut at a central facility and packaged in boxes, which are then delivered to the grocery store instead of whole carcasses or part carcasses. This lowers the amount of truck space required and hence the cost of transportation. However, it does make it more difficult for a consumer to have a particular piece of meat custom cut.

Donor cow stands behind some of her 20 offspring. By means of superovulation the cow produced 28 fertilized embryos, which were transplanted into other cows with a 71% success rate.

Courtesy, B. W. Pickett, Colorado State University

Foods for the future. As of 1979 there were only 2,000 llamas in the United States, but they were reported to be thriving, especially on ranges at high altitudes in the Rocky Mountain region. The highly desirable wool they produce is in constant demand. There were not enough of them to be used as food-producing animals as yet, but their potential for the future was significant. Owners said there was one problem in using llamas for food-production; they have attractive personalities, and it is very easy to become emotionally tied to them as pets.

In addition to providing raw material for clothing, a cotton plant has been developed that yields an excellent food product. The glandless cottonseed can be dehulled to produce a nutlike product with a flavor between that of a peanut and a cashew. The principal research was conducted at Texas A&M University, and thus the nut product is called Tamunut.

The key scientific breakthrough in the breeding of a glandless cottonseed was the elimination of gossypol, the cottonseed's major contaminant. Gossypol contains a metabolic inhibitor which is undesirable, and flour made from ordinary cottonseeds is yellow in color. Flour from glandless cottonseeds is nearly white and has excellent quality protein. The addition of as little as 5 parts of such cottonseed flour to 95 parts of wheat flour doubles the protein content of a loaf of bread, and mixtures of up to 20% cottonseed flour can provide high-protein bread, cookies, and other bakery goods. This is especially significant for people whose diets are generally low-protein or protein-deficient. The cottonseed also has a pleasant odor.

Once FDA requirements have been met, vegetables, meat entrees, delicate sauces, and almost anything that now comes in a can or bottle will be sterilized in thin aluminum foil or a plasticlike envelope, using a fraction of the time and much less energy than are required for canning. The technique involves the use of retortable pouches and is essentially canning without the can. Since the so-called retort foods do not have to be refrigerated and have a shelf life of up to ten years, it provides yet another mechanism for storing and shipping food. Furthermore, the possible saving of energy is appealing. Research at the U.S. Army Research and Development Command laboratories at Natick, Mass., indicates that the total energy expended in production, processing, and delivery is 60% higher for frozen vegetables than for the retortable pouches and at least 15% higher for canned goods. There are also savings in weight, storage space, and disposal of the packages. Retort foods can be eaten cold, heated in a microwave oven, or dropped in a pan of boiling water for three to five minutes. In addition, foods prepared in retortable pouches are said to be truer in taste, firmer in texture, and fresher in flavor than comparable canned or frozen products.

Another new process involves compressing foods.

This is essentially a form of freeze-drying which removes most of the water and thus most of the bulk weight of food products. With the addition of water the compressed food regains its original shape, color, taste, and texture.

—John Patrick Jordan

Nutrition

The United Nations designated 1979 as the International Year of the Child. Much attention was to be focused on health problems that originate early in life, even prior to birth.

Nutrition education. Who has the responsibility or the right to tell people what to eat? All consumers, regardless of age, life-style, and cultural and socioeconomic background need nutrition education. But U.S. consumers generally want freedom of choice in what to believe and what to eat. "Can nutrition educators present scientifically based nutrition information in such a way that its authenticity is recognized and acted upon?" asked Neige Todhunter of Vanderbilt University in a review of 50 years of effort to inform the public about its nutritional needs.

Present-day consumers have increasing numbers of questions about nutrition, in part because more meals are being eaten away from home, children and young people have greater freedom to choose their own diets, and unusual dietary practices are frequently recommended in conflict with research findings and advice from health and medical authorities. The public must be provided information on nutrition and food values and given ways to apply this information in making wise food choices. Consumers also want to know in what ways food may be related to childhood and adult obesity, diabetes, hypertension, coronary heart disease, cancer, and other health problems.

Norman Borlaug, credited with the development and initiation of the "Green Revolution" in which grain production was greatly increased, expressed his concerns about the current conflict between natural fertilizers and chemical fertilizers for food production. He stated in "Nature's Way Isn't Good Enough," published in *American Forests*, that "The use of organic fertilizer is wonderful for growing six rose bushes in your back yard and three tomato plants, but it is no damned good at all for trying to feed four billion people." Borlaug stated that "high yield production in agriculture is dependent upon changing the first basic obstacle to increased yield—poor soil. Much of the land in many of these food deficient, densely populated nations is deficient in one or more nutrients." He complained that some people think plant geneticists should develop varieties of grains "that wouldn't need fertilizer." This is no more possible than to produce a person who will need no food to grow and be healthy. "Nature's way is not good enough with the population that we have right now." Much stress must be placed on realism when considering solutions to world food problems as well as in developing strong nutrition education programs.

Nutrition education and services should be an integral part of all health delivery systems, including home health care services. Unfortunately, the programs designed for home health care often do not provide funds for the services of a dietitian/nutritionist. Legislation to provide these funds is needed.

Some of the social welfare programs with a nutrition component were considered ineffective because there was no way of evaluating how well they were achieving their goals. For example, an evaluation of the use of donated foods should include an assessment of developmental changes in the growth of infants and children receiving those foods. Many nutrition education programs have failed because their administrators did not understand the complexity and importance of community and family traditions of low-income families. Nutrition education must work with the family as an entire unit and not focus only on a child who needs help.

Child nutrition. The Kaiser-Permanente Medical Center in San Francisco initiated a long-range study of pregnant women entering the center. The researchers identified the following high-risk factors in pregnancy: chronic hypertension, tendency toward fetal loss (spontaneous abortion), heart disease, heavy smoking (a half-pack or more daily), being out of wedlock, short stature (under 62 in), low weight (15% or more below average), and previous babies with low birth weight. Of 294 eligible pregnant women 227 accepted the invitation to participate in a study of diet supplementation to improve the outcome of pregnancy, but only 102 completed the study through delivery. Of 100 single births among these women only three low-birth-weight babies were delivered (5.5 lb or less); of the 16 women who had previously had low-birth-weight babies only

one did so again. No significant association was found with the three supplements (high protein, low protein, or only vitamin-mineral complex) and birth weights. This finding was attributed to the fact that all nutrient intakes were at least 75% of the recommended allowance.

More than 90% of 61 lactating women interviewed in Pennsylvania and Indiana said that they ate differently than when not nursing their baby. They said they had a higher liquid intake, tried to eat a balanced diet, and avoided junk foods, certain vegetables (cabbage, beans, garlic, and onions), chocolate, alcoholic drinks, and carbonated beverages. Nearly all considered their health and diet good or excellent, even though two-thirds indicated that they wanted to lose weight. More than half chose foods advertised as "organic, natural, or health food," which included whole cereals, bran, wheat germ, honey, and yogurt.

The American College of Obstetricians and Gynecologists was taking the position that the physician as head of the health team has the ultimate responsibility for ensuring a high-quality nutrition component in maternity-care services. A survey of physicians in British Columbia, Canada, revealed that general practitioners who were most involved in achieving this role had these characteristics; they were female, consulted a dietitian/nutritionist, had advanced training, attended continuing education programs, had nutrition education in their medical school curricula, and had been in medical practice for ten years or less. These data supported those from U.S. surveys.

Studies of dietary intakes, eating patterns, and development of young children in the U.S. indicated that protein intakes are extremely high, with 83% of the children at all ages having intakes above the Recommended Daily Allowance. Such high intakes do not necessarily ensure an adequate diet, and the general

Warning that saccharin has caused cancer in laboratory animals and may be hazardous to human health is posted in a grocery store. The U.S. Food and Drug Administration began a nationwide study in 1978 on the possible role of the sweetener in promoting bladder cancer.

public may have been oversold on protein. Furthermore, the use of dietary supplements without assessment of need can result in complications if nutrient intakes are excessive over an extended period of time (during infancy and preschool years). Data show that preschool children with adequate diets often take diet supplements. These data indicate a need for effective nutrition education programs for parents and their preschool children.

The strong urge to eat sweet-tasting foods and beverages, combined with the ban on cyclamates and the questionable safety of saccharin, contributed to an investigation of nutritive sweeteners other than glucose and sucrose, especially those that can be used safely by diabetics. Uncommonly used nutritive sweeteners being considered were fructose and such sugar-alcohols as sorbitol and xylitol. These have absorption rates and metabolic pathways different from glucose and thus do not contribute to as rapid a rise in the level of blood sugar. These compounds, however, have energy value and therefore cannot be used as substitutes for saccharin in weight reduction diets or in noncaloric beverages.

Consumer influence caused some changes in the composition of infant foods. These included reduced sodium content because of lower levels of salt and monosodium glutamate, increased levels of iron and copper to aid in prevention of infant anemias, and in some cases lower sugar levels. The revised edition of Handbook No. 8, compiled by the U.S. Department of Agriculture, will have a section describing the composition of baby food products.

Nutrition during cancer treatment. The National Conference on Nutrition in Cancer, held in late June 1978 in Seattle, Wash., emphasized nutrition and nutrition therapy. The conference determined that oral feeding of cancer patients is preferable, and that whenever the gastrointestinal tract is involved tube feeding can supplement or replace oral food intake. Both of these methods are less strenuous on the patient and less costly than intravenous feeding.

The major emphasis of the conference was that the patient must be fed on a regular schedule; weight loss is a serious danger signal and must be prevented or corrected. Feeding was regarded as the therapy that supports the life system while the body is being subjected to treatments required to combat the cancer. Obviously the preferences and attitudes of patients toward food must be considered when planning with them to meet their dietary needs. The conference stressed the urgent need to achieve effective teamwork between dietitians, nurses, and physicians in order to convince patients that they should eat as long as their gastrointestinal tracts are functioning.

Recently Joseph A. Migliozzi published a report of his research on tumor development in the *British Journal of Cancer*. After implanting tumors in guinea

Courtesy, Du Pont Company

Permasep permeator developed by the Du Pont Co. removes 98.5% of the salts in typical seawater by reverse osmosis and requires only about half the energy used by other methods of desalination.

pigs he fed them for 20 weeks with diets having varying levels of ascorbic acid. The tumors regressed completely in 55% of the guinea pigs receiving 0.3 mg of ascorbic acid per kilogram of food each day; tumors showed no regression in guinea pigs receiving 10 mg/kg daily; and tumors grew without any retardation when the pigs received 1 g/kg daily. When guinea pigs received ascorbic acid many times in excess of their dietary need, their tumors responded by enhanced growth. These findings completely contradicted claims made by those who advocated massive doses of ascorbic acid to combat cancer.

Food fortification. A major dispute involves the extent to which nutrients in food should be increased for increased health benefits. For example, the iron content in the premix used to enrich breads and flour has been under scrutiny, with proponents supporting an increase to as much as three times the original amount added in 1940. The U.S. Food and Drug Administration had the proposal under consideration for seven years before rejecting the superenrichment concept, stating that the need for more iron had not been established, that enrichment had not been shown as a useful remedy for anemia, and that high levels of iron may do more harm than good.

A problem with food fortification is that people not needing the nutrient may be the chief consumers of that food. For example, in the case of bread and flour products men at all ages are the chief consumers. They, however, have adequate iron stores with rare cases of anemia, and so iron fortification of bread would not benefit them. On the other hand women during childbearing years avoid these foods to be slender, thus becoming deficient in iron and contributing to anemias in their infants and young children.

—Mina W. Lamb

Life sciences

During the year investigators in the life sciences deepened their understanding of the interrelationship between temperature and the structure and biochemistry of plants; the process by which disease-producing bacteria adhere to human tissue; and the role of the cell membrane in cell energetics, growth regulation, and sperm-egg interaction. Controversy over warm-bloodedness in dinosaurs was freshly fueled, and the popularity of various theories concerning the genetic origins of antibodies rose and fell with new evidence from several laboratories.

Botany

The relationship of plants and temperature served as the focus for several important botanical studies during 1978. The growth-inhibiting effects of insect attack on Australian trees were explored, and well-preserved elm leaves that had lived perhaps 17–25 million years in the past presented botanists with a unique opportunity for microscopic and chemical analyses.

Big trees. The American Forestry Association (AFA) *National Register of Big Trees* became a reality in 1978, having been preceded by AFA big-tree lists of various kinds since 1940. The *Register* consists of a list of the largest recorded specimen of each of some 661 species found in the conterminous United States. Each champion must be nominated by an individual or a group, which submits measurements of trunk circumference, height, and spread to support the nomination. Some of the newly crowned champions in 1978 were *Fraxinus profunda* (pumpkin ash; circumference 18 ft 3 in, height 86 ft), *Thuja plicata* (western red cedar; 61 ft, 178 ft), *Ulmus alata* (winged elm; 11 ft 1 in, 116 ft), *Acer macrophyllum* (big-leaf maple; 34 ft 11 in, 101 ft), *Acer saccharum* (sugar maple; 21 ft 3 in, 78 ft) and *Quercus lyrata* (overcup oak; co-champion at 21 ft 5 in, 116 ft).

Recently two biogeographers attempted to determine why big trees are located in a particular part of their species range. Although many factors combine to determine this, Vernon Meentemeyer of the University of Georgia and Wallace M. Elton of Middlebury (Vt.) College proposed that a certain combination of water and energy availability might predict the location of big trees. Contrary to expectation the champions are not necessarily found in regions of highest precipitation but tend to appear in the cooler parts of their species range, where loss of water through leaves is comparatively low.

Fossil leaves. Although nearly countless fossils of seed plants have been collected and studied in past years, relatively few have yielded to detailed study of cellular structure. Any reported structure has been gleaned from observation with the light microscope and has not yielded much information on cellular substructure. The besetting problems lie in the process of fossilization itself, which usually leaves the material in a form that is difficult to prepare for and interpret by electron microscopy.

Preserved leaf of Zelkova (left), a genus of the elm family, lies as it was found in a bed of volcanic ash at least 16.7 million years old. Low-power scanning electron micrograph of leaf cross section (right) reveals distinct structural details including tissue layers and midrib.

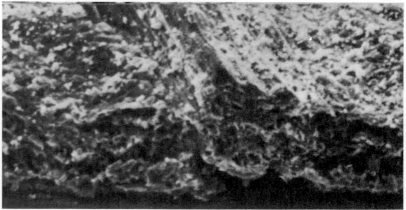

Photos, Karl J. Niklas, Division of Biological Sciences, Cornell University

Karl J. Niklas of the New York Botanical Garden, New York City, and his associates discovered some leaves of a species of tree of the elm family which had been fossilized in such a way that study by electron microscope was possible. Materials collected from the Succor Creek Formation, a Middle Miocene deposit found in eastern Oregon and dated at a minimum of 25–16.7 million years before the present, had been preserved in rapidly falling volcanic ash that prevented microbial decay and somehow stabilized the cellular structure. Studies with transmission and scanning electron microscopes yielded identifiable images of cell walls, nuclei, and chloroplasts (in which light absorption and photosynthesis take place) with their lamellar structures. Cuticle was detected on the outer surfaces of both upper and lower epidermis. Other structures were identified as well, and various organic substances were detected by chemical analysis. These researchers felt that the preservation of cellular substructure and associated organic compounds was possible because of rapid burial without heat damage, rapid dehydration and cell shrinkage, release of plant compounds that acted to preserve the structure of cells, and gradual mineralization of cavities before structural changes could take place.

Plants and temperature. Several new findings were reported concerning the relationship of plant structure, function, and distribution to temperature. One concerns the studies of a University of Wyoming botanist, William K. Smith, who added another way that leaf size may be important to desert plants. As a consequence of their adaptation to high heat and aridity, such plants are expected to possess small leaves, lowered water loss through transpiration, and maintenance of temperature within the leaves that is close to air temperature. In an examination of several perennial plants from the Coachella Valley of California, Smith discovered some with low internal temperatures and high transpiration rates. It happens that these plants also have larger leaves than expected.

Computer simulations using measurements secured in the field indicated some of the advantages of large leaves. First, their internal temperature is more responsive to changes in the amount of sunlight than that of small leaves, giving them a greater potential to be cool, particularly in the shaded, inner part of the plant canopy. Second, the internal temperature of large leaves is more sensitive to rates of transpiration; hence, these leaves would benefit more from the higher rates of transpiration that were found. The overall effect of lowered temperature seems to favor photosynthesis in these plants. Whereas many desert plants have developed optimal photosynthetic rates at higher internal leaf temperatures, these larger leaved plants seem to have taken advantage of lower leaf temperatures by maximizing photosynthetic rates at these temperatures. The latter combination enables a plant to derive

Vernon Ahmadjian, Clark University

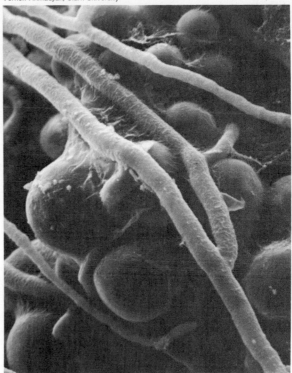

Magnified view of developing lichen thallus shows thick tubular fungal hyphae in contact with spherical algal cells. A veil of binding substance produced by the algae stretches between the two organisms.

particular benefit from periodic rainfall by carrying out rapid photosynthesis afterward.

Botanists also continued to be interested in the effects of temperature on the distribution of plants. A new discovery on the relation of temperature to natural distribution of closely related plants came from the laboratory of J. D. MacFarlane and Kenneth A. Kershaw of McMaster University, Hamilton, Ont. Their research demonstrated that two closely related lichens respond to certain temperature levels by a difference that would explain in part why these lichens occupy different habitats.

It has long been taught that lichens are resistant to heat stress when dried out, as they often are in natural environments. MacFarlane and Kershaw subjected dried *Peltigera canina* variant *praetextata* and *P. canina* variant *rufescens* to various temperatures under controlled conditions in a growth chamber. They checked the activity of the enzyme nitrogenase (which is involved in nitrogen fixation) as well as photosynthetic and respiration rates. It was found that *rufescens* maintained nitrogenase, photosynthetic, and respiratory activities at 45° C (113° F) similar to those at 25° C (77° F). By contrast, *praetextata* experienced a marked drop in these activities under similar conditions. The investigators suggested that the response differences of these lichens correlate with their environment: *praetextata* is found in woodlands in southern Ontario where internal temperatures of the lichen seldom rise above 30° C (86° F), whereas *rufescens* may be found on roadsides where internal temperatures can rise to 60° C (140° F). They also pointed to other evidence that Arctic and subarctic lichens are more sensitive to heat stress than the temperate species they investigated. Overall, they felt that thermal sensitivity is an outstanding factor in the distribution of lichens.

Lichen assembly. Lichens are well-known plant pioneers, often found in such habitats as rock surfaces where other plants cannot grow. Actually each species of lichen is made up of cells of two different organisms that are intimately associated. The main part of the lichen body, or thallus, consists most often of filaments of an ascomycete fungus in which are embedded individual cells of a blue-green alga. The fungus provides water and other nutrients, and the alga provides products of photosynthesis in a symbiotic relationship called mutualism, in which both species benefit. Reproduction is accomplished by chance distribution of dried pieces of thallus by wind; thus alga and fungus are transferred together.

The specific relationship of alga and fungus has been subject to much interest and some experimentation. Although there has been some success at reconstituting lichens from previously separated and cultured parts, how reassociation occurs is little known. Vernon Ahmadjian of Clark University, Worcester,

Mass., and his associates studied the events of reassociation with a scanning electron microscope. They isolated the component species of the lichen *Lecidea albocaerulescens* and cultured them separately for about one year before recombining them in an incubated and lighted culture.

The first effect noted following combination was a change to a dark green color in the alga, which had tended to be yellow in isolated cultures. Then, as the fungal filaments, or hyphae, grew toward the algae, they tended to form appressoria over them, one hypha forming appressoria over several algal cells. An appressorium is a flat structure that attaches to an algal cell and penetrates it with many peglike substructures called haustoria. This arrangement, which provides for direct alga-fungus exchange of materials, involved about 40% of the algal cells, similar to the proportion in the natural lichen. Further events necessary to complete the matlike thallus were not verified by observation but were believed to involve formation of a tissue-like structure called the pseudoparenchyma to bind the algal cells.

Algal "muscle." Several decades ago microscopists were able to identify striated rootlike structures attached to the bases of flagella (whiplike appendages used for locomotion) inside certain green algae. In fact, some rather old drawings show these structures, and they came to be called rhizoplasts ("root bodies") because of their appearance. Yet their structure remained uncertain. Within the last decade it became generally agreed that rhizoplasts seemed to be an-

A single raw fiber from a cotton garment (left) and one subjected to laundering abrasion (right) are compared in scanning electron micrographs. Such direct visualization assists in evaluating the physical characteristics of the fibers and their interaction with chemical textile finishes.

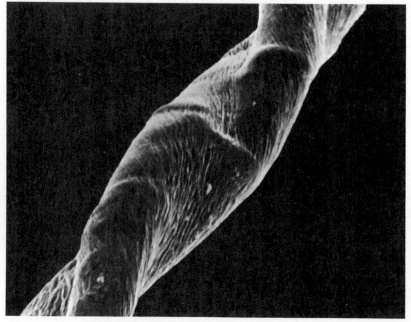
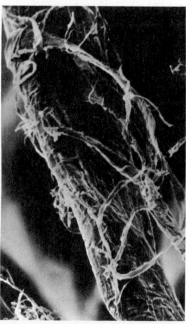

Photos, courtesy, Science and Education Administration, USDA

choring structures to absorb the stress of flagellar movement. Some workers went further to speculate that the striated appearance of rhizoplasts resembled that of myofibrils in skeletal animal muscle and that rhizoplasts might be able to contract like muscle.

Recently two Ohio State University botanists, J. L. Salisbury and G. L. Floyd, were able to show that rhizoplasts are indeed capable of contraction. They photographed different cells of a green alga, *Platymonas subcordiformis,* in an electron microscope and saw rhizoplasts in various stages of contraction. Moreover, they found that they could produce the contracted state by adding calcium chloride ($CaCl_2$) to the cells before preparation for viewing. Because calcium is necessary for muscle contraction, another similarity was established. By adding $CaCl_2$ to the algae under a light microscope, the investigators were actually able to view the effects of contraction, the main one of which is to aid movement of the flagella by tugging on their basal bodies. To date, examination of the microfibril (finest filament) structure of rhizoplasts had not shown it to be identical to muscle; thus how contraction actually works was still not clear.

Chloroplast genetics. Associated with the very rapid expansion of knowledge about structure and function of genetic material in all cells was the discovery that other specialized cellular parts (organelles) besides nuclei could have chromosomes. Chloroplasts are among these organelles in maize (corn) cells having a chromosome large enough to carry instructions for the synthesis of more than 100 different gene products. It would be reasonable for genes on chloroplast chromosomes to control processes in the chloroplasts themselves. Past reports had shown that genes for the production of ribosomal RNA (a constituent of ribosomes, the sites of protein synthesis) and transfer RNA (important to protein assembly in the ribosomes) were present, as was the gene for at least one enzyme involved in photosynthesis.

During the past year a team of researchers from Harvard University and the Massachusetts Institute of Technology reported that the chloroplast chromosome in maize contains genes that may be involved in the development of the organelle itself. Chloroplast development is light dependent; mature membrane structure, chlorophyll accumulation, and certain kinds of enzyme production are only observed when light has been available to developing leaves. By employing a number of commonly used techniques such as DNA-RNA hybridization, gel electrophoresis, and radio-isotope labeling on preparations made from both green seedlings and etiolated seedlings (grown in the dark), these investigators found that certain segments of messenger RNA are formed only in chloroplasts of green seedlings. Because messenger RNA carries the necessary code between gene and ribosome for the sequence of amino acids in protein, some protein or proteins associated with the light-dependent development and function of the chloroplast are expected to be encoded by chloroplast-located genes. As of early 1979 the specific proteins were yet to be identified.

Insects and plants. Many studies have shown that insect outbreaks can cause radical decrease in growth rate and other aspects of productivity in trees. Some have documented decrease in radial growth in several species, as shown in the width of tree rings. Two U.S. researchers, P. A. Morrow and Valmore C. LaMarche, Jr., went to the Snowy Mountains of southeastern Australia to study growth in two species of *Eucalyptus* under continual insect attack. It was known that 48 species of insects attack *Eucalyptus stellulata* and 39 attack *E. pauciflora;* more than half of the insect species feed on these hosts alone. Insect damage in 1975 and 1976 was extensive; *E. stellulata* lost 96% of its shoots and 50.5% of its leaf area to chewing insects, while *E. pauciflora* lost 76.8% of its shoots and 36.7% of its leaf area.

To assess the effect of such continual attack on lateral stem growth, Morrow and LaMarche sprayed a sample of trees in 1972 and 1973 as follows. They temporarily covered all branches but one on three trees of each species while spraying the exposed branch of each tree with the insecticide Thiodane. Sprayings were repeated weekly from December 1972 to March 1973. Enhanced canopy development not only of the sprayed branch but of the whole tree resulted the next year. Trees were observed for three years, and cross-sections were cut from sprayed branches, spray-protected branches, and branches from untreated control trees. The investigators noted large increases in ring width on the sprayed branches, somewhat smaller but definite increases in the spray-protected branches, and no increases in control branches. Hence, the protection afforded one branch on the tree had benefited productivity in the whole tree, which was seen to decline steadily until it reached the original insect-suppressed rate in about five years.

The investigators felt that some variation in ring growth of insect-susceptible trees could be due to natural insect population fluctuations and that this information should be considered when tree rings are used to analyze climatic conditions of the past. Because insect population fluctuations are also affected by weather, an indirect link between tree growth and climate could be established.

See also Feature Article: THE SCIENCE OF GROWING A TREE.

—Albert J. Smith

Microbiology

Steady advances continued to be made across the broad front of microbiology during 1978. Legionnaires' disease was one of the more "popular" topics that

Courtesy, J. L. Bump and I. L. Roth, Department of Microbiology, The University of Georgia, Athens

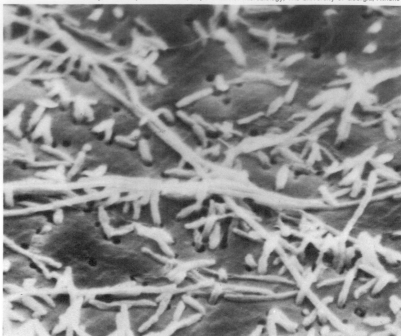

Under high magnification cells of the bacterium responsible for Legionnaires' disease display a diversity of lengths. Some are as short as 0.5 micrometers (about two hundred-thousandths of an inch), whereas others are 100 times as long. The perforated surface below the bacteria is part of the porous membrane used to filter the organisms for examination.

carried over from the recent past. Legionnaires' disease, a severe, febrile, respiratory illness, was first recognized as a hitherto undocumented disease during an outbreak in the summer of 1976 among participants at an American Legion convention in Philadelphia. There were 29 deaths among the 182 cases reported. Workers at the Center for Disease Control in Atlanta, Ga., subsequently isolated the bacterium considered to be responsible for the disease. It was thought to be a member of a new bacterial genus and recently was given the tentative name of *Legionella pneumophila.* (See *1979 Yearbook of Science and the Future* Feature Article: LEGIONNAIRES' DISEASE: STALKING A KILLER EPIDEMIC.)

Since the outbreak in Philadelphia, dozens of other sporadic and widely disseminated cases of Legionnaires' disease have been reported. As of early 1979, sporadic cases had been diagnosed in 13 countries on three continents. Moreover, it has become evident that an appreciable number of past cases of undiagnosed pneumonia, thought to have been caused by viruses because bacteria could not be isolated, were actually Legionnaires' disease. This conclusion is based on evidence that antibodies which react specifically with *L. pneumophila* were detected in blood serums taken from these patients during their illness and preserved by freezing. It is clear that these patients had Legionnaires' disease because the specific antibodies could have been formed by these patients only if they had been in contact with *L. pneumophila.*

Legionnaires' disease occurs most often in patients with other underlying health disorders. Similarly, per-

sons who are heavy smokers, who are elderly, or who are on immunosuppressive drugs are also more predisposed toward the illness. There is no strong evidence, however, for person-to-person spread; instead, many cases appear to have been contracted from contact with water associated with air-conditioning cooling towers and condenser systems.

Disease-producing bacteria must colonize, or adhere to and grow upon, specific cells or tissues in the body—not just to cells or tissues in general—before they can exert their harmful effect. What factors are involved in the selective adherence of bacteria to specific cells has been the subject of much recent study. Although the phenomenon was not clearly understood in all cases, it is certain that bacterial adherence is a cell-surface phenomenon.

In some instances, experimental data to explain bacterial adherence were reported. For example, adherence of certain toxigenic types of *Escherichia coli* (*i.e.,* those that cause diarrheal diseases) to the intestinal lining, or mucosa, was thought to be brought about by pili. Pili are hairlike appendages, composed mostly of protein, that originate from the bacterial cell membrane and extend through the cell wall for a distance as much as ten times the diameter of the bacterial cell. In addition to bacterial adherence pili are also involved in cell-to-cell contact during bacterial mating, or conjugation. The recent evidence that pili are involved in adherence of disease-producing bacteria to specific cells extends previous evidence for the adhesive properties of pili.

The organism that causes Asiatic cholera, *Vibrio*

cholerae, adheres to the small intestine. Recent work indicated that this organism contains a "lectin" on its surface that permits it to attach to small intestinal cells. Lectin is the term used to describe any of a class of proteins produced by certain living cells that bind to specific sugar-containing components on the surface of other cells.

It is interesting that both the *Vibrio cholerae* lectin and *Escherichia coli* pili belong to another category of substances called hemagglutinins. This is in keeping with recent evidence that bacterial hemagglutinins are lectins. Hemagglutinins are the agents that endow certain microorganisms with the ability to cause red blood cells to agglutinate, or clump. It is debatable whether hemagglutination itself plays a role in the bacterial disease-producing effect, but this common ability in lectins and pili may point to a biochemical similarity in the way they are involved in bacterial adherence.

Most bacteria in nature produce a slimy, fibrous layer called the glycocalyx, which is composed chiefly of complex, sugar-containing compounds. This layer is thought to allow aquatic bacteria to adhere to submerged surfaces and to allow specific bacteria to form an adherent population on the surface of particular plant and animal cells. This type of bacterial adherence may also play a role in the disease-producing process because recent investigation showed that *Vibrio parahaemolyticus* attaches to intestinal cells by such a surface layer. This bacterium causes a type of food poisoning that is usually acquired from eating contaminated raw or inadequately prepared seafood.

Infections by group A streptococci are implicated in the development of acute rheumatic fever when these bacteria are present in the pharynx (that part of the throat between the mouth cavity and the esophagus) for a prolonged period of time. Recent experimental evidence indicated that certain individuals may be prone to develop rheumatic fever because the streptococci adhere avidly to their pharyngeal cells. On the other hand, those individuals who are not prone to develop rheumatic fever were thought to be protected because of the lower propensity of their pharyngeal cells to bacterial adherence. Although the surface components in streptococci and pharyngeal cells involved in adherence have yet to be positively identified, it became apparent that the recognition mechanism involves specific sugars in the cell surface of the streptococci.

It was also postulated that an initial step in dental plaque formation leading to dental cavities is adherence of *Streptococcus* bacteria to the salivary pellicle that coats the enamel surface of the teeth. The pellicle is formed from glycoproteins, which are protein molecules that contain sugars. Tooth decay results from the effect of acids produced by plaque bacteria on the tooth enamel.

Plants get a form of cancer known as crown gall disease. The bacterium that causes crown gall disease, or plant tumors, is *Agrobacterium tumefaciens.* The transformation of plant cells to the tumorous state proceeds only after attachment of the organisms to the plant cells. The next step in the disease-producing process is the transfer of DNA from the bacteria to the plant cells, a phenomenon that may be viewed as a form of "natural" genetic engineering. Adherence of the bacteria to the plant cell walls depends on a recognition factor: the polysaccharide portion (a large complex molecule composed of sugars) of lipopolysaccharide

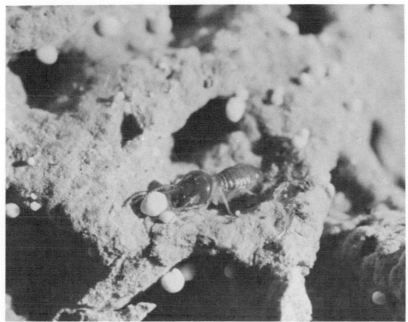

Termite of the species Macrotermes natalensis *tends to its fungus garden, a spongelike comb made of chewed plant fragments dotted with the white, globular spores of a particular fungus. Consumption of the fungus provides the termite species with enzymes that aid in the complete digestion of cellulosic plant materials.*

Courtesy, Robin Crewe, University of the Witwatersrand

molecules ("lipo" means fatty substances) on the outer surface of the microorganisms.

It recently came to light that some cases of sudden infant death syndrome (SIDS), a mysterious malady that strikes sleeping babies usually less than a year old, may be caused by an infectious form of botulism resulting from swallowing spores of *Clostridium botulinum,* the causative agent of botulism. Surprisingly, the bacteria can grow in the intestinal tract of infants and produce toxin. Botulism is usually associated with food poisoning received from eating inadequately preserved foods in which the bacteria have grown. More light was expected to be shed on SIDS in the near future because the suckling mouse had been found to be a satisfactory animal model for its study.

In the late 1970s the U.S. continued to experience widespread cases of sexually transmitted diseases. Gonorrhea, the most common of these afflictions, is caused by the gonococcus, or *Neisseria gonorrhoeae,* and the primary site of infection is the lining of the urethra, the passage that conducts urine from the bladder to the outside. A common and serious complication of untreated gonorrhea in women is acute salpingitis, a form of pelvic inflammatory disease (PID). This problem occurs when the microorganisms spread into the lower peritoneal cavity in the abdomen. Recently it was found that gonococci which cause PID are more resistant to antibiotics than those from uncomplicated cases, thus making treatment of gonococcal PID more difficult.

Another recent observation, but seemingly contrary to the preceding, was that a significant fraction of *N. gonorrhoeae* isolated in the laboratory and the clinic contains mutant strains that show increased susceptibility to antibiotics. The explanation seemed to be that, although antibiotic usage promotes growth of drug-resistant organisms, poorer growth characteristics in some of these mutants have given the selective advantage to other mutations that grow well but have an increased susceptibility to antibiotics. Hence, antibiotic usage paradoxically may be selecting for both greater antibiotic resistance and greater antibiotic sensitivity. (See *1979 Yearbook of Science and the Future* Feature Article: THE MICROBES FIGHT BACK.)

Glucan, a large carbohydrate isolated from the cell wall of bakers' yeast and other fungi, was shown experimentally to have potential use in the treatment of microbial diseases. As of early 1979 its mode of action was not entirely clear, but it appeared to stimulate the reticuloendothelial system, which in turn increases the number and activity of those body cells that make up this system; *i.e.,* most of the phagocytes that engulf and remove invading microorganisms. Another chemical agent that showed promise in the treatment of disease is trisodium phosphonoformate. This agent exerts an antiviral effect by acting on an enzyme that is involved in the synthesis of viral DNA.

The digestive tracts of many animals, both vertebrates and invertebrates, carry microorganisms that break down cellulosic materials. A new dimension to this relationship was added with discovery of a species of termite that acquires cellulose-digesting enzymes from fungi that grow in its nests. The termites feed both upon wood, the source of their dietary cellulose, and upon the fungi. This find suggests that acquisition of digestive enzymes from microorganisms may be a widespread phenomenon among invertebrates that feed upon litter, detritus, and dead wood. By contrast, certain marine and terrestrial wood-boring crustaceans, which also are invertebrates, maintain a gut completely free of microorganisms. It was thought that these animals produce their own cellulose-digesting enzymes, but the mechanisms by which the crustaceans maintain a bacteria-free digestive system remained unexplained.

Polychlorinated biphenyls (PCB's), a group of industrial chemicals, have been implicated in the past few years as environmental hazards. Although aquatic environments are widely contaminated by these chemicals, it had been generally assumed that significant PCB degradation did not occur in these habitats. Recent evidence, however, suggested that significant reduction of PCB levels occurred in one month both in a laboratory model and in a reservoir due to microbial uptake and digestion of the chemical.

—Robert G. Eagon

Molecular biology

Proponents of experiments that exploit the powerful methods of recombinant DNA technology had another good year in 1978. These experiments brought closer to realization earlier promises of both practical benefits and fundamental knowledge of the structure of genes of complex organisms. On the other hand, none of the perils thought by some to attend the experiments materialized, and it grew more widely accepted that the hazards of recombinant DNA experiments had been exaggerated. Accordingly, on Jan. 1, 1979, the U.S. National Institutes of Health promulgated revised guidelines for recombinant DNA experiments. In general, the new guidelines lower the physical and biological containment required for the experiments, so even faster progress can be expected in the near future.

Recombinant DNA generally consists of two or more segments of DNA joined in a single continuous molecule capable of replication in a suitable host organism; for example, the bacterium *Escherichia coli.* (See *1979 Yearbook of Science and the Future* Year in Review: LIFE SCIENCES: *Molecular biology* for a complete description of recombinant DNA methods.) One segment is derived from either a bacterial plasmid (a circular DNA molecule that replicates independently of the bacterial chromosome) or a bacterial virus. Some viruses, such as the one called lambda, contain some DNA that can be removed without interfering with viral replication. When lambda is the entity chosen for the construction of recombinant DNA, the dispensable segment is cut out, or excised, with a restriction endonuclease, an enzyme that cuts DNA only at certain specified nucleotide sequences. The lambda segment is then replaced with a DNA fragment of choice. This fragment can be obtained in a number of ways: cut from the chromosomal DNA of an organism using the same restriction endonuclease; synthesized as a DNA copy using messenger RNA (mRNA) as template for the enzyme called reverse transcriptase; or synthesized chemically. All three methods have been used successfully.

Infection with a bacterial virus usually results in the death of the bacterial host with concomitant release of several hundred progeny virus particles. Therefore, lambda is useful as a vector, or carrier agent, for recombinant DNA in order to amplify and to produce the DNA itself on a large scale. If the object is to engineer bacterial strains that produce useful materials (e.g., rare mammalian hormones) following the instructions carried by the recombinant DNA, then plasmid vectors, which do not kill their bacterial hosts, are more suitable. In 1977 one such plasmid vector, called pMB9, was used to clone (insert and replicate) the DNA copy of the mRNA for rat insulin in E. coli. This plasmid carries a gene that confers resistance to the antibiotic tetracycline to the bacterium harboring the plasmid.

Subsequently, Francisco Bolivar and others at the University of California, San Francisco, constructed an improved vector called pBR322, which contains genes for resistance to ampicillin as well as to tetracycline. By 1979 this plasmid was in very wide use for the following reason: for each of the restriction endonucleases called *Pst*I and *Hin*dIII there exists one and only one site for cutting pBR322 DNA. The *Pst*I site is in the gene for ampicillin resistance, whereas the *Hin*dIII site is in the gene for tetracycline resistance. Insertion of DNA segments into either site inactivates the gene for resistance to that particular antibiotic. Therefore, the sensitivity with which one can detect bacteria that contain recombinant DNA plasmids is increased tremendously; if the *Pst*I site is used, for example, the recipient bacteria will be resistant to tetracycline but sensitive to ampicillin.

An extra dividend was obtained from the development of this cloning system because it became possible to engineer bacteria that secrete desirable proteins. Normally bacteria keep all the proteins they make to themselves. Bacteria that manufacture such useful proteins as insulin would have to be grown in batch culture, harvested, and killed in order to extract starting material for purification of the final product. If the bacteria could be persuaded to secrete the protein of interest, they could be grown in continuous culture and the desired product purified from the culture fluid.

It turns out that the enzyme penicillinase, the product of the *amp*^r gene that confers ampicillin resistance to bacteria, is secreted. As is the case with many mammalian proteins that are secreted from the cells in which they are synthesized (including insulin), penicillinase is synthesized in the form of a precursor protein that contains a small number of extra amino acids not found in the mature enzyme. These amino acids are found at the N-terminal region of the precursor protein and are called the leader sequence. (N terminal and C terminal are terms used to distinguish between the beginning and end of a protein chain.) The leader sequence interacts in some way with the cell membrane with the result that the leader is clipped off and the remainder of the protein is secreted, *i.e.*, transported across the cell membrane to the outside.

Admittedly, an enzyme that destroys penicillin and ampicillin is not a particularly desirable product. However, studies in the laboratory of Walter Gilbert at Harvard University showed how these properties could be put to good use. A reverse transcript (a DNA copy) of mRNA for rat proinsulin (insulin precursor) was cloned into the *Pst*I site in pBR322. It was reasoned that, because the site is inside the gene for penicillinase (*amp*^r), a DNA fragment inserted at that site might be transcribed into RNA and translated into protein as though it were part of the penicillinase molecule. Of greater importance, if all went well, the new protein fragment would get a free ride across the cell membrane thanks to the leader sequence of the penicillinase precursor. The experiment worked. Taking advantage of an extremely sensitive immunological technique developed by Stephanie Broome of Harvard, Gilbert and co-workers isolated a recombinant DNA plasmid that directs the synthesis of a chimeric protein, which is secreted, with the antigenic properties of both penicillinase and insulin. Although a great deal of engineering remained to be done, the road seemed clear to the production of significant quantities of mammalian hormones in bacteria, thanks to recombinant DNA.

One of the most exciting developments in the molecular biology of gene expression in eucaryotic cells (cells of all but the most primitive organisms) began several years ago with the discovery of spliced mRNA in two virus-infected cell systems. Experiments done at roughly the same time in half a dozen laboratories indicated that different mRNA's (transcripts of different genes) found in the cytoplasm of cells infected with adenovirus all contained the same sequence of nucleotides at their 5′ ends. (The opposite ends of DNA and RNA strands are differentiated by the symbols 3′ and 5′.) When strands of such mRNA's were annealed to strands of adenovirus DNA and examined in the electron microscope, the resulting RNA-DNA duplex structure was found to contain one or more single-stranded DNA loops that had no matching RNA stretches. The interpretation of these structures was that the mRNA

L. T. Chow, R. E. Gelinas, T. R. Broker, and R. J. Roberts, *Cell*, Vol. 12, pp. 1–8, 1977

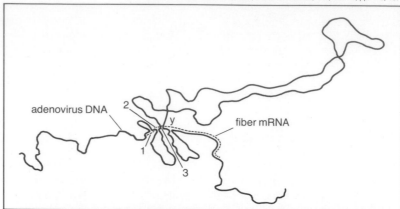

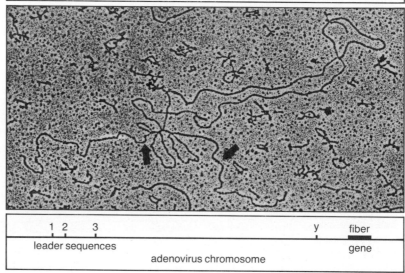

Revealed under high magnification, a long single strand of adenovirus DNA annealed to a shorter strand of fiber messenger RNA (mRNA) produces a duplex structure (region between arrow tips) that contains four single-stranded loops of DNA. Such loops provide evidence that the mRNA was spliced together from comparatively short RNA fragments (see drawing at top; dashed sections 1, 2, 3, y, and the remaining unlabeled stretch) of a longer RNA molecule derived from a comparably long stretch of the adenovirus chromosome. The sections of chromosome actually represented in the fiber mRNA are diagrammed below the photomicrograph. The intervening sections account for the observed loops.

consisted of spliced fragments from what must have originally been a longer transcript. (Such a splicing mechanism also explained how the same nucleotide sequence could appear at the 5′ ends of different mRNA's.) Subsequent experiments showed this interpretation to be correct. It has been possible to isolate, from nuclei, giant RNA molecules that contain all the nucleotides of a complete transcript of a portion of adenovirus DNA. It also has been possible to find a series of somewhat smaller RNA molecules, some of which, when annealed to adenovirus DNA, produce one, two, or three single-stranded DNA loops. These RNA's appear to be intermediates in the removal of extra RNA present in the nuclear transcript but not wanted in the cytoplasmic mRNA.

The nucleotide sequences present in the chromosomal DNA and its initial RNA transcript but missing from the cytoplasmic mRNA have been termed intervening sequences. Excision of intervening sequences is clearly an important feature of the processing of eucaryotic RNA. Such intervening sequences have turned up in a wide number of places, many of which were discovered by comparing recombinant DNA made from a reverse

transcript of mRNA with recombinant DNA made from the corresponding chromosomal fragment. This proved to be the case for the genes for globin (the protein part of hemoglobin), for immunoglobulins, and for ovalbumin. It was also found to be true for several of the genes for transfer RNA (tRNA) in yeast and certain genes for ribosomal RNA (rRNA).

The biochemistry of the excision process, which must also involve the linking, or ligation, of the cut ends of RNA to be preserved, remained a mystery as of early 1979. So far it has been possible to observe splicing (excision and ligation) in vitro in a very crude system from yeast, which removes a 14-nucleotide segment from the interior of a precursor to a yeast tRNA molecule. Similar RNA processing also occurs in procaryotes (primitive, principally bacterial cells), but so far appears to be restricted to excision; no examples of ligation of RNA have been reported. Excision is required in bacteria to cut individual ribosomal RNA's from a precursor that contains both of two specific RNA sequences called 16S and 23S. One of the excision events recently was shown to be carried out by an enzyme called ribonuclease III, discovered some years ago to degrade specifically double-stranded RNA. Most ribonucleases do not cut double-stranded RNA at all. Ribonuclease III, by contrast, requires at least nine paired nucleotides on either side of the cutting site. In the case of the ribosomal RNA precursor of *E. coli*, it was recently shown by Richard Young and Joan Steitz of Yale University that the 16S molecule is excised by action of ribonuclease III on a double-stranded stem of a lollipop-shaped RNA precursor. The circular section of the precursor consists of a single-stranded loop more than 1,700 nucleotides long, which contains the 16S molecule, whereas the stem is created from the pairing of two complementary sequences 26 nucleotides long that are located on either side of the 16S molecule. This is a bit of a surprise since one imagines it to be easier in nature to pair two single strands to form two stems with a loop between them—each stem containing a target for ribonuclease III—than to form a loop with one stem by bringing together opposite ends of one single strand that are separated from each other by 1,700 nucleotides. The relationship between ribonuclease III excision events in *E. coli* and the processing of intervening sequences in eucaryotes was unknown.

One of the most intriguing examples of intervening sequences in eucaryotic genes is that found in the genes coding for immunoglobulin. Immunoglobulins, or antibodies, are complex proteins consisting of equal numbers of two kinds of polypeptides (chains of amino acids) called light and heavy chains. The antibody specificity of an immunoglobulin molecule (*i.e.*, its tailor-made ability to react with only a specific chemical substance, called its antigen) is determined by a site formed from the N-terminal half of a light chain and the N-terminal fourth of a heavy chain. Amino-acid sequence determinations of a number of different antibody molecules indicate that the N-terminal sequences are variable in composition (V regions) whereas the C-terminal sequences are relatively constant (C regions). In the very well-studied case of the mouse light chain (well-studied because there are tumor cell lines available that produce so-called myeloma proteins, which are single classes of immunoglobulin proteins), about 95% have identical C regions, called kappa. The remaining 5% of the mouse light chains contain one of two related lambda sequences. On the other hand, there are probably approximately 10,000 different V-region sequences.

Since the light chain is a covalently continuous polypeptide, a major problem in molecular immunology has been to determine how the V regions and C regions are brought together. A second, related problem has been to determine the genetic basis for V-region diversity in amino-acid sequences. Considerable progress, though not complete solutions to both problems, appeared last year.

Based on a combination of amino-acid–sequence and genetic data, it was suggested some years ago by

Sidney Harris

"Why, it must be somatotropin, the growth hormone!"

William Dreyer and J. C. Bennett, both then of the California Institute of Technology, that the V and C regions are coded by separate genes (V genes and C genes) brought together by a genetic translocation event during the development of an antibody-producing cell. Subsequent gene-counting experiments, which are basically measurements of the amount of chromosomal DNA capable of annealing with either light-chain mRNA or with a DNA reverse transcript of that mRNA, showed that the mouse germ line contained only a few C genes but many more V genes. Because every V gene could not have a C gene next to it and a subtle genetic argument ruled out somatic mutation (changes to genes contained in body cells rather than to those in the germ line) as the origin of all V gene diversity, it seemed likely that gene transposition did bring V and C genes together. However, when Susumu Tonegawa and colleagues of the Basel (Switz.) Institute for Immunology annealed a recombinant DNA molecule containing a cloned myeloma V+C gene to mRNA from the same myeloma cells, they found that the gene contained a 1,200-nucleotide–pair intervening sequence, right between the V and C genes. Subsequently, the same group cloned a chromosomal fragment containing a mouse germ-line gene that corresponds to one of the lambda C regions. This fragment also contains a V gene, and its complete structure was determined. It

Adapted from "Rearrangement of Genetic Information May Produce Immunoglobulin Diversity," M. Weigert et al, *Nature*, Vol. 276, No. 5690, pp. 785–790, 21/28 December 1978

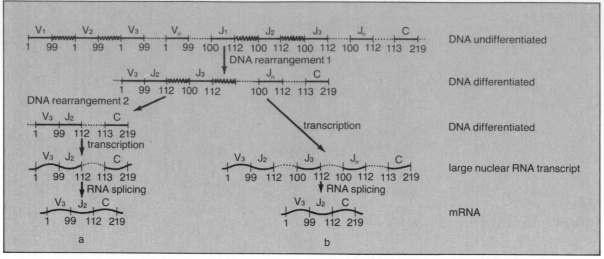

Diagram presents two models for the rearrangement of mouse antibody genes during differentiation of individual lymphocytes. Undifferentiated DNA contains several hundred variable, or V, genes (providing amino acids 1–99) and perhaps 10–20 joining segments, or J genes (providing amino acids 100–112), separated by other regions of DNA. Rearrangement begins with fusion of a specific V gene with a specific J gene (e.g., V_3 with J_2). Subsequently the process can follow one of at least two pathways (a or b) that result in fusion of the J gene with a constant segment, or C gene. In a, this occurs by means of a second rearrangement of DNA, followed by transcription of the DNA to RNA and final joining at this level via RNA splicing. In b, the DNA following initial rearrangement is transcribed, and all further joining occurs at the RNA level.

contains 45 nucleotide pairs coding for the lambda leader sequence (the antibody molecule is secreted), 306 nucleotide pairs coding for 102 amino acids of the V region, more than 4,500 nucleotide pairs of intervening DNA, then (surprisingly) 39 nucleotide pairs coding for 13 amino acids of the V region, then the 1,200 nucleotide pairs of intervening sequence found in the myeloma gene, and finally 312 nucleotide pairs coding for 104 amino acids of the C region. Apparently, in cells producing lambda light chains, a V gene is fused to the 39 nucleotide fragment, eliminating the 4,500 nucleotide intervening sequence. Tonegawa calls the 39 nucleotide fragment the J region because it participates in joining the V and C genes.

A related picture emerged from detailed study of amino-acid sequences of the V regions of a class of mouse kappa light chains. Twenty-two different proteins were sequenced by the groups of Martin Weigert at The Institute for Cancer Research in Philadelphia and of Leroy Hood at the California Institute of Technology. The V region was known from previous studies not to be equally variable over its entire length. Most of the amino-acid differences between different kappa chains are found in stretches of amino acids numbered 24–38, 53–60, or 93–102. These three segments are called hypervariable regions 1, 2, and 3, respectively. Analysis of their sequences suggested that the 22 kappa proteins could be assigned to six families, each of which derived from a different kappa V gene. It turned out that annealing experiments to count this class of kappa V genes were consistent with six genes for that particular class.

The sequences for amino acids 100–112 needed to be considered separately. For this part of the protein there were eight different sequences that appeared to be attached more or less randomly to the six families found for amino acids 1–99. Significantly, residues 100–112, formerly considered to be part of the V region, correspond exactly to the J segment described above. The number of different J segment genes in the mouse is unknown, but it seems to be greater than 13.

The picture emerging from these and other studies is the following: the mouse germ line contains several hundred V genes (of all classes), perhaps 10–20 J genes, and a few C genes. Development of an antibody-producing cell involves rearrangement of genes, specifically fusion of a V gene (providing amino acids 1–99) with a J gene (or several J genes, of which only one is not in the region of intervening sequence) providing amino acids 100–112, followed by intervening sequence and the C gene. It is not yet clear whether the combinational joining (a term coined by Weigert and Hood) of V and J genes can account for all of the known diversity of V regions or whether somatic mutation in the hypervariable regions must still be invoked.

See also Year in Review: CHEMISTRY: *Applied chemistry.*

—Robert Haselkorn

Zoology

Reports that cell membranes function in energy transduction (transformation from one form to another), regulation of growth, and in fertilization expanded understanding of cellular zoology during the past year. Neurobiologists reported a number of biochemical and morphological correlates with animal behavior. Progress was made in controlling sleeping sickness in Africa, basic research studies indicated that the extremely fertile oceans of the Antarctic could lead to their exploitation as a source of protein, and paleobiologists continued to debate whether dinosaurs were warm- or cold-blooded animals.

Cellular zoology. The 1978 Nobel Prize for Chemistry (see SCIENTISTS OF THE YEAR) was given to a man who proposed an explanation of the way living cells derive useful energy from oxidative metabolism. Operating from a private laboratory in Cornwall, England, Peter Mitchell developed his chemiosmotic theory in 1961; since then this concept has directed the field of bioenergetics away from the simple notion that the only way energy is transferred within the cell is when chemical groups move from one molecule to another. Emphasizing instead the role of structural-chemical differences across membranes, his theory proposes that protons, or hydrogen ions (H^+), are transported across the membranes of plant chloroplasts during photosynthesis or across the membranes of mitochondria—found in both plant and animal cells—during aerobic respiration, thus creating an ion gradient. The potential energy created by the ion gradient is changed into chemical bond energy, which becomes stored in the common energy currency adenosine triphosphate (ATP) when the ions bind with a carrier group and pass back across the membrane. The model is unique in that it stresses the necessity both for membranes, so that ion gradients may develop, and for vectorial (one-way) carriers in energy-transducing systems. All oxidative reactions in living organisms that channel energy into the formation of ATP are known to occur on membranes, and proof is being sought for the presence of vectorial carriers.

Membranes and associated structures, once thought to be only passive barriers, not only function in energy transduction but may actually regulate cellular growth. Judah Folkman and colleagues of the Harvard Medical School showed that changes in the shape of cells being cultured in the laboratory are highly correlated with the cells' ability to synthesize DNA and grow. Cancer researchers have long been concerned with altered properties of cell membranes in malignant transformations. M. E. Bramwell and Henry Harris of the University of Oxford compared the proteins and glycoproteins (sugar-containing proteins) of cell membranes from a variety of normal and tumor cells. They found that the only reproducible difference was associated with the presence in malignant cells of a glycoprotein with a molecular weight of 100,000. This was an exciting discovery that needed confirmation because, if there is a general membrane difference in malignancy, it might be possible to develop simple diagnoses, therapies that "home in" on this difference, and possibly an understanding of the mechanisms of malignancy.

Developmental biology. For years the morphological events occurring at fertilization have been known, but only recently were the biochemical events described. Victor Vacquier and colleagues of the University of California at Davis studied sea urchins as an easily manipulated experimental fertilization system. They isolated a species-specific protein, called bindin,

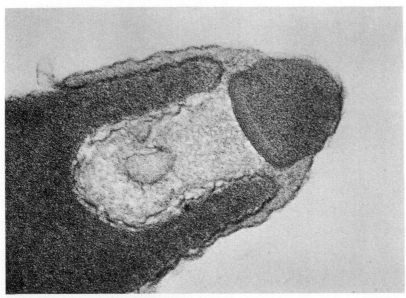

Microscopic view of the head of a sea urchin sperm cell shows a dark, acorn-shaped body called the acrosome granule at the very tip end. The major component of the acrosome granule is bindin, a species-specific protein that functions during fertilization to bind the sperm to receptor sites on the egg surface.

Victor D. Vacquier, Scripps Institution of Oceanography

from sea urchin sperm that functions in binding sperm to receptor sites on the egg surface. Similar events are thought to occur in mammals, and hence this work has obvious implications for new methods of birth control. Vacquier suggested that if a human bindin could be identified or if the human-egg receptor protein could be isolated, women could be immunized against sperm or possibly against their own eggs so that their antibodies would prevent egg-sperm binding and fertilization.

Although a single egg binds with thousands of sperm, only one actually fertilizes the egg. Once fertilized, the egg apparently activates defense mechanisms blocking further sperm entry. Larinda Jaffe of Woods Hole (Mass.) Marine Biological Laboratory described a voltage change that occurs across the sea urchin egg membrane at fertilization. The potential changes sharply from -60 mV (millivolts; thousandths of a volt) to $+10$ mV. When Jaffe deliberately raised the potential of unfertilized eggs to $+5$ mV with microelectrodes, the eggs remained unfertilized; once the current was turned off, however, fertilization occurred. Apparently the immediate defense to multiple sperm penetration is a positive electrical potential. Other workers demonstrated that the change of potential at fertilization is due to altered membrane characteristics, which allow a sudden influx of positively charged sodium ions to the egg.

Following these events, small sacs at the egg surface release enzymes that destroy the binding sites for sperm. These enzymes also produce hydrogen peroxide, which forms cross-links between glycoproteins present on the surface to cause a hardening of the egg's jellylike outer coatings. The formation of peroxide probably accounts for the almost instantaneous increase of oxygen consumption seen in eggs at fertilization. Several workers believed that these changes are initiated by massive releases of stored calcium by the sperm when it penetrates the egg. As a demonstration experiment, if unfertilized fish eggs are injected with aequorin, a chemical that fluoresces in proportion to calcium ion concentration, they give off a low luminescence. When activated by sperm, the light output increases 15,000 times and can actually be seen with the naked eye as a flash of light. Extrusion of hydrogen ions from the egg then leads to a gradual increase of alkalinity within, which results in a turning on of synthetic functions that start the process of embryonic development.

The interest in fertilization events was more than academic, and by early 1979 successful "test-tube" fertilization methods had been developed for several mammals. Biologists understood the methods needed to harvest eggs and store sperm, the conditions needed for fertilization, and the procedures for implanting the fertilized egg in the uterus. Perhaps this technique reached its highest point in July 1978 when two British researchers announced the birth of a test-tube baby—

apparently the first such of a human conceived in a culture dish. The event raised a number of ethical, legal, and societal questions about the implications of this form of reproduction, ones that will be of growing concern to scientists and nonscientists alike as scientific discovery exerts an ever greater influence on the human condition.

Neurobiology and behavior. The structural and biochemical basis of behavior remained a topic of interest. A research team in West Germany reported the successful transferral of time memory from one honeybee to another. After donor bees were trained to fly to a food source each day, each insect was decapitated and the mushroom body near the brain was removed and implanted in a space near the brain of a recipient bee. Within a few days the recipient bees began to appear at feeding stations according to the trained donors' schedule. There were no changes in the feeding habits of control bees, which underwent a surgical procedure that did not involve implantation. Subsequent microscopic examination of the recipient bees indicated that no nerve connections had developed between the implant and the recipient's brain. The researchers concluded that an unknown chemical factor was cyclically produced and carried to the brain by the hemolymph (invertebrate "blood") to cause the change in behavior. This observation added to the growing body of evidence that neurosecretions modify basic behaviors in invertebrates and vertebrates.

It is a basic premise of zoology that structure reflects function. Behavior then must have a structural correlation in the brain, and indeed researchers have found that nerve cells grow and change shape as a result of processing information. Using young jewel fish reared apart from visual and tactile contact with members of their own species, Richard G. Coss and Albert Globus of the University of California at Davis found that nerve cells in the optic tectum region of the brain had fewer and shorter cytoplasmic extensions (branches and spines) near the cell body compared with nerve cells of community-raised fish. The spines are sites of information transmission from one cell to another, and their poor development suggests that nerve cells build additional circuits in response to activity demands. Because these young socially deprived fish demonstrated abnormal behavior in social situations, the differences noted in their neuronal structure may be related to learning.

Bats are among the best known animals that use ultrasonic pulses to obtain information about the external world. Using species-specific cries, they can gauge the size, distance, and velocity of prey by interpreting echoes. It is estimated that a hunting bat can gather 500 insects in an hour; hence, there is little doubt that this perceptual mode is efficient and highly developed. Information about the distance of an object perceived by echolocation is processed by cells in the midbrain.

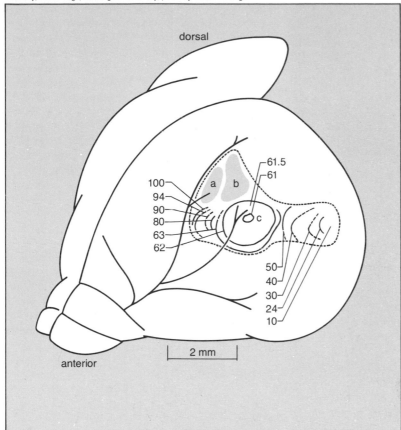

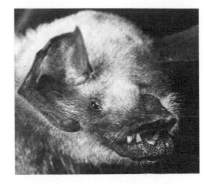

Studies of the mustache bat (above) have revealed much about the way its brain responds to components of its emitted cry and their Doppler-shifted echoes. Diagram of the left cerebrum (left) maps major processing areas in the primary auditory cortex (region enclosed by dashed line) that differ in the kinds of sounds to which they best respond: (a) combinations of constant-frequency (CF) signals, (b) combinations of frequency-modulated (FM) signals, and (c) single, Doppler-shifted CF signals. Numbered areas show distributions of best frequency response in kHz of nerve cells.

A group of nerve cells in this area discharges only when an ultrasonic pulse that resembles the animal's cry is followed by an echo. Specific cells of the group are active depending on the time interval between cry and echo. Consequently, the activity of an individual nerve cell is a measure of a specific distance.

In addition to measuring distance, the returning echo carries information about the prey's speed and direction of movement. Nobuo Suga and his colleagues at Washington University in St. Louis, Mo., showed that much of the auditory cortex of the bat brain is devoted to detecting a Doppler shift; *i.e.,* a slight difference in frequency between the returning echo and the emitted cry that is due to relative motion between the bat and its prey. Cells in the auditory cortex are arranged in a three-dimensional array for processing incoming signals from the ears. Nerve cells responding to different frequencies between 61–63 kHz (thousands of cycles per second) are arranged in concentric rings, with different sectors of each ring responding best to different loudnesses. Thus, activity in a given area corresponds both to the Doppler shift, which gives information about directional movement, and to loudness, which gauges distance and direction. When echoes are faint, nerve cells located on the lower cortex respond, with inputs coming from both ears. As the echoes become suffi-

ciently loud to carry useful information about direction, nerve cells located on the upper cortex respond. These cells are driven by an input from the ear located farther from the echo source and inhibited by input from the nearer ear. The bat brain thus represents a graphic picture of a prey's position and movement, a map that guides the animal in feeding.

Man is often thought to be the only animal capable of communicating abstractly. This assumption, however, was being challenged by studies with other primates. Research at the Yerkes Regional Primate Research Center at Emory University in Atlanta, Ga., and Georgia State University demonstrated that symbolic communication is possible between chimpanzees and humans. Francine (Penny) Patterson at Stanford University showed that gorillas also can be taught to communicate. In 1972 Patterson adopted Koko, a female gorilla. Although gorillas do not have the complex vocal apparatus required to talk, it proved possible to teach Koko sign language. With an acquired auditory keyboard linked to a computer, Koko demonstrated her ability to produce spoken words as well. Recently she learned to rhyme words in sign language, such as wash with squash, and to interpret many different objects in terms of her own limited vocabulary; *e.g.,* a mask is an "eye hat" and a Pinocchio doll is an "elephant baby."

Chimpanzee Sherman selects bread morsel for friend Austin behind window and then passes it to him. Sherman responded to a geometric symbol from Austin for bread in tests that demonstrated the ability of nonhuman primates to communicate symbolically.

Patterson obtained a mate for Koko and expected to be able to maintain communication with her if and when she has young.

Many studies have shown that animals have biological clocks, and a major effort is under way to identify their physiological basis. In birds, the pineal body, a small, light-sensitive, neurosecretory structure in the brain, may control daily cyclical activity. Michael Menaker at the University of Texas at Austin found that if sparrows are surgically deprived of the pineal gland (pinealectomized) and then kept in darkness, their normal cycle of activity becomes random. However, if the pineal is not removed but only cut off from nervous contact with the rest of the brain, there is no loss of

normal rhythms, implicating a chemically transmitted factor. In fact, normal rhythm can be restored in pinealectomized sparrows by transplanting a pineal into the anterior eye chamber. Here the tissue thrives without nervous connection and can secrete chemical messages. When this type of experiment is repeated using two groups of donors whose cycles are diametrically out of synchrony, the pinealectomized recipient adopts the cycle of the donor and the two recipient groups become diametrically out of phase. It appeared, therefore, that the avian pineal could be the master clock that controls activity and perhaps other circadian rhythms through chemical secretion.

Organismic zoology. In the oceans different species of fish live at different depths, and many shallow-water species cannot tolerate high pressures. This phenomenon raises the question of the adaptations necessary for deep-water colonization. Investigators at the Scripps Institution of Oceanography, La Jolla, Calif., examined two species of rockfish (*Sebastolobus*) that have similar appearances and life histories but are found at different depths. One species lives at depths of 180–440 m (590–1,440 ft) and the other at 550–1,300 m (1,800–4,260 ft). The deep-water species was found to have an important skeletal muscle enzyme, lactate dehydrogenase (LDH), that is pressure insensitive; that is, its ability to catalyze the reaction for which it exists—the reduction of pyruvic acid to lactic acid—is not changed by increasing pressure. The LDH from the shallow-water species proved more sensitive and consequently less efficient under pressure.

When other species of rockfish were examined, pressure insensitivity was a general characteristic of the enzymes from deep-water forms. Hence, physiological barriers apparently prevent shallow-water species from invading deep water, but factors other than enzyme structure must prevent the reverse type of colonization.

In tropical Africa the tsetse fly (*Glossina* species) carries the protozoan parasite *Trypanosoma* and can transmit it to mammals by biting. The parasite causes sleeping sickness in humans and a similar disease called nagana in domesticated animals. It is estimated that the threat of nagana has kept 4.5 million sq mi of grazing land, capable of supporting 125 million cattle, out of productive use within the heart of a developing, protein-starved continent. The only possible control methods are elimination of the tsetse fly or development of immunization against the parasite.

In Tanzania researchers supported by U.S. funds set up a facility to rear genetically deficient male tsetse flies, which are sterilized by radiation and released to infiltrate the endogenous population. This technique also was used to rid the southern U.S. of the screwworm, a cattle pest, and depends on the life history of the species involved: males must normally copulate more than once while females mate only once. Both of

Tsetse fly swells with blood as its sucks from a human victim. The insect's needlelike labium, which it uses to penetrate the skin, also provides a route of entry and exit for protozoans called trypanosomes, the causative agent of sleeping sickness in man.

these characteristics fit the tsetse fly life cycle. The female stores the sperm from her single mating whether they are viable or not and uses them to fertilize eggs, which are laid every ten days for approximately three months. Eggs fertilized by sperm from irradiated males do not develop. The logistics of operating a rearing facility are complex and involve feeding adults blood meals, collecting larvae and identifying them by sex, and releasing adult flies. In preliminary trials on a 100-sq-mi ranch, local fly populations were reduced but surrounding populations moved in. Eventual eradication of the tsetse fly will probably occur as a result of several combined techniques: use of insecticides, sterile-male release, and use of recently identified and synthesized chemical sex attractants.

The trypanosomes, however, are the actual disease agent. When taken in by a fly feeding on an infected mammal, they undergo a complicated cycle of development ultimately ending up in the insect's salivary glands. When the insect bites another mammal, parasites flow into the wound and invade nervous tissue with debilitating effects. Theoretically mammals should be afforded protection by immunization. It has been impossible, however, to develop a vaccine because the trypanosomes have the ability to change the chemical composition of their glycoprotein surface coats. As the host develops antibodies against one form of glycoprotein, the parasite thrives by changing, thus staying one step ahead of the host's immune system. Research on the surface composition of the parasites has been difficult because it has been impossible to culture the parasite outside of the natural host. Recently, however, investigators managed to grow mature forms in a test tube, an advance that should allow

the unraveling of the perplexing problem of changing chemical identities.

Environmental zoology. Biologists consider low numbers in natural populations dangerous because of a consequent reduction in genetic diversity, which is essential for a species to adapt to new situations. Two examples recently appeared in the popular press: the California condor population was reported at its lowest level, with 16 counted in 1978, and the International Whaling Commission expressed concern that sperm-whale populations were too low and too widely dispersed for successful mating.

In 1973 the U.S. Congress faced the problem of small populations by passing the Endangered Species Act, which forbade federal agencies to participate in or fund projects that would jeopardize the continued existence of species that occur in small populations in critical habitats. The most publicized use of this act was a political move to stop the building of the Tellico Dam in Tennessee. Although opponents claimed that the sole habitat of a fish, the snail darter, would be destroyed, many of them were more interested in stopping the dam in order to force a reexamination of water use policy. The issue was taken all the way to the

Los Angeles Zoo resident Topa-Topa, the only captive California condor, stoically awaits implementation of plans for a breeding center for the bird and several of the very few wild California condors known to exist.

Nothomyrmecia macrops, a species of Australian ant not seen since its first description from two collected specimens in 1934, was rediscovered in October 1977. Now the subject of international study, the insect has been recognized as the most generalized and, hence, the most primitive living ant known. It is likely a near copy of a species that throve at least 60 million years ago.

Supreme Court, which ruled in June 1978 against further dam construction.

During 1978 the Endangered Species Act of 1973 was reviewed by Congress. Subsequently a bill was submitted and passed under which a Cabinet-level Endangered Species Committee could be petitioned to exempt specific projects from the act's provisions but only if an otherwise irreversible conflict exists, if the project is of regional or national importance, and if the benefits of the project clearly outweigh the benefits of preserving a species or habitat. In January 1979 the committee voted to deny the Tellico Dam project an exemption from compliance with the act. In the future, economic importance clearly will be weighed against biological ramifications.

As these developments occurred, the Tecopa pupfish became the first species removed from the endangered species list for reasons of extinction. The small fish had lived in the Amargosa River near Death Valley, Calif., but rechanneling of the river and the introduction of bluegills, which acted as competitors, were thought to have led to its demise.

An ecosystem in which the environment and populations are as yet largely undisturbed by man's intervention occurs in Antarctica, but this situation may not remain so. Nations are becoming aware that the oceans of this region are highly productive because upwelling currents bring nutrients to the surface, where they stimulate growth of phytoplankton, despite the cold temperatures and low-light intensities during the Antarctic winter. John H. Ryther of Woods Hole (Mass.)

Oceanographic Institution commented on the role of phytoplankton as the foundation of relatively short food chains, which allow minimal energy losses between the phytoplankton and predators higher up the chain. Consequently, relatively large populations of phytoplankton consumers exist in the ecosystem, the most common macroscopic animals being the shrimplike krill—the primary food for many fish, marine mammals, and birds. Before any harvesting is done, the population dynamics, physiology, and behavior of the major species in this ecosystem need to be surveyed. In the late 1970s the U.S. National Science Foundation was supporting work of this type, and several investigators, notably Mary Alice McWhinnie of DePaul University in Chicago, were studying the basic biology of krill and other species. Understanding the ecosystem before disturbance should allow an intelligent and efficient harvest later.

Despite this sentiment an estimated 50,000 metric tons of krill were already being taken annually and harvested as food products by the Soviet Union, Poland, Japan, and most recently East and West Germany. Chile, which earlier had tested krill catch and processing technology, was expected to return, and several nations were reportedly considering the construction of on-site processing plants. Meanwhile, scientists from a dozen countries doing research in the Antarctic joined forces to form a program for the Biological Investigation of Marine Antarctic Systems and Stocks (BIOMASS). Their goal is to gain a deeper understanding of the structure and dynamic functioning of

340

the Antarctic as a basis for the future management of this living resource. (*See also* Feature Article: ANTARCTICA—THE LIVING LEGACY.)

Evolutionary zoology. Early in 1979 a discovery was described that constituted an evolutionary revolution for those interested in the exact nature of human origins. Donald C. Johanson of the Cleveland (Ohio) Museum of Natural History announced identification of a new species of apelike man after several years of meticulous study of fossils from East Africa. The new species, named *Australopithecus afarensis,* is intermediate between human and ape, having walked erect like a human but possessing the primitive teeth and small skull of an ape. The 350 bone fragments examined, thought to be more than three million years old, came from two locations: the Laetolil site in Tanzania and the Hadar region of Ethiopia. This material represents the oldest and most primitive of hominid remains known to science.

For several years the evolution of body temperature regulation has been a controversial topic. In 1965 Loris S. Russell (then with the Royal Ontario Museum) claimed that dinosaurs were warm-blooded (endothermic) and generated their body heat solely through metabolism as do modern endotherms; *i.e.,* mammals and birds. Present-day reptiles are considered ectotherms and regulate their body temperatures by basking in warm environments or finding shade. At the 1978 meeting of the American Association for the Advancement of Science, paleontologists debated the topic, presenting what are of necessity correlation arguments. For example, among living vertebrates the only animals that walk erect are endotherms; all ectotherms have a sprawling lizardlike posture. From the shape of bones and the narrow width of fossil tracks, dinosaurs are considered to have walked erect. Erect posture and high head height require a high blood pressure and a four-chambered heart, two conditions found in modern animals only among endotherms. Therefore, the argument concludes, dinosaurs must have been endotherms. Unfortunately the only evidence for this debate was inference from fossils, and despite the fervor of the proponents, the existence of endothermy in dinosaurs was far from proved.

—Warren D. Dolphin

Materials sciences

A cement formulation that offered considerable energy savings, a novel family of photosensitive glasses, and new ceramic surgical implants highlighted progress during the past year in the field of materials sciences. Investigators also achieved a better understanding of the heat transfer process taking place inside rotary kilns and continued their search for ways to test the quality of high-performance structural ceramics.

Ceramics

The cement industry is one of the top ten energy consumers in the U.S.; in 1971, in fact, cement production accounted for 1.6% of world energy consumption. Conversion to dry processing had already reduced the energy used in removing water that once had been required for ease in mixing raw materials. Recently a composition change developed by P. Kumar Mehta of the University of California at Berkeley offered a 25% reduction in the energy still consumed in portland cement production. Most of that energy is used in heating the raw materials, generally limestone and clay, to 1,370°–1,480° C (2,500°–2,700° F). During this process the limestone ($CaCO_3$) decomposes to form lime (CaO), an essential ingredient of the compounds generally present in portland cement. Because Mehta's composition contains more iron oxide but about 25% less lime, it can be produced with much less energy input. The modified cement also appears to develop its strength more rapidly than ordinary cement.

Corning Glass Works, Corning, N.Y., announced discovery of a family of "polychromatic glasses," in which a full range of transparent or opaque colors could be developed photographically. Starting materials are es-

Sample of Corning Glass Works' polychromatic glass demonstrates the versatility of this new medium. Areas of color were developed photographically by selective exposure to ultraviolet light and heat.

Courtesy, Corning Glass Works

sentially photosensitive opal glasses based on sodium silicate. The new glasses, however, also contain several halides, including significant amounts of fluorine, bromine, chlorine, or iodine ions or combinations thereof, and several sensitizers, including silver, cerium, tin, and antimony. To produce the colors, two sets of ultraviolet-light exposures and heat treatments are needed. The first exposure and heat treatment is essentially a nucleation process, in which a mixture of cubic and highly elongated pyramidal crystals of alkali halide forms and grows on nuclei of silver ions. In this stage silver ions appear to concentrate into clusters at the pyramid tips. The second, more extreme ultraviolet exposure and heat treatment completes the silver precipitation and reduces the silver ions at the pyramid apexes to metallic particles of silver. Color is apparently controlled by the ratio of the dimensions of the silver particles at the pyramid tips, and this in turn by the details of the nucleation process. The size of the tiny alkali halide crystals determines whether the colored region will be transparent or opaque, the larger sizes causing light scattering and opacity. It is apparently also possible to control the depth of coloration in the glass so that three-dimensional images can be formed. Although no commercial applications for these polychromatic glasses had been announced by early 1979, they could represent the first color photographic medium having true color permanence.

Significant progress in magnetic-bubble memory devices was made, and applications that promised to revolutionize the use of computers appeared quite likely. These devices, invented at Bell Laboratories, Murray Hill, N.J., utilize tiny regions of magnetization, called microdomains or bubbles, in a thin film of a magnetic ceramic to store information in a form that is useful for a computer memory. The magnetic bubbles can be created and moved by application of a magnetic field. Their presence or absence at a given point then comprises the "zero" or "one" binary system used for computer information processing. Because the domains even in the first generation of these devices are very small, of the order of three microns in diameter (one micron is one-millionth of a meter), a great deal of information can be stored in a very small volume. For example, a bubble memory device of this type can accommodate about 70,000 bits of information in the same volume occupied by a semiconductor memory device storing 16,000 bits. In 1978 Western Electric was making these devices commercially for its first Bell System application, a mass memory for use in central telephone offices to record, store, and deliver standard "call assist" messages. The system would convert speech to digital information that could be stored in the magnetic-bubble memory, to be retrieved and reconverted to speech as needed.

In a further development of this technology IBM scientists announced successful fabrication of a device that contains all the elements needed to read, write, and store information in a bubble lattice. Whereas in a normal magnetic-bubble device the bubbles must be kept several diameters apart to prevent their interference, in a bubble lattice device every location in the lattice contains a bubble and the information is stored in extremely thin walls between bubbles. Although the first IBM experimental bubble lattice device contained a 32-by-32 bubble array for 1,024 bits of storage, storage density can be more than five million bits per square inch. In a very recent development IBM researchers showed that magnetic-bubble diameter can be reduced from three to five microns to as little as 0.4 microns, allowing the next generation of magnetic-bubble devices a potential 100 million bits of information.

Use of glass and graphite fiber grew dramatically in the past year as applications for fiber-reinforced plastic expanded. Nearly 910,000,000 kg (2,000,000,000 lb) were used in 1978, about one-quarter in the automotive industry where weight, cost, and fuel savings were becoming increasingly important. Their use in body, chassis, and power-train components could save 70% of the weight of conventional steel parts. Only about one-tenth of fiber-reinforced plastics was used specifically for such corrosion-resistant products as pipes,

Small armor-piercing projectile lies embedded in the polycarbonate back layer of a sapphire-glass-plastic sandwich developed by Sandia Laboratories to protect vehicles that transport radioactive materials.

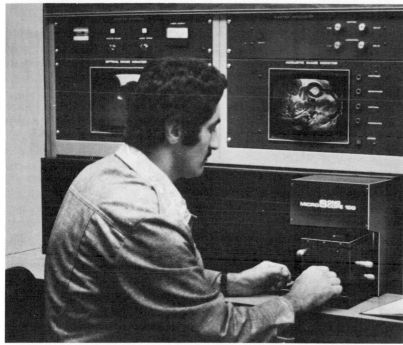

Technician adjusts on-screen sample of material under examination in a scanning laser acoustic microscope developed by Sonoscan Inc. Acoustic microscopy was becoming increasingly important in evaluating the mechanical properties of ceramics and detecting minute defects nondestructively.

containers, and pressure vessels. These applications were almost certain to increase greatly in the future, however, driven by the soaring cost of corrosion and the need for material conservation. Although glass fibers were still by far the most common reinforcement, use of graphite in high-performance composites also increased, and some graphite fiber costs were reduced by 10–20%.

Some initial applications of graphite fibers were slowed by indications that accidental release into the atmosphere of these light, electrically conductive fibers could cause interference with electronic equipment. Recent studies in the U.S., however, showed that with reasonable precautions such incidents should be extremely unlikely, and future applications of high-strength and high-stiffness graphite fibers were certain to grow.

For a number of years research has been conducted on ceramic materials specially formulated for use as surgical implants, and many ceramics have been found to be compatible with human tissue. Battelle Memorial Institute researchers in Frankfurt am Main, West Germany, recently announced development of biologically active sintered calcium phosphate materials that have advantages over the biologically inert metallic and plastic materials ordinarily used. The bioactive ceramic materials form an intimate bond with bone and can be made in forms such that they dissolve gradually in the body as they are replaced by new, healthy bone tissue. Future applications could include the bridging of bone defects and use as implantable tooth roots. Battelle Columbus (Ohio) Laboratories was producing dense

alumina for artificial roots, and the Ohio State University Dental Clinic successfully implanted them experimentally in baboons. The ceramic roots stabilize within two or three months after implantation in the jaw, with dense natural bone growing around the artificial root. A metal post is then inserted into each root for attachment of an artificial crown. This procedure might be ready for human use within the next several years.

As the use of ceramics for high-temperature applications in heat engines was becoming increasingly likely, means were being sought of assuring the quality of ceramic components. Ceramics generally have very low fracture toughnesses, failing commonly because of rapid propagation of cracks from defects or machining damage introduced during their manufacture. Components containing large, strength-limiting flaws need to be identified and eliminated to avoid their failure in service. Although nondestructive evaluation (NDE) of ceramics is not new, its application to high-performance structural ceramics has introduced a new class of problems. Internal pores or inclusions and surface cracks, often as small as 25 microns in diameter, must be found. Current efforts on NDE in ceramics were addressing the techniques needed both to detect the presence of such defects and to determine their type, size, and orientation.

Microfocus X-ray methods use a small-diameter, carefully collimated beam of X-rays to improve the resolution over that obtained by conventional X-ray techniques. When combined with image enlargement and modern image-enhancement techniques, microfocus X-rays have been demonstrated to be quite useful for the NDE of structural ceramics, particularly for the detection of dense inclusions. Unfortunately, some defects such as residual silicon inclusions did not show up well in radiographs.

Use of reflected ultrasonic waves for the detection and characterization of defects has been one of the mainstays of NDE. Although in the late 1970s their use for ceramics was still in an early stage of development, researchers at Stanford University recently showed that 200–500 MHz signals (one megahertz is one million hertz) can be generated and detected in dense, fine-grained ceramics without excessive absorption. Although much remained to be done in developing equipment and solving complex contact problems, the technique appeared to be especially powerful for defect characterization.

A number of other techniques that could be particularly useful for the detection of very small flaws in ceramics were just emerging. Studies at Stanford Research Institute, Menlo Park, Calif., showed that 100 GHz microwave signals (one gigahertz is 1,000,000,-000 hertz) can be used in much the same way as ultrasonic waves, but without many of the contact problems associated with ultrasonics. The technique was also especially sensitive to silicon inclusions. Acoustic microscopy, under development since 1971, and the scanning laser acoustic microscope introduced recently by Sonoscan, Inc., Bensenville, Ill., reveal microscopic variations in such physical properties as elastic modulus and density that determine the propagation rate of sound in a specimen.

Several other techniques, including laser photoacoustic spectroscopy, acoustic emission, holography, and high-frequency eddy currents were also being developed for use in detecting flaws in ceramics. Researchers believe that their use could significantly improve the reliability of ceramics in future, more efficient heat engines.

—Norman M. Tallan

Metallurgy

During the past few years metallurgists have become increasingly involved with attempts to understand the factors that determine the efficiencies of various metallurgical operations. Recently significant progress has been made in understanding the factors that contribute to the efficient use of energy in rotary kiln gas-solid reactors. Rotary kilns are employed in a wide variety of operations involving endothermic (heat-absorbing) reactions; their primary function being to heat the solid reactants to the temperature at which the reaction begins and to supply the heat necessary to sustain the reaction. Typical endothermic reactions that have been conducted in rotary kilns include the calcination of carbonates, dehydration of hydrates, and the reduction of oxides.

In concept the rotary kiln is a fairly simple piece of equipment, comprising a long, slightly inclined, rotating insulated tube into which the solid reactants are fed at the high end and hot combustion gases introduced at the low end. The solids, moving downward continuously as a bed through the kiln, are heated by the stream of gases flowing in the opposite direction. In spite of this simplicity, the mechanisms of heat transfer within the kiln are very complex, involving the inner wall of the kiln as well as the gas and solids. The situation is further complicated by the occurrence of dust and flames in the gas and by the cyclic variation in the temperature of the inside wall of the rotating kiln as it is repeatedly covered by solids and then exposed to hot gas.

Although the transfer of heat is very often the rate-limiting step in reactions occurring in rotary kilns, it has been poorly understood. This situation is due mainly to the considerable experimental difficulties encountered in making measurements in a rotating vessel under industrial conditions. Consequently the lack of experimental data has severely hampered attempts to determine the extent to which these processes can be described by mathematical models. Hence, the evolution of many rotary kiln processes has depended mainly on rule-of-thumb empiricism.

Within the past year a significant increase in the understanding of these heat flow processes was achieved as the result of a three-year research program conducted at the University of British Columbia (Vancouver). In the program a pilot-scale rotary kiln, fitted with 52 temperature-measuring devices called thermocouples, was used to measure the influence of such operating variables as speed of rotation of the kiln, average depth of the bed of solids (expressed as the percentage filling of the kiln), rate of fuel consumption (expressed as firing rate), and rate of movement of the bed through the kiln (expressed as solids feed rate) on variations in the temperatures with distance along the inner wall of the kiln, the bed of solids, and the gas. In these experiments the bed of solids, which was heated by combustion of natural gas, was composed of closely sized particles of silica sand. Measurement of the temperatures of the inner wall, the bed of solids, and the gas permitted accurate derivation of the rates of heat flow from the gas to the inner wall and from the gas to the bed of solids.

It was found that the rate of heat flow from the gas to the inner wall is a function only of the local temperatures and that the influences on this heat flux of firing rate, speed of rotation, and percentage filling of the kiln are due simply to the influences of these variables on the temperature field within the kiln. For example, an increase in the speed of rotation at a fixed firing rate causes an increase in the solids feed rate and hence an increase in the thermal burden on the kiln. This, in turn, produces a decrease in the local temperatures

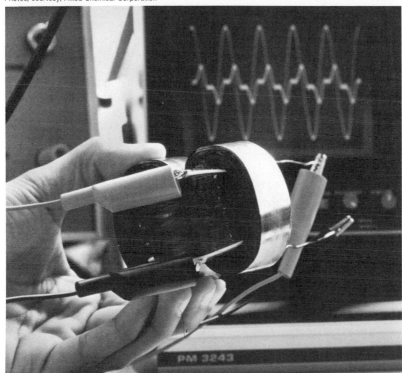 

Transformer core components (left) and magnetic shielding (right) are two promising applications for metallic glass, a noncrystalline form of metal. Its magnetic and electrical properties and corrosion resistance are preferred in many cases to those of steel and other crystalline metals.

and thus decreases the rate of transfer of heat from the gas to the wall. From this observation it was found that the heat flow between gas and inner wall can be adequately described by a simple radiation model.

On the other hand it was learned that, under identical kiln conditions, the rate of heat flow from the gas to the bed of solids is as much as ten times greater than that of the flow from the gas to the wall, an observation that could not be accounted for in terms of conventional heat transfer theory. Furthermore, it was seen that, whereas an increase in the speed of rotation of the kiln decreases the rate of heat flow from the gas to the wall, it increases the flow from the gas to the bed of solids. It was determined that the solids feed rate is the important variable controlling the rate of transfer of heat from the gas to the bed of solids, with the rate of transfer increasing to a certain limit with increasing solids feed rate. In this case the significant influences of rotation speed and percentage filling of the kiln on heat flow are exerted on the solids feed rate and not on the local temperature. The large discrepancy between the measured heat flow from the gas to the bed of solids and that calculated from heat transfer theory indicated that convection accounts for 70–80% of this transfer of heat; by contrast, radiation accounts for nearly all of the heat flow from the gas to the wall.

The observation that the rate of flow of heat from the gas to the bed increases to a certain limit with increasing solids feeding rate provided valuable confirmation of a theory, suggested in 1955, of the controlling steps in the transfer of heat from a gas to a bed of solids. It also correlated well with observations of the modes of motion of beds of solids in rotary kilns. Three types of motion of the surface of a bed of solids can be distinguished: (1) "slumping," a repeating process in which the surface particles near the rising edge of the rotating bed remain motionless relative to the inner wall until, at a critical level, they slump down en masse to a lower level; (2) "rolling," in which the surface particles continuously tumble downward from the uppermost point of contact of the bed with the kiln wall; and (3) a transition stage in which both rolling and slumping occur.

For a fixed percentage filling of the kiln, slumping occurs at low speeds of rotation, rolling occurs at high speeds, and the transition from slumping to rolling occurs at intermediate speeds. Thus, in a slumping bed the rate of transfer of heat from the gas to the bed is limited by the extent to which mixing of the solids occurs and is independent of the temperature of the gas. As the speed of rotation of the kiln is increased (and hence, as the solids feed rate increases), the extent of mixing of the solids increases and consequently the rate of transfer of heat increases. This effect continues with increasing speed of rotation until a fully rolling bed is developed in which the extent of mixing of the solids is maximized. At and beyond this point the temperature of the gas is the factor controlling the heat flow, which then becomes independent of the solids feed rate. In this manner the observed variation of the heat flow with solids feed rate is fully explained.

This study, the results of which are of great importance to the achievement of optimum heat flow conditions in rotary kilns, was being continued in early 1979 in investigations of such variables as particle size and size distribution, wall roughness, stickiness of the solids, and kiln diameter.

See also Feature Article: Corrosion—The Silent Scourge.

—David R. Gaskell

Mathematics

The most prestigious award in mathematics is the Fields Medal, presented every four years at the International Congress of Mathematicians "in recognition of work already done and as an encouragement for further achievements." In contrast to the comparable but more widely known Nobel Prizes, the Fields Medals are traditionally awarded to mathematicians under the age

Three-dimensional model of the image on the Shroud of Turin consists of sheets of cardboard cut according to computer-generated profiles. Many believe the image on the cloth to be that of Christ.

© Joseph Hanlon

of 40 who have made major contributions to research early in their careers. Thus, the Fields Medals not only signal past achievement but also spotlight individuals who will be among the leaders of mathematical research in future decades.

In 1978 four young mathematicians received Fields Medals at the August meeting of the International Congress of Mathematicians in Helsinki, Fin.: Pierre Deligne of the Institut des Hautes Études Scientifiques in France; Charles Fefferman of Princeton University in Princeton, N.J.; Gregory Margulis of the Soviet Union; and Daniel Quillen of the Massachusetts Institute of Technology (MIT) at Cambridge, Mass. These awards brought to 24 the total number of Fields Medals conferred since 1936 when the awards were established as a bequest from the Canadian mathematician J. C. Fields.

Deligne. Pierre Deligne, a 34-year-old Belgian mathematician who has spent most of his mathematical career in France, was awarded a Fields Medal primarily for his solution in 1973 of certain long-standing conjectures of André Weil, one of France's leading mathematicians. These conjectures concern the solution of algebraic equations, such as $y^2 - x^3 + 1 = 0$, similar to those studied in high school algebra. But, like most of Deligne's work, they address the heart of algebraic geometry, one of the most overpowering and austere subjects in the core of modern mathematics.

There are several domains in which one might search for solutions to equations such as $y^2 - x^3 + 1 = 0$. One can seek solutions that are integers (thereby entering the study of what are called Diophantine Equations, after the 3rd century AD arithmetician Diophantus of Alexandria); or solutions that are real numbers (positive and negative whole numbers, fractions, and irrational numbers); or solutions that are complex numbers (such as $3 + 2i$, where i is the "imaginary" square root of -1). Quite commonly, mathematicians seek solutions in one of the modular (or "clock") arithmetics in which numbers repeat (such as 1, 2, 3, 1, 2, 3, 1, 2, 3. . .) after reaching a specific level.

Many years ago Weil discovered in some simple examples certain unexpected connections between the solutions of algebraic equations in modular arithmetic and the geometry of the surfaces that arise in the solutions using complex numbers. These connections pointed to profound relations between arithmetic and geometry, the two oldest branches of mathematics. Motivated in this work by suggestions in Carl Friedrich Gauss's monumental *Disquisitiones Arithmeticae,* itself inspired by the *Arithmetica* of Diophantus, Weil guessed at the general pattern from these few concrete examples.

A quarter century later Deligne proved that the Weil conjectures were correct by a virtuoso interpretation of diverse themes drawn not only from contemporary French algebraic geometry but also from British and

Sidney Harris

"But Gershon, you can't call it Gershon's Equation if everyone has known it for ages."

Japanese elaborations on the works of the largely self-taught early 20th-century Indian mathematician Srinivara Ramanujan. Deligne's work orchestrated themes from 3rd-century Alexandria, 19th-century Germany, early 20th-century India, mid-20th-century Britain, and late-20th-century France, Japan, and the United States; it is no wonder that the announcement of his proof caused a worldwide sensation in mathematical circles.

Fefferman. Charles Fefferman, at 29 the youngest of 1978's four Fields medalists, had been a mathematical prodigy. Entering college at age 14, Fefferman received his Ph.D. at age 20 from Princeton University, and at age 22 became a full professor at the University of Chicago, the youngest person ever to achieve that rank in the history of U.S. higher education. In 1976 he received the first Waterman Award from the National Science Foundation as the most promising researcher in all of U.S. science.

Fefferman's work is in classical subjects such as harmonic and complex analysis and partial differential equations. He has shown extraordinary insight into problems involving many variables. For example, in 1974 Fefferman showed that one of the key properties of functions of a single complex variable (a variable that assumes complex numbers as values) remains true for functions of several complex variables—namely, that functions acting on a region with a smooth boundary (like a circle or an oval) will not disturb the smoothness of the boundary. This theorem had been conjectured for many years, but could not be easily proved because many of the tools essential to the single-variable case were not applicable in the higher-dimensional setting. Fefferman's proof is exceedingly

complex and has so far resisted all efforts by mathematicians at simplification.

Another of Fefferman's favorite arenas is the theory of Fourier series, sums of trigonometric and exponential functions named after the 19th-century French scientist Joseph Fourier. These series enable mathematicians and scientists to break down complex functions into constituent components, just as musical tones can be acoustically decomposed into a sum of simple pure tones. Indeed, this analogy is so strong that the mathematical study of Fourier series is traditionally known as "harmonic" analysis.

Fefferman is one of the few mathematicians who has thoroughly explored harmonic analysis in high dimensions. He discovered that several important theorems of the one-dimensional subject simply are not true in higher dimensions. For example, Fourier series for rather simple continuous functions in dimension two need not converge properly, and even when they do converge they may not have properties corresponding to their one-dimensional analogues. The subject Fefferman studies is so difficult that very few have dared to challenge it, yet it is vitally important in the study of differential equations that arise in routine scientific and engineering problems.

Margulis. Gregory Margulis received his Fields Medal for "breathtaking" results in the theory of Lie groups, results that help relate two of the most fundamental structures of mathematics—the discrete and the continuous. Lie groups, named after 19th-century Norwegian mathematician Sophus Lie, are abstract mathematical objects that unite in one structure models for both continuous processes and discrete change. Lie introduced them in his study of solutions of differential equations; now they are fundamental and useful tools of pure and applied mathematics.

The two-dimensional coordinate plane of high-school analytic geometry is a simple example of Lie group; on it one can do continuous things like calculus, as well as discrete things such as reflections, inversions, and 90° rotations. This Lie group has a special discrete subgroup consisting of "lattice" points, the coordinates of which are both integers. The lattice points in the plane form a subgroup, which, so to speak, demarcates a repeating pattern of squares; the entire plane is like a wall covered with wallpaper that has a repeated pattern determined by the lattice points. Thus the structure of the lattice subgroup is an essential ingredient in the structure of the Lie group, one that must be understood in order to extrapolate from localized information to the global pattern of the entire Lie group.

Margulis's accomplishment was to discover (and prove) the relationship between continuous Lie groups and their discrete lattice subgroups. From 1969 to 1974 he developed a proof of a conjecture posed by Atle Selberg, a Norwegian mathematician who re-

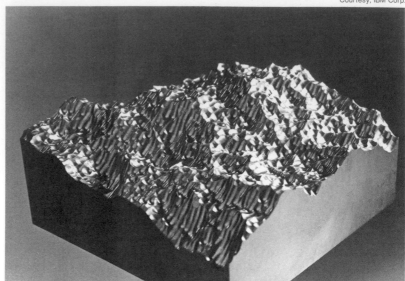

Fractal surface was produced by a computer-driven machine tool. It is an example of a family of irregular but well-defined mathematical shapes used to model forms observed in nature, such as mountains, coastlines, galaxy clusters, and the shapes of large polymer molecules in dilution.

ceived the Fields Medal in 1950. Selberg's conjecture covered only one of the two types of lattice subgroups; little was known—there were not even good conjectures—about the other type. But in 1974 Margulis cracked the second case as well, by transporting the lattice from its original to a more tractable setting. This strategy enabled him to complete the analysis of the lattice subgroups, thereby providing totally fresh insight into the structure of one of the oldest and most important objects in mathematics. Margulis was only 28 when he solved the lattice subgroup problem, and was 32 at the time he received his Fields Medal.

Quillen. A 38-year-old professor at MIT, Daniel Quillen received his Fields Medal for creating the exotic but useful "K-theory," which helps unify diverse parts of algebra and topology. Quillen's K-theory extends enormously the enterprise begun 40 years earlier by such mathematicians as Samuel Eilenberg of Columbia University in New York City and Saunders MacLane of the University of Chicago to translate difficult problems in geometry into easier problems in algebra. Quillen's theory enables mathematicians to reduce many problems of high-dimensional geometry to routine, though still difficult, algebraic calculations.

As René Descartes and Pierre de Fermat introduced algebraic methods into classical geometry in the 17th century, thereby paving the way for the development of calculus, so 20th-century mathematicians have discovered various ways of relating algebraic structures (called groups) to surfaces arising in high-dimensional geometry and topology. (Topology is the study of geometric properties of surfaces as they are bent and distorted.) The theories that accomplish this are known as homology or cohomology (from a Greek word meaning "agreeing").

The specific basis for Quillen's K-theory is a struc-

ture introduced by Alexander Grothendieck of the Institut des Hautes Études Scientifiques in France and Michael Atiyah of Oxford University in Great Britain. Grothendieck and Atiyah, both winners of Fields Medals in 1966, studied a group called K(X), the structure of which "agreed" with a surface X (called an algebraic variety) that arises as the solution to an algebraic equation. Similarly, it is possible to define a group K the structure of which "agrees" with that of a family of functions defined on a surface. Doing this permits advanced study of functions as well as of surfaces.

Earlier homology studies had shown that homology theory emerged from the group K(X) by creation of a whole sequence of groups called $K_0(X)$, $K_1(X)$, $K_2(X)$, ..., of which K(X) was only the first. (This process of extension and generalization, so characteristic of mathematics, is crucial to all scientific studies: as one learns much about the Earth, for example, by studying Venus and Mars, so mathematicians can learn about the "planet" K(X) by studying the "solar system" $K_n(X)$.) Yet despite major efforts by several leading algebraists virtually no progress had been made in "algebraic" K-theory, the homology theory corresponding to functions. Not a single nontrivial example of the higher groups K_n could be calculated, nor was there any agreement on the appropriate definition of these higher groups. Research on the basic group K was stymied for lack of a coherent theory into which it could fit.

Then in 1972 Quillen defined the higher K groups, developed their theory, and showed how their structure could be effectively computed. One mathematician described his novel methods as like "a new and friendly mathematical planet. One meets there not only new theorems and new methods, but new mathematical creatures and a complete paradigm of gestures for dealing with them."

Prime numbers and ticktacktoe. Two other achievements of 1978 were not deep enough for medals but were nonetheless worth recording. In October two high school students, Laura Nickel and Curt Noll, used a computer at California State University at Hayward to find a prime number (one not divisible by any integer other than itself and one) larger than any previously discovered. This number, $2^{21,701} - 1$, has 6,533 digits and required several hundred hours of computer time to discover and verify.

Also, Oren Patashnik at Bell Laboratories in Murray Hill, N.J., succeeded by an ingenious combination of analysis and extensive computer search to analyze fully the $4 \times 4 \times 4$ game of three-dimensional ticktacktoe. This game, marketed commercially as Qubic, had previously resisted all attempts at analysis. Patashnik proved that the first player in Qubic can always win, if he remembers the appropriate combination of billions of possible moves.

—Lynn Arthur Steen

Medical sciences

Among the many developments in the medical sciences during 1978 was the birth of the first "test-tube baby." This achievement was viewed by many as a means of offering some infertile couples the chance to have a child. Human insulin was produced in the laboratory for the first time, a significant achievement because of the dwindling supplies of animal-extracted insulin. Research continued on the relationship between certain behavior patterns and the likelihood of suffering from coronary heart disease.

General medicine

Perhaps the year's most dramatic medical breakthrough took place on July 25, 1978, in the form of one 5-lb 12-oz baby named Louise Joy Brown, born to Gilbert and Lesley Brown in Oldham, England. She was delivered by cesarean section at Oldham General Hospital; the doctors responsible for her birth were Patrick C. Steptoe, a gynecologist and president of the International Federation of Fertility Societies, and Robert G. Edwards, an obstetrician and reproduction specialist at the University of Cambridge.

An egg had been taken from Lesley Brown, fertilized by sperm from her husband, and then reimplanted, a procedure called in vitro fertilization. The specifics of the techniques were not made known immediately, although Steptoe and Edwards did reveal some information in preliminary correspondence with the British medical journal *The Lancet* and in interviews. In early 1979 they reported specific details to the Royal College of Obstetricians and Gynaecologists and international fertility societies.

Only a single egg was removed on Nov. 10, 1977, from Louise's mother, Lesley, 31, and it was done by laparoscopy, a small surgical entrance into the abdomen. The egg was then fertilized with fresh sperm from Gilbert Brown. After two and a half days—in its eight-cell stage—the embryo was reimplanted into the mother. Sixteen weeks into the pregnancy amniocentesis indicated a normally developing 46XX fetus—in lay terms, a baby girl.

The announcement of Louise Brown's birth elicited a full range of praise and criticism. Some hailed it as a means of offering certain infertile couples a chance to have a child; others anticipated the beginning of a "Brave New Medical World" in which abuses of in vitro fertilization could become commonplace. Moralists argued that man was tampering with nature's own power, while others warned that the technique was being used before adequate testing had been done. Still others maintained that science was taking the mystique out of motherhood by manufacturing made-to-order babies in a laboratory.

In vitro fertilization, in fact, works only for certain cases of infertility. Lesley Brown suffered from defec-

The world's first test-tube baby, Louise Joy Brown, was conceived when an egg was removed from her mother's body and fertilized by her father's sperm (left and center). The egg was then reimplanted in the mother, and the baby was born by cesarean section. At the right is Louise Brown at seven months.

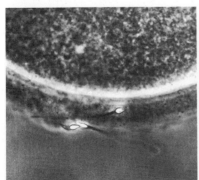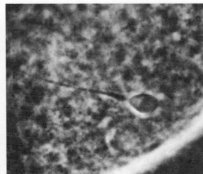

(Above left, center) Central Press/Pictorial Parade; (right) Wide World

tive oviducts, or fallopian tubes, which, if normal, would have carried an egg from the ovaries to the uterus each month. It is normally during this passage that fertilization takes place. Twenty-five percent or more of all the female infertility problems in the world are, like Lesley Brown's, caused by defective fallopian tubes, and a wide range of congenital and infectious ailments can account for the malformation or malfunction of these tubes. There are a number of surgical approaches to correcting the problem. Sometimes the very methods used in diagnosis (passing carbon dioxide gas into the tubes and inserting dyes for the purpose of X-ray, for example) will correct the blockage. Particularly over the past two years a growing number of physicians have had success with microsurgery in the reconstruction of blocked fallopian tubes, a tedious operation that takes about four hours. In this procedure a microscope is used to magnify the surgical field 4–25 times, enabling surgeons to identify clearly the three layers of tubes and remove the obstructions. Then very small needles and superfine sutures are used to sew up each layer of the tube.

Exact data on the success of microsurgical reconstruction of the tubes are not available. It is estimated that only about half of the women with tubal obstructions can be treated with microsurgery. The best candidates are those who have been sterilized by methods that produce a clean break with which to rejoin the ends. In vitro fertilizations and reimplantations are designed, it is hoped by Steptoe and Edwards, for those women whose tubes are so badly damaged that they cannot be surgically reconstructed.

According to the researchers techniques for achieving in vitro fertilization and reimplantation have been improved even since the birth of Louise Brown. While only one in 100 fertilizations was successfully implanted at the time of her birth, now approximately one in ten is successful. As of early 1979 Steptoe's and Edwards's method had produced four pregnancies; two ended in miscarriage, while the other two produced Louise Brown and a second baby, Alastair Montgomery, born in January 1979.

In their long-awaited report to the fertility societies the doctors credited their pair of successes to a greater adherence to nature. They abandoned artificially induced superovulation, the production of more than a single egg cell, and instead harvested a single egg during the natural menstrual cycle. In their procedure the egg and the husband's fresh sperm are placed in a fertilization medium immediately after inspection for defects; then after approximately 12 to 14 hours they are transferred to another medium for cell division. The embryo is then transplanted into the uterus via the vagina and cervix. Interestingly, the doctors found that pregnancies were more likely to occur when the fertilized eggs were transplanted late in the evening rather than in the morning. The doctors also abandoned hormonal therapy to suppress rejection of the fertilized egg, although they continued to contemplate its use.

Studies done at the University of Alabama in Birmingham had shown that rhesus monkey embryos implanted even after only one or two cell divisions could survive. It is believed that this finding led to the reimplantation of the Brown embryo after two and a half days rather than the four to four and a half that had been tried earlier. Perhaps earlier tries had failed because the embryos had existed too long in an artificial environment.

Interferon, a substance manufactured in the body, is placed in microwell plates that contain cells to which a test virus has been added. Researchers then determine whether the interferon has protected the cells from destruction by the virus.

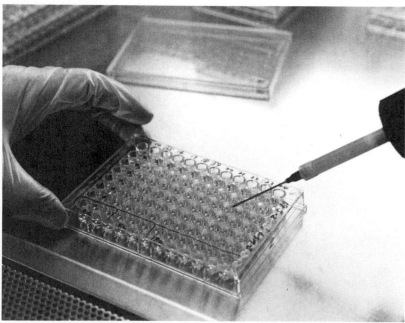

Courtesy, Memorial Sloan-Kettering Cancer Center & The American Cancer Society

It was also believed that drugs to bring on superovulation upset or overwhelmed the natural system. Normally when an egg is released from its sac in the ovary, a special tissue called corpus luteum forms there. Hormones essential to pregnancy are then manufactured. If fertility is achieved, the embryo gives the signal for hormone production to continue; if not, the corpus luteum regresses and menstruation occurs. If an embryo is inserted at that time, the signal to the corpus luteum to regress may cause the embryo to be expelled.

In a recent interview Steptoe said that in vitro fertilization also has been used to overcome infertility in men. In order for normal fertilization to take place several hundred million sperm must be ejaculated. In test-tube fertilizations, however, fewer are needed. Thus men whose infertility is a result of low sperm count could father a child by this method.

Interferon. In 1957 two virologists at the National Institute for Medical Research in London, Alick Isaacs and Jean Lindenmann, discovered why a person seldom contracts two viral infections at the same time. The body, they found, manufactures a substance that interferes with development of multiviral infections. The two researchers appropriately dubbed that substance "interferon." In 1978 clinical trials began in the U.S. using interferon on cancer victims, raising the hope stimulated by isolated studies around the world that interferon might become a therapeutic tool against the three forms of cancer—sarcoma, carcinoma, and hematological malignancy.

While the exact mechanism of interferon's antiviral activity is not known, it is believed to be the body's first line of defense against the spread of viral infections. Almost any cell being attacked by a virus can manufacture interferon, which then quickly spreads to neighboring cells of the same tissue-type in an effort to protect them from invasion by that virus and a range of others. Only a small amount of the substance is manufactured by the cells because that is all that is needed. Moreover, interferon is species-specific, which means that only human interferon can be used successfully to treat human ailments. These two factors cause production of the substance to be expensive and time-consuming. (The chief source of it is the highly organized National Blood Bank in Helsinki, Finland.) Despite its scarcity and cost, however, scientists are hoping to develop methods of making large quantities of human interferon for further studies of its function in the body and for experimental use as a drug.

For years scientists have been baffled by the problem of viruses, which, unlike bacteria, are resistant to most drugs. The few drugs that are effective are so only against a few kinds of viruses. Interferon, on the other hand, promises to be an ideal antiviral drug. It is a natural substance produced by the human body; it seems to have no serious side effects; and it appears to be effective against all viruses.

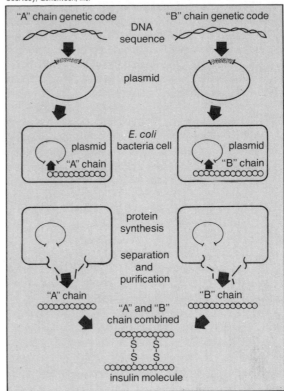

Human insulin was produced by the common bacteria Escherichia coli *in the procedure illustrated above. Large-scale production for testing purposes is expected to begin soon.*

Initial studies indicated that interferon has promise in the control of tumor growth and of the concurrent viral infections that sometimes plague cancer victims. Other investigators envisage a potential use for interferon as an agent that improves the body's defenses against the development of cancer after exposure to some viruses and carcinogenic substances. The antiviral effect is thought to be largely the inhibition of protein synthesis by neighboring cells, which might explain in part the power of the interferon to prevent proliferation of malignant cells.

Interferon's critics say that the dosages necessary to bring about tumor regression may be potent against normal cells as well. But other researchers say that its inhibition of cell division is specific to cancer cells alone. At any rate interferon is promising enough to have prompted the American Cancer Society to fund a $2 million clinical trial of human interferon from Finland to be used on carefully selected cancer patients in the U.S. Some 150 patients will be treated at ten centers throughout the country. Only patients with advanced cases of the disease who have not been helped by established modes of therapy will be admitted to the trial treatments.

Bacterially made insulin. Insulin, the protein hormone produced in the pancreas and used by the body to metabolize sugar and other carbohydrates, is too complex a molecule to be synthesized industrially. Therefore, millions of diabetics who take daily injections of the protein must rely on insulin extracted from the pancreatic glands of slaughtered pigs and cattle. Clinicians have long feared that the annual 6% increase in the incidence of diabetes in the U.S. will soon cause the number of diabetics to exceed the available animal quantities of insulin. Consequently, scientists have been searching for a way to develop human insulin in a laboratory.

During the summer of 1978 two groups of researchers—one in Massachusetts and one in California—worked feverishly to become the first to produce laboratory human insulin. Each team was working with controversial recombinant DNA techniques that they hoped would coax a special laboratory strain of the bacteria *Escherichia coli*—commonly found in the intestines of man—to produce human insulin.

DNA (deoxyribonucleic acid), the substance of which genes are composed, contains the chemical record in which all genetic information is encoded. Recombinant DNA—popularly called gene slicing—is the process of taking pieces of the DNA of one organism and combining it with the DNA of another organism to produce a third; in this case it would involve taking the genetic material that codes for the production of insulin and joining it with the genetic material of the bacteria. The newly coded bacteria then could make insulin, and when the bacteria reproduce, more and more insulin would be manufactured. The bacteria thus would become virtually an insulin factory.

Early in the summer of 1978 the scientists at Harvard Biological Laboratories, Cambridge, Mass., and the Joslin Diabetes Foundation, Boston, succeeded in inducing bacteria to make rat proinsulin, the immediate precursor of rat insulin. But these still were animal experiments; no human insulin had yet been made.

In September, though, Genentech, Inc., and the City of Hope National Medical Center, a private research institution and a hospital, both in California, announced that they indeed had produced human insulin. Their success promised to be a significant advancement for the millions of diabetics who have been relying on the dwindling supplies of animal-extracted insulin injections for survival. Also, it marked the first time that recombinant DNA research has led to potentially practical human application.

In the production of the hormone researchers combined synthetic rather than natural genes for each of two amino acid chains of insulin with the necessary control mechanisms, called plasmids. These are extrachromosomal circular strands of DNA found in cells that have had an appropriate "chunk" taken out. The newly constructed plasmid hybrids (containing the remaining

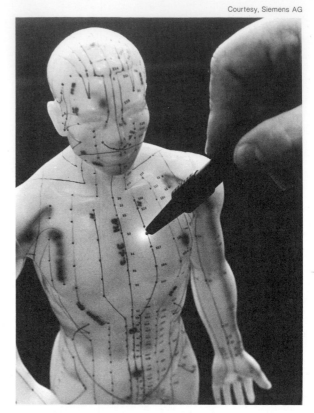

Acupuncture by laser is demonstrated by training a laser gun on a manikin "tattooed" with the traditional acupuncture points. Such treatment is both aseptic and painless.

DNA plus the new synthetic gene that carried the code for human insulin) were then inserted into a laboratory strain of *E. coli.* Once inside the bacteria the genes were "switched on," translating the code to produce the "A" and "B" protein chains of insulin. The separate chains then were joined to construct complete insulin molecules. This new technique could potentially provide not only enough insulin for everyone's needs, but also would help overcome the problems of allergic responses some diabetics have to animal insulin.

Antiplatelet therapy. In February 1978 U.S. and Canadian researchers reported that a drug used for the treatment of gout halved the incidence of sudden cardiac deaths among patients who had previously suffered one heart attack. The drug, sulfinpyrazone (its brand name is Anturane), thus presented itself as a possible new therapy for victims of heart attacks. Previously there was no medicine that could prevent a heart attack patient from dying of a second attack. Each year some one million people in the U.S. suffer their first attack; of those, about half die quickly and about 400,-000 survive. About 47,000 of the latter, however, usually die of another heart attack within one year.

In the first study of the effects of Anturane on subsequent heart attacks, patients at 26 medical centers in

Canada and the U.S. took part. It was headed by Sol Sherry of the medical school of Temple University in Philadelphia. At their first office visit to their physician, usually 25 to 35 days following their first heart attack, the patients were given either Anturane or a placebo (a pill of a medically inactive substance).

Of the 1,475 patients in the study, 733 took Anturane and 742 took the placebo. After 8.4 months of treatment the preliminary results showed that there were 68 deaths from heart conditions in the two groups: 44 in the placebo group but only 24 in the Anturane group. Of the 68 deaths, 42 were sudden: 29 in the placebo group and 13 in the Anturane group. The others were due to myocardial infarctions: 9 in the Anturane group (there were 2 cardiac deaths for other reasons) and 12 in the placebo group. The annual death rate then was 9.5% in the placebo group and 4.9% in the Anturane group, a reduction of 48.5%. The annual rate of sudden death was 6.3% for the placebo group and 2.7% for the Anturane group, a reduction of 57.2%.

There were 41 nonfatal heart attacks among the placebo group and 31 among the Anturane group. Furthermore, 25 of the placebo group but only 14 of the Anturane group were hospitalized for serious heart-rhythm abnormalities. The original purpose of the study was to see if Anturane could reduce the incidence of recurrent heart attack. This it seemed unable to do (although a longer, larger study may reveal that it does). But the researchers did find a significant reduction in deaths from a second heart attack.

It is not certain how Anturane protects patients, probably because physicians are unsure of what precisely causes a heart attack. Does a clot obstruct an artery after or before an attack? Do microscopic clots disrupt the heart's electrical system and lead to sudden deaths? These and other questions need to be answered: How long will Anturane protect against a second fatal attack? When is the best time to begin treatment? Could it be used prophylactically in anyone at risk to even a first attack? Does it protect against sudden deaths caused by heart-rhythm disturbances?

Other researchers found that aspirin, which like Anturane is an antiplatelet or anticlotting agent, helps reduce the risk of developing a disabling or fatal stroke in men who have experienced transient ischemic attacks (TIA's). Temporary symptoms caused by poor blood flow (ischemia) to the brain, TIA's precede about 10% of all strokes. They are fleeting episodes of one or more symptoms such as fainting, stumbling, numbness, paralysis of limbs, blurred vision, and loss of speech. People who experience such symptoms are four to ten times more likely to have a stroke than those who do not.

The study on reducing the risk of stroke among patients with TIA's was conducted by the Canadian Cooperative Study Group. A total of 585 patients with at least one cerebral or retinal ischemic attack in the three preceding months were studied for an average of 1,003 days (about 33 months). Patients were given either aspirin or Anturane, singly or in combination. Patients who were given aspirin with or without Anturane had a 31% reduction in stroke or death. Those receiving Anturane with or without aspirin had a nonsignificant 10% reduction. Patients on both drugs had a

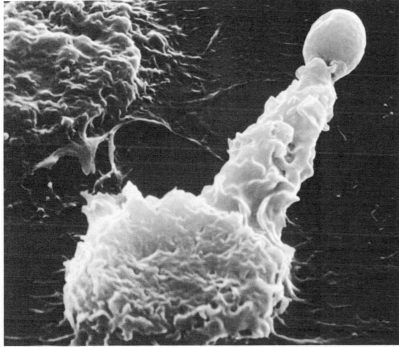

Alveolar macrophage cell extends outward to engulf and digest a foreign object inhaled into the lung, in this case a yeast particle. By forming these extensions a macrophage can clean an area in the lung up to 40 times its own diameter.

Battelle Pacific Northwest Laboratories

lower risk of stroke or death than those on aspirin alone, but the difference was not considered significant. In total 85 patients had a stroke, 52 of whom died.

Aspirin reduced the risk of stroke or death in men by 48%, but women taking aspirin did not experience any significant reduction. Why aspirin should protect men and not women is unknown. Based on this study, physicians recommended that men with TIA's be treated with aspirin if they can tolerate it.

The placebo effect. Physicians have known since the 19th century that medically inactive substances can have dramatic positive effects on those receiving them if they are believed to be real medicines. In fact, so strong is this response to placebos (Latin for "I shall please") that researchers, when testing any new drug, must anticipate an improvement in as many as one-third of the patients in the control group that is given the classic placebo "sugar pill" instead of the experimental drug.

Patient whose cancer is being treated by subjecting it to beams of pions is monitored at the Los Alamos (N.M.) Scientific Laboratory. Some tumors have regressed as a result of the therapy.

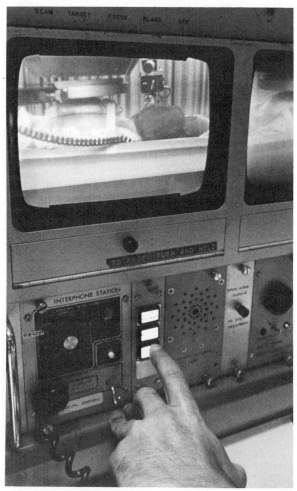

The placebo effect is usually considered a psychological response. But during the summer of 1978 investigators at the University of California at San Francisco found a physiological link between thinking something will help you and its actually doing so. It seems that some people can release pain-relieving substances in their own bodies. Neuroscientists Jon D. Levine and Howard L. Fields and oral surgeon Newton C. Gordon found that for those patients whose pain subsided after they were given a placebo, a single dose of a drug called naloxone would cause the pain to begin again. Naloxone, an opiate blocker, is known neither to increase nor to diminish pain.

Researchers concluded that the placebo's effect was to reduce pain by stimulating the production of natural pain relievers in the body—opiatelike substances called enkephalins and endorphins. First detected in the mid-1970s, these substances act on specific pain receptors in the brain and spinal cord just as morphine and other narcotics do. Naloxone, which has been used to counteract overdoses of heroin, appears in some related way to counteract the narcoticlike enkephalins and endorphins produced by the body after taking the placebo.

The experiment was described in Montreal at the Second World Congress on Pain. Fifty patients who just had had their molar teeth removed were given either a placebo or naloxone. On the average those who got naloxone reported considerably more postoperative pain than those who took the placebo. Then the patients who had received the placebo were divided into two groups: those whose pain was not relieved by the placebo and those whose pain had been reduced. Both these groups were then given naloxone.

Those who had not responded to the placebo in the first place experienced no additional pain with naloxone. But those whose pain had lessened after taking the placebo experienced sudden increases in pain after taking naloxone.

The next phase of the experiment is to find out why placebos trigger the release of endorphins in some people and not in others. Perhaps other psychological approaches to disease, such as biofeedback or relaxation training, may also have direct physiological effects on the nervous system.

Saccharin. In March 1977 the U.S. Food and Drug Administration (FDA) proposed that the artificial sweetener saccharin be banned as a food additive, based on animal experiments showing that in high doses it produces cancer. Intense public response to the FDA's proposal prompted the U.S. Congress to order a study on the sweetener by the National Academy of Sciences (NAS).

The NAS response came in November 1978, when it issued its fifth report since 1955 on saccharin. Its conclusion was that saccharin does pose a potential carcinogenic risk—though a small one—to humans and that, moreover, saccharin may act as a co-carcinogen; that is, it may promote the development of cancer initiated by other substances.

The NAS report agreed with a 1977 study by the Canadian government which concluded that saccharin is carcinogenic in rats. The saccharin and soft-drink industries had criticized this study for alleged inaccuracies, in reply to which the NAS said simply, "Further laboratory studies to establish the carcinogenicity of saccharin are not needed under existing law."

The NAS did say, however, that more precise studies should be made, ones that could quantitatively apply animal test results to humans. For example, current knowledge is insufficient to predict the number of human bladder cancer cases that could result from continued exposure to saccharin.

The NAS targeted several groups that it believed to be at greater risk from saccharin than others. In particular it noted children under ten, one-third of whom have increased their consumption of saccharin-containing products 160% since 1970. The NAS noted that the amount these youngsters consume in relation to body weight makes them the group with the greatest exposure. The other group mentioned as frequent consumers of saccharin was women 20 to 39 years old.

In response to the NAS report the American Diabetes Association reconfirmed its statement of the summer of 1978 that, based on available evidence, there appeared to be little justification for placing further government restrictions on the use of saccharin by the U.S. public. The association said, "Although the NAS report noted no scientific evidence concerning the positive benefits from the use of saccharin by diabetic patients, we believe that much subjective good from the use of nonnutritive sweeteners does accrue to those diabetic people who must avoid sugars and other sweets because of their disease."

Gene mapping. The word "gene" was coined almost a century ago. Only recently, however, has much research on the gene been possible. It was some years ago that scientists, trying to determine where genes are located on specific chromosomes, were able to "map" genes, in the hope of determining which ones are linked to human hereditary diseases. As of 1979 scientists had mapped precisely about 250 genes, more than half of which are located on the X chromosome, the female sex chromosome.

Aided by other techniques in molecular biology such as cell fusion, recombinant DNA research, and cell hybridization, gene mapping may go beyond determining whether an unborn child will inherit a certain disease; it actually promises to correct many genetic disorders. If, for example, a defective gene could be removed and another normal gene inserted in its place on the map of human chromosomes, many genetic disorders could be prevented.

—Dalma Heyn

Stress and illness

Psychological and biomedical researchers generally acknowledge that stress may threaten human welfare and contribute to illness, yet there is little agreement on a precise definition of stress. For some, it is an external stimulus that places heavy demands on an individual's capacity to carry out routine activities. For others, stress is an unpleasant inner state, and for still others it is an observable response to a particular stimulus or situation. Despite these differing conceptions there is agreement that stress is a generic term for an area of study concerned with how physiological, psychological, and social processes interact when individuals deal with potentially threatening demands that tax their adaptive resources.

Theories of stress. Hans Selye, an influential contributor to theory and research on stress and disease, proposed that the body's reactions to noxious agents or "stressors" are part of a general pattern of physiological response called the General Adaptation Syndrome (GAS). The GAS is considered a nonspecific reaction, for it is supposed to function in the same way regardless of the type of stressor confronting the individual. It consists of three stages: alarm, resistance, and exhaustion. Each stage involves somewhat different neuroendocrine reactions, although Selye's model places heavy emphasis on the role of ACTH (adrenocorticotrophic hormone) in stimulating the adrenal cortex to release its corticoid hormones and thus initiate general stress reactivity. If the noxious conditions and the body's defenses mobilized against them continue for some time, various forms of tissue damage occur that are called "diseases of adaptation."

John W. Mason and Richard S. Lazarus proposed alternatives to Selye's proposition that stress is a nonspecific physiological response. These authors pointed out that the body's response varies with the particular type of stressor stimulus and the context in which that stimulus occurs. According to Lazarus, for example, the arousal of stress can be determined by the anticipation of a harmful or threatening event. Once a stimulus is appraised as threatening, coping processes are aroused that have the function of reducing or avoiding the anticipated harm. A person can cope by taking direct action to reduce aversive stimulation, or by using psychological defenses that permit a reappraisal of the stressor as less dangerous. The end result of the coping process is reduced stress response. However, stress response will remain unaltered if environmental demands are excessive and/or the individual is unsuccessful in his coping efforts. Disease can be an outcome of undiminished stress. A case in point is the recent work on life change and illness.

Life events such as retirement, financial loss, and death of a loved one constitute a class of stressful situations to which many people are exposed. It appears that such events can play a role in the occurrence of illness. Thomas H. Holmes and Richard H. Rahe developed a self-report measure of life change called the Schedule of Recent Experience. This measure was scaled so that changes requiring the greatest

Social Readjustment Rating Scale	
Life Event	Mean Value
1. Death of spouse	100
2. Divorce	73
3. Marital separation	65
4. Jail term	63
5. Death of close family member	63
6. Personal injury or illness	53
7. Marriage	50
8. Loss of job due to firing	47
9. Marital reconciliation	45
10. Retirement	45
11. Change in health of family member	44
12. Pregnancy	40
13. Sex difficulties	39
14. Gain of new family member	39
15. Business readjustment	39
16. Change in financial state	38
17. Death of close friend	37
18. Change to different line of work	36
19. Change in number of arguments with spouse	35
20. Taking on mortgage over $10,000	31
21. Foreclosure of mortgage or loan	30
22. Change in responsibilities at work	29
23. Son or daughter leaving home	29
24. Trouble with in-laws	29
25. Outstanding personal achievement	28
26. Wife beginning or stopping work	26
27. Beginning or ending school	26
28. Change in living conditions	25
29. Revision of personal habits	24
30. Trouble with boss	23
31. Change in work hours or conditions	20
32. Change in residence	20
33. Change in schools	20
34. Change in recreation	19
35. Change in church activities	19
36. Change in social activities	18
37. Taking on mortgage or loan less than $10,000	17
38. Change in sleeping habits	16
39. Change in number of family get-togethers	15
40. Change in eating habits	15
41. Vacation	13
42. Christmas	12
43. Minor violations of the law	11

Adapted from T. H. Holmes and R. H. Rahe: The Social Readjustment Rating Scale, *Journal of Psychosomatic Research*, Vol. 11, pp. 213–218, 1967

effort of readjustment (such as divorce) were given higher values than events requiring lesser adjustment (such as a change in work habits). Holmes, Rahe, and their co-workers then conducted extensive research, which indicated that high life-change scores typically precede major illness.

Moderators of life stress. Recent analysis of the life change-illness pathway indicates that physiological reactions to stressful events may depend upon the success or failure of various coping mechanisms, as well as the manner in which these events are appraised. Appraisal is influenced, in turn, by a number of antecedents, including the perception of control or lack of control over the stressor. Perceived control may be defined as the felt ability to escape and/or avoid threatening stimuli. The work of Martin E. P. Seligman suggests that a psychological state of helplessness results when one encounters aversive events about which one can do nothing. A range of motivational, cognitive, and emotional disturbances results from such a situation.

The role of uncontrollability and helplessness in heightening stress responses has figured prominently in psychosomatic research. Indeed, several investigators proposed a state of helplessness as a general precursor to physical disease. In one study illustrative of this point a group of women who were required to report for a biopsy to determine if they had cervical cancer were interviewed. These women, who were without symptoms at the time of interview, were asked questions designed to identify feelings of helplessness and hopelessness. The investigators found that helpless or depressive feelings and attitudes were significantly associated with biopsy findings indicative of cervical cancer.

A state of helplessness has been implicated in the deterioration of the health of institutionalized aged people. One study found that providing elderly residents with the ability to control aspects of the institutional environment and enhancing their sense of choice and responsibility for rather routine events could result in heightened happiness, activity, and well-being. Helplessness can also impede recovery from disease. Favorable outcomes such as reduced complications, shortened stay in the hospital, and reduced invalidism may be fostered by environmental and treatment interventions that bolster a patient's sense of competence and control.

The notion of social support has been suggested as a moderator of the impact of life stressors. Social support is defined as "information leading the individual to believe that he/she is cared for, esteemed and a member of a network of mutual obligations." The effects of social support are illustrated in a study of pregnant women before and after they came to a hospital to deliver their children. The women were given two questionnaires, one designed to measure life change before

Elderly people who are institutionalized often suffer from feelings of helplessness that appear to affect their health adversely. When such people are allowed to control some aspects of their environment, the result, according to one study, is an improvement in their activity and sense of well-being.

and during pregnancy and a second designed to measure "psychosocial asset," or social support as defined above. Women with high life-change scores both before and during pregnancy and low social support scores experienced a high number of complications during pregnancy. By contrast, women with high life change and high social support experienced fewer complications.

Another demonstration of the stress-reducing effects of social support comes from a study of coping and recovery from surgery. One group of patients was given supporting care by the anesthetist, and another group not receiving this support served as a control. Although the physicians did not know which patients had received which treatment, the supportive-care group requested substantially less medication for pain and were discharged on the average several days earlier from the hospital. Further research is needed to clarify exactly how social support moderates life stress.

Stress and cardiovascular disease. Cardiovascular diseases such as hypertension and coronary heart disease are major health hazards in our society. These illnesses have complex etiologies involving an interplay of hereditary factors, metabolic and hormonal alterations, and an individual's life-style. Because the role of environmental stress in cardiovascular pathology has received extensive study over the past few decades, the remainder of this discussion will consider this topic.

Hypertension. Hypertension is a condition in which the blood vessels throughout the body are constricted or contracted, thereby raising arterial pressure. A specific cause for this condition, called peripheral resistance, cannot be found in most patients. In the very early stages of hypertension there is evidence that

blood pressure elevations are associated with excessive pumping of blood from the heart (cardiac output), but over the years there is a change toward increased peripheral resistance with a normal or decreased cardiac output.

Evidence of a linkage between environmental stress and hypertension comes from several sources, although racial, dietary, and other factors are often plausible explanations. Epidemiological research has shown that urban populations have higher blood pressure and hypertensive mortality rates than neighboring nonurban populations. It is also known that black people in the United States have higher mean blood pressures than whites. Because studies outside the U.S. do not consistently detect black-white differences, this variation is probably attributable as much to environmental as genetic factors. Moreover, black populations in "high stress" neighborhoods are reported to have higher blood-pressure levels than blacks in more benign, middle-class neighborhoods. Various life-threatening events (such as combat conditions) have been associated with blood-pressure elevations, as have such situations demanding rapid cultural change as urbanization and migration. In one study higher mean blood pressures were found in Zulu adults who had recently migrated to an urban setting as compared with those who had remained in their original rural settlement areas.

Stressful aspects of the physical environment may also be linked to blood-pressure elevations. For example, one study found that children attending schools under the flight path of an airport had higher chronic blood pressures (measured during quiet) than children attending schools not exposed to aircraft noise. Experimental studies in animals also suggested that noxious

357

Adapted from R. H. Rosenman, *et al*, "The central nervous system and coronary heart disease," *Hospital Practice*, Vol. 6, pp. 87–97, 1971, by permission

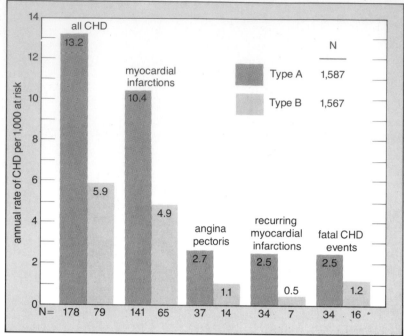

The annual rate of all types of coronary heart disease (CHD) is higher for those people exhibiting the Type A behavior pattern (characterized by extremes of competitiveness, a strong sense of time urgency, and hostility) than for Type B persons. The 3,154 subjects were studied for eight and a half years. N equals the number of cases of the particular disease.

environmental stressors (such as electric shock) can produce sustained elevations in blood pressure.

The notion of a "hypertensive personality" has been proposed by a number of investigators who have made attempts to find consistent relationships between sustained high blood pressure and suppressed hostility, anger, anxiety, and tightly controlled emotions. On balance, studies that have attempted to identify such a hypertensive personality have produced inconclusive results.

Coronary heart disease. Coronary heart disease is the general term for a clinical disorder resulting from damage to the coronary arteries (atherosclerosis). Myocardial infarction or heart attack is one of the most common forms of clinical coronary disease. Although epidemiologists identify an array of risk factors for coronary heart disease (elevated blood lipids, smoking, and hypertension), the best combination of these factors still fails to identify most new cases of the disease. Therefore, investigators have turned to an examination of psychological factors that might enhance the risk of coronary disease. Among the most promising variables are psychological stress and an overt behavior pattern called Type A. There is some evidence that these factors, which will be discussed below, independently and in conjunction with one another contribute to increased risk of developing coronary heart disease.

Several classes of psychological stressors have been studied in connection with coronary disease. The first is life dissatisfactions related to jobs, as well as to marital and interpersonal relations. Although a number of studies have reported that coronary patients are critical and irritated with their lives, it is difficult to infer that illness was preceded by dissatisfaction since virtually all of this research was conducted on persons who had already experienced an infarction.

Chronic stress such as excessive work and responsibility has also been implicated in the development of coronary heart disease. For example, feelings that job demands are beyond a person's control (work overload) have been linked to elevated serum cholesterol and to the incidence of coronary heart disease. Acutely stressful events, such as death of a close relative, appear to increase the likelihood of death in next of kin due to coronary disease. In addition, recent studies indicate that rejection by a loved one or a sudden loss of self-esteem sometimes precedes an acute heart attack.

Consistent with the earlier discussion of illness and stressful life events, one team of investigators reported that sudden death due to coronary heart disease may be linked to feelings of helplessness and depression. Male patients who died suddenly were the focus of their study. Data obtained from medical records and from interviews with the surviving next of kin indicated that a substantial majority of the deceased patients were reported to have had clinical symptoms of depression for a week up to several months prior to death. These depressions were precipitated either by sudden losses or by life events over which the individual had little control.

Recent research indicates some of the physiological mechanisms by which stress may enhance the development of coronary disease. These include increases in such factors as serum cholesterol and blood pressure, acceleration of the rate of damage to the coronary arteries over time, and facilitation of the aggregation of blood platelets (substances that are important to blood coagulation and clotting). Stress can also contribute to heart disease through the body's general reaction to aversive stimulation. It is widely agreed that this reaction involves heightened activity of the sympathetic nervous system and the discharge of such catecholamines as adrenalin and noradrenalin. These substances may have a special significance in the development of coronary disease. It appears that they can accelerate the rate of arterial damage, induce myocardial lesions, and produce sudden cardiac arrhythmias.

Perhaps the most thoroughly investigated psychosocial factor contributing to coronary heart disease is the Type A behavior pattern. Type A, described initially by Ray H. Rosenman and Meyer Friedman in 1959, is characterized by extremes of competitiveness, a strong sense of time urgency, and hostility. A contrasting Type B pattern is defined as the relative absence of these characteristics. Although several studies documented an association between individuals manifesting Type A behavior and coronary disease, the

Crowding, as seen below on a subway train, may be one of the stressful events that induces in susceptible individuals Type A behavior by threatening their sense of control.

Donald C. Dietz—Stock, Boston

most convincing evidence came from an investigation called the Western Collaborative Group Study. In this research more than 3,000 initially well men, from 39 to 59 years old, were assessed at intake for a comprehensive array of social, dietary, biochemical, clinical, and behavioral variables. An eight and one-half year follow-up study showed that subjects exhibiting Type A behavior at intake were about twice as likely as Type B subjects to develop clinical coronary disease. This difference occurred independently of other risk factors such as serum cholesterol and cigarette smoking.

David C. Glass suggested that Type A behavior is elicited in susceptible individuals only by appropriately stressful situations. Type A people work hard to succeed, exhibit rapid pacing of their activities, and express hostility when slowed. The Type A pattern might, therefore, be described as a characteristic style of responding to environmental stressors that threaten an individual's sense of control. Glass presented evidence that Type A individuals, in contrast to Type B's, do indeed exert enhanced efforts to cope with stressors that they perceive as uncontrollable. However, after prolonged exposure to uncontrollable stress, Type A individuals are more likely than Type B persons to give up efforts at control and show a passivity that has been termed helplessness. This leads to the speculation that continual alternation between enhanced coping efforts and passivity is accompanied by physiological processes (increases and decreases of catecholamines and sympathetic nervous system activity) that potentiate atherosclerotic deposits in the coronary artery walls over time. It is also hypothesized that infarctions and cardiac arrhythmias may be induced by abrupt changes in catecholamine levels generated by the alternations in Type A behavior.

Conclusions and future directions. In reviewing possible linkages between stress and illness, this discussion has emphasized the point that human response to stress is mediated by sociopsychological factors such as social support and beliefs concerning one's ability to control the environment. A current focus of stress research is the examination of physiological mechanisms linking these factors to health outcomes. For example, investigators are now examining psychological influences on the immune response and on brain regulation of the autonomic nervous system.

Research on stress and illness has obvious implications for prevention and cure. For example, researchers are attempting to develop programs designed to change beliefs about the controllability of the environment in an effort to lessen the impact of stressful events on individual health. Considerable attention is also being given to attempts to modify Type A behavior. It is hoped that such modification, in conjunction with dietary and other life-style changes, will reduce deaths and disability from coronary heart disease.

—David C. Glass and David S. Krantz

Dentistry

During 1978 the dental profession continued to place strong emphasis on the expansion of so-called access programs, focusing in particular on providing services for denture patients. At its annual session in October in Anaheim, Calif., the American Dental Association (ADA) urged all state dental societies to establish denture referral programs. Such programs, ADA officials noted, would strengthen organized dentistry's position on improving access to dental care and would constitute the "strongest offense against the encroachment of denturism." Denturists are dental laboratory personnel who make dentures for patients without the supervision of a dentist. By the end of 1978, the ADA said, there were 52 access programs in 25 states.

At the same meeting the ADA altered its *Principles of Ethics* to make it conform with the U.S. Supreme Court's historic decisions on advertising by professionals. Under the changed version "a dentist may advertise the availability of his services and the fees that he charges for routine procedures." However, the ADA noted that advertising that is false, fraudulent, misleading, or deceptive is excluded from constitutional protection.

In a more scientifically related matter the ADA told the Federal Communications Commission and the Federal Trade Commission investigating children's television programming and advertising practices that such advertising is "heavily slanted toward encouraging youngsters to buy and consume highly sugared food items." Sugar has been identified by scientists as a direct cause of dental decay, and children are an especially vulnerable audience because they lack the ability to make sound judgments of advertising claims. As a countermeasure the ADA suggested that positive health education messages on nutrition and dental hygiene should be featured on children's programs in the form of both public service announcements (which have been produced by the association for many years) and as part of product advertising.

Dental fillings. Experiments with invisible tooth-colored plastic dental fillings offer hope for developing materials of impressive wear resistance and color stability, two U.S. Public Health Service dental researchers reported. Development of invisible tooth-colored filling materials that are as safe and durable as previously used conventional metallic restorative agents has long been a goal of modern dentistry, according to Joseph Moffa and Wayne Jenkins, both of San Francisco. Speaking at the annual meeting of the International Association for Dental Research in Washington, D.C., they noted that although plastic can be made to simulate tooth structure in appearance, previous attempts to utilize plastics for the restoration of back teeth have met with failure because of wear, leakage, and a high decay rate.

A microdrill bores tiny wells in a sample of tooth enamel. Studies indicate that tooth decay usually begins in the enamel just below the tooth's surface.

A three-year study of an experimental glass-filled composite material proved it to be physically superior when compared with a similar plastic material with regard to color stability and wear resistance. At the end of four years 91% of the experimental material examined exhibited no detectable wear, compared with only 25% for the other substance.

Gum surgery. Tetracycline, a popular antibiotic, seems to enhance results of surgery and bone grafts in treating gum disease, suggested a State University of New York at Buffalo dental researcher. Robert Genco of Buffalo said that his studies suggest that therapy involving tetracycline could be a useful adjunct to conventional periodontal surgery or surgery combined with bone grafts. The latter treatment is needed for severe cases of periodontal disease in which the bone structure supporting the teeth is weakened. If not treated, such a disorder can result in tooth loss.

Tetracycline was selected for the study because it is believed to have some affinity to bone and is effective against certain bacteria found in large numbers in the mouths of periodontitis patients. There is also evidence from animal studies that it is effective against gum destruction.

Genetics and tooth decay. A new study at the Medical College of Virginia may have opened the door to gene experimentation that could eventually lead to a reduction of tooth decay. Francis Macrina of Richmond, Va., spent more than two years gathering evidence to learn if there are in the mouth *Streptococcus mutans* that carry specific pieces of genetic information called plasmids. *Streptococcus mutans* are organisms generally thought to contribute to the development of cavities.

Macrina screened nearly 100 isolated strains of *Streptococcus mutans*, most of which were taken from human dental plaque obtained from individuals in the U.S. and U.K. Plaque is a soft substance that constantly forms on the teeth and that is considered a major contributing factor in tooth decay. "In studying genetic composition of a bacterial cell, two kinds of determinants are clinically important—those which make the cell antibiotic resistant and those which make the cell virulent or able to cause disease," he explained. "There's no evidence that plasmids in the *Streptococcus mutans* make them virulent or resistant to antibiotics." However, his study uncovered that the plasmids found in the *Streptococcus mutans* are receptive to genetic engineering experiments, thus paving the way for gene experimentation for curbing tooth decay.

Fluoride gel and mouth rinse. A regimen of supervised self-administered fluoride gel applications and fluoride mouth rinsing by schoolchildren produced additional evidence that such programs can provide significant protection against new tooth decay even when the decay rate is already low because of community water fluoridation. These findings were reported by Stanley Heifetz of the National Institute of Dental Research based on a 30-month field trial involving 416 children in Stickney, Ill., a Chicago suburb with fluoridated water. A test group of fifth graders in 15 schools applied fluoride gel to their teeth daily for five days three times during the first year and used a fluoride mouth rinse once a week during all 30 months, under the supervision of public health nurses. A control group of children used only an inactive mouth rinse weekly. New tooth decay occurring in the test group of children was about 30% less than the new decay detected among the control group during the 30 months.

For the mouth-rinsing procedure alone the cost was only 42 cents for each child per year. The cost of the fluoride gel applications was much greater because professional dental teams used denture liner materials and vinyl holders to make two custom-fitted mouthpieces for each child in the test group. If an inexpensive disposable mouthpiece now commercially available

Electron microscopy reveals circular plasmid DNA molecules obtained from a strain of Streptococcus mutans. *Such plasmids are expected to be useful in gene experiments aimed at reducing the incidence of tooth decay.*

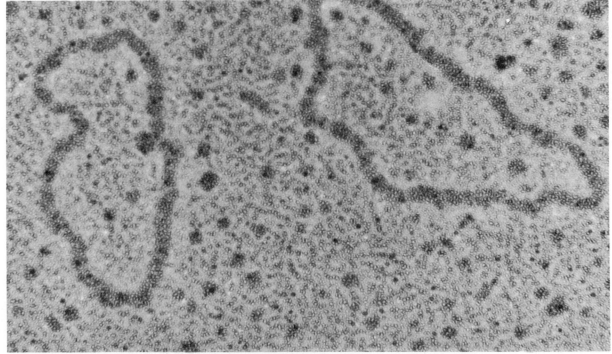

can be effectively used in place of the individually fitted ones, this self-administered preventive procedure may become more practical and economical.

Plant substances. Substances derived from ordinary plant tissue such as grass, leaves, peanut shells, and potato peelings have shown a remarkable ability to inhibit dental plaque, reported two Indiana University dental researchers. Simon Katz and I. C. Park of Indianapolis said that their preliminary findings were encouraging but emphasized that the substances have not yet been tested in humans.

To determine the antiplaque potential of these substances, which were extracted from plant tissues by concentrated alkali, plaque was grown on small glass plates incubated with *Streptococcus mutans* in a sucrose-containing medium to which minute amounts of the extracts had been added. Control specimens were incubated in the same medium but without the extracts. Plaque accumulations on the plates were then measured by analyzing the amount of light absorbed from a beam that passed through the plaque. Plaque reductions between 90 and 100% were found with all extracts. Additional experiments with sugar beet pulp suggest that it may be possible to obtain plant extracts that would be capable of blocking the two main stages in the development of tooth decay, plaque accumulation and acid formation.

Self-test for oral cancer. A quick, simple ten-step self-examination can substantially aid in the detection of oral cancer, which is often painless in the early stages but can be treated most successfully at that time. Helene Bednarsh, a dental community development specialist at the Indian Health Service dental branch in Rapid City, S.D., said that the mouth provides easy visual access and early detection of precancerous changes. Of the 24,000 new cases of oral cancer diagnosed annually, only an approximate 35% survive

five years. This happens because about 50% of all oral cancers have already spread from the primary site to the lymph nodes at the time a diagnosis is made. This factor, as well as the size of the tumor, lessens the probability of five-year survival. The chance of surviving five years with a small lesion is 59% but drops to 17% with larger lesions, according to Bednarsh.

In examining the mouth, head, and neck, Bednarsh listed the following symptoms to look for: a swelling or lump, any sore that does not heal in two weeks, numbness or tingling, white scaly patches or red velvet areas, bleeding or loose teeth for no apparent reason, prolonged hoarseness or sore throat, and difficulty in swallowing or opening the mouth.

—Lou Joseph

Veterinary medicine

Results of a major survey of U.S. veterinary manpower needs from 1978 to 1990, published in 1978, indicated that an oversupply of veterinarians was probably imminent. Commissioned by the American Veterinary Medical Association (AVMA), the so-called Little Report (based on a study by Arthur D. Little, Inc.) determined the supply of and demand for veterinarians in private practice to be in balance nationally in 1977, when the number totaled about 32,000. An insufficient number with postgraduate training resulted in a slight shortage of teachers and researchers in educational institutions and a substantial shortage in industry.

With the present 22 veterinary schools and the two expected to begin operation shortly, there would be about 49,900 active veterinarians by 1990, or 51,100 if four other projected schools should become operational. The predicted demand in 1990 was for only about 41,600 veterinarians, leaving a projected surplus of at least 8,300, and a surplus of about 3,900 by 1985 if 24

A steer wears boots containing measuring devices that can determine at any moment the animal's weight with a margin of error within one pound in a thousand. An FM radio in the backpack on the animal transmits the data from the boots to a minicomputer for processing.

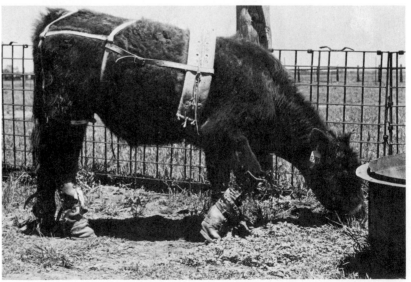

schools were in operation. The demand for veterinarians with postgraduate training, however, was expected to rise more steeply than that for those with only a D.V.M. (or V.M.D.) degree.

These figures were in sharp contrast to those reported in 1971 on the basis of a two-year study by the National Research Council of the National Academy of Sciences, also commissioned by the AVMA. It had determined that there were about 25,900 veterinarians in the U.S. in 1970 compared with a projected need for 42,000 by 1980. This was substantially more than the educational system could produce during that time, despite the opening of four new schools and an increase in enrollment at most of the others, from 1,436 first-year students in 1970 to 1,977 in 1977.

As summarized in the *Journal of the AVMA* the principal basis given in the Little Report for the predicted "significant oversupply" of veterinarians was "the increasing influence of certain noneconomic factors which could render the market less responsive to the normal competitive forces of supply and demand." Federal measures in the economic-animal sector were cited as another factor. This general statement was supported only by recognition that the numbers of purebred dogs had become static rather than increasing as they had prior to 1970 and that the number of dairy cattle was decreasing, though beef cattle numbers were increasing.

In order "to preserve a competitive pattern in the market for veterinary services and thereby minimize the possibility of a misallocation of resources resulting from an oversupply of veterinarians," the Little Report made several suggestions.

One was to increase the awareness of the future oversupply, which was expected to discourage prospective students whose interests in veterinary medicine were least intense.

A second recommendation was regionalization of veterinary schools. This would lessen the continuing pressures to establish schools in states now lacking them, together with broadening interstate compacts whereby one school agrees to accept up to a specified number of qualified students from certain states lacking schools.

The Little Report also urged that federal and state government programs revise their policy of encouraging schools to proliferate or expand and instead concentrate on preparing veterinarians for food-animal practice.

Finally, the report advocated the expansion of post-professional education in order to increase opportunities for specialized employment. An increase in funding for training in research related to human health and ecological problems was termed desirable.

Critics of the Little Report argued that it failed to take into account many changes in veterinary practice during recent years. In the companion-animal area these included a large decrease in hours worked, expanded technology, increased specialization, and the advent of emergency hospitals, group practices, and centralized hospitals; all of these developments had the effect of requiring an expanded work force. A 400% increase in the number of "Veterinarian Wanted" advertisements in professional journals during the past ten years reflected certain of these changes. Critics also pointed out that veterinary services have long been underutilized by livestock producers, even for overt disease problems.

Adequate attention to these largely disregarded problems would require many more practitioners and advisers with specialized training in preventive herd health.

The Little Report was not expected to have much impact on plans to establish new veterinary schools in

Swine infected with hog cholera. A vaccine has eliminated the disease in the U.S., but it exists along with related forms of swine fever in other parts of the world.

Wisconsin, Virginia, and North Carolina, and the announcement of two regional plans predated the report. In a cooperative arrangement students from Washington, Oregon, and Idaho will rotate instruction at existing and new facilities at those state universities, with particular emphasis on food-animal medicine. A new school at Tufts University, to serve the New England states, accepted 35 students for instruction beginning in 1979.

Since the inception of state-supported veterinary schools in Iowa in 1879, the preference extended to residents of those states has hampered the opportunity of prospective students from other states. Five states (California, Mississippi, Oklahoma, Tennessee, and Texas) accepted only residents in 1977, and five others accounted for a total of only 47 nonresidents. With the cost of veterinary instruction approaching $20,000 per student per year and with as little as $150 to as much as $6,000 coming from student fees, more states were expected to consider regional compacts.

Growth promoters. A proposal made in 1977 by the U.S. Food and Drug Administration (FDA) to prohibit or severely restrict the use of certain antibiotics as growth promoters in animal feeds was vigorously protested by veterinary organizations and livestock producers. As a result the FDA announced in August 1978 that it would not implement the proposed regulations, and Congress directed deferment of any action until the results of additional research on possible health hazards to man were available, probably in 1980.

Diethylstilbestrol (DES), used as a growth promoter in cattle, has been believed to have a potential for causing cancer in persons eating meat from such animals. In 1972–73 the FDA banned its use for that purpose because there was no way to prevent miniscule residues of DES in meat, even though no human cases of DES-residue-related cancer had been documented. These bans were later overturned, but following a hearing on the matter the FDA in September 1978 proposed reinstating the ban. Another concern of the FDA was that of sulfonamide residues in meat from animals treated with these drugs. However, an AVMA study concluded: "No realistic evidence exists that sulfonamides are even potentially toxic to human beings at the infinitesimal levels present in swine tissues."

Drug approval. Acting upon the increasing concern of veterinarians over the availability of drugs for animal use, the AVMA proposed a number of changes in FDA procedures. To expedite approval of new drugs it was recommended that this process be handled by the Bureau of Veterinary Medicine alone rather than in conjunction with the Bureau of Foods as at present. Animal-oriented criteria for approving a drug were urged in lieu of those used for approval of human drugs. Since veterinary practitioners are considered well qualified to evaluate the efficacy and safety of drugs for animals, making a drug that is awaiting approval available for

field testing would greatly shorten the time required for marketing a safe and effective final product. Also, the AVMA objected to FDA reclassification of an "old" drug as "new" whenever a new use for it was claimed, thus depriving veterinarians of the drug for any use until it could be approved.

In June 1978 Lester Crawford, formerly on the veterinary faculty of the University of Georgia, became director of the FDA Bureau of Veterinary Medicine. In January 1979, Crawford indicated that the FDA may go part way in broadening drug availability, as urged by the AVMA.

Disease outbreaks. After contagious equine metritis, a venereal disease transmitted by infected stallions to mares, was discovered in Great Britain, Ireland, and France in 1977, importation of horses from those countries and Australia to the U.S. was banned. However, the disease occurred in Kentucky during early 1978. The breeding season was temporarily interrupted, and a quarantine affecting some 400 mares appeared to have brought the disease under control without reducing the 1979 foal crop.

In June 1978 African swine fever was found in Brazil, and by August it had spread to 10 of that country's 24 states. A separate outbreak in the Dominican Republic in July was attributed to virus in pork discarded from an airliner and fed to hogs. Puerto Rico was considered to be at high risk because nearly all of its hogs are garbage-fed, and the swine industry there and in Florida was placed under close surveillance. Because there is no vaccine for prevention and no treatment once the disease exists, import regulations and inspection procedures were tightened at all U.S. ports of entry. The disease resembles hog cholera ("classical" swine fever), which has been eradicated in the U.S., but diagnosis is more difficult in countries where both exist. African swine fever, long present throughout much of Africa, spread to southern Europe about 20 years ago. In 1971 the disease appeared in Cuba, where about one-third of the swine population died before it was eradicated by slaughter.

—J. F. Smithcors

Optical engineering

During the past year the most dramatic advances in optical engineering resulted from the combination of new electronic and computer capabilities with recent optical developments. As always, advances in one area of optical engineering furnished the impetus for advances in other areas. For example, developments in adaptive optics and atmospheric turbulence correction increased the interest in large-aperture telescopes. In turn, the interest in producing large-aperture telescopes and high-energy lasers generated needs for advances in optical fabrication and testing tech-

Observatory on the top of Mt. Hopkins in Arizona houses the first multiple-mirror telescope (MMT). Composed of six separate 1.8-meter-diameter telescopes with one common focus, the MMT has a combined light-collecting area equal to that of a 4.5-meter telescope.

nology. Likewise, developments in fiber-optic communication techniques were used to solve data transmission requirements in laser fusion systems. The interaction among the different technologies is almost endless.

Multiple-mirror telescope. The multiple-mirror telescope (MMT) recently installed at the top of Mt. Hopkins, Ariz., is the first example of a novel optical design that could pave the way for the construction of telescopes much larger than any now in existence. Consisting of six separate 1.8-m-diameter telescopes with one common focus, the MMT has a combined light-collecting area equal to that of a 4.5-m telescope. There are two major reasons for designing large telescopes. First there is the need to collect more photons, especially for spectroscopy of faint and distant objects. The second reason is to manifest the increased resolution that corresponds to the diffraction limit (the extent to which images with angular separations can be produced) of a large aperture. Increased resolution via increased aperture can be realized in a space telescope or on the ground for infrared wavelengths greater than approximately ten micrometers. At shorter wavelengths the deformation of wavefronts by atmospheric inhomogeneities limits the clarity of actual images formed by all telescopes to about one arcsecond. The diffraction limit of existing telescopes for visible light is already far below this value, however, due to new technology such as speckle interferometry and adaptive optics (see below); the technology for being able to see details as small as the diffraction limit set by the telescope size is fast approaching.

The primary reason for building a multiple-mirror

telescope rather than one with a single large mirror is an approximate two-thirds reduction in cost. These savings result because of the shorter tube length of the individual telescopes and because of the reduction in weight over a solid monolithic mirror. Also, the MMT can be housed in a building considerably smaller than that required for a conventional domed telescope. The drawback of the MMT is that the individual components must be controlled by servomechanisms so that they operate together.

The basic idea of the control system is to monitor the three-dimensional positions of each of the six images of the sky by the use of 12 laser beams. The error signals from the laser-beam detectors are fed back to the individual secondary mirrors, which have focus and two-axis tilt controls. Initial results indicated that extremely good repeatability in fixing positions to within 0.5 arcsecond was being achieved without operation of the servomechanisms. If progress continues at that rate, the MMT will lead the way toward construction of much larger telescopes using similar principles. By 1979 planning for two such projects had already started. The University of California branches at Berkeley, Los Angeles, San Diego, and Santa Cruz were studying possible designs for a ten-meter telescope, and a group at Kitt Peak National Observatory in Arizona was investigating the feasibility of a telescope with an aperture of 25 m.

Adaptive optics. Adaptive optics is defined as optical systems that measure and correct wavefront aberrations in real time. This possibility of improving the performance of an optical system has many applications for both passive imaging systems and laser sys-

Courtesy, Laboratory for Laser Energetics, College of Engineering and Applied Science, University of Rochester

Target chamber of the first stage of the University of Rochester's Omega 24 laser system. The needlelike stalk seen through the open port holds the tiny target, atoms of hydrogen isotopes. In October six laser beams entered the chamber symmetrically around its circumference and irradiated the target with a peak power of 2.5 million megawatts.

tems. For example, as mentioned above, adaptive optics offers the possibility of removing the effect of atmospheric turbulence and allowing diffraction-limited images from the ground. It can also compensate for the degrading effects of the atmosphere in transmitting laser radiation. Active corrections and controls are necessary for the construction of the next generation of large telescopes, which will be likely to consist of many smaller optical elements.

Working adaptive systems consist of three basic components. A wavefront sensor is required to sense the aberration or wavefront error that must be corrected. A wavefront corrector, which is generally a deformable or "rubber" mirror, is used to correct the aberrations. Finally, electronic components, often including a computer, convert the information obtained from the wavefront sensor into a form that can control the rubber mirror.

Of the many types of wavefront sensors being used, the most common is a lateral shear interferometer that compares the received wavefront with a shifted version of itself. The received light beam is broken up into several smaller beams, and the wavefront sensor measures the error in the direction of arrival of each of these small beams.

The wavefront corrector (rubber mirror) corrects for this error in the direction of arrival of each of these smaller beams. Some rubber mirrors consist of a large mirror with a discrete array of pushers or pullers (actuators) attached to the back surface of the mirror that deform the shape of the mirror to the appropriate shape required to compensate for wavefront errors. Other rubber mirrors are small monolithic mirrors made of a piezoelectric material that deforms when the appropriate voltages are applied. Several electrodes are implanted within these monolithic piezoelectric mirrors, and when an appropriate array of voltage is applied to these electrodes the piezoelectric material will expand and contract the required amount to produce the desired mirror shape. The larger mirrors with discrete actuators are most useful when large amounts of correction are required, while the smaller monolithic mirrors are most useful when high-frequency response is required.

While adaptive optics systems have been used for correction of simulated aberrations produced by a high-power laser system and for some correction of atmospheric turbulence, such demonstrations have been mostly academic. This, however, should change in the near future. In 1979 the Itek Corp. was completing its adaptive optics system, intended to correct for atmospheric turbulence for a 1.5-m-diameter telescope. The system is to consist of a wavefront sensor detector and rubber mirror correcting elements spaced every 11 cm across the telescope diameter. It is designed to work with sources as faint as the ninth or eleventh magnitude. With this system it will be possible to demonstrate the operating limits of an adaptive optics atmospheric compensating correction system.

Laser fusion systems. During the past year the laser fusion facilities at the University of Rochester's Laboratory for Laser Energetics, Lawrence Livermore Laboratory, and Los Alamos Scientific Laboratory all made progress in the development of lasers for fusion. The University of Rochester laser obtained its goal of a power output of three terawatts (3,000,000 megawatts), and both Lawrence Livermore and Los Alamos reached their goal of at least ten kilojoules in a pulse of less than one-billionth of a second (nanosecond).

When these laser outputs are focused on a target,

they produce plasma densities and temperatures comparable with those found in the envelope of white dwarf stars and the interiors of cool helium white dwarfs. Thus, laboratory simulations of these astronomical conditions have become possible for the first time.

Both the University of Rochester and Lawrence Livermore laboratories were making pulsed neodymium glass lasers for laser fusion research. The University of Rochester's Omega 24 is a 24-beam, 30-terawatt laser. Six beams of the Omega were first fired in October. They irradiated a 123-micrometer target with a peak power of 2.5 terawatts and an energy of 117 joules. The Livermore's Shiva is a 20-beam laser that by the end of the year was producing ten kilojoules in a single optical pulse of less than a nanosecond.

The Los Alamos Scientific Laboratory approached laser fusion by using a carbon-dioxide laser that operated in the nine- to ten-micrometer wavelength region. In the short-pulse CO_2 laser system the short-pulse generator produces a nanosecond millijoule pulse that is amplified in a series of preamplifiers to energies required for optimum energy extraction. For the eight-beam ten-kilojoule system completed during the past year the eight 40-cm output beams are focused onto the target by use of parabolic mirrors.

A six-laser 100-kilojoule CO_2 laser system (Antares) was also under construction at Los Alamos. For this system the power amplifier was to consist of 12 trapezoidal-shaped sectors arranged in a ring. The size of each sector was limited to approximately 45 cm in diameter due to existing fabrication technology for sodium chloride windows. The 12 beams from each laser were to form a ringlike configuration with an outside diameter of 200 cm and an inside diameter of 150 cm. Each beam would be displaced to a smaller diameter by the use of a periscope and then directed onto a focusing mirror by several turning mirrors. The 72 beams produced by the six lasers would supply a total output energy of 100 kilojoules.

The need for high-power lasers both for laser fusion and for weapons has produced, and is in the process of producing, some radical changes in the old, established optical fabrication technology. The glass disks used for the neodymium-glass laser and the sodium chloride windows for the CO_2 lasers have required new polishing techniques to obtain both the desired quality and quantity. The metal focusing optics for the laser systems have required vast improvements in diamond turning (see *1978 Yearbook of Science and the Future* Year in Review: OPTICAL ENGINEERING). Testing of the optics has required the development of new laser interferometric techniques, generally coupled with computer processing of the test results. The need for more high-power lasers is expected to result in vast changes in optical fabrication technology during the next decade.

Laser fusion systems have also required the use of technology developed for fiber-optic communication. The electromagnetic interference level inside a laser fusion facility, such as the 100-kilojoule Antares laser at Los Alamos, is comparable to that produced by 13,-000 citizens band radios. Not only will a fiber-optic system work well in such a hostile environment without requiring expensive means for error checking and correction, but also the fibers will provide protection from high voltage because the data transmission is through a medium that does not conduct electricity.

—James C. Wyant

Aluminum disk of true optical quality was produced without polishing. The diamond-point machine tool at the left, workpiece spindle at the right, and a system of computer controls were used together to achieve the ultrasmooth surface. High-quality, inexpensive solar collectors are possible applications for the material.

Courtesy, Battelle Pacific Northwest Laboratories

Physics

Research in physics during the year was rewarded with several significant advances and discoveries, including a deeper understanding of the surface physics of semiconductors and of the reactor design characteristics necessary for successful plasma fusion. Nuclear scientists continued to create and examine increasingly exotic combinations of protons and neutrons in their exploration of atomic nuclei far from stability. The most important event in particle physics was the announcement of strong experimental support for a theory that sought to unify the weak force and electromagnetism, two of the four fundamental interactions known to exist in nature.

General developments

Understanding fundamental processes of energy production, both within the confines of a plasma fusion reactor and within the active centers of distant galaxies, continued as major pursuits in physics during the past year. A mathematical model of the expanding universe was developed, and U.S. researchers reported success in momentarily compressing hydrogen to a metallic state.

Plasma physics. The pursuit of controlled thermonuclear fusion is a major factor in all long-term energy plans. Since the early 1950s, when uncontrolled fusion gave rise to the hydrogen bomb, laboratory attempts to tame fusion have met with fundamental roadblocks. To ignite deuterium, an isotope of hydrogen, in quantity demands that it be in a high-temperature ionized state, or plasma, contained long enough to allow many individual collisions and fusions to occur among the deuterium nuclei. The hot plasma is contained inside a webbing of magnetic fields, like jello held by a net of rubber bands.

In August 1978 workers at Princeton University announced that a tokamak or doughnut-shaped device, the Princeton Large Torus, had attained the record-breaking temperature of about 55 million degrees Celsius, near the fusion threshold. Excitement greeted this news because theory had claimed that the device would produce an unstable plasma at this ion temperature. When it began operation in 1975, the Princeton Large Torus was called by some the "Princeton Large Turkey," because first results were discouraging. At that time, hot plasma held at the core of the magnetic doughnut contained many impurities (significantly, iron nuclei) which radiated energy very efficiently, cooling the plasma. These impurities appeared when the plas-

Princeton Large Torus, a nuclear fusion test machine, used four neutral-beam heating devices to achieve record-breaking temperatures near the fusion threshold for deuterium.

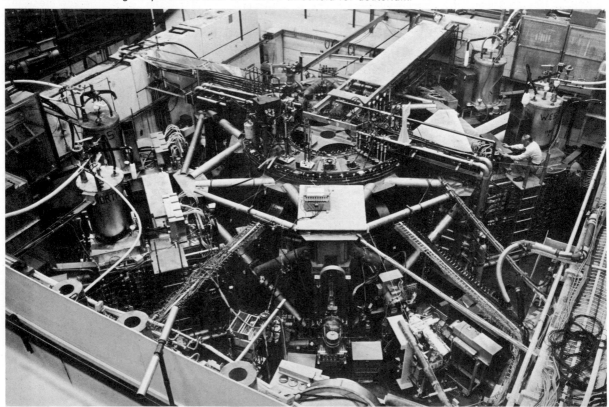

Workers at the Lawrence Livermore Laboratory in California inspect power supply for the recently completed Rotating Target Neutron Source-II, presently the world's most intense continuous supply of fusion-generated neutrons. Interaction of a beam of deuterium nuclei with a rapidly spinning metal target imbedded with tritium nuclei produces a beam of energetic neutrons, which will be used to study the behavior of materials being considered for use in future fusion-power generators, where neutron bombardment will be intense.

ma bombarded the stainless steel wall of the surrounding vacuum chamber, causing iron nuclei to sputter into the chamber. Engineers solved this problem by coating the chamber wall with sputter-resistant titanium. This coat prevents both light impurities (*e.g.,* oxygen) and iron, which radiates well, from invading the central plasma.

The high temperatures were achieved by injecting high-energy beams of neutral atoms into the plasma. These beams collide with the plasma trapped inside the magnetic doughnut, slow down rapidly, and become ionized themselves. Their kinetic energy is converted into thermal energy without destroying the delicately adjusted magnetic confinement of the plasma as a whole. The resulting plasma density (n) was 4.5×10^{13} nuclei/cc and the hot temperatures lasted a time τ of 20×10^{-3} seconds. The quantity $n\tau$, called the crucial fusion parameter, was thus about 10^{12} nuclei-seconds/cc. The "break-even" condition for a fusion reactor (*i.e.,* fusion energy generated equals heating energy consumed) demands an $n\tau$ of 200 times this. Nonetheless, the achievement raised expectations that the next large machine, the Tokamak Fusion Test Reactor, would attain the plasma densities and longer confinement times needed to reach break-even. All that seems to be needed thereafter are higher energy neutral-atom beams from devices now under construction, so that the plasma inside the doughnut can be heated further.

The Soviet-developed tokamak design has been a central focus of the U.S. program since 1970. The results at Princeton proved that the design could confine plasma, giving both the high temperatures and plasma purity requirements of a working reactor. Ironically, by 1979 the Soviet fusion program lagged far behind U.S. and European efforts, primarily because of a surge of U.S. interest during the last decade and better overall engineering.

In the race to fusion a dark horse has moved forward most impressively in the last few years; the magnetic mirror machine. New advances have made these devices the principal alternative to the tokamak. Mirror machines produce open-ended "magnetic bottles" resembling the glass chimney of an oil lamp, with hot ions confined between two relative highs in magnetic-field strength. A serious drawback of early mirror devices was that, as the ions cycled back and forth between the two magnetic highs, they were scattered by collisions and gained the momentum needed to escape. Recently the magnetic instabilities that give rise to such scattering were understood and suppressed, leading to renewed interest in mirror devices. Certain magnetic characteristics of the open-ended types, which have field lines that leave the plasma volume, make these machines theoretically capable of high efficiency. In addition, the open field lines offer a convenient way to dispose of charged waste products, and particles that do escape can be slowed electrostatically in such a way as to directly convert their kinetic energy to electricity, adding to the machine's total energy output.

Ordinary collisions between ions, however, still set a limit on confinement. Two ways around this were advanced in 1978. One idea, the "tandem" mirror concept, is to cut the mirror machine at the middle and insert a long section with a straight magnetic field. The two halves of the field produced by the old mirror device then form "plugs" at the ends. The relatively poor ion confinement at the plugs is compensated by the fact that ions will spend much of their time in the long, straight section, where they are contained well. Testing of this principle began in late 1978 at the Lawrence Livermore Laboratory in California.

A second, more fundamental approach was investigated in a series of experiments using currents of injected relativistic (near-light-speed) electron beams. These spinning ring-shaped currents act to close the lines of magnetic flux deep inside the plasma, while leaving the field lines open near the plasma surface. Plasma cannot escape easily from such interior magnetic wells. To produce such wells without intruding external conductors into the plasma offers the stabilizing advantages of closed configurations, such as the tokamak, with the economies of open mirror-type designs. Several laboratories created these configurations in 1978 and found that the deep magnetic well was produced within the plasma and did stabilize the bulk of the plasma. The major remaining basic physics question is how to ensure that the interior well is truly isolated from the outside.

Diagrams of varying scale for the radio source surrounding galaxy NGC 6251 *show the total source as two vast radio lobes (top), one of which includes a large nuclear jet (center). Recently radio astronomers discovered a much smaller jet (bottom) that lies within and parallel to the first.*

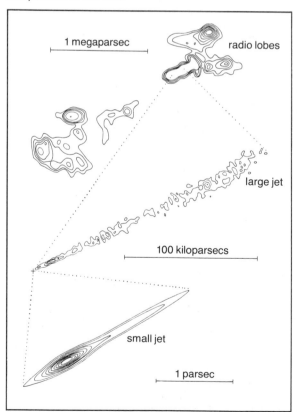

Adapted from "A Jet in the Nucleus of NGC6251," A. C. S. Readhead, M. H. Cohen, and R. D. Blandford, *Nature,* Vol. 272, No. 5649, p. 133, March 9, 1978

Black hole physics. The active centers of galaxies and quasars are far too bright to be explained by fusion reactions. Clues about the small, violent cores of these objects recently emerged in detailed radio maps of the radio source surrounding the galaxy NGC 6251. In 1977 radio astronomers at Cambridge, England, announced their discovery of vast lobes of radio-frequency emission around the elliptical galaxy. The lobes are much larger than the galaxy, and inside one lobe is a 200-kiloparsec radio jet. (A parsec is 3.26 light-years.) Double lobes are common, but such jets are rare. All that have been discovered to date are aligned perpendicular to the galactic major axis. They emit a particular kind of radiation called synchrotron radiation, which is produced by relativistic electrons moving along curved paths through intergalactic magnetic fields.

In 1978 Anthony C. S. Readhead, Marshall H. Cohen, and Roger Blandford at the California Institute of Technology in Pasadena announced the discovery of a much smaller, 1.7-parsec jet inside the first, coming from the central galaxy itself. This was the first discovery of the same phenomenon on two different length scales. Such narrow structure over such huge distances implies that a beam of particles is being ejected from the compact galactic center. The central source probably is able to maintain, or "remember," the same axis of ejection over long periods of time because it is the rotation axis of the massive galactic nucleus. Such long-term memory seems to rule out sporadic ejections of matter. How a massive core can focus these beams and supply energy steadily is a subject of much theoretical controversy, hinting at significant "new" physics involving extremely condensed and massive states of stellar matter called black holes.

For NGC 6251 and for galaxies showing jets in both the optical and radio spectrum, notably galaxy M87, the observed flux of X-rays is consistent with a simple black hole model. This picture envisions a disk of gas at the center of the galaxy, rotating about the hole. Stars passing near the hole will be broken up by gravitational effects, feeding matter into the disk. As the disk gas spirals inward, it radiates X-rays and optical and radio emissions. A kind of electrodynamic effect may also occur, because the disk may be a good electrical conductor. If a magnetic field is caught in this conductor as the gas sweeps inward, the disk becomes a vast dynamo and produces currents. These may in turn lead to acceleration of charged particles near the hole, forcing particles out along the axis of rotation of the hole. Thus, two beams of focused particles could emerge in opposite directions, making the jets and feeding the large radio lobes that have been observed.

If this is the basic mechanism, it points to a process by which gravitational energy is converted directly into electrically induced acceleration. This in turn could explain high-energy cosmic rays and other violent cosmic

The Kitt Peak National Observatory

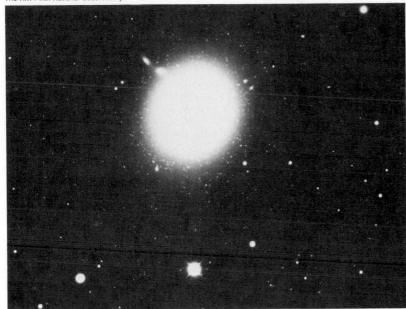

Elliptical galaxy M87 is known to have an energetically active nucleus and to possess an extended jet of matter that is detectable at both optical and radio wavelengths. Studies published in 1978 presented evidence for a large concentration of nuclear matter equivalent in mass to 5,000,000,000 Suns and for a concentration of stars that appear gravitationally bound to a large central mass. Some astronomers and physicists believed that such evidence points to the existence of a black hole in the galactic nucleus.

activity on the scale of supermassive black holes (with masses approaching 10^8 solar masses). Such models may work on much smaller scales as well, for "ordinary" black holes of a few solar masses. Important discoveries may follow if this connection between radio jets and black holes can be made secure.

Cosmology. Numerical methods have been used to simulate many physical systems. In 1978 astrophysicists simulated not simply a single isolated system but the entire universe. A transcontinental collaboration between workers at the University of Cambridge, England, and at Harvard and Princeton universities in the U.S. began by randomly placing 4,000 masses, each representing a galaxy, in an expanding spherical volume. The gravitational force of each galaxy on all the others was computed using Newtonian principles, and general effects consistent with relativity theory determined the behavior of the galaxies in space and time. Each "run" of the simulation took eight hours and followed expansion of the galaxies soon after a "big-bang" beginning into a volume of space that would be 300 million light-years across at present. These pocket universes expanded about 20 times during a run.

The cosmic microwave background radiation discovered by Arno A. Penzias and Robert W. Wilson in 1965 (*see* SCIENTISTS OF THE YEAR) gave evidence of an earlier hot, uniform universe. A major question in cosmology is how the lumpy, nonuniform distribution of galaxies observed today came about. The simulations showed how small statistical fluctuations grow by means of gravitational instability to form groups, clusters, and finally superclusters of galaxies. The final clustering patterns were remarkably similar to those in the present universe. According to the simulation, individual galaxies appear to have formed about 15,000,000,000 years ago, 3,000,000,000 years after the big bang. (*See also* Feature Article: THE STRUCTURE OF THE UNIVERSE.)

Metallic hydrogen? Theories of dense matter imply that the lightest element, hydrogen, should become a metal if it is sufficiently compressed. Until recently, however, experiments using pressures as high as a million bars (one megabar) gave no indication of a shift toward the metallic phase. In October 1978 physicists at the Lawrence Livermore Laboratory announced that they had achieved transitory pressures of about two megabars and had evidence of metallic hydrogen.

To create the immense pressures exploding TNT was used to crush a cylinder containing a magnetic field. As the cylinder collapsed, its metal walls compressed the field, increasing it from five tesla to more than a thousand tesla. This field pressure in turn compressed a cylindrical silver sample containing hydrogen. Keeping the hydrogen in at the ends of the sample were two conical anvils, one of which was an insulator and the other a conductor. At maximum compression the hydrogen density rose to at least 0.96 g/cc, about as dense as water. There was an abrupt decrease in the sample resistivity, as measured by the conducting anvil, indicating transition to a highly conducting, metallic phase. Some recent theory suggested that hydrogen might become conducting in the less dense, molecular phase, so it was not certain that the observed resistivity drop signaled the appearance of metallic hydrogen. By comparison, theory indicated that neon should remain an insulator until at least 20 megabars of pressure, and the experimenters indeed found that five megabars did not change neon from an insulator.

Stanford University's two-mile-long linear accelerator served as the scene for experiments that demonstrated the existence of a parity-nonconserving force in inelastic electron scattering. The results supported a theory that sought to unify weak and electromagnetic interactions.

The metallic phase of hydrogen is important in several subfields of physics, most obviously in the study of giant gaseous planets. Much of Jupiter's deep interior may be composed of metallic hydrogen, which implies much about its production of magnetic fields and its evolution.

—Gregory Benford

High-energy physics

The most important development in high-energy physics in 1978 was the demonstration that a parity-non-conserving force—one that changes sign when the mirror image of the physical system in which the force operates is considered—exists between electrons and nucleons (protons and neutrons) in addition to the usual electromagnetic force. This was shown in a beautiful experiment performed at the Stanford Linear Accelerator Center (SLAC) in California by a group of physicists from various laboratories, headed by Charles Y. Prescott, Vernon W. Hughes, and Richard C. Taylor. The strength of the force as measured is in good agreement with a prediction based on a theory uniting weak and electromagnetic interactions, proposed in 1967 by Steven Weinberg and soon thereafter by Abdus Salam. By year's end most physicists regarded this theory to be essentially confirmed by the new result. This experiment marked the first time that parity-nonconserving forces were observed in a particle interaction in which an electron remains an electron after scattering. They

had previously been observed in processes in which an electron is created from another particle, say, in the scattering of a neutrino by a nucleon. Their existence in processes in which electrons do not change their nature is a hallmark of the Weinberg-Salam theory.

The most direct way to detect the existence of a parity-nonconserving force is to compare the value of two quantities that would have to be equal in the absence of such a force. In the SLAC experiment these quantities were the scattering cross sections of polarized electrons scattered by nuclei of hydrogen-2 (deuterium), which contain a neutron and a proton. The cross section is a measure of the probability of scattering, or deflection through some angle, when the electron passes near the nucleus. The electrons begin with a high energy of 16–22 GeV (one GeV is 1,000,000,000 electron volts). When they scatter, the deuterium nucleus usually breaks up, and additional particles are produced as well. As a result, the electron loses some of its energy and emerges with 12.5–17 GeV. This phenomenon is known as inelastic scattering, as opposed to elastic scattering in which the electron emerges with the same energy that it had at the start.

Producing polarized electrons. The development that made this experiment possible was a technique for producing intense beams of high-energy, longitudinally polarized electrons. Like protons and neutrons, electrons carry a type of intrinsic angular momentum, called spin, corresponding to a rotation around an axis through the particle, much like the Earth's rotation. The magnitude of this spin is fixed, but its direction can vary. In particular, it may point either with (parallel to) or against (antiparallel to) the direction of motion of the electron through space (see figure 1). Ordinarily, a beam of electrons will contain equal numbers of electrons with either spin direction and is said to be unpolarized. A beam made up of electrons whose spin points in one of these two alternative possibilities is said to be longitudinally polarized.

In order to produce longitudinally polarized electrons, the experimenters began with linearly polarized light from an intense laser and then converted it into longitudinally polarized light in a device called a Pockels cell. With the Pockels cell it is possible to produce light with either parallel or antiparallel longitudinal polarization. The longitudinally polarized light is allowed to hit a gallium arsenide crystal, causing it to emit electrons of one state of longitudinal polarization or the other, depending on the polarization of the light. These electrons have very low energy, however, and for the experiment needed to be accelerated by the SLAC linear electron accelerator. Acted upon by electric forces, they emerge from the accelerator with a speed near that of light and an energy of as much as 22 GeV. If longitudinally polarized electrons are inserted at one end of the accelerator, they remain so at the other end.

If longitudinally polarized particles could be viewed in a mirror that is perpendicular to their direction of motion, they would appear to have opposite longitudinal polarization. This is because direction of motion reverses in a mirror, whereas spin direction remains the same (see figure 2). Therefore, the mirror image of an experiment in which a longitudinally polarized particle is scattered by an unpolarized particle is an experiment in which a particle having opposite longitudinal polarization but the same energy is scattered. In the absence

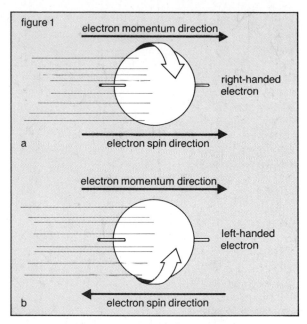

Seen from behind, a right-handed electron (a) and a left-handed electron (b) rotate in opposite directions. The first is said to be polarized with its spin direction parallel to its momentum; the second, with spin direction antiparallel to momentum.

of parity-nonconserving forces, the scattering cross sections in these two experiments would have to be equal. Thus, by measuring these cross sections and comparing them, the presence or absence of parity-nonconserving forces can be determined.

The experiment. The difficulty of the experiment lies in the fact that the two cross sections are expected to be very nearly equal, differing by only about one part in 10,000. Therefore, very small effects must be ob-

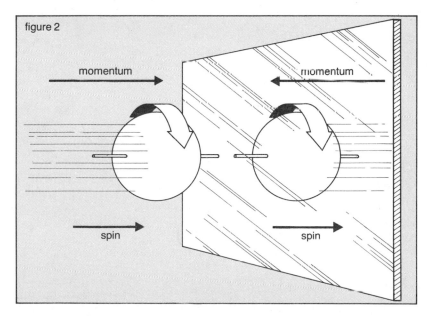

A right-handed electron viewed in a mirror perpendicular to its motion would appear to have opposite longitudinal polarization; its direction of motion reverses, but its spin direction remains the same. Seen from behind, the mirror image is identical with the left-handed electron shown in figure 1.

served to detect the difference. When such small effects must be measured, it is necessary to ensure that subtle sources of error are not present, for example, a minute energy difference between the electrons of opposite polarization. Because the cross section is known to depend on the electron energy, such an energy difference would appear as a difference in cross section that is unrelated to parity nonconservation. Because it is not feasible to measure the energy of each electron to the required precision, the experimenters measured the average energy of accelerated electrons of each polarization type in groups of 10^{11} and found that these averages were very close to each other. They then corrected the observed cross sections for the slight difference due to the energy dependence of the cross section. Similar procedures were followed for other properties of the electrons that might affect the cross section. A further check that was carried out involved comparing the scattering cross sections from two beams of electrons that were polarized in another way that does not reverse in a mirror. In this case the cross sections were expected to be the same for the two beams, and in fact they were within very small experimental errors.

Data were collected at a number of different energies of the incident electron beam, at several energies of the scattered electrons, and at a fixed angle of scattering of the electrons. The specific quantity of interest was the asymmetry parameter, that is, the difference in cross sections for the two types of longitudinal polarization, divided by the sum of the cross sections. This difference, averaged over a number of the experimental conditions, came out to be approximately 10^{-4}, with a possible experimental error of about 15%. This means that the probability of scattering of left-handed electrons, those whose spin and momentum point in the opposite directions, is greater by about one part in 10,000 than that for right-handed electrons, those whose spin and momentum point in the same direction. The fact that the observed effect was so much larger than the experimental error seemed to leave no doubt that the effect of a parity-nonconserving force was really seen.

The experimenters also carried out a similar experiment using hydrogen nuclei (protons) as a target and obtained a similar value for the asymmetry. In this case, however, the experimental error was somewhat greater and thus the effect less certain.

Implications for the Weinberg-Salam theory. Although the SLAC experiment was extremely important in its own right, demonstrating a new physical effect, it had further importance in providing a key piece of evidence for a far-reaching theory that unifies electromagnetism, known for over a century, with weak interactions, a set of processes involved in radioactive decay that have been intensively studied only in the past 20 years. To see the relevance of the SLAC experiment to this unification, it first must be said that the parity-nonconserving force is thought to arise by means of the exchange between electron and nucleon of a yet undiscovered particle called the Z^0 intermediate boson. This is in direct analogy with the mechanism for generating electromagnetic forces—by means of the exchange of a known particle, the photon.

The relative strength of the two kinds of force is a result of two factors. One of these is the probability of emission and absorption of the exchanged particle, and this probability is thought to be approximately the

In 1978 a collaboration of scientists from five U.S. institutions reported a unique neutrino-induced collision event producing four leptons, three of which were electrons. Recorded photographically in a neon- and hydrogen-filled bubble chamber at the Fermi National Accelerator Laboratory near Batavia, Ill., the event produced one positive muon (μ^+), one positive electron (or positron; e^+), and two negative electrons (e^-), as well as an additional neutral kaon (K_s^0; see inset for magnified view of collision region) that quickly decayed into two oppositely charged pions (π^+, π^-).

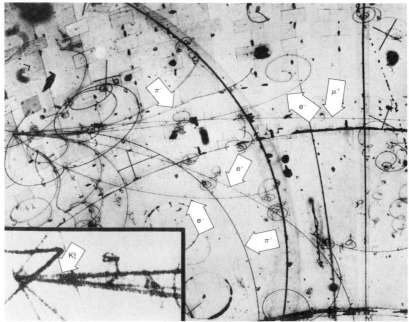

same for Z^0 bosons and for photons. The other factor is the rest mass of the exchanged particle. Here a tremendous difference exists: the photon is known to have zero rest mass, whereas the Z^0 particle probably has a rest mass almost 100 times that of the proton. A result of this difference in rest mass is that at very low energies, for example, those encountered in atomic physics, the force due to Z^0 exchange is 10^{16} times smaller than electromagnetic forces and very difficult to observe. At the 20-GeV energy of the SLAC experiment, the relative strength of the Z^0-exchange force has increased, and the measured asymmetry factor of 10^{-4} indicates the relative strength of the forces at this energy. In future electron-scattering experiments that may be carried out at 100 GeV or more, the two types of force should become comparable in strength.

In the Weinberg-Salam theory there is a precise relationship among the ways both electrons and nucleons interact with the photon, the Z^0 particle, and two other massive, yet unobserved particles called W^+ and W^-. The effect of the photons has been known for a century and those of the W^+ and W^- for 20 years, but the unified theory was able to predict, in terms of these known effects, fairly precise values for the previously unobserved effect of the Z^0 particle. One such effect was observed in 1973: the scattering of a neutrino by a nucleon in which the neutrino remains a neutrino. This scattering was observed with about the cross section predicted by the theory and was certainly evidence for Z^0-induced effects.

However, the neutrino-scattering experiments did not distinguish completely between the Weinberg-Salam theory and other theories that also included Z^0 particles but did not include parity-nonconserving forces. Several experiments that attempted to detect parity-nonconserving forces in atomic-physics experiments, which would distinguish among the various theories, gave somewhat ambiguous results. For that reason most physicists welcomed the unambiguous result of the SLAC experiment, which pointed very strongly to the Weinberg-Salam theory. This theory presently describes accurately all of the known data on neutrino scattering, as well as the SLAC electron-scattering data, and it is likely that, when atomic-physics experiments eventually give unambiguous results, they will also follow the theoretical predictions.

The remaining questions about the unified theory mainly involve actual production of Z^0 and W particles for extended times, rather than for the extremely short times during which they exist when they are exchanged. The rest mass of these particles is too high for them to be produced in experiments using existing accelerators. Collisions between a moving proton and a proton at rest would require the moving proton to possess an energy of 2,500–5,000 GeV in order to produce a single W or Z^0 particle, and such energetic protons will not be available until the 1990s. More

promising are collisions between two particles traveling in opposite directions. Such collisions require only 50 GeV each for the colliding particles to produce a W or Z^0 particle. Accelerators to provide such energetic colliding beams—either of protons or of electrons and positrons—may become available by 1985. If the W and Z^0 are produced in such experiments and if their masses turn out as predicted, it will constitute a dramatic confirmation of the Weinberg-Salam theory.

—Gerald Feinberg

Nuclear physics

The domain of nuclear physics, its frontiers, and its future directions appear naturally in a "map" of the kind shown in figure 1. Here, instead of latitude and longitude, one plots the number of protons (Z) and the number of neutrons (N) present in a given nucleus. All nuclear species having the same Z (a horizontal line through the map) are isotopes of the same element, while all those having the same N (a vertical line through the map) are called isotones.

There are only 300 naturally occurring nuclear species; these are shown as the black squares in the figure. In the half century since its beginning, nuclear science has identified and studied about 1,300 unstable or radioactive species, making a total of about 1,600 in all. This total is included within the jagged-edged area, which also encloses the black squares. Nevertheless, nuclear scientists confidently predict that this total will rise to encompass nearly 10,000 different species as the result of experiments using new heavy-ion accelerators presently under construction which will bombard uranium targets with uranium projectiles possessing an energy of several GeV (1 GeV is 1,000,000,000 electron volts). Indeed they also predict that all the species included within the outermost boundaries of the central region of this map will be stable against instantaneous dissociation. In the case of uranium (U), for example, all isotopes from mass 195 to mass 302, each having 92 protons and a neutron number between 103 and 210, would be expected to have finite lifetimes; of this total of 108 different isotopes, only 15 were known as of early 1979. Corresponding stretches of isotopes are also shown in the figure for the cases of calcium (Ca) and tin (Sn).

Were one to consider this map in a geographical sense, then the most stable nuclei—those with the tightest binding—would lie at the bottom of a very deep valley running diagonally across the map, a valley in which depth is proportional to the binding energy of the nucleus. Attempting to describe and understand all the possible nuclear species shown on this map from the measured characteristics of those already studied would be comparable to attempting a detailed description of U.S. geography following only a study of the floor of the Grand Canyon!

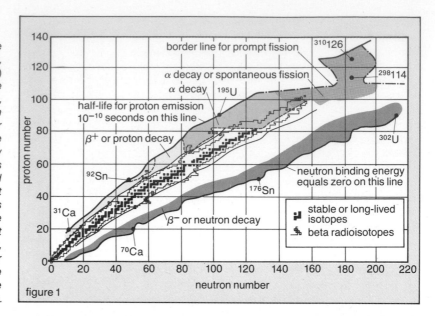

Figure 1 presents a map of the nuclear domain. For light nuclei, those in which proton number (Z) equals neutron number (N) are most stable. As Z increases, however, electrostatic repulsion between protons favors stability for nuclei having larger N than Z. The lowermost boundary is defined by the condition that any species below the boundary would instantly "drip" neutrons until it transformed itself into a species lying on the boundary. The definition of the uppermost boundary is more complex, depending upon whether spontaneous fission, alpha particle decay, or proton emission is the most probable decay mechanism.

figure 1

Three definite frontiers appear in this map. The first is in the direction of ever heavier nuclei. As more protons are added, their mutual electrostatic repulsion acts to destroy the nucleus and leads to spontaneous fission; it is this tendency that limits naturally occurring species to proton numbers less than 94. Effectively the valley of stability becomes ever more shallow with increasing proton number. To date accelerators have produced species as high as $Z = 106$ and possibly 107, but for these latter the valley is so shallow that the

Figure 2, a representation of the display screen of the Berkeley detector, plots fragments of argon nuclei in terms of nuclear charge (Z) and mass number (Z + N). Detection of ^{28}Ne and ^{35}Al (in boxes) calls for revision of previous stability limit (solid line).

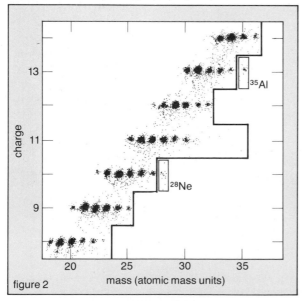

figure 2

lifetimes are measured in millionths of seconds.

As measurements on the heaviest stable nuclei near lead ($Z = 82$) become more detailed and more precise, nuclear scientists can extrapolate with increasing confidence to ever heavier regions beyond those that are thought ever to have existed in nature. And such extrapolations predict possible stable pits or deep small-diameter holes in the map near $Z = 114$ and 126. It has been suggested that if one could arrange to make these new superheavy species, they might be entirely stable or at least have long lifetimes. Because these would represent entirely new realms of physics and chemistry, they have been sought widely both in nature, where they might have remained as relics of some primordial cataclysm, and in the products of heavy-ion collisions induced by the largest of present-day accelerators. Extensive searches by groups led by Albert Ghiorso at the University of California at Berkeley, Georgi N. Flerov at Dubna in the Soviet Union, Peter Armbruster at the GSI facility in Darmstadt, West Germany, and Robert Gentry at the Oak Ridge (Tenn.) National Laboratory yielded negative results, but they were being continued with considerable optimism.

A second frontier is approached by climbing laterally out of the valley and moving to very neutron-rich (large N) or very proton-rich (large Z) isotopes. Two primary mechanisms have been developed for producing these unusual species. In the first, pursued by Vadim V. Volkov and his collaborators in the Soviet Union, massive nuclei are collided at the maximum possible energies in the expectation that they will fuse and that the massive fused system subsequently will fission to yield the desired fragments. In the second mechanism, pioneered by Andrew Poskanzer and his associates at Berkeley, very high-energy protons (hydrogen nuclei) are used to chip fragments away from heavy target nuclei in so-called spallation reactions. Although both mechanisms have been successful, their yields of desired species into any given detector are exceedingly low, and consequently very large amounts of accelerator time are required to identify any new species.

Recently David Scott and his associates at Berkeley evolved a very ingenious variant of this second mechanism wherein they bombard a light target (carbon-12 in the initial measurements) with the heaviest possible projectile (argon-40) at the highest available energy (205 MeV [million electron volts] per mass unit) from the Berkeley Bevalac. The advantage in this case is that the fragments from the dissociating argon projectile all continue to move essentially together in the original beam direction after the collision so that all of the products enter a detector placed behind the target; this greatly increases the detection efficiency. By using a very sophisticated, many-segmented solid-state detector fabricated by Frederick Goulding and his associates at Berkeley, these fragments can be both detected and identified. Figure 2 depicts a small section of the output display of this new system showing evidence for the creation of light, neutron-rich species and specifically the first evidence ever obtained for the existence of neon-28 and aluminum-35. Proton-rich species were also detected, but the corresponding data had yet to be analyzed. Clearly, when heavier projectiles become available, this new technique will permit rapid exploration of the unknown regions of the nuclear map out to the limits of stability. This venture will provide a very stringent test of present-day knowledge of nuclear structure, because it is in this region, at the limits of stability, where disruptive forces and very small variations in the strength of the binding can force the species either way across the stability limit.

An elegant demonstration of the influence of the shape of nuclei in their fusion probability was obtained by Robert Stokstad of the Oak Ridge National Laboratory and his collaborators at the Weizmann Institute of Science, Israel, in their study of the fusion of oxygen nuclei with the different isotopes of samarium. Oxygen is known to be spherical in shape, but samarium is unique in that at mass 148 it too is spherical whereas at mass 154 it has a pronounced football shape. Stokstad's group found that at high energies the probability of fusion was independent of shape but at low energies near the Coulomb barrier (the electrostatic repulsion that must be overcome for two nuclei to fuse), the probability of oxygen fusing to football-shaped ^{154}Sm was more than ten times greater than that to spherical ^{148}Sm. They interpreted this observation to reflect the fact that the Coulomb barrier is thinner at the ends of the football and thus more likely to permit fusion when the available energy is near the barrier.

The third frontier in figure 1 is penetrated by adding internal energy to each nuclear species and moving up away from the surface of the map—toward the "nu-

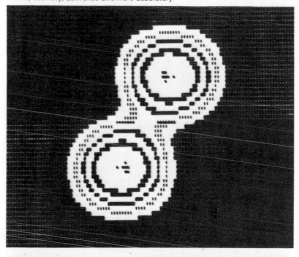

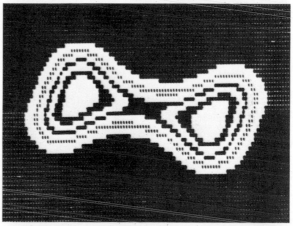

The collision of two oxygen-16 nuclei at an energy of 52.5 MeV is depicted in three of a series of computer images based on a mathematical model developed by scientists at the Lawrence Livermore Laboratory in California. Contour lines represent intervals of nuclear density. Viewed in their entire sequence, the two nuclei repeatedly coalesce, rebound, and revolve about each other for an appreciable time.

377

olcal stratosphere." Thus far, detailed measurements have been limited largely to the region very close to the surface, *i.e.,* near the nuclear ground state, where the discrete energy levels, or quantum states, to which the nuclei are confined are well separated and easily accessible. But the question of what happens when energy is added to the nuclear quantum system is a fundamental one in many-body physics. From a study of quantum states in light isobars (nuclei that have identical mass numbers but different proton numbers) Peter Parker and his associates at Yale University concluded that with each additional million electron volts of energy the typical nucleus expands its radius by about 1%; *i.e.,* when heated they expand!

Fortunately this is not all that happens; some of the additional energy takes the form of increased nuclear spin. Several years ago Stanley Thompson and Norman Glendenning of Berkeley and their associates discovered very special states—recently dubbed yrast traps—which are spinning so fast that they have no simple way to get rid of their excess energy while still conserving angular momentum; consequently they exist an anomalously long time before emitting an alpha particle or fissioning spontaneously. In 1979 scientists in several countries were devoting much effort to studies of these rapidly spinning states. Presumably the total angular momentum that a nucleus can sustain before it flies apart under centrifugal forces is limited; it will be important to determine this limit.

Russell Betts and his collaborators at Yale recently found an entirely new class of nuclear excitations— now called pairing isomers—in reactions in which a projectile removes two (or four) nucleons from a target. (Collectively protons and neutrons are termed nucleons.) In the past it had been assumed that the picked-up nucleons were always taken from the target surface and, therefore, that the reaction characteristics would depend upon structural details of that surface and upon the characteristics of the least bound nucleon orbits, which define the so-called Fermi surface. Obviously these orbits differ from one kind of target nucleus to another. Betts's group found that under appropriate circumstances nucleons could be extracted from tightly bound orbits well below the Fermi surface and that the resultant configurations were all very similar, provided that the target nuclei were in the same general mass region.

It has become clear that nuclear molecular configurations, long considered a curiosity following their discovery by Allan Bromley and his collaborators at the Chalk River (Ont.) Nuclear Laboratories in 1960, are a ubiquitous aspect of nuclear structure and dynamics, and their study was one of the most active endeavors of nuclear science during the past year. When certain selected energies are added to nuclei, the nucleons present have been found to readily arrange themselves into a limited number of subclusters that have

very simple motions with respect to one another and are thus reminiscent of atoms in simple chemical molecules. Long ago U.S. physicist Edward Teller and others showed how chemical molecules are bound through appropriate exchange and sharing of electrons. Understanding how the binding of nuclear molecules arises correspondingly from nucleon effects was just beginning to emerge in the late 1970s.

What has become very apparent, however, is that with each increase in the ability of physicists to probe higher and higher into the nuclear stratosphere—to increasingly high-energy quantum excitations—new and surprising modes of nuclear behavior have appeared. Fortunately, new precision accelerators under construction around the world have been designed to probe these new regions with the delicacy and precision essential to understanding this behavior. There were perhaps more machines under construction during the past year than at any time since immediately after World War II, with most of them outside of the U.S. This is a reflection of the vitality of international experimental nuclear science and the extent to which initiative in this field is passing out of the U.S.

It is in some sense a fortunate circumstance that substantial parallel progress has been made very recently in the theoretical understanding of nuclear structure and dynamics. It has long been characteristic of nuclear physics that often wildly contradictory models —*e.g.,* independent-particle shell models in which nucleons moved freely versus liquid-drop models wherein the nucleon mean free path was substantially less than the nuclear radius—could coexist to describe nuclear phenomena, depending upon which of their many facets were being modeled. A new model, developed originally by Franco Iachello of Yale and Herman Feshbach of the Massachusetts Institute of Technology and subsequently refined by Iachello in collaboration with Igal Talmi of the Weizmann Institute, Akito Arima of the University of Tokyo, and others, shows considerable promise not only of unifying all these models but also of describing successfully many other static and dynamic facets of nuclear behavior that had eluded earlier models.

Fundamental to this new Iachello model is the concept that nuclear neutrons and protons bind together pairwise to form stable entities (bosons), which in turn are the building blocks for nuclei. It can readily be shown that in these pairs the nucleons have either zero or two units of angular momentum; hence, there are only two kinds of paired entities. The new model automatically accounts for both independent-particle and collective aspects of nuclear behavior. The former arise when the nucleons move entirely independently, whereas the latter reflect coherent participation of many nucleons to yield either vibrations or rotations of the nuclear surface. Iachello and his co-workers showed that the nucleons first form pairs, which then cooperate to yield coherent collective behavior—hence the name "interacting boson model." As an increasingly large number of pairs cooperate, the features of a liquid drop appear.

Of great interest has been the discovery that in evolving coherent cooperation the pairs display both simple and complex symmetries readily described by that branch of mathematics known as group theory, which has already proved to be a powerful tool in elucidating many physical systems. The model predicts three quite distinct types of symmetries in nuclei, and all three finally have been observed. During the past year Richard Casten and his collaborators at the Brookhaven (N.Y.) National Laboratory found the last of the predicted three types in systematic studies on the highly excited states of heavy nuclei.

Quite apart from correlating a vast body of previously disparate data, the model also makes a wealth of predictions that await experimental test. Moreover, in contrast to some of the fashionable very large computer-based shell models, calculations using the new model are sufficiently simple and transparent that the underlying intuitive physics is not submerged.

—D. Allan Bromley

Solid-state physics

Certain developments of considerable long-range consequence not only to solid-state physics but to the balance of power in the world became apparent in 1978. To place these events in perspective, it will be helpful to review the important interaction between solid-state physics and the growth of the electronics industry. In turn, the development of the electronics industry should be considered with regard to international competition.

Since World War II, U.S. leadership in electronics has been due principally to massive wartime development efforts and to the invention and development of the transistor and a host of other solid-state electronic devices in the decades that followed. Completely intertwined with the development of a basic understanding of the behavior of electrons in semiconductors, the invention of the transistor not only ushered in a technological revolution but also brought a branch of physics, semiconductor physics, from obscurity to a place of major importance. Basic work in the 1950s and 1960s treated the semiconductor in bulk; that is, as an infinite solid without the surfaces or interfaces that limit performance in real semiconductors. As might be expected, the electronics industry grew on a similar basis; practical devices depended on electron behavior in bulk, and empirical methods were found to neutralize the effects of the surface.

The first solid-state devices were discrete, single-function items that replaced the much larger vacuum tubes in electronic circuits on a one-for-one basis. They were followed by "hybrid" units that combined several solid-state devices on a single "chip" of silicon crystal. In the 1970s a revolutionary new step was taken, in which complete electronic systems, called integrated circuits (IC's), were fabricated on a single wafer of silicon. As the size of each element was reduced so that more elements (as many as 100,000) could be placed on one small chip (several millimeters square), the term large-scale integration (LSI) was coined. In the forefront of present research is yet the next step, called very large-scale integration (VLSI), which aims at in-

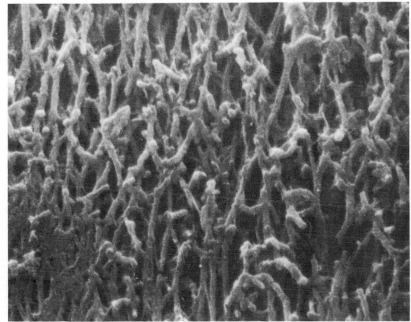

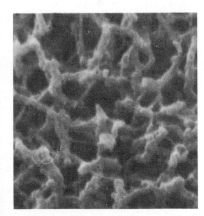

Photomicrographs reveal structural differences between normal, random-fiber polyacetylene film (above) and a modified form whose aligned fibers (left) have much higher electrical conductivities. This polymer can also be doped to yield the electronic properties of a semiconductor.

Photos, courtesy, Alan G. MacDiarmid, University of Pennsylvania

figure 1

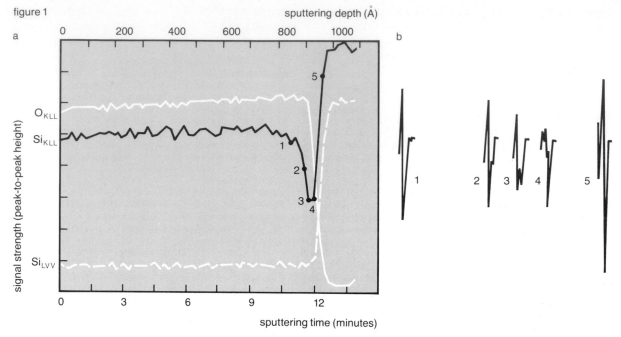

sputtering depth (Å)

a

b

O$_{KLL}$

Si$_{KLL}$

signal strength (peak-to-peak height)

Si$_{LVV}$

1 2 3 4 5

sputtering time (minutes)

creasing the density of elements in the circuit tenfold or as much as a hundredfold by a reduction in the size of each element.

It is well known that, as the size of a body decreases, the ratio of its surface area to its bulk volume increases. Hence, for VLSI, in which critical dimensions are in thousands of angstroms or less (one angstrom, Å, is 10^{-8} cm), surfaces play a new and dominant role in device operation. And therein lies an important frontier for solid-state physics.

International aspects. The long lead of the U.S. in electronics has many important ramifications. One is that the U.S. computer industry has dominated the world market and generates an important fraction of foreign revenues. Another is that, because the U.S. is losing ground to other countries with respect to less sophisticated military technology, its defense posture will depend increasingly on continued leadership in advanced computer and communications capabilities, which VLSI will make possible.

Other countries—most notably Japan—which have kept pace perhaps a decade behind the U.S. in electronics technology, are moving impressively and ambitiously to "leap frog" the U.S. and lead in the development of VLSI. Such competition is not only weakening the U.S. position but also is straining the very strong interactions that have been built up in past years between Japanese and U.S. engineers and scientists. It also has become clear that the needs of defense and civilian sectors for electronics are diverging and that the military can no longer depend simply on civilian developments. In addition, the Soviet Union recently has been advancing much faster than expected in military electronics.

Need for new knowledge. As emphasized above, a comprehensive knowledge of semiconductor surfaces and interfaces is essential to the development of VLSI. Although integrated circuits in the past were exclusively of silicon (Si), another class of materials began to appear in IC's in recent months. These are the 3-5 compounds, so called because they are made from elements in the third and fifth columns of the periodic table. Gallium arsenide (GaAs) is an example. Such "binary" compounds are more difficult to work with than elementary crystalline silicon; thus, 3-5 devices must have superior performance to justify their use. The key areas of superiority are due to the differences in electronic structure; for example, it is often easier to move electrons through 3-5s than through silicon. In a paper presented in December 1978, Dick Eden of Rockwell International Corp. reported device measurements on GaAs IC's, showing both increased speed of response and reduced dissipation of power. Eden emphasized that these advantages increase as one progresses to the small dimensions of VLSI.

Fabrication of 3-5 device structures, however, has presented a much more difficult problem than those of silicon, principally because of the difficulty in growing "native" oxides on the surface of 3-5 materials. (By native oxide is meant an oxide formed from the semiconductor material itself. If a clean semiconductor is exposed to air, it will be adversely affected and cannot be used for device purposes. The easiest solution to this problem is to grow a sufficiently thin (about 1000 Å) layer of native oxide to exclude the effect of air exposure but not prevent the device from working.) For silicon this oxide is simply SiO_2; however, for the two-component 3-5 semiconductors, things are much more complicated. For example, a complex variety of oxides can be formed from gallium arsenide—(GaAs)O$_4$, Ga$_2$O$_3$, As$_2$O$_3$, As$_2$O$_5$, and others. The kind of oxide is important principally because material perfection is required at the semiconductor/oxide interface. Imperfections at this interface—for instance, in the form of missing atoms or unsatisfied chemical bonds—produce states that can trap electrons and thus slow electron transport. The complexity of native oxide growth on 3-5s leads to such a high density of interface trapping states that, to date, it has proved impractical to make devices with these oxide interfaces. Rather, a configuration is used involving a metal/semiconductor interface of a certain type called a Schottky barrier. The Schottky barrier forms a rectifying diode that will pass current when biased (when a small control voltage is applied) in one direction but will not when biased in the reverse direction. To make optimum 3-5 devices, it will be necessary to conquer the oxide interface problem, and physicists currently are making a large effort in this direction. Understanding the oxidation of 3-5 surfaces and consequent formation of defects can speed the process.

As mentioned above, the Si-SiO$_2$ interface has not been a serious problem to date. However, a desire for greater fundamental knowledge of this interface is growing because, as dimensions are decreased to produce VLSI, surface-to-volume ratio will increase and stronger demands will be made on the oxide. For example, size constraints may demand a smaller oxide thickness, which may have different interfacial properties than the optimum oxides now in use. In addition, even with conventional oxides, there is a desire to exert increasingly tighter control on the detailed fabrication procedures.

Probing the Si-SiO$_2$ interface. Classically, the Si-SiO$_2$ interface has been investigated by electrical measurements, which give results closely related to device performance. However, such measurements provide little insight into the reasons for this performance, i.e., the material topology at the interface. For example, one could ask if there is an abrupt transition between silicon and SiO$_2$ or if there is a connective region of silicon suboxides, where silicon is oxidized to a lesser degree. Is the silicon/oxide junction abrupt and planar or rough and uneven? How do the oxidation parameters, such as temperature of oxidation, affect these

characteristics? Do the added impurities, or dopants, that give silicon its desired electronic properties tend to become concentrated at the interface? The answers to these closely related questions are essential to an understanding of the cause and control of electronic defects at the interface.

In the last few years, new tools have been applied to the problem and older tools have been refined. One example of a relatively new tool is ion sputter etching used in conjunction with Auger electron spectroscopy (AES). From AES one can gain information on the abundance and chemical state of elements. However, it only "sees" the top few atomic layers on a surface, whereas the Si-SiO$_2$ interface is typically buried beneath 1000 Å of SiO$_2$. To reach the interface, the excess SiO$_2$ must be removed without seriously distorting the underlying layer. This is done by bombarding the surface with rare-gas ions, which remove SiO$_2$, in a process called sputter etching. The Auger measurement is made simultaneously with sputtering to determine chemical composition and state as a function of depth.

A group at Stanford University and the firm of Varian Associates in Palo Alto, Calif., improved sputtering techniques so that sputtering damage did not invalidate the Auger results. Figure 1 shows the Auger data obtained as one sputters through the oxide into the interface. Figure 1a shows the strength of three signals, the signal from oxygen in the oxide and two silicon signals. The first silicon signal involves electronic energy states characteristic of tightly bound silicon atoms. This is labeled Si$_{KLL}$. The second silicon signal, labeled Si$_{LVV}$, also involves chemical bonding states. The Si$_{LVV}$ signal recorded in these measurements only occurs

figure 3

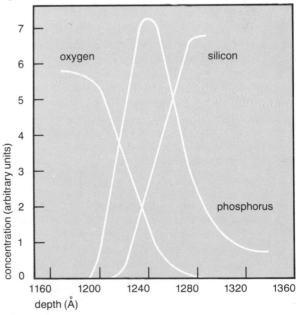

figure 2

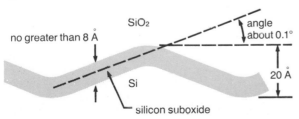

from unoxidized silicon. Making use of the two silicon signals, one can determine the chemical state as well as the amount of silicon present as a function of depth.

Figure 1b indicates the details of the Si_{KLL} signal taken at various depths versus energy. The energy of the Si_{KLL} signal varies depending on the number of oxygen atoms bonded to a given silicon atom. The spectrum labeled 1 (taken at the depth indicated in figure 1a) is characteristic of silicon atoms in SiO_2; that labeled 5, of unoxidized silicon. By examining the details of such spectra, it was determined that there was, at most, 8 Å of suboxide between the unoxidized silicon and SiO_2. Further, by the rate of rise of the Si_{LVV} signal and fall of the oxygen peak, it could be determined that the transition region, averaged over a comparatively wide area parallel to the interface, was about 20 Å or greater. This led to the model shown in figure 2. Based on new techniques, results published late in 1978 showed that the Si-SiO_2 transition takes place over only one or two atomic layers; i.e., it is almost as abrupt as possible. It has also been found that details of the Si-SiO_2 transition depend on the growth parameters of the oxide, such as the temperature of growth.

Figure 3 shows a different type of result; these are data reduced from detailed analysis of an interface resulting from oxidation of silicon doped with about 1% of phosphorus. As can be seen, there is a very large concentration of phosphorus on the silicon side of the interface (almost eight times the bulk doping). It is essential to have information on such concentrations in order to predict the kind of device performance that will result from specific processing.

—W. E. Spicer

Psychology

The year 1979 marks the centennial celebration of psychology's emergence as a formal discipline. It was especially fitting, therefore, that during 1978, the last year of psychology's first century, one of the most vigorously debated issues was the role that verbal reports can or should play in psychological research. This issue is noteworthy because introspection was the major, and in many cases the exclusive, research technique utilized by the early psychologists such as Wilhelm Wundt and E. B. Titchener.

Important as it was in the early days of psychology, introspection soon went under a cloud as the behavioristic system developed and increasingly large numbers of psychologists were persuaded that overt behavior was the only meaningful kind of event to observe and manipulate. The founder of the behavioristic school, John B. Watson, was willing to accept verbal report as a form of behavior. Nevertheless, during the long dominance of behaviorism in U.S. psychology, few efforts were made to utilize such measures, even in conjunc-

tion with observations of other, more "objective" behaviors. However, with the recent return to scientific respectability of mental phenomena and, especially, cognitive processes, renewed interest was being expressed in the use of verbal reports as supplements to the more traditional forms of observation.

The validity of verbal reports was vigorously challenged in a paper published in 1977 by Richard E. Nisbett and Timothy D. Wilson. The focus of the paper was the repeated failure of subjects, in retrospective verbal reports requested after completion of the standard data-collection phase of an experiment, to admit —let alone spontaneously identify—the significance of certain events that appeared to have played a crucial role in determining their behavior. An example of such an event would be the taking of a pill, in reality a placebo but with falsely attributed psychological effects, which did indeed produce large behavioral differences between such experimental subjects and control subjects who were not given pills.

Prominent among the responses to the Nisbett-Wilson paper were 1978 "working papers" by K. A. Ericsson and Herbert A. Simon. (Simon, who received the 1978 Nobel Prize for Economics for work on decision-making by business executives done two decades earlier, had since been involved mainly in research on problem solving, largely in collaboration with A. Newell.) Ericsson and Simon present a plausible and finely

Brain wave amplitudes of two subjects, E.S. and L.N., in reaction to light stimuli are larger during the television news program "Face the Nation" than during the TV showing of an erotic movie.

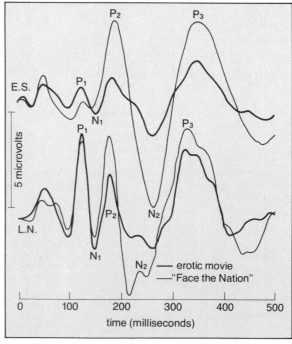

Edward W. P. Schafer, *International Journal of Neuroscience*

conceived "model" incorporating the concepts of short-term and long-term memory stores to account for most of the concurrent and retrospective verbal reports that have been used. In their response they conclude that ". . . when the conditions specified by the information processing model of verbalization are satisfied, we must accept the genuineness of verbalized information. The time has come to use protocols and retrospective reports, in appropriately designed studies, as a rich source of empirical data for revealing human cognitive processes, and for testing theories of such processes."

Assessment of the individual. Psychologists, along with other behavioral scientists, continued to develop new criteria and practices in a large number of problem areas bearing upon everyday-life situations. One of the most far-reaching examples concerned the growing trend toward deinstitutionalization in the treatment of persons with behavior disorders. In a pioneering step the state of New York was implementing an ambitious plan for transferring many of its 26,000 chronically disabled individuals from state mental hospitals to long-term local-care facilities, with $13.7 million already earmarked for this purpose.

The heart of the program was a relatively new concept called "level of care" (LOC). Individual data covering a wide variety of personal characteristics were fed into a computer which was programmed to indicate the most appropriate level of care for each person. The first results of the LOC survey surprised some of the officials in charge of the program. More than 17% of the institutionalized persons were diagnosed as capable of either independent or sheltered independent life and another 10% as suited to nursing-home care, making a total of more than 27% not really requiring institutionalization in a mental hospital.

Another problem of even wider concern is how to rear children so that they will attain a high degree of maturity and happiness as young adults. An unusual follow-up of an earlier study, done a quarter of a century ago, was carried out by a Harvard University research team led by psychologist David C. McClelland. The original study, also performed by Harvard psychologists (Robert Sears, Eleanor Maccoby, and Harry Levin), attempted to discover the effect of various child-rearing techniques on personality development. This research group interviewed 379 mothers of kindergarten children in two towns in the vicinity of Boston. Each of the mothers was rated on approximately 150 specific practices (*e.g.*, whether the mother controlled the child's behavior by physical means, deprivation of privileges, or withdrawal of love). Major weaknesses in this study were that the researchers depended for their data on the mother's impressions of their children rather than their own direct study, and that there was no way at the time of assessing the long-term effects of the various practices.

The latter gap was in part redressed by the new research team. Focusing on families previously categorized as "middle class," the McClelland team found and interviewed 78 of the children (now in their early 30s) from the earlier survey, 49 of whom had children of their own. After being told that the researchers were interested in comparing their views on child rearing with those of their parents, these young adults were interviewed and given psychological tests. The overall conclusion was that specific child-rearing techniques themselves, at least as practiced within the first five years of a child's life, have little influence upon how the children think and behave when they are grown. However, two intangible factors were found to have had a substantial effect. The highest levels of social and moral maturity were found in those persons whose mothers had shown genuine love for the children and whose parents had tolerated the general messiness of children rather than maintaining what the researchers labeled an "adult-centered home."

Two developmental psychologists, Edward Zigler

Sidney Harris

"What with the primary mental ability test and the differential aptitude test and the reading readiness test and the basic skills test and the I.Q. test and the sequential tests of educational progress and the mental maturity test, we haven't been learning anything at school."

and Penelope Trickett of Yale University, called for replacement of the standard intelligence test as the exclusive or major measure used in assessment of early childhood intervention programs. Arguing that social competence should be the primary measure used in this kind of assessment, they suggested an appropriate social-competence index composed of a number of key component measures (physical health, IQ, school achievement, motivational and emotional status, and certain social variables such as school attendance and juvenile delinquency).

A somewhat different approach to the same problem, but centered on the older child and young adult, was proposed by psychologists Lee Cronbach and Richard Snow of Stanford University in their book *Aptitudes and Instructional Methods: A Handbook for Research on Interactions.* Their theme is that more attention needs to be paid to the interactions between individual attributes and abilities and instructional variations in educational endeavors. Again, one notes a new degree of concern for the individual qua individual and a condemnation of the more traditional practice of setting arbitrary standards.

One final example comes from an unexpected source, the relatively new field of environmental psychology, in this instance interacting with the more traditional field of architecture. Psychologist/psychiatrist Carl Eisdorfer of the University of Washington spoke up strongly for greater concern for the consumer in all fields and, specifically, in architecture. At a conference on the design of mental health facilities, Eisdorfer exclaimed that "Whether you're a psychologist or a psychiatrist or a social worker or . . . an architect, you're really an applied behavioral scientist." He pointed out that the latest stage in the design of mental health facilities is the "barrier-free" movement—toward greater consumer access and control.

Architect Herbert McLaughlin, who had participated in the designing of more than 20 hospitals, admitted that architects have tended to keep both clients (who pay the bills) and users (who suffer the consequence of faulty design) from active participation in the design process, but he emphasized that architects are now trying to learn more from the users. He also pointed out that mental health professionals in the past have not contributed positively on the side of the user; rather, they either have been neutral or have accepted some of the old stereotyped notions, such as that psychiatric patients should not have too much environmental stimulation.

Behaviorism and humanism. Much of this concern for the individual could be attributed to the growing power of a kind of humanistic interest in psychology, often identified as the "third force" in contradistinction to the more traditional forces of behaviorism and psychoanalysis. During the year intensified, specific attention was paid to this growing humanistic concern. In

one of the significant instances of this trend, Leonard Krasner, himself closely identified with the behaviorists, found evidence of the approaching convergence of the behavioristic and humanistic movements within psychology.

Looking at the roots of both movements in the post-World War II period, Krasner concluded that they actually have a high degree of commonality; for example, both derive from the motivation to make a better world. This is true despite the adversarial role that each has played in relation to the other, as in the much-publicized running dialogues between behaviorist B. F. Skinner and humanist Carl Rogers. Moreover, Krasner points to the rapid development of new models, conceptualizations, and research approaches, such as the increasing use of "natural environments" as behavioral research settings and the convergence of the research roles of the former "subject" and "investigator" into the "participant-observer."

That Krasner's perspective may be overly optimistic, however, is suggested by the article that followed his in the September 1978 issue of *American Psychologist.* In that article Samuel Deitz forcefully raised questions about the growing tendency of researchers in applied behavioral analysis to concentrate on socially important behaviors and on "cure." In this emphasis "the investigative, analytic aspects of applied behavioral analysis are subordinated to its useful, applicable aspects." Deitz concluded that this shift has been too rapid and is premature; it must be checked if psychologists are to avoid the seriously detrimental consequences of ignoring normal scientific procedures in their quest for utility.

Sex differences. The study of sex differences has had a long and stormy history. Few topics have been more subject to bias and prejudice. Only recently have relatively dispassionate investigations begun to be the norm rather than the exception.

Among the most active facets of this general problem area currently under investigation is the study of fundamental differences in how the brain functions in males and females. If important congenital differences in brain function are demonstrated, a significant step forward will have been taken in the long-standing debate between those investigators who emphasize biological determinants as causal factors in observed sex differences in behavior and those who point to cultural determinants.

A proposition that is emerging from a variety of brain research—mainly from work on differential effects of sex hormones by Diane McGuinness and Karl Pribram at Stanford and on differential electrical activity for various mental functions by a Harvard group headed by psychologist Richard Davidson—is that females are better able to shift from one hemispheric function to another while males perform more effectively when the two hemispheres are not competing. McGuinness and

Pribram thus characterize males as more "manipulative," expressing themselves more through actions, and females as more "communicative," more characterized by memory and transmission of signs. Moreover, they claim to find support for this distinction in their reading of primate behavior, which is relatively unaffected by cultural factors.

Behavioral investigations also continued to produce suggestions of basic sex differences. Thus in Melvin Marx's research, female subjects consistently have been found to learn better when observing—simply being shown correct and incorrect responses—than when performing, selecting responses, and then being informed of their correctness. This advantage has been found in female subjects from elementary school through college. Males, on the other hand, generally seem to repeat their own responses, whether correct or incorrect, more than females, and there is some evidence suggesting that they tend more than females to transfer correct responses to new situations.

All of these differences, of course, must be recognized as matters of degree and in no sense absolute. It is especially important to keep all of the reported differences in proper perspective and to guard against overgeneralization.

Sociobiology. In recent years the strongest emphasis on genetic determinants of behavior has been made by the new and rapidly growing field of sociobiology. Foremost among proponents of this view, which in essence is an attempt to generalize from animal observations to human problems, is Harvard entomologist Edward O. Wilson. It was his 1975 book, *Sociobiology: The New Synthesis*, that spearheaded the movement. In 1978 he published another, more clearly human-oriented work, *On Human Nature*, which promised to be even more controversial. One indication of the intense interest stirred by this newest version of genetic determinism was the report that at least ten additional books on sociobiology, most of them supportive of the general theme, were in the making.

—Melvin H. Marx

Space exploration

Probes of the surface and atmosphere of Venus and a new record for a manned mission were highlights of the year in space exploration. In other developments the United States continued to test the shuttle orbiter, and the Soviets introduced unmanned craft to carry supplies to space stations.

Manned flight

U.S. Pres. Jimmy Carter outlined his new space policy in an October speech at Kennedy Space Center in Florida. It centered on maximum utilization of the shut-

Forward assembly of a booster rocket for the U.S. space shuttle is lowered into place on top of the other rocket sections at the Marshall Space Flight Center in Huntsville, Ala.

tle space transportation system in an expanded operation of communications, Earth resources, and military satellites. Carter ruled out any new projects such as space factories, solar power satellites, or large space platforms. "It is too early to commit the nation to such projects," he said.

Space shuttle. Although the U.S. space shuttle was scheduled for its first orbital flight in the fall of 1979, the outlook early in the year for accomplishing this in 1979 was dismal. The major setback occurred on Dec. 27, 1978, when one of three main engines destined for the first flight exploded during a test firing in Mississippi.

The development of the main engines had been plagued by fires and explosions in turbopumps and other engine components. But despite delays for rework and redesign more than 400 minutes of firing time had been logged by September 1978, including several of the eight and a half-minute full-duration firings that will be needed to boost the shuttle orbiter into space. The orbiter carries three of these 470,000-lb-thrust engines, which are fed by an external liquid oxygen-liquid hydrogen tank.

Similar testing of the smaller orbiter maneuvering and attitude rocket engines was begun in 1978 at Johnson Space Center's White Sands Test Facility in New

U.S. space shuttle "Enterprise" is hoisted to a dynamic test stand at the Marshall Space Flight Center in Alabama to undergo a series of ground vibration tests.

Mexico. Also, the recoverable solid-propellant booster rocket was test-fired three times in Utah.

The shuttle orbiter "Enterprise," flown in glide-to-landing tests during 1977, was ferried in March from California to Alabama atop a Boeing 747 carrier aircraft. In Alabama at the U.S. National Aeronautics and Space Administration (NASA) Marshall Space Flight Center, "Enterprise" was hoisted into a test stand formerly used for Saturn rockets and joined with the external tank and solid rockets for extensive structural and vibration tests.

"Enterprise" seems destined to become a tourist exhibit after its service as a ground-test spacecraft is completed, because the expense of modifying it for spaceflight is considered too high. An orbiter originally built only for structural tests was to be upgraded to spaceflight status to replace the "Enterprise."

Names were selected for the rest of the orbiters in the planned shuttle fleet. They were "Columbia," "Challenger," "Discovery," and "Atlantis." "Columbia," near completion at the assembly plant in Palmdale, Calif., was moved overland in March 1979 through the streets of Palmdale and Lancaster to NASA's nearby Dryden Flight Research Center. A Boeing 747 aircraft then would ferry it from Dryden to the Kennedy Space Center for the first orbital flight.

Space veteran John W. Young and rookie Robert L. Crippen were named to pilot "Columbia" in its first orbital flight. The mission was scheduled to be launched from the refurbished Apollo Pad 39 at Kennedy Space Center and to land at Edwards Air Force Base, Calif., after a 54-hour shakedown flight. The backup landing site for the orbital test flights is the dry lake bed at White Sands Missile Range in New Mexico. Six orbital flight tests were planned; after the fourth flight, landings were to be on the shuttle runway at Kennedy Space Center.

Two engineers wearing space suits move and fit together beams in the simulated weightlessness of the Neutral Buoyancy Simulator at the Marshall Space Flight Center. Other divers accompany the engineers for purposes of safety and assistance. The tests are aimed at learning how to assemble large structures in space.

Crew cockpit trainers and the Mission Control Center near Houston, Texas, were to be linked together in mid-1979 for joint orbital flight simulations. Modifications to Mission Control's data-handling system were under way to permit simultaneous operation of shuttle scientific and industrial payloads as well as classified military payloads. The U.S. Air Force was to have bought two shuttle orbiters and built a separate control center, but budgetary limitations forced combined civilian and military payload operations.

A yearlong recruiting drive for additional astronauts and mission specialists ended in January 1978 with the selection of 35 candidates—20 mission specialists and 15 pilot-astronauts. Six of the mission specialist candidates were women. The candidates entered a two-year training course at the Johnson Space Center near Houston. After completing it, in July 1980, they will be available for shuttle flight assignments.

Candidates were also named for mission and payload specialist crew assignments on the European-built Spacelab, scheduled for orbital flight in the shuttle orbiter's cargo bay during the 1980s. At the year's end more than 150 industrial and educational organizations had reserved cargo-bay space on shuttle flights for some 250 scientific and industrial payloads.

Skylab. Meanwhile, like the "Flying Dutchman," space station Skylab came back to haunt space planners. Launched in May 1973 and manned for 171 days by three U.S. crews during 1973–74, Skylab then was predicted to remain in orbit for ten years. However, its orbit began "wearing out" more rapidly than expected because of a high level of solar flares that bulged portions of the Earth's atmosphere outward to the space station's altitude.

Faced with this problem, NASA began work on the Teleoperator Retrieval System, a television-guided rocket tug that could dock with the derelict space station to either boost it to a safer orbit or plunge it into the atmosphere for a fiery funeral at a selected remote location. Flight controllers in Houston awakened Skylab after a four-year sleep and stabilized it from random drifting flight. Skylab's giant solar panels began feeding electrical power into banks of dead batteries.

By the end of 1978, however, NASA abandoned the plan to deorbit Skylab with the teleoperator because only one of the space station's three stabilizing gyroscopes was reliable and most of the attitude-control nitrogen gas was gone. Instead, the flight controllers planned to try to influence Skylab's atmospheric entry by using the remaining attitude gas. The space station was expected to reenter the Earth's atmosphere in mid-summer 1979.

Soviet flights. Soviet manned spaceflight activities during 1978 focused upon the technology and logistics needed for continuously manned space stations. A new craft introduced during the year was the Progress resupply spacecraft, basically a stripped-down Soyuz

Soviet unmanned space freighter Progress 1 is launched in January 1978 to provide fresh supplies for the cosmonauts in Salyut 6.

that carried food, water, fuel, and even a guitar up to the Salyut 6 space station. Driven into one of Salyut's docking ports by Soviet ground control using television guidance, the Progress spacecraft could deliver two and a half tons of supplies to the space station. This included rocket fuel for Salyut's maneuvering engines, the first in-flight fuel transfers in space.

During a record-breaking 139-day stay aboard Salyut 6, Soyuz 29 cosmonauts Vladimir V. Kovalenok and Aleksandr S. Ivanchenkov were resupplied three times by Progress space freighters. After their missions the empty Progress spacecraft were jettisoned to vaporize during atmospheric reentry over the Pacific Ocean.

Progress 1, the first use of an unmanned space freighter, brought consumables to Salyut 6 in January 1978 to aid the Soyuz 26 crew of Yuri V. Romanenko and Georgy M. Grechko to set a new space endurance record of 96 days. Romanenko and Grechko returned to Earth on March 16, 1978.

The dual docking ports of Salyut 6 allowed docking either by Progress resupply barges or visits by second crews in Soyuz spacecraft. One such visit to Romanenko and Grechko was by Soyuz 28 crewmen Aleksey A. Gubarev of the U.S.S.R. and Vladimir Remek of

Largest of the four probes of Pioneer Venus 2 is readied for launch on Aug. 8, 1978. Four months later the probe measured constituents and dynamics of the atmosphere of Venus as it plunged toward the surface of the planet.

Czechoslovakia. Remek was the first person other than one from the U.S. or Soviet Union to enter space.

Two more international crews brought mail, newspapers, and supplies to Kovalenok and Ivanchenkov during their 139-day stay aboard Salyut 6. Soyuz 30, with Soviet cosmonaut Pyotr Klimuk and Polish cosmonaut Miroslaw Hermaszewski, spent eight days docked with the space station, and Soyuz 31, with Soviet cosmonaut Valery Bykovsky and Sigmund Jaehn from East Germany, stayed there seven days.

As each visiting crew left Salyut, they returned to Earth in the previously docked spacecraft, leaving the "freshest" Soyuz for the next crew. Kovalenok and Ivanchenkov left Salyut in Soyuz 31, landing in Soviet Asia on Nov. 2, 1978, after preparing the space station for dormant flight. Salyut 6 later was boosted by Soviet ground control into a higher parking orbit to await future cosmonaut crews.

Scientific investigations conducted aboard the Salyut ranged from space physics and astronomy to biomedical and Earth resources survey experiments. The Salyut cosmonauts conducted more than 50 materials-processing experiments and formed metallic alloys in the weightlessness of orbit.

In regard to future manned spacecraft, the Soviet Union was reported to be building a long, hard-surfaced runway near the Tyuratam Cosmodrome. This would be used for landing the U.S.S.R.'s reusable shuttle spacecraft.

—Terry White

Space probes

Venus again received the attention of scientific probes during 1978. The planet was visited by two U.S. and two Soviet craft in its most extensive scientific investi-

gation to date. Other probes continued to study Mars and to journey toward Saturn.

Probing Venus. On May 20, 1978, Pioneer Venus 1 was launched by an Atlas Centaur from the Kennedy Space Center. The 581-kg (1,280-lb) probe was scheduled to arrive at Venus in December and to orbit the planet for one Venusian sidereal day (243 Earth days, later extended to 486 days).

The craft had the mission of mapping the Venusian clouds, atmosphere, and ionosphere by means of remote-sensing instruments. It also carried a side-looking radar that was to be used for mapping the planetary surface. Additionally, the orbiter was instrumented to study irregularities in the gravitational field of Venus and carried a scientific instrument designed to pinpoint the location of sources of gamma-ray bursts in interplanetary space.

As the probe passed through the Earth's magnetosphere on its way to Venus, instruments aboard it made measurements. On June 1 mission controllers at the California-based Ames Research Center (ARC) of NASA fired the orbiter's rocket engines to change its course. The maneuver insured that the probe would arrive at Venus six and a half hours earlier than planned on December 4.

During the journey through interplanetary space a gamma-ray detector aboard Pioneer Venus 1 began reporting extremely powerful "bursts" of such radiation. The phenomenon, unknown until 1973, occurs about once a month, originating from as yet undetermined sources or causes. Typical of the bursts was a two-second pulse when the probe was only 565,110 km (351,000 mi) from the Earth. The same burst was reported by a Vela satellite of the U.S. Department of Energy and the Helios 2 scientific satellite orbiting the Sun.

On August 8 Pioneer Venus 2 was launched from the Kennedy Space Center, also by an Atlas Centaur. The 903-kg (1,990-lb) craft carried one large and three small probes designed to plunge into the Venusian atmosphere and make quantitative and qualitative measurements before reaching the surface and being destroyed in the process. The main part of the craft was instrumented to make measurements in the upper atmosphere as it plunged toward the surface. The large probe weighed 316 kg (695 lb) and contained seven scientific experiments to identify gaseous constituents of the atmosphere and to make measurements of its clouds, circulation, structure, and energy distribution. The probe was targeted to enter the atmosphere over the Venusian equator. It featured a 13.5-karat precision optical window made from a 205-karat, industrial-grade diamond that permitted passage of infrared energy but withstood the great heat and pressures associated with the planet's atmosphere.

The three small probes each weighed 91 kg (200 lb). They were instrumented to measure the atmospheric structure (pressure, temperature, and probe acceleration, from which altitude and density could be determined) as well as cloud particles and heat distribution within the atmosphere. Two of the probes were targeted to impact on the night side of the planet, one at a high-northern and the other at a mid-southern latitude. The third was aimed at a point on the day side in the mid-southern latitudes. On August 16 Pioneer Venus 2 was given a course change which insured that its probes would land in their designated areas.

As the two U.S. probes were on the way to Venus in the fall of 1978, they were joined by Venera 11 and Venera 12, two Soviet probes. They were nearly identical to Venera 9 and 10, launched in 1975, and were scheduled to reach Venus in December. Venera 11 was launched on September 9 from the space complex at Tyuratam. It was instrumented, as was the Pioneer Venus 1, to make physical measurements in interplanetary space of the solar wind, cosmic rays, and other radiation. A special gamma-ray burst detector, developed by French scientists, also was aboard. The similarly instrumented Venera 12 was launched on September 14.

Throughout October mission controllers at ARC tested various systems aboard the two Pioneer Venus probes. On October 10 the orbiter began measuring light from Venus. Beginning on November 15 the four probes of Pioneer Venus 2 successfully detached themselves from the main craft and entered trajectories toward their target areas on Venus. A month later Pioneer Venus 1 went into an orbit about the planet that ranged in altitude from 378 km (235 mi) to 64,672 km (40,169 mi), later changed to 233 km (145 mi) and 66,010 km (41,000 mi). Each complete orbit took 23 hours and 11 minutes. An ion-mass spectrometer in the orbiter reported the presence of atomic oxygen, molecular oxygen, hydrogen, helium, nitrogen, and carbon dioxide and that they were abundant in the upper atmosphere.

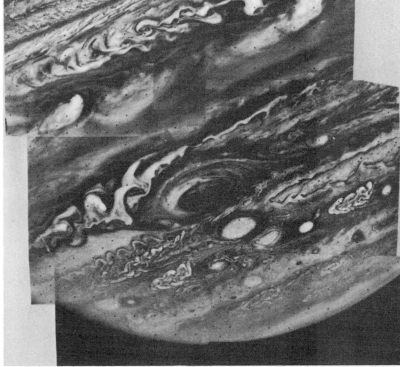

Clouds above Jupiter are revealed in a mosaic assembled from images obtained by the U.S. space probe Voyager 1 at a distance of about four million miles from the planet. The swirling vortex motion in the Great Red Spot, just below the center of the mosaic, can also be seen in the nearby white clouds. The smallest clouds in the mosaic are only about 70 miles across.

Courtesy, NASA

The probes of Pioneer Venus 2 entered the Venusian atmosphere, as planned, on December 9. The small probe that landed on the day side of the planet surprised mission controllers and its designers and builders by remaining operational on the surface in a temperature of 480° C (900° F) and transmitting data for 67 minutes. Among the most surprising findings were the presence of argon-36 in the atmosphere and the fact that the cloud-top temperatures on the night side of the planet were warmer than those on the day side. Instruments also reported that the planet's upper atmosphere is cooler than previously supposed. Water vapor both above the clouds and below them was scarce.

On December 14 Venera 12 received commands to make a slight course correction, and two days later its lander capsule detached from the orbiter and headed for an impact on the far side of the planet. The lander touched down on December 21 and transmitted environmental data for 110 minutes. On December 22 the Soviet publication *Gudok* stated that the Venera 12 lander had "an automatic camera that began operating 30 seconds after landing." It also reported a special device that tested the Venusian soil by digging into it and then chemically analyzing the sample. By early 1979, however, no surface pictures had been released by the Soviets.

As the Venera 12 lander penetrated the Venusian atmosphere, instruments aboard the craft analyzed it for chemical components and made a spectral analysis of solar radiation diffused by the atmosphere. Once on the surface the probe reported that the atmospheric pressure at the landing site was 88 atm, slightly lower than readings reported by the U.S. probes. (One atmosphere, 14.7 psi, is the pressure of the air at sea level on the Earth.) The temperature was given as 460° C (860° F), which was in general agreement with findings of the U.S. probes.

Venera 11's lander touched down on December 25 at a point some 773 km (480 mi) away from its sister probe. It had separated two days earlier and begun its plunge through the Venusian atmosphere. After landing it reported a temperature of 446° C (835° F) and a pressure of 88 atm. The probe transmitted data for 95 minutes. Both landers reported the presence of argon-36, as did their U.S. counterparts; however, there were discrepancies in values reported by the various probes, and further study was required.

Some data returned by the Venera landers caused concern among U.S. scientists. For example, the probes reported the presence of carbon monoxide in the lower atmosphere. While the Pioneer Venus probes detected the compound in the upper atmosphere, they did not in the lower, although they were instrumented to do so. In commenting, Lawrence Colin, a Pioneer Venus project scientist, said, "One would not

Arsia Mons, one of the three Tharsis volcanoes on Mars, is seen in a mosaic of pictures taken from the Viking Orbiter 1 at an altitude of 3,700 miles. Considered among the youngest of the Martian surface features, the volcano stands about 12 miles above the surrounding terrain and has a central caldera measuring some 75 miles across.

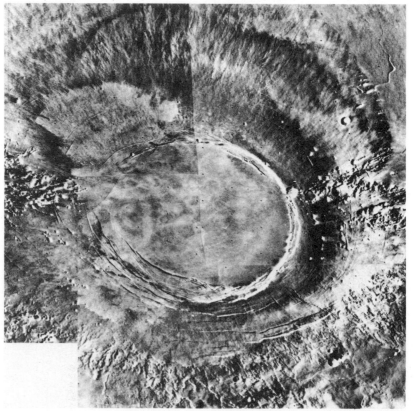

Courtesy, NASA

expect carbon monoxide in the lower atmosphere. . . [It] could only come from the [photodissociation] of carbon dioxide, and you'd expect that to happen at high altitudes.'' The apparent discrepancy was placed on the agenda for a joint meeting to be held with Soviet scientists at a later date.

As the year ended problems with the side-looking radar in the Pioneer Venus 1 led to an investigation by engineers at ARC. Data returned by it were often scrambled and unusable. Nonetheless, the radar had succeeded in mapping about 4% of the planet's surface that is largely unobservable by Earth-based radars. Hopes were that the problems were not serious because the experiment was a major mission objective.

On to Jupiter and Saturn. The U.S. probes Voyager 1 and 2 continued on their way through interplanetary space for a rendezvous first with Jupiter and later Saturn. On February 22 the scan platform of Voyager 1 malfunctioned as it was being exercised, stopping in a fixed position at 43°. However, during the following month mission controllers were able to free it. In early April Voyager 2 developed problems in both of its radio receivers and would not respond to commands from mission controllers at the Jet Propulsion Laboratory (JPL) in Pasadena, Calif. Luckily, one of the receivers became functional and the mission continued.

Voyager 1 entered the asteroid belt between Mars and Jupiter on Dec. 10, 1977, and emerged unscathed from it on Sept. 8, 1978. Its sister probe exited unharmed from the belt on Oct. 21, 1978. Both probes remained on course. Voyager 1 was scheduled to pass within 286,580 km (178,000 mi) of Jupiter on March 5, 1979. Voyager 2 was to pass the giant planet at an altitude of 642,390 km (399,000 mi) in July 1979. If the mission then continues as planned, Voyager 1 will arrive at Saturn in November 1980 and Voyager 2 will pass the ringed planet in August 1981.

Data from Mars. On March 3 mission controllers at the JPL successfully ejected the bioshield that had remained attached to Viking Orbiter 2 since Viking Lander 2 separated from the Orbiter on Sept. 3, 1976. The shield had been left in place although it degraded performance of the Orbiter 2 because of uncertainties in the probe's gyrostabilization system. However, in view of the enormous amount of data already obtained from Viking Lander 2, mission controllers believed that the risk was worth the chance. Casting off the shield nearly tripled the field of view of the probe's scan platform, on which were mounted the Orbiter's cameras and other scientific instruments.

On July 25, however, Viking Orbiter 2 was silenced forever. In February a leaking attitude-control valve had begun depleting the probe's limited supply of gas. By midsummer it had to be shut down. The craft by then had completed 706 orbits of the planet and returned approximately 19,000 pictures of it to Earth. Originally designed for a lifetime of only 150 days, it had been circling Mars since Aug. 7, 1976.

Despite the loss of Viking Orbiter 2, the remaining probes of the mission continued functioning. As 1978 ended, NASA planned to continue the Viking mission until September 1979 in order to give scientists enough time to finish their studies. However, Viking Landers 1 and 2 and Viking Orbiter 1 would transmit data only through February 1979.

As a footnote to the successful Viking program, NASA reminded the public that both of the orbiters had been designed to circle Mars for 50 years before entering its tenuous atmosphere. An international treaty required that they be so built and orbited so as to avoid any possible contamination of Mars by bacteria from the Earth, since the two craft were not sterilized as were the two landers. Thus, the silent Viking Orbiter 2 should continue to circle the planet until the year 2019.

Probing the Sun. On August 12 the 469-kg (1,033-lb) International Sun Earth Explorer 3 (ISEE 3) was launched by a Delta rocket from the Kennedy Space Center. It was aimed at a target never before visited by a scientific probe from Earth, an imaginary point in space one million miles from Earth in a straight line to the Sun. This is called a libration point, a place where the gravity of two celestial bodies, in this case the Sun and the Earth, cancel each other. An object precisely placed there would never fall by gravity into either body. On November 20 ISEE 3 was placed into a ''halo orbit'' that circled the libration point. The probe had a period of six months, rising and falling some 150,060 km (93,205 mi) through the ecliptic plane. It carried enough station-keeping propellant to insure that it would have a lifetime of at least ten years.

ISEE 3 was instrumented to monitor the solar wind and solar flares as an ''early warning'' craft, detecting such phenomena about an hour before they reach near-Earth space. Data so gathered were to be compared with similar data from the ISEE 1, ISEE 2, and Geos 2 spacecraft, which were orbiting in the magnetosphere of Earth. Those sister spacecraft were launched in October 1977.

The Pioneer missions. In April a scientific instrument aboard Pioneer 11, en route to Saturn since its launching on April 5, 1973, suddenly returned to life after being considered dead since 1975. Designed to measure the solar wind in interplanetary space, the instrument had functioned well during the 21-month, 620 million-mi journey from the Earth to Jupiter, which the probe reached in December 1974. To restore it to operation, mission controllers literally shocked the instrument into operation by applying high voltages to some of its electrical circuits.

On its voyage from Jupiter to Saturn, Pioneer 11 moved through an electrical ''current sheet'' and into the Sun's northern magnetic hemisphere. Data from the probe led scientists to believe that the Sun has a simple dipole magnetic field, similar to that of the Earth.

Drawing shows the proposed solar polar mission. Two space probes would be launched so that in swinging past Jupiter they would be thrown out of the ecliptic, the solar equatorial plane in which the planets lie, and into orbit over the poles of the Sun.

A final course correction was made to Pioneer 11 on July 23. It insured that the probe would encounter Saturn on Sept. 1, 1979, and then move to within 28,980 km (18,000 mi) of the planet's outer ring and pass under it to within 24,150 km (15,000 mi) of its surface, taking color pictures as it did so.

As 1978 ended, Pioneer 10, launched on March 2, 1972, was estimated to be 1.6 billion mi from Earth on its way to Saturn. The probe reported that at that distance the behavior of cosmic radiation becomes erratic. Its finding may indicate that the probe was approaching the heliospheric boundary, where the Sun's influence gives way to that of galactic space. All of its instruments, like those of its sister probe, were functioning perfectly at the time.

A note on the Moon. After reconsidering data from earlier lunar probes and unmanned roving vehicles, Soviet scientists during 1978 hypothesized that there might be dust storms on the Moon despite the fact that it has no atmosphere. Members of the A. F. Ioffe Physical-Technical Institute in Leningrad proposed such phenomena based in part on data from Lunokhod 2,

which had observed a luminescence on the lunar horizon after sunset. Instead of an atmospheric wind, the force on the Moon that could lift and suspend particles of matter several fractions of a micron in size could consist of an electrostatic field created by sunlight and ultraviolet radiation. Such particles could remain suspended for periods up to 300 hours, the Soviet scientists contended.

Probing the future. As 1978 ended, the always hopeful and optimistic NASA had any dreams for a brave new venture into space dashed by the administration of President Carter. Faced with the necessity for reducing the federal budget, the administration was vague on what the future would be and how it would be funded. Definitely eliminated were plans for a probe to be launched in August 1985 that would have swung by Halley's Comet in November 1985 and ejected a subprobe toward it while the craft went on for a rendezvous with Comet Tempel II in July 1988. The probe and the comet could have stayed close together for many days in matched orbits, or, alternately, the probe could have landed on the comet itself. Dreams for roving vehicles on Mars faded, also.

Still presumably viable at the end of the year was Project Galileo, a combined orbiter and lander mission to Jupiter. Launch was scheduled for January 1982 using the space shuttle vehicle. The probe was scheduled to pass Mars at an altitude of only 165 mi and be swung by that planet's gravity toward Jupiter, where it should arrive on March 14, 1985. The probe would use the same technique to fly past several of the moons of Jupiter.

Still planned for launch in 1983, but not funded by Congress, was a probe for a solar polar mission, a joint undertaking of NASA and the European Space Agency. Planning continued for two probes, one from each agency, that would be launched by the space shuttle. The two would be placed on trajectories so that in swinging past Jupiter they would be placed in orbits that would pass them over the poles of the Sun. Approximately 30 scientific experiments were selected for the mission.

Also as 1978 ended, the U.S. National Research Council (NRC) recommended to the Carter administration that the U.S. and U.S.S.R. undertake a joint unmanned mission to Venus and a mission to the Moon to return a soil sample from that body's far side. While there was no assurance that the Soviets would concur in such a project, the proposal showed that someone in the U.S. other than NASA was thinking of the nation's future in space.

NRC suggestions notwithstanding, the U.S.S.R. went ahead with plans for future lunar probes on its own. Typical of these were a lunar polar orbiter and a soil-sample return probe from the far side of the Moon without U.S. participation.

—Mitchell R. Sharpe

Transportation

The major influences on technological developments in transportation during 1978 continued to be the fuel price/supply problem and the continuing pressures exerted by environmental and safety regulations imposed by various governmental agencies. The list of innovations being tested and applied to help conserve petroleum-based fuels continued to grow. Individually, most of the innovations were not strikingly impressive, but collectively they brought about sizable savings. Aircraft engines for the new generation of jet transports promised fuel savings of 30% or more over comparable existing engines. Redesigned radial tires resulted in claimed savings in fuel of about 5% for millions of motor vehicles. More over-the-road trucks were equipped with aerodynamically designed bodies to cut down on drag. New carbon-fiber plastic composites were being used in both military and commercial aircraft construction to reduce weight. Rail piggyback flatcars were being skeletonized to cut weight, and one innovation, the bimodal Roadrailer, was designed to operate without any flatcars.

In the safety area manufacturers of motor vehicles intensified their research programs to meet new brake and bumper standards, and airports were required to install new sophisticated aircraft landing and airway safety aids. In addition, all carriers of hazardous materials had to adjust their packaging and shipping practices in order to comply with ever stricter rules.

In the environmental field aircraft builders stepped up their research and development so that their planes would be able to meet tough noise reduction requirements. Motor vehicle manufacturers tested innovations designed to meet upcoming fuel exhaust emission standards, and shipbuilders faced the problem of redesigning ships to minimize spillage.

Air transport. With hundreds of aging first-generation jet transports approaching the ends of their productive lives, concern about rising fuel costs played a major role in new air transport designs. A major benefit of the next-generation transports was expected to be a possible 30–35% reduction in fuel consumption—based on comparable passenger-mile performance of present-day transports—as a result of a variety of innovations. One of these is the use of longer wings that provide added lift and less drag and that contain what the industry calls "active" controls, the ability to adjust control surfaces automatically so as to distribute the stresses more evenly.

Also contributing to the fuel savings will be the weight reduction of airframes as a result of the use of new, lighter aluminum alloys and strong composite materials. One aircraft manufacturer, the LearAvia

A-300 Airbuses under construction in France. These widebody jets, available in several configurations, represent a European challenge to U.S. domination of the passenger airliner market.

Pelletan—Sipa Press/Black Star

Quiet short-haul research aircraft (QSRA) is rolled out for tests by the Boeing Co. Featuring above-wing engines, it is designed to land at half the speed of conventional airplanes and therefore to require comparatively short runways.

Corp., reported the development of a novel propeller-driven corporate plane with an airframe composed almost entirely of molded graphite epoxy that it said would reduce the craft's overall weight by 40–50% compared with a like-capacity turboprop.

The Boeing Co. announced the start of its next-generation jet transports after receiving a $1.2 billion order from United Air Lines, Inc., for 30 B-767s, a sufficient number to schedule production. The 767 is a wide-body, twin-engine transport with a capacity of approximately 200 persons and a range of 2,200 mi. Boeing claimed that the new craft would be 35% more fuel-efficient than current transports of like size and would feature high-bypass engines, an advanced-technology thick wing with innovative controls to achieve low speeds on landing approaches, and extensive use of aluminum and composite materials to reduce weight. First deliveries were scheduled for mid-1982.

Boeing also received orders, 21 from Eastern Air Lines, Inc., and 19 from British Airways, for another new-generation transport. This was the B-757, a narrow-body derivative of its widely used 727. It would carry about 175 passengers and feature new fuel-efficient Rolls-Royce engines and high-technology wings for 30% better fuel economy than the 727. Its range was to be 2,000–2,500 mi, with the first rollouts scheduled for 1983–84.

Airbus Industries, the European consortium that competes in the commercial aircraft manufacturing field with its twin-engine widebody A-300, announced plans to develop shortened versions to compete in the market for 200–245 passengers. Its A-310-100 would have a 2,100-mi range, and the higher capacity A-310-200 a 2,920-mi range. The A-310s would have smaller, thicker wings and shorter fuselages than the basic A-300s and would offer maximum fuel efficiency.

The entry of Lockheed Aircraft Corp. in the field of

planes carrying 200–230 passengers was to be a redesigned L-1011-400. The McDonnell Douglas Corp., on the other hand, dropped plans to compete in this market and concentrated on its 350-seat, stretched DC-10, with a range of 3,200–5,400 mi and its ongoing program to build the smaller DC-9 Super 80.

The U.S. National Aeronautics and Space Administration (NASA) announced plans to award the three major U.S. aircraft manufacturing firms—Boeing, Lockheed, and McDonnell Douglas—contracts totaling $48 million (partially funded by the companies) for the second phase of an eight-year, $450 million aircraft energy-efficiency program. The first phase stressed fuel-saving technologies such as winglets, wing-tip extensions, laminar-flow airfoils, active controls, computers and autothrottles, supercritical wings (those redesigned for less drag and shock to permit lighter weight and fuel economy), and low-speed, high-lift concepts. Phase two was to refine developments in the areas mentioned above and add wing-load alleviation devices, use of composite materials in controls structures, and extensive wind-tunnel testing of supercritical wings. The program was seeking to make transports 50% more fuel-efficient by the late 1980s.

A Microwave Landing System (MLS) designed by the United States and Australia was chosen by the International Civil Aviation Organization to replace the Instrument Landing System (ILS) in use since 1949. The new system would use a scanning microwave beam to sweep a wedge-shaped area, providing approaching aircraft with position-fixing information five times a second. It was chosen over the British-sponsored Doppler MLS, which utilizes pulsating waves to enable planes to fix their positions. Advantages of the MLS over the ILS include a sweeping microwave beam that allows greater directional flexibility in approach paths without suffering the bottleneck created by the ILS's single narrow beam; also, microwaves are less susceptible to interference and to distortion by terrain, which can render the ILS unusable in mountainous areas.

The Boeing Co. rolled out for tests its quiet short-haul research aircraft (QSRA), built under a $21 million NASA contract. The four-jet experimental short-take-off-and-landing craft, designed for use at medium-sized and small airports, featured a supercritical wing and above-wing engines that provide upper-surface blowing to boost lift.

Boeing claimed that the QSRA can utilize runways less than half as long as those required by current airliners and that it can land at half the speed of conventional aircraft. The manufacturer also maintained that even with the "highest lift capacity of any airplane" the QSRA is the quietest jet plane ever flown, making only about one-thirtieth the noise of a B-727.

Motor vehicles. The U.S. Department of Energy (DOE) launched a $160 million program to promote acceptance and use of electric vehicles. The DOE planned to subsidize part of the purchase of both electric and electric-gasoline hybrids by dealers and fleet operators to evaluate reliability, performance, efficiency, user acceptance, and operating and maintenance costs.

The DOE selected five private companies to start its program and established tough performance standards. These included: maximum speed of 50 mph for five minutes; range of 31 mi for electric and 125 mi for hybrid vehicles; acceleration from 0 to 31 mph in 15 seconds; battery recharge capability in ten hours from an 80% discharge; and, after 12 months or 9,320 mi, a battery that retained 75% of its power without suffering any loss in acceleration or gradability.

The major obstacle to the development of electric vehicles remained the low-energy density of lead-acid batteries, which limits travel range and requires low acceleration and speed compared with gasoline-powered vehicles. Most electric vehicles must be heated or air-conditioned by supplemental power sources because of the drain on batteries. While major research efforts in many laboratories around the world continued to seek an advanced type of battery, no significant breakthrough, from a cost-benefit standpoint, was announced during the year.

Innovations being studied to boost the battery's range included a system of braking to recover energy through a motor generator. More promising was the possible recovery of energy generated by braking through use of a flywheel mechanism, a development tested successfully on two New York City subway cars, which reportedly recovered about 30% of the energy needed for their propulsion.

The U.S. Environmental Protection Agency (EPA) threatened to place a major roadblock on the route that a number of auto manufacturers were taking to meet future federal fuel economy requirements—the use of the diesel engine. The EPA announced plans to propose standards that would require 1981–82 model diesel cars and light-duty diesel trucks to emit 0.6 g or less of particulate matter for each mile driven and only 0.2 g for 1983 models. The EPA claimed that diesel cars produce from 30 to 70 times as much particulate pollution as gasoline-powered cars, and it warned that very small particulates in auto soot can penetrate deeply into a person's lungs. Auto manufacturers seriously questioned their technological ability to meet the proposed standards, particularly the second round,

Experimental subcompact-sized electric car designed by the General Electric Co. contains a 24-horsepower traction motor (center), solid-state controller and power conditioner, and a blower for cooling the motor and electronic components. The 12-volt battery at the left powers fans, headlights, and other accessories. The 18 six-volt batteries that power the car are slung beneath it.

Courtesy, General Electric Research and Development Center

and said that turbochargers may be needed at costs ranging from $130 to $285 per vehicle. The EPA countered by claims that much of the added cost would be absorbed by the fuel savings made possible by the turbochargers.

The promotion of gasohol, usually 90% unleaded gasoline and 10% alcohol, was stepped up. The DOE created a special task force to study the "state of the art" and to seek the removal of remaining obstacles to more widespread acceptance of such blended fuels. The Illinois Bell Telephone Co. began a six-month trial of gasohol in 15 of its vehicles in the Peoria area, with the 10% alcohol portion made from corn. According to a spokesman for the firm gasohol prices in that area were higher than those for regular unleaded gas but lower than those for premium unleaded gas.

California's Energy Commission also announced a yearlong test of a varied mixture of alcohol and gasoline on four Hondas with stratified engines, which it claimed would be widely used in the U.S. during the 1980s. Such engines contain two combustion chambers, one using a rich mixture for ignition purposes and the other a leaner mixture to provide propulsion. Advantages were said to be increased mileage per gallon of fuel, reduced emission problems, and lower maintenance costs.

In the safety area the U.S. Department of Transportation (DOT) took delivery of its Large Research Safety Vehicle (LRSV), which was developed by Minicars, Inc. under a $250,000 contract with the DOT's National Highway Traffic Safety Administration. Called "the ideal family car of the future," the LRSV was built from a 1977 Chevrolet Impala six-passenger sedan but was redesigned to be safer, more fuel-efficient, and less polluting than conventional family cars. A trans-

versely mounted four-cylinder Volvo engine powers the front wheels through a five-speed manual transmission to provide a boost in fuel economy to an expected average of 27.5 mpg. Despite a weight reduction of 1,000 lb the LRSV was designed to provide crash protection in 40-mph frontal collisions and 30-mph side collisions by means of inclusion of high-strength, box-like steel structures and by filling doors with energy-absorbing plastic foam.

The use of computers to balance truck loads and thus reduce empty back hauls by as much as 25% was introduced by a division of the American Trucking Associations. Called the Computerized Interchange Substituted Service, it was designed to increase fuel economy and efficiency, with potential savings of 35 million gallons of diesel fuel annually and about $122 million in operating costs. Truck lines with imbalanced loads would supply data via the computer terminal in their dispatch offices to a centralized computer in Washington, D.C., for match-ups with the load data of other truck lines. The carrier advertising the load would deliver the sealed trailer to the matching carrier's terminal for hauling for a fixed fee per mile. It, in turn, would seek another carrier's loaded trailer for delivery on routes in the direction of its home base.

Computers in automobiles were being offered by the Cadillac division of General Motors to provide a wide range of information to drivers, including the car's miles per gallon, average speed, total elapsed trip time, range in miles on remaining fuel supply, miles to destination, estimated arrival time, time of day, engine temperature, and system voltage. The information is flashed on a dashboard screen. The first cars to get the computers were the Seville models. A more advanced computer was designed to expand into such areas as

"Solar Surrey" obtains its power from 484 silicon solar cells placed over the cab of the vehicle. The cells convert sunlight into electricity, which is then used to charge an automobile battery. The surrey can travel as far as six miles at up to 11 miles per hour on one sunny day's charge of electricity.

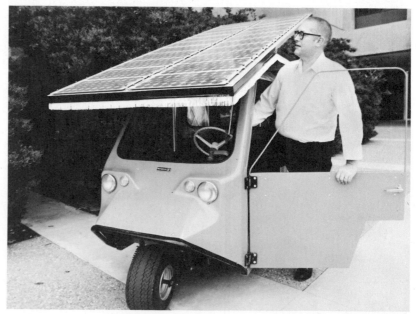

carburetor control, electronic fuel injection, exhaust gas recirculation, spark selection, transmission control, air conditioning, cruise control, and theft-deterrent systems.

Another technological challenge to the transportation industry was introduced by the DOT's decision that all federally funded public transit vehicles, both rail and bus, must be accessible to both the elderly and handicapped by Sept. 30, 1979. This directive was applicable nationwide because virtually all urban transit vehicles were purchased on a joint basis, with the U.S. paying about 80% of the cost. The major impact, from a design point of view, was on bus operators, because new buses must be able to "kneel" to 18 inches for boarding or discharging and also must include wheelchair lifts or ramps. Operators expressed considerable concern about not only the added costs—which overall could run into billions of dollars—but also the potential liability from injuries, the very small use that will be made of the complicated lifts and ramps, and the adverse impact they will have on the vast majority of riders that must accept the operating delays in boarding and discharging such persons. They claimed that a far better choice would be to provide small vehicles exclusively designed for transporting the elderly and handicapped with door-to-door service. Such special

services were rejected, however, because they failed to meet the test of across-the-board accessibility that present law requires for all transportation facilities receiving federal funding.

Pipelines. Further advances in deepwater pipelining were promised from a joint program supported by 33 oil and gas companies and conducted by the Battelle Memorial Institute. The first phase of the program was to establish technical requirements for laying pipelines 1,000–3,000 ft under water; computer programs were developed by the Battelle researchers to evaluate buckling and collapse, ship motion, and actions of the pipelines during offshore placement. In the proposed second phase actions of pipelines during abandonment and recovery were to be analyzed.

A consortium of advocates of coal-slurry pipelines formed the Energy Transition Corp. (ETCO) to overcome the strong opposition to such pipelines because of their heavy use of the scarce water supplies of the western states of the U.S. To solve this problem ETCO planned to turn part of the West's low-sulfur coal into methanol and use it as the liquid carrier to be mixed with finely crushed coal. The company claimed that each 4.4 tons of mined coal would produce two tons of pulverized coal for shipment and one ton of methanol, with the remaining 1.4 tons being used to supply the

Double-stacked container car carries two 40-foot shipping containers. The design reduces the weight of the equipment needed to handle containers by up to 45% compared with single-level flatcars.

Tom Lea—Southern Pacific Transportation Company

Prototype of the High-Speed Surface Transport (HSST) developed by Japan Air Lines made its first public test run on a track near Tokyo in May 1978. The vehicle uses magnetic levitation to lift it about ten millimeters above the track. With a 120-seat capacity the HSST is designed to reach a speed of about 190 miles per hour.

energy used in the conversion process.

ETCO announced plans to transport the mixture to generating stations in the Southeast or West Coast and then separate it, with coal used to feed a generating station and the methanol used as a fuel for a combined-cycle gas turbine electrical generator. ETCO estimated that the cost of a conversion facility to produce 5,000 tons of methanol and 10,000 tons of pulverized coal a day would be $750 million; yet it maintained that operating costs would be lower because the entire mix could be used as fuel and because existing oil and gas pipelines could be utilized rather than building a new line.

The Slurry Transport Association, the major organization promoting coal-slurry lines, viewed the ETCO plan with reservations, noting that it may take more water to make the methanol than to slurry the coal. Other energy spokesmen pointed to the technological problem of separating the coal and methanol as well as the strong railroad opposition to any form of slurry line that would carry the railroads' major and most promising source of traffic, coal.

Rail transport. Amtrak announced that it had started a four-year program to resurface more than 400 mi of track in the Boston-to-Washington Northeast Corridor. To expedite the program, it was using an automatic track laying system (TLS). The TLS, which is run by a 160-man crew, consists of 15 machines that can completely renew track and ballast about 3½ times as fast as conventional equipment. The heart of the TLS is a $1.5-million track laying machine (TLM), which can replace old rail and ties with continuous welded rail and concrete ties at a rate of 1,200 ft an hour.

Preceding the TLM, at the front of a train that stretches a mile and a half, is a machine that lifts the track with electromagnets, cleans and replaces the ballast, and then realigns the track with a laser beam. Next come men and machines to pull spikes and anchors, followed by cars carrying enough ties for a mile of track.

Behind the tie cars is the TLS, its front riding on the old rail and its rear on the new rail. The machine picks up old ties and moves them forward by an overhead conveyor to a tie exchange car, where a crane picks them up and carries them to a flatcar. The crane returns with new ties for the tie exchange car, from which they are conveyed to the TLM for placement. The TLM pushes the old rail to the shoulders, places the new ties, and, after workers have placed tie pads on the ties, threads the new rail onto the pads. Behind the TLM men and machines install rail clips and insulators, add new ballast, tamp the roadbed, and align the track.

Two western U.S. railroads continued tests on new rail flatcars for moving trailers and containers. Stressing reduction in the weight of the cars so that they can carry larger payloads and still reduce consumption of fuel, the Atchison Topeka & Santa Fe Railway Co. successfully tested a skeleton-type car and announced plans to build a train of them. The train will consist of 11 of the articulated cars, each carrying ten trailers and/or containers. Fuel savings of up to 15% were predicted because the train would weigh about 35% less than conventional piggyback trains. The highly specialized cars would not be designed for interchange with other roads, and thus would serve Santa Fe routes with a potential for high-volume merchandise traffic.

The Southern Pacific Transportation Co. ran tests of a specialized type of flatcar which would be able to carry two 40-ft containers one on top of the other. It is about 45% lighter and much shorter than present trailer and container flatcars. The bottom container rests in a recessed well, and the top of the upper container is no higher than an auto carrier, thus avoiding any road clearance problems.

Another highly specialized type of railroad car designed to replace conventional equipment is the Roadrailer, a truck trailer able to operate on rails as well as highways through use of a dual steel rubber-tired wheel system. Built by the Bi-Modal Corp., the trailers are linked together to form a train and thus do not require flatcars. By eliminating the latter, Bi-Modal claimed sizable savings in train weight, equipment costs, and fuel consumption. Extensive tests of two Roadrailers were completed at the DOT Test Center at Pueblo, Colo., and actual on-the-road operations with one or more trains were scheduled for 1979 provided clearance could be obtained from the Federal Railroad Administration to operate under an exemption from normal rail freight train safety rules.

Canadian Pacific Ltd. announced that it was installing a closed-circuit television system to allow clerks at a Toronto yard to read railway car numbers with better than 95% accuracy in trains moving at up to 60 mph. Unlike standard closed-circuit television systems, which tend to blur numbers at speeds above six to eight miles per hour, the new one uses videotape to record the car numbers in frames of $1/1,000$ second each. The clerk can then view the tape when he needs the information, stopping it at any frame. The system will cost the railroad $900,000 for installation and a five-year lease and maintenance contract, but it is expected to save $225,000 a year in labor and car detention costs.

Water transport. A number of innovations were reported as part of an effort to extend the navigation season on the Great Lakes and the St. Lawrence Seaway. One was the use of ice booms, which consist of floating wooden timbers connected by chains to a steel cable anchored to the river bottom and installed several hundred feet apart along ship channels. They confine icepacks close to the shore and also help to promote formation along the channels of a stable ice cover that can more easily be broken by icebreakers and cargo ships equipped for cold-weather navigation. The St. Lawrence Seaway Development Corp., using a 422-ft by 80-ft scale model filled with 130,000 gal of water and built to represent a 13-mi section of the St. Lawrence River, demonstrated how such ice booms work.

Another innovation, as reported in an analysis by the U.S. Army Corps of Engineers, is the use of air-bubblers, submerged perforated pipes that release air under low pressure. The bubbling effect keeps the ice from consolidating along channels, especially at turns and in docking areas. The analysis by the Corps also proposed consideration of fixed all-weather navigation aids (towers with lights and radar transponders and reflectors) to replace floating aids that have to be removed in winter; a long-range radio navigation system (which was being installed); emergency vessel-location transmitters; airborne radar; and the use of satellite imagery.

A new cold-weather ship promises extended navigation in the arctic regions to four months, compared with the normal six weeks or less. The Canadian icebreaker cargo ship "N/V Arctic" scheduled trips during July through October to haul lead-zinc concentrate from mines on Baffin Island to The Netherlands. Double-hulled and equipped with an air-bubbler system to

Liquefied natural gas (LNG) tanker built by General Dynamics Corp. returns from successful sea trials in the Atlantic Ocean. The 936-foot, 125,000-cubic meter ship was scheduled to carry LNG between Indonesia and Japan.

reduce the friction of ice on its hull, the $38 million ship also was equipped with a ducted controllable-pitch propeller, which enabled it to travel through ice up to two feet thick. It also had a landing pad to permit use of helicopters for reconnaissance purposes. During winter it was scheduled to be used in the upper Great Lakes.

The U.S. Maritime Administration introduced the design of a new multipurpose ship that would have the capability of handling roll-on/off, lift-on/off, containerized, and oversized cargoes. The agency claimed a high degree of confidence in the design to meet U.S. military requirements, but the question of its commercial feasibility must still be answered. One commercial market could be the growing intermodal trade with less developed nations, which generally did not have the terminal facilities to handle large container ships.

The basic design of the ship called for a capacity of 16,550 deadweight tons, a speed of 20.7 knots, adjustable stern ramps, and interior between-deck ramps for roll-on/off cargo. It would be equipped with five cranes for containers and heavy-lift freight, as well as hatches on all lower decks for container storage. Its container capacity would be 926 units measuring 20 ft by 8 ft by 8 ft. A jumbo model, with a 110-ft supplemental midsection, could handle 1,286 such containers and would be fitted with a gantry and large roll-on/off ramps. An austere version would have a straight ramp but no interior ramps, giving it a capacity of 1,064 containers.

Seeking to break a virtual monopoly by the British in the large amphibious hovercraft market, a French firm, Sedam, built a $30 million, 70-mph hovercraft to compete in the heavy-volume, passenger/auto ferry business across the English Channel between France and the U.K. Called the N-500, it could carry 400 passengers and 60 autos, and Sedam claimed that it employs an improved skirt system for better entrapment of the air beneath its hull.

Earlier during the year, the British Hovercraft Corp. inaugurated cross-channel ferry service with its SRN 4 Mk 3, a 300-ton craft with a new flexible skirt to provide a ride on a cushion of air more than ten feet thick, thus permitting rough-weather operations. With a beam of 94 ft and length of 185 ft, the manufacturer claimed a more comfortable ride for its passengers than on smaller hovercraft. Power was provided by four Rolls-Royce marine proteus gas turbines for lift, plus a large variable-pitch propeller engine for directional control.

—Frank A. Smith

U.S. science policy

Two conflicting themes characterized U.S. science policy in 1978. On the one hand, government officials —from the president down—sought to draw attention to the generous support that the Carter administration was providing for the conduct of research and development, especially fundamental research. Indeed, the level of funding had risen after a decade of declining support, although the actual turnaround had taken place in the administration of Gerald Ford. On the other hand, the academic community—responsible for the conduct of most basic research in the United States— was voicing grave concerns about a variety of government restraints on the conduct of research on university campuses.

Two faces of federal policy. Some of the significant trends in federal support of research—both favorable and unfavorable—were spelled out in the first annual report on science and technology, submitted to the U.S. Congress in October 1978 by the National Science Foundation and the President's Office of Science and Technology Policy. The report noted that while federal support of research and development (R and D) had declined 17% in constant dollars between 1969 and 1975, it had climbed 14% in the three succeeding years. The increase in federal support of basic research (again in constant dollars) had risen even faster—25% since 1976.

Giving especially generous support to basic research in order to compensate for the alarming deficits of the 1966–76 decade was the proclaimed policy of the Carter administration. This was evident in its budget for fiscal year (FY) 1979, which provided an increase of 5% in constant dollars over FY 1978. The overall increase in federal support of R and D barely outpaced inflation, however—1% in constant dollars, compared with a 3% growth rate from 1977 to 1978. The largest increases in R and D went to national defense, space research and technology, transportation, and health.

In proposing ample increases in federal funds for basic research, the Office of Management and Budget recognized the severe pressures that had recently come to bear on the academic research community. The administration's budget for basic research, OMB said, was intended to "assist in ameliorating some of the problems currently associated with the performance of research in colleges and universities, including the growing obsolescence of equipment and the lack of opportunities for young investigators."

It seemed to a number of university administrators, however, that what the government was disbursing with one hand, it was taking away with the other. Particularly galling were recent OMB decisions to disallow certain university expenses as not falling within the category of reimbursable expenditures and to impose new, onerous reporting requirements.

Nowhere were these concerns more angrily expressed than at the annual meeting of the National Council of University Research Administrators in Washington, D.C. The effect was all the greater in that the speaker was Jerome Wiesner, president of the

Massachusetts Institute of Technology and the widely respected science adviser to Pres. John F. Kennedy. "The basic relationship between the federal government and the research community, after nearly three decades of the most fruitful partnership, is floundering," he said. "Indeed, it has begun to deteriorate and come apart so badly that we have reached a point of crisis. . . ."

Wiesner ticked off the major concerns of the university scientific community. There was a prevailing suspicion that since the research budget was in the "discretionary" portion of the federal budget, it would be among the first victims of any administration cutbacks in the fight against inflation. Because federal support mechanisms were spread throughout many federal agencies, there was, on one hand, not enough money to provide research support for good young scientists and, on the other, a shortage of good researchers to exploit promising areas of research. The proliferation of government regulations concerning increased accountability, protection of human subjects, equal employment opportunity, environmental pollution, and the like was so great that research investigators were forced to spend more and more time filling out forms. The growing unwillingness of the Department of Health, Education, and Welfare (under OMB pressure) to share the costs of maintaining essential nonlaboratory facilities, such as research libraries, forced universities to divert an increasing amount of their budgets to campus facilities that previous administrations had en-couraged them to build. Additional strains on university budgets developed as the result of a congressional mandate that forbade the National Science Foundation to reimburse universities for faculty salaries at a rate higher than the top range of civil service employees in federal agencies.

Wiesner also agreed with the administration's own science report that laboratory instruments available to do research were rapidly growing obsolete. He estimated that the current deficit in laboratory equipment on university campuses was in the neighborhood of $150 million–200 million. Even more alarming, there was beginning to be a deficit in basic research itself.

The distinction between basic and applied research is partly a matter of semantics. In the main, basic research is the search for new knowledge rather than for the solution to a specific problem encountered in the development of, for example, a product or a medical treatment. Most basic research is performed in universities with support from the federal government. During the last several decades a substantial fraction of basic research has been conducted in high-technology industry, principally electronics, communications, and materials. But from management's viewpoint basic research is a long-term investment, and in times of high interest rates the attractiveness of long-term investments diminishes. Accordingly, many sectors of industry have terminated their basic-research activities.

At the same time, Wiesner pointed out, the federal government has become wedded to the concept of the

U.S. government science officials (left) meet with their Chinese counterparts in Peking. The meetings opened the way for closer intergovernmental science relations between the two countries.

Courtesy, Executive Office of the President, Office of Science & Technology Policy

quick payoff. He noted subtle policy changes at a number of granting agencies, the net result of which has been an increase in funding for applied research at the expense of basic research. Uppermost in Wiesner's mind—and in the minds of many other university administrators—was the fear that some fundamental shift was taking place in the relationship between the universities and the federal government, a partnership that over the course of recent decades had brought science in the United States to a position of undisputed world leadership.

The scientific community received sympathy from an unexpected quarter. Sen. William Proxmire (Dem., Wis.) had earned a fearsome reputation among the recipients of federal grants through his periodic dispensation, from his powerful position on the Senate Appropriations Committee, of "Golden Fleece" awards to research projects he found particularly undeserving. But in his committee's report on an appropriations bill for independent agencies was the following statement: "The committee is concerned that to many knowledgeable observers the federal research project system appears to have become overly complex, burdensome, and less responsive to the needs of the nation. . . . In the committee's view, it is time for a comprehensive, objective review of the funding relationships between the federal government and the research universities. . . ." To many outside Washington, it seemed evident that the comprehensive review could well begin with the U.S. Congress. Many of the most restrictive regulations imposed by federal granting agencies had been mandated by legislative actions.

Changing science faculties. Still another concern among the leaders of the scientific enterprise was the changing nature of science faculties. The rapid growth of federal support for academic research during the period 1958–68 led to an increase in the number of graduate students in science and a concomitant enlargement of the science faculties. Many or most faculty members were receiving at least part of their salaries from research-support funds, and, in what turned out to be misplaced optimism, universities awarded tenure generously to their burgeoning science departments. But with the falling off in federal research funds and the subsequent decrease in the number of graduate students, the universities found themselves with a superfluity of tenured faculty, many of them relatively young. It was apparent to all that there would be few new faculty positions until mandatory retirement forced out the older professors. Panic began to set in when Congress enacted legislation postponing mandatory retirement until age 70.

By 1978 one result was already apparent. A report issued near year's end by the National Research Council provided clear evidence that universities were hiring increasing numbers of scientists and engineers in temporary research appointments that were not part of the

regular tenure track. According to the data gathered by the council, the number of Ph.D. scientists holding postdoctoral appointments, research staff positions, and other nonfaculty appointments grew considerably faster than the number of faculty members during 1973–77. While the nonfaculty segment rose 16% from 1973 to 1975 and 19% from 1975 to 1977, total science and engineering faculties grew 14% and 8%, respectively.

The data also showed that the nonfaculty staff were younger than their faculty counterparts, earned considerably less, but did a great deal more research. While chemists in doctoral research staff positions, for instance, devoted 86.6% of their time to research and 3.9% to teaching, chemistry faculty members spent 43.6% of their time on research and 42.2% on teaching. Of the nontenured chemists on research staffs more than 85% received federal support, compared with a little more than 50% of the tenured faculty.

The implications for the future of the U.S. research program were all too clear. The heart of the U.S. research enterprise, in contrast to its European counterparts, has been the linking of basic research programs with graduate education in the sciences, enabling students to conduct legitimate research in the context of their university training and science faculties to maintain their research skills while benefiting from continuing interaction with bright young students. Now it appeared that this successful structure was beginning to fall apart through lack of attention.

Partly because of this shifting structure in academic science, a group of experts was assembled by the National Academy of Sciences toward the end of 1978 to help the government anticipate funding needs over the next five years. Their major findings:

Total undergraduate enrollment in U.S. colleges and universities will enter a period of decline during the next five years, chiefly because of the fall in the birthrate. Graduate-school enrollment, however, will continue to grow in both the scientific and nonscientific fields.

Somewhat paradoxically, the total number of doctorates to be awarded over the next five years will decline gradually, despite an increase in the number of graduate students. Declining undergraduate enrollments will mean a reduction in the need for new faculty members with doctoral degrees. A substantial part of the decline in doctorates will be accounted for in the fields of physics, chemistry, mathematics, and engineering.

The relative unavailability of university faculty openings will cause a greater number of persons with postgraduate education in the sciences to seek positions in industry, government, and nonprofit research organizations. Special measures may be required to ensure the retention of scientists in the academic world.

The rapid growth in the relative number of female graduate students and in the number of female holders of doctoral degrees will slacken somewhat. There will

"That's it? That's peer review?"

be a slow but continuing increase in the numbers of women in the sciences and engineering. The declining need for faculty members will limit the job prospects for women with recent doctoral degrees. The outlook for minority students, particularly blacks and those of Latin-American ancestry, is for continued slow improvement in the number of doctoral recipients.

Although federal assistance for academic science has increased modestly in recent years and may continue to do so, the universities will be under growing pressure to raise their share of the funding, which currently amounts to more than 20%. The decline in federal funding during the period 1968–74, combined with inflation and the rising number of scientific investigators within the universities, ensures that the years ahead will be a time of frugality within academic science. Universities and government will have to find ways to cope with the problems of aging buildings, obsolescent equipment, and rising support costs.

The DNA controversy. In 1978 as in previous years, some of the liveliest public debates about science policy centered on ethical and moral considerations inherent in scientific research: the protection of human subjects in experimental situations, fetal research, and so-called genetic engineering through the application of recombinant DNA techniques. Of all these subjects,

the last continued to be the most controversial. It had been a matter of public debate since 1974, when a committee of scientists asked for a worldwide moratorium on certain kinds of laboratory experiments in which the hereditary material of one organism was transferred to another. The researchers asked their colleagues to go slowly until there was assurance that the work would not produce some highly virulent new pathogen entirely resistant to natural or man-made controls.

Because the appeal was made publicly and because subsequent discussions of the subject received wide coverage in the media, considerable public concern was generated over the issue. By 1978, however, it had become evident that the likelihood of some new lethal strain being developed was almost zero. The organisms used in the experiments could not, it appeared, survive outside the laboratory. Even more important, it became clear that any new strains that could be developed would be far less hazardous than some of the organisms handled routinely in any modern hospital. Some scientists who had originally argued against the need for restrictions—including Nobel laureate James D. Watson—now trumpeted their scorn for the cautious approach of their colleagues. Some began to wonder whether the mistake had lain not in worrying about the

Children with hearing impairments are often integrated with normal children in classrooms, a procedure described as "mainstreaming." This controversial practice is a response to the Education for All Handicapped Children Act of 1975.

potential hazards of the technique but in worrying about them publicly.

Sen. Adlai E. Stevenson III (Dem., Ill.), chairman of the Senate Subcommittee on Science, Technology, and Space, strongly rejected this view: "Since 1974, a great many scientists have come to doubt their own wisdom or that of their colleagues in questioning the safety of recombinant DNA research and making it a public issue. This attitude is both regrettable and largely unfounded. Scientists should derive a great deal of satisfaction from the recent course of events. Congress has not passed restrictive legislation of the sort once contemplated. States and communities have acted responsibly. Research proceeds at an increasingly rapid and productive pace. Most importantly, the recombinant DNA debate has been exceedingly instructive for dealing with future technologies promising significant scientific and social benefits but possibly at some risk."

Reports from the National Institutes of Health suggested that recombinant DNA research was indeed proceeding apace. The number of NIH research projects using recombinant DNA techniques had more than doubled to nearly 500; bacteria had been artificially refashioned to produce small amounts of such enormously valuable biological products as insulin and somatostatin; and a number of pharmaceutical houses were preparing to enter the field on a commercial basis.

Dissident Soviet scientists. One issue that aroused a fair amount of relatively well-mannered debate within the scientific community in 1978 had to do with the plight of a small number of Soviet scientists. The issue was more or less limited to scientists who worked at the higher levels of international collabora-

tion in research projects, but those who were concerned were fiercely concerned, and a growing number of them took action.

Their focus was a series of repressive measures used by the Soviet government against a small number of scientists who had sought to call attention to alleged Soviet violations of the Helsinki agreement on human rights. These included harsh prison sentences meted out at trials from which U.S. correspondents were excluded. A number of U.S. scientists scheduled to attend scientific conferences in the Soviet Union suddenly canceled their plans. A few U.S. government delegations did likewise.

Despite the intensity of the U.S. scientists' feelings, the U.S. scientific community was by no means unanimous in believing that such boycotts were useful. Even among scientists with the gravest concerns in this area, there was almost an even split over whether the boycotts might not be counterproductive. Those in favor of the boycotts argued that, since the U.S.S.R. had more to gain from scientific exchange than the U.S., the coupling of scientific exchange with protests against repression would have positive effects. If the exchanges continued at their current level, the Soviets would be unlikely to take verbal protests seriously.

Scientists who opposed the boycotts argued that the best way to reduce tension between the two countries was through continuation of the exchange program, and that the more Soviet scientists learn about the U.S., the more sensitive they will be to repression in their own country. Finally and perhaps most persuasively, they pointed out that boycotts were opposed by the dissident Soviet scientists themselves.

—Howard J. Lewis

404

Scientists of the Year

Honors and awards

The following is a selective list of recent awards and prizes in the areas of science and technology.

Anthropology

Distinguished Service Award. The American Anthropological Association presented 1978 Distinguished Service Awards to William W. Howells and to Nathalie F. S. Woodbury. Howells, emeritus professor of anthropology and curator of somatology at the Peabody Museum of Harvard University, was cited for fundamental research and for technical writings on human growth, biological variations, and evolution. Woodbury, who has held many elective and appointive offices in learned societies and high editorial positions with scholarly journals, was honored for "creative and caring leadership" and for "an unsurpassed contribution" to the profession of anthropology.

Stirling Award. The American Anthropological Association presented its 1978 Stirling Award in Culture and Personality Studies to Susan Abbott and Ruben Klein as co-authors of a paper entitled "Symptoms of Depression and Anxiety Among Rural Kikuyu in Kenya." Abbott is a postdoctoral fellow at the University of California, Berkeley, on leave from the University of Kentucky. Klein, an associate professor at the Instituto de Matematica Pura e Aplicada in his native Brazil, has expertise in data analysis, contingency tables, and multivariate analysis.

Architecture and civil engineering

Brown Medal. The Franklin Institute of Philadelphia presented its 1978 Frank P. Brown Medal to Henry J. Degenkolb, a consulting engineer whose company is based in San Francisco. Degenkolb was honored for his leadership in designing earthquake-resistant structures and for his part in having provisions for earthquake resistance incorporated into building codes.

Honor Awards. In 1978 Honor Awards were extended to 15 structures or complexes by the American Institute of Architects. The list includes a private residence on eastern Long Island, N.Y. (Howard Barnstone, Morey & Hollenbeck, William Chafee); Kearns/Daynes/Alley Annex in Salt Lake City, Utah (Boyd A. Blackner & Associates); Center Stage in Baltimore, Md. (James R. Grieves Associates, Inc.); Institute of Contemporary Art in Boston (Graham Gund Associ-

ates, Inc.); the Robert Elliott house in Chevy Chase, Md. (Hugh Newell Jacobsen); Cooper-Hewitt Museum in New York City (Hardy Holzman Pfeiffer Associates); Turtle Bay Towers in New York City (Bernard Rothzeid & Partners); Faneuil Hall Marketplace in Boston (Benjamin Thompson & Associates, Inc.); Sixty-01 apartments in Redmond, Wash. (George Bissell/Frank August and Associates); a private residence in Geyserville, Calif. (Chester Bowles, Jr.); the Art-Drama-Music Complex of Columbia Basin Community College in Pasco, Wash. (Brooks Hensley Creager Architects); IBM Santa Teresa Laboratory in San Jose, Calif. (MBT [McCue Boone Tomsick] Associates); the Yale Center for British Art in New Haven, Conn. (Louis I. Kahn; design and construction completed by Pellecchia and Meyers Architects); the Art Institute of Chicago (Skidmore, Owings & Merrill); and Three "H" Services Center in Houston, Texas (John Zemanek).

P/A Awards. Over 900 projects were submitted to *Progressive Architecture* for its annual awards. Among the structures that received special commendation for outstanding architectural design was the highly unusual Ruck-A-Chucky Bridge, commissioned by the U.S. Bureau of Reclamation for a site some 35 mi from Sacramento, Calif. The most striking feature of

Ruck-A-Chucky Bridge

Hedrich Blessing

Eugene N. Parker

the bridge, which spans 1,300 ft across a reservoir, is its high-strength steel cables arranged to create an array of spidery tensile forces that produce pure axial compression in the curved deck. The vertical-force components of the cables balance the weight of the deck, and the support cables come directly out of the hillside from between the trees. The structural engineering was done by T. Y. Lin International; Hanson Engineers Inc. served as engineering consultants and Skidmore, Owings & Merrill as architects.

Astronomy

Arctowski Medal. The National Academy of Sciences presented the 1978 Henryk Arctowski Medal and a $5,000 honorarium to John R. Winckler of the University of Minnesota for his work on solar modulation and acceleration of high-energy particles, and for his discovery of solar-flare gamma rays and auroral X-rays.

Cannon Award. Paula Szkody, an astrophysicist at the University of Washington and a visiting researcher at the California Institute of Technology, received the 1978–79 Annie Jump Cannon Award in Astronomy from the American Association of University Women. Szkody, credited with the first observations of photometric eclipses in AM Herculis, conducted research in visible and infrared photometry of dwarf novae and related close binary systems.

Eddington Medal. The Royal Astronomical Society, London, bestowed its Eddington Medal on William A. Fowler of the California Institute of Technology for his contributions to nuclear astrophysics. The citation called special attention to Fowler's pioneering work "on the origin of the chemical elements; element production in massive objects; the role of the universal fireball and the production of helium; and the importance of entropy considerations."

Einstein Award. The Albert Einstein Award, which consists of a gold medal and an honorarium of $15,000 supplied by the Lewis and Rosa Strauss Memorial Fund, was given in 1978 to Stephen W. Hawking, an astrophysicist and mathematician at the University of Cambridge. Hawking was honored for his studies of black holes and exceptionally strong gravitational fields.

Hale Prize. Eugene N. Parker was named first recipient of the biennial George Ellery Hale Prize by the solar physics division of the American Astronomical Society. Parker, a professor at the Enrico Fermi Institute for Nuclear Studies of the University of Chicago, was cited "for his imaginative and stimulating contributions in which plasma and magnetohydrodynamical physics have been applied to astronomy." Specific research focused on the origin and propagation of galactic cosmic rays; the expansion of solar and stellar winds; the interaction of the solar wind with the terrestrial magnetic field; the formation of sunspots; and the origins of solar, stellar, and cosmic magnetic fields.

Oppenheimer Prize. The Center for Theoretical Studies at the University of Miami in Florida bestowed its 1978 J. Robert Oppenheimer Memorial Prize on Jocelyn Bell Burnell, a research scientist at the Mullard Space Science Laboratory of University College, London. Burnell, the first woman to receive the award since its inauguration in 1969, was selected for her role in discovering pulsating radio sources (pulsars).

Pierce Prize. James M. Moran, Jr., an astronomer associated with Harvard University and the Smithsonian Astrophysical Observatory, received the 1978 Newton Lacy Pierce Prize from the American Astronomical Society for his contributions to very-long-baseline interferometry. The citation noted his "development of powerful data-handling methods, the planning and execution of many VLBI observations, and the mapping of interstellar maser sources with sub-milliarc-second resolution.''

Russell Lecture. Maarten Schmidt, director of the Hale Observatories in California, received the most prestigious award of the American Astronomical Society when he was named Henry Norris Russell Lecturer for 1978. Schmidt's citation noted that he was "the first to recognize the significance of the peculiar spectra of the quasi-stellar radio sources: that they were 'normal' spectral features highly red-shifted.'' The discovery opened an entire new field in astronomy.

Warner Prize. The 1978 Helen B. Warner Prize of the American Astronomical Society was presented to David N. Schramm of the Enrico Fermi Institute of the University of Chicago for his "incisive and energetic application of nuclear physics to a wide range of astrophysical problems . . . from the elemental composition of the solar system to the age—and future—of the universe.''

Chemistry

Cresson Medal. The Franklin Institute presented a 1978 gold Elliott Cresson Medal to Herbert C. Brown and to Frank H. Stillinger. Brown, professor emeritus of Purdue University and an international figure in his field, was honored for synthesis of diborane and borohydrides, and for the discovery of hydroboration as a method for the synthesis of organic compounds. Stillinger, who heads the chemical physics research department of Bell Laboratories in Murray Hill, N.J., was commended for developing a model for liquid water, which indicates that water is composed of a disorderly, but not totally random, network of molecules. This research not only benefited Bell, but also was successfully applied in meteorology (to predict the severity of thunderstorms and to stimulate rain), in biology (to determine how water influences protein molecules), in pharmacology (to predict the potential effectiveness of new drugs in the human body's aqueous environment), and in solar energy technology (to explain the conversion of light to energy in liquid-junction solar cells).

Franklin Medal. The 1978 Franklin Medal was awarded to Elias J. Corey of Harvard University "for development of reagents and methods for the synthesis of complex organic molecules, including a number of natural products never before synthesized, and for development of computer-assisted approaches to organizing the logic of synthesis. The first achievement has made available valuable natural products (including such rare therapeutic drugs as the prostaglandins) from inexpensive and abundant raw materials; the second has provided researchers with an invaluable tool for planning organic synthesis. Professor Corey is considered one of the world's foremost organic chemists. His name is synonymous with the discovery and exploi-

tation of numerous versatile synthetic reagents; his work has increased understanding of the vital forces maintaining life.''

Inventor of the Year. The Association for the Advancement of Invention and Innovation named Barbara S. Askins Inventor of the Year for 1978. Askins, a chemist at the Marshall Space Flight Center in Alabama, devised a method for intensifying underexposed photographic images. The process has proved its value in astronomy, medical radiology, and biological research. Askins's autoradiographic intensification process has been employed, for example, to salvage far-ultraviolet photographs of the nebula in Orion that had been drastically underexposed.

Nobel Prize. The Royal Swedish Academy of Sciences named Peter Mitchell recipient of the 1978 Nobel Prize for Chemistry. The British biochemist, whose Nobel honorarium amounted to $165,000, was honored for working out a plausible theory of how the cells of living creatures transfer the energy available in oxygen and sunlight into the essential compound adenosine triphosphate (ATP). The formation of ATP during intracellular chemical reactions is a way in which an organism conserves some of the energy liberated in those reactions instead of setting it free as heat that would be dissipated to its surroundings. The energy saved in the form of ATP can be recovered by the cells when the ATP takes part in reactions that require an external supply of energy in producing substances essential to the organism. In the animal cell a special structure, the mitochondrion—sometimes called the

Peter Mitchell

powerhouse of the cell—channels the energy from oxygen molecules into the formation of molecules of ATP; in the plant cell the chloroplast performs a similar function, obtaining the necessary energy from the photons of light. Though a great deal remains to be learned about the workings of this intricate apparatus, Mitchell's ideas have already shown their value by unifying and refocusing the research being conducted on this crucial problem in biochemistry.

Potts Medal. Michael Szwarc, director of the Polymer Research Center at the State University of New York College of Environmental Science and Forestry in Syracuse, was given the 1978 Howard N. Potts Medal by the Franklin Institute. Szwarc, a pioneer in the field of kinetics and thermodynamics of polymerization, inspired the development of new products, including new families of polystyrenes of controlled molecular sizes and synthetic rubbers that can be melted and injection-molded.

Priestley Medal. The American Chemical Society named Glenn T. Seaborg recipient of its prestigious 1979 Priestley Medal. The annual award, first bestowed in 1923, paid tribute to Seaborg's lifelong contributions to science and society. His fundamental work in expanding the periodic table and in making many new radioactive forms of elements has taken on vast importance in research, medicine, and energy-related fields. He and his colleagues discovered more than 100 isotopes and demonstrated that slow neutron bombardment induces the fission of plutonium-239 and uranium-233, which unlock, respectively, the energy stored in nonfissionable uranium-238 and thorium-232. Seaborg shared a Nobel Prize in 1951 for his research concerning the chemistry of the transuranium elements.

Rumford Medal. The Rumford Medal of the Royal Society was presented in 1978 to Sir George Porter, director of the Royal Institution of Great Britain. He was honored for developing the technique of flash photolysis, which permits the study of ultrafast chemical reactions. Unstable excited states are induced by very short but intense bursts of light. The properties of these short-lived species may then be measured by analyzing the spectrum produced when they are exposed to a second brief beam of light. Porter was also selected to deliver the 1978 Howard P. Robertson Memorial Lecture.

Welch Award. E. Bright Wilson of Harvard University received a gold medal and a $100,000 honorarium as recipient of the fourth Robert A. Welch Award in Chemistry. Wilson, one of the inventors of microwave spectroscopy, was selected by the Welch Foundation "for his pioneering theoretical and experimental contributions to molecular structure." His current work concerns conformation problems in hydrogen-bonded molecules.

Wetherill Medal. The Franklin Institute's 1978 John Price Wetherill Medal was presented to William A. Klemperer of Harvard University for his development of molecular beam techniques for understanding molecular structure. His theoretical and experimental work has proved valuable in such areas as biochemistry, petroleum refining, and atmospheric pollution.

Wolf Prize. Carl Djerassi of Stanford University, a leader in the development of oral contraceptives, was named first recipient of the Wolf Prize in chemistry. The Wolf Foundation in Israel also supplied a $100,000 honorarium for Wolf awards in the fields of agriculture, mathematics, medicine, and physics.

Earth sciences

AAAS-Rosenstiel Award. Henry M. Stommel, an oceanographer at the Massachusetts Institute of Technology, was presented with a $5,000 honorarium as recipient of the 1977 American Association for the Advancement of Science-Rosenstiel Award in Oceanographic Science. Stommel has specialized in currents, tides, eddies, and oceanic turbulence and circulation, and has developed the use of infrared photography for instantaneous recording of ocean water circulation.

Bowie Medal. The American Geophysical Union presented its annual William Bowie Medal to Helmut E. Landsberg in 1978 for his outstanding contributions to fundamental geophysics. Landsberg, professor emeritus at the University of Maryland, was cited for a lifetime of scientific achievements that have encompassed "the fields of geophysics, seismology, meteorology, climatology, air pollution, biometeorology, medical climatology, and urban meteorology."

Day Medal. The Geological Society of America presented its 1978 Arthur L. Day Medal to Samuel Epstein, a professor of geochemistry at the California Institute of Technology. His techniques of isotope measurements have been applied to such diverse fields of science as meteorology, hydrology, glaciology, petrology, biochemistry, plant physiology, climatology, and paleontology.

Day Prize and Lecture. John Verhoogen of the University of California at Berkeley received a $10,000 honorarium from the National Academy of Sciences as winner of the 1978 Arthur L. Day Prize and Lectureship. Verhoogen was specifically honored for his work on the thermodynamics of the Earth's core and mantle and in general for his overall contributions to Earth sciences.

Ewing Medal. The third annual Maurice Ewing Medal, jointly awarded by the U.S. Navy and the American Geophysical Union, was presented in 1978 to Sir Edward Bullard. After retiring from the University of Cambridge, Bullard was welcomed to the University of California's Scripps Institution of Oceanography as a leading authority on the geology of the oceans and on the Earth's magnetic field and upper mantle.

Jacques Nihoul

Francqui Prize. Jacques Nihoul of the universities of Liège and Louvain in Belgium was awarded the Francqui Prize, Belgium's highest scientific award, "for his contribution to the fundamental theory of hydrodynamic phenomena in oceans." The 1978 prize included an honorarium worth one million Belgian francs (about $30,000). From 1971 to 1976 Nihoul coordinated a comprehensive program designed to improve knowledge of the marine environment of the North Sea.

IMO Prize. The International Meteorological Organization, which annually honors an individual for outstanding scientific work and international collaboration, presented its 1978 award to Alf E. G. E. Nyberg, former director general of the Swedish Meteorological and Hydrological Institute.

Meisinger Award. The annual Meisinger Award of the American Meteorological Society is given for research that at least in part deals with the phenomena of the free air as revealed by kites, balloons, airplanes, and clouds. The 1979 recipient was John C. Wyngaard, who was cited "for his experimental and theoretical studies of turbulent processes in the boundary layer." Wyngaard is associated with the Cooperative Institute for Research in Environmental Sciences (CIRES) at the University of Colorado and with the Wave Propagation Laboratory of the National Oceanic and Atmospheric Administration (NOAA) in Boulder, Colo.

Penrose Medal. Robert M. Garrels of Northwestern University was named by the Geological Society of America recipient of its 1978 Penrose Medal. Garrels's most recent publication on the global nitrogen cycle and man was preceded by nearly a hundred other contributions that won him international recognition and numerous honors.

Rossby Medal. The 1979 Carl-Gustaf Rossby Research Medal, the highest honor of the American Meteorological Society, was awarded to Herbert Riehl, who was cited "for his outstanding analyses of tropical phenomena, ranging from studies of individual clouds, tropical depressions and hurricanes, to the trade wind inversion and the Hadley circulation." Riehl took leave from the National Center for Atmospheric Research to serve as senior scientist at CIRES and NOAA.

Second Half Century Award. The 1979 Second Half Century Award of the American Meteorological Society was given to J. Murray Mitchell, Jr., a senior research climatologist with the Environmental Data and Information Service of NOAA. Mitchell was cited "for his broad fundamental contributions to the study of climate and climate change, ranging in scope from ice ages to the effects of urbanization."

Electronics and information sciences

Goode Award. The American Federation of Information Processing Societies presented its 1978 Harry Goode Memorial Award to Gordon E. Moore and Robert N. Noyce, founders of Intel Corp. The two were cited for "their original contributions to semiconductor integrated circuit technology, their pioneering achievements in using this technology for the development and production of microprocessors and many other computer system components, and their distinguished leadership of and insight in computer science and technology, which have revolutionized the information processing field."

NAE Founder's Medal. John R. Pierce, a professor of engineering at the California Institute of Technology, was named by the National Academy of Engineering as recipient of its Founder's Medal. Pierce was chosen for his contributions to the development of electronic communications.

Pecora Award. Since 1974 the U.S. Department of the Interior and the National Aeronautics and Space Administration (NASA) have honored individuals or organizations that have made outstanding contributions in the field of remote sensing. The 1978 recipient of the William T. Pecora Award was David S. Johnson, director of the National Environmental Satellite Service of the Department of Commerce. The citation noted that Johnson "has devoted a major portion of his scientific and managerial life to the development and implementation of remote sensing systems designed to observe weather patterns, impacts of weather and man on our environment, the climatological trends of the Earth, and in the process eliminated or alleviated loss of property and life as a result of natural disasters."

Turing Award. The Association for Computing Machinery presented its 1978 A. M. Turing Award to Robert W. Floyd of Stanford University. He was cited for his contributions to "methodologies for the creation of efficient and reliable software" and for "helping to found the following important subfields of computer science: the theory of parsing, the semantics of programming languages, automatic program verification, automatic program synthesis, and analysis of algorithms."

Energy

Clark Medal. The 1978 Walton Clark Medal of the Franklin Institute was given to Paul N. "Red" Adair, president of Red Adair Co. Inc., in Houston, Texas. He was honored for the "development and use of advanced techniques in fighting oil- and gas-well fires, in capping wild wells, and in reducing the time required to control offshore blowouts." The Clark Medal was established in 1926 to call attention to notable advances in any phase of the technologies of combustible gases and other fuels or sources of energy.

Lawrence Award. The Ernest Orlando Lawrence Award was established in 1959 to honor scientists under the age of 46 for outstanding contributions to all areas of the sciences related to nuclear power. At a White House ceremony, 1977 awards were presented to James D. Bjorken of the Stanford Linear Accelerator Center for his "elegant theoretical contributions to elementary-particle physics, including the concept of scaling and the introduction of charm"; to John L. Emmett of the Lawrence Livermore Laboratory for his leadership in "the development of laser science and technology and . . . their application to the generation of nuclear and thermonuclear energy"; to F. William Studier of the Brookhaven National Laboratory for his work on the characterization of the genetic structure of the virus bacteriophage T7, which is linked to nuclear-power generation by the insights it offers to radiation-damage processes; to Gareth Thomas of the Lawrence Berkeley Laboratory for his "pioneering work in applying transmission electron microscopy to materials science and engineering"; and to Dean A. Waters of the Oak Ridge Gaseous Diffusion Plant for "his leadership and engineering inventiveness in the development of gas-centrifuge systems for the enrichment of uranium."

Environment

Getty Prize. The $50,000 J. Paul Getty Wildlife Conservation Prize for 1979 was given to Boonsong Lekagul by the World Wildlife Fund. The 71-year-old retired physician was described as "a lone voice in the wilderness, leading the fight for wildlife preservation, helping to create a national park system for Thailand, stimulating conservation education, and above all, inspiring young people to help safeguard their country's rich wildlife heritage." Boonsong was still a practicing physician in 1951 when he founded the Association for Conservation of Wildlife.

NWF Award. The National Wildlife Federation presented a special award in 1978 to Col. Donald A. Wisdom, district engineer for the Army Corps of Engineers at Jacksonville, Fla. Wisdom was lauded for "outstanding skill and leadership and his strong enforcement of Section 404 of the Water Pollution Control Act, [which] have resulted in the preservation of thousands of acres of precious wetlands which will benefit the public for years to come."

Tyler Award. The $150,000 John and Alice Tyler Ecology Award for 1977 was given to Russell E. Train, president of the World Wildlife Fund-U.S. His efforts to raise funds for conserving ecosystems, habitats, and species were described as great contributions to mankind. Train was the first chairman of the Council of Environmental Quality and served as administrator of the Environmental Protection Agency.

Zimmermann Award. Dean F. Martin of the University of South Florida was named recipient of the 1978 F. J. Zimmermann Award in Environmental Science. His many environmentally oriented projects include research on the encroachment of aquatic weeds that are clogging Florida lakes and streams and studies on ways in which to manage the health hazards that result from outbreaks of red tide, the discoloration of water caused by the presence of organisms called dinoflagellates in densities fatal to some forms of marine life.

Food and agriculture

Assinsel Award. The International Plant Breeders Association for the Protection of New Plant Varieties (Assinsel) presented its first quadrennial award to André C. Gallais of France. The new award is given for basic research that significantly improves methods of plant breeding for the benefit of agriculture and horticulture. Gallais was chosen for his biometrical study on heterosis in an allogamic autotetraploid species (alfalfa).

Borden Award. Hamish N. Munro of the Massachusetts Institute of Technology received the 1978 Borden Award in Nutrition. He was honored by the American Institute of Nutrition for his work on mammalian protein metabolism and nutrition.

Corson Medal and Elvehjem Award. The 1978 Bolton L. Corson Medal of the Franklin Institute was awarded to Jean Mayer, president of Tufts University in Massachusetts. Mayer, who was cited for his role as a scientist, writer, and administrator in furthering knowledge and understanding of human nutrition, has been associated with the UN Food and Agriculture Organization, the World Health Organization, and the President's Commission on World Hunger. The American Institute of Nutrition also honored Mayer by bestowing on him its 1978 Conrad A. Elvehjem Award.

Goldberger Award. The American Medical Association named Lloyd J. Filer, Jr., recipient of its 1978 Joseph B. Goldberger Award in Clinical Nutrition. Filer, the author of more than 100 publications, is widely recognized as an authority on the nutritional requirements of infants. A professor with the University of Iowa College of Medicine, he has also served with numerous agencies, including the National Institutes of Health and the U.S.-Japan Cooperative Medical Science Program.

Humboldt Award. The 1978 Alexander von Humboldt Award was given to Carl H. Norris for his development of infrared reflectance spectroscopy, a simple, flexible, precise, and inexpensive method for measuring the chemical composition of seeds and many other plant materials. Norris's achievement is viewed as a major breakthrough in agricultural research and is likely to revolutionize the analysis of the protein of cereal grains and oilseeds. The equipment he developed measures the amount of reflected infrared light and automatically computes oil, protein, moisture, and other chemical components in less than two minutes. Norris, a member of the U.S. Department of Agriculture's Science and Education Administration, is chief of the Beltsville (Md.) Agricultural Center's Instrumentation Research Laboratory.

McCormick Medal. The American Society of Agricultural Engineers presented its 1978 Cyrus Hall McCormick Medal to Russell R. Poynor "for exceptional and meritorious engineering achievement in agriculture." Before his retirement Poynor was safety manager of the agricultural equipment division of International Harvester Co.

Osborne and Mendel Award. The American Institute of Nutrition presented the 1978 Osborne and Mendel Award of the Nutrition Foundation to Donald B. McCormick of Cornell University for his fundamental research concerning the metabolism and metabolic functions of coenzymes derived from essential micronutrients.

Life sciences

BSA Merit Award. The Botanical Society of America presented 1978 Merit Awards to Lyman D. Benson of Pomona College in California for outstanding teaching and taxonomic research on the flora of North America; to Theodore Delevoryas of the University of Texas for contributions to Mesozoic paleobotany; to Warren H. Wagner, Jr., of the University of Michigan for work on the morphology, classification, and evolution of ferns; and to W. Gordon Whaley of the University of Texas for his pioneering role in the elucidation of the cellular biology of plants.

Gairdner Awards. The Gairdner Foundation of Willowdale, Ont., presented three $10,000 prizes and two $5,000 prizes to scientists in 1978 for outstanding research in the life sciences. Sydney Brenner of the MRC Laboratory of Molecular Biology in Cambridge, England, received $10,000 for "his highly original and

conceptual contributions to molecular biology, and to the understanding of how genetic information is read and translated." Donald S. Fredrickson, director of the National Institutes of Health in Maryland, received a similar honorarium "for his contributions to our understanding of the genetic, biochemical and clinical aspects of the hyperlipoproteinemias." A $10,000 prize also went to Edwin G. Krebs of the University of Washington "for elucidating fundamental biochemical mechanisms related to glycogen breakdown, pioneer work that has enhanced our knowledge of hormone action." Lars Terenius of Uppsala University in Sweden and Jean-Pierre Changeux of the Institut Pasteur in France shared a $10,000 prize. Terenius was cited "for his development of radioreceptor methods, their application to opiates and the detection of an endogenous opiate-like substance in the nervous system." Changeux was honored for "his pioneering work in purifying and elucidating the mechanisms of the cholinergic receptor."

Lasker Award. Three persons shared the 1978 Albert Lasker Basic Medical Research Award "for contributions in the pharmacology of mechanisms involved in pain and its relief." Solomon H. Snyder of the Johns Hopkins School of Medicine was honored for discovering opiate receptors and locating their sites in the brain, research that "lies at the heart of attempts to solve the major human problems of the relief of pain, and the counteracting of narcotic addiction." Hans W. Kosterlitz of the University of Aberdeen, Scotland, and John Hughes of the Imperial College of Science and Technology in London shared the award for their research on the "newly discovered relationship between brain chemistry and nerve functions as they affect pain, narcotic addiction, and emotional behavior." Stimulated by Snyder's finds, Kosterlitz and Hughes isolated and characterized the structure of a new kind of brain chemical, which they named enkephalin. It mimics the actions of opiates on receptor sites and appears to modulate sensations and emotional reactions. It appears possible that abnormal concentrations of receptors or enkephalins can change the brain's control of other neurochemicals, leaving it vulnerable to aberrant chemical behavior and possibly producing emotional dysfunction.

Life Sciences Award. As recipient of the 3M Life Sciences Award for 1978, Leon A. Heppel of Cornell University was presented with a $15,000 honorarium. The Federation of American Societies for Experimental Biology cited Heppel's contributions to the understanding of active transport, bioenergetics, and nucleic acid structure. It also called attention to other work by Heppel, such as that on synthetic RNA and cyclic AMP, which laid the groundwork for research that resulted in Nobel Prizes for others.

Neuberg Medal. Ines Mandl, professor of reproductive biochemistry at Columbia University's College of

Physicians and Surgeons, was selected to receive the Carl Neuberg Medal by the Virchow-Pirquet Medical Society. Mandl, an authority on protein chemistry, was especially commended for her studies of collagen and elastin and the specific enzymes that degrade these proteins.

Passano Award. The Passano Foundation presented its 1978 award to Michael S. Brown and Joseph L. Goldstein of the University of Texas Health Science Center at Dallas. The co-recipients of the $12,000 honorarium were chosen because of their "brilliant work which unraveled the heretofore impenetrable yarn of blood cholesterol at levels of molecular physiology, human pathology, and genetics."

Rosenstiel Award. Barbara McClintock of the Cold Spring Harbor Laboratory in New York received the seventh annual Lewis Rosenstiel Award for Distinguished Work in Basic Medical Research from Brandeis University for pioneer work in genetic research that focused on the mechanics of chromosome separation and segregation. She found that the chromosomes of maize acquire different genetic control properties when they break and reassort.

Superior Service Award. T. Kent Kirk of the Forest Products Laboratory in Wisconsin received a Superior Service Award from the U.S. Department of Agriculture for his research project on the degradation of lignin by microorganisms. Lignin, the gluelike substance that binds the cellulose fibers of plants to one another, is now removed by mechanical or chemical means when plant materials are converted into paper and other products. Using microorganisms to degrade the lignin promises to reduce energy needs and pollution.

U.S. Steel Award. The National Academy of Sciences presented a $5,000 honorarium to Günter Blobel as recipient of the 1978 U.S. Steel Foundation Award in Molecular Biology. A professor of cell biology at Rockefeller University, Blobel was cited for his research on mechanisms by which secreted proteins pass into and across membranes.

Wakeman Award. Viktor Hamburger of Washington University, St. Louis, Mo., received the 1978 Wakeman Award for his research on the development of the nervous system. The award was established in 1971 to aid paraplegics by encouraging neurobiological research on the regeneration of the central nervous system.

Waksman Award. The National Academy of Sciences presented the 1978 Selman A. Waksman Award in Microbiology to Howard Green of the Massachusetts Institute of Technology. Green, who received a $5,000 honorarium, is well known for his research on cell differentiation, genetics, and cancer.

Wolf Prize. A $100,000 honorarium supplied by the Wolf Foundation was shared by George F. Sprague of the University of Illinois and John C. Walker of the University of Wisconsin. Sprague was selected for his work with hybrid corn, including the development of

mathematical models for corn genetics. He demonstrated that protein nourishment in corn was amenable to genetic manipulation. Walker was cited for his research on plant diseases and the role of soil and other environmental factors in their incidence.

Materials sciences

Extractive Metallurgy Science Award. The Metallurgical Society named J. Paul Pemsler and Carl Wagner recipients of the 1978 Extractive Metallurgy Science Award. Pemsler, director of new technology at EIC Corp. in Massachusetts, was cited for his extensive work "in extractive metallurgy of copper and nickel, thermodynamics, kinetics, materials science and energy technology." The award to Wagner was given posthumously. Before his death he was associated with the Max Planck Institute for Biophysical Chemistry in West Germany.

Extractive Metallurgy Technology Award. The 1978 Extractive Metallurgy Technology Award of the Metallurgical Society was presented to Takashi Suzuki and to Takeshi Nagano. Suzuki, an employee of Mitsubishi Metals Corp., is general manager of the Naoshima Smelter, which he helped design before taking charge of its operation. Nagano was involved in the development of a new injection smelting process, which was adopted by Mitsubishi for its continuous smelting and converting process at Naoshima.

Hume-Rothery Award. Karl A. Gschneidner, Jr., assistant program director for metallurgy and ceramics at the Ames Laboratory and director of the Rare-Earth Information Center (both at Iowa State University), received the 1978 William Hume-Rothery Award of the Metallurgical Society. He has done extensive research on the physical metallurgy of plutonium and of cerium-base alloys.

Mathewson Medal. The 1978 Champion H. Mathewson Gold Medal of the Metallurgical Society was given to C. Marvin Wayman. The University of Illinois professor was cited for his book on the crystallography of martensitic transformations and for numerous other writings that include such topics as electron microscopy.

Mathematics

Fields Medal. In 1978, during the quadrennial meeting of the International Congress of Mathematicians, Fields Medals were presented to four mathematicians under the age of 40. Pierre Deligne of the Institut des Hautes Études Scientifiques in France was honored for solving the Weil conjectures and for introducing a new strategy called weights theory, which has important applications in differential equations. Charles Fefferman of Princeton University was selected for several innovations in classical analysis that opened up new

Left, left to right, Pierre Deligne, Charles Fefferman, Daniel Quillen; above, Gregory A. Margulis

areas of study in the interface of harmonic analysis, complex analysis, and differential equations. Gregory A. Margulis, a Soviet mathematician, was cited for his analysis of Lie groups, which combine algebraic, geometric, and analytical structures into a single object. Lie groups have become a powerful tool in applied mathematics. Daniel Quillen of the Massachusetts Institute of Technology was chosen because he was chief architect of a new field known as algebraic K-theory, which has employed geometric and topological tools to solve major problems from algebra. For an extended discussion of the works of these four men, *see* Year in Review: MATHEMATICS.

Whitehead Prize. The London Mathematical Society awarded its third biennial Whitehead Prize to I. Mackenzie James in 1978. The Savilian Professor of Geometry at the University of Oxford was honored for his work in algebraic topology, particularly in homotopy theory.

Wolf Prize. Izrail M. Gelfand of Moscow State University and Carl L. Siegel of the Georg August University of Göttingen in West Germany shared a $100,000 honorarium as joint recipients of the 1978 Wolf Prize in the field of mathematics. Whereas Gelfand was selected for pioneer work in functional analysis, Siegel was chosen for significant contributions to the theory of numbers, celestial mechanics, and complex variables.

Medical sciences

Beaumont Award. H. Belton P. Meyer of Phoenix, Ariz., was named by the American Medical Association as recipient of its 1978 Dr. William Beaumont Award in Medicine. Meyer was selected for his contributions as a clinician, medical administrator, and innovator in transporting high-risk newborns from remote rural areas to special-care urban centers.

Bristol-Myers Award. James A. and Elizabeth C. Miller, a husband and wife team working at the McArdle Laboratory for Cancer Research at the University of Wisconsin, received the first annual $25,000 Bristol-Myers Award for Distinguished Achievement in Cancer Research. They were chosen for discovering that most chemicals must first be activated within the body before they can cause cancer.

Coolidge Award. Lawrence H. Lanzl of the University of Chicago was chosen by the American Association of Physicists in Medicine to receive the 1978 William D. Coolidge Award. Lanzl's credits include involvement in the removal of the electron beam from the betatron and its development for radiation therapy, and the use of computers for calculating dose distributions.

Distinguished Older American Award. In 1978 the American Aging Association named Russel V. A. Lee first recipient of its Distinguished Older American Award. Lee's achievements included the establishment of the Palo Alto (Calif.) Clinic, which became the prototype for group medical practice in small communities, and of Channing House, the widely copied retirement home in Palo Alto. He also wrote such books as *No Gravy on the Vest: The Art of Growing Old in Style.*

Distinguished Service Award. In 1978 the American Medical Association gave its Distinguished Service Award to William P. Longmire, Jr., of Los Angeles. In presenting its highest award the AMA noted Longmire's international reputation as a distinguished surgeon, clinician, and educator. It also lauded his many years of service on the editorial boards of such publications as *American Surgeon, Advances in Surgery, The Journal of Surgical Research, Surgery, Annals of Surgery,* and *The Journal of Surgical Technique.*

Gairdner Awards. The Gairdner Foundation of Ontario presented 1978 Gairdner Awards to four scien-

Werner Arber (left), Daniel Nathans (center), Hamilton Smith (right)

tists for outstanding medical research. Samuel O. Freedman and Phil Gold, both of McGill University, Montreal, shared a $10,000 prize for "their discovery of carcinoembryonic antigen, and for studies which elucidated its biological and clinical significance." James A. and Elizabeth C. Miller of the University of Wisconsin McArdle Laboratory for Cancer Research were named joint winners of a $10,000 prize for "their many important contributions to our understanding of how environmental chemicals, both naturally occurring and man made, induce cancer."

Herrick Award. The 1978 James B. Herrick Award, sponsored each year by the Council on Clinical Cardiology of the American Heart Association, was given to W. Proctor Harvey, director of cardiology at the Georgetown University School of Medicine.

Jacobi Award. The American Medical Association and the American Academy of Pediatrics presented the 1978 Abraham Jacobi Memorial Award to Sydney S. Gellis, chairman of the department of pediatrics at Tufts University School of Medicine.

Lasker Award. The 1978 Albert Lasker Clinical Medical Research Award of $15,000 was shared by three scientists for their roles in developing new vaccines. Michael Heidelberger of the New York University School of Medicine was cited for immunochemistry research that laid the groundwork for purified vaccines made from bacterial substances called polysaccharides. Robert Austrian of the University of Pennsylvania School of Medicine was honored for developing a vaccine against pneumococci bacteria. Emil C. Gotschlich of Rockefeller University received his award for developing a vaccine against meningitis, a brain inflammation caused by bacterial infection.

Nobel Prize. The 1978 Nobel Prize for Physiology or Medicine was shared by three microbiologists, Werner

Arber of Switzerland and Daniel Nathans and Hamilton O. Smith of the U.S. They were selected for the discovery and application of enzymes that break the giant molecules of DNA into manageable pieces, small enough to be separated for individual study but large enough to retain bits of the genetic information inherent in the sequence of units that make up the original substance.

Arber was born in 1929 and studied at the Swiss Federal Institute of Technology in Zürich, the University of Geneva, and the University of Southern California. Since 1970 he has been a professor at the University of Basel. He continued the work of Salvador Luria, who had observed that bacteriophages (viruses that infect bacteria) not only induce hereditary mutations in their bacterial hosts but at the same time undergo hereditary mutations themselves. Arber gathered evidence that the effects stemmed from the action of protective enzymes present in the bacterium that modified the DNA of the infecting virus. One of these, the restriction enzyme, restricts the growth of the bacteriophage by cutting the molecules of its DNA to pieces.

Smith was born in 1931 and attended the University of California at Berkeley and Johns Hopkins University. In 1973 he joined the faculty of the school of medicine at Johns Hopkins. Smith and his colleagues isolated a restriction enzyme that, unlike those studied by Arber, not only recognizes a specific region in a DNA molecule, but always breaks the DNA at that very site. This has made it uniquely valuable in molecular genetics.

Nathans was born in 1928 and attended the University of Delaware and Washington University. He joined Johns Hopkins in 1967. His investigation centered on the structure of the DNA of simian virus 40 (SV40), the simplest virus known to induce cancerous tumors. He found that Smith's enzyme broke the SV40 molecule into 11 fragments; he then used two other similar enzymes to break the viral DNA at other positions. He was thus able to deduce its entire constitution. This construction of a genetic map of a virus marked the first application of the new enzymes to the problem of identifying the molecular basis of cancer.

Order of Culture. Takashi Sugimura, a professor at the University of Tokyo and director of the Research Institute at Japan's National Cancer Centre, was awarded the Order of Culture in 1978. Sugimura was honored as the first research scientist to produce stomach cancer by chemical means.

Prix Griffuel. The 1978 Prix Griffuel, the highest scientific award offered by the government of France, was presented to Ludwik Gross, chief of cancer research at the Bronx Veterans Administration Hospital. He was honored for elucidating the concept that cancerous diseases, including leukemia and lymphomas, are caused by viruses that usually remain latent but may be triggered into action by radiation or carcinogenic chemicals.

Research Award. Kenneth R. Brizzee was named 1978 recipient of the American Aging Association's first annual Research Award. Brizzee was honored for developing "highly sophisticated and automated morphometric methods for quantitative evaluation of cell populations and lipofusin accumulation in the brain. This singular and outstanding achievement has made it possible to carry out a variety of studies of age-dependent alterations in sensory, learning, memory, and motor functions in relation to cell loss and lipofusin accumulation in specific regions of the brain."

Scientific Achievement Award. The American Medical Association named F. Mason Sones recipient of its 1978 Scientific Achievement Award. He was cited for his role in "the development of new and improved techniques for exploring the heart with special catheters and defining the morphology of the central circulation using high speed X-ray motion picture photography known as cine cardioangiography. He was the first to selectively opacify [cause to become opaque] and define the morphology of the coronary artery circulation in a living human."

WAS Award. The Washington Academy of Sciences Annual Award for scientific achievement in biological sciences was given in 1978 to John W. Kebabian of the National Institute of Neurological and Communicative Disorders and Stroke. He was cited for "demonstration of dopamine-sensitive adenyl cyclase in the mammalian striatum." Kebabian and his colleagues performed enzyme assays that demonstrated the presence and elucidated certain characteristics of two of five known types of cellular sites of dopamine action in the brain. Kebabian's work may lead to the development of improved antipsychotic drugs and to the control of Parkinson's disease.

Weicker Award. Ernest Bueding of Johns Hopkins University was named first recipient of the annual $10,-000 Theodore Weicker Memorial Award. The American Society for Pharmacology and Experimental Therapeutics, which administers the award for the Weicker Foundation, called attention to Bueding's internationally known research on filariasis and schistosomiasis, two major parasitic diseases.

Wolf Prize. Three persons shared the $100,000 Wolf Prize in medicine, one of five such prizes awarded by the Wolf Foundation in five different fields. The recipients were George D. Snell of the Jackson Laboratory in Maine, Jean Dausset of France, and Johannes J. Van Rood of The Netherlands. All three were honored for their research on antigens that figure in the immune response of humans and animals, including resistance to transplanted tissue.

Optical engineering

Creative Invention Award. The American Chemical Society presented its 1978 Award for Creative Invention to Legrand G. Van Uitert of Bell Laboratories. Van Uitert was cited for his work in polycrystalline ferrites, laser and fluorescent materials, nonlinear optical materials, single-crystal magnetic materials, and optical fibers. This research "brought into being the new generation of ferrites, garnets, and niobates upon which the recent laser, fluorescence, and magnetics technology has been based."

Industrial Applications of Physics Prize. The American Institute of Physics presented its first Industrial Applications of Physics Prize to Robert D. Maurer of the Corning Glass Works in New York. He was cited for contributions "made to the practical application of optical communications through the understanding and discovery of materials and techniques for the fabrication of glass fiber waveguides."

Ives Medal. The 1978 Frederic Ives Medal of the Optical Society of America was given to Harold H. Hopkins of the University of Reading, England. Hopkins was honored for his many contributions to optics, including advances in aberration theory, optical design, image evaluation, coherence theory, interferometry, and fiber optics.

Physics

Achievement in Physics Medal. John M. Robson of McGill University was named by the Canadian Association of Physicists recipient of the 1978 Medal for Achievement in Physics. After initial research on free neutron decay at Canada's National Research Council Atomic Energy Project, he conducted experiments that "made a substantial contribution to our knowledge of weak-interaction physics." More recently Robson's research has been in the areas of attenuation of neutrons and gamma rays in shielding materials, nuclear reactions, and the properties of ultracold neutrons.

Bingham Medal. The Society of Rheology awarded the 1978 Bingham Medal to Thor L. Smith, an IBM research scientist working in California. Smith has studied the rheological properties of rubbers, glassy polymers, dispersions, composites, and other types of materials, and has successfully related mechanical behavior in small deformations to phenomena observed in large deformations and to mechanical failure and rupture.

Boys Prize. The Institute of Physics in London named R. A. Sherlock of the University of Waikato in New Zealand and Adrian F. G. Wyatt of the University of Exeter in England recipients of the Charles Vernon Boys Prize for their work on the propagation of phonons in liquid and solid helium.

Comstock Prize. At intervals of five or more years, the National Academy of Sciences awards the Cyrus B. Comstock Prize to a resident of North America who is judged to have made the most important discovery or conducted the most important research involving electricity, magnetism, or radiant energy. In 1978 the $5,000 prize was given to Raymond Davis, Jr., of the Brookhaven National Laboratory for determining the intensity of neutrino radiation reaching the Earth.

Davisson-Germer Prize. Vernon W. Hughes of Yale University was awarded the 1978 Davisson-Germer Prize by the American Physical Society for his pioneering experiments on muonium (an "atom" composed of a positive muon nucleus orbited by an electron) and for his measurements of fundamental atomic properties and tests of quantum electrodynamics.

Europhysics Prize. The European Physical Society presented the 1978 Hewlett-Packard Europhysics Prize to Zhores I. Alferov of the A. F. Ioffe Physical-Technical Institute in Leningrad. Alferov, who received an honorarium worth about $13,000, was selected for his contribution to the development of a new type of semiconducting material that can be used to produce, among other things, highly efficient solar cells and lasers with continuous output.

Herzberg Medal. The Canadian Association of Physicists presented its 1978 Herzberg Medal to Walter N. Hardy of the University of British Columbia. His research interests include molecular and solid-state physics.

Hughes Medal. The Royal Society in London awarded the 1978 Hughes Medal to William Cochran of the University of Edinburgh for his contributions to crystallography and lattice dynamics. "He realized the importance of electron density distribution in solids, developed the necessary techniques and performed the first successful experiments in this field."

MacRobert Award. The £25,000 MacRobert Award, administered by the Council of Engineering Institutions, acknowledges outstanding contributions in engineering or physical technology that serve to enhance the prestige or prosperity of the United Kingdom. The 1977 award was given to a five-person team for developing the Malvern Correlator, an extremely sensitive instrument for measuring the movement of particles and molecules. Sharing the prize were Eric Jakeman, Robin Jones, Christopher Oliver, and Roy Pike, all members of the Royal Signals and Radar Establishment, and Stephen Trudgill of the Malvern Instruments Co.

Nobel Prize. The 1978 Nobel Prize for Physics was awarded jointly to a Soviet scientist and two Americans. Half of the honorarium was given to Pyotr Kapitsa of the Soviet Academy of Sciences for his research on the liquefaction of helium and the unusual qualities of helium in a liquid state. Kapitsa's work ushered in a

Left, left to right, Robert W. Wilson, Arno A. Penzias. Above, Pyotr Kapitsa

new era in low-temperature experimentation. The other half of the Nobel honorarium was shared equally by Arno A. Penzias and Robert W. Wilson, who together provided additional evidence for the so-called big-bang theory of the origin of the universe when they detected faint electromagnetic radiation that seems to permeate the entire universe.

Kapitsa was born in 1894 near what is now Leningrad. He studied at the Polytechnic Institute there, but spent the 1920s and early 1930s at the University of Cambridge, where he investigated the properties of materials subjected to extremely low temperatures or to intense magnetic fields. Kapitsa enlarged the boundaries of modern physics by building a magnet that produced a field of 500,000 gauss and by developing a machine that produced liquid helium, the most difficult of all gases to condense, at the unprecedented rate of two liters per hour. The machine was the prototype of helium liquefiers now used worldwide in cryogenic laboratories. Kapitsa continued to study liquid helium in the U.S.S.R. and found that at temperatures below 2.2 K it loses practically all resistance to flow and acquires unique properties in its "superfluid" state.

Penzias was born in Germany in 1933 and studied at the City College of New York and Columbia University before joining Bell Laboratories in 1961. Wilson was born in Texas in 1936 and joined Bell Laboratories after studying at Rice University and the California Institute of Technology. The two first refined a large antenna that had been used to detect radio waves reflected from the Echo satellites orbited by NASA in 1960 and 1964. They then used this radio telescope to study the intensity of radio waves emitted from the gaseous halo that surrounds our Galaxy. The microwave radiation that they detected in all directions was more intense than that emitted from any known natural source. Their finding added weight to the big-bang theory of the origin of the universe, namely, that some 10 billion to 20 billion years ago all matter and energy were compressed in a dense, hot ball that exploded and expanded in all directions.

Order of Culture. In 1978 the Japanese government awarded the Order of Culture to Yoichiro Nambu, a professor of physics at the University of Chicago. Nambu was honored for research that used an analogy of superconductivity theory to study the structure of elementary particles, and for being one of the first to introduce the concept of color into the quark model.

Schottky Prize. Bernhard Authier and Horst Fischer of West Germany shared the 1978 Walter Schottky Prize for Solid State Research. The German Physical Society honored the pair for their work on a new process that cuts the cost of producing semiconductor materials for solar cells. The "directional freezing" of a poured melt of silicon produces a block containing columnar single crystals oriented perpendicularly to the surface. These oriented polycrystals are not only economical to produce but when used in silicon solar cells have relatively high efficiencies.

Waterman Award and TIF Founders' Medal. In 1975 the U.S. Congress established the annual Alan T. Waterman Award to honor and encourage outstanding U.S. scientists who are not more than 35 years of age. The recipient is given a total grant of $150,000 over a three-year period to conduct scientific research. In 1978 the award went to Richard A. Muller of the Lawrence Berkeley Laboratory "for his highly original and innovative research, which has led to important discoveries and inventions in diverse areas of physics, including astrophysics, radioisotope dating, and optics." Muller was also given a $35,000 honorarium from the Texas Instruments Foundation as recipient of its 1977 Founders' Medal.

Wolf Prize. The Wolf Foundation of Israel presented a $100,000 Wolf Prize in physics to Chien-Shiung Wu of Columbia University. Wu was honored for demonstrating that certain symmetries of behavior that are generally typical of physics do not apply in the case of radioactive decay.

Psychology

Applications in Psychology Award. The American Psychological Association named Alphonse Chapanis recipient of the 1978 Distinguished Contribution for Applications in Psychology Award. Chapanis, president of the International Ergonomics Association and a founder of the field of engineering psychology, was lauded for his wide range of contributions, including "research on work-station design and man-machine systems relations."

Professional Contribution Award. Arthur L. Benton, professor emeritus at the University of Iowa, received the 1978 Distinguished Professional Contribution Award from the American Psychological Association for being "a leader and one of the principal architects of neuropsychology."

Scientific Contribution Award. Three psychologists were named recipients of the 1978 Distinguished Scientific Contribution Award by the American Psychological Association. Julian Hochberg of Columbia University was cited "for his insightful recognition that the central problem of human perception is to explain how that perception is organized, and for highly significant theoretical contributions toward greater understanding of this central problem." Philip Teitelbaum of the University of Illinois was honored for his analysis of how the brain works. "A common thread of ideas runs through his work ranging from hypothalamic control of feeding and motivation, and their sensory control, to the operant control of reflexes and the nature of voluntary response." Robert B. Zajonc of the University of Michigan received his prize for demonstrating that social processes are most profitably analyzed by the concepts and methods of experimental and mathematical psychology.

Sheen Award. The $10,000 Dr. Rodman E. Sheen and Thomas G. Sheen Award of the American Medical Association was presented in 1978 to Karl A. Menninger, co-founder of the Menninger Foundation in Kansas. During his long and distinguished career Menninger "has achieved international recognition as a psychiatrist, medical educator, and researcher into the basic concepts in personality, psychosomatic relationships, and unconscious self-destructive trends."

Space exploration

NAE Founders Medal. The National Academy of Engineering presented its 1978 Founders Medal to George M. Low, president of Rensselaer Polytechnic Institute in Troy, N.Y., for "playing a central technical and management role in the U.S. space program and especially for his leadership in one of mankind's most complex and dramatic enterprises which culminated in man's footsteps on the moon."

NASA Medal. Olin E. Teague, then U.S. representative from Texas, received a 1978 Distinguished Public Service Medal from NASA for "his consistent and unswerving faith in the value and virtue of a dynamic and imaginative space program."

Transportation

Propulsion Award. William J. Blatz of the McDonnell Aircraft Co. received the 1978 Air Breathing Propulsion Award from the American Institute of Aeronautics and Astronautics "for his meritorious accomplishments of technical leadership in developing unique propulsion and airframe concepts for the F-15 tactical fighter."

RAS Medals. The Royal Aeronautical Society in London presented its 1978 Gold Medal to Ludwig Bölkow, consultant engineer for Messerschmitt-Bölkow-Blohm; its Silver Medal to J. C. Wimpenny, executive director of research for the British Aerospace Aircraft Group; and its Bronze Medal to Lieut. Comdr. D. R. Taylor, the inventor of the Harrier ski-jump technique.

Wyld Award. The American Institute of Aeronautics and Astronautics gave the 1978 Wyld Propulsion Award to William C. Rice of the Marshall Space Flight Center "for his outstanding contributions to the development of solid propellent rocket motors."

Science journalism

AIP-U.S. Steel Award. Robert C. Cowen, a science writer and editor for the *Christian Science Monitor,* was named the 1979 winner of the American Institute of Physics-U.S. Steel Foundation Science-Writing Award in Physics and Astronomy. Cowen was selected as top science journalist for "The New Astronomy," a

series of three articles that appeared in the *Christian Science Monitor* on Dec. 19–21, 1978. Edwin C. Krupp, director of the Griffith Observatory in California, was given a 1978 prize as the author of a book entitled *In Search of Ancient Astronomies.* Each author received an honorarium of $1,500.

Bernard Award. Two writers were named recipients of 1977 Claude Bernard Science Journalism Awards. Donald C. Drake, medical writer for the *Philadelphia Inquirer,* was selected for a series of articles entitled "The Breath of Life." Arthur Fisher, employed by *Popular Science* as group editor for science and engineering, was chosen for his article "Slow Viruses: Biological Time Bombs," which appeared in Time-Life's *Nature/Science Annual.* Each received $1,000 from the National Society for Medical Research, which sponsors the awards.

Technology Writers' Award. The 1977 Technology Writers' Award was given to Richard Casement of *The Economist* for his article "The Brainstorm Technology," and to David Fishlock of the *Financial Times* for his article "TV's Bird High in the Sky."

Washburn Award. The Museum of Science in Boston presented the 1978 Bradford Washburn Award, which consists of a gold medal and a $5,000 honorarium, to Carl Sagan of Cornell University. He was honored for contributing to public understanding of science, notably through such books as *The Cosmic Connection,* which won the 1974 John W. Campbell Memorial Award as the best science book of the year, and *The Dragons of Eden: Speculations on the Evolution of Human Intelligence,* which won the 1978 Pulitzer Prize for nonfiction.

Miscellaneous

Fahrney Medal. Simon Ramo, chairman of the science and technology committee of TRW Inc., received the 1978 Delmer S. Fahrney Medal of the Franklin Institute "for outstanding leadership of major scientific and technological projects of national and international importance."

Kalinga Prize. Each year since 1952 the Kalinga Prize for the Popularization of Science has been given to individuals for distinguished careers of public service that involved interpreting science as writers, editors, speakers, or radio program directors. In 1977 UNESCO selected Fernand Séguin, a French-speaking scientist and television broadcaster in Canada. Since 1954 he has contributed to more than 800 television broadcasts, has published eight popular science books and two medical texts, and has undertaken research that led to a biochemical diagnosis of schizophrenia from spinal ribonucleic acids. The £1,000 honorarium is supplied by Bijoyananda Patnaik, an Indian industrialist. The recipient is expected to spend a month or more in India studying its life and culture.

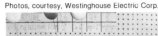

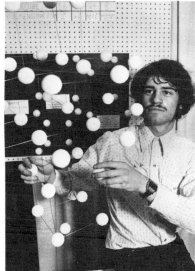

Ron K. Unz (top left), David N. Shykind (top right), Eileen Chang (left).

Science Talent Awards. The 38th annual Science Talent Search, sponsored by the Westinghouse Educational Foundation and administered by Science Service, produced the following 1979 winners. The first-place award, a $12,000 scholarship, was given to Ron K. Unz of North Hollywood High School in California. His project in theoretical physics related to the possible effects of gravitational fields on electromagnetic interactions. The second-place $10,000 scholarship went to David N. Shykind of Silver Spring, Md., who conducted detailed immunochemical research at the Naval Medical Research Institute in Bethesda, Md. He attempted to locate and statistically analyze specific chemical sites on a class of antibodies from normal human blood that may produce allergic or similar complicating factors during blood transfusions. Winner of the third-place $10,000 scholarship was Eileen Chang of New York City. She found that when large doses of precocene II, a botanically derived compound, are applied to mosquito larvae, the breeding and the growth of mosquitoes are affected. Precocene II may prove to be an effective means of controlling mosquito populations. Three other winners each received a $7,500 scholarship: David J. LePoire of Michigan for developing a computer program to carry out calculations dealing with electron densities and energies in two states of matter; Geoffrey C. Frank of Mississippi for an environmental microbiological project centered on the effects of crude oil in microflora in a saltwater environment; and Gregory Sorkin of New York for his study of graph theory in advanced mathematics. Four others received scholarships of $5,000: Michael Urciuoli of New York for an advanced mathematics distribution problem involving sub-semi-groups of positive integers or natural numbers; Julia E. Little of West Virginia for a fertility-related analysis of boar sperm; Ernest M. Moy of New York for his studies of hemoglobin; and Ashfaq Abdulrehman Munshi of New York for a model which represented impurities in the subatomic structure of glass.

Obituaries

The following persons, all of whom died in recent months, were widely recognized for their scientific accomplishments.

Bergier, Jacques (Aug. 8, 1912—Nov. 23, 1978), French science writer, was one of the select group that first studied the properties of polonium, the very rare radioactive element discovered by Pierre and Marie Curie in 1898. Bergier and his colleagues also registered the first patent for the electronic cooling of nuclear batteries. During the 1930s Bergier studied physics, chemistry, and engineering, but after France fell to the Nazis in 1940 he set up an underground organization, named Marco Polo, to fight the Vichy regime in France. He also developed a radio network and such gadgetry as a blowgun for shooting poison needles and the letter bomb, so thin it could be slipped under a door without detonating. Using data transmitted by Bergier's group, Britain's Royal Air Force bombed Peenemünde, the place where the Germans assembled their V-2 rockets. Though tortured and confined to a concentration camp, Bergier steadfastly refused to reveal any information. After his release he became a part-time consultant to French intelligence, but spent the major portion of his time writing. A favorite topic was espionage, applied to politics, industry, and other areas. His scientific books included *L'Energie H* and *Merveilles de la chimie.* Bergier was also a founder of *Planète*, a magazine concerned with scientific speculation.

Best, Charles Herbert (Feb. 27, 1899—March 31, 1978), Canadian physiologist, was still an undergraduate when he and Frederick Banting, in 1921, using a University of Toronto laboratory made available to them by J. J. R. Macleod, discovered insulin and its use in treating diabetes. Operating on a shoestring budget of $100, Best and Banting bought stray dogs for one dollar each and, after several weeks and countless failures, prepared an extract that lowered the blood sugar of depancreatized dogs. In 1923 the Nobel Prize for Physiology or Medicine was jointly awarded to Macleod and Banting for this discovery; Best's contributions were passed over in silence. This omission prompted Macleod to remark that he was being honored for discovering Best, and Banting manifested his outrage by giving half his prize money to his colleague. Besides saving millions of lives, this find stimulated public support of research, attracted students to laboratory research, and gave hope to both doctors and patients. Best introduced the use of the complex carbohydrate heparin to inhibit blood clotting during surgery. He was head of the University of Toronto's physiology department (1929–65) and director of the Banting and Best department of medical research (1941–67) established at the university in 1923.

Conant, James Bryant (March 26, 1893—Feb. 11, 1978), U.S. chemist and educator, had a multifaceted career as a research scientist, educational reformer, and public servant. Three years after earning (1916) his Ph.D. from Harvard University, Conant returned to his alma mater as instructor of organic chemistry and was soon made a full professor. Besides his research on the chemical structure of chlorophyll, Conant, together with N. F. Hall, introduced the concept of superacidity for solutions of strong acids in nonaqueous solvents, and initiated the quantitative study of organic reactions. For two decades (1933–53) he served as president of Harvard University and formulated an educational philosophy that called for a balance between academic and vocational programs in high schools and a diversified general curriculum for colleges. He became a central figure in organizing U.S. science policy for World War II, including the testing and development of the atomic bomb. After the war he served as a senior adviser to the National Science Foundation and to the Atomic Energy Commission. In 1955 he became the first U.S. ambassador to West Germany. Conant returned to the U.S. in 1957 and resumed his public education studies. His writings include *The American High School Today* (1959) and *Slums and Suburbs* (1961). He also published two textbooks, *Practical Chemistry* (with N. H. Black; 1920) and *The Chemistry of Organic Compounds* (1933).

Du Vigneaud, Vincent (May 18, 1901—Dec. 11, 1978), U.S. biochemist, was awarded the 1955 Nobel Prize for Chemistry for the isolation and synthesis of

Vincent Du Vigneaud

420

the pituitary hormones vasopressin, an antidiuretic, and oxytocin, the principal uterus-contracting agent in labor and milk-releasing agent after childbirth. After receiving (1927) a Ph.D. from the University of Rochester, N.Y., Du Vigneaud studied at Johns Hopkins University, Baltimore, Md., the Kaiser Wilhelm Institute, Dresden, Germany, and the University of Edinburgh, Scotland, before serving (1932–38) as head of the department of biochemistry at George Washington University School of Medicine in Washington, D.C. In 1938 he became professor and head of the biochemistry department at the medical school of Cornell University in New York City. Under his direction the Cornell laboratories contributed to such major achievements as the synthesis of penicillin and the isolation and development of the structure of the sulfur-bearing vitamin biotin, as well as examining many other sulfur-containing organic compounds. From 1967 to 1975 Du Vigneaud was professor of chemistry at Cornell University in Ithaca, N.Y.

Gödel, Kurt (April 28, 1906—Jan. 14, 1978), Czech-born mathematician, earned a permanent niche in the history of mathematics with the celebrated theorem that bears his name. Gödel, who was regarded as one of the world's foremost logicians, set forth a philosophical principle (consistency theorem) stating that in any formal system utilizing number theory there exists a proposition that cannot be proved or disproved on the basis of the axioms within that system. His doctoral dissertation, which was published in 1930, was devoted to a completeness theorem stating that everything that logically follows from a given statement can be derived from that statement by using first order predicate logic. His consistency theory laid the foundations for 20th-century mathematical advancement because it implied that a computer could never be programmed to answer all mathematical questions and that human ingenuity rather than mechanical programming would always be needed to produce new mathematical axioms. After earning his Ph.D. from the University of Vienna, Gödel was on the faculty of his alma mater (1933–38) before serving as longtime (1953–76) professor at the Institute for Advanced Study in New Jersey. His work *Consistency of the Axiom of Choice and of the Generalized Continuum-Hypothesis with the Axioms of Set Theory* (1940; rev. ed., 1958) is a classic in modern mathematics. Gödel received the National Medal of Science in 1974.

Goudsmit, Samuel Abraham (July 11, 1902—Dec. 4, 1978), Dutch-born physicist, co-discovered (1925) with George E. Uhlenbeck that electrons possess an intrinsic characteristic called spin. This discovery proved to be of great importance in modern quantum theory because spin and such other basic properties as charge and mass serve to identify and relate subatomic particles. Moreover, each of these quantum properties must usually be conserved or accounted for after

two or more particles interact. After earning (1927) a Ph.D. in physics from the University of Leiden in The Netherlands, Goudsmit traveled to the U.S. and assumed a post as lecturer at the University of Michigan. He became professor of physics there in 1932 and remained on the faculty until 1946 even though he conducted wartime research at the Radiation Laboratory at the Massachusetts Institute of Technology, and undertook (1944) a scientific intelligence mission to Europe for the War Department during World War II. "Alsos," the code name of the mission, followed the invasion forces into Europe to determine if German physicists were preparing an atomic bomb. Goudsmit and his colleagues sampled water from the Rhine River to see if its radioactivity indicated bomb preparations upstream. The group found that attempts to develop a bomb had been abandoned. Besides serving as senior physicist (1948–52), chairman (1952–60), and deputy chairman (1960–67) at Brookhaven National Laboratory in New York, Goudsmit was editor (1951–62) of *The Physical Review*; managing editor (1951–65) and editor in chief (1966–74) of *The American Physical Society*; and founder (1958) and editor (1958–74) of *Physical Review Letters.* He was the coauthor of two scientific books: *The Structure of Line Spectra* and *Atomic Energy.*

Hasselblad, Victor (March 8, 1906—Aug. 5, 1978), Swedish inventor, developed (1941) for the Swedish Air Force a camera that appeared commercially in 1948 as the world's first 2¼ in by 2¼ in single-lens reflex camera with interchangeable lenses and magazines. The Hasselblad camera, which earned a reputation as the Rolls-Royce of its field, was widely used by

Victor Hasselblad

professional photographers and was later adopted by the U.S. National Aeronautics and Space Administration for the first photographs of the Moon. On July 20, 1969, Apollo astronaut Neil Armstrong used a Hasselblad camera for this purpose. Hasselblad, who studied camera making at the offices of Eastman Kodak Co. in both France and the U.S., was also president (1944–66) of his own photography company, Hasselblad Photography, Inc., before he sold the controlling interests to a Swedish industrial group in 1967.

Keldysh, Mstislav Vsevolodovich (Feb. 10 [Jan. 28, old style], 1911—June 24, 1978), Soviet mathematician, became in effect czar of science when he was unanimously elected (1961) president of the Soviet Academy of Sciences. During the 14 years he held office, the Soviet space program flourished under his direction. After graduating (1931) from the state university in Moscow, Keldysh joined the faculty of its Central Institute of Aerohydrodynamics, where he conducted pioneering research into the theory of vibration analysis of such aircraft structures as wings and landing gear wheels. Keldysh was reportedly named (1943) director of the secret Research Institute No. 1 of the Ministry of Aircraft Industry, where he continued to advance the study of vibrational analysis, and three years later became a member of the Academy of Sciences of the U.S.S.R. In 1947 he served on a special committee of Soviet scientists who evaluated the feasibility of developing a manned space glider proposed by German engineer Eugen Saenger during World War II. He later became (1953) director of the Institute of Applied Mathematics of the Academy of Sciences and, together with such noted colleagues as V. A. Yegorov, was instrumental in developing the trajectories for the first Soviet lunar and space probes. A member of the Central Committee of the Communist Party of the Soviet Union, he was buried in the wall of the Kremlin.

Kessler, Henry H. (April 10, 1896—Jan. 18, 1978), U.S. physician, was an orthopedic surgeon especially noted for devising ingenious ways for attaching artificial limbs to the body. Kessler, who was credited with the development of cineplasty, a surgical technique for the muscular control of prosthetic equipment, was also deeply involved in establishing rehabilitation services for the physically handicapped. After receiving (1919) his medical degree from Cornell University Medical School in New York, he set up a private practice and served on the staff of Newark City Hospital, Beth Israel, and the Hospital for Crippled Children, all in Newark, N.J. In 1949 he was a founder of the Kessler Institute for Rehabilitation in West Orange, the first such center in New Jersey. Later, Kessler became a consultant to the World Health Organization, an agency of the United Nations, offering advice on rehabilitation facilities in foreign countries that included Yugoslavia (1951), Indonesia (1954), and the Philippines (1955–56); he was also a consultant to the World Veterans Federation.

His published works include: *Accidental Injuries* (1931), *Occupational Disability Legislation* (1932), *The Crippled and the Disabled* (1934), and *Cineplasty* (1947). Kessler's autobiography, *The Knife is Not Enough,* appeared in 1968.

Lear, William Powell (June 26, 1902—May 14, 1978), U.S. industrialist, produced such diverse inventions as the car radio, the eight-track stereo cartridge, and the automatic pilot for aircraft. Lear, who never graduated from high school, held some 150 patents in the fields of electronics, aviation technology, and auto engineering. He also pioneered the first corporate jet aircraft. In 1939 he founded Lear, Inc., which sold $100 million worth of equipment to the U.S. armed forces during World War II, but he sold (1962) his shares in the company when the board of directors refused to approve plans for a low-priced jet airplane. He then established Lear Jet Corp., which rolled the first "baby jet" off the assembly line in 1963. In 1967 he sold his interest in Lear Jet Corp. for $28 million, but his retirement was only temporary; he soon undertook plans to develop a steam-powered automobile and a new rear-engine turboprop business jet at his company, Lear Avia, in Reno, Nev.

Mallowan, Sir Max Edgar Lucien (May 6, 1904—Aug. 19, 1978), British archaeologist, supervised large-scale excavations in Iraq, notably in Tell Brak (1937–38) and Nimrud (1949–58), and thereby continued a tradition of British archaeological discovery in Mesopotamia that began with Sir Henry Layard in 1842. Mallowan worked with Leonard Woolley at Ur of the Chaldees (1925–30) after graduating from New College, Oxford, and later directed (1931–32) expeditions with R. Campbell Thompson at the ancient city of Nineveh in Iraq. After World War II Mallowan served as director (1947–61), chairman (1966–70), and president (from 1970) of the British School of Archaeology, in Iraq. He was professor of Western Asiatic archaeology, University of London (1947–62), and a fellow of All Souls College, Oxford (1962–71). He also served as editor (1948–65) of the Near Eastern and West Asiatic series of Penguin Books and editor (1948–71) of the Baghdad School journal *Iraq.* Mallowan, who was knighted in 1968, was the husband of mystery writer Dame Agatha Christie.

Mead, Margaret (Dec. 16, 1901—Nov. 15, 1978), U.S. anthropologist, was internationally known both as an authority on various literate and illiterate cultures and as an irrepressible propagandist for her own ideas. A woman of seemingly limitless energy, she never tired of lecturing the public, formally and informally, on such far-ranging topics as population control, space probes, environmental pollution, world hunger, adolescence, mental health, human sexuality, primitive art, city planning, women's liberation, drug use, child rearing, and tribal customs. Though fellow scientists were sometimes disturbed that Mead felt the need to air her views

Margaret Mead

monoplane prototype of the Me 109 won the world air speed record at 469 mph (755 kph) in April 1939, and some 35,000 Me 109s were produced during the war. Besides the Me 262 he designed the Me 163, a swept-back-wing, rocket-driven plane. After the war Messerschmitt was detained for two years by the U.S. occupation authorities, and during the postwar ban on fighter aircraft construction he manufactured prefabricated houses, sewing machines, and enclosed motor-tricycles. In the late 1960s Messerschmitt was named honorary chairman of Messerschmitt-Bölkow-

Willy E. Messerschmitt

on subjects unrelated to anthropology, the attention she attracted also redounded to the benefit of their profession. In 1923 Mead entered the graduate school of Columbia University, where, under the guidance of Franz Boas, she obtained a Ph.D. in 1929. During a 1925 field trip in Samoa she gathered material for the first of her 23 books, *Coming of Age in Samoa* (1928), a perennial best-seller and a characteristic example of her reliance on observation rather than statistics for data. Other works include *Growing Up in New Guinea* (1930), *Sex and Temperament in Three Primitive Societies* (1935), *Balinese Character: A Photographic Analysis* (with Gregory Bateson; 1942), *Continuities in Cultural Evolution* (1964), and *A Rap on Race* (with James Baldwin; 1971). During her many years with the American Museum of Natural History in New York City she successively served as assistant curator (1926–42), associate curator (1942–64), and curator (1964–69) of ethnology. Her contributions to science received special recognition when, at the age of 72, she was elected to the presidency of the American Association for the Advancement of Science. In 1979 Margaret Mead was posthumously awarded the Presidential Medal of Freedom, the United States' highest civilian honor.

Messerschmitt, Willy E. (June 26, 1898—Sept. 17, 1978), German aeronautical engineer, was the designer of the feared Me 109 fighter, Germany's principal aerial defense against Allied bombers during World War II; the Me 110 two-man fighter-bomber, which was used primarily as an attack aircraft and as a night fighter; and the twin-engined Me 262, the first operational jet fighter, which saw action during the last days of the Third Reich. Educated at the Munich Institute of Technology, Messerschmitt also gained useful knowledge about aircraft construction as a gliding enthusiast. His

Blohm, Ltd. In the late 1970s the company employed more than 20,000 workers, who constructed satellites and missiles as well as the Franco-West German airbus and the West German share of the Tornado combat aircraft for the North Atlantic Treaty Organization.

Newson, Henry Winston (Nov. 26, 1909—May 14, 1978), U.S. physicist, was one of a group of distinguished experimental physicists, who, under the direction of Enrico Fermi, were present at the first controlled nuclear chain reaction at the University of Chicago's Stagg Field in 1942. Together with his colleagues Newson invented an overall control system that is still used in modern nuclear reactors. He also was a participant in the Manhattan Project, which produced the first atomic bombs at Los Alamos (N.M.) Scientific Laboratory and helped develop a cyclotron at Lawrence Radiation Laboratory at the University of California.

Newson, who was the first to observe neutron disintegration of fluorine, predicted the discovery of induced radioactivity. After receiving (1934) a Ph.D. in chemistry from the University of Chicago, Newson was associated with several scientific laboratories before becoming (1948) a professor at Duke University in Durham, N.C. His book *Fast Neutron Physics* (Part I, 1960, Part II, 1963) was written in collaboration with J. H. Gibbons.

Nobile, Umberto (Jan. 21, 1885—July 30, 1978), Italian airship designer and explorer, designed and piloted the airship "Norge," which carried explorer Roald Amundsen and his American companion, Lincoln Ellsworth, from Svalbard (Spitsbergen) over the North Pole to Alaska in 1926 in the first exploration flight to cross the Arctic Ocean. Nobile was rewarded with the rank of general in the Italian Air Service, but, when Amundsen criticized his technical skills, a bitter controversy developed. Two years later Nobile set out for the North Pole in the dirigible "Italia." The ship crashed northeast of Svalbard, throwing Nobile and other crew members onto the ice, but then took off again with the rest of the crew, who were never seen again. Amundsen also disappeared in a rescue attempt, and Nobile, severely criticized by a subsequent inquiry, was forced to resign. The controversy continued, and Nobile defended himself in a book about his Arctic adventures, *Gli italiani al Polo Nord* (1959; *My Polar Flights,* 1961). After spending some years designing aircraft for the Soviet Union, he returned to Italy, and in 1945 he was reinstated as a general in the Air Service.

Norrish, Ronald George Wreyford (Nov. 9, 1897—June 7, 1978), British physical chemist, shared the

Ronald Norrish

Keystone

1967 Nobel Prize for Chemistry with his co-workers (Sir) George Porter and Manfred Eigen for studies of extremely fast chemical reactions. As director of the department of physical chemistry at the University of Cambridge (1937–65), Norrish developed research techniques of flash photolysis and flash spectroscopy to measure and study the rapid reactions of free atoms and radicals. He was able to stop chemical reactions at intervals approaching one-thousandth of a millionth of a second and to study the intermediate stages of the progressive changes. Most experiments involved atoms of chlorine as they exist in an equilibrium of other atoms and molecules. The gas mixture was irradiated with high-intensity sparks of extremely short duration to disturb the equilibrium, and then the speed at which the normal balance was regained was measured. Norrish's investigations were detailed in more than 200 scientific papers. He was elected to the Royal Society in 1936 and served as president of the Faraday Society (1953–55).

Oka, Kiyoshi (April 19, 1901—March 1, 1978), Japanese mathematician, was internationally known for his contribution to the theory of functions of several complex variables. He entered the physics department of Kyoto University in 1922 but in the following year switched to mathematics. While holding the position of lecturer at the university, he realized he could not do original research if he remained in Japan. In 1929 he enrolled at the Poincaré Institute in France, where he became absorbed in unsolved problems in the theory of functions of several complex variables. He returned to Japan in 1932 and taught a few years in Hiroshima. Five years later Oka returned to his parents' home in Wakayama and for a time supported his family by farming. In 1949 he was appointed professor at Nara Women's College, where he remained until his retirement in 1963. The bulk of his contributions to mathematics consisted of ten papers published between 1936 and 1963 under the title "Sur les fonctions de plusieurs variables." They included solutions to Cousin's problem and Hartog's inverse problem, and the introduction of the concept of holomorphic ideals of indeterminate domains. During these years Oka became interested in philosophy, delving deeply into Japanese haiku poetry and Zen philosophy in an effort to confront his own existence. Later in life he lectured on the Japanese race and published a number of essays on nonmathematical subjects. He received the Japan Academy Award in 1951 and the Order of Culture in 1960.

Poulter, Thomas Charles (March 3, 1897—June 14, 1978), U.S. explorer, was second in command and chief scientist on Richard E. Byrd's second Antarctic expedition (1933–35), aimed at mapping and claiming land in the region of the South Pole. Poulter led the rescue party that revived Byrd, who was near death after spending five months alone in the Bolling Advance Base weather station. In addition to holding more than 75 other patents, Poulter designed the 33-ton "Snow Cruiser" used by Byrd to traverse glacier chasms during his third expedition. Early in his career Poulter headed the departments of chemistry (1925–27) and physics (1927–32) at Iowa Wesleyan College, his alma mater, where he taught James Van Allen, the discoverer of radiation belts around the Earth. After returning from Byrd's Antarctic expeditions, Poulter served as director (1948–54) of the Stanford Research Institute and director of Stanford's Poulter Laboratories (1954–60). At the time of his death he was experimenting with implants to aid the deaf.

Quick, Armand James (July 18, 1894—Jan. 26, 1978), U.S. hematologist, developed (1932) a prothrombin time test (Quick test) that assesses the clotting ability of a patient's blood. The test is used to determine the dosage of blood-thinning drugs and to diagnose liver diseases. Quick, who was recognized as one of the leading experts of the 20th century on blood diseases, also devised a prothrombin consumption time test that is helpful in diagnosing hemophilia, a hereditary defect in the blood-clotting function that promotes excessive bleeding. His research also led to the discovery of warfarin and dicumarol, used as blood-thinning drugs. He was also one of the first to recognize aspirin's effects on the blood-clotting process. Quick served as professor of biochemistry and chairman of the department (1944–66) at Marquette University School of Medicine (now Medical College of Wisconsin) after receiving (1928) his M.D. from Cornell University. A prolific writer, Quick wrote some 300 papers and numerous books, including *Hemorrhagic Diseases* (1957) and *Bleeding Problems in Clinical Medicine* (1970).

Roberts, Sir Gilbert (Feb. 18, 1899—Jan. 1, 1978), British civil engineer, pioneered new design and construction methods in a series of major bridges including the 3,300-ft (1,006-m) Firth of Forth highway bridge in Scotland, the seventh longest in the world. After graduating from the University of London, he became a civil engineer and worked on the Sydney Harbour Bridge and on the Otto Beit suspension bridge across the Zambezi in what was then Southern Rhodesia. A brilliant designer, he adopted new welding methods and the use of high-tensile steel and introduced box columns and girders in the construction of power stations, thereby using less steel. Roberts's designs, which called for lighter construction, better stability, and lower cost, were implemented in such engineering masterpieces as the Severn River Bridge in western England, the Auckland Harbour Bridge in New Zealand, the Volta Bridge in Ghana, and the suspension bridge across the Bosporus in Turkey. Roberts also developed all-welded ships in World War II and designed the Dome of Discovery for the Festival of Britain in 1951, the Babcock 500-ton Goliath crane, and a 210-ft- (64-m-) diameter radio telescope in Australia. In

1965 he was knighted and elected a fellow of the Royal Society.

Siegbahn, Karl Manne Georg (Dec. 3, 1886—Sept. 26, 1978), Swedish physicist, won (1924) the Nobel Prize for Physics for his discoveries and investigations in X-ray spectroscopy. In 1916 Siegbahn discovered a

Karl Manne Siegbahn

new group of spectral lines, the M-series. He also developed equipment and techniques that enabled him to determine accurately the wavelengths of X-rays. Siegbahn designed X-ray tubes and a crystal spectrograph, and he improved the vacuum technique that previously had presented experimental problems for researchers. After receiving (1911) a Ph.D. from the University of Lund, he took a teaching position at his alma mater and eventually became head of the physics department. While teaching physics at Uppsala University, he and his associates proved (1924) that X-rays are refracted when they pass through prisms, just as light is. In 1937 he was appointed director of the newly created Nobel Institute of Physics in Stockholm and also became professor of physics at the University of Stockholm. From 1939 to 1962 Siegbahn served as a member of the International Committee on Weights and Measures. His volume, *Spectroscopy of X-rays* (1924) was a classic in the field.

Shields, James (Nov. 21, 1918—June 20, 1978), British geneticist, was internationally acclaimed for his research on twins and on the genetics of mental disorder. In 1947 Shields began his work in the Psychiatric Genetics Unit at Maudsley Hospital in London, where he compiled case histories of twins and conducted research on the role of genetics in social environment and upbringing. His classic volume *Monozygotic Twins Brought up Apart and Brought up Together* (1962) was based on the largest collection ever made of separated twins. Later, Shields collaborated with Irving Gottesman on papers dealing with genetics and schizophrenia. In 1972 they conclusively reported that genetic factors specific to schizophrenia are involved in its etiology. Shields, who spent the greater part of his professional career at the University of London, also studied anxiety states, neuroses, homosexuality, alcoholism, and adoption in relation to schizophrenia. At the time of his death he was reader in psychiatric genetics at the Institute of Psychiatry of the University of London.

Stone, Edward Durell (March 9, 1902—Aug. 6, 1978), U.S. architect, designed (1937) with Philip Goodwin the Museum of Modern Art in New York City, the first major U.S. public building in the International Style. After studying at Harvard University and the Massachusetts Institute of Technology, Stone toured Europe, where he encountered new architectural trends. He won praise for the lavish Art-Deco interiors he designed (1932) for New York City's Radio City Music Hall. Stone had growing doubts about the enduring appeal of the International Style with its stark glass and aluminum structures. After World War II, in which he served as chief of planning and design for the U.S. Army Air Corps, he was associate professor of architecture at Yale University from 1946 to 1952. In 1946 he designed the El Panama Hotel in Panama City, then turned to such traditional materials as concrete, stone, and marble and claimed his first architectural triumph, the U.S. embassy in New Delhi (1954). The templelike structure was perched on a raised platform fronted by a lavish reflecting pool and enclosed by a lacy concrete grill, one of his trademarks. Although critics described his work as overly romantic, Stone received a steady flow of commissions, including the American Pavilion constructed for the Brussels World's Fair of 1958, the Nuclear Research Center (1966) near Islamabad, Pakistan, and the Huntington Hartford Gallery of Modern Art (1959; now the New York Cultural Center) in New York City. In Washington, D.C. his works include the National Geographic Society headquarters (1961) and the John F. Kennedy Center for the Performing Arts (1964). After the publication of his autobiography, *The Evolution of an Architect* (1962), Stone completed designs (1964 and 1969) for the 50-story General Motors tower in New York City and the 80-story Standard Oil Building in Chicago.

Täckholm, Vivi Laurent (Jan. 7, 1898—May 3, 1978), Swedish botanist, was instrumental in establishing one of the largest herbaria and finest botanical libraries in Africa during her 50 years of research at the University of Cairo in Giza. After obtaining (1921) a degree in botany from the University of Stockholm, Vivi Laurent traveled to the U.S. where she undertook an assortment of odd jobs and began a writing career. Besides publishing *Vivi's Journey* (1923) Laurent wrote for several Stockholm newspapers and produced the children's classic, *The Saga of Snipp, Snapp, Sorum* (1926). In the same year she married Gunnar Vilhelm Täckholm, who then joined the University of Cairo and founded a department of botany in a newly established faculty of science. They ran the department together during the next three years and made a number of major field trips to collect botanical material for the completion of *Flora of Egypt*. During the following years the couple studied and classified their specimens in Switzerland, Germany, England, and Sweden. After the death (1933) of her husband, Vivi Täckholm continued to collaborate with Mohammed Drar. *Flora of Egypt* was published in four volumes, the first appearing in 1941.

Thackeray, Andrew David (1910—Feb. 21, 1978), British astrophysicist, discovered with A. J. Wesselink that the two galactic systems (Magellanic Clouds) closest to the Galaxy are twice as far from Earth as originally believed. This find, together with similar results obtained by Walter Baade in his study of the Andromeda galaxy, indicated that the Universe was twice its previously presumed age, thereby resolving a paradox: the Earth was not after all older than the Universe. Thackeray also showed that both old and young stars existed in the Magellanic Clouds, contrary to earlier suppositions. His work on the Sculptor galaxy was largely responsible for establishing that spheroidal galaxies consist entirely of old stars. Through his spectroscopic studies of stars in the Magellanic Clouds, Thackeray determined that an upper limit to stellar brightness is about a million times the solar luminosity. While in Pretoria, South Africa, he made extensive radial velocity measurements of stars in the southern Milky Way, which led to new determinations of the constants of galactic rotation and an estimate of the distance to the galactic center. Thackeray, who was educated at Eton and Kings College, Cambridge, joined the staff of the Solar Physics Observatory at Cambridge before traveling to South Africa, where he was chief assistant (1948–50) and director (1950–74) of the Radcliffe Observatory in Pretoria. When the observatory closed in 1974, the 74-inch Radcliffe reflector, which was the largest telescope in the Southern Hemisphere for many years, was acquired by the South African Astronomical Observatory for use at Sutherland, Cape Province. Thackeray then became Radcliffe Professor of Astronomy at the University of Cape Town.

Contributors to the Science Year in Review

C. Melvin Aikens *Archaeology.* Professor of Anthropology, University of Oregon, Eugene.

Joseph Ashbrook *Astronomy.* Editor, *Sky and Telescope* magazine, Cambridge, Mass.

Fred Basolo *Chemistry: Inorganic chemistry.* Professor of Chemistry, Northwestern University, Evanston, Ill.

Louis J. Battan *Earth sciences: Atmospheric sciences.* Director, Institute of Atmospheric Physics, University of Arizona, Tucson.

Gregory Benford *Physics: General developments.* Associate Professor of Physics, University of California, Irvine.

Harold Borko *Electronics and information sciences: Information systems and services.* Professor, Graduate School of Library and Information Science, University of California, Los Angeles.

D. Allan Bromley *Physics: Nuclear physics.* Henry Ford II Professor and Director, Wright Nuclear Structure Laboratory, Yale University, New Haven, Conn.

Marjorie C. Caserio *Chemistry: Organic chemistry.* Professor of Chemistry, University of California, Irvine.

Warren D. Dolphin *Life sciences: Zoology.* Associate Professor of Zoology and Executive Officer of Biology, Iowa State University, Ames.

F. C. Durant III *Electronics and information sciences: Satellite systems.* Assistant Director, National Air and Space Museum, Smithsonian Institution, Washington, D.C.

Robert G. Eagon *Life sciences: Microbiology.* Professor of Microbiology, University of Georgia, Athens.

Gerald Feinberg *Physics: High-energy physics.* Professor of Physics, Columbia University, New York, N.Y.

Lawrence E. Fisher *Anthropology.* Assistant Professor of Anthropology, University of Illinois at Chicago Circle.

David R. Gaskell *Materials sciences: Metallurgy.* Associate Professor of Metallurgy, University of Pennsylvania, Philadelphia.

Robert Geddes *Architecture and civil engineering.* Dean, School of Architecture and Urban Planning, Princeton University, Princeton, N.J.

David C. Glass *Medical sciences: Stress and illness.* Professor of Psychology, City University of New York.

Robert Haselkorn *Life sciences: Molecular biology.* F. L. Pritzker Professor and Chairman of the Department of Biophysics and Theoretical Biology, University of Chicago.

Dalma Heyn *Medical sciences: General medicine.* Editor, *Family Health* magazine, New York, N.Y.

John Patrick Jordan *Food and agriculture: Agriculture.* Director, Colorado State University Experiment Station, Fort Collins.

Lou Joseph *Medical sciences: Dentistry.* Manager of Media Relations, Bureau of Public Information, American Dental Association, Chicago, Ill.

Bruce R. Julian *Earth sciences: Geophysics.* Geophysicist, U.S. Geological Survey, Golden, Colo.

George B. Kauffman *Chemistry: Applied chemistry.* Professor of Chemistry, California State University, Fresno.

David B. Kitts *Earth sciences: Geology and geochemistry.* Professor of Geology and Geophysics and of the History of Science, University of Oklahoma, Norman.

David S. Krantz *Medical sciences: Stress and illness.* Assistant Professor of Medical Psychology, University of Health Sciences, Bethesda, Md.

Mina W. Lamb *Food and agriculture: Nutrition.* Professor emeritus, Department of Food and Nutrition, Texas Tech University, Lubbock.

Howard J. Lewis *U.S. science policy.* Director, Office of Information, National Academy of Sciences, Washington, D.C.

Melvin H. Marx *Psychology.* Research Professor of Psychology, University of Missouri, Columbia.

Arthur L. Robinson *Chemistry: Physical chemistry.* Research News Writer, *Science* magazine, Washington, D.C.

Saul Rosen *Electronics and information sciences: Computers.* Director, Computing Center, Purdue University, West Lafayette, Ind.

Arthur H. Seidman *Electronics and information sciences: Electronics.* Professor of Electrical Engineering, Pratt Institute, Brooklyn, N.Y.

Mitchell R. Sharpe *Space exploration: Space probes.* Historian, Alabama Space and Rocket Center, Huntsville.

Albert J. Smith *Life sciences: Botany.* Professor of Biology, Wheaton College, Wheaton, Ill.

Frank A. Smith *Transportation.* Senior Vice-President, Transportation Association of America, Washington, D.C.

J. F. Smithcors *Medical sciences: Veterinary medicine.* Editor, American Veterinary Publications, Santa Barbara, Calif.

W. E. Spicer *Physics: Solid-state physics.* Stanley W. Ascherman Professor of Engineering, Stanford University, Stanford, Calif.

Lynn Arthur Steen *Mathematics.* Professor of Mathematics, St. Olaf College, Northfield, Minn.

Robert F. Steen *Electronics and information sciences: Communications systems.* Technical Adviser to the Vice-President and Chief Scientist, IBM Corp., Armonk, N.Y.

Norman M. Tallan *Materials sciences: Ceramics.* Acting Chief, Metals and Ceramics Division, Air Force Materials Laboratory, Wright-Patterson Air Force Base, Ohio.

William A. Vogely *Energy.* Professor and Chairman of the Department of Mineral Economics, Pennsylvania State University, University Park.

Kenneth E. F. Watt *Environment.* Professor of Zoology and Environmental Studies, University of California, Davis.

Terry White *Space exploration: Manned flight.* Public Information Specialist, NASA Johnson Space Center, Houston, Texas.

Eric F. Wood *Earth sciences: Hydrology.* Assistant Professor of Civil Engineering, Princeton University, Princeton, N.J.

Warren S. Wooster *Earth sciences: Oceanography.* Professor of Marine Studies and Fisheries, University of Washington, Seattle.

James C. Wyant *Optical engineering.* Associate Professor of Optical Sciences, University of Arizona, Tucson.

Index

This is a three-year cumulative index. Index entries to feature and review articles in this and previous editions of the *Yearbook of Science and the Future* are set in boldface type, *e.g.,* **Astronomy.** Entries to other subjects are set in lightface type, *e.g.,* Radiation. Additional information on any of these subjects is identified with a subheading and indented under the entry heading. The numbers following headings and subheadings indicate the year (boldface) of the edition and the page number (lightface) on which the information appears.

Astronomy 80–255; **79**–262; **78**–263
    black hole physics **80**–370
    climatology **79**–148; **78**–282
    computer simulated galaxies il. **80**–297
    cosmology **80**–88
    Einstein's theories **80**–79
    honors **80**–406; **79**–410; **78**–413
    laser use in simulation **80**–367
    Native American influence **79**–214
    Other Civilizations in Space: The Search
        for Extraterrestrial Life **78**–282

All entry headings, whether consisting of a single word or more, are treated for the purpose of alphabetization as single complete headings and are alphabetized letter by letter up to the punctuation. The abbreviation "il." indicates an illustration.

Acknowledgments

6   Photographs and illustrations by (left to right, top to bottom) W. Ostgathe—Leo de Wys, Inc.; Rob Sauber; Kinuyo Y. Craft; Stephen Dalton—Natural History Photographic Agency; Wm. Franklin McMahon; John Youssi

12, 15, 17, 30–31, 34, 38   Illustrations by John Draves

92   Adapted from Allan Sandage, ASTROPHYSICAL JOURNAL, Vol. 178, p. 12, November 15, 1972 © The American Astronomical Society. All rights reserved

96   Chart adapted from NEW SCIENTIST, London, November 16, 1978, p. 506. The weekly review of Science & Technology

100   Adapted from "Will the Universe Expand Forever?", J. Richard Gott III et al. © March 1976 by SCIENTIFIC AMERICAN INC. All rights reserved

109, 111, 113   Illustrations by John Craig

175, 179, 180   Adapted from P. T. Haskell, "The Future of Locust and Grasshopper Control", OUTLOOK ON AGRICULTURE, Vol. 6, No. 4, 1970, pp. 166–174

203   Adapted from John L. Mero, THE MINERAL RESOURCES OF THE SEA, p. 87, 1965, Elsevier Publishing Co., Amsterdam-London-New York

210   Adapted from "The Original of Metal Deposits in the Oceanic Lithosphere", Enrico Bonatti © February 1978 by SCIENTIFIC AMERICAN INC. All rights reserved

17 68

To extend the tradition of excellence of your Encyclopaedia Britannica educational program, you may also avail yourself of other aids for your home reference center.

The following pages feature two companion products—the Britannica 3 bookcase and the Britannica Reading Achievement Program—that are designed to help you and your family.

Should you wish to order them, or to obtain further information, please write to us at

Britannica Home Library Service
Attn: Year Book Department
P. O. Box 4928
Chicago, Illinois 60680

Britannica 3
custom-designed
BOOKCASE

- requires less than 1 x 3-ft. floor space

- laminated pecan finish resists burns, stains, scratches

- Early American styling enriches any setting

- case size: 35$\frac{3}{4}$" wide, 9$\frac{3}{4}$" deep, 27$\frac{5}{8}$" high